THE COMPLETE
Cosori
AIR FRYER OVEN
Cookbook 2021

JOHN BROWN

TABLE OF CONTENTS

First Printing Edition, 2021

Printed in the United States of America
Available from Amazon.com and other retail outlets

INTRODUCTION

This Air Fryer Oven Cookbook contains easy, delicious and healthy recipes that can be made in minutes.

Even if you have never tried the Cosori Air Fryer Oven before, it promises you one thing, after receiving this cookbook, you will feel guilty for not discovering it sooner.

It will prompt you to empty your kitchen of all the other useless appliances that only take up space and you will start putting your air fryer oven to good use. The oven with air fryer will give you lots of joy, time and, above all, tasty dishes. Feel free to modify and adapt these recipes, or simply let yourself be inspired to make your own personalized dishes!

The oven with air fryer will make your life much easier, both for you and for your family. This cookbook will share many different recipes to provide a complete guide to all regular users of the oven. With the latest functions of the air fryer oven, you can fry, dehydrate, grill, toast, roast and bake all kinds of dishes. Relax and let your imagination run wild by following the delicious recipes that you will find listed in the following chapters that will help you add more color and flavor to your dining table using the oven with air fryer.

WHY USE AN AIR FRYER OVEN?

The popularity of this appliance exploded when we began to realize the enormous benefits it had for the health of users. Convenience and ease of use offer a very simple choice for anyone who wants to enjoy a healthy and delicious meal that is not too time-consuming. Here is a list of the fantastic benefits you will enjoy with this magical oven!

Excellent for cooking solidified foods without oil and special or preheated foods.

Due to the smaller containers, food cooks faster than ovens and no preheating is required.

The type of food is brilliant because the heat gives it a pleasantly cool appearance and does not burn.

Perfect for two individuals or smaller segments. There are such a significant number of larger models out there for cooking larger parts for more individuals. The potential results are invaluable.

It is a healthier way to cook fried or crunchy foods. In general, you can use substantially less oil to get crunchy, crunchy finished foods.

Everything is pleasantly contained inside the air fryer during cooking.

The food is cooked fresh due to the smaller cooking zone and the heating element is closer to the food.

There is no need to heat the house in the summer when you want something hot, roasted or fried in a pan.

CLEANING AND MAINTENANCE

Remember to clean the air fryer oven and accessories according to the instructions and safety precautions after every kitchen adventure. Like any household appliance, maintenance is necessary to maintain the correct functioning of the device in the long term. Any tool used for food preparation must be kept perfectly clean. Don't let dirt build up and clean the fryer environment frequently, so you get great results when using the air fryer oven. You have to make sure you remember this, "keep it clean and keep it" to get the best results efficiently because your appliance care will last longer and longer. We provide you with some cleaning tips; however, it is not difficult.

The external and internal parts could be cleaned relatively easily and should be done frequently. In the heating coil situation, do this a couple of times a year only. After cleaning it properly, move on to finally enjoy the delicious recipes in this fantastic cookbook!

This cookbook offers a step-by-step guide to cooking various meals ranging from breakfast, poultry, meat, vegetables, snacks and so much more. Get this latest air fryer oven cookbook and bring convenience to your kitchen floor right away. If you had an oven with an air fryer and don't know what to cook, now you do - with all the recipes at their best!

what are you still waiting for? Start cooking in your air fryer oven and enjoy all the foods you thought were unhealthy!

BREAKFAST

I. VEGETABLE EGG CUPS

Basic Recipe
Preparation Time: 10 minutes
Cooking Time: 20 minutes

Servings: 4
INGREDIENTS:

- 4 eggs
- 1 tbsp cilantro, chopped
- 4 tbsp half and half
- 1 cup cheddar cheese, shredded
- 1 cup vegetables, diced
- Pepper
- Salt

DIRECTIONS:
Sprinkle four ramekins with cooking spray and set aside.
In a mixing bowl, whisk eggs with cilantro, half and half, vegetables, 1/2 cup cheese, pepper, and salt.
Pour egg mixture into the four ramekins.
Place ramekins in air fryer basket and cook at 300 F for 12 minutes
Top with remaining 1/2 cup cheese and cook for 2 minutes more at 400 F.
Serve and enjoy.
NUTRITION: Calories 194 Fat 11.5 g Carbs 6 g Protein 13 g

2. SAVORY CHEESE AND BACON MUFFINS

Basic Recipe
Preparation Time: 5 minutes
Cooking Time: 17 minutes
Servings: 4
INGREDIENTS:

- 1 ½ cup of all-purpose flour
- 2 teaspoons of baking powder
- ½ cup of milk
- 2 eggs
- 1 tablespoon of freshly chopped parsley
- 4 cooked and chopped bacon slices
- 1 thinly chopped onion
- ½ cup of shredded cheddar cheese
- ½ teaspoon of onion powder
- 1 teaspoon of salt
- 1 teaspoon of black pepper

DIRECTIONS:
Turn on your air fryer to 360 degrees Fahrenheit.
Using a large bowl, add and stir all the ingredients until it mixes properly.
Then grease the muffin cups with a nonstick cooking spray or line it with a parchment paper. Pour the batter proportionally into each muffin cup.
Place it inside your air fryer and bake it for 15 minutes
Thereafter, carefully remove it from your air fryer and allow it to chill.
Serve and enjoy!
NUTRITION: Calories 180 Fat 18g Carbs 16g Protein 15g

3. BEST AIR-FRIED ENGLISH BREAKFAST

Basic Recipe
Preparation Time: 5 minutes
Cooking Time: 20 minutes
Servings: 4
INGREDIENTS:

- 8 sausages
- 8 bacon slices
- 4 eggs
- 1 (16-ounce) can of baked beans
- 8 slices of toast

DIRECTIONS:

Add the sausages and bacon slices to your air fryer and cook them for 10 minutes at a 320 degrees Fahrenheit.
Using a ramekin or heat-safe bowl, add the baked beans, then place another ramekin and add the eggs and whisk.
Increase the temperature to 290 degrees Fahrenheit.
Place it inside your air fryer and cook it for an additional 10 minutes or until everything is done.
Serve and enjoy!
NUTRITION: Calories 850 Fat 40g Carbs 20g Protein 48g

4. AIR FRYER BAKED EGGS

Prep time: 5 minutes | Cook time: 6 to 7 minutes | Serves 2

- 2 large eggs
- 2 tablespoons half-and-half
- 2 teaspoons shredded Cheddar cheese
- Salt and freshly ground black pepper, to taste
- Cooking spray

Spritz 2 ramekins lightly with cooking spray. Crack an egg into each ramekin.
Top each egg with 1 tablespoon of half-and-half and 1 teaspoon of Cheddar cheese. Sprinkle with salt and black pepper. Stir the egg mixture with a fork until well combined.
Select Bake, set temperature to 330ºF (166ºC), and set time to 6 minutes. Select Start to begin preheating.
Once preheated, place the ramekins in the oven.
When cooking is complete, the eggs should be set. Check for doneness and continue cooking for 1 minute more as needed. Allow to cool for 5 minutes before removing and serving.

5. SPINACH FRITTATA

Basic Recipe
Preparation Time: 5 minutes
Cooking Time: 8 minutes
Servings: 1
INGREDIENTS:

- 3 eggs
- 1 cup spinach, chopped
- 1 small onion, minced
- 2 tbsp mozzarella cheese, grated
- Pepper
- Salt

DIRECTIONS:
Preheat the air fryer to 350 F. Spray air fryer pan with cooking spray.
In a bowl, whisk eggs with remaining ingredients until well combined.
Pour egg mixture into the prepared pan and place pan in the air fryer basket.
Cook frittata for 8 minutes or until set. Serve and enjoy.
NUTRITION: Calories 384 Fat 23.3 g Carbs 10.7 g
Protein 34.3 g

b. SAUSAGE AND EGG BREAKFAST BURRITO

Basic Recipe
Preparation Time: 5 minutes
Cooking Time: 30 minutes
Servings: 6
INGREDIENTS:

- 6 eggs
- Salt
- Pepper
- Cooking oil
- ½ cup chopped red bell pepper
- ½ cup chopped green bell pepper
- 8 ounces ground chicken sausage
- ½ cup salsa

- 6 medium (8-inch) flour tortillas
- ½ cup shredded Cheddar cheese

DIRECTIONS:

In a medium bowl, whisk the eggs. Add salt and pepper to taste.

Place a skillet on medium-high heat. Spray with cooking oil. Add the eggs. Scramble for 2 to 3 minutes, until the eggs are fluffy. Remove the eggs from the skillet and set aside.

If needed, spray the skillet with more oil. Add the chopped red and green bell peppers. Cook for 2 to 3 minutes, once the peppers are soft.

Add the ground sausage to the skillet. Break the sausage into smaller pieces using a spatula or spoon. Cook for 3 to 4 minutes, until the sausage is brown.

Add the salsa and scrambled eggs. Stir to combine. Remove the skillet from heat.

Spoon the mixture evenly onto the tortillas.

To form the burritos, fold the sides of each tortilla in toward the middle and then roll up from the bottom. You can secure each burrito with a toothpick. Or you can moisten the outside edge of the tortilla with a small amount of water. I prefer to use a cooking brush, but you can also dab with your fingers.

Spray the burritos with cooking oil and place them in the air fryer. Do not stack. Cook the burritos in batches if they do not all fit in the basket. Cook for 8 minutes

Open the air fryer and flip the burritos. Heat it for an additional 2 minutes or until crisp.

If necessary, repeat steps 8 and 9 for the remaining burritos.

Sprinkle the Cheddar cheese over the burritos. Cool before serving.

NUTRITION: Calories 236 Fat 13g Carbs 16g Protein 15g

7.   HOME-FRIED POTATOES

Basic Recipe

Preparation Time: 5 minutes

Cooking Time: 25 minutes

Servings: 4

INGREDIENTS:

- 3 large russet potatoes
- 1 tablespoon canola oil
- 1 tablespoon extra-virgin olive oil
- 1 teaspoon paprika
- Salt
- Pepper
- 1 cup chopped onion
- 1 cup chopped red bell pepper
- 1 cup chopped green bell pepper

DIRECTIONS:

Cut the potatoes into ½-inch cubes. Place the potatoes in a large bowl of cold water and allow them to soak for at least 30 minutes, preferably an hour.

Dry out the potatoes and wipe thoroughly with paper towels. Return them to the empty bowl.

Add the canola and olive oils, paprika, and salt and pepper to flavor. Toss to fully coat the potatoes.

Transfer the potatoes to the air fryer. Cook for 20 minutes, shaking the air fryer basket every 5 minutes (a total of 4 times).

Put the onion and red and green bell peppers to the air fryer basket. Fry for an additional 3 to 4 minutes, or until the potatoes are cooked through and the peppers are soft.

Cool before serving.

NUTRITION: Calories 279 Fat 8g Carbs 50g Protein 6g

8.   FRIED CHICKEN AND WAFFLES

Basic Recipe

Preparation Time: 10 minutes

Cooking Time: 30 minutes

Servings: 4

INGREDIENTS:

- 8 whole chicken wings
- 1 teaspoon garlic powder
- Chicken seasoning or rub
- Pepper
- ½ cup all-purpose flour
- Cooking oil
- 8 frozen waffles
- Maple syrup (optional)

DIRECTIONS:

In a medium bowl, spice the chicken with the garlic powder and chicken seasoning and pepper to flavor.

Put the chicken to a sealable plastic bag and add the flour. Shake to thoroughly coat the chicken.

Sprinkle the air fryer basket with cooking oil.

With the use of tongs, put the chicken from the bag to the air fryer. It is okay to pile the chicken wings on top of each other. Sprinkle them with cooking oil. Heat for five minutes

Unlock the air fryer and shake the basket. Presume to cook the chicken. Keep shaking every 5 minutes until 20 minutes has passed and the chicken is completely cooked.

Take out the cooked chicken from the air fryer and set aside.

Wash the basket and base out with warm water. Put them back to the air fryer.

Ease the temperature of the air fryer to 370°F.

Put the frozen waffles in the air fryer. Do not pile. Depends on how big your air fryer is, you may need to cook the waffles in batches. Sprinkle the waffles with cooking oil. Cook for 6 minutes

If necessary, take out the cooked waffles from the air fryer, then repeat step 9 for the leftover waffles.

Serve the waffles with the chicken and a bit of maple syrup if desired.

NUTRITION: Calories 461 Fat 22g Carbs 45g Protein 28g

9.   SAUSAGE AND CREAM CHEESE BISCUITS

Basic Recipe

Preparation Time: 5 minutes

Cooking Time: 15 minutes

Serving: 5

INGREDIENTS:

- 12 ounces chicken breakfast sausage
- 1 (6-ounce) can biscuits
- ⅛ cup cream cheese

DIRECTION:

Form the sausage into 5 small patties.

Place the sausage patties in the air fryer. Cook for 5 minutes

Open the air fryer. Flip the patties. Cook for an additional 5 minutes

Remove the cooked sausages from the air fryer.

Separate the biscuit dough into 5 biscuits.

Place the biscuits in the air fryer. Cook for 3 minutes

Open the air fryer. Flip the biscuits. Cook for an additional 2 minutes

Remove the cooked biscuits from the air fryer.

Split each biscuit in half. Spread 1 teaspoon of cream cheese onto the bottom of each biscuit. Top with a sausage patty and the other half of the biscuit, and serve.

NUTRITION: Calories 24g Fat 13g Carbs 20g Protein 9g

10.   SPINACH AND BACON ENGLISH MUFFINS

Prep time: 5 minutes | Cook time: 10 minutes | Serves 4

- 2 strips turkey bacon, cut in half crosswise
- 2 whole-grain English muffins, split
- 1 cup fresh baby spinach, long stems removed
- ¼ ripe pear, peeled and thinly sliced
- 4 slices Provolone cheese

Put the turkey bacon strips in a perforated pan.

Select Air Fry. Set temperature to 390ºF (199ºC) and set time to 6 minutes. Select Start to begin preheating.

Once preheated, slide the pan into the oven. Flip the strips halfway through the cooking time.

When cooking is complete, the bacon should be crisp.

Remove from the oven and drain on paper towels. Set aside.

Put the muffin halves in the perforated pan.

Select Air Fry and set time to 2 minutes. Place the pan back to the oven. When done, the muffin halves will be lightly browned.

Remove the pan from the oven. Top each muffin half with ¼ of the baby spinach, several pear slices, a strip of turkey bacon, followed by a slice of cheese.

Select Bake. Set temperature to 360ºF (182ºC) and set time to 2 minutes. Place the pan back to the oven. When done, the cheese will be melted.

Serve warm.

11. HOMEMADE CHERRY BREAKFAST TARTS
Basic Recipe
Preparation Time: 15 minutes
Cooking Time: 20 minutes
Servings: 6
INGREDIENTS:
For the tarts:
- 2 refrigerated piecrusts
- ⅓ Cup cherry preserves
- 1 teaspoon cornstarch
- Cooking oil
For the frosting:
- ½ cup vanilla yogurt
- 1-ounce cream cheese
- 1 teaspoon stevia
- Rainbow sprinkles

DIRECTIONS:
To make the tarts:
Place the piecrusts on a flat surface. Make use of a knife or pizza cutter, cut each piecrust into 3 rectangles, for 6 in total. (I discard the unused dough left from slicing the edges.)

In a small bowl, combine the preserves and cornstarch. Mix well.

Scoop 1 tablespoon of the preserve mixture onto the top half of each piece of piecrust.

Fold the bottom of each piece up to close the tart. Press along the edges of each tart to seal using the back of a fork.

Sprinkle the breakfast tarts with cooking oil and place them in the air fryer. I do not recommend piling the breakfast tarts. They will stick together if piled. You may need to prepare them in two batches. Cook for 10 minutes

Allow the breakfast tarts to cool fully before removing from the air fryer.

If needed, repeat steps 5 and 6 for the remaining breakfast tarts.

To make the frosting:
In a small bowl, mix the yogurt, cream cheese, and stevia. Mix well.

Spread the breakfast tarts with frosting and top with sprinkles, and serve.

NUTRITION: Calories 119 Fat 4g Carbs 19g Protein 2g

12. OMELET FRITTATA
Basic Recipe
Preparation Time: 10 minutes
Cooking Time: 6 minutes
Servings: 2

INGREDIENTS:
- 3 eggs, lightly beaten
- 2 tbsp cheddar cheese, shredded
- 2 tbsp heavy cream
- 2 mushrooms, sliced
- 1/4 small onion, chopped
- 1/4 bell pepper, diced
- Pepper
- Salt

DIRECTIONS:
In a bowl, whisk eggs with cream, vegetables, pepper, and salt.

Preheat the air fryer to 400 F.

Pour egg mixture into the air fryer pan. Place pan in air fryer basket and cook for 5 minutes

Add shredded cheese on top of the frittata and cook for 1 minute more.

Serve and enjoy.

NUTRITION: Calories 160 Fat 10 g Carbs 4 g Protein 12 g

13. CLASSIC HASH BROWNS
Basic Recipe
Preparation Time: 15 minutes
Cooking Time: 20 minutes
Servings: 4
INGREDIENTS:
- 4 russet potatoes
- 1 teaspoon paprika
- Salt
- Pepper
- Cooking oil

DIRECTIONS:
Peel the potatoes using a vegetable peeler. Using a cheese grater shred the potatoes. If your grater has different-size holes, use the area of the tool with the largest holes.

Put the shredded potatoes in a large bowl of cold water. Let sit for 5 minutes Cold water helps remove excess starch from the potatoes. Stir to help dissolve the starch.

Dry out the potatoes and dry with paper towels or napkins. Make sure the potatoes are completely dry.

Season the potatoes with the paprika and salt and pepper to taste.

Spray the potatoes with cooking oil and transfer them to the air fryer. Cook for 20 minutes and shake the basket every 5 minutes (a total of 4 times).

Cool before serving.

NUTRITION: Calories 150 Sodium: 52mg Carbs 34g Fiber 5g Protein 4g

14. DELICIOUS BREAKFAST SOUFFLE
Basic Recipe
Preparation Time: 5 minutes
Cooking Time: 15 minutes
Servings: 4
INGREDIENTS:
- 6 eggs
- 1/3 of cup of milk
- ½ cup of shredded mozzarella cheese
- 1 tablespoon of freshly chopped parsley
- ½ cup of chopped ham
- 1 teaspoon of salt
- 1 teaspoon of black pepper
- ½ teaspoon of garlic powder

DIRECTIONS:
Grease 4 ramekins with a nonstick cooking spray. Preheat your air fryer to 350 degrees Fahrenheit.

Using a large bowl, add and stir all the ingredients until it mixes properly.

Pour the egg mixture into the greased ramekins and place it inside your air fryer.

Cook it inside your air fryer for 8 minutes. Then carefully remove the soufflé from your air fryer and allow it to cool off.

Serve and enjoy!

NUTRITION: Calories 195 Fat 15g Carbs 6g Protein 9g

15. FRIED CHEESE GRITS

Prep time: 10 minutes | Cook time: 11 minutes | Serves 4

- ⅔ cup instant grits
- 1 teaspoon salt
- 1 teaspoon freshly ground black pepper
- ¾ cup whole or 2% milk
- 3 ounces (85 g) cream cheese, at room temperature
- 1 large egg, beaten
- 1 tablespoon butter, melted
- 1 cup shredded mild Cheddar cheese
- Cooking spray

Mix the grits, salt, and black pepper in a large bowl. Add the milk, cream cheese, beaten egg, and melted butter and whisk to combine. Fold in the Cheddar cheese and stir well.

Spray a baking pan with cooking spray. Spread the grits mixture into the baking pan.

Select Air Fry. Set temperature to 400ºF (205ºC) and set time to 11 minutes. Select Start to begin preheating.

Once preheated, place the pan into the oven. Stir the mixture halfway through the cooking time.

When done, a knife inserted in the center should come out clean. Rest for 5 minutes and serve warm.

16. BREAKFAST CHEESE SANDWICHES

Prep time: 5 minutes | Cook time: 8 minutes | Serves 2

- 1 teaspoon butter, softened
- 4 slices bread
- 4 slices smoked country ham
- 4 slices Cheddar cheese
- 4 thick slices tomato

Spoon ½ teaspoon of butter onto one side of 2 slices of bread and spread it all over.

Assemble the sandwiches: Top each of 2 slices of unbuttered bread with 2 slices of ham, 2 slices of cheese, and 2 slices of tomato. Place the remaining 2 slices of bread on top, butter-side up.

Lay the sandwiches in a perforated pan, buttered side down.

Select Bake, set temperature to 370ºF (188ºC), and set time to 8 minutes. Select Start to begin preheating.

Once preheated, slide the pan into the oven. Flip the sandwiches halfway through the cooking time.

When cooking is complete, the sandwiches should be golden brown on both sides and the cheese should be melted. Remove from the oven. Allow to cool for 5 minutes before slicing to serve.

17. CANADIAN BACON MUFFIN SANDWICHES

Prep time: 5 minutes | Cook time: 8 minutes | Serves 4

- 4 English muffins, split
- 8 slices Canadian bacon
- 4 slices cheese
- Cooking spray

Make the sandwiches: Top each of 4 muffin halves with 2 slices of Canadian bacon, 1 slice of cheese, and finish with the remaining muffin half.

Put the sandwiches in a perforated pan and spritz the tops with cooking spray.

Select Bake, set temperature to 370ºF (188ºC), and set time to 8 minutes. Select Start to begin preheating.

Once preheated, slide the pan into the oven. Flip the sandwiches halfway through the cooking time.

When cooking is complete, remove the pan from the oven. Divide the sandwiches among four plates and serve warm.

18. SPICY CAULIFLOWER RICE

Basic Recipe
Preparation Time: 10 minutes
Cooking Time: 22 minutes
Servings: 2
INGREDIENTS:

- 1 cauliflower head, cut into florets
- 1/2 tsp cumin
- 1/2 tsp chili powder
- 6 onion spring, chopped
- 2 jalapenos, chopped
- 4 tbsp olive oil
- 1 zucchini, trimmed and cut into cubes
- 1/2 tsp paprika
- 1/2 tsp garlic powder
- 1/2 tsp cayenne pepper
- 1/2 tsp pepper
- 1/2 tsp salt

DIRECTIONS:

Preheat the air fryer to 370 F.

Add cauliflower florets into the food processor and process until it looks like rice.

Transfer cauliflower rice into the air fryer baking pan and Drizzle with half oil.

Place pan in the air fryer and cook for 12 minutes, stir halfway through.

Heat the remaining oil in a small pan over medium heat.

Add zucchini and cook for 5-8 minutes

Add onion and jalapenos and cook for 5 minutes

Add spices and stir well. Set aside.

Add cauliflower rice in the zucchini mixture and stir well.

 Serve and enjoy.

NUTRITION: Calories 254 Fat 28 g Carbs 12.3 g Protein 4.3 g

19. CHEESY TATER TOT BREAKFAST BAKE

Basic Recipe
Preparation Time: 5 minutes
Cooking Time: 20 minutes
Servings: 4
INGREDIENTS:

- 4 eggs
- 1 cup milk
- 1 teaspoon onion powder
- Salt
- Pepper
- Cooking oil
- 12 ounces ground chicken sausage
- 1-pound frozen tater tots
- ¾ cup shredded Cheddar cheese

DIRECTIONS:

In a medium bowl, whisk the eggs. Add the milk, onion powder, and salt and pepper to taste. Stir to combine.

Spray a skillet with cooking oil and set over medium-high heat. Add the ground sausage. Using a spatula or spoon, break the sausage into smaller pieces. Cook for 3 to 4 minutes, until the sausage is brown. Remove from heat and set aside.

Spray a barrel pan with cooking oil. Make sure to cover the bottom and sides of the pan.

Place the tater tots in the barrel pan. Cook for 6 minutes

Open the air fryer and shake the pan, then add the egg mixture and cooked sausage. Cook for an additional 6 minutes. Open the air fryer and sprinkle the cheese over the tater tot bake. Cook for an additional 2 to 3 minutes

Cool before serving.

NUTRITION: Calories 518 Fat 30g Carbs 31g Protein 30g

20. BREAKFAST SCRAMBLE CASSEROLE

Basic Recipe
Preparation Time: 20 minutes
Cooking Time: 10 minutes
Servings: 4
INGREDIENTS:
- 6 slices bacon
- 6 eggs
- Salt
- Pepper
- Cooking oil
- ½ cup chopped red bell pepper
- ½ cup chopped green bell pepper
- ½ cup chopped onion
- ¾ cup shredded Cheddar cheese

DIRECTIONS:
In a pan, over medium-high heat, cook the bacon, 5 to 7 minutes, flipping to evenly crisp. Dry out on paper towels, crumble, and set aside. In a medium bowl, whisk the eggs. Add salt and pepper to taste.
Spray a barrel pan with cooking oil. Make sure to cover the bottom and sides of the pan. Add the beaten eggs, crumbled bacon, red bell pepper, green bell pepper, and onion to the pan. Place the pan in the air fryer. Cook for 6 minutes Open the air fryer and sprinkle the cheese over the casserole. Cook for an additional 2 minutes. Cool before serving.
NUTRITION: Calories 348 Fat 26g Carbs 4g Protein 25g

21. RADISH HASH BROWNS
Basic Recipe
Preparation Time: 10 minutes
Cooking Time: 13 minutes
Servings: 4
INGREDIENTS:
- 1 lb. radishes, washed and cut off roots
- 1 tbsp olive oil
- 1/2 tsp paprika
- 1/2 tsp onion powder
- 1/2 tsp garlic powder
- 1 medium onion
- 1/4 tsp pepper
- 3/4 tsp sea salt

DIRECTIONS:
Slice onion and radishes using a mandolin slicer.
Add sliced onion and radishes in a large mixing bowl and toss with olive oil.
Transfer onion and radish slices in air fryer basket and cook at 360 F for 8 minutes Shake basket twice.
Return onion and radish slices in a mixing bowl and toss with seasonings.
Again, cook onion and radish slices in air fryer basket for 5 minutes at 400 F. Shake the basket halfway through.
Serve and enjoy.
NUTRITION: Calories 62 Fat 3.7 g Carbs 7.1 g Protein 1.2 g

22. ASPARAGUS FRITTATA
Basic Recipe
Preparation Time: 10 minutes
Cooking Time: 10 minutes
Servings: 4

INGREDIENTS:
- 6 eggs
- 3 mushrooms, sliced
- 10 asparagus, chopped
- 1/4 cup half and half
- 2 tsp butter, melted
- 1 cup mozzarella cheese, shredded
- 1 tsp pepper
- 1 tsp salt

DIRECTIONS:
Toss mushrooms and asparagus with melted butter and add into the air fryer basket. Cook mushrooms and asparagus at 350 F for 5 minutes Shake basket twice.
Meanwhile, in a bowl, whisk together eggs, half and half, pepper, and salt. Transfer cook mushrooms and asparagus into the air fryer baking dish. Pour egg mixture over mushrooms and asparagus.
Place dish in the air fryer and cook at 350 F for 5 minutes or until eggs are set. Slice and serve.
NUTRITION: Calories 211 Fat 13 g Carbs 4 g Protein 16 g

23. BREAKFAST TATER TOT CASSEROLE
Prep time: 5 minutes | Cook time: 17 to 18 minutes | Serves 4

- 4 eggs
- 1 cup milk
- Salt and pepper, to taste
- 12 ounces (340 g) ground chicken sausage
- 1 pound (454 g) frozen tater tots, thawed
- ¾ cup grated Cheddar cheese
- Cooking spray

Whisk together the eggs and milk in a medium bowl. Season with salt and pepper to taste and stir until mixed. Set aside.
Place a skillet over medium-high heat and spritz with cooking spray. Place the ground sausage in the skillet and break it into smaller pieces with a spatula or spoon. Cook for 3 to 4 minutes until the sausage starts to brown, stirring occasionally. Remove from heat and set aside.
Coat a baking pan with cooking spray. Arrange the tater tots in the baking pan.
Select Bake. Set temperature to 400°F (205°C) and set time to 14 minutes. Select Start to begin preheating.
Once preheated, slide the pan into the oven.
After 6 minutes, remove the pan from the oven. Stir the tater tots and add the egg mixture and cooked sausage. Return the pan to the oven and continue cooking.
After 6 minutes, remove the pan from the oven. Scatter the cheese on top of the tater tots. Return the pan to the oven and continue to cook another 2 minutes.
When done, the cheese should be bubbly and melted.
Let the mixture cool for 5 minutes and serve warm.

24. MINI BROWN RICE QUICHES
Prep time: 10 minutes | Cook time: 14 minutes | Serves 6

- 4 ounces (113 g) diced green chilies
- 3 cups cooked brown rice
- 1 cup shredded reduced-fat Cheddar cheese, divided
- ½ cup egg whites
- ⅓ cup fat-free milk
- ¼ cup diced pimiento
- ½ teaspoon cumin
- 1 small eggplant, cubed
- 1 bunch fresh cilantro, finely chopped
- Cooking spray

Spritz a 12-cup muffin pan with cooking spray.
In a large bowl, stir together all the ingredients, except for ½ cup of the cheese.
Scoop the mixture evenly into the muffin cups and sprinkle the remaining ½ cup of the cheese on top.
Select Bake. Set temperature to 400°F (205°C) and set time to 14 minutes. Select Start to begin preheating.
Once the unit has preheated, slide the pan into the oven.
When cooking is complete, remove the pan and check the quiches. They

should be set.

Carefully transfer the quiches to a platter and serve immediately.

25. BREAKFAST GRILLED HAM AND CHEESE

Basic Recipe

Preparation Time: 5 minutes

Cooking Time: 10 minutes

Servings: 2

INGREDIENTS:

• 1 teaspoon butter
• 4 slices bread
• 4 slices smoked country ham
• 4 slices Cheddar cheese
• 4 thick slices tomato

DIRECTIONS:

Spread ½ teaspoon of butter onto one side of 2 slices of bread. Each sandwich will have 1 slice of bread with butter and 1 slice without.

Assemble each sandwich by layering 2 slices of ham, 2 slices of cheese, and 2 slices of tomato on the unbuttered pieces of bread. Top with the other bread slices, buttered side up.

Place the sandwiches in the air fryer buttered-side down. Cook for 4 minutes

Open the air fryer. Flip the grilled cheese sandwiches. Cook for an additional 4 minutes

Cool before serving. Cut each sandwich in half and enjoy.

NUTRITION: Calories 525 Fat 25g Carbs 34g Protein 41g

26. GLAZED STRAWBERRY TOAST

Prep time: 5 minutes | Cook time: 8 minutes | Makes 4 toasts

• 4 slices bread, ½-inch thick
• 1 cup sliced strawberries
• 1 teaspoon sugar
• Cooking spray

On a clean work surface, lay the bread slices and spritz one side of each slice of bread with cooking spray.

Place the bread slices in a perforated pan, sprayed side down. Top with the strawberries and a sprinkle of sugar.

Select Air Fry, set temperature to 375°F (190°C), and set time to 8 minutes. Select Start to begin preheating.

Once preheated, slide the pan into the oven.

When cooking is complete, the toast should be well browned on each side. Remove from the oven to a plate and serve.

27. TURKEY BREAKFAST SAUSAGE PATTIES

Prep time: 5 minutes | Cook time: 10 minutes | Serves 4

• 1 tablespoon chopped fresh thyme
• 1 tablespoon chopped fresh sage
• 1¼ teaspoons kosher salt
• 1 teaspoon chopped fennel seeds
• ¾ teaspoon smoked paprika
• ½ teaspoon onion powder
• ½ teaspoon garlic powder
• ⅛ teaspoon crushed red pepper flakes
• ⅛ teaspoon freshly ground black pepper
• 1 pound (454 g) 93% lean ground turkey
• ½ cup finely minced sweet apple (peeled)

Thoroughly combine the thyme, sage, salt, fennel seeds, paprika, onion powder, garlic powder, red pepper flakes, and black pepper in a medium bowl.

Add the ground turkey and apple and stir until well incorporated. Divide the mixture into 8 equal portions and shape into patties with your hands, each about ¼ inch thick and 3 inches in diameter.

Place the patties in a perforated pan in a single layer.

Select Air Fry, set temperature to 400°F (205°C), and set time to 10 minutes. Select Start to begin preheating.

Once preheated, slide the pan into the oven. Flip the patties halfway through the cooking time.

When cooking is complete, the patties should be nicely browned and cooked through. Remove from the oven to a plate and serve warm.

28. CHEESE SOUFFLÉS

Basic Recipe

Preparation Time: 10 minutes

Cooking Time: 6 minutes

Servings: 8

INGREDIENTS:

• 6 large eggs, separated
• 3/4 cup heavy cream
• 1/4 tsp cayenne pepper
• 1/2 tsp xanthan gum
• 1/2 tsp pepper
• 1/4 tsp cream of tartar
• 2 tbsp chives, chopped
• 2 cups cheddar cheese, shredded
• 1 tsp salt

DIRECTIONS:

Preheat the air fryer to 325 F.

Spray eight ramekins with cooking spray. Set aside.

In a bowl, whisk together almond flour, cayenne pepper, pepper, salt, and xanthan gum.

Slowly add heavy cream and mix to combine.

Whisk in egg yolks, chives, and cheese until well combined.

In a large bowl, add egg whites and cream of tartar and beat until stiff peaks form.

Fold egg white mixture into the almond flour mixture until combined.

Pour mixture into the prepared ramekins. Divide ramekins in batches.

Place the first batch of ramekins into the air fryer basket.

Cook soufflé for 20 minutes

Serve and enjoy.

NUTRITION: Calories 210 Fat 16 g Carbs 1 g Protein 12 g

29. VEGETABLE EGG SOUFFLÉ

Basic Recipe

Preparation Time: 10 minutes

Cooking Time: 20 minutes

Servings: 4

INGREDIENTS:

• 4 large eggs
• 1 tsp onion powder
• 1 tsp garlic powder
• 1 tsp red pepper, crushed
• 1/2 cup broccoli florets, chopped
• 1/2 cup mushrooms, chopped

DIRECTIONS:

Sprinkle four ramekins with cooking spray and set aside.

In a bowl, whisk eggs with onion powder, garlic powder, and red pepper. Add mushrooms and broccoli and stir well.

Pour egg mixture into the prepared ramekins and place ramekins into the air fryer basket.

Cook at 350 F for 15 minutes Make sure soufflé is cooked if soufflé is not cooked then cook for 5 minutes more.

Serve and enjoy.

NUTRITION: Calories 91 Fat 5.1 g Carbs 4.7 g Protein 7.4 g

30. FRENCH TOAST STICKS

Basic Recipe

Preparation Time: 5 minutes
Cooking Time: 15 minutes
Servings: 12
INGREDIENTS:
- 4 slices Texas toast (or any thick bread, such as challah)
- 1 tablespoon butter
- 1 egg
- 1 teaspoon stevia
- 1 teaspoon ground cinnamon
- ¼ cup milk
- 1 teaspoon vanilla extract
- Cooking oil

DIRECTIONS:
Cut each slice of bread into 3 pieces (for 12 sticks total).
Place the butter in a small, microwave-safe bowl. Heat for 15 seconds, or until the butter has melted.
Remove the bowl from the microwave. Add the egg, stevia, cinnamon, milk, and vanilla extract. Whisk until fully combined.
Sprinkle the air fryer basket with cooking oil.
Dredge each of the bread sticks in the egg mixture.
Place the French toast sticks in the air fryer. It is okay to stack them.
Spray the French toast sticks with cooking oil. Cook for 8 minutes
Open the air fryer and flip each of the French toast sticks. Cook for an additional 4 minutes, or until the French toast sticks are crisp.
Cool before serving.
NUTRITION: Calories 52 Fat 2g Carbs 7g Protein 2g

31. YUMMY BREAKFAST ITALIAN FRITTATA
Basic Recipe
Preparation Time: 5 minutes
Cooking Time: 10 minutes
Servings: 6
INGREDIENTS:
- 6 eggs
- 1/3 cup of milk
- 4-ounces of chopped Italian sausage
- 3 cups of stemmed and roughly chopped kale
- 1 red deseeded and chopped bell pepper
- ½ cup of a grated feta cheese
- 1 chopped zucchini
- 1 tablespoon of freshly chopped basil
- 1 teaspoon of garlic powder
- 1 teaspoon of onion powder
- 1 teaspoon of salt
- 1 teaspoon of black pepper

DIRECTIONS:
Turn on your air fryer to 360 degrees Fahrenheit.
Grease the air fryer pan with a nonstick cooking spray.
Add the Italian sausage to the pan and cook it inside your air fryer for 5 minutes
While doing that, add and stir in the remaining ingredients until it mixes properly.
Add the egg mixture to the pan and allow it to cook inside your air fryer for 5 minutes
Thereafter carefully remove the pan and allow it to cool off until it gets chill enough to serve.
Serve and enjoy!
NUTRITION: Calories 225 Fat 14g Carbs 4.5g Protein 20g

32. CINNAMON SWEET POTATO CHIPS
Prep time: 5 minutes | Cook time: 8 minutes | Makes 6 to 8 slices

- 1 small sweet potato, cut into ⅜ inch-thick slices
- 2 tablespoons olive oil
- 1 to 2 teaspoon ground cinnamon

Add the sweet potato slices and olive oil in a bowl and toss to coat. Fold in the cinnamon and stir to combine.
Lay the sweet potato slices in a single layer in a perforated pan.
Select Air Fry, set temperature to 390ºF (199ºC), and set time to 8 minutes. Select Start to begin preheating.
Once preheated, slide the pan into the oven. Stir the potato slices halfway through the cooking time.
When cooking is complete, the chips should be crisp. Remove the pan from the oven. Allow to cool for 5 minutes before serving.

33. SPINACH AND BACON ROLL-UPS
Prep time: 5 minutes | Cook time: 8 to 9 minutes | Serves 4

- 4 flour tortillas (6- or 7-inch size)
- 4 slices Swiss cheese
- 1 cup baby spinach leaves
- 4 slices turkey bacon

Special Equipment:
4 toothpicks, soak in water for at least 30 minutes

On a clean work surface, top each tortilla with one slice of cheese and ¼ cup of spinach, then tightly roll them up.
Wrap each tortilla with a strip of turkey bacon and secure with a toothpick.
Arrange the roll-ups in a perforated pan, leaving space between each roll-up.
Select Air Fry, set temperature to 390ºF (199ºC), and set time to 8 minutes. Select Start to begin preheating.
After 4 minutes, remove the pan from the oven. Flip the roll-ups with tongs and rearrange them for more even cooking. Return to the oven and continue cooking for another 4 minutes.
Once preheated, slide the pan into the oven.
When cooking is complete, the bacon should be crisp. If necessary, continue cooking for 1 minute more. Remove the pan from the oven. Rest for 5 minutes and remove the toothpicks before serving.

34. CANADIAN BACON AND CHEESE ENGLISH MUFFINS
Basic Recipe
Preparation Time: 5 minutes
Cooking Time: 10 minutes
Servings: 4
INGREDIENTS:
- 4 English muffins
- 8 slices Canadian bacon
- 4 slices cheese
- Cooking oil

DIRECTIONS:
Split each English muffin. Assemble the breakfast sandwiches by layering 2 slices of Canadian bacon and 1 slice of cheese onto each English muffin bottom. Put the other half on top of the English muffin. Place the sandwiches in the air fryer. Spray the top of each with cooking oil. Cook for 4 minutes
Open the air fryer and flip the sandwiches. Cook for an additional 4 minutes
Cool before serving.
NUTRITION: Calories 333 Fat 14g Carbs 27g Protein 24g

35. EGG IN A HOLE

Prep time: 5 minutes | Cook time: 5 minutes | Serves 1

- 1 slice bread
- 1 teaspoon butter, softened
- 1 egg
- Salt and pepper, to taste
- 1 tablespoon shredded Cheddar cheese
- 2 teaspoons diced ham

On a flat work surface, cut a hole in the center of the bread slice with a 2½-inch-diameter biscuit cutter.

Spread the butter evenly on each side of the bread slice and transfer to a baking dish.

Crack the egg into the hole and season as desired with salt and pepper. Scatter the shredded cheese and diced ham on top.

Select Bake, set temperature to 330°F (166°C), and set time to 5 minutes. Select Start to begin preheating.

Once preheated, place the baking dish in the oven.

When cooking is complete, the bread should be lightly browned and the egg should be set. Remove from the oven and serve hot.

36. WESTERN OMELET

Prep time: 5 minutes | Cook time: 20 minutes | Serves 2

- ¼ cup chopped bell pepper, green or red
- ¼ cup chopped onion
- ¼ cup diced ham
- 1 teaspoon butter
- 4 large eggs
- 2 tablespoons milk
- ⅛ teaspoon salt
- ¾ cup shredded sharp Cheddar cheese

Put the bell pepper, onion, ham, and butter in a baking pan and mix well.

Select Air Fry. Set temperature to 390°F (199°C) and set time to 5 minutes. Select Start to begin preheating.

Once the oven has preheated, slide the pan into the oven.

After 1 minute, remove the pan from the oven. Stir the mixture. Return the pan to the oven and continue to cook another 4 minutes.

When done, the veggies should be softened.

Whisk together the eggs, milk, and salt in a bowl. Pour the egg mixture over the veggie mixture.

Select Bake. Set temperature to 360°F (182°C) and set time to 15 minutes. Place the pan in the oven.

After 14 minutes, remove the pan from the oven. Scatter the omelet with the shredded cheese. Return the pan to the oven and continue to cook another 1 minute.

When cooking is complete, the top will be lightly golden browned, the eggs will be set and the cheese will be melted.

Let the omelet cool for 5 minutes before serving.

37. CHEESY HASH BROWN CUPS

Prep time: 10 minutes | Cook time: 9 minutes | Serves 6

- 4 eggs, beaten
- 2¼ cups frozen hash browns, thawed
- 1 cup diced ham
- ½ cup shredded Cheddar cheese
- ½ teaspoon Cajun seasoning
- Cooking spray

Lightly spritz a 12-cup muffin tin with cooking spray.

Combine the beaten eggs, hash browns, diced ham, cheese, and Cajun seasoning in a medium bowl and stir until well blended.

Spoon a heaping 1½ tablespoons of egg mixture into each muffin cup.

Select Bake. Set temperature to 350°F (180°C) and set time to 9 minutes. Select Start to begin preheating.

Once preheated, place the muffin tin into the oven.

When cooked, the muffins will be golden brown.

Allow to cool for 5 to 10 minutes on a wire rack and serve warm.

38. HAM AND CHEESE TOAST

Prep time: 5 minutes | Cook time: 6 minutes | Serves: 1

- 1 slice bread
- 1 teaspoon butter, at room temperature
- 1 egg
- Salt and freshly ground black pepper, to taste
- 2 teaspoons diced ham
- 1 tablespoon grated Cheddar cheese

On a clean work surface, use a 2½-inch biscuit cutter to make a hole in the center of the bread slice with about ½-inch of bread remaining.

Spread the butter on both sides of the bread slice. Crack the egg into the hole and season with salt and pepper to taste. Transfer the bread to a perforated pan.

Select Air Fry, set temperature to 325°F (163°C), and set time to 6 minutes. Select Start to begin preheating.

Once preheated, slide the pan into the oven.

After 5 minutes, remove the pan from the oven. Scatter the cheese and diced ham on top and continue cooking for an additional 1 minute.

When cooking is complete, the egg should be set and the cheese should be melted. Remove the toast from the oven to a plate and let cool for 5 minutes before serving.

39. VANILLA GRANOLA

Prep time: 5 minutes | Cook time: 40 minutes | Serves 4

- 1 cup rolled oats
- 3 tablespoons maple syrup
- 1 tablespoon sunflower oil
- 1 tablespoon coconut sugar
- ¼ teaspoon vanilla
- ¼ teaspoon cinnamon
- ¼ teaspoon sea salt

Mix together the oats, maple syrup, sunflower oil, coconut sugar, vanilla, cinnamon, and sea salt in a medium bowl and stir to combine. Transfer the mixture to a baking pan.

Select Bake. Set temperature to 248°F (120°C) and set time to 40 minutes. Select Start to begin preheating.

Once preheated, slide the pan into the oven. Stir the granola four times during cooking.

When cooking is complete, the granola will be mostly dry and lightly browned.

Let the granola stand for 5 to 10 minutes before serving.

40. EASY BUTTERMILK BISCUITS

Prep time: 5 minutes | Cook time: 18 minutes | Makes 16 biscuits

- 2½ cups all-purpose flour
- 1 tablespoon baking powder
- 1 teaspoon kosher salt
- 1 teaspoon sugar
- ½ teaspoon baking soda
- 8 tablespoons (1 stick) unsalted butter, at room temperature
- 1 cup buttermilk, chilled

Stir together the flour, baking powder, salt, sugar, and baking powder in a large bowl.

Add the butter and stir to mix well. Pour in the buttermilk and stir with a rubber spatula just until incorporated.

Place the dough onto a lightly floured surface and roll the dough out to a disk, ½ inch thick. Cut out the biscuits with a 2-inch round cutter and re-roll any scraps until you have 16 biscuits.

Arrange the biscuits in a perforated pan in a single layer.

Select Bake. Set temperature to 325ºF (163ºC) and set time to 18 minutes. Select Start to begin preheating.

Once preheated, place the pan into the oven.

When cooked, the biscuits will be golden brown.

Remove from the oven to a plate and serve hot.

41.   PEPPERED MAPLE BACON KNOTS
Prep time: 5 minutes | Cook time: 7 to 8 minutes | Serves 6

- 1 pound (454 g) maple smoked center-cut bacon
- ¼ cup maple syrup
- ¼ cup brown sugar
- Coarsely cracked black peppercorns, to taste

On a clean work surface, tie each bacon strip in a loose knot.

Stir together the maple syrup and brown sugar in a bowl. Generously brush this mixture over the bacon knots.

Place the bacon knots in a perforated pan and sprinkle with the coarsely cracked black peppercorns.

Select Air Fry, set temperature to 390ºF (199ºC), and set time to 8 minutes. Select Start to begin preheating.

Once preheated, slide the pan into the oven.

After 5 minutes, remove the pan from the oven and flip the bacon knots. Return the pan to the oven and continue cooking for 2 to 3 minutes more. When cooking is complete, the bacon should be crisp. Remove from the oven to a paper towel-lined plate. Let the bacon knots cool for a few minutes and serve warm.

42.   CRUSTLESS   BROCCOLI QUICHE
Prep time: 5 minutes | Cook time: 10 minutes | Serves 4

- 1 cup broccoli florets
- ¾ cup chopped roasted red peppers
- 1¼ cups grated Fontina cheese
- 6 eggs
- ¾ cup heavy cream
- ½ teaspoon salt
- Freshly ground black pepper, to taste
- Cooking spray

Spritz a baking pan with cooking spray

Add the broccoli florets and roasted red peppers to the pan and scatter the grated Fontina cheese on top.

In a bowl, beat together the eggs and heavy cream. Sprinkle with salt and pepper. Pour the egg mixture over the top of the cheese. Wrap the pan in foil.

Select Air Fry. Set temperature to 325ºF (163ºC) and set time to 10 minutes. Select Start to begin preheating.

Once preheated, slide the pan into the oven.

After 8 minutes, remove the pan from the oven. Remove the foil. Return the pan to the oven and continue to cook another 2 minutes.

When cooked, the quiche should/will be golden brown.

Rest for 5 minutes before cutting into wedges and serve warm.

43.   SIMPLE EGG SOUFFLÉ
Basic Recipe
Preparation Time: 5 minutes

Cooking Time: 8 minutes
Servings: 2
INGREDIENTS:
- 2 eggs
- 1/4 tsp chili pepper
- 2 tbsp heavy cream
- 1/4 tsp pepper
- 1 tbsp parsley, chopped
- Salt

DIRECTIONS:
In a bowl, whisk eggs with remaining gradients.

Spray two ramekins with cooking spray.

Pour egg mixture into the prepared ramekins and place into the air fryer basket.

Cook soufflé at 390 F for 8 minutes

Serve and enjoy.

NUTRITION: Calories 116 Fat 10 g Carbs 1.1 g Protein 6 g

44.   OLIVES, KALE, AND PECORINO BAKED EGGS
Prep time: 5 minutes | Cook time: 11 minutes | Serves 2

- 1 cup roughly chopped kale leaves, stems and center ribs removed
- ¼ cup grated pecorino cheese
- ¼ cup olive oil
- 1 garlic clove, peeled
- 3 tablespoons whole almonds
- Kosher salt and freshly ground black pepper, to taste
- 4 large eggs
- 2 tablespoons heavy cream
- 3 tablespoons chopped pitted mixed olives

Place the kale, pecorino, olive oil, garlic, almonds, salt, and pepper in a small blender and blitz until well incorporated.

One at a time, crack the eggs in a baking pan. Drizzle the kale pesto on top of the egg whites. Top the yolks with the cream and swirl together the yolks and the pesto.

Select Bake. Set temperature to 300ºF (150ºC) and set time to 11 minutes. Select Start to begin preheating.

Once preheated, place the pan into the oven.

When cooked, the top should begin to brown and the eggs should be set. Allow the eggs to cool for 5 minutes. Scatter the olives on top and serve warm.

45.   CORNMEAL PANCAKE
Prep time: 10 minutes | Cook time: 6 minutes | Serves 4

- 1½ cups yellow cornmeal
- ½ cup all-purpose flour
- 2 tablespoons sugar
- 1 teaspoon salt
- 1 teaspoon baking powder
- 1 cup whole or 2% milk
- 1 large egg, lightly beaten
- 1 tablespoon butter, melted
- Cooking spray

Line a perforated pan with parchment paper.

Stir together the cornmeal, flour, sugar, salt, and baking powder in a large bowl. Mix in the milk, egg, and melted butter and whisk to combine.

Drop tablespoonfuls of the batter onto the parchment paper for each pancake. Spray the pancakes with cooking spray.

Select Bake. Set temperature to 350ºF (180ºC) and set time to 6 minutes. Select Start to begin preheating.

Once the oven has preheated, slide the pan into the oven. Flip the pancakes and spray with cooking spray again halfway through the cooking time.

When cooking is complete, remove the pancakes from the oven to a plate.

Cool for 5 minutes and serve immediately.

46. SAUSAGE AND CHEESE QUICHE

Prep time: 5 minutes | Cook time: 25 minutes | Serves 4

12 large eggs
1 cup heavy cream
Salt and black pepper, to taste
12 ounces (340 g) sugar-free breakfast sausage
2 cups shredded Cheddar cheese
Cooking spray

Coat a casserole dish with cooking spray.

Beat together the eggs, heavy cream, salt and pepper in a large bowl until creamy. Stir in the breakfast sausage and Cheddar cheese.

Pour the sausage mixture into the prepared casserole dish.

Select Bake. Set temperature to 375ºF (190ºC) and set time to 25 minutes. Select Start to begin preheating.

Once the oven has preheated, slide the pan into the oven.

When done, the top of the quiche should be golden brown and the eggs will be set.

Remove from the oven and let sit for 5 to 10 minutes before serving.

47. BANANA AND OAT BREAD PUDDING

Prep time: 10 minutes | Cook time: 16 minutes | Serves 4

• 2 medium ripe bananas, mashed
• ½ cup low-fat milk
• 2 tablespoons maple syrup
• 2 tablespoons peanut butter
• 1 teaspoon vanilla extract
• 1 teaspoon ground cinnamon
• 2 slices whole-grain bread, cut into bite-sized cubes
• ¼ cup quick oats
• Cooking spray

Spritz a baking dish lightly with cooking spray.

Mix the bananas, milk, maple syrup, peanut butter, vanilla, and cinnamon in a large mixing bowl and stir until well incorporated.

Add the bread cubes to the banana mixture and stir until thoroughly coated. Fold in the oats and stir to combine.

Transfer the mixture to the baking dish. Wrap the baking dish in aluminum foil.

Select Air Fry. Set temperature to 350ºF (180ºC) and set time to 16 minutes. Select Start to begin preheating.

Once the oven has preheated, slide the pan into the oven.

After 10 minutes, remove the pan from the oven. Remove the foil. Return the pan to the oven and continue to cook another 6 minutes.

When done, the pudding should be set.

Let the pudding cool for 5 minutes before serving.

48. BOURBON VANILLA FRENCH TOAST

Prep time: 15 minutes | Cook time: 6 minutes | Serves 4

• 2 large eggs
• 2 tablespoons water
• ⅔ cup whole or 2% milk
• 1 tablespoon butter, melted
• 2 tablespoons bourbon
• 1 teaspoon vanilla extract
• 8 (1-inch-thick) French bread slices
• Cooking spray

Line a perforated pan with parchment paper and spray it with cooking spray.

Beat the eggs with the water in a shallow bowl until combined. Add the milk, melted butter, bourbon, and vanilla and stir to mix well.

Dredge 4 slices of bread in the batter, turning to coat both sides evenly. Transfer the bread slices onto the parchment paper.

Select Bake. Set temperature to 320ºF (160ºC) and set time to 6 minutes. Select Start to begin preheating.

Once the oven has preheated, slide the pan into the oven. Flip the slices halfway through the cooking time.

When cooking is complete, the bread slices should be nicely browned.

Remove from the oven to a plate and serve warm.

49. TOMATO-CORN FRITTATA WITH AVOCADO DRESSING

Prep time: 10 minutes | Cook time: 20 minutes | Serves 2 or 3

• ½ cup cherry tomatoes, halved
• Kosher salt and freshly ground black pepper, to taste
• 6 large eggs, lightly beaten
• ½ cup fresh corn kernels
• ¼ cup milk
• 1 tablespoon finely chopped fresh dill
• ½ cup shredded Monterey Jack cheese
• Avocado Dressing:
• 1 ripe avocado, pitted and peeled
• 2 tablespoons fresh lime juice
• ¼ cup olive oil
• 1 scallion, finely chopped
• 8 fresh basil leaves, finely chopped

Put the tomato halves in a colander and lightly season with salt. Set aside for 10 minutes to drain well. Pour the tomatoes into a large bowl and fold in the eggs, corn, milk, and dill. Sprinkle with salt and pepper and stir until mixed.

Pour the egg mixture into a baking pan.

Select Bake. Set temperature to 300ºF (150ºC) and set time to 15 minutes. Select Start to begin preheating.

Once the oven has preheated, slide the pan into the oven.

When done, remove the pan from the oven. Scatter the cheese on top.

Select Bake. Set temperature to 315ºF (157ºC) and set time to 5 minutes. Return the pan back to the oven.

When cooking is complete, the frittata will be puffy and set.

Meanwhile, make the avocado dressing: Mash the avocado with the lime juice in a medium bowl until smooth. Mix in the olive oil, scallion, and basil and stir until well incorporated.

Let the frittata cool for 5 minutes and serve alongside the avocado dressing.

50. RICE, SHRIMP, AND SPINACH FRITTATA

Prep time: 15 minutes | Cook time: 16 minutes | Serves 4

• 4 eggs
• Pinch salt
• ½ cup cooked rice
• ½ cup chopped cooked shrimp
• ½ cup baby spinach
• ½ cup grated Monterey Jack cheese
• Nonstick cooking spray

Spritz a baking pan with nonstick cooking spray.

Whisk the eggs and salt in a small bowl until frothy.

Place the cooked rice, shrimp, and baby spinach in the baking pan. Pour in the whisked eggs and scatter the cheese on top.

Select Bake. Set temperature to 320ºF (160ºC) and set time to 16 minutes. Select Start to begin preheating.

Once the oven has preheated, slide the pan into the oven.

When cooking is complete, the frittata should be golden and puffy.

Let the frittata cool for 5 minutes before slicing to serve.

51. CHEESY BREAKFAST CASSEROLE

Prep time: 10 minutes | Cook time: 16 minutes | Serves 4

- 6 slices bacon
- 6 eggs
- Salt and pepper, to taste
- Cooking spray
- ½ cup chopped green bell pepper
- ½ cup chopped onion
- ¾ cup shredded Cheddar cheese

Place the bacon in a skillet over medium-high heat and cook each side for about 4 minutes until evenly crisp. Remove from the heat to a paper towel-lined plate to drain. Crumble it into small pieces and set aside.

Whisk the eggs with the salt and pepper in a medium bowl.

Spritz a baking pan with cooking spray.

Place the whisked eggs, crumbled bacon, green bell pepper, and onion in the prepared pan.

Select Bake. Set temperature to 400ºF (205ºC) and set time to 8 minutes. Select Start to begin preheating.

Once preheated, place the pan into the oven.

After 6 minutes, remove the pan from the oven. Scatter the Cheddar cheese all over. Return the pan to the oven and continue to cook another 2 minutes.

When cooking is complete, let sit for 5 minutes and serve on plates.

52. MIXED BERRY DUTCH BABY PANCAKE

Prep time: 10 minutes | Cook time: 14 minutes | Serves 4

- 1 tablespoon unsalted butter, at room temperature
- 1 egg
- 2 egg whites
- ½ cup 2% milk
- ½ cup whole-wheat pastry flour
- 1 teaspoon pure vanilla extract
- 1 cup sliced fresh strawberries
- ½ cup fresh raspberries
- ½ cup fresh blueberries

Grease a baking pan with the butter.

Using a hand mixer, beat together the egg, egg whites, milk, pastry flour, and vanilla in a medium mixing bowl until well incorporated.

Pour the batter into the pan.

Select Bake. Set temperature to 330ºF (166ºC) and set time to 14 minutes. Select Start to begin preheating.

Once the oven has preheated, slide the pan into the oven.

When cooked, the pancake should puff up in the center and the edges should be golden brown

Allow the pancake to cool for 5 minutes and serve topped with the berries.

53. BACON AND EGG BREAD CUPS

Prep time: 10 minutes | Cook time: 10 minutes | Serves 4

- 4 (3-by-4-inch) crusty rolls
- 4 thin slices Gouda or Swiss cheese mini wedges
- 5 eggs
- 2 tablespoons heavy cream
- 3 strips precooked bacon, chopped
- ½ teaspoon dried thyme
- Pinch salt

- Freshly ground black pepper, to taste

On a clean work surface, cut the tops off the rolls. Using your fingers, remove the insides of the rolls to make bread cups, leaving a ½-inch shell. Place a slice of cheese onto each roll bottom.

Whisk together the eggs and heavy cream in a medium bowl until well combined. Fold in the bacon, thyme, salt, and pepper and stir well.

Scrape the egg mixture into the prepared bread cups.

Select Bake. Set temperature to 330ºF (166ºC) and set time to 10 minutes. Select Start to begin preheating.

Once preheated, place the bread cups into the oven.

When cooked, the eggs should be cooked to your preference.

Serve warm.

54. MEXICAN BREAKFAST PEPPER RINGS

Basic Recipe

Preparation Time: 5 minutes

Cooking Time: 10 minutes

Serving : 4

INGREDIENTS:

- Olive oil
- 1 large red, yellow, or orange bell pepper, cut into four ¾-inch rings
- 4 eggs
- Salt
- Freshly ground black pepper
- 2 teaspoons salsa

DIRECTIONS:

Lightly spray a small round air fryer–friendly pan with olive oil.

Place 2 bell pepper rings on the pan. Crack one egg into each bell pepper ring. Season it with salt and black pepper.

Spoon ½ teaspoon of salsa on top of each egg. Place the pan in the fryer basket. Air fry until the yolk is slightly runny, 5 to 6 minutes or until the yolk is fully cooked, 8 to 10 minutes

Repeat with the remaining 2 pepper rings. Serve hot.

Pair It With: Turkey sausage or turkey bacon make this a heartier morning meal.

Air Fry Like A Pro: Use a silicone spatula to easily move the rings from the pan to your plate.

NUTRITION: Calories 84 Fat 5g Saturated Fat 2g Cholesterol 186mg Carbs 3g Protein 7g Fiber 1g Sodium: 83mg

55. SIMPLE MONKEY BREAD

Prep time: 5 minutes | Cook time: 8 minutes | Serves 4

- 1 (8-ounce / 227-g) can refrigerated biscuits
- 3 tablespoons melted unsalted butter
- ¼ cup white sugar
- 3 tablespoons brown sugar
- ½ teaspoon cinnamon
- ⅛ teaspoon nutmeg

On a clean work surface, cut each biscuit into 4 pieces.

In a shallow bowl, place the melted butter. In another shallow bowl, stir together the white sugar, brown sugar, cinnamon, and nutmeg until combined.

Dredge the biscuits, one at a time, in the melted butter, then roll them in the sugar mixture to coat well. Spread the biscuits evenly in a baking pan.

Select Bake. Set temperature to 350ºF (180ºC) and set time to 8 minutes. Select Start to begin preheating.

Once the oven has preheated, place the pan into the oven.

When cooked, the biscuits should be golden brown.

Cool for 5 minutes before serving.

56. WHOLE-WHEAT BLUEBERRY SCONES

Prep time: 5 minutes | Cook time: 20 minutes | Serves 14

- ½ cup low-fat buttermilk
- ¾ cup orange juice
- Zest of 1 orange
- 2¼ cups whole-wheat pastry flour
- ⅓ cup agave nectar
- ¼ cup canola oil
- 1 teaspoon baking soda
- 1 teaspoon cream of tartar
- 1 cup fresh blueberries

In a small bowl, stir together the buttermilk, orange juice and orange zest.

In a large bowl, whisk together the flour, agave nectar, canola oil, baking soda and cream of tartar.

Add the buttermilk mixture and blueberries to the bowl with the flour mixture. Mix gently by hand until well combined.

Transfer the batter onto a lightly floured baking sheet. Pat into a circle about ¾ inch thick and 8 inches across. Use a knife to cut the circle into 14 wedges, cutting almost all the way through.

Select Bake. Set temperature to 375ºF (190ºC) and set time to 20 minutes. Select Start to begin preheating.

Once the unit has preheated, slide the baking sheet into the oven.

When cooking is complete, remove the pan and check the scones. They should be lightly browned.

Let rest for 5 minutes and cut completely through the wedges before serving.

57. FRENCH TOAST STICKS

Prep time: 5 minutes | Cook time: 12 minutes | Serves 4

- 3 slices low-sodium whole-wheat bread, each cut into 4 strips
- 1 tablespoon unsalted butter, melted
- 1 tablespoon 2 percent milk
- 1 tablespoon sugar
- 1 egg, beaten
- 1 egg white
- 1 cup sliced fresh strawberries
- 1 tablespoon freshly squeezed lemon juice

Arrange the bread strips on a plate and drizzle with the melted butter.

In a bowl, whisk together the milk, sugar, egg and egg white.

Dredge the bread strips into the egg mixture and place on a wire rack to let the batter drip off. Arrange half the coated bread strips on the sheet pan.

Select Air Fry. Set temperature to 380ºF (193ºC) and set time to 6 minutes. Select Start to begin preheating.

Once preheated, slide the pan into the oven.

After 3 minutes, remove the pan from the oven. Use a tong to turn the strips over. Rotate the pan and return the pan to the oven to continue cooking.

When cooking is complete, the strips should be golden brown. Repeat with the remaining strips.

In a small bowl, mash the strawberries with a fork and stir in the lemon juice. Serve the French toast sticks with the strawberry sauce.

58. MAPLE WALNUT PANCAKE

Prep time: 10 minutes | Cook time: 20 minutes | Serves 4

- 3 tablespoons melted butter, divided
- 1 cup flour
- 2 tablespoons sugar
- 1½ teaspoons baking powder
- ¼ teaspoon salt
- 1 egg, beaten
- ¾ cup milk
- 1 teaspoon pure vanilla extract

- ½ cup roughly chopped walnuts
- Maple syrup or fresh sliced fruit, for serving

Grease a baking pan with 1 tablespoon of melted butter.

Mix together the flour, sugar, baking powder, and salt in a medium bowl.

Add the beaten egg, milk, the remaining 2 tablespoons of melted butter, and vanilla and stir until the batter is sticky but slightly lumpy.

Slowly pour the batter into the greased baking pan and scatter with the walnuts.

Select Bake. Set temperature to 330ºF (166ºC) and set time to 20 minutes. Select Start to begin preheating.

Once preheated, place the pan into the oven.

When cooked, the pancake should/will be golden brown and cooked through.

Let the pancake rest for 5 minutes and serve topped with the maple syrup or fresh fruit, if desired.

59. VEGGIE FRITTATA

Prep time: 10 minutes | Cook time: 12 minutes | Serves 4

- ½ cup chopped red bell pepper
- ⅓ cup grated carrot
- ⅓ cup minced onion
- 1 teaspoon olive oil
- 1 egg
- 6 egg whites
- ⅓ cup 2% milk
- 1 tablespoon shredded Parmesan cheese

Mix together the red bell pepper, carrot, onion, and olive oil in a baking pan and stir to combine.

Select Bake. Set temperature to 350ºF (180ºC) and set time to 12 minutes. Select Start to begin preheating.

Once preheated, place the pan into the oven.

After 3 minutes, remove the pan from the oven. Stir the vegetables. Return the pan to the oven and continue cooking.

Meantime, whisk together the egg, egg whites, and milk in a medium bowl until creamy.

After 3 minutes, remove the pan from the oven. Pour the egg mixture over the top and scatter with the Parmesan cheese. Return the pan to the oven and continue cooking for additional 6 minutes.

When cooking is complete, the eggs will be set and the top will be golden around the edges.

Allow the frittata to cool for 5 minutes before slicing and serving.

60. BREAKFAST BLUEBERRY COBBLER

Prep time: 5 minutes | Cook time: 15 minutes | Serves 4

- ¾ teaspoon baking powder
- ⅓ cup whole-wheat pastry flour
- Dash sea salt
- ⅓ cup unsweetened nondairy milk
- 2 tablespoons maple syrup
- ½ teaspoon vanilla
- Cooking spray
- ½ cup blueberries
- ¼ cup granola
- Nondairy yogurt, for topping (optional)

Spritz a baking pan with cooking spray.

Mix together the baking powder, flour, and salt in a medium bowl. Add the milk, maple syrup, and vanilla and whisk to combine.

Scrape the mixture into the prepared pan. Scatter the blueberries and granola on top.

Select Bake. Set temperature to 347ºF (175ºC) and set time to 15 minutes. Select Start to begin preheating.

Once preheated, place the pan into the oven.

When done, the top should begin to brown and a knife inserted in the center should come out clean.

Let the cobbler cool for 5 minutes and serve with a drizzle of nondairy yogurt.

61. WHOLE-WHEAT MUFFINS WITH BLUEBERRIES

Prep time: 5 minutes | Cook time: 25 minutes | Makes 8 muffins

- ½ cup unsweetened applesauce
- ½ cup plant-based milk
- ½ cup maple syrup
- 1 teaspoon vanilla extract
- 2 cups whole-wheat flour
- ½ teaspoon baking soda
- 1 cup blueberries
- Cooking spray

Spritz a 8-cup muffin pan with cooking spray.

In a large bowl, stir together the applesauce, milk, maple syrup and vanilla extract. Whisk in the flour and baking soda until no dry flour is left and the batter is smooth. Gently mix in the blueberries until they are evenly distributed throughout the batter.

Spoon the batter into the muffin cups, three-quarters full.

Select Bake. Set temperature to 375°F (190°C) and set time to 25 minutes. Select Start to begin preheating.

When cooking is complete, remove the pan and check the muffins. You can stick a knife into the center of a muffin and it should come out clean. Let rest for 5 minutes before serving.

62. EGGS IN BELL PEPPER RINGS

Prep time: 5 minutes | Cook time: 7 minutes | Serves 4

- 1 large red, yellow, or orange bell pepper, cut into four ¾-inch rings
- 4 eggs
- Salt and freshly ground black pepper, to taste
- 2 teaspoons salsa
- Cooking spray

Coat a baking pan lightly with cooking spray.

Put 4 bell pepper rings in the prepared baking pan. Crack one egg into each bell pepper ring and sprinkle with salt and pepper. Top each egg with ½ teaspoon of salsa.

Select Air Fry. Set temperature to 350°F (180°C) and set time to 7 minutes. Select Start to begin preheating.

Once preheated, place the pan into the oven.

When done, the eggs should be cooked to your desired doneness.

Remove the rings from the pan to a plate and serve warm.

63. SPINACH, LEEK AND CHEESE FRITTATA

Prep time: 10 minutes | Cook time: 22 minutes | Serves 2

- 4 large eggs
- 4 ounces (113 g) baby bella mushrooms, chopped
- 1 cup (1 ounce / 28-g) baby spinach, chopped
- ½ cup (2 ounces / 57-g) shredded Cheddar cheese
- ⅓ cup (from 1 large) chopped leek, white part only
- ¼ cup halved grape tomatoes
- 1 tablespoon 2% milk
- ¼ teaspoon dried oregano
- ¼ teaspoon garlic powder
- ½ teaspoon kosher salt
- Freshly ground black pepper, to taste
- Cooking spray

Lightly spritz a baking dish with cooking spray.

Whisk the eggs in a large bowl until frothy. Add the mushrooms, baby spinach, cheese, leek, tomatoes, milk, oregano, garlic powder, salt, and pepper and stir until well blended. Pour the mixture into the prepared baking dish.

Select Bake. Set temperature to 300°F (150°C) and set time to 22 minutes. Select Start to begin preheating.

Once the oven has preheated, slide the pan into the oven.

When cooked, the center will be puffed up and the top will be golden brown.

Let the frittata cool for 5 minutes before slicing to serve.

64. CHEESY HASH BROWN CASSEROLE

Prep time: 15 minutes | Cook time: 30 minutes | Serves 4

- 3½ cups frozen hash browns, thawed
- 1 teaspoon salt
- 1 teaspoon freshly ground black pepper
- 3 tablespoons butter, melted
- 1 (10.5-ounce / 298-g) can cream of chicken soup
- ½ cup sour cream
- 1 cup minced onion
- ½ cup shredded sharp Cheddar cheese
- Cooking spray

Put the hash browns in a large bowl and season with salt and black pepper. Add the melted butter, cream of chicken soup, and sour cream and stir until well incorporated. Mix in the minced onion and cheese and stir well.

Spray a baking pan with cooking spray.

Spread the hash brown mixture evenly into the baking pan.

Select Bake. Set temperature to 325°F (163°C) and set time to 30 minutes. Select Start to begin preheating.

Once the oven has preheated, place the pan into the oven.

When cooked, the hash brown mixture will be browned.

Cool for 5 minutes before serving.

65. PEANUT BUTTER–PUMPKIN MUFFINS

Prep time: 10 minutes | Cook time: 25 minutes | Serves 2

- 2 tablespoons powdered peanut butter
- 2 tablespoons finely ground flaxseeds
- 2 tablespoons coconut flour
- 1 tablespoon dried cranberries
- 1 teaspoon pumpkin pie spice
- ½ teaspoon baking powder
- ½ cup water
- 1 cup canned pumpkin
- 2 large eggs
- ½ teaspoon vanilla extract
- Cooking spray

In a bowl, stir together the powdered peanut butter, flaxseeds, coconut flour, dried cranberries, pumpkin pie spice, baking powder and water.

In another bowl, stir together the pumpkin and eggs until smooth.

Add the pumpkin mixture to the peanut butter mixture. Stir to combine.

Add the vanilla extract to the bowl. Mix together well.

Spritz 2 ramekins with cooking spray. Spoon half of the batter into each ramekin. Place the ramekins on the sheet pan.

Select Bake. Set temperature to 350°F (180°C) and set time to 25 minutes. Select Start to begin preheating.

Once the unit has preheated, slide the pan into the oven.

When cooking is complete, a toothpick inserted in the center should come out clean. Serve immediately.

66. EGG AND AVOCADO BURRITO

Prep time: 10 minutes | Cook time: 4 minutes | Serves 4

- 4 low-sodium whole-wheat flour tortillas

Filling:
- 1 hard-boiled egg, chopped
- 2 hard-boiled egg whites, chopped
- 1 ripe avocado, peeled, pitted, and chopped
- 1 red bell pepper, chopped
- 1 (1.2-ounce / 34-g) slice low-sodium, low-fat American cheese, torn into pieces
- 3 tablespoons low-sodium salsa, plus additional for serving (optional)

Special Equipment:

4 toothpicks (optional), soaked in water for at least 30 minutes

Make the filling: Combine the egg, egg whites, avocado, red bell pepper, cheese, and salsa in a medium bowl and stir until blended.

Assemble the burritos: Arrange the tortillas on a clean work surface and place ¼ of the prepared filling in the middle of each tortilla, leaving about 1½-inch on each end unfilled. Fold in the opposite sides of each tortilla and roll up. Secure with toothpicks through the center, if needed. Transfer the burritos to a perforated pan.

Select Air Fry. Set temperature to 390°F (199°C) and set time to 4 minutes. Select Start to begin preheating.

Once the oven has preheated, slide the pan into the oven.

When cooking is complete, the burritos should be crisp and golden brown.

Allow to cool for 5 minutes and serve with salsa, if desired.

67. FRIED POTATOES WITH PEPPERS AND ONIONS

Prep time: 10 minutes | Cook time: 35 minutes | Serves 4

- 1 pound (454 g) red potatoes, cut into ½-inch dices
- 1 large red bell pepper, cut into ½-inch dices
- 1 large green bell pepper, cut into ½-inch dices
- 1 medium onion, cut into ½-inch dices
- 1½ tablespoons extra-virgin olive oil
- 1¼ teaspoons kosher salt
- ¾ teaspoon sweet paprika
- ¾ teaspoon garlic powder
- Freshly ground black pepper, to taste

Mix together the potatoes, bell peppers, onion, oil, salt, paprika, garlic powder, and black pepper in a large mixing and toss to coat.

Transfer the potato mixture to a perforated pan.

Select Air Fry. Set temperature to 350°F (180°C) and set time to 35 minutes. Select Start to begin preheating.

Once preheated, slide the pan into the oven. Stir the potato mixture three times during cooking.

When done, the potatoes should be nicely browned.

Remove from the oven to a plate and serve warm.

68. ASPARAGUS AND CHEESE STRATA

Prep time: 10 minutes | Cook time: 17 minutes | Serves 4

- 6 asparagus spears, cut into 2-inch pieces
- 1 tablespoon water
- 2 slices whole-wheat bread, cut into ½-inch cubes
- 4 eggs
- 3 tablespoons whole milk
- 2 tablespoons chopped flat-leaf parsley
- ½ cup grated Havarti or Swiss cheese
- Pinch salt
- Freshly ground black pepper, to taste
- Cooking spray

Add the asparagus spears and 1 tablespoon of water in a baking pan.

Select Bake. Set temperature to 330°F (166°C) and set time to 4 minutes. Select Start to begin preheating.

Once preheated, place the pan into the oven.

When cooking is complete, the asparagus spears will be crisp-tender. Remove the asparagus from the pan and drain on paper towels.

Spritz the pan with cooking spray. Place the bread and asparagus in the pan.

Whisk together the eggs and milk in a medium mixing bowl until creamy. Fold in the parsley, cheese, salt, and pepper and stir to combine. Pour this mixture into the baking pan.

Select Bake and set time to 13 minutes. Place the pan back to the oven. When done, the eggs will be set and the top will be lightly browned.

Let cool for 5 minutes before slicing and serving.

69. BAKED AVOCADO WITH EGGS

Prep time: 5 minutes | Cook time: 9 minutes | Serves 2

- 1 large avocado, halved and pitted
- 2 large eggs
- 2 tomato slices, divided
- ½ cup nonfat Cottage cheese, divided
- ½ teaspoon fresh cilantro, for garnish

Line the sheet pan with the aluminium foil.

Slice a thin piece from the bottom of each avocado half so they sit flat. Remove a small amount from each avocado half to make a bigger hole to hold the egg.

Arrange the avocado halves on the pan, hollow-side up. Break 1 egg into each half. Top each half with 1 tomato slice and ¼ cup of the Cottage cheese.

Select Bake. Set temperature to 425°F (220°C) and set time to 9 minutes. Select Start to begin preheating.

Once the unit has preheated, slide the pan into the oven.

When cooking is complete, remove the pan from the oven. Garnish with the fresh cilantro and serve.

70. CARROT BANANA MUFFIN

Prep time: 10 minutes | Cook time: 20 minutes | Serves 12

- 1½ cups whole-wheat flour
- 1 cup grated carrot
- 1 cup mashed banana
- ½ cup bran
- ½ cup low-fat buttermilk
- 2 tablespoons agave nectar
- 2 teaspoons baking powder
- 1 teaspoon vanilla
- 1 teaspoon baking soda
- ½ teaspoon nutmeg
- Pinch cloves
- 2 egg whites

Line a muffin pan with 12 paper liners.

In a large bowl, stir together all the ingredients. Mix well, but do not over beat.

Scoop the mixture into the muffin cups.

Select Bake. Set temperature to 400°F (205°C) and set time to 20 minutes. Select Start to begin preheating.

Once the unit has preheated, slide the pan into the oven.

When cooking is complete, remove the pan and let rest for 5 minutes.

Serve warm or at room temperature.

71. CHOCOLATE BANANA BREAD

Prep time: 10 minutes | Cook time: 30 minutes | Serves 4

- ¼ cup cocoa powder

- 6 tablespoons plus 2 teaspoons all-purpose flour, divided
- ½ teaspoon kosher salt
- ¼ teaspoon baking soda
- 1½ ripe bananas
- 1 large egg, whisked
- ¼ cup vegetable oil
- ½ cup sugar
- 3 tablespoons buttermilk or plain yogurt (not Greek)
- ½ teaspoon vanilla extract
- 6 tablespoons chopped white chocolate
- 6 tablespoons chopped walnuts

Mix together the cocoa powder, 6 tablespoons of the flour, salt, and baking soda in a medium bowl.

Mash the bananas with a fork in another medium bowl until smooth. Fold in the egg, oil, sugar, buttermilk, and vanilla, and whisk until thoroughly combined. Add the wet mixture to the dry mixture and stir until well incorporated.

Combine the white chocolate, walnuts, and the remaining 2 tablespoons of flour in a third bowl and toss to coat. Add this mixture to the batter and stir until well incorporated. Pour the batter into a baking pan and smooth the top with a spatula.

Select Bake. Set temperature to 310ºF (154ºC) and set time to 30 minutes. Select Start to begin preheating.

Once the oven has preheated, slide the pan into the oven.

When done, a toothpick inserted into the center of the bread should come out clean.

Remove from the oven and allow to cool on a wire rack for 10 minutes before serving.

72. COCONUT BROWN RICE PORRIDGE WITH DATES

Prep time: 5 minutes | Cook time: 23 minutes | Serves 1 or 2

- ½ cup cooked brown rice
- 1 cup canned coconut milk
- ¼ cup unsweetened shredded coconut
- ¼ cup packed dark brown sugar
- 4 large Medjool dates, pitted and roughly chopped
- ½ teaspoon kosher salt
- ¼ teaspoon ground cardamom
- Heavy cream, for serving (optional)

Place all the ingredients except the heavy cream in a baking pan and stir until blended.

Select Bake. Set temperature to 375ºF (190ºC) and set time to 23 minutes. Select Start to begin preheating.

Once the oven has preheated, slide the pan into the oven. Stir the porridge halfway through the cooking time.

When cooked, the porridge will be thick and creamy.

Remove from the oven and ladle the porridge into bowls.

Serve hot with a drizzle of the cream, if desired.

73. CHICKEN BREAKFAST SAUSAGES

Prep time: 15 minutes | Cook time: 10 minutes | Makes 8 patties

- 1 Granny Smith apple, peeled and finely chopped
- 2 tablespoons apple juice
- 2 garlic cloves, minced
- 1 egg white
- ⅓ cup minced onion
- 3 tablespoons ground almonds
- ⅛ teaspoon freshly ground black pepper
- 1 pound (454 g) ground chicken breast

Combine all the ingredients except the chicken in a medium mixing bowl

and stir well.

Add the chicken breast to the apple mixture and mix with your hands until well incorporated.

Divide the mixture into 8 equal portions and shape into patties. Arrange the patties in a perforated pan.

Select Air Fry. Set temperature to 330ºF (166ºC) and set time to 10 minutes. Select Start to begin preheating.

Once the oven has preheated, slide the pan into the oven.

When done, a meat thermometer inserted in the center of the chicken should reach at least 165ºF (74ºC).

Remove from the oven to a plate. Let the chicken cool for 5 minutes and serve warm.

74. SPICY APPLE TURNOVERS

Prep time: 10 minutes | Cook time: 20 minutes | Serves 4

- 1 cup diced apple
- 1 tablespoon brown sugar
- 1 teaspoon freshly squeezed lemon juice
- 1 teaspoon all-purpose flour, plus more for dusting
- ¼ teaspoon cinnamon
- ⅛ teaspoon allspice
- ½ package frozen puff pastry, thawed
- 1 large egg, beaten
- 2 teaspoons granulated sugar

Whisk together the apple, brown sugar, lemon juice, flour, cinnamon and allspice in a medium bowl.

On a clean work surface, lightly dust with the flour and lay the puff pastry sheet. Using a rolling pin, gently roll the dough to smooth out the folds, seal any tears and form it into a square. Cut the dough into four squares. Spoon a quarter of the apple mixture into the center of each puff pastry square and spread it evenly in a triangle shape over half the pastry, leaving a border of about ½ inch around the edges of the pastry. Fold the pastry diagonally over the filling to form triangles. With a fork, crimp the edges to seal them. Place the turnovers on the sheet pan, spacing them evenly.

Cut two or three small slits in the top of each turnover. Brush with the egg. Sprinkle evenly with the granulated sugar.

Select Bake. Set temperature to 350ºF (180ºC) and set time to 20 minutes. Select Start to begin preheating.

Once the unit has preheated, slide the pan into the oven.

After 10 to 12 minutes, remove the pan from the oven. Check the pastries. If they are browned unevenly, rotate the pan. Return the pan to the oven and continue cooking.

When cooking is complete, remove the pan from the oven. The turnovers should be golden brown and the filling bubbling. Let cool for about 10 minutes before serving.

75. ZUCCHINI MUFFINS

Basic Recipe
Preparation Time: 10 minutes
Cooking Time: 20 minutes
Servings: 8
INGREDIENTS:
- 6 eggs
- 4 drops stevia
- 1/4 cup Swerve
- 1/3 cup coconut oil, melted
- 1 cup zucchini, grated
- 3/4 cup coconut flour
- 1/4 tsp ground nutmeg
- 1 tsp ground cinnamon
- 1/2 tsp baking soda

DIRECTIONS:
Preheat the air fryer to 325 F.
Add all ingredients except zucchini in a bowl and mix well.

Add zucchini and stir well.

Pour batter into the silicone muffin molds and place into the air fryer basket.

Cook muffins for 20 minutes

Serve and enjoy.

NUTRITION: Calories 136 Fat 12 g Carbs 1 g Protein 4 g

76. EGG FLORENTINE WITH SPINACH

Prep time: 10 minutes | Cook time: 15 minutes | Serves 4

- 3 cups frozen spinach, thawed and drained
- 2 tablespoons heavy cream
- ¼ teaspoon kosher salt
- ⅛ teaspoon freshly ground black pepper
- 4 ounces (113 g) Ricotta cheese
- 2 garlic cloves, minced
- ½ cup panko bread crumbs
- 3 tablespoons grated Parmesan cheese
- 2 teaspoons unsalted butter, melted
- 4 large eggs

In a medium bowl, whisk together the spinach, heavy cream, salt, pepper, Ricotta cheese and garlic.

In a small bowl, whisk together the bread crumbs, Parmesan cheese and butter. Set aside.

Spoon the spinach mixture on the sheet pan and form four even circles.

Select Roast. Set temperature to 375ºF (190ºC) and set time to 15 minutes. Select Start to begin preheating.

Once the unit has preheated, slide the pan into the oven.

After 8 minutes, press Cancel and remove the pan. The spinach should be bubbling. With the back of a large spoon, make indentations in the spinach for the eggs. Crack the eggs into the indentations and sprinkle the panko mixture over the surface of the eggs.

Return the pan to the oven and press Start to continue cooking.

When cooking is complete, remove the pan from the oven. Serve hot.

77. CORNED BEEF HASH WITH EGGS

Prep time: 10 minutes | Cook time: 25 minutes | Serves 4

- 2 medium Yukon Gold potatoes, peeled and cut into ¼-inch cubes
- 1 medium onion, chopped
- ⅓ cup diced red bell pepper
- 3 tablespoons vegetable oil
- ½ teaspoon dried thyme
- ½ teaspoon kosher salt, divided
- ½ teaspoon freshly ground black pepper, divided
- ¾ pound (340 g) corned beef, cut into ¼-inch pieces
- 4 large eggs

In a large bowl, stir together the potatoes, onion, red pepper, vegetable oil, thyme, ¼ teaspoon of the salt and ¼ teaspoon of the pepper. Spread the vegetable mixture on the sheet pan in an even layer.

Select Roast. Set temperature to 375ºF (190ºC) and set time to 25 minutes. Select Start to begin preheating.

Once the unit has preheated, slide the pan into the oven.

After 15 minutes, remove the pan from the oven and add the corned beef. Stir the mixture to incorporate the corned beef. Return the pan to the oven and continue cooking.

After 5 minutes, remove the pan from the oven. Using a large spoon, create 4 circles in the hash to hold the eggs. Gently crack an egg into each circle. Season the eggs with the remaining ¼ teaspoon of the salt and ¼ teaspoon of the pepper. Return the pan to the oven. Continue cooking for 3 to 5 minutes, depending on how you like your eggs.

When cooking is complete, remove the pan from the oven. Serve immediately.

78. EASY FRENCH TOAST CASSEROLE

Prep time: 5 minutes | Cook time: 12 minutes | Serves 6

- 3 large eggs, beaten
- 1 cup whole milk
- 1 tablespoon pure maple syrup
- 1 teaspoon vanilla extract
- ¼ teaspoon cinnamon
- ¼ teaspoon kosher salt
- 3 cups stale bread cubes
- 1 tablespoon unsalted butter, at room temperature

In a medium bowl, whisk together the eggs, milk, maple syrup, vanilla extract, cinnamon and salt. Stir in the bread cubes to coat well.

Grease the bottom of the sheet pan with the butter. Spread the bread mixture into the pan in an even layer.

Select Roast. Set temperature to 350ºF (180ºC) and set time to 12 minutes. Select Start to begin preheating.

Once the unit has preheated, slide the pan into the oven.

After about 10 minutes, remove the pan and check the casserole. The top should be browned and the middle of the casserole just set. If more time is needed, return the pan to the oven and continue cooking.

When cooking is complete, serve warm.

79. CHEESY ARTICHOKE-MUSHROOM FRITTATA

Prep time: 10 minutes | Cook time: 15 minutes | Serves 6

- 8 eggs
- ½ teaspoon kosher salt
- ¼ cup whole milk
- ¾ cup shredded Mozzarella cheese, divided
- 2 tablespoons unsalted butter, melted
- 1 cup coarsely chopped artichoke hearts
- ¼ cup chopped onion
- ½ cup mushrooms
- ¼ cup grated Parmesan cheese
- ¼ teaspoon freshly ground black pepper

In a medium bowl, whisk together the eggs and salt. Let rest for a minute or two, then pour in the milk and whisk again. Stir in ½ cup of the Mozzarella cheese.

Grease the sheet pan with the butter. Stir in the artichoke hearts and onion and toss to coat with the butter.

Select Roast. Set temperature to 375ºF (190ºC) and set time to 12 minutes. Select Start to begin preheating.

Once the unit has preheated, slide the pan into the oven.

After 5 minutes, remove the pan. Spread the mushrooms over the vegetables. Pour the egg mixture on top. Stir gently just to distribute the vegetables evenly. Return the pan to the oven and continue cooking for 5 to 7 minutes, or until the edges are set. The center will still be quite liquid.

Select Broil. Set temperature to Low and set time to 3 minutes. Press Start to begin. After 1 minute, remove the pan and sprinkle the remaining ¼ cup of the Mozzarella and Parmesan cheese over the frittata. Return the pan to the oven and continue cooking for 2 minutes.

When cooking is complete, the cheese should be melted with the top completely set but not browned. Sprinkle the black pepper on top and serve.

80. MINI CINNAMON ROLLS

Prep time: 5 minutes | Cook time: 25 minutes | Makes 18 rolls

- ⅓ cup light brown sugar
- 2 teaspoons cinnamon
- 1 (9-by-9-inch) frozen puff pastry sheet, thawed
- All-purpose flour, for dusting
- 6 teaspoons unsalted butter, melted, divided

In a small bowl, stir together the brown sugar and cinnamon.

On a clean work surface, lightly dust with the flour and lay the puff pastry sheet. Using a rolling pin, press the folds together and roll the dough out in one direction so that it measures about 9 by 11 inches. Cut it in half to form two squat rectangles of about 5½ by 9 inches.

Brush 2 teaspoons of the butter over each pastry half. Sprinkle with 2 tablespoons of the cinnamon sugar. Pat it down lightly with the palm of your hand to help it adhere to the butter.

Starting with the 9-inch side of one rectangle. Using your hands, carefully roll the dough into a cylinder. Repeat with the other rectangle. To make slicing easier, refrigerate the rolls for 10 to 20 minutes.

Using a sharp knife, slice each roll into nine 1-inch pieces. Transfer the rolls to the center of the sheet pan. They should be very close to each other, but not quite touching. Drizzle the remaining 2 teaspoons of the butter over the rolls and sprinkle with the remaining cinnamon sugar.

Select Bake. Set temperature to 350°F (180°C) and set time to 25 minutes. Select Start to begin preheating.

Once the unit has preheated, slide the pan into the oven.

When cooking is complete, remove the pan and check the rolls. They should be puffed up and golden brown.

Let the rolls rest for 5 minutes and transfer them to a wire rack to cool completely. Serve.

81. BROCCOLI STUFFED PEPPERS

Basic Recipe
Preparation Time: 10 minutes
Cooking Time: 40 minutes
Servings: 2

INGREDIENTS:

- 4 eggs
- 1/2 cup cheddar cheese, grated
- 2 bell peppers cut in half and remove seeds
- 1/2 tsp garlic powder
- 1 tsp dried thyme
- 1/4 cup feta cheese, crumbled
- 1/2 cup broccoli, cooked
- 1/4 tsp pepper
- 1/2 tsp salt

DIRECTIONS:

Preheat the air fryer to 325 F.

Stuff feta and broccoli into the bell peppers halved.

Beat egg in a bowl with seasoning and pour egg mixture into the pepper halved over feta and broccoli.

Place bell pepper halved into the air fryer basket and cook for 35-40 minutes

Top with grated cheddar cheese and cook until cheese melted.

Serve and enjoy.

NUTRITION: Calories 340 Fat 22 g Carbs 12 g Protein 22 g

82. BLUEBERRY BREAKFAST COBBLER

Basic Recipe
Preparation Time: 5 minutes
Cooking Time: 15 minutes
Servings: 4

INGREDIENTS:

- ⅓ cup whole-wheat pastry flour
- ¾ teaspoon baking powder
- Dash sea salt
- ½ cup 2% milk
- 2 tablespoons pure maple syrup
- ½ teaspoon vanilla extract
- Cooking oil spray
- ½ cup fresh blueberries
- ¼ cup Granola, or plain store-bought granola

DIRECTIONS:

In a medium bowl, whisk the flour, baking powder, and salt. Add the milk, maple syrup, and vanilla and gently whisk, just until thoroughly combined.

Preheat the unit by selecting BAKE, setting the temperature to 350°F, and setting the time to 3 minutes Select START/STOP to start.

Spray a 6-by-2-inch round baking pan with cooking oil and pour the batter into the pan. Top evenly with the blueberries and granola.

Once the unit is preheated, place the pan into the basket.

Select BAKE, set the temperature to 350°F, and set the time to 15 minutes Select START/STOP to begin.

When the cooking is complete, the cobbler should be nicely browned and a knife inserted into the middle should come out clean. Enjoy plain or topped with a little vanilla yogurt.

NUTRITION: Calories 112 Fat 1g Carbs 23g Protein 3g

83. 32 GRANOLA

Intermediate Recipe
Preparation Time: 5 minutes
Cooking Time: 40 minutes
Servings: 2

INGREDIENTS:

- 1 cup rolled oats
- 3 tablespoons pure maple syrup
- 1 tablespoon sugar
- 1 tablespoon neutral-flavored oil, such as refined coconut, sunflower, or safflower
- ¼ teaspoon sea salt
- ¼ teaspoon ground cinnamon
- ¼ teaspoon vanilla extract

DIRECTIONS:

Insert the crisper plate into the basket and the basket into the unit. Preheat the unit by selecting BAKE, setting the temperature to 250°F, and setting the time to 3 minutes Select START/STOP to start.

In a medium bowl, stir together the oats, maple syrup, sugar, oil, salt, cinnamon, and vanilla until thoroughly combined. Transfer the granola to a 6-by-2-inch round baking pan.

Once the unit is preheated, place the pan into the basket.

Select BAKE, set the temperature to 250°F and set the time to 40 minutes Select START/STOP to begin. After 10 minutes, stir the granola well. Resume cooking, stirring the granola every 10 minutes, for a total of 40 minutes, or until the granola is lightly browned and mostly dry.

Place the granola on a plate to cool, when the cooking is complete. It will become crisp as it cools. Store the completely cooled granola in an airtight container in a cool, dry place for 1 to 2 weeks.

Variation Tip: You can change this recipe to include some of your favorite granola ingredients, such as dried fruits, different types of nuts, and even goodies such as chocolate chips. Stir them in after the granola is done, but before it's completely cool.

NUTRITION: Calories 165 Fat 5g Carbs 27g Protein 3g

84. SWEET BANANA BREAD PUDDING

Prep time: 10 minutes | Cook time: 18 minutes | Serves 4

- 2 medium ripe bananas, mashed
- ½ cup low-fat milk
- 2 tablespoons maple syrup
- 2 tablespoons peanut butter
- 1 teaspoon vanilla extract
- 1 teaspoon ground cinnamon
- 2 slices whole-grain bread, torn into bite-sized pieces
- ¼ cup quick oats
- Cooking spray

Spritz the sheet pan with cooking spray.

In a large bowl, combine the bananas, milk, maple syrup, peanut butter, vanilla extract and cinnamon. Use an immersion blender to mix until well combined.

Stir in the bread pieces to coat well. Add the oats and stir until everything is combined.

Transfer the mixture to the sheet pan. Cover with the aluminum foil.

Select Air Fry. Set temperature to 375°F (190ºC) and set time to 18 minutes. Select Start to begin preheating.

Once the unit has preheated, slide the pan into the oven.

After 10 minutes, remove the foil and continue to cook for 8 minutes. Serve immediately.

85. MIXED BERRY MUFFINS
Basic Recipe
Preparation Time: 15 minutes
Cooking Time: 15 minutes
Servings: 8

INGREDIENTS:
- 1⅓ cups plus 1 tablespoon all-purpose flour, divided
- ¼ cup granulated sugar
- 2 tablespoons light brown sugar
- 2 teaspoons baking powder
- 2 eggs
- ⅔ Cup whole milk
- ⅓ Cup safflower oil
- 1 cup mixed fresh berries

DIRECTIONS:
In a medium bowl, stir together 1⅓ cups of flour, the granulated sugar, brown sugar, and baking powder until mixed well.

In a small bowl, whisk the eggs, milk, and oil until combined. Mix the egg mixture into the dry ingredients just until combined.

In another small bowl, toss the mixed berries with the left over 1 tablespoon of flour until coated. Gently stir the berries into the batter.

Two times the 16 foil muffin cups to make 8 cups.

Insert the crisper plate into the basket and the basket into the unit. Preheat the unit by selecting BAKE, setting the temperature to 315°F, and setting the time to 3 minutes Select START/STOP to start.

Once the unit is preheated, place 4 cups into the basket and fill each three-quarter full with the batter.

Select BAKE, set the temperature to 315°F, and set the time for 17 minutes Select START/STOP to begin.

After about 12 minutes, check the muffins. If they spring back when lightly touched with your finger, they are done. If not, resume cooking. When the cooking is done, transfer the muffins to a wire rack to cool.

Repeat steps 6, 7, and 8 with the remaining muffin cups and batter. Let the muffins cool for 10 minutes before serving.

NUTRITION: Calories 230 Fat 11g Carbs 30g Protein 4g

86. CASHEW GRANOLA WITH CRANBERRIES
Prep time: 5 minutes | Cook time: 12 minutes | Serves 6

- 3 cups old-fashioned rolled oats
- 2 cups raw cashews
- 1 cup unsweetened coconut chips
- ½ cup honey
- ¼ cup vegetable oil
- ⅓ cup packed light brown sugar
- ¼ teaspoon kosher salt
- 1 cup dried cranberries

In a large bowl, stir together all the ingredients, except for the cranberries. Spread the mixture on the sheet pan in an even layer.

Select Bake. Set temperature to 325ºF (163ºC) and set time to 12 minutes. Select Start to begin preheating.

Once the unit has preheated, slide the pan into the oven.

After 5 to 6 minutes, remove the pan and stir the granola. Return the pan to the oven and continue cooking.

When cooking is complete, remove the pan. Let the granola cool to room temperature. Stir in the cranberries before serving.

87. WAFFLES AND CHICKEN
Basic Recipe
Preparation Time: 15 minutes
Cooking Time: 30 minutes
Servings: 4

INGREDIENTS:
- 8 whole chicken wings
- 1 teaspoon garlic powder
- Chicken seasoning, for preparing the chicken
- Freshly ground black pepper
- ½ cup all-purpose flour
- Cooking oil spray
- 8 frozen waffles
- Pure maple syrup, for serving (optional)

DIRECTIONS:
In a medium bowl, combine the chicken and garlic powder and season with chicken seasoning and pepper. Toss to coat.

Transfer the chicken to a re-sealable plastic bag and add the flour. Seal the bag and shake it to coat the chicken thoroughly.

Insert the crisper plate into the basket and the basket into the unit. Preheat the unit by selecting AIR FRY, setting the temperature to 400°F, and setting the time to 3 minutes Select START/STOP to begin.

Once the unit is preheated, spray the crisper plate with cooking oil. Using tongs, transfer the chicken from the bag to the basket. It is okay to stack the chicken wings on top of each other. Spray them with cooking oil.

Select air fry, set the temperature to 400°F, and set the time to 20 minutes Select start/stop to begin.

After 5 minutes, remove the basket and shake the wings. Reinsert the basket to resume cooking. Remove and shake the basket every 5 minutes until the chicken is fully cooked.

When the cooking is complete, remove the cooked chicken from the basket; cover to keep warm.

Rinse the basket and crisper plate with warm water. Insert them back into the unit.

Select air fry, set the temperature to 360°F, and set the time to 3 minutes Select start/stop to begin.

Once the unit is preheated, spray the crisper plate with cooking spray. Work in batches, place the frozen waffles into the basket. Do not stack them. Spray the waffles with cooking oil.

elect air fry, set the temperature to 360°F, and set the time to 6 minutes Select start/stop to begin.

Repeat steps 10 and 11 with the remaining waffles when the cooking is complete.

Serve the waffles with the chicken and a touch of maple syrup, if desired.

NUTRITION: Calories 461 Fat 22g Carbs 45g Protein 28g

88. CHOCOLATE-FILLED DOUGHNUT HOLES
Basic Recipe
Preparation Time: 10 minutes
Cooking Time: 30 minutes
Servings: 12

INGREDIENTS:
- 1 (8-count) can refrigerated biscuits
- Cooking oil spray
- 48 semisweet chocolate chips
- 3 tablespoons melted unsalted butter
- ¼ cup confectioners' sugar

DIRECTIONS:
Separate the biscuits and cut each biscuit into thirds, for 24 pieces.

Flatten each biscuit piece slightly and put 2 chocolate chips in the center. Wrap the dough around the chocolate and seal the edges well.

Insert the crisper plate into the basket and the basket into the unit. Preheat the unit by selecting air fry, setting the temperature to 330°F, and setting the time to 3 minutes Select start/stop to begin.

Once the unit is preheated, spray the crisper plate with cooking oil. Brush each doughnut hole with a bit of the butter and place it into the basket. Select air fry, set the temperature to 330°F, and set the time between 8 and 12 minutes Select start/stop to begin.

The doughnuts are done when they are golden brown. When the cooking is complete, place the doughnut holes on a plate and dust with the confectioners' sugar. Serve warm.

NUTRITION: Calories 393 Fat 17g Carbs 55g Protein 5g

89. BLUEBERRY CAKE

Prep time: 5 minutes | Cook time: 10 minutes | Serves 8

- 1½ cups Bisquick
- ¼ cup granulated sugar
- 2 large eggs, beaten
- ¾ cup whole milk
- 1 teaspoon vanilla extract
- ½ teaspoon lemon zest
- Cooking spray
- 2 cups blueberries

Stir together the Bisquick and sugar in a medium bowl. Stir together the eggs, milk, vanilla and lemon zest. Add the wet ingredients to the dry ingredients and stir until well combined.

Spritz the sheet pan with cooking spray and line with the parchment paper, pressing it into place. Spray the parchment paper with cooking spray. Pour the batter on the pan and spread it out evenly. Sprinkle the blueberries evenly over the top.

Select Bake. Set temperature to 375°F (190°C) and set time to 10 minutes. Select Start to begin preheating.

Once the unit has preheated, slide the pan into the oven.

When cooking is complete, the cake should be pulling away from the edges of the pan and the top should be just starting to turn golden brown. Let the cake rest for a minute before cutting into 16 squares. Serve immediately.

90. MUSHROOM FRITTATA

Basic Recipe
Preparation Time: 10 minutes
Cooking Time: 13 minutes
Servings: 1
INGREDIENTS:

- 1 cup egg whites
- 1 cup spinach, chopped
- 2 mushrooms, sliced
- 2 tbsp parmesan cheese, grated
- Salt

DIRECTIONS:

Sprinkle pan with cooking spray and heat over medium heat. Add mushrooms and sauté for 2-3 minutes Add spinach and cook for 1-2 minutes or until wilted.

Transfer mushroom spinach mixture into the air fryer pan. Beat egg whites in a mixing bowl until frothy. Season it with a pinch of salt.

Pour egg white mixture into the spinach and mushroom mixture and sprinkle with parmesan cheese. Place pan in air fryer basket and cook frittata at 350 F for 8 minutes

Slice and serve.

NUTRITION: Calories 176 Fat 3 g Carbs 4 g Protein 31 g

91. EASY MAPLE-GLAZED DOUGHNUTS

Basic Recipe
Preparation Time: 10 minutes
Cooking Time: 14 minutes
Servings: 8

INGREDIENTS:

- 1 (8-count) can jumbo flaky refrigerator biscuits
- Cooking oil spray
- ½ cup light brown sugar
- ¼ cup butter
- 3 tablespoons milk
- 2 cups confectioners' sugar, plus more for dusting (optional)
- 2 teaspoons pure maple syrup

DIRECTIONS:

Insert the crisper plate into the basket and the basket into the unit. Preheat the unit by selecting air fry, setting the temperature to 350°F, and setting the time to 3 minutes Select start/stop to begin.

Remove the biscuits from the tube and cut out the center of each biscuit with a small, round cookie cutter.

Once the unit is preheated, spray the crisper plate with cooking oil. Work it in batches, place 4 doughnuts into the basket.

Select air fry, set the temperature to 350°F, and set the time to 5 minutes Select start/stop to begin.

When the cooking is complete, place the doughnuts on a plate. Repeat steps 3 and 4 with the remaining doughnuts.

In a small saucepan over medium heat, combine the brown sugar, butter, and milk. Heat until the butter is melted and the sugar is dissolved, about 4 minutes

Remove the pan from the heat and whisk in the confectioners' sugar and maple syrup until smooth.

Dip the slightly cooled doughnuts into the maple glaze. Place them on a wire rack and dust with confectioners' sugar (if using). Let rest just until the glaze sets. Enjoy the doughnuts warm.

NUTRITION: Calories 219 Fat 10g Carbs 30g Protein 2g

92. JALAPENO BREAKFAST MUFFINS

Preparation Time: 10 minutes
Cooking Time: 15 minutes
Servings: 8
INGREDIENTS:

- 5 eggs
- 1/3 cup coconut oil, melted
- 2 tsp baking powder
- 3 tbsp erythritol
- 3 tbsp jalapenos, sliced
- 1/4 cup unsweetened coconut milk
- 2/3 cup coconut flour
- 3/4 tsp sea salt

DIRECTIONS:

Preheat the air fryer to 325 F.

In a large bowl, mix together coconut flour, baking powder, erythritol, and sea salt.

Stir in eggs, jalapenos, coconut milk, and coconut oil until well combined.

Pour batter into the silicone muffin molds and place into the air fryer basket.

Cook muffins for 15 minutes

Serve and enjoy.

NUTRITION: Calories 125 Fat 12 g Carbs 7 g Protein 3 g

93. CAJUN BREAKFAST MUFFINS

Intermediate Recipe
Preparation Time: 10 minutes
Cooking Time: 10 minutes
Serving : 6
INGREDIENTS:

- Olive oil
- 4 eggs, beaten
- 2¼ cups frozen hash browns, thawed
- 1 cup diced ham
- ½ cup shredded Cheddar cheese

- ½ teaspoon Cajun seasoning

DIRECTIONS:

Lightly spray 12 silicone muffin cups with olive oil.

In a medium bowl, mix together the eggs, hash browns, ham, Cheddar cheese, and Cajun seasoning in a medium bowl.

Spoon a heaping 1½ tablespoons of hash brown mixture into each muffin cup.

Place the muffin cups in the fryer basket.

Air fry until the muffins are golden brown on top and the center has set up, 8 to 10 minutes

Make It Even Lower Calorie: Reduce or eliminate the cheese.

NUTRITION: Calories 178 Fat 9g Saturated Fat 4gCholesterol 145mg Carbs 13g Protein 11g Fiber 2g Sodium: 467mg

94. HOMEMADE STRAWBERRY BREAKFAST TARTS

Basic Recipe
Preparation Time: 15 minutes
Cooking Time: 20 minutes
Servings: 6

INGREDIENTS:

- 2 refrigerated piecrusts
- ½ cup strawberry preserves
- 1 teaspoon cornstarch
- Cooking oil spray
- ½ cup low-fat vanilla yogurt
- 1-ounce cream cheese, at room temperature
- 3 tablespoons confectioners' sugar
- Rainbow sprinkles, for decorating

DIRECTIONS:

Place the piecrusts on a flat surface. Cut each piecrust into 3 rectangles using a knife or pizza cutter, for 6 in total. Discard any unused dough from the piecrust edges.

In a small bowl, stir together the preserves and cornstarch. Mix well, ensuring there are no lumps of cornstarch remaining.

Scoop 1 tablespoon of the strawberry mixture onto the top half of each piece of piecrust.

Fold the bottom of each piece up to enclose the filling. Press along the edges of each tart to seal using the back of a fork.

Insert the crisper plate into the basket and the basket into the unit. Preheat the unit by selecting bake, setting the temperature to 375°F, and setting the time to 3 minutes Select start/stop to start.

Once the unit is preheated, spray the crisper plate with cooking oil. Work in batches, spray the breakfast tarts with cooking oil and place them into the basket in a single layer. Do not stack the tarts.

Select bake, set the temperature to 375°F, and set the time to 10 minutes Select start/stop to begin.

When the cooking is complete, the tarts should be light golden brown. Let the breakfast tarts cool fully before removing them from the basket. Repeat steps 5, 6, 7, and 8 for the remaining breakfast tarts.

In a small bowl, stir together the yogurt, cream cheese, and confectioners' sugar. Spread the breakfast tarts with the frosting and top with sprinkles.

NUTRITION: Calories 408 Fat 20.5g Carbs 56g Protein 1g

95. CREAMY QUESADILLAS WITH BLUEBERRIES

Prep time: 5 minutes | Cook time: 4 minutes | Serves 2

- ¼ cup nonfat Ricotta cheese
- ¼ cup plain nonfat Greek yogurt
- 2 tablespoons finely ground flaxseeds
- 1 tablespoon granulated stevia
- ½ teaspoon cinnamon
- ¼ teaspoon vanilla extract

- 2 (8-inch) low-carb whole-wheat tortillas
- ½ cup fresh blueberries, divided

Line the sheet pan with the aluminum foil.

In a small bowl, whisk together the Ricotta cheese, yogurt, flaxseeds, stevia, cinnamon and vanilla.

Place the tortillas on the sheet pan. Spread half of the yogurt mixture on each tortilla, almost to the edges. Top each tortilla with ¼ cup of blueberries. Fold the tortillas in half.

Select Bake. Set temperature to 400°F (205°C) and set time to 4 minutes. Select Start to begin preheating.

Once the unit has preheated, slide the pan into the oven.

When cooking is complete, remove the pan from the oven. Serve immediately.

96. EGG MUFFINS

Basic Recipe
Preparation Time: 10 minutes
Cooking Time: 15 minutes
Servings: 12

INGREDIENTS:

- 9 eggs
- 1/2 cup onion, sliced
- 1 tbsp olive oil
- 8 oz ground sausage
- 1/4 cup coconut milk
- 1/2 tsp oregano
- 1 1/2 cups spinach
- 3/4 cup bell peppers, chopped
- Pepper
- Salt

DIRECTIONS:

Preheat the air fryer to 325 F.

Add ground sausage in a pan and sauté over medium heat for 5 minutes

Add olive oil, oregano, bell pepper, and onion and sauté until onion is translucent.

Put spinach to the pan and cook for 30 seconds.

Remove pan from heat and set aside.

In a mixing bowl, whisk together eggs, coconut milk, pepper, and salt until well beaten.

Add sausage and vegetable mixture into the egg mixture and mix well.

Pour egg mixture into the silicone muffin molds and place into the air fryer basket. (Cook in batches)

Cook muffins for 15 minutes

 Serve and enjoy.

NUTRITION: Calories 135 Fat 11 g Carbs 1.5 g Protein 8 g

97. EARLY MORNING STEAK AND EGGS

Basic Recipe
Preparation Time: 10 minutes
Cooking Time: 30 minutes

Servings: 4

INGREDIENTS:

- Cooking oil spray
- 4 (4-ounce) New York strip steaks
- 1 teaspoon granulated garlic, divided
- 1 teaspoon salt, divided
- 1 teaspoon freshly ground black pepper, divided
- 4 eggs
- ½ teaspoon paprika

DIRECTIONS:

Insert the crisper plate into the basket and the basket into the unit. Preheat the unit by selecting air fry, setting the temperature to 360°F, and setting the time to 3 minutes Select start/stop to begin.

Once the unit is preheated, spray the crisper plate with cooking oil. Place

2 steaks into the basket; do not oil or season them at this time.

Select air fry, set the temperature to 360°F, and set the time to 9 minutes Select start/stop to begin.

After 5 minutes, open the unit and flip the steaks. Sprinkle each with ¼ teaspoon of granulated garlic, ¼ teaspoon of salt, and ¼ teaspoon of pepper. Resume cooking until the steaks register at least 145°F on a food thermometer.

When the cooking is complete, transfer the steaks to a plate and tent with aluminum foil to keep warm. Repeat steps 2, 3, and 4 with the remaining steaks.

Spray 4 ramekins with olive oil. Crack 1 egg into each ramekin. Sprinkle the eggs with the paprika and remaining ½ teaspoon each of salt and pepper. Work in batches, place 2 ramekins into the basket.

Select BAKE, set the temperature to 330°F, and set the time to 5 minutes Select start/stop to begin. When the cooking is complete and the eggs are cooked to 160°F, remove the ramekins and repeat step 7 with the remaining 2 ramekins.

Serve the eggs with the steaks.

NUTRITION: Calories 304 Fat 19g Carbs 2g Protein 31g

98. HEARTY BLUEBERRY OATMEAL

Intermediate Recipe
Preparation Time: 10 minutes
Cooking Time: 25 minutes
Serving : 6

INGREDIENTS:
- 1½ cups quick oats
- 1¼ teaspoons ground cinnamon, divided
- ½ teaspoon baking powder
- Pinch salt
- 1 cup unsweetened vanilla almond milk
- ¼ cup honey
- 1 teaspoon vanilla extract
- 1 egg, beaten
- 2 cups blueberries
- Olive oil
- 1½ teaspoons sugar, divided
- 6 tablespoons low-fat whipped topping (optional)

DIRECTIONS:

In a large bowl, mix together the oats, 1 teaspoon of cinnamon, baking powder, and salt.

In a medium bowl, whisk together the almond milk, honey, vanilla and egg.

Pour the liquid ingredients into the oats mixture and stir to combine. Fold in the blueberries.

Lightly spray a round air fryer–friendly pan with oil.

Add half the blueberry mixture to the pan.

Sprinkle ⅛ teaspoon of cinnamon and ½ teaspoon sugar over the top.

Cover the pan with aluminum foil and place gently in the fryer basket.

Air fry for 20 minutes remove the foil and air fry for an additional 5 minutes Transfer the mixture to a shallow bowl.

Repeat with the remaining blueberry mixture, ½ teaspoon of sugar, and ⅛ teaspoon of cinnamon.

To serve, spoon into bowls and top with whipped topping.

NUTRITION: Calories 170 Fat 3g Saturated Fat 1g Cholesterol 97mg Carbs 34g Protein 4g Fiber 4g Sodium: 97mg

99. GREEK FRITTATA

Intermediate Recipe
Preparation Time: 10 minutes
Cooking Time: 20 minutes
Serving : 4

INGREDIENTS:
- Olive oil
- 5 eggs
- ¼ teaspoon salt

- ⅛ Teaspoon freshly ground black pepper
- 1 cup baby spinach leaves, shredded
- ½ cup halved grape tomatoes
- ½ cup crumbled feta cheese

DIRECTIONS:

Spray a small round air fryer-friendly pan with olive oil.

In a medium bowl, whisk together eggs, salt, and pepper and whisk to combine.

Add the spinach and stir to combine.

Pour ½ cup of the egg mixture into the pan.

Sprinkle ¼ cup of the tomatoes and ¼ cup of the feta on top of the egg mixture.

Cover the pan with aluminum foil and secure it around the edges.

Place the pan carefully into the fryer basket.

Air fry for 12 minutes

Remove the foil from the pan and cook until the eggs are set, 5 to 7 minutes

Remove the frittata from the pan and place on a serving platter. Repeat with the remaining ingredients.

NUTRITION: Calories 146 Fat 10g Saturated Fat 5g Cholesterol 249mg Carbs 3g Protein 11g Fiber 1g Sodium: 454mg

100. PUFFED EGG TARTS

Basic Recipe
Preparation Time: 10 minutes
Cooking Time: 20 minutes
Servings: 4

INGREDIENTS:
- ⅓ Sheet frozen puff pastry, thawed
- Cooking oil spray
- ½ cup shredded Cheddar cheese
- 2 eggs
- ¼ teaspoon salt, divided
- 1 teaspoon minced fresh parsley (optional)

DIRECTIONS:

Insert the crisper plate into the basket and the basket into the unit. Preheat the unit by selecting bake, setting the temperature to 390°F, and setting the time to 3 minutes Select start/stop to begin.

Lay the puff pastry sheet on a piece of parchment paper and cut it in half. Once the unit is preheated, spray the crisper plate with cooking oil. Transfer the 2 squares of pastry to the basket, keeping them on the parchment paper.

Select bake, set the temperature to 390°F, and set the time to 20 minutes Select start/stop to begin.

After 10 minutes, use a metal spoon to press down the center of each pastry square to make a well. Divide the cheese equally between the baked pastries. Carefully crack an egg on top of the cheese, and sprinkle each with the salt. Resume cooking for 7 to 10 minutes

When the cooking is complete, the eggs will be cooked through. Sprinkle each with parsley (if using) and serve.

NUTRITION: Calories 322 Fat 24g Carbs 12g Protein 15g

101. ZUCCHINI NOODLES

Intermediate Recipe
Preparation Time: 10 minutes
Cooking Time: 44 minutes
Servings: 3

INGREDIENTS:
- 1 egg
- 1/2 cup parmesan cheese, grated
- 1/2 cup feta cheese, crumbled
- 1 tbsp thyme
- 1 garlic clove, chopped
- 1 onion, chopped
- 2 medium zucchinis, trimmed and spiralized

- 2 tbsp olive oil
- 1 cup mozzarella cheese, grated
- 1/2 tsp pepper
- 1/2 tsp salt

DIRECTIONS:

Preheat the air fryer to 350 F.

Add spiralized zucchini and salt in a colander and set aside for 10 minutes. Wash zucchini noodles and pat dry with a paper towel.

Heat the oil in a pan over medium heat. Add garlic and onion and sauté for 3-4 minutes

Add zucchini noodles and cook for 4-5 minutes or until softened.

Add zucchini mixture into the air fryer baking pan. Add egg, thyme, cheeses. Mix well and season.

Place pan in the air fryer and cook for 30-35 minutes

Serve and enjoy.

NUTRITION: Calories 435 Fat 29 g Carbs 10.4 g Protein 25 g

102. BREAKFAST POTATOES

Basic Recipe
Preparation Time: 10 minutes
Cooking Time: 20 minutes
Serving: 6

INGREDIENTS:
- 1½ teaspoons olive oil, divided, plus more for misting
- 4 large potatoes, skins on, cut into cubes
- 2 teaspoons seasoned salt, divided
- 1 teaspoon minced garlic, divided
- 2 large green or red bell peppers, cut into 1-inch chunks
- ½ onion, diced

DIRECTIONS:

Lightly mist the fryer basket with olive oil.

In a medium bowl, toss the potatoes with ½ teaspoon of olive oil. Sprinkle with 1 teaspoon of seasoned salt and ½ teaspoon of minced garlic. Stir to coat.

Place the seasoned potatoes in the fryer basket in a single layer.

Cook for 5 minutes Shake the basket and cook for another 5 minutes Meanwhile, in a medium bowl, toss the bell peppers and onion with the remaining ½ teaspoon of olive oil.

Sprinkle the peppers and onions with the remaining 1 teaspoon of seasoned salt and ½ teaspoon of minced garlic. Stir to coat.

Add the seasoned peppers and onions to the fryer basket with the potatoes.

Cook for 5 minutes Shake the basket and cook for an additional 5 minutes

NUTRITION: Calories 199 Fat 1g Carbs 43g Protein 5g

103. EVERYTHING BAGELS

Basic Recipe
Preparation Time: 10 minutes
Cooking Time: 10 minutes
Servings: 2

INGREDIENTS:
- ½ cup self-rising flour, plus more for dusting
- ½ cup plain Greek yogurt
- 1 egg
- 1 tablespoon water
- 4 teaspoons everything bagel spice mix
- Cooking oil spray
- 1 tablespoon butter, melted

DIRECTIONS:

In a large bowl, using a wooden spoon, stir together the flour and yogurt until a tacky dough forms. Transfer the dough to a lightly floured work surface and roll the dough into a ball.

Cut the dough into 2 pieces and roll each piece into a log. Form each log into a bagel shape, pinching the ends together.

In a small bowl, whisk the egg and water. Brush the egg wash on the bagels.

Sprinkle 2 teaspoons of the spice mix on each bagel and gently press it into the dough.

Insert the crisper plate into the basket and the basket into the unit. Preheat the unit by selecting bake, setting the temperature to 330°F, and setting the time to 3 minutes Select start/stop to begin.

Once the unit is preheated, spray the crisper plate with cooking spray. Drizzle with the bagels with the butter and place them into the basket.

Select BAKE, set the temperature to 330°F, and set the time to 10 minutes Select START/STOP to begin.

When the cooking is complete, the bagels should be lightly golden on the outside. Serve warm.

NUTRITION: Calories 271 Fat 13g Carbs 28g Protein 10g

104. DELICIOUS ORIGINAL HASH BROWNS

Basic Recipe
Preparation Time: 15 minutes
Cooking Time: 20 minutes
Servings: 4

INGREDIENTS:
- 4 russet potatoes, peeled
- 1 teaspoon paprika
- Salt
- Freshly ground black pepper
- Cooking oil spray

DIRECTIONS:

Using a box grater or food processor, shred the potatoes. If your grater has different hole sizes, use the largest holes.

Place the shredded potatoes in a large bowl of cold water. Let it sit for 5 minutes (Cold water helps remove excess starch from the potatoes.) Stir them to help dissolve the starch.

Insert the crisper plate into the basket and the basket into the unit. Preheat the unit by selecting air fry, setting the temperature to 360°F, and setting the time to 3 minutes Select start/stop to begin.

Dry out the potatoes and pat them with paper towels until the potatoes are completely dry. Season the potatoes with the paprika, salt, and pepper.

Once the unit is preheated, spray the crisper plate with cooking oil. Spray the potatoes with the cooking oil and place them into the basket.

Select air fry, set the temperature to 360°F, and set the time to 20 minutes Select start/stop to begin.

After 5 minutes, remove the basket and shake the potatoes. Reinsert the basket to resume cooking. Continue shaking the basket every 5 minutes (a total of 4 times) until the potatoes are done.

When the cooking is complete, remove the hash browns from the basket and serve warm.

NUTRITION: Calories 150 Fat 0g Carbs 34g Protein 4g

105. MINI SHRIMP FRITTATA

Intermediate Recipe
Preparation Time: 15 minutes
Cooking Time: 20 minutes
Serving : 4

INGREDIENTS:
- 1 teaspoon olive oil, plus more for spraying
- ½ small red bell pepper, finely diced
- 1 teaspoon minced garlic
- 1 (4-ounce) can of tiny shrimp, Dry out
- Salt
- Freshly ground black pepper
- 4 eggs, beaten
- 4 teaspoons ricotta cheese

DIRECTIONS:

Spray four ramekins with olive oil. In a medium skillet over medium-low heat, heat 1 teaspoon of olive oil. Add the bell pepper and garlic and

sauté until the pepper is soft, about 5 minutes
Add the shrimp, season with salt and pepper, and cook until warm, 1 to 2 minutes Remove from the heat.
Add the eggs and stir to combine. Pour one quarter of the mixture into each ramekin.
Place 2 ramekins in the fryer basket and cook for 6 minutes. Remove the fryer basket from the air fryer and stir the mixture in each ramekin. Top each frittata with 1 teaspoon of ricotta cheese. Return the fryer basket to the air fryer and cook until eggs are set and the top is lightly browned, 4 to 5 minutes
Repeat with the remaining two ramekins.
NUTRITION: Calories 114 Fat 7g Carbs 1g Protein 12g

106. SPINACH AND MUSHROOM MINI QUICHE

Intermediate Recipe
Preparation Time: 10 minutes
Cooking Time: 15 minutes
Serving: 4
INGREDIENTS:
*   1 teaspoon olive oil, plus more for spraying
*   1 cup coarsely chopped mushrooms
*   1 cup fresh baby spinach, shredded
*   4 eggs, beaten
*   ½ cup shredded Cheddar cheese
*   ½ cup shredded mozzarella cheese
*   ¼ teaspoon salt
*   ¼ teaspoon black pepper

DIRECTIONS:
Spray 4 silicone baking cups with olive oil and set aside. In a medium sauté pan over medium heat, warm 1 teaspoon of olive oil. Add the mushrooms and sauté until soft, 3 to 4 minutes
Add the spinach and cook until wilted, 1 to 2 minutes Set aside.
In a medium bowl, whisk together the eggs, Cheddar cheese, mozzarella cheese, salt, and pepper. Gently fold the mushrooms and spinach into the egg mixture.
Pour ¼ of the mixture into each silicone baking cup. Place the baking cups into the fryer basket and air fry for 5 minutes Stir the mixture in each ramekin slightly and air fry until the egg has set, an additional 3 to 5 minutes
NUTRITION: Calories 183 Fat 13g Saturated Fat 7g Cholesterol 206mg Carbs 3g Protein 14g Fiber 1g Sodium: 411mg

107. ITALIAN EGG CUPS

Basic Recipe
Preparation Time: 5 minutes
Cooking Time: 10 minutes
Serving: 4
INGREDIENTS:
*   Olive Oil
*   1 cup marinara sauce
*   4 eggs
*   4 tablespoons shredded mozzarella cheese
*   4 teaspoons grated Parmesan cheese
*   Salt
*   Freshly ground black pepper
*   Chopped fresh basil, for garnish

DIRECTIONS:
Lightly spray 4 individual ramekins with olive oil.
Pour ¼ cup of marinara sauce into each ramekin.
Crack one egg into each ramekin on top of the marinara sauce.
Sprinkle 1 tablespoon of mozzarella and 1 tablespoon of Parmesan on top of each egg. Season it with salt and pepper.
Cover each ramekin with aluminum foil. Place two of the ramekins in the fryer basket.
Air fry for 5 minutes and remove the aluminum foil. Air fry until the top is lightly browned and the egg white is cooked, another 2 to 4 minutes If you prefer the yolk to be firmer, cook for 3 to 5 more minutes

Repeat with the remaining two ramekins. Garnish with basil and serve.
NUTRITION: Calories 135 Fat 8g Saturated Fat 3g Cholesterol 191mg Carbs 6g Protein 10g Fiber 1g Sodium: 407mg

108. BAKED POTATO BREAKFAST BOATS

Basic Recipe
Preparation Time: 10 minutes
Cooking Time: 20 minutes
Serving: 4
INGREDIENTS:
*   2 large russet potatoes, scrubbed
*   Olive oil
*   Salt
*   Freshly ground black pepper
*   4 eggs
*   2 tablespoons chopped, cooked bacon
*   1 cup shredded cheddar cheese

DIRECTIONS:
Poke holes in the potatoes with a fork and microwave on full power for 5 minutes. Turn potatoes over and cook an additional 3 to 5 minutes, or until the potatoes are fork tender.
Cut the potatoes in half lengthwise and use a spoon to scoop out the inside of the potato. Be careful to leave a layer of potato so that it makes a sturdy "boat."Lightly spray the fryer basket with olive oil. Spray the skin side of the potatoes with oil and sprinkle with salt and pepper to taste.
Place the potato skins in the fryer basket skin side down. Crack one egg into each potato skin.
Sprinkle ½ tablespoon of bacon pieces and ¼ cup of shredded cheese on top of each egg. Sprinkle with salt and pepper to taste.
Air fry until the yolk is slightly runny, 5 to 6 minutes, or until the yolk is fully cooked, 7 to 10 minutes
NUTRITION: Calories 338 Fat15g Saturated Fat 8g Cholesterol 214mg Carbs 35g Protein 17g Fiber 3g Sodium: 301mg

LUNCH RECIPES

109. MAPLE CHICKEN THIGHS

Servings: 4
Cooking Time: 30 Minutes
INGREDIENTS:
*   4 large chicken thighs, bone-in
*   2 tablespoons French mustard
*   2 tablespoons Dijon mustard
*   1 clove minced garlic
*   1/2 teaspoon dried marjoram
*   2 tablespoons maple syrup

DIRECTIONS:
Mix chicken with everything in a bowl and coat it well.
Place the chicken along with its marinade in the baking pan.
Press "Power Button" of Air Fry Oven and turn the dial to select the "Bake" mode.
Press the Time button and again turn the dial to set the cooking time to 30 minutes.
Now push the Temp button and rotate the dial to set the temperature at 370 degrees F.
Once preheated, place the baking pan inside and close its lid.
Serve warm.
Nutrition Info: Calories 301 Total Fat 15.8 g Saturated Fat 2.7 g Cholesterol 75 mg Sodium 189 mg Total Carbs 31.7 g Fiber 0.3 g Sugar 0.1 g Protein 28.2 g

110. PERSIMMON TOAST WITH SOUR CREAM & CINNAMON

Servings: 1

Cooking Time: 5 Minutes

INGREDIENTS:
- 1 slice of wheat bread
- 1/2 persimmon
- Sour cream to taste
- Sugar to taste
- Cinnamon to taste

DIRECTIONS:

Spread a thin layer of sour cream across the bread.

Slice the persimmon into 1/4 inch pieces and lay them across the bread.

Sprinkle cinnamon and sugar over persimmon.

Toast in toaster oven until bread and persimmon begin to brown.

Nutrition Info: Calories: 89, Sodium: 133 mg, Dietary Fiber: 2.0 g, Total Fat: 1.1 g, Total Carbs: 16.5 g, Protein: 3.8 g.

III.   DUCK BREAST WITH FIGS

Servings: 2

Cooking Time: 45 Minutes

INGREDIENTS:
- 1 pound boneless duck breast
- 6 fresh figs, halved
- 1 tablespoon fresh thyme, chopped
- 2 cups fresh pomegranate juice
- 2 tablespoons lemon juice
- 3 tablespoons brown sugar
- 1 teaspoon olive oil
- Salt and black pepper, as required

DIRECTIONS:

Preheat the Air fryer to 400 degree F and grease an Air fryer basket.

Put the pomegranate juice, lemon juice, and brown sugar in a medium saucepan over medium heat.

Bring to a boil and simmer on low heat for about 25 minutes.

Season the duck breasts generously with salt and black pepper.

Arrange the duck breasts into the Air fryer basket, skin side up and cook for about 14 minutes, flipping once in between.

Dish out the duck breasts onto a cutting board for about 10 minutes.

Meanwhile, put the figs, olive oil, salt, and black pepper in a bowl until well mixed.

Set the Air fryer to 400 degree F and arrange the figs into the Air fryer basket.

Cook for about 5 more minutes and dish out in a platter.

Put the duck breast with the roasted figs and drizzle with warm pomegranate juice mixture.

Garnish with fresh thyme and serve warm.

Nutrition Info: Calories: 699, Fat: 12.1g, Carbohydrates: 90g, Sugar: 74g, Protein: 519g, Sodium: 110mg

II2.   TURKEY-STUFFED PEPPERS

Servings: 6

Cooking Time: 35 Minutes

INGREDIENTS:
- 1 pound lean ground turkey
- 1 tablespoon olive oil
- 2 cloves garlic, minced
- 1/3 onion, minced
- 1 tablespoon cilantro (optional)
- 1 teaspoon garlic powder
- 1 teaspoon cumin powder
- 1/2 teaspoon salt
- Pepper to taste
- 3 large red bell peppers
- 1 cup chicken broth
- 1/4 cup tomato sauce
- 1-1/2 cups cooked brown rice
- 1/4 cup shredded cheddar

- 6 green onions

DIRECTIONS:

Start by preheating toaster oven to 400°F.

Heat a skillet on medium heat.

Add olive oil to the skillet, then mix in onion and garlic.

Sauté for about 5 minutes, or until the onion starts to look opaque.

Add the turkey to the skillet and season with cumin, garlic powder, salt, and pepper.

Brown the meat until thoroughly cooked, then mix in chicken broth and tomato sauce.

Reduce heat and simmer for about 5 minutes, stirring occasionally.

Add the brown rice and continue stirring until it is evenly spread through the mix.

Cut the bell peppers lengthwise down the middle and remove all of the seeds.

Grease a pan or line it with parchment paper and lay all peppers in the pan with the outside facing down.

Spoon the meat mixture evenly into each pepper and use the back of the spoon to level.

Bake for 30 minutes.

Remove pan from oven and sprinkle cheddar over each pepper, then put it back in for another 3 minutes, or until the cheese is melted.

While the cheese melts, dice the green onions. Remove pan from oven and sprinkle onions over each pepper and serve.

Nutrition Info: Calories: 394, Sodium: 493 mg, Dietary Fiber: 4.1 g, Total Fat: 12.9 g, Total Carbs: 44.4 g, Protein: 27.7 g.

II3.   RANCH CHICKEN WINGS

Servings: 3

Cooking Time: 10 Minutes

INGREDIENTS:
- 1/4 cup almond meal
- 1/4 cup flaxseed meal
- 2 tablespoons butter, melted
- 6 tablespoons parmesan cheese, preferably freshly grated
- 1 tablespoon Ranch seasoning mix
- 2 tablespoons oyster sauce
- 6 chicken wings, bone-in

DIRECTIONS:

Start by preheating your Air Fryer to 370 degrees F.

In a resealable bag, place the almond meal, flaxseed meal, butter, parmesan, Ranch seasoning mix, andoyster sauce. Add the chicken wings and shake to coat on all sides.

Arrange the chicken wings in the Air Fryer basket. Spritz the chicken wings with a nonstick cooking spray.

Cook for 11 minutes. Turn them over and cook an additional 11 minutes. Serve warm with your favorite dipping sauce, if desired. Enjoy!

Nutrition Info: 285 Calories; 22g Fat; 3g Carbs; 12g Protein; 5g Sugars; 6g Fiber

II4.   PARMESAN CHICKEN MEATBALLS

Servings: 4

Cooking Time: 12 Minutes

INGREDIENTS:
- 1-lb. ground chicken
- 1 large egg, beaten
- ½ cup Parmesan cheese, grated
- ½ cup pork rinds, ground
- 1 teaspoon garlic powder
- 1 teaspoon paprika
- 1 teaspoon kosher salt
- ½ teaspoon pepper
- Crust:
- ½ cup pork rinds, ground

DIRECTIONS:

Toss all the meatball Ingredients: in a bowl and mix well.

Make small meatballs out this mixture and roll them in the pork rinds.
Place the coated meatballs in the air fryer basket.
Press "Power Button" of Air Fry Oven and turn the dial to select the "Bake" mode.
Press the Time button and again turn the dial to set the cooking time to 12 minutes.
Now push the Temp button and rotate the dial to set the temperature at 400 degrees F.
Once preheated, place the air fryer basket inside and close its lid.
Serve warm.
Nutrition Info: Calories 529 Total Fat 17 g Saturated Fat 3 g Cholesterol 65 mg Sodium 391 mg Total Carbs 55 g Fiber 6 g Sugar 8 g Protein 41g

115. EASY TURKEY BREASTS WITH BASIL
Servings: 4
Cooking Time: 10 Minutes
INGREDIENTS:
• 2 tablespoons olive oil
• 2 pounds turkey breasts, bone-in skin-on
• Coarse sea salt and ground black pepper, to taste
• 1 teaspoon fresh basil leaves, chopped
• 2 tablespoons lemon zest, grated
DIRECTIONS:
Rub olive oil on all sides of the turkey breasts; sprinkle with salt, pepper, basil, and lemon zest.
Place the turkey breasts skin side up on a parchment-lined cooking basket.
Cook in the preheated Air Fryer at 330 degrees F for 30 minutes. Now, turn them over and cook an additional 28 minutes.
Serve with lemon wedges, if desired.
Nutrition Info: 416 Calories; 26g Fat; 0g Carbs; 49g Protein; 0g Sugars; 2g Fiber

116. TOMATO AND AVOCADO
Servings: 4
Cooking Time: 12 Minutes
INGREDIENTS:
• ½ lb. cherry tomatoes; halved
• 2 avocados, pitted; peeled and cubed
• 1 ¼ cup lettuce; torn
• 1/3 cup coconut cream
• A pinch of salt and black pepper
• Cooking spray
DIRECTIONS:
Grease the air fryer with cooking spray, combine the tomatoes with avocados, salt, pepper and the cream and cook at 350°F for 5 minutes shaking once
In a salad bowl, mix the lettuce with the tomatoes and avocado mix, toss and serve.
Nutrition Info: Calories: 226; Fat: 12g; Fiber: 2g; Carbs: 4g; Protein: 8g

117. ONION OMELET
Servings: 2
Cooking Time: 15 Minutes
INGREDIENTS:
• 4 eggs
• ¼ teaspoon low-sodium soy sauce
• Ground black pepper, as required
• 1 teaspoon butter
• 1 medium yellow onion, sliced
• ¼ cup Cheddar cheese, grated
DIRECTIONS:
In a skillet, melt the butter over medium heat and cook the onion and cook for about 8-10 minutes.
Remove from the heat and set aside to cool slightly.

Meanwhile, in a bowl, add the eggs, soy sauce and black pepper and beat well.
Add the cooked onion and gently, stir to combine.
Place the zucchini mixture into a small baking pan.
Press "Power Button" of Air Fry Oven and turn the dial to select the "Air Fry" mode.
Press the Time button and again turn the dial to set the cooking time to 5 minutes.
Now push the Temp button and rotate the dial to set the temperature at 355 degrees F.
Press "Start/Pause" button to start.
When the unit beeps to show that it is preheated, open the lid.
Arrange pan over the "Wire Rack" and insert in the oven.
Cut the omelet into 2 portions and serve hot.
Nutrition Info: Calories: 222 Cal Total Fat: 15.4 g Saturated Fat: 6.9 g Cholesterol: 347 mg Sodium: 264 mg Total Carbs: 6.1 g Fiber: 1.2 g Sugar: 3.1 g Protein: 15.3 g

118. PARMIGIANO REGGIANO AND PROSCIUTTO TOASTS WITH BALSAMIC GLAZE
Servings: 8
Cooking Time: 15 Minutes

INGREDIENTS:
• 3 ounces thinly sliced prosciutto, cut crosswise into 1/4-inch-wide strips
• 1 (3-ounce) piece Parmigiano Reggiano cheese
• 1/2 cup balsamic vinegar
• 1 medium red onion, thinly sliced
• 1 loaf ciabatta, cut into 3/4-inch-thick slices
• 1 tablespoon extra-virgin olive oil
• 1 clove garlic
• Black pepper to taste
DIRECTIONS:
Preheat toaster oven to 350°F.
Place onion in a bowl of cold water and let sit for 10 minutes.
Bring vinegar to a boil, then reduce heat and simmer for 5 minutes.
Remove from heat completely and set aside to allow the vinegar to thicken.
Drain the onion.
Brush the tops of each bun with oil, rub with garlic, and sprinkle with pepper.
Use a vegetable peeler to make large curls of Parmigiano Reggiano cheese and place them on the bun.
Bake for 15 minutes or until the bread just starts to crisp.
Sprinkle prosciutto and onions on top, then drizzle vinegar and serve.
Nutrition Info: Calories: 154, Sodium: 432 mg, Dietary Fiber: 1.0 g, Total Fat: 5.6 g, Total Carbs: 17.3 g, Protein: 8.1 g.

119. SWEET POTATO CHIPS
Servings: 2
Cooking Time: 40 Minutes
INGREDIENTS:
• 2 sweet potatoes
• Salt and pepper to taste
• Olive oil
• Cinnamon
DIRECTIONS:
Start by preheating toaster oven to 400°F.
Cut off each end of potato and discard.
Cut potatoes into 1/2-inch slices.
Brush a pan with olive oil and lay potato slices flat on the pan.
Bake for 20 minutes, then flip and bake for another 20.
Nutrition Info: Calories: 139, Sodium: 29 mg, Dietary Fiber: 8.2 g, Total Fat: 0.5 g, Total Carbs: 34.1 g, Protein: 1.9 g.

120. CHICKEN PARMESAN

Servings: 4
Cooking Time: 10 Minutes
INGREDIENTS:

- 2 (6-oz.boneless, skinless chicken breasts
- 1 oz. pork rinds, crushed
- ½ cup grated Parmesan cheese, divided.
- 1 cup low-carb, no-sugar-added pasta sauce.
- 1 cup shredded mozzarella cheese, divided.
- 4 tbsp. full-fat mayonnaise, divided.
- ½ tsp. garlic powder.
- ¼ tsp. dried oregano.
- ½ tsp. dried parsley.

DIRECTIONS:

Slice each chicken breast in half lengthwise and lb. out to 3/4-inch thickness. Sprinkle with garlic powder, oregano and parsley

Spread 1 tbsp. mayonnaise on top of each piece of chicken, then sprinkle ¼ cup mozzarella on each piece.

In a small bowl, mix the crushed pork rinds and Parmesan. Sprinkle the mixture on top of mozzarella

Pour sauce into 6-inch round baking pan and place chicken on top. Place pan into the air fryer basket. Adjust the temperature to 320 Degrees F and set the timer for 25 minutes

Cheese will be browned and internal temperature of the chicken will be at least 165 Degrees F when fully cooked. Serve warm.

Nutrition Info: Calories: 393; Protein: 32g; Fiber: 1g; Fat: 28g; Carbs: 8g

121. PARMESAN-CRUSTED PORK LOIN

Servings: 4
Cooking Time: 20 Minutes
INGREDIENTS:

- 1 pound pork loin
- 1 teaspoon salt
- 1/2 tablespoon garlic powder
- 1/2 tablespoon onion powder
- 2 tablespoons parmesan cheese
- 1 tablespoon olive oil

DIRECTIONS:

Start by preheating toaster oven to 475°F.

Place pan in the oven and let it heat while the oven preheats.

Mix all ingredients in a shallow dish and roll the pork loin until it is fully coated.

Remove pan and sear the pork in the pan on each side.

Once seared, bake pork in the pan for 20 minutes.

Nutrition Info: Calories: 334, Sodium: 718 mg, Dietary Fiber: 0 g, Total Fat: 20.8 g, Total Carbs: 1.7 g, Protein: 33.5 g.

122. CHICKEN & RICE CASSEROLE

Servings: 6
Cooking Time: 40 Minutes
INGREDIENTS:

- 2 lbs. bone-in chicken thighs
- Salt and black pepper
- 1 teaspoon olive oil
- 5 cloves garlic, chopped
- 2 large onions, chopped
- 2 large red bell peppers, chopped
- 1 tablespoon sweet Hungarian paprika
- 1 teaspoon hot Hungarian paprika
- 2 tablespoons tomato paste
- 2 cups chicken broth
- 3 cups brown rice, thawed
- 2 tablespoons parsley, chopped

- 6 tablespoons sour cream

DIRECTIONS:

Mix broth, tomato paste, and all the spices in a bowl.

Add chicken and mix well to coat.

Spread the rice in a casserole dish and add chicken along with its marinade.

Top the casserole with the rest of the Ingredients:.

Press "Power Button" of Air Fry Oven and turn the dial to select the "Bake" mode.

Press the Time button and again turn the dial to set the cooking time to 40 minutes.

Now push the Temp button and rotate the dial to set the temperature at 350 degrees F.

Once preheated, place the baking pan inside and close its lid.

Serve warm.

Nutrition Info: Calories 440 Total Fat 7.9 g Saturated Fat 1.8 g Cholesterol 5 mg Sodium 581 mg Total Carbs 21.8 g Sugar 7.1 g Fiber 2.6 g Protein 37.2 g

123. ROASTED BEET SALAD WITH ORANGES & BEET GREENS

Servings: 6
Cooking Time: 1-1/2 Hours
INGREDIENTS:

- 6 medium beets with beet greens attached
- 2 large oranges
- 1 small sweet onion, cut into wedges
- 1/3 cup red wine vinegar
- 1/4 cup extra-virgin olive oil
- 2 garlic cloves, minced
- 1/2 teaspoon grated orange peel

DIRECTIONS:

Start by preheating toaster oven to 400°F.

Trim leaves from beets and chop, then set aside.

Pierce beets with a fork and place in a roasting pan.

Roast beets for 1-1/2 hours.

Allow beets to cool, peel, then cut into 8 wedges and put into a bowl.

Place beet greens in a sauce pan and cover with just enough water to cover. Heat until water boils, then immediately remove from heat.

Drain greens and press to remove liquid from greens, then add to beet bowl.

Remove peel and pith from orange and segment, adding each segment to the bowl.

Add onion to beet mixture. In a separate bowl mix together vinegar, oil, garlic and orange peel.

Combine both bowls and toss, sprinkle with salt and pepper.

Let stand for an hour before serving.

Nutrition Info: Calories: 214, Sodium: 183 mg, Dietary Fiber: 6.5 g, Total Fat: 8.9 g, Total Carbs: 32.4 g, Protein: 4.7 g.

124. ZUCCHINI AND CAULIFLOWER STEW

Servings: 4
Cooking Time: 12 Minutes
INGREDIENTS:

- 1 cauliflower head, florets separated
- 1 ½ cups zucchinis; sliced
- 1 handful parsley leaves; chopped.
- ½ cup tomato puree
- 2 green onions; chopped.
- 1 tbsp. balsamic vinegar
- 1 tbsp. olive oil
- Salt and black pepper to taste.

DIRECTIONS:

In a pan that fits your air fryer, mix the zucchinis with the rest of the ingredients except the parsley, toss, introduce the pan in the air fryer and cook at 380°F for 20 minutes

Divide into bowls and serve for lunch with parsley sprinkled on top.

Nutrition Info: Calories: 193; Fat: 5g; Fiber: 2g; Carbs: 4g; Protein: 7g

125. SPICY AVOCADO CAULIFLOWER TOAST

Servings: 2

Cooking Time: 15 Minutes

INGREDIENTS:

- 1/2 large head of cauliflower, leaves removed
- 3 1/4 teaspoons olive oil
- 1 small jalapeño
- 1 tablespoon chopped cilantro leaves
- 2 slices whole grain bread
- 1 medium avocado
- Salt and pepper
- 5 radishes
- 1 green onion
- 2 teaspoons hot sauce
- 1 lime

DIRECTIONS:

Start by preheating toaster oven to 450°F.

Cut cauliflower into thick pieces, about 3/4-inches-thick, and slice jalapeño into thin slices.

Place cauliflower and jalapeño in a bowl and mix together with 2 teaspoons olive oil.

Add salt and pepper to taste and mix for another minute.

Coat a pan with another teaspoon of olive oil, then lay the cauliflower mixture flat across the pan.

Cook for 20 minutes, flipping in the last 5 minutes.

Reduce heat to toast.

Sprinkle cilantro over the mix while it is still warm, and set aside.

Brush bread with remaining oil and toast until golden brown, about 5 minutes.

Dice onion and radish.

Mash avocado in a bowl, then spread on toast and sprinkle salt and pepper to taste.

Put cauliflower mix on toast and cover with onion and radish. Drizzle with hot sauce and serve with a lime wedge.

Nutrition Info: Calories: 359, Sodium: 308 mg, Dietary Fiber: 11.1 g, Total Fat: 28.3 g, Total Carbs: 26.4 g, Protein: 6.6 g.

126. CHICKEN LEGS WITH DILLED BRUSSELS SPROUTS

Servings: 2

Cooking Time: 10 Minutes

INGREDIENTS:

- 2 chicken legs
- 1/2 teaspoon paprika
- 1/2 teaspoon kosher salt
- 1/2 teaspoon black pepper
- 1/2 pound Brussels sprouts
- 1 teaspoon dill, fresh or dried

DIRECTIONS:

Start by preheating your Air Fryer to 370 degrees F.

Now, season your chicken with paprika, salt, and pepper. Transfer the chicken legs to the cooking basket. Cook for 10 minutes.

Flip the chicken legs and cook an additional 10 minutes. Reserve.

Add the Brussels sprouts to the cooking basket; sprinkle with dill. Cook at 380 degrees F for 15 minutes, shaking the basket halfway through.

Serve with the reserved chicken legs.

Nutrition Info: 365 Calories; 21g Fat; 3g Carbs; 36g Protein; 2g Sugars; 3g Fiber

127. SWEET POTATO AND PARSNIP SPIRALIZED LATKES

Servings: 12

Cooking Time: 20 Minutes

INGREDIENTS:

- 1 medium sweet potato
- 1 large parsnip
- 4 cups water
- 1 egg + 1 egg white
- 2 scallions
- 1/2 teaspoon garlic powder
- 1/2 teaspoon sea salt
- 1/2 teaspoon ground pepper

DIRECTIONS:

Start by spiralizing the sweet potato and parsnip and chopping the scallions, reserving only the green parts.

Preheat toaster oven to 425°F.

Bring 4 cups of water to a boil. Place all of your noodles in a colander and pour the boiling water over the top, draining well.

Let the noodles cool, then grab handfuls and place them in a paper towel; squeeze to remove as much liquid as possible.

In a large bowl, beat egg and egg white together. Add noodles, scallions, garlic powder, salt, and pepper, mix well.

Prepare a baking sheet; scoop out 1/4 cup of mixture at a time and place on sheet.

Slightly press down each scoop with your hands, then bake for 20 minutes, flipping halfway through.

Nutrition Info: Calories: 24, Sodium: 91 mg, Dietary Fiber: 1.0 g, Total Fat: 0.4 g, Total Carbs: 4.3 g, Protein: 0.9 g.

128. HERBED RADISH SAUTÉ

Servings: 4

Cooking Time: 12 Minutes

INGREDIENTS:

- 2 bunches red radishes; halved
- 2 tbsp. parsley; chopped.
- 2 tbsp. balsamic vinegar
- 1 tbsp. olive oil
- Salt and black pepper to taste.

DIRECTIONS:

Take a bowl and mix the radishes with the remaining ingredients except the parsley, toss and put them in your air fryer's basket.

Cook at 400°F for 15 minutes, divide between plates, sprinkle the parsley on top and serve as a side dish

Nutrition Info: Calories: 180; Fat: 4g; Fiber: 2g; Carbs: 3g; Protein: 5g

129. HERB-ROASTED CHICKEN TENDERS

Servings: 2

Cooking Time: 10 Minutes

INGREDIENTS:

- 7 ounces chicken tenders
- 1 tablespoon olive oil
- 1/2 teaspoon Herbes de Provence
- 2 tablespoons Dijon mustard
- 1 tablespoon honey
- Salt and pepper

DIRECTIONS:

Start by preheating toaster oven to 450°F.

Brush bottom of pan with 1/2 tablespoon olive oil.

Season the chicken with herbs, salt, and pepper.

Place the chicken in a single flat layer in the pan and drizzle the remaining olive oil over it.

Bake for about 10 minutes.

While the chicken is baking, mix together the mustard and honey for a tasty condiment.

Nutrition Info: Calories: 297, Sodium: 268 mg, Dietary Fiber: 0.8 g, Total Fat: 15.5 g, Total Carbs: 9.6 g, Protein: 29.8 g.

130. AIR FRIED STEAK SANDWICH

Servings: 4
Cooking Time: 16 Minutes
INGREDIENTS:
• Large hoagie bun, sliced in half
• 6 ounces of sirloin or flank steak, sliced into bite-sized pieces
• ½ tablespoon of mustard powder
• ½ tablespoon of soy sauce
• 1 tablespoon of fresh bleu cheese, crumbled
• 8 medium-sized cherry tomatoes, sliced in half
• 1 cup of fresh arugula, rinsed and patted dry

DIRECTIONS:
Preparing the ingredients. In a small mixing bowl, combine the soy sauce and onion powder; stir with a fork until thoroughly combined.
Lay the raw steak strips in the soy-mustard mixture, and fully immerse each piece to marinate.
Set the instant crisp air fryer to 320 degrees for 10 minutes.
Arrange the soy-mustard marinated steak pieces on a piece of tin foil, flat and not overlapping, and set the tin foil on one side of the instant crisp air fryer basket. The foil should not take up more than half of the surface.
Lay the hoagie-bun halves, crusty-side up and soft-side down, on the other half of the air-fryer.
Air frying. Close air fryer lid.
After 10 minutes, the instant crisp air fryer will shut off; the hoagie buns should be starting to crisp and the steak will have begun to cook.
Carefully, flip the hoagie buns so they are now crusty-side down and soft-side up; crumble a layer of the bleu cheese on each hoagie half.
With a long spoon, gently stir the marinated steak in the foil to ensure even coverage.
Set the instant crisp air fryer to 360 degrees for 6 minutes.
After 6 minutes, when the fryer shuts off, the bleu cheese will be perfectly melted over the toasted bread, and the steak will be juicy on the inside and crispy on the outside.
Remove the cheesy hoagie halves first, using tongs, and set on a serving plate; then cover one side with the steak, and top with the cherry-tomato halves and the arugula. Close with the other cheesy hoagie-half, slice into two pieces, and enjoy.
Nutrition Info: Calories 284 Total fat 7.9 g Saturated fat 1.4 g Cholesterol 36 mg Sodium 704 mg Total carbs 46 g Fiber 3.6 g Sugar 5.5 g Protein 17.9 g

131. DIJON AND SWISS CROQUE MONSIEUR

Servings: 2
Cooking Time: 13 Minutes
INGREDIENTS:
• 4 slices white bread
• 2 tablespoons unsalted butter
• 1 tablespoon all-purpose flour
• 1/2 cup whole milk
• 3/4 cups shredded Swiss cheese
• 1/4 teaspoon freshly ground black pepper
• 1/8 teaspoon salt
• 1 tablespoon Dijon mustard
• 4 slices ham

DIRECTIONS:
Start by cutting crusts off bread and placing them on a pan lined with parchment paper.
Melt 1 tablespoon of butter in a sauce pan, then dab the top sides of each piece of bread with butter.
Toast bread in oven for 3-5 minutes until each piece is golden brown.
Melt the second tablespoon of butter in the sauce pan and add the flour, mix together until they form a paste.
Add the milk and continue to mix until the sauce begins to thicken.

Remove from heat and mix in 1 tablespoon of Swiss cheese, salt, and pepper; continue stirring until cheese is melted.
Flip the bread over in the pan so the untoasted side is facing up.
Set two slices aside and spread Dijon on the other two slices.
Add ham and sprinkle 1/4 cup Swiss over each piece.
Broil for about 3 minutes.
Top the sandwiches off with the other slices of bread, soft-side down.
Top with sauce and sprinkle with remaining Swiss. Toast for another 5 minutes or until the cheese is golden brown.
Serve immediately.
Nutrition Info: Calories: 452, Sodium: 1273 mg, Dietary Fiber: 1.6 g, Total Fat: 30.5 g, Total Carbs: 19.8 g, Protein: 24.4 g.

132. BUTTERY ARTICHOKES

Servings: 4
Cooking Time: 20 Minutes
INGREDIENTS:
• 4 artichokes, trimmed and halved
• 3 garlic cloves, minced
• 1 tablespoon olive oil
• Salt and black pepper to the taste
• 4 tablespoons butter, melted
• ¼ teaspoon cumin, ground
• 1 tablespoon lemon zest, grated

DIRECTIONS:
In a bowl, combine the artichokes with the oil, garlic and the other Ingredients:, toss well and transfer them to the air fryer's basket.
Cook for 20 minutes at 370 degrees F, divide between plates and serve as a side dish.
Nutrition Info: Calories 214, fat 5, fiber 8, carbs 12, protein 5

133. CRISPY BREADED PORK CHOP

Servings: 6
Cooking Time: 12 Minutes
INGREDIENTS:
• olive oil spray
• 6 3/4-inch thick center-cut boneless pork chops, fat trimmed
• (5 oz each)
• kosher salt
• 1 large egg, beaten
• 1/2 cup panko crumbs, check labels for GF
• 1/3 cup crushed cornflakes crumbs
• 2 tbsp grated parmesan cheese
• 1 1/4 tsp sweet paprika
• 1/2 tsp garlic powder
• 1/2 tsp onion powder
• 1/4 tsp chili powder
• 1/8 tsp black pepper

DIRECTIONS:
Preheat the Instant Pot Duo Crisp Air Fryer for 12 minutes at 400°F.
On both sides, season pork chops with half teaspoon kosher salt.
Then combine cornflake crumbs, panko, parmesan cheese, 3/4 tsp kosher salt, garlic powder, paprika, onion powder, chili powder, and black pepper in a large bowl.
Place the egg beat in another bowl. Dip the pork in the egg & then crumb mixture.
When the air fryer is ready, place 3 of the chops into the Instant Pot Duo Crisp Air Fryer Basket and spritz the top with oil.
Close the Air Fryer lid and cook for 12 minutes turning halfway, spritzing both sides with oil.
Set aside and repeat with the remaining.
Nutrition Info: Calories 281, Total Fat 13g, Total Carbs 8g, Protein 33g

134. ROASTED STUFFED PEPPERS

Servings: 4

Cooking Time: 20 Minutes

INGREDIENTS:

- 4 ounces shredded cheddar cheese
- ½ tsp. Pepper
- ½ tsp. Salt
- 1 tsp. Worcestershire sauce
- ½ c. Tomato sauce
- 8 ounces lean ground beef
- 1 tsp. Olive oil
- 1 minced garlic clove
- ½ chopped onion
- 2 green peppers

DIRECTIONS:

Preparing the ingredients. Ensure your instant crisp air fryer is preheated to 390 degrees. Spray with olive oil.

Cut stems off bell peppers and remove seeds. Cook in boiling salted water for 3 minutes.

Sauté garlic and onion together in a skillet until golden in color.

Take skillet off the heat. Mix pepper, salt, Worcestershire sauce, ¼ cup of tomato sauce, half of cheese and beef together.

Divide meat mixture into pepper halves. Top filled peppers with remaining cheese and tomato sauce.

Place filled peppers in the instant crisp air fryer.

Air frying. Close air fryer lid. Set temperature to 390°f, and set time to 20 minutes, bake 15-20 minutes.

Nutrition Info: Calories: 295; Fat: 8g; Protein:23g; Sugar:2g

135. SWEET POTATO ROSTI

Servings: 2

Cooking Time: 15 Minutes

INGREDIENTS:

- ½ lb. sweet potatoes, peeled, grated and squeezed
- 1 tablespoon fresh parsley, chopped finely
- Salt and ground black pepper, as required
- 2 tablespoons sour cream

DIRECTIONS:

In a large bowl, mix together the grated sweet potato, parsley, salt, and black pepper.

Press "Power Button" of Air Fry Oven and turn the dial to select the "Air Fry" mode.

Press the Time button and again turn the dial to set the cooking time to 15 minutes.

Now push the Temp button and rotate the dial to set the temperature at 355 degrees F.

Press "Start/Pause" button to start.

When the unit beeps to show that it is preheated, open the lid and lightly grease the sheet pan.

Arrange the sweet potato mixture into the "Sheet Pan" and shape it into an even circle.

Insert the "Sheet Pan" in the oven.

Cut the potato rosti into wedges.

Top with the sour cream and serve immediately.

Nutrition Info: Calories: 160 Cal Total Fat: 2.7 g Saturated Fat: 1.6 g Cholesterol: 5 mg Sodium: 95 mg Total Carbs: 32.3 g Fiber: 4.7 g Sugar: 0.6 g Protein: 2.2 g

136. TOMATO FRITTATA

Servings: 2

Cooking Time: 30 Minutes

INGREDIENTS:

- 4 eggs
- ¼ cup onion, chopped
- ½ cup tomatoes, chopped
- ½ cup milk
- 1 cup Gouda cheese, shredded
- Salt, as required

DIRECTIONS:

In a small baking pan, add all the ingredients and mix well.

Press "Power Button" of Air Fry Oven and turn the dial to select the "Air Fry" mode.

Press the Time button and again turn the dial to set the cooking time to 30 minutes.

Now push the Temp button and rotate the dial to set the temperature at 340 degrees F.

Press "Start/Pause" button to start.

When the unit beeps to show that it is preheated, open the lid.

Arrange the baking pan over the "Wire Rack" and insert in the oven.

Cut into 2 wedges and serve.

Nutrition Info: Calories: 247 Cal Total Fat: 16.1 g Saturated Fat: 7.5 g Cholesterol: 332 mg Sodium: 417 mg Total Carbs: 7.30 g Fiber: 0.9 g Sugar: 5.2 g Protein: 18.6 g

137. BBQ CHICKEN BREASTS

Servings: 4

Cooking Time: 15 Minutes

INGREDIENTS:

- 4 boneless skinless chicken breast about 6 oz each
- 1-2 Tbsp bbq seasoning

DIRECTIONS:

Cover both sides of chicken breast with the BBQ seasoning. Cover and marinate the in the refrigerator for 45 minutes.

Choose the Air Fry option and set the temperature to 400°F. Push start and let it preheat for 5 minutes.

Upon preheating, place the chicken breast in the Instant Pot Duo Crisp Air Fryer basket, making sure they do not overlap. Spray with oil.

Cook for 13-14 minutes .flipping halfway.

Remove chicken when the chicken reaches an internal temperature of 160°F. Place on a plate and allow to rest for 5 minutes before slicing.

Nutrition Info: Calories 131, Total Fat 3g, Total Carbs 2g, Protein 24g

138. GARLIC CHICKEN POTATOES

Servings: 4

Cooking Time: 30 Minutes

INGREDIENTS:

- 2 lbs. red potatoes, quartered
- 3 tablespoons olive oil
- 1/2 teaspoon cumin seeds
- Salt and black pepper, to taste
- 4 garlic cloves, chopped
- 2 tablespoons brown sugar
- 1 lemon (1/2 juiced and 1/2 cut into wedges)
- Pinch of red pepper flakes
- 4 skinless, boneless chicken breasts
- 2 tablespoons cilantro, chopped

DIRECTIONS:

Place the chicken, lemon, garlic, and potatoes in a baking pan.

Toss the spices, herbs, oil, and sugar in a bowl.

Add this mixture to the chicken and veggies then toss well to coat.

Press "Power Button" of Air Fry Oven and turn the dial to select the "Bake" mode.

Press the Time button and again turn the dial to set the cooking time to 30 minutes.

Now push the Temp button and rotate the dial to set the temperature at 400 degrees F.

Once preheated, place the baking pan inside and close its lid.

Serve warm.

Nutrition Info: Calories 545 Total Fat 36.4 g Saturated Fat 10.1 g Cholesterol 200 mg Sodium 272 mg Total Carbs 40.7 g Fiber 0.2 g Sugar 0.1 g Protein 42.5 g

139. ROASTED GARLIC

Servings: 12 Cloves

Cooking Time: 12 Minutes

INGREDIENTS:

- 1 medium head garlic
- 2 tsp. avocado oil

DIRECTIONS:

Remove any hanging excess peel from the garlic but leave the cloves covered. Cut off ¼ of the head of garlic, exposing the tips of the cloves Drizzle with avocado oil. Place the garlic head into a small sheet of aluminum foil, completely enclosing it. Place it into the air fryer basket. Adjust the temperature to 400 Degrees F and set the timer for 20 minutes. If your garlic head is a bit smaller, check it after 15 minutes

When done, garlic should be golden brown and very soft

To serve, cloves should pop out and easily be spread or sliced. Store in an airtight container in the refrigerator up to 5 days.

You may also freeze individual cloves on a baking sheet, then store together in a freezer-safe storage bag once frozen.

Nutrition Info: Calories: 11; Protein: 2g; Fiber: 1g; Fat: 7g; Carbs: 0g

140. CHICKEN WITH VEGGIES AND RICE

Servings: 3

Cooking Time: 20 Minutes

INGREDIENTS:

- 3 cups cold boiled white rice
- 1 cup cooked chicken, diced
- ½ cup frozen carrots
- ½ cup frozen peas
- ½ cup onion, chopped
- 6 tablespoons soy sauce
- 1 tablespoon vegetable oil

DIRECTIONS:

Preheat the Air fryer to 360 degree F and grease a 7" nonstick pan.

Mix the rice, soy sauce, and vegetable oil in a bowl.

Stir in the remaining ingredients and mix until well combined.

Transfer the rice mixture into the pan and place in the Air fryer.

Cook for about 20 minutes and dish out to serve immediately.

Nutrition Info: Calories: 405, Fat: 6.4g, Carbohydrates: 63g, Sugar: 3.5g, Protein: 21.7g, Sodium: 1500mg

141. TURKEY MEATLOAF

Servings: 4

Cooking Time: 20 Minutes

INGREDIENTS:

- 1 pound ground turkey
- 1 cup kale leaves, trimmed and finely chopped
- 1 cup onion, chopped
- ½ cup fresh breadcrumbs
- 1 cup Monterey Jack cheese, grated
- 2 garlic cloves, minced
- ¼ cup salsa verde
- 1 teaspoon red chili powder
- ½ teaspoon ground cumin
- ½ teaspoon dried oregano, crushed
- Salt and ground black pepper, as required

DIRECTIONS:

Preheat the Air fryer to 400 degree F and grease an Air fryer basket.

Mix all the ingredients in a bowl and divide the turkey mixture into 4 equal-sized portions.

Shape each into a mini loaf and arrange the loaves into the Air fryer basket.

Cook for about 20 minutes and dish out to serve warm.

Nutrition Info: Calories: 435, Fat: 23.1g, Carbohydrates: 18.1g, Sugar: 3.6g, Protein: 42.2g, Sodium: 641mg

142. FRIED PAPRIKA TOFU

Servings:

Cooking Time: 12 Minutes

INGREDIENTS:

- 1 block extra firm tofu; pressed to remove excess water and cut into cubes
- 1/4 cup cornstarch
- 1 tablespoon smoked paprika
- salt and pepper to taste

DIRECTIONS:

Line the Air Fryer basket with aluminum foil and brush with oil. Preheat the Air Fryer to 370 - degrees Fahrenheit.

Mix all ingredients in a bowl. Toss to combine. Place in the Air Fryer basket and cook for 12 minutes.

143. BBQ PORK RIBS

Basic Recipe

Preparation Time: 10 minutes

Cooking Time: 12 minutes

Servings: 6

INGREDIENTS:

- 1 slab baby back pork ribs, cut into pieces
- ½ cup BBQ sauce
- ½ tsp paprika
- Salt

DIRECTIONS:

Add pork ribs in a mixing bowl. Add BBQ sauce, paprika, and salt over pork ribs and coat well and set aside for 30 minutes

Preheat the Cosori air fryer oven to 350 F. Arrange marinated pork ribs on Cosori air fryer oven pan and cook for 10-12 minutes Turn halfway through.

Serve and enjoy.

NUTRITION: Calories 145 Fat 7 g Carbs 10 g Protein 9 g

144. SPICE-ROASTED ALMONDS

Servings: 32

Cooking Time: 10 Minutes

INGREDIENTS:

- 1 tablespoon chili powder
- 1 tablespoon olive oil
- 1/2 teaspoon salt
- 1/2 teaspoon ground cumin
- 1/2 teaspoon ground coriander
- 1/4 teaspoon ground cinnamon
- 1/4 teaspoon black pepper
- 2 cups whole almonds

DIRECTIONS:

Start by preheating toaster oven to 350°F.

Mix olive oil, chili powder, coriander, cinnamon, cumin, salt, and pepper. Add almonds and toss together.

Transfer to a baking pan and bake for 10 minutes.

Nutrition Info: Calories: 39, Sodium: 37 mg, Dietary Fiber: 0.8 g, Total Fat: 3.5 g, Total Carbs: 1.4 g, Protein: 1.3 g.

145. ROASTED FENNEL, DITALINI, AND SHRIMP

Servings: 4

Cooking Time: 30 Minutes

INGREDIENTS:

- 1 pound extra large, thawed, tail-on shrimp
- 1 teaspoon fennel seeds
- 1 teaspoon salt
- 1 fennel bulb, halved and sliced crosswise
- 4 garlic cloves, chopped
- 2 tablespoons olive oil

- 1/2 teaspoon freshly ground black pepper
- Grated zest of 1 lemon
- 1/2 pound whole wheat ditalini

DIRECTIONS:

Start by preheating toaster oven to 450°F.

Toast the seeds in a medium pan over medium heat for about 5 minutes, then toss with shrimp.

Add water and 1/2 teaspoon salt to the pan and bring the mixture to a boil.

Reduce heat and simmer for 30 minutes.

Combine fennel, garlic, oil, pepper, and remaining salt in a roasting pan.

Roast for 20 minutes, then add shrimp mixture and roast for another 5 minutes or until shrimp are cooked.

While the fennel is roasting, cook pasta per the directions on the package, drain, and set aside.

Remove the shrimp mixture and mix in pasta, roast for another 5 minutes.

Nutrition Info: Calories: 420, Sodium: 890 mg, Dietary Fiber: 4.2 g, Total Fat: 10.2 g, Total Carbs: 49.5 g, Protein: 33.9 g.

146. VEGETARIAN PHILLY SANDWICH

Servings: 2
Cooking Time: 20 Minutes
INGREDIENTS:

- 2 tablespoons olive oil
- 8 ounces sliced portabello mushrooms
- 1 vidalia onion, thinly sliced
- 1 green bell pepper, thinly sliced
- 1 red bell pepper, thinly sliced
- Salt and pepper
- 4 slices 2% provolone cheese
- 4 rolls

DIRECTIONS:

Preheat toaster oven to 475°F.

Heat the oil in a medium sauce pan over medium heat.

Sauté mushrooms about 5 minutes, then add the onions and peppers and sauté another 10 minutes.

Slice rolls lengthwise and divide the vegetables into each roll.

Add the cheese and toast until the rolls start to brown and the cheese melts.

Nutrition Info: Calories: 645, Sodium: 916 mg, Dietary Fiber: 7.2 g, Total Fat: 33.3 g, Total Carbs: 61.8 g, Protein: 27.1 g.

147. DELICIOUS CHICKEN BURGERS

Servings: 4
Cooking Time: 30 Minutes
INGREDIENTS:

- 4 boneless, skinless chicken breasts
- 1¾ ounces plain flour
- 2 eggs
- 4 hamburger buns, split and toasted
- 4 mozzarella cheese slices
- 1 teaspoon mustard powder
- ½ teaspoon paprika
- 1 teaspoon Worcestershire sauce
- ¼ teaspoon dried parsley
- ¼ teaspoon dried tarragon
- ¼ teaspoon dried oregano
- 1 teaspoon dried garlic
- 1 teaspoon chicken seasoning
- ½ teaspoon cayenne pepper
- Salt and black pepper, as required

DIRECTIONS:

Preheat the Air fryer to 355 degree F and grease an Air fryer basket.

Put the chicken breasts, mustard, paprika, Worcestershire sauce, salt, and black pepper in a food processor and pulse until minced.

Make 4 equal-sized patties from the mixture.

Place the flour in a shallow bowl and whisk the egg in a second bowl.

Combine dried herbs and spices in a third bowl.

Coat each chicken patty with flour, dip into whisked egg and then coat with breadcrumb mixture.

Arrange the chicken patties into the Air fryer basket in a single layer and cook for about 30 minutes, flipping once in between.

Place half bun in a plate, layer with lettuce leaf, patty and cheese slice.

Cover with bun top and dish out to serve warm.

Nutrition Info: Calories: 562, Fat: 20.3g, Carbohydrates: 33g, Sugar: 3.3g, Protein: 58.7g, Sodium: 560mg

148. FLAVORFUL STEAK

Basic Recipe
Preparation Time: 10 minutes
Cooking Time: 18 minutes
Servings: 2
INGREDIENTS:

- 2 steaks, rinsed and pat dry
- ½ tsp garlic powder
- 1 tsp olive oil
- Pepper
- Salt

DIRECTIONS:

Rub steaks with olive oil and season with garlic powder, pepper, and salt.

Preheat the Cosori air fryer oven to 400 F.

Place steaks on air fryer oven pan and air fry for 10-18 minutes turn halfway through.

Serve and enjoy.

NUTRITION: Calories 361 Fat 10.9 g Carbs 0.5 g Protein 61.6 g

149. SAUCY CHICKEN WITH LEEKS

Servings: 6
Cooking Time: 10 Minutes
INGREDIENTS:

- 2 leeks, sliced
- 2 large-sized tomatoes, chopped
- 3 cloves garlic, minced
- ½ teaspoon dried oregano
- 6 chicken legs, boneless and skinless
- ½ teaspoon smoked cayenne pepper
- 2 tablespoons olive oil
- A freshly ground nutmeg

DIRECTIONS:

In a mixing dish, thoroughly combine all ingredients, minus the leeks.

Place in the refrigerator and let it marinate overnight.

Lay the leeks onto the bottom of an Air Fryer cooking basket. Top with the chicken legs.

Roast chicken legs at 375 degrees F for 18 minutes, turning halfway through. Serve with hoisin sauce.

Nutrition Info: 390 Calories; 16g Fat; 2g Carbs; 59g Protein; 8g Sugars; 4g Fiber

150. LAMB GYRO

Servings: 4
Cooking Time: 25 Minutes
INGREDIENTS:

- 1 pound ground lamb
- ¼ red onion, minced
- ¼ cup mint, minced
- ¼ cup parsley, minced
- 2 cloves garlic, minced
- ½ teaspoon salt

- ⅛ teaspoon rosemary
- ½ teaspoon black pepper
- 4 slices pita bread
- ¾ cup hummus
- 1 cup romaine lettuce, shredded
- ½ onion sliced
- 1 Roma tomato, diced
- ½ cucumber, skinned and thinly sliced
- 12 mint leaves, minced
- Tzatziki sauce, to taste

DIRECTIONS:

Mix ground lamb, red onion, mint, parsley, garlic, salt, rosemary, and black pepper until fully incorporated.

Select the Broil function on the COSORI Air Fryer Toaster Oven, set time to 25 minutes and temperature to 450°F, then press Start/Cancel to preheat.

Line the food tray with parchment paper and place ground lamb on top, shaping it into a patty 1-inch-thick and 6 inches in diameter.

Insert the food tray at top position in the preheated air fryer toaster oven, then press Start/Cancel.

Remove when done and cut into thin slices.

Assemble each gyro starting with pita bread, then hummus, lamb meat, lettuce, onion, tomato, cucumber, and mint leaves, then drizzle with tzatziki.

Serve immediately.

Nutrition Info: Calories: 409 kcal Total Fat: 14.6 g Saturated Fat: 0 g Cholesterol: 0 mg Sodium: 0 mg Total Carbs: 29.9 g Fiber: 0 g Sugar: 0 g Protein: 39.4 g

151. LIME AND MUSTARD MARINATED CHICKEN

Servings: 4
Cooking Time: 10 Minutes

INGREDIENTS:

- 1/2 teaspoon stone-ground mustard
- 1/2 teaspoon minced fresh oregano
- 1/3 cup freshly squeezed lime juice
- 2 small-sized chicken breasts, skin-on
- 1 teaspoon kosher salt
- 1teaspoon freshly cracked mixed peppercorns

DIRECTIONS:

Preheat your Air Fryer to 345 degrees F.

Toss all of the above ingredients in a medium-sized mixing dish; allow it to marinate overnight.

Cook in the preheated Air Fryer for 26 minutes.

Nutrition Info: 255 Calories; 15g Fat; 7g Carbs; 33g Protein; 8g Sugars; 3g Fiber

152. OKRA CASSEROLE

Servings: 4
Cooking Time: 12 Minutes

INGREDIENTS:

- 2 red bell peppers; cubed
- 2 tomatoes; chopped.
- 3 garlic cloves; minced
- 3 cups okra
- ½ cup cheddar; shredded
- ¼ cup tomato puree
- 1 tbsp. cilantro; chopped.
- 1 tsp. olive oil
- 2 tsp. coriander, ground
- Salt and black pepper to taste.

DIRECTIONS:

Grease a heat proof dish that fits your air fryer with the oil, add all the ingredients except the cilantro and the cheese and toss them really gently

Sprinkle the cheese and the cilantro on top, introduce the dish in the fryer

and cook at 390°F for 20 minutes.

Divide between plates and serve for lunch.

Nutrition Info: Calories: 221; Fat: 7g; Fiber: 2g; Carbs: 4g; Protein: 9g

153. CRISP CHICKEN CASSEROLE

Servings: 4
Cooking Time: 15 Minutes

INGREDIENTS:

- 3 cup chicken, shredded
- 12 oz bag egg noodles
- 1/2 large onion
- 1/2 cup chopped carrots
- 1/4 cup frozen peas
- 1/4 cup frozen broccoli pieces
- 2 stalks celery chopped
- 5 cup chicken broth
- 1 tsp garlic powder
- salt and pepper to taste
- 1 cup cheddar cheese, shredded
- 1 package French's onions
- 1/4 cup sour cream
- 1 can cream of chicken and mushroom soup

DIRECTIONS:

Place the chicken, vegetables, garlic powder, salt and pepper, and broth and stir. Then place it into the Instant Pot Duo Crisp Air Fryer Basket.

Press or lightly stir the egg noodles into the mix until damp/wet.

Select the option Air Fryer and cook for 4 minutes.

Stir in the sour cream, can of soup, cheese, and 1/3 of the French's onions.

Top with the remaining French's onions and close the Air Fryer lid and cook for about 10 more minutes.

Nutrition Info: Calories 301, Total Fat 17g, Total Carbs 17g, Protein 20g

154. ROASTED MINI PEPPERS

Servings: 6
Cooking Time: 15 Minutes

INGREDIENTS:

- 1 bag mini bell peppers
- Cooking spray
- Salt and pepper to taste

DIRECTIONS:

Start by preheating toaster oven to 400°F.

Wash and dry the peppers, then place flat on a baking sheet.

Spray peppers with cooking spray and sprinkle with salt and pepper.

Roast for 15 minutes.

Nutrition Info: Calories: 19, Sodium: 2 mg, Dietary Fiber: 1.3 g, Total Fat: 0.3 g, Total Carbs: 3.6 g, Protein: 0.6 g.

155. ORANGE CHICKEN RICE

Servings: 4
Cooking Time: 55 Minutes

INGREDIENTS:

- 3 tablespoons olive oil
- 1 medium onion, chopped
- 1 3/4 cups chicken broth
- 1 cup brown basmati rice
- Zest and juice of 2 oranges
- Salt to taste
- 4 (6-oz.) boneless, skinless chicken thighs
- Black pepper, to taste
- 2 tablespoons fresh mint, chopped
- 2 tablespoons pine nuts, toasted

DIRECTIONS:

Spread the rice in a casserole dish and place the chicken on top.

Toss the rest of the Ingredients: in a bowl and liberally pour over the chicken.

Press "Power Button" of Air Fry Oven and turn the dial to select the "Bake" mode.

Press the Time button and again turn the dial to set the cooking time to 55 minutes.

Now push the Temp button and rotate the dial to set the temperature at 350 degrees F.

Once preheated, place the casserole dish inside and close its lid.

Serve warm.

Nutrition Info: Calories 231 Total Fat 20.1 g Saturated Fat 2.4 g Cholesterol 110 mg Sodium 941 mg Total Carbs 30.1 g Fiber 0.9 g Sugar 1.4 g Protein 14.6 g

156. CREAMY GREEN BEANS AND TOMATOES

Servings: 4
Cooking Time: 20 Minutes
INGREDIENTS:
- 1 pound green beans, trimmed and halved
- ½ pound cherry tomatoes, halved
- 2 tablespoons olive oil
- 1 teaspoon oregano, dried
- 1 teaspoon basil, dried
- Salt and black pepper to the taste
- 1 cup heavy cream
- ½ tablespoon cilantro, chopped

DIRECTIONS:
In your air fryer's pan, combine the green beans with the tomatoes and the other Ingredients:, toss and cook at 360 degrees F for 20 minutes. Divide the mix between plates and serve.

Nutrition Info: Calories 174, fat 5, fiber 7, carbs 11, protein 4

157. PECAN CRUNCH CATFISH AND ASPARAGUS

Servings: 4
Cooking Time: 12 Minutes
INGREDIENTS:
- 1 cup whole wheat panko breadcrumbs
- 1/4 cup chopped pecans
- 3 teaspoons chopped fresh thyme
- 1-1/2 tablespoons extra-virgin olive oil, plus more for the pan
- Salt and pepper to taste
- 1-1/4 pounds asparagus
- 1 tablespoon honey
- 4 (5- to 6-ounce each) catfish filets

DIRECTIONS:
Start by preheating toaster oven to 425°F.

Combine breadcrumbs, pecans, 2 teaspoons thyme, 1 tablespoon oil, salt, pepper and 2 tablespoons water.

In another bowl combine asparagus, the rest of the thyme, honey, salt, and pepper.

Spread the asparagus in a flat layer on a baking sheet. Sprinkle a quarter of the breadcrumb mixture over the asparagus.

Lay the catfish over the asparagus and press the rest of the breadcrumb mixture into each piece. Roast for 12 minutes.

Nutrition Info: Calories: 531, Sodium: 291 mg, Dietary Fiber: 6.1 g, Total Fat: 30.4 g, Total Carbs: 31.9 g, Protein: 34.8 g.

158. OREGANO CHICKEN BREAST

Servings: 6
Cooking Time: 25 Minutes
INGREDIENTS:
  2 lbs. chicken breasts, minced
  1 tablespoon avocado oil
  1 teaspoon smoked paprika
  1 teaspoon garlic powder

1 teaspoon oregano
1/2 teaspoon salt
Black pepper, to taste
DIRECTIONS:
Toss all the meatball Ingredients: in a bowl and mix well.

Make small meatballs out this mixture and place them in the air fryer basket.

Press "Power Button" of Air Fry Oven and turn the dial to select the "Air Fry" mode.

Press the Time button and again turn the dial to set the cooking time to 25 minutes.

Now push the Temp button and rotate the dial to set the temperature at 375 degrees F.

Once preheated, place the air fryer basket inside and close its lid.

Serve warm.

Nutrition Info: Calories 352 Total Fat 14 g Saturated Fat 2 g Cholesterol 65 mg Sodium 220 mg Total Carbs 15.8 g Fiber 0.2 g Sugar 1 g Protein 26 g

159. EASY ITALIAN MEATBALLS

Servings: 4
Cooking Time: 13 Minutes
INGREDIENTS:
- 2-lb. lean ground turkey
- ¼ cup onion, minced
- 2 cloves garlic, minced
- 2 tablespoons parsley, chopped
- 2 eggs
- 1½ cup parmesan cheese, grated
- ½ teaspoon red pepper flakes
- ½ teaspoon Italian seasoning Salt and black pepper to taste

DIRECTIONS:
Toss all the meatball Ingredients: in a bowl and mix well.

Make small meatballs out this mixture and place them in the air fryer basket.

Press "Power Button" of Air Fry Oven and turn the dial to select the "Air Fry" mode.

Press the Time button and again turn the dial to set the cooking time to 13 minutes.

Now push the Temp button and rotate the dial to set the temperature at 350 degrees F.

Once preheated, place the air fryer basket inside and close its lid.

Flip the meatballs when cooked halfway through.

Serve warm.

Nutrition Info: Calories 472 Total Fat 25.8 g Saturated Fat .4 g Cholesterol 268 mg Sodium 503 mg Total Carbs 1.7 g Fiber 0.3 g Sugar 0.6 g Protein 59.6 g

160. PORTOBELLO PESTO BURGERS

Servings: 4
Cooking Time: 26 Minutes
INGREDIENTS:
- 4 portobello mushrooms
- 1/4 cup sundried tomato pesto
- 4 whole-grain hamburger buns
- 1 large ripe tomato
- 1 log fresh goat cheese
- 8 large fresh basil leaves

DIRECTIONS:
Start by preheating toaster oven to 425°F.

Place mushrooms on a pan, round sides facing up.

Bake for 14 minutes.

Pull out tray, flip the mushrooms and spread 1 tablespoon of pesto on each piece.

Return to oven and bake for another 10 minutes.

Remove the mushrooms and toast the buns for 2 minutes.

Remove the buns and build the burger by placing tomatoes, mushroom, 2 slices of cheese, and a sprinkle of basil, then topping with the top bun.
Nutrition Info: Calories: 297, Sodium: 346 mg, Dietary Fiber: 1.8 g, Total Fat: 18.1 g, Total Carbs: 19.7 g, Protein: 14.4 g.

161. CRISPY MEATBALLS
Basic Recipe
Preparation Time: 10 minutes
Cooking Time: 12 minutes
Servings: 8
INGREDIENTS:
• 1 lb. ground pork
• 1 lb. ground beef
• 1 tbsp Worcestershire sauce
• ½ cup feta cheese, crumbled
• ½ cup breadcrumbs
• 2 eggs, lightly beaten
• ¼ cup fresh parsley, chopped
• 1 tbsp garlic, minced
• 1 onion, chopped
• ¼ tsp pepper
• 1 tsp salt
DIRECTIONS:
Add all ingredients into the mixing bowl and mix until well combined.
Spray air fryer oven tray pan with cooking spray.
Make small balls from meat mixture and arrange on a pan and air fry t 400 F for 10-12 minutes
Serve and enjoy.
NUTRITION: Calories 263 Fat 9 g Carbs 7.5 g Protein 35.9 g

162. HONEY MUSTARD PORK TENDERLOIN
Basic Recipe
Preparation Time: 10 minutes
Cooking Time: 26 minutes
Servings: 4
INGREDIENTS:
• 1 lb. pork tenderloin
• 1 tsp sriracha sauce
• 1 tbsp garlic, minced
• 2 tbsp soy sauce
• 1 ½ tbsp honey
• ¾ tbsp Dijon mustard
• 1 tbsp mustard
DIRECTIONS:
Add sriracha sauce, garlic, soy sauce, honey, Dijon mustard, and mustard into the large zip-lock bag and mix well.
Add pork tenderloin into the bag. Seal bag and place in the refrigerator for overnight. Preheat the Cosori air fryer oven to 380 F.Spray Cosori air fryer tray with cooking spray then place marinated pork tenderloin on a tray and air fry for 26 minutes Turn pork tenderloin after every 5 minutes. Slice and serve.
NUTRITION: Calories 195 Fat 4.1 g Carbs 8 g Protein 30.5 g

163. EASY ROSEMARY LAMB CHOPS
Basic Recipe
Preparation Time: 10 minutes
Cooking Time: 6 minutes
Servings: 4
INGREDIENTS:
• 4 lamb chops
• 2 tbsp dried rosemary
• ¼ cup fresh lemon juice
• Pepper
• Salt
DIRECTIONS:

In a small bowl, mix together lemon juice, rosemary, pepper, and salt.
Brush lemon juice rosemary mixture over lamb chops.
Place lamb chops on air fryer oven tray and air fry at 400 F for 3 minutes.
Turn lamb chops to the other side and cook for 3 minutes more. Serve and enjoy.
NUTRITION: Calories 267 Fat 21.7 g Carbs 1.4 g Protein 16.9 g

164. SKINNY BLACK BEAN FLAUTAS
Servings: 10
Cooking Time: 25 Minutes
INGREDIENTS:
• 2 (15-ounce) cans black beans
• 1 cup shredded cheddar
• 1 (4-ounce) can diced green chilies
• 2 teaspoons taco seasoning
• 10 (8-inch) whole wheat flour tortillas
• Olive oil
DIRECTIONS:
Start by preheating toaster oven to 350°F.
Drain black beans and mash in a medium bowl with a fork.
Mix in cheese, chilies, and taco seasoning until all ingredients are thoroughly combined.
Evenly spread the mixture over each tortilla and wrap tightly.
Brush each side lightly with olive oil and place on a baking sheet.
Bake for 12 minutes, turn, and bake for another 13 minutes.
Nutrition Info: Calories: 367, Sodium: 136 mg, Dietary Fiber: 14.4 g, Total Fat: 2.8 g, Total Carbs: 64.8 g, Protein: 22.6 g.

165. JUICY STEAK BITES
Basic Recipe
Preparation Time: 10 minutes
Cooking Time: 9 minutes
Servings: 4
INGREDIENTS:
• 1 lb. sirloin steak, cut into bite-size pieces
• 1 tbsp steak seasoning
• 1 tbsp olive oil
• Pepper
• Salt
DIRECTIONS:
Preheat the Cosori air fryer oven to 390 F.
Add steak pieces into the large mixing bowl. Add steak seasoning, oil, pepper, and salt over steak pieces and toss until well coated.
Transfer steak pieces on Cosori air fryer pan and air fry for 5 minutes
Turn steak pieces to the other side and cook for 4 minutes more.
Serve and enjoy.
NUTRITION: Calories 241 Fat 10.6 g Carbs 0 g Protein 34.4 g

166. GREEK LAMB CHOPS
Basic Recipe
Preparation Time: 10 minutes
Cooking Time: 10 minutes
Servings : 4
INGREDIENTS:
• 2 lbs. lamb chops
• 2 tsp garlic, minced
• 1 ½ tsp dried oregano
• ¼ cup fresh lemon juice
• ¼ cup olive oil
• ½ tsp pepper
• 1 tsp salt
DIRECTIONS:
Add lamb chops in a mixing bowl. Add remaining ingredients over the lamb chops and coat well.

Arrange lamb chops on the air fryer oven tray and cook at 400 F for 5 minutes

Turn lamb chops and cook for 5 minutes more.

Serve and enjoy.

NUTRITION: Calories 538 Fat 29.4 g Carbs 1.3 g Protein 64 g

167. HERB BUTTER RIB-EYE STEAK

Basic Recipe

Preparation Time: 10 minutes

Cooking Time: 14 minutes

Servings: 4

INGREDIENTS:

- 2 lbs. rib eye steak, bone-in
- 1 tsp fresh rosemary, chopped
- 1 tsp fresh thyme, chopped
- 1 tsp fresh chives, chopped
- 2 tsp fresh parsley, chopped
- 1 tsp garlic, minced
- ¼ cup butter softened
- Pepper
- Salt

DIRECTIONS:

In a small bowl, combine together butter and herbs.

Rub herb butter on rib-eye steak and place it in the refrigerator for 30 minutes

Place marinated steak on Cosori air fryer oven pan and cook at 400 F for 12-14 minutes

Serve and enjoy.

NUTRITION: Calories 416 Fat 36.7 g Carbs 0.7 g Protein 20.3 g

168. CLASSIC BEEF JERKY

Basic Recipe

Preparation Time: 10 minutes

Cooking Time: 4 hours

Servings: 4

INGREDIENTS:

- 2 lbs. London broil, sliced thinly
- 1 tsp onion powder
- 3 tbsp brown sugar
- 3 tbsp soy sauce
- 1 tsp olive oil
- 3/4 tsp garlic powder

DIRECTIONS:

Add all ingredients except meat in the large zip-lock bag.

Mix until well combined. Add meat in the bag.

Seal bag and massage gently to cover the meat with marinade.

Let marinate the meat for 1 hour.

Arrange marinated meat slices on Cosori air fryer tray and dehydrate at 160 F for 4 hours.

NUTRITION: Calories 133 Fat 4.7 g Carbs 9.4 g Protein 13.4 g

169. SEASONED BEEF ROAST

Basic Recipe

Preparation Time: 10 minutes

Cooking Time: 45 minutes

Servings: 10

INGREDIENTS:

- 3 pounds beef top roast
- 1 tablespoon olive oil
- 2 tablespoons Montreal steak seasoning

DIRECTIONS:

Coat the roast with oil and then rub with the seasoning generously.

With kitchen twines, tie the roast to keep it compact. Arrange the roast onto the cooking tray.

Arrange the drip pan in the bottom of Cosori plus Air Fryer Oven cooking chamber.

Select "Air Fry" and then adjust the temperature to 360 degrees F. Set the timer for 45 minutes and press the "Start".

When the display shows "Add Food" insert the cooking tray in the center position.

When the display shows "Turn Food" do nothing.

When cooking time is complete, remove the tray from Vortex and place the roast onto a platter for about 10 minutes before slicing. With a sharp knife, cut the roast into desired sized slices and serve.

NUTRITION: Calories 269 Fat 9.9 g Carbs 0 g Fiber 0 g

170. CREAMY CHICKEN TENDERS

Servings: 8

Cooking Time: 20 Minutes

INGREDIENTS:

- 2 pounds chicken tenders
- 1 cup feta cheese
- 4 tablespoons olive oil
- 1 cup cream
- Salt and black pepper, to taste

DIRECTIONS:

Preheat the Air fryer to 340 degree F and grease an Air fryer basket.

Season the chicken tenders with salt and black pepper.

Arrange the chicken tenderloins in the Air fryer basket and drizzle with olive oil.\

Cook for about 15 minutes and set the Air fryer to 390 degree F.

Cook for about 5 more minutes and dish out to serve warm.

Repeat with the remaining mixture and dish out to serve hot.

Nutrition Info: Calories: 344, Fat: 21.1g, Carbohydrates: 1.7g, Sugar: 1.4g, Protein: 35.7g, Sodium: 317mg

171. SIMPLE BEEF PATTIES

Basic Recipe

Preparation Time: 10 minutes

Cooking Time: 13 minutes

Servings: 4

INGREDIENTS:

- 1 lb. ground beef
- ½ tsp garlic powder
- ¼ tsp onion powder
- Pepper
- Salt

DIRECTIONS:

Preheat the Cosori air fryer oven to 400 F.

Add ground meat, garlic powder, onion powder, pepper, and salt into the mixing bowl and mix until well combined.

Make even shape patties from meat mixture and arrange on air fryer pan.

Place pan in Cosori air fryer oven.

Cook patties for 10 minutes Turn patties after 5 minutes

Serve and enjoy.

NUTRITION: Calories 212 Fat 7.1 g Carbs 0.4 g Protein 34.5 g

172. LEMON GARLIC LAMB CHOPS

Basic Recipe

Preparation Time: 10 minutes

Cooking Time: 6 minutes

Servings : 6

INGREDIENTS:

- 6 lamb loin chops
- 2 tbsp fresh lemon juice
- 1 ½ tbsp lemon zest
- 1 tbsp dried rosemary

- 1 tbsp olive oil
- 1 tbsp garlic, minced
- Pepper
- Salt

DIRECTIONS:

Add lamb chops in a mixing bowl. Add remaining ingredients on top of lamb chops and coat well.

Arrange lamb chops on air fryer oven tray and air fry at 400 F for 3 minutes. Turn lamb chops to another side and air fry for 3 minutes more. Serve and enjoy.

NUTRITION: Calories 69 Fat 6 g Carbs 1.2 g Protein 3 g

173. BEEF BURGERS

Basic Recipe
Preparation Time: 15 minutes
Cooking Time: 18 minutes
Servings: 4

INGREDIENTS:

For Burgers:
- 1-pound ground beef
- ½ cup panko breadcrumbs
- ¼ cup onion, chopped finely
- 3 tablespoons Dijon mustard
- 3 teaspoons low-sodium soy sauce
- 2 teaspoons fresh rosemary, chopped finely
- Salt, to taste

For Topping:
- 2 tablespoons Dijon mustard
- 1 tablespoon brown sugar
- 1 teaspoon soy sauce
- 4 Gruyere cheese slices

DIRECTIONS:

In a large bowl, add all the ingredients and mix until well combined.

Make 4 equal-sized patties from the mixture.

Arrange the patties onto a cooking tray.

Arrange the drip pan in the bottom of Cosori Plus Air Fryer Oven cooking chamber.

Select "Air Fry" and then adjust the temperature to 370 degrees F.

Set the timer for 15 minutes and press the "Start".

When the display shows "Add Food" insert the cooking rack in the center position.

When the display shows "Turn Food" turn the burgers.

Meanwhile, for sauce: in a small bowl, add the mustard, brown sugar and soy sauce and mix well.

When cooking time is complete, remove the tray from Vortex and coat the burgers with the sauce.

Top each burger with 1 cheese slice.

Return the tray to the cooking chamber and select "Broil".

Set the timer for 3 minutes and press the "Start".

When cooking time is complete, remove the tray from Vortex and serve hot.

NUTRITION: Calories 402 Fat 18 g Carbs 6.3 g Protein 44.4 g

174. JUICY PORK CHOPS

Basic Recipe
Preparation Time: 10 minutes
Cooking Time: 16 minutes
Servings: 4

INGREDIENTS:
- 4 pork chops, boneless
- 2 tsp olive oil
- ½ tsp celery seed
- ½ tsp parsley
- ½ tsp granulated onion
- ½ tsp granulated garlic
- ¼ tsp sugar
- ½ tsp salt

DIRECTIONS:

In a small bowl, mix together oil, celery seed, parsley, granulated onion, granulated garlic, sugar, and salt.

Rub seasoning mixture all over the pork chops.

Place pork chops on the air fryer oven pan and cook at 350 F for 8 minutes

Turn pork chops to other side and cook for 8 minutes more.

Serve and enjoy.

NUTRITION: Calories 279 Fat 22.3 g Carbs 0.6 g Protein 18.1 g

175. SWEET & SOUR PORK

Servings: 4
Cooking Time: 27 Minutes

INGREDIENTS:
- 2 pounds Pork cut into chunks
- 2 large Eggs
- 1 teaspoon Pure Sesame Oil (optional)
- 1 cup Potato Starch (or cornstarch)
- 1/2 teaspoon Sea Salt
- 1/4 teaspoon Freshly Ground Black Pepper
- 1/16 teaspoon Chinese Five Spice
- 3 Tablespoons Canola Oil
- Oil Mister

DIRECTIONS:

In a mixing bowl, combine salt, potato starch, Chinese Five Spice, and peppers.

In another bowl, beat the eggs & add sesame oil.

Then dredge the pieces of Pork into the Potato Starch and remove the excess. Then dip each piece into the egg mixture, shake off excess, and then back into the Potato Starch mixture.

Place pork pieces into the Instant Pot Duo Crisp Air Fryer Basket after spray the pork with oil.

Close the Air Fryer lid and cook at 340°F for approximately 8 to12 minutes (or until pork is cooked), shaking the basket a couple of times for evenly distribution.

Nutrition Info: Calories 521, Total Fat 21g, Total Carbs 23g, Protein 60g

176. EASY BEEF ROAST

Basic Recipe
Preparation Time: 10 minutes
Cooking Time: 45 minutes
Servings: 6

INGREDIENTS:
- 2 ½ lbs. beef roast
- 2 tbsp Italian seasoning

DIRECTIONS:

Arrange roast on the rotisserie spite.

Rub roast with Italian seasoning then insert into the Cosori air fryer oven.

Air fry at 350 F for 45 minutes or until the internal temperature of the roast reaches to 145 F.

Slice and serve.

NUTRITION: Calories 365 Fat 13.2 g Carbs 0.5 g Protein 57.4 g

177. EASY PROSCIUTTO GRILLED CHEESE

Servings: 1
Cooking Time: 5 Minutes

INGREDIENTS:
- 2 slices muenster cheese
- 2 slices white bread
- Four thinly-shaved pieces of prosciutto
- 1 tablespoon sweet and spicy pickles

DIRECTIONS:

Set toaster oven to the Toast setting.

Place one slice of cheese on each piece of bread.

Put prosciutto on one slice and pickles on the other.

Transfer to a baking sheet and toast for 4 minutes or until the cheese is melted.

Combine the sides, cut, and serve.

Nutrition Info: Calories: 460, Sodium: 2180 mg, Dietary Fiber: 0 g, Total Fat: 25.2 g, Total Carbs: 11.9 g, Protein: 44.2 g.

178. TURKEY AND BROCCOLI STEW

Servings: 4

Cooking Time: 12 Minutes

INGREDIENTS:

- 1 broccoli head, florets separated
- 1 turkey breast, skinless; boneless and cubed
- 1 cup tomato sauce
- 1 tbsp. parsley; chopped.
- 1 tbsp. olive oil
- Salt and black pepper to taste.

DIRECTIONS:

In a baking dish that fits your air fryer, mix the turkey with the rest of the ingredients except the parsley, toss, introduce the dish in the fryer, bake at 380°F for 25 minutes

Divide into bowls, sprinkle the parsley on top and serve.

Nutrition Info: Calories: 250; Fat: 11g; Fiber: 2g; Carbs: 6g; Protein: 12g

179. CHICKEN CAPRESE SANDWICH

Servings: 2

Cooking Time: 3 Minutes

INGREDIENTS:

- 2 leftover chicken breasts, or pre-cooked breaded chicken
- 1 large ripe tomato
- 4 ounces mozzarella cheese slices
- 4 slices of whole grain bread
- 1/4 cup olive oil
- 1/3 cup fresh basil leaves
- Salt and pepper to taste

DIRECTIONS:

Start by slicing tomatoes into thin slices.

Layer tomatoes then cheese over two slices of bread and place on a greased baking sheet.

Toast in the toaster oven for about 2 minutes or until the cheese is melted. Heat chicken while the cheese melts.

Remove from oven, sprinkle with basil, and add chicken.

Drizzle with oil and add salt and pepper.

Top with other slice of bread and serve.

Nutrition Info: Calories: 808, Sodium: 847 mg, Dietary Fiber: 5.2 g, Total Fat: 43.6 g, Total Carbs: 30.7 g, Protein: 78.4 g.

180. SIMPLE BEEF SIRLOIN ROAST

Basic Recipe

Preparation Time: 10 minutes

Cooking Time: 50 minutes

Servings: 8

INGREDIENTS:

- 2½ pounds sirloin roast
- Salt and ground black pepper, as required

DIRECTIONS:

Rub the roast with salt and black pepper generously.

Insert the rotisserie rod through the roast.

Insert the rotisserie forks, one on each side of the rod to secure the rod to the chicken.

Arrange the drip pan in the bottom of Cosori Plus Air Fryer Oven cooking chamber.

Select "Roast" and then adjust the temperature to 350 degrees F.

Set the timer for 50 minutes and press the "Start".

When the display shows "Add Food" press the red lever down and load the left side of the rod into the Vortex.

Now, slide the rod's left side into the groove along the metal bar so it doesn't move. Then, close the door and touch "Rotate". Press the red lever to release the rod when cooking time is complete.

Remove from the Vortex and place the roast onto a platter for about 10 minutes before slicing. With a sharp knife, cut the roast into desired sized slices and serve.

NUTRITION: Calories 201 Fat 8.8 g Carbs 0 g Protein 28.9 g

181. SEASONED PORK TENDERLOIN

Basic Recipe

Preparation Time: 10 minutes

Cooking Time: 45 minutes

Servings : 5

INGREDIENTS:

- 1½ pounds pork tenderloin
- 2-3 tablespoons BBQ pork seasoning

DIRECTIONS:

Rub the pork with seasoning generously. Insert the rotisserie rod through the pork tenderloin.

Insert the rotisserie forks, one on each side of the rod to secure the pork tenderloin.

Arrange the drip pan in the bottom of Cosori plus Air Fryer Oven cooking chamber.

Select "Roast" and then adjust the temperature to 360 degrees F.

Set the timer for 45 minutes and press the "Start".

When the display shows "Add Food" press the red lever down and load the left side of the rod into the Vortex.

Now, slide the rod's left side into the groove along the metal bar so it doesn't move.

Then, close the door and touch "Rotate".

Press the red lever to release the rod when cooking time is complete.

Remove the pork from Vortex and place onto a platter for about 10 minutes before slicing.

With a sharp knife, cut the roast into desired sized slices and serve.

NUTRITION: Calories 195 Fat 4.8 g Carbs 0 g Protein 35.6 g

182. GLAZED PORK TENDERLOIN

Basic Recipe

Preparation Time: 15 minutes

Cooking Time: 20 minutes

Servings: 3

INGREDIENTS:

- 1-pound pork tenderloin
- 2 tablespoons Sriracha
- 2 tablespoons honey
- Salt, as required

DIRECTIONS:

Insert the rotisserie rod through the pork tenderloin.

Insert the rotisserie forks, one on each side of the rod to secure the pork tenderloin.

In a small bowl, add the Sriracha, honey and salt and mix well.

Brush the pork tenderloin with honey mixture evenly.

Arrange the drip pan in the bottom of Cosori Plus Air Fryer Oven cooking chamber.

Select "Air Fry" and then adjust the temperature to 350 degrees F.

Set the timer for 20 minutes and press the "Start".

When the display shows "Add Food" press the red lever down and load the left side of the rod into the Vortex.

Now, slide the rod's left side into the groove along the metal bar so it doesn't move.

Then, close the door and touch "Rotate".

Press the red lever to release the rod when cooking time is complete.

Remove the pork from Vortex and place onto a platter for about 10 minutes before slicing.

With a sharp knife, cut the roast into desired sized slices and serve.

NUTRITION: Calories 269 Fat 5.3 g Carbs 13.5 g Protein 39.7 g

183. DUCK ROLLS

Servings: 3

Cooking Time: 40 Minutes

INGREDIENTS:

- 1 pound duck breast fillet, each cut into 2 pieces
- 3 tablespoons fresh parsley, finely chopped
- 1 small red onion, finely chopped
- 1 garlic clove, crushed
- 1½ teaspoons ground cumin
- 1 teaspoon ground cinnamon
- ½ teaspoon red chili powder
- Salt, to taste
- 2 tablespoons olive oil

DIRECTIONS:

Preheat the Air fryer to 355 degree F and grease an Air fryer basket.

Mix the garlic, parsley, onion, spices, and 1 tablespoon of olive oil in a bowl.

Make a slit in each duck piece horizontally and coat with onion mixture.

Roll each duck piece tightly and transfer into the Air fryer basket.

Cook for about 40 minutes and cut into desired size slices to serve.

Nutrition Info: Calories: 239, Fats: 8.2g, Carbohydrates: 3.2g, Sugar: 0.9g, Proteins: 37.5g, Sodium: 46mg

184. PARMESAN SHRIMP

Basic Recipe

Preparation Time: 10 minutes

Cooking Time: 10 minutes

Servings: 6

INGREDIENTS

- 2 pounds jumbo shrimp, wild-caught, peeled, deveined
- 2 tablespoons minced garlic
- 1 teaspoon onion powder
- 1 teaspoon basil
- 1 teaspoon ground black pepper
- 1/2 teaspoon dried oregano
- 2 tablespoons olive oil
- 2/3 cup grated parmesan cheese, reduced Fat
- 2 tablespoons lemon juice

DIRECTIONS:

Switch on the air fryer, insert fryer basket, grease it with olive oil, then shut with its lid, set the fryer at 350 degrees F and preheat for 5 minutes

Meanwhile, place cheese in a bowl, add remaining ingredients except for shrimps and lemon juice and stir until combined.

Add shrimps and then toss until well coated.

Open the fryer, add shrimps in it, spray oil over them, close with its lid and cook for 10 minutes until nicely golden and crispy, shaking halfway through the frying. When air fryer beeps, open its lid, transfer chicken onto a serving plate, Drizzle with lemon juice and serve.

NUTRITION: Calories 307 Cal Carbs 12g Fat 16.4g Protein 27.6g

185. BREADED PORK CHOPS

Basic Recipe

Preparation Time: 15 minutes

Cooking Time: 28 minutes

Servings : 2

INGREDIENTS:

- 2 (5-ounce) boneless pork chops
- 1 cup buttermilk
- ½ cup flour
- 1 teaspoon garlic powder
- Salt and ground black pepper, as required

- Olive oil cooking spray

DIRECTIONS:

In a bowl, place the chops and buttermilk and refrigerate, covered for about 12 hours.

Remove the chops from the bowl of buttermilk, discarding the buttermilk.

In a shallow dish, mix together the flour, garlic powder, salt, and black pepper.

Coat the chops with flour mixture generously.

Place the pork chops onto the cooking tray and spray with the cooking spray.

Arrange the drip pan in the bottom of Cosori Plus Air Fryer Oven cooking chamber.

Select "Air Fry" and then adjust the temperature to 380 degrees F.

Set the timer for 28 minutes and press the "Start".

When the display shows "Add Food" insert the cooking tray in the center position.

When the display shows "Turn Food" turn the pork chops.

When cooking time is complete, remove the tray from Vortex and serve hot.

NUTRITION: Calories 370 Fat 6.4 g Carbs 30.7 g Protein 44.6 g

186. SEASONED PORK CHOPS

Basic Recipe

Preparation Time: 10 minutes

Cooking Time: 12 minutes

Servings: 4

INGREDIENTS:

- 4 (6-ounce) boneless pork chops
- 2 tablespoons pork rub
- 1 tablespoon olive oil

DIRECTIONS:

Coat both sides of the pork chops with the oil and then, rub with the pork rub.

Place the pork chops onto the lightly greased cooking tray.

Arrange the drip pan in the bottom of Cosori Plus Air Fryer Oven cooking chamber.

Select "Air Fry" and then adjust the temperature to 400 degrees F.

Set the timer for 12 minutes and press the "Start".

When the display shows "Add Food" insert the cooking tray in the center position.

When the display shows "Turn Food" turn the pork chops.

When cooking time is complete, remove the tray from Vortex and serve hot.

NUTRITION: Calories 285 Fat 9.5 g Carbs 1.5 g Protein 44.5 g

187. JICAMA FRIES

Servings: 4

Cooking Time: 12 Minutes

INGREDIENTS:

- 1 small jicama; peeled.
- ¼ tsp. onion powder.
- ¾tsp. chili powder
- ¼ tsp. ground black pepper
- ¼ tsp. garlic powder.

DIRECTIONS:

Cut jicama into matchstick-sized pieces.

Place pieces into a small bowl and sprinkle with remaining ingredients.

Place the fries into the air fryer basket

Adjust the temperature to 350 Degrees F and set the timer for 20 minutes. Toss the basket two or three times during cooking. Serve warm.

Nutrition Info: Calories: 37; Protein: 8g; Fiber: 7g; Fat: 1g; Carbs: 7g

188. CRUSTED RACK OF LAMB

Intermediate Recipe
Preparation Time: 15 minutes
Cooking Time: 19 minutes
Servings: 4

INGREDIENTS:
- 1 rack of lamb, trimmed all fat and frenched
- Salt and ground black pepper, as required
- 1/3 cup pistachios, chopped finely
- 2 tablespoons panko breadcrumbs
- 2 teaspoons fresh thyme, chopped finely
- 1 teaspoon fresh rosemary, chopped finely
- 1 tablespoon butter, melted
- 1 tablespoon Dijon mustard

DIRECTIONS:
Insert the rotisserie rod through the rack on the meaty side of the ribs, right next to the bone.
Insert the rotisserie forks, one on each side of the rod to secure the rack.
Season the rack with salt and black pepper evenly.
Arrange the drip pan in the bottom of Cosori Plus Air Fryer Oven cooking chamber.
Select "Air Fry" and then adjust the temperature to 380 degrees F.
Set the timer for 12 minutes and press the "Start".
When the display shows "Add Food" press the red lever down and load the left side of the rod into the Vortex.
Now, slide the rod's left side into the groove along the metal bar so it doesn't move.
Then, close the door and touch "Rotate".
Meanwhile, in a small bowl, mix together the remaining ingredients except the mustard.
Press the red lever to release the rod when cooking time is complete..
Remove the rack from Vortex and brush the meaty side with the mustard.
Then, coat the pistachio mixture on all sides of the rack and press firmly.
Now, place the rack of lamb onto the cooking tray, meat side up.
Select "Air Fry" and adjust the temperature to 380 degrees F.
Set the timer for 7 minutes and press the "Start".
When the display shows "Add Food" insert the cooking tray in the center position.
When the display shows "Turn Food" do nothing.
When cooking time is complete, remove the tray from Vortex and place the rack onto a cutting board for at least 10 minutes
Cut the rack into individual chops and serve.
NUTRITION: Calories 824 Fat 39.3 g Carbs 10.3 g Protein 72 g

189. SHRIMP SCAMPI

Basic Recipe
Preparation Time: 5 minutes
Cooking Time: 12 minutes
Servings: 4

INGREDIENTS:
- 1-pound shrimp, peeled, deveined
- 1 tablespoon minced garlic
- 1 tablespoon minced basil
- 1 tablespoon lemon juice
- 1 teaspoon dried chives
- 1 teaspoon dried basil
- 2 teaspoons red pepper flakes
- 4 tablespoons butter, unsalted
- 2 tablespoons chicken stock

DIRECTIONS:
Switch on the air fryer, insert fryer pan, grease it with olive oil, then shut with its lid, set the fryer at 330 degrees F and preheat for 5 minutes
Add butter in it along with red pepper and garlic and cook for 2 minutes or until the butter has melted.
Then add remaining ingredients in the pan, stir until mixed and continue cooking for 5 minutes until shrimps have cooked, stirring halfway

through.
When done, remove the pan from the air fryer, stir the shrimp scampi, let it rest for 1 minute and then stir again.
Garnish shrimps with basil leaves and serve.
NUTRITION: Calories 221 Cal Carbs 1g Fat 13g Protein 23g

190. SPICED PORK SHOULDER

Basic Recipe
Preparation Time: 15 minutes
Cooking Time: 55 minutes
Servings: 6

INGREDIENTS:
- 1 teaspoon ground cumin
- 1 teaspoon cayenne pepper
- 1 teaspoon garlic powder
- Salt and ground black pepper, as required
- 2 pounds skin-on pork shoulder
-

DIRECTIONS:
In a small bowl, mix together the spices, salt and black pepper.
Arrange the pork shoulder onto a cutting board, skin-side down.
Season the inner side of pork shoulder with salt and black pepper.
With kitchen twines, tie the pork shoulder into a long round cylinder shape.
Season the outer side of pork shoulder with spice mixture.
Insert the rotisserie rod through the pork shoulder.
Insert the rotisserie forks, one on each side of the rod to secure the pork shoulder.
Arrange the drip pan in the bottom of Cosori Plus Air Fryer Oven cooking chamber.
Select "Roast" and then adjust the temperature to 350 degrees F.
Set the timer for 55 minutes and press the "Start".
When the display shows "Add Food" press the red lever down and load the left side of the rod into the Vortex.
Now, slide the rod's left side into the groove along the metal bar so it doesn't move.
Then, close the door and touch "Rotate".
Press the red lever to release the rod when cooking time is complete.
Remove the pork from Vortex and place onto a platter for about 10 minutes before slicing.
With a sharp knife, cut the pork shoulder into desired sized slices and serve.
NUTRITION: Calories 445 Fat 32.5 g Carbs 0.7 g Protein 35.4 g

191. SHRIMP WITH LEMON AND CHILE

Basic Recipe
Preparation Time: 5 minutes
Cooking Time: 12 minutes
Servings: 2

INGREDIENTS:
- 1-pound shrimp, wild-caught, peeled, deveined
- 1 lemon, sliced
- 1 small red chili pepper, sliced
- ½ teaspoon ground black pepper
- 1/2 teaspoon garlic powder
- 1 teaspoon salt
- 1 tablespoon olive oil

DIRECTIONS:
Switch on the air fryer, insert fryer basket, grease it with olive oil, then shut with its lid, set the fryer at 400 degrees F and preheat for 5 minutes
Meanwhile, place shrimps in a bowl, add garlic, salt, black pepper, oil, and lemon slices and toss until combined. Open the fryer, add shrimps and lemon in it close with its lid and cook for 5 minutes, shaking halfway through the frying. Then add chili slices, shake the basket until mixed and continue cooking for 2 minutes or until shrimps are opaque and crispy. When air fryer beeps, open its lid, transfer shrimps and lemon

slices onto a serving plate and serve.
NUTRITION: Calories 112.5 Cal Carbs 1g Fat 1g Protein 2g

192. TILAPIA

Basic Recipe
Preparation Time: 5 minutes
Cooking Time: 12 minutes
Servings: 2
INGREDIENTS:
- 2 tilapia fillets, wild-caught, 1 ½ inch thick
- 1 teaspoon old bay seasoning
- ¾ teaspoon lemon pepper seasoning
- ½ teaspoon salt

DIRECTIONS:
Switch on the air fryer, insert fryer basket, grease it with olive oil, then shut with its lid, set the fryer at 400 degrees F and preheat for 5 minutes Meanwhile, spray tilapia fillets with oil and then season with salt, lemon pepper, and old bay seasoning until evenly coated. Open the fryer, add tilapia in it, close with its lid and cook for 7 minutes until nicely golden and cooked, turning the fillets halfway through the frying. When air fryer beeps, open its lid, transfer tilapia fillets onto a serving plate and serve.
NUTRITION: Calories 36 Cal Carbs 0g Fat 0.75g Protein 7.4g

193. SPICY EGG AND GROUND TURKEY BAKE

Servings: 6
Cooking Time: 10 Minutes

INGREDIENTS:
- 1½ pounds ground turkey
- 6 whole eggs, well beaten
- 1/3 teaspoon smoked paprika
- 2 egg whites, beaten
- Tabasco sauce, for drizzling
- 2 tablespoons sesame oil
- 2 leeks, chopped
- 3 cloves garlic, finely minced
- 1 teaspoon ground black pepper
- 1/2 teaspoon sea salt

DIRECTIONS:
Warm the oil in a pan over moderate heat; then, sweat the leeks and garlic until tender; stir periodically.
Next, grease 6 oven safe ramekins with pan spray. Divide the sautéed mixture among six ramekins.
In a bowl, beat the eggs and egg whites using a wire whisk. Stir in the smoked paprika, salt and black pepper; whisk until everything is thoroughly combined. Divide the egg mixture among the ramekins.
Air-fry approximately 22 minutes at 345 degrees F. Drizzle Tabasco sauce over each portion and serve.
Nutrition Info: 298 Calories; 16g Fat; 4g Carbs; 16g Protein; 9g Sugars; 7g Fiber

194. BACON WRAPPED FILET MIGNON

Basic Recipe
Preparation Time: 10 minutes
Cooking Time: 15 minutes
Servings: 2
INGREDIENTS:
- 2 bacon slices
- 2 (4-ounce) filet mignon
- Salt and ground black pepper, as required
- Olive oil cooking spray

DIRECTIONS:
Wrap 1 bacon slice around each filet mignon and secure with toothpicks. Season the filets with the salt and black pepper lightly.
Arrange the filet mignon onto a coking rack and spray with cooking spray.
Arrange the drip pan in the bottom of Cosori plus Air Fryer Oven cooking chamber.
Select "Air Fry" and then adjust the temperature to 375 degrees F.
Set the timer for 15 minutes and press the "Start".
When the display shows "Add Food" insert the cooking rack in the center position.
When the display shows "Turn Food" turn the filets.
When cooking time is complete, remove the rack from Vortex and serve hot.
NUTRITION: Calories 360 Fat 19.6 g Carbs 0.4 g Protein 42.6 g

195. MARINATED PORK CHOPS

Basic Recipe
Preparation Time: 10 minutes
Cooking Time: 30 minutes
Servings: 2
INGREDIENTS:
- 2 pork chops, boneless
- 1 tsp garlic powder
- ½ cup flour
- 1 cup buttermilk
- Pepper
- Salt

DIRECTIONS:
Add pork chops and buttermilk in a zip-lock bag. Seal bag and place in the refrigerator for overnight.
In another zip-lock bag add flour, garlic powder, pepper, and salt.
Remove marinated pork chops from buttermilk and add in flour mixture and shake until well coated.
Preheat the Cosori air fryer oven to 380 F.
Spray air fryer tray with cooking spray.
Arrange pork chops on a tray and air fryer for 28-30 minutes Turn pork chops after 18 minutes
Serve and enjoy.
NUTRITION: Calories 424 Fat 21.3 g Carbs 30.8 g
Protein 25.5 g

196. TOMATO BASIL SCALLOPS

Basic Recipe
Preparation Time: 5 minutes
Cooking Time: 15 minutes
Servings: 2
INGREDIENTS:
- 8 jumbo sea scallops, wild-caught
- 1 tablespoon tomato paste
- 12 ounces frozen spinach, thawed and dry outed
- 1 tablespoon chopped fresh basil
- 1 teaspoon ground black pepper
- 1 teaspoon minced garlic
- 1 teaspoon salt
- 3/4 cup heavy whipping cream, reduced Fat

DIRECTIONS:
Switch on the air fryer, insert fryer basket, grease it with olive oil, then shut with its lid, set the fryer at 350 degrees F and preheat for 5 minutes Meanwhile, take a 7 inches baking pan, grease it with oil and place spinach in it in an even layer.
Spray the scallops with oil, sprinkle with ½ teaspoon each of salt and black pepper and then place scallops over the spinach.
Place tomato paste in a bowl, whisk in cream, basil, garlic, and remaining salt and black pepper until smooth, and then pour over the scallops.
Open the fryer, place the pan in it, close with its lid and cook for 10 minutes until thoroughly cooked and sauce is hot.
Serve straight away.
NUTRITION: Calories 359 Cal Carbs 6g Fat 33g Protein 9g

197. GARLICKY PORK TENDERLOIN

Basic Recipe
Preparation Time: 15 minutes
Cooking Time: 20 minutes
Servings : 5
INGREDIENTS:
- 1½ pounds pork tenderloin
- Nonstick cooking spray
- 2 small heads roasted garlic
- Salt and ground black pepper, as required

DIRECTIONS:
Lightly, spray all the sides of pork with cooking spray and then, season with salt and black pepper.

Now, rub the pork with roasted garlic. Arrange the roast onto the lightly greased cooking tray.

Arrange the drip pan in the bottom of Cosori plus Air Fryer Oven cooking chamber.

Select "Air Fry" and then adjust the temperature to 400 degrees F. Set the timer for 20 minutes and press the "Start".

When the display shows "Add Food" insert the cooking tray in the center position.

When the display shows "Turn Food" turn the pork.

When cooking time is complete, remove the tray from Vortex and place the roast onto a platter for about 10 minutes before slicing. With a sharp knife, cut the roast into desired sized slices and serve.

NUTRITION: Calories 202 Fat 4.8 g Carbs 1.7 g Protein 35.9 g

198. RICOTTA TOASTS WITH SALMON

Servings: 2
Cooking Time: 4 Minutes

INGREDIENTS:
- 4 bread slices
- 1 garlic clove, minced
- 8 oz. ricotta cheese
- 1 teaspoon lemon zest
- Freshly ground black pepper, to taste
- 4 oz. smoked salmon

DIRECTIONS:
In a food processor, add the garlic, ricotta, lemon zest and black pepper and pulse until smooth.

Spread ricotta mixture over each bread slices evenly.

Press "Power Button" of Air Fry Oven and turn the dial to select the "Air Fry" mode.

Press the Time button and again turn the dial to set the cooking time to 4 minutes.

Now push the Temp button and rotate the dial to set the temperature at 355 degrees F.

Press "Start/Pause" button to start.

When the unit beeps to show that it is preheated, open the lid and lightly, grease the sheet pan.

Arrange the bread slices into "Air Fry Basket" and insert in the oven.

Top with salmon and serve.

Nutrition Info: Calories: 274 Cal Total Fat: 12 g Saturated Fat: 6.3 g Cholesterol: 48 mg Sodium: 1300 mg Total Carbs: 15.7 g Fiber: 0.5 g Sugar: 1.2 g Protein: 24.8 g

199. JUICY TURKEY BURGERS

Servings: 8
Cooking Time: 25 Minutes
INGREDIENTS:
- 1 lb ground turkey 85% lean / 15% fat
- ¼ cup unsweetened apple sauce
- ½ onion grated
- 1 Tbsp ranch seasoning

- 2 tsp Worcestershire Sauce
- 1 tsp minced garlic
- ¼ cup plain breadcrumbs
- Salt and pepper to taste

DIRECTIONS:
Combine the onion, ground turkey, unsweetened apple sauce, minced garlic, breadcrumbs, ranch seasoning, Worchestire sauce, and salt and pepper. Mix them with your hands until well combined. Form 4 equally sized hamburger patties with them.

Place these burgers in the refrigerator for about 30 minutes to have them firm up a bit.

While preparing for cooking, select the Air Fry option. Set the temperature of 360°F and the cook time as required. Press start to begin preheating.

Once the preheating temperature is reached, place the burgers on the tray in the Air fryer basket, making sure they don't overlap or touch. Cook on for 15 minutes
flipping halfway through.

Nutrition Info: Calories 183, Total Fat 3g, Total Carbs 11g, Protein 28g

200. FISH STICKS

Basic Recipe
Preparation Time: 5 minutes
Cooking Time: 15 minutes
Servings: 4
INGREDIENTS
- 1-pound cod, wild-caught
- ½ teaspoon ground black pepper
- 3/4 teaspoon Cajun seasoning
- 1 teaspoon salt
- 1 1/2 cups pork rind
- 1/4 cup mayonnaise, reduced Fat
- 2 tablespoons water
- 2 tablespoons Dijon mustard

DIRECTIONS:
Switch on the air fryer, insert fryer basket, grease it with olive oil, then shut with its lid, set the fryer at 400 degrees F and preheat for 5 minutes
Meanwhile, place mayonnaise in a bowl and then whisk in water and mustard until blended.

Place pork rinds in a shallow dish, add Cajun seasoning, black pepper and salt and stir until mixed.

Cut the cod into 1 by 2 inches pieces, then dip into mayonnaise mixture and then coat with pork rind mixture.

Open the fryer; add fish sticks in it, spray with oil, close with its lid and cook for 10 minutes until nicely golden and crispy, flipping the sticks halfway through the frying.

When air fryer beeps, open its lid, transfer fish sticks onto a serving plate and serve.

NUTRITION: Calories 263 Cal Carbs 1g Fat 16g Protein 26.4g

201. LEMON CHICKEN BREASTS

Servings: 4
Cooking Time: 30 Minutes
INGREDIENTS:
- 1/4 cup olive oil
- 3 tablespoons garlic, minced
- 1/3 cup dry white wine
- 1 tablespoon lemon zest, grated
- 2 tablespoons lemon juice
- 1 1/2 teaspoons dried oregano, crushed
- 1 teaspoon thyme leaves, minced
- Salt and black pepper
- 4 skin-on boneless chicken breasts
- 1 lemon, sliced

DIRECTIONS:

Whisk everything in a baking pan to coat the chicken breasts well.

Place the lemon slices on top of the chicken breasts.

Spread the mustard mixture over the toasted bread slices.

Press "Power Button" of Air Fry Oven and turn the dial to select the "Bake" mode.

Press the Time button and again turn the dial to set the cooking time to 30 minutes.

Now push the Temp button and rotate the dial to set the temperature at 370 degrees F.

Once preheated, place the baking pan inside and close its lid.

Serve warm.

Nutrition Info: Calories 388 Total Fat 8 g Saturated Fat 1 g Cholesterol 153mg sodium 339 mg Total Carbs 8 g Fiber 1 g Sugar 2 g Protein 13 g

202. BBQ PORK CHOPS

Basic Recipe

Preparation Time: 10 minutes

Cooking Time: 7 minutes

Servings: 4

INGREDIENTS:
- 4 pork chops
- For rub:
- ½ tsp allspice
- ½ tsp dry mustard
- 1 tsp ground cumin
- 1 tsp garlic powder
- ½ tsp chili powder
- ½ tsp paprika
- 1 tbsp brown sugar
- 1 tsp salt

DIRECTIONS:

In a small bowl, mix together all rub ingredients and rub all over pork chops.

Arrange pork chops on air fryer tray and air fry at 400 F for 5.

Turn pork chops to other side and air fry for 2 minutes more.

Serve and enjoy.

NUTRITION: Calories 273 Fat 20.2 g Carbs 3.4 g Protein 18.4 g

203. SALMON CAKES

Basic Recipe

Preparation Time: 5 minutes

Cooking Time: 12 minutes

Servings: 2

INGREDIENTS:
- ½ cup almond flour
- 15 ounces cooked pink salmon
- ¼ teaspoon ground black pepper
- 2 teaspoons Dijon mustard
- 2 tablespoons chopped fresh dill
- 2 tablespoons mayonnaise, reduced Fat
- 1 egg, pastured
- 2 wedges of lemon

DIRECTIONS:

Switch on the air fryer, insert fryer basket, grease it with olive oil, then shut with its lid, set the fryer at 400 degrees F and preheat for 5 minutes

Meanwhile, place all the ingredients in a bowl, except for lemon wedges, stir until combined and then shape into four patties, each about 4-inches.

Open the fryer, add salmon patties in it, spray oil over them, close with its lid and cook for 12 minutes until nicely golden and crispy, flipping the patties halfway through the frying.

When air fryer beeps, open its lid, transfer salmon patties onto a serving plate and serve.

NUTRITION: Calories 517 Cal Carbs 15g Fat 27g Protein 52g

204. HERBED DUCK LEGS

Servings: 2

Cooking Time: 30 Minutes

INGREDIENTS:
- ½ tablespoon fresh thyme, chopped
- ½ tablespoon fresh parsley, chopped
- 2 duck legs
- 1 garlic clove, minced
- 1 teaspoon five spice powder
- Salt and black pepper, as required

DIRECTIONS:

Preheat the Air fryer to 340 degree F and grease an Air fryer basket.

Mix the garlic, herbs, five spice powder, salt, and black pepper in a bowl.

Rub the duck legs with garlic mixture generously and arrange into the Air fryer basket.

Cook for about 25 minutes and set the Air fryer to 390 degree F.

Cook for 5 more minutes and dish out to serve hot.

Nutrition Info: Calories: 138, Fat: 4.5g, Carbohydrates: 1g, Sugar: 0g, Protein: 25g, Sodium: 82mg

205. LAMB BURGERS

Intermediate Recipe

Preparation Time: 15 minutes

Cooking Time: 8 minutes

Servings: 6

INGREDIENTS:
- 2 pounds ground lamb
- 1 tablespoon onion powder
- Salt and ground black pepper, as required

DIRECTIONS:

In a bowl, add all the ingredients and mix well.

Make 6 equal-sized patties from the mixture.

Arrange the patties onto a cooking tray.

Arrange the drip pan in the bottom of Cosori Plus Air Fryer Oven cooking chamber.

Select "Air Fry" and then adjust the temperature to 360 degrees F.

Set the timer for 8 minutes and press the "Start".

When the display shows "Add Food" insert the cooking rack in the center position.

When the display shows "Turn Food" turn the burgers.

When cooking time is complete, remove the tray from Vortex and serve hot.

NUTRITION: Calories 285 Fat 11.1 g Carbs 0.9 g Protein 42.6 g

206. AIR FRYER SALMON

Basic Recipe

Preparation Time: 5 minutes

Cooking Time: 12 minutes

Servings : 2

INGREDIENTS
- 2 salmon fillets, wild-caught, each about 1 ½ inch thick
- 1 teaspoon ground black pepper
- 2 teaspoons paprika
- 1 teaspoon salt
- 2 teaspoons olive oil

DIRECTIONS:

Switch on the air fryer, insert fryer basket, grease it with olive oil, then shut with its lid, set the fryer at 390 degrees F and preheat for 5 minutes.

Meanwhile, rub each salmon fillet with oil and then season with black pepper, paprika, and salt.

Open the fryer, add seasoned salmon in it, close with its lid and cook for 7 minutes until nicely golden and cooked, flipping the fillets halfway through the frying. When air fryer beeps, open its lid, transfer salmon onto a serving plate and serve.

NUTRITION: Calories 288 Cal Carbs 1.4g Fat 18.9g Protein 28.3g

207. SWEET & SPICY MEATBALLS

Basic Recipe
Preparation Time: 20 minutes
Cooking Time: 30 minutes
Servings: 8

INGREDIENTS:

For Meatballs:
- 2 pounds lean ground beef
- 2/3 cup quick-cooking oats
- ½ cup Ritz crackers, crushed
- 1 (5-ounce) can evaporated milk
- 2 large eggs, beaten lightly
- 1 teaspoon honey
- 1 tablespoon dried onion, minced
- 1 teaspoon garlic powder
- 1 teaspoon ground cumin
- Salt and ground black pepper, as required

For Sauce:
- 1/3 cup orange marmalade
- 1/3 cup honey
- 1/3 cup brown sugar
- 2 tablespoons cornstarch
- 2 tablespoons soy sauce
- 1-2 tablespoons hot sauce
- 1 tablespoon Worcestershire sauce

DIRECTIONS:

For meatballs: in a large bowl, add all the ingredients and mix until well combined.

Make 1½-inch balls from the mixture.

Arrange half of the meatballs onto a cooking tray in a single layer.

Arrange the drip pan in the bottom of Cosori Plus Air Fryer Oven cooking chamber.

Select "Air Fry" and then adjust the temperature to 380 degrees F.

Set the timer for 15 minutes and press the "Start".

When the display shows "Add Food" insert the cooking tray in the center position.

When the display shows "Turn Food" turn the meatballs.

When cooking time is complete, remove the tray from Vortex.

Repeat with the remaining meatballs.

Meanwhile, for sauce: in a small pan, add all the ingredients over medium heat and cook until thickened, stirring continuously.

Serve the meatballs with the topping of sauce.

NUTRITION: Calories 411 Fat 11.1 g Carbs 38.8 g Protein 38.9 g

208. KALE AND PINE NUTS

Servings: 4
Cooking Time: 12 Minutes

INGREDIENTS:
- 10 cups kale; torn
- 1/3 cup pine nuts
- 2 tbsp. lemon zest; grated
- 1 tbsp. lemon juice
- 2 tbsp. olive oil
- Salt and black pepper to taste.

DIRECTIONS:

In a pan that fits the air fryer, combine all the ingredients, toss, introduce the pan in the machine and cook at 380°F for 15 minutes

Divide between plates and serve as a side dish.

Nutrition Info: Calories: 121; Fat: 9g; Fiber: 2g; Carbs: 4g; Protein: 5g

209. SEASON AND SALT-CURED BEEF

Intermediate Recipe
Preparation Time: 15 minutes
Cooking Time: 3 hours

Servings: 4

INGREDIENTS:
- 1½ pounds beef round, trimmed
- ½ cup Worcestershire sauce
- ½ cup low-sodium soy sauce
- 2 teaspoons honey
- 1 teaspoon liquid smoke
- 2 teaspoons onion powder
- ½ teaspoon red pepper flakes
- Ground black pepper, as required

DIRECTIONS:

In a zip-top bag, place the beef and freeze for 1-2 hours to firm up.

Place the meat onto a cutting board and cut against the grain into 1/8-¼-inch strips.

In a large bowl, add the remaining ingredients and mix until well combined.

Add the steak slices and coat with the mixture generously.

Refrigerate to marinate for about 4-6 hours.

Remove the beef slices from bowl and with paper towels, pat dry them.

Divide the steak strips onto the cooking trays and arrange in an even layer.

Select "Dehydrate" and then adjust the temperature to 160 degrees F.

Set the timer for 3 hours and press the "Start".

When the display shows "Add Food" insert 1 tray in the top position and another in the center position.

After 1½ hours, switch the position of cooking trays.

Meanwhile, in a small pan, add the remaining ingredients over medium heat and cook for about 10 minutes, stirring occasionally.

When cooking time is complete, remove the trays from Vortex.

NUTRITION: Calories 372 Fat 10.7 g Carbs 12 g Protein 53.8 g

210. AIR FRYER BEEF STEAK

Servings: 4
Cooking Time: 15 Minutes

INGREDIENTS:
- 1 tbsp. Olive oil
- Pepper and salt
- 2 pounds of ribeye steak

DIRECTIONS:

Preparing the ingredients. Season meat on both sides with pepper and salt.

Rub all sides of meat with olive oil.

Preheat instant crisp air fryer to 356 degrees and spritz with olive oil.

Air frying. Close air fryer lid. Set temperature to 356°f, and set time to 7 minutes. Cook steak 7 minutes. Flip and cook an additional 6 minutes.

Let meat sit 2-5 minutes to rest. Slice and serve with salad.

Nutrition Info: Calories: 233; Fat: 19g; Protein:16g; Sugar:0g

211. CHILI CHICKEN SLIDERS

Servings: 4
Cooking Time: 10 Minutes

INGREDIENTS:
- 1/3 teaspoon paprika
- 1/3 cup scallions, peeled and chopped
- 3 cloves garlic, peeled and minced
- 1 teaspoon ground black pepper, or to taste
- 1/2 teaspoon fresh basil, minced
- 1 ½ cups chicken,minced
- 1 ½ tablespoons coconut aminos
- 1/2 teaspoon grated fresh ginger
- 1/2 tablespoon chili sauce
- 1 teaspoon salt

DIRECTIONS:

Thoroughly combine all ingredients in a mixing dish. Then, form into 4 patties.

Cook in the preheated Air Fryer for 18 minutes at 355 degrees F.
Garnish with toppings of choice.
Nutrition Info: 366 Calories; 6g Fat; 4g Carbs; 66g Protein; 3g Sugars; 9g Fiber

212. TURMERIC MUSHROOM
Servings: 4
Cooking Time: 12 Minutes
INGREDIENTS:
• 1 lb. brown mushrooms
• 4 garlic cloves; minced
• ¼ tsp. cinnamon powder
• 1 tsp. olive oil
• ½ tsp. turmeric powder
• Salt and black pepper to taste.
DIRECTIONS:
In a bowl, combine all the ingredients and toss.
Put the mushrooms in your air fryer's basket and cook at 370°F for 15 minutes
Divide the mix between plates and serve as a side dish.
Nutrition Info: Calories: 208; Fat: 7g; Fiber: 3g; Carbs: 5g; Protein: 7g

213. MUSHROOM MEATLOAF
Servings: 4
Cooking Time: 25 Minutes
INGREDIENTS:
• 14-ounce lean ground beef
• 1 chorizo sausage, chopped finely
• 1 small onion, chopped
• 1 garlic clove, minced
• 2 tablespoons fresh cilantro, chopped
• 3 tablespoons breadcrumbs
• 1 egg
• Salt and freshly ground black pepper, to taste
• 2 tablespoons fresh mushrooms, sliced thinly
• 3 tablespoons olive oil
DIRECTIONS:
Preparing the ingredients. Preheat the instant crisp air fryer to 390 degrees f.
In a large bowl, add all ingredients except mushrooms and mix till well combined.
In a baking pan, place the beef mixture.
With the back of spatula, smooth the surface.
Top with mushroom slices and gently, press into the meatloaf.
Drizzle with oil evenly.
Air frying. Arrange the pan in the instant crisp air fryer basket, close air fryer lid and cook for about 25 minutes.
Cut the meatloaf in desires size wedges and serve.
Nutrition Info: Calories 284 Total fat 7.9 g Saturated fat 1.4 g Cholesterol 36 mg Sodium 704 mg Total carbs 46 g Fiber 3.6 g Sugar 5.5 g Protein 17.9 g

214. GLAZED LAMB CHOPS
Servings: 4
Cooking Time: 15 Minutes
INGREDIENTS:
• 1 tablespoon Dijon mustard
• ½ tablespoon fresh lime juice
• 1 teaspoon honey
• ½ teaspoon olive oil
• Salt and ground black pepper, as required
• 4 (4-ounce) lamb loin chops
DIRECTIONS:
In a black pepper large bowl, mix together the mustard, lemon juice, oil, honey, salt, and black pepper.

Add the chops and coat with the mixture generously.
Place the chops onto the greased "Sheet Pan".
Press "Power Button" of Ninja Foodi Digital Air Fry Oven and turn the dial to select the "Air Bake" mode.
Press the Time button and again turn the dial to set the cooking time to 15 minutes.
Now push the Temp button and rotate the dial to set the temperature at 390 degrees F.
Press "Start/Pause" button to start.
When the unit beeps to show that it is preheated, open the lid.
Insert the "Sheet Pan" in oven.
Flip the chops once halfway through.
Serve hot.
Nutrition Info: Calories: 224 kcal Total Fat: 9.1 g Saturated Fat: 3.1 g Cholesterol: 102 mg Sodium: 169 mg Total Carbs: 1.7 g Fiber: 0.1 g Sugar: 1.5 g Protein: 32 g

215. BUTTER FISH WITH SAKE AND MISO
Servings: 4
Cooking Time: 11 Minutes
INGREDIENTS:
• 4 (7-ounce) pieces of butter fish
• 1/3 cup sake
• 1/3 cup mirin
• 2/3 cup sugar
• 1 cup white miso
DIRECTIONS:
Start by combining sake, mirin, and sugar in a sauce pan and bring to a boil.
Allow to boil for 5 minutes, then reduce heat and simmer for another 10 minutes.
Remove from heat completely and mix in miso.
Marinate the fish in the mixture for as long as possible, up to 3 days if possible.
Preheat toaster oven to 450°F and bake fish for 8 minutes.
Switch your setting to Broil and broil another 2-3 minutes, until the sauce is caramelized.
Nutrition Info: Calories: 529, Sodium: 2892 mg, Dietary Fiber: 3.7 g, Total Fat: 5.8 g, Total Carbs: 61.9 g, Protein: 53.4 g.

216. BASIC ROASTED TOFU
Servings: 4
Cooking Time: 45 Minutes
INGREDIENTS:
• 1 or more (16-ounce) containers extra-firm tofu
• 1 tablespoon sesame oil
• 1 tablespoon soy sauce
• 1 tablespoon rice vinegar
• 1 tablespoon water
DIRECTIONS:
Start by drying the tofu: first pat dry with paper towels, then lay on another set of paper towels or a dish towel.
Put a plate on top of the tofu then put something heavy on the plate (like a large can of vegetables). Leave it there for at least 20 minutes.
While tofu is being pressed, whip up marinade by combining oil, soy sauce, vinegar, and water in a bowl and set aside.
Cut the tofu into squares or sticks. Place the tofu in the marinade for at least 30 minutes.
Preheat toaster oven to 350°F. Line a pan with parchment paper and add as many pieces of tofu as you can, giving each piece adequate space.
Bake 20–45 minutes; tofu is done when the outside edges look golden brown. Time will vary depending on tofu size and shape.
Nutrition Info: Calories: 114, Sodium: 239 mg, Dietary Fiber: 1.1 g, Total Fat: 8.1 g, Total Carbs: 2.2 g, Protein: 9.5 g

217. COUNTRY STYLE PORK TENDERLOIN

Basic Recipe
Preparation Time: 15 minutes
Cooking Time: 25 minutes
Servings: 3

INGREDIENTS:
- 1-pound pork tenderloin
- 1 tablespoon garlic, minced
- 2 tablespoons soy sauce
- 2 tablespoons honey
- 1 tablespoon Dijon mustard
- 1 tablespoon grain mustard
- 1 teaspoon Sriracha sauce

DIRECTIONS:

In a large bowl, add all the ingredients except pork and mix well.
Add the pork tenderloin and coat with the mixture generously.
Refrigerate to marinate for 2-3 hours.
Remove the pork tenderloin from bowl, reserving the marinade.
Place the pork tenderloin onto the lightly greased cooking tray.
Arrange the drip pan in the bottom of Cosori Plus Air Fryer Oven cooking chamber.
Select "Air Fry" and then adjust the temperature to 380 degrees F.
Set the timer for 25 minutes and press the "Start".
When the display shows "Add Food" insert the cooking tray in the center position.
When the display shows "Turn Food" turn the pork and oat with the reserved marinade.
When cooking time is complete, remove the tray from Vortex and place the pork tenderloin onto a platter for about 10 minutes before slicing.
With a sharp knife, cut the pork tenderloin into desired sized slices and serve.
NUTRITION: Calories 277 Fat 5.7 g Carbs 14.2 g Protein 40.7 g

218. DELIGHTFUL TURKEY WINGS

Servings: 4
Cooking Time: 26 Minutes

INGREDIENTS:
- 2 pounds turkey wings
- 4 tablespoons chicken rub
- 3 tablespoons olive oil

DIRECTIONS:

Preheat the Air fryer to 380 degree F and grease an Air fryer basket.
Mix the turkey wings, chicken rub, and olive oil in a bowl until well combined.
Arrange the turkey wings into the Air fryer basket and cook for about 26 minutes, flipping once in between.
Dish out the turkey wings in a platter and serve hot.
Nutrition Info: Calories: 204, Fat: 15.5g, Carbohydrates: 3g, Sugar: 0g, Protein: 12g, Sodium: 465mg

219. PORK STEW

Servings: 4
Cooking Time: 12 Minutes

INGREDIENTS:
- 2 lb. pork stew meat; cubed
- 1 eggplant; cubed
- ½ cup beef stock
- 2 zucchinis; cubed
- ½ tsp. smoked paprika
- Salt and black pepper to taste.
- A handful cilantro; chopped.

DIRECTIONS:

In a pan that fits your air fryer, mix all the ingredients, toss, introduce in your air fryer and cook at 370°F for 30 minutes
Divide into bowls and serve right away.

Nutrition Info: Calories: 245; Fat: 12g; Fiber: 2g; Carbs: 5g; Protein: 14g

220. TURKEY AND ALMONDS

Servings: 2
Cooking Time: 10 Minutes

INGREDIENTS:
- 1 big turkey breast, skinless; boneless and halved
- 2 shallots; chopped
- 1/3 cup almonds; chopped
- 1 tbsp. sweet paprika
- 2 tbsp. olive oil
- Salt and black pepper to taste.

DIRECTIONS:

In a pan that fits the air fryer, combine the turkey with all the other ingredients, toss.
Put the pan in the machine and cook at 370°F for 25 minutes
Divide everything between plates and serve.
Nutrition Info: Calories: 274; Fat: 12g; Fiber: 3g; Carbs: 5g; Protein: 14g

221. TOMATO AVOCADO MELT

Servings: 2
Cooking Time: 4 Minutes

INGREDIENTS:
- 4 slices of bread
- 1-2 tablespoons mayonnaise
- Cayenne pepper
- 1 small Roma tomato
- 1/2 avocado
- 8 slices of cheese of your choice

DIRECTIONS:

Start by slicing avocado and tomato and set aside.
Spread mayonnaise on the bread.
Sprinkle cayenne pepper over the mayo to taste.
Layer tomato and avocado on top of cayenne pepper.
Top with cheese and put on greased baking sheet.
Broil on high for 2–4 minutes, until the cheese is melted and bread is toasted.
Nutrition Info: Calories: 635, Sodium: 874 mg, Dietary Fiber: 4.1 g, Total Fat: 50.1 g, Total Carbs: 17.4 g, Protein: 30.5 g.

222. LEMON PEPPER TURKEY

Servings: 6
Cooking Time: 45 Minutes

INGREDIENTS:
- 3 lbs. turkey breast
- 2 tablespoons oil
- 1 tablespoon Worcestershire sauce
- 1 teaspoon lemon pepper
- 1/2 teaspoon salt

DIRECTIONS:

Whisk everything in a bowl and coat the turkey liberally.
Place the turkey in the Air fryer basket.
Press "Power Button" of Air Fry Oven and turn the dial to select the "Air Fry" mode.
Press the Time button and again turn the dial to set the cooking time to 45 minutes.
Now push the Temp button and rotate the dial to set the temperature at 375 degrees F.
Once preheated, place the air fryer basket inside and close its lid.
Serve warm.
Nutrition Info: Calories 391 Total Fat 2.8 g Saturated Fat 0.6 g Cholesterol 330 mg Sodium 62 mg Total Carbs 36.5 g Fiber 9.2 g Sugar 4.5 g Protein 6.6

223. KALAMTA MOZARELLA PITA MELTS

Servings: 2
Cooking Time: 5 Minutes
INGREDIENTS:
- 2 (6-inch) whole wheat pitas
- 1 teaspoon extra-virgin olive oil
- 1 cup grated part-skim mozzarella cheese
- 1/4 small red onion
- 1/4 cup pitted Kalamata olives
- 2 tablespoons chopped fresh herbs such as parsley, basil, or oregano

DIRECTIONS:
Start by preheating toaster oven to 425°F.
Brush the pita on both sides with oil and warm in the oven for one minute.
Dice onions and halve olives.
Sprinkle mozzarella over each pita and top with onion and olive.
Return to the oven for another 5 minutes or until the cheese is melted.
Sprinkle herbs over the pita and serve.
Nutrition Info: Calories: 387, Sodium: 828 mg, Dietary Fiber: 7.4 g, Total Fat: 16.2 g, Total Carbs: 42.0 g, Protein: 23.0 g.

DINNER RECIPES

224. BLUEBERRY OVERLOAD FRENCH TOAST
Basic Recipe
Preparation Time: 5 minutes
Cooking Time: 40minutes
Serving: 5
INGREDIENTS:
- 1 (8 ounce) package cream cheese, cut into 1-inch cubes
- 1 cup fresh blueberries, divided
- 1 cup milk
- 1 tablespoon cornstarch
- 1/2 cup water
- 1/2 cup white sugar
- 1/2 teaspoon vanilla extract
- 1-1/2 teaspoons butter
- 2 tablespoons and 2 teaspoons maple syrup
- 6 eggs, beaten
- 6 slices day-old bread, cut into 1-inch cubes

DIRECTIONS:
Lightly grease baking pan of air fryer with cooking spray.
Evenly spread half of the bread on bottom of pan. Sprinkle evenly the cream cheese and ½ cup blueberries. Add remaining bread on top.
In a large bowl, whisk well eggs, milk, syrup, and vanilla extract. Pour over bread mixture.
Cover air fryer baking pan with foil and refrigerate overnight.
Preheat air fryer to 330oF.
Cook for 25 minutes covered in foil, remove foil and cook for another 20 minutes or until middle is set.
Meanwhile, make the sauce by mixing cornstarch, water, and sugar in a saucepan and bring to a boil. Stir in remaining blueberries and simmer until thickened and blueberries have burst.
Serve and enjoy with blueberry syrup.
NUTRITION: Calories 492 Carbs 51.9g Protein 15.1g Fat 24.8g

225. THYME TURKEY BREAST
Preparation Time: 10 minutes
Cooking Time: 40 minutes
Serving: 4
INGREDIENTS:
- 2 lb. turkey breast
- Salt, to taste
- Black pepper, to taste
- 4 tablespoon butter, melted
- 3 cloves garlic, minced
- 1 teaspoon thyme, chopped
- 1 teaspoon rosemary, chopped

DIRECTIONS:
Mix butter with salt, black pepper, garlic, thyme, and rosemary in a bowl.
Rub this seasoning over the turkey breast liberally and place in the Air Fryer basket.
Turn the dial to select the "Air Fry" mode.
Hit the Time button and again use the dial to set the cooking time to 40 minutes
Now push the Temp button and rotate the dial to set the temperature at 375 degrees F.
Once preheated, place the Air fryer basket inside the oven
Slice and serve fresh.
NUTRITION: Calories 334 Fat 4.7 g Carbs 54.1 g Protein 26.2 g

226. EASY ITALIAN MEATBALLS
Basic Recipe
Preparation Time: 10 minutes
Cooking Time: 13 minutes
Serving: 4

INGREDIENTS:
- 2-lb. lean ground turkey
- ¼ cup onion, minced
- 2 cloves garlic, minced
- 2 tablespoons parsley, chopped
- 2 eggs
- 1½ cup parmesan cheese, grated
- ½ teaspoon red pepper flakes
- ½ teaspoon Italian seasoning
- Salt and black pepper to taste

DIRECTIONS:
Toss all the meatball ingredients in a bowl and mix well. Make small meatballs out this mixture and place them in the air fryer basket.
Press "Power Button" of Air Fry Oven and turn the dial to select the "Air Fry" mode. Press the Time button and again turn the dial to set the cooking time to 13 minutes. Now push the Temp button and rotate the dial to set the temperature at 350 degrees F.
Once preheated, place the air fryer basket inside and close its lid.
Flip the meatballs when cooked halfway through.
Serve warm.
NUTRITION: Calories 472 Fat 25.8 Carbs 1.7 g Protein 59.6 g

227. OREGANO CHICKEN BREAST
Basic Recipe
Preparation Time: 10 minutes
Cooking Time: 25 minutes
Serving: 6
INGREDIENTS:
- 2 lbs. chicken breasts, minced
- 1 tablespoon avocado oil
- 1 teaspoon smoked paprika
- 1 teaspoon garlic powder
- 1 teaspoon oregano
- 1/2 teaspoon salt
- Black pepper, to taste

DIRECTIONS:
Toss all the meatball ingredients in a bowl and mix well. Make small meatballs out this mixture and place them in the air fryer basket.
Press "Power Button" of Air Fry Oven and turn the dial to select the "Air Fry" mode. Press the Time button and again turn the dial to set the cooking time to 25 minutes
Now push the Temp button and rotate the dial to set the temperature at 375 degrees F.
Once preheated, place the air fryer basket inside and close its lid.

Serve warm.
NUTRITION: Calories 352 Fat 14 g Carbs: 15.8 g Protein 26 g

228. LEMON CHICKEN BREASTS

Basic Recipe
Preparation Time: 10 minutes
Cooking Time: 30 minutes
Serving: 4
INGREDIENTS:
- 1/4 cup olive oil
- 3 tablespoons garlic, minced
- 1/3 cup dry white wine
- 1 tablespoon lemon zest, grated
- 2 tablespoons lemon juice
- 1 1/2 teaspoons dried oregano, crushed
- 1 teaspoon thyme leaves, minced
- Salt and black pepper
- 4 skin-on boneless chicken breasts
- 1 lemon, sliced

DIRECTIONS:
Whisk everything in a baking pan to coat the chicken breasts well.
Place the lemon slices on top of the chicken breasts.
Spread the mustard mixture over the toasted bread slices.
Press "Power Button" of Air Fry Oven and turn the dial to select the "Bake" mode.
Press the Time button and again turn the dial to set the cooking time to 30 minutes
Now push the Temp button and rotate the dial to set the temperature at 370 degrees F.
Once preheated, place the baking pan inside and close its lid.
Serve warm.
NUTRITION: Calories 388 Fat 8 g Carbs 8 g Protein 13 g

229. CAJUN SALMON

Basic Recipe
Preparation Time: 5 minutes
Cooking Time: 10 minutes
Serving: 2
INGREDIENTS:
- 2 Salmon steaks
- 2 tbsp cajun seasoning

DIRECTIONS:
Rub the salmon steaks with the Cajun seasoning evenly. Set aside for about 10 minutes. Arrange the salmon steaks onto the greased cooking tray. Arrange the drip pan in the bottom of the Cosori Air Fryer Oven cooking chamber. Select "Air Fry" and then adjust the temperature to 390 °F. Set the time for 8 minutes and press "Start". When the display shows "Add Food" insert the cooking tray in the center position. When the display shows "Turn Food" turn the salmon steaks. When the cooking time is complete, remove the tray from the Vortex Oven. Serve hot.
NUTRITION: Calories 225 Carbs 0g Fat 10.5g Protein 22.1g

230. CRUSTED CHICKEN DRUMSTICKS

Basic Recipe
Preparation Time: 10 minutes
Cooking Time: 10 minutes
Serving: 4
INGREDIENTS:
- 1 lb. chicken drumsticks
- 1/2 cup buttermilk
- 1/2 cup panko breadcrumbs
- 1/2 cup flour
- 1/4 teaspoon baking powder
- Spice Mixture:
- 1/2 teaspoon salt

- 1/2 teaspoon celery salt
- 1/4 teaspoon oregano
- 1/4 teaspoon cayenne
- 1 teaspoon paprika
- 1/4 teaspoon garlic powder
- 1/4 teaspoon dried thyme
- 1/2 teaspoon ground ginger
- 1/2 teaspoon white pepper
- 1/2 teaspoon black pepper
- 3 tablespoon butter melted

DIRECTIONS:
Soak chicken in the buttermilk and cover to marinate overnight in the refrigerator. Mix spices with flour, breadcrumbs, and baking powder in a shallow tray.
Remove the chicken from the milk and coat them well with the flour spice mixture
Place the chicken drumsticks in the Air fryer basket of the Ninja Oven.
Pour the melted butter over the drumsticks
Turn the dial to select the "Air fry" mode. Hit the Time button and again use the dial to set the cooking time to 10 minutes
Now push the Temp button and rotate the dial to set the temperature at 425 degrees F.
Once preheated, place the baking tray inside the oven
Flip the drumsticks and resume cooking for another 10 minutes
Serve warm.
NUTRITION: Calories 331 Fat 2.5 g Carbs 69 g Protein 28.7g

231. BLACKENED CHICKEN BAKE

Basic Recipe
Preparation Time: 10 minutes
Cooking Time: 18 minutes
Serving: 4
INGREDIENTS:
- 4 chicken breasts
- 2 teaspoon olive oil
- Seasoning:
- 1 1/2 tablespoon brown sugar
- 1 teaspoon paprika
- 1 teaspoon dried oregano
- 1/4 teaspoon garlic powder
- 1/2 teaspoon salt and pepper
- Garnish:
- Chopped parsley

DIRECTIONS:
Mix olive oil with brown sugar, paprika, oregano, garlic powder, salt, and black pepper in a bowl.
Place the chicken breasts in the baking tray of the Ninja Oven.
Pour and rub this mixture liberally over all the chicken breasts.
Turn the dial to select the "Bake" mode.
Hit the Time button and again use the dial to set the cooking time to 18 minutes
Now push the Temp button and rotate the dial to set the temperature at 425 degrees F.
Once preheated, place the baking tray inside the oven
Serve warm.
NUTRITION: Calories 412 Fat 24.8 g Carbs 43.8 g Protein 18.9 g

232. GROUND CHICKEN MEATBALLS

Basic Recipe
Preparation Time: 10 minutes
Cooking Time: 10 minutes
Serving: 4
INGREDIENTS:
- 1-lb. ground chicken
- 1/3 cup panko

- 1 teaspoon salt
- 2 teaspoons chives
- 1/2 teaspoon garlic powder
- 1 teaspoon thyme
- 1 egg

DIRECTIONS:

Toss all the meatball ingredients in a bowl and mix well. Make small meatballs out this mixture and place them in the air fryer basket.

Press "Power Button" of Air Fry Oven and turn the dial to select the "Air Fry" mode. Press the Time button and again turn the dial to set the cooking time to 10 minutes

Now push the Temp button and rotate the dial to set the temperature at 350 degrees F. Once preheated, place the air fryer basket inside and close its lid. Serve warm.

NUTRITION: Calories 453 Fat 2.4 g Carbs 18 g Protein 23.2 g

233. LEMONY SALMON

Basic Recipe
Preparation Time: 5 minutes
Cooking Time: 10 minutes
Serving: 2
INGREDIENTS:

- 1 tbsp. of fresh lemon juice
- ½ tbsp olive oil
- Salt and ground black pepper, as required
- 1 garlic clove, minced
- ½ tsp. fresh thyme leaves, chopped
- 2 (7-oz) Salmon fillets

DIRECTIONS:

In a bowl, add all ingredients except the salmon and mix well. Add the salmon fillets and coat with the mixture generously. Arrange the salmon fillets onto a lightly greased cooking rack, skin-side down. Arrange the drip pan in the bottom of the Cosori Air Fryer Oven cooking chamber. Select "Air Fry" and then adjust the temperature to 400 °F. Set the time for 10 minutes and press "Start". When the display shows "Add Food" insert the cooking rack in the bottom position. When the display shows "Turn Food" turn the fillets. When the cooking time is complete, remove the tray from the Vortex Oven. Serve hot.

NUTRITION: Calories 297 Carbs 0.8g Fat 15.8g Protein 38.7g

234. ROASTED DUCK

Intermediate Recipe
Preparation Time: 10 minutes
Cooking Time: 3 hours
Serving: 12
INGREDIENTS:

- 6 lb. whole Pekin duck
- Salt
- 5 garlic cloves chopped
- 1 lemon, chopped
- Glaze
- 1/2 cup balsamic vinegar
- 1 lemon, juiced
- 1/4 cup honey

DIRECTIONS:

Place the Pekin duck in a baking tray and add garlic, lemon, and salt on top.

Whisk honey, vinegar, and honey in a bowl.

Brush this glaze over the duck liberally.

Marinate overnight in the refrigerator.

Remove the duck from the marinade and fix it on the rotisserie rod in the Air fryer oven

Turn the dial to select the "Air Roast" mode.

Hit the Time button and again use the dial to set the cooking time to 3 hours.

Now push the Temp button and rotate the dial to set the temperature at

350 degrees F.

Close its lid and allow the duck to roast.

Serve warm.

NUTRITION: Calories 387 Fat 6 g Carbs 37.4 g Protein 14.6 g

235. LEMON PEPPER TURKEY

Intermediate Recipe
Preparation Time: 10 minutes
Cooking Time: 45 minutes
Serving: 6
INGREDIENTS:

- 3 lbs. turkey breast
- 2 tablespoons oil
- 1 tablespoon Worcestershire sauce
- 1 teaspoon lemon pepper
- 1/2 teaspoon salt

DIRECTIONS:

Whisk everything in a bowl and coat the turkey liberally.

Place the turkey in the Air fryer basket.

Press "Power Button" of Air Fry Oven and turn the dial to select the "Air Fry" mode.

Press the Time button and again turn the dial to set the cooking time to 45 minutes

Now push the Temp button and rotate the dial to set the temperature at 375 degrees F.

Once preheated, place the air fryer basket inside and close its lid.

Serve warm.

NUTRITION: Calories 391 Fat 2.8 g Carbs 36.5 g Protein 6.6

236. MISO GLAZED SALMON

Basic Recipe
Preparation Time: 5 minutes
Cooking Time: 10 minutes
Serving: 4
INGREDIENTS:

- 1/3 cup sake
- ¼ cup sugar
- ¼ cup red miso
- 1 tbsp low-sodium soy sauce
- 2 tbsp vegetable oil
- 4 (5-oz) Skinless salmon fillets, (1-inch thick)

DIRECTIONS:

Place the sake, sugar, miso, soy sauce and oil into a bowl and beat until thoroughly combined. Rub the salmon fillets with the mixture generously. In a plastic zip lock bag, place the salmon fillets with any remaining miso mixture. Seal the bag and refrigerate to marinate for about 30 minutes Grease a baking dish that will fit in the Vortex Air Fryer Oven. Remove the salmon fillets from bag and shake off the excess marinade. Arrange the salmon fillets into the prepared baking dish. Arrange the drip pan in the bottom of the Cosori Air Fryer Oven cooking chamber. Select "Broil" and Set the time for 5 minutes. When the display shows "Add Food" insert the baking dish in the center position. When the display shows "Turn Food" do not turn food. When cooking time is complete, remove the baking dish from the Vortex Oven. Serve hot.

NUTRITION: Calories 335 Carbs 18.3g Fat 16.6g Protein 29.8g

237. SPICED TILAPIA

Basic Recipe
Preparation Time: 5 minutes
Cooking Time: 12 minutes
Serving: 2
INGREDIENTS:

- ½ Tsp lemon pepper seasoning
- ½ tsp. Garlic powder
- ½ tsp onion powder

- Salt and ground black pepper, as required
- 2 (6-oz) tilapia fillets
- 1 tbsp olive oil

DIRECTIONS:

In a small bowl, mix together the spices, salt and black pepper. Coat the tilapia fillets with oil and then rub with spice mixture. Arrange the tilapia fillets onto a lightly greased cooking rack, skin-side down. Arrange the drip pan in the bottom of the Cosori Air Fryer Oven cooking chamber. Select "Air Fry" and then adjust the temperature to 360 °F. Set the time for 12 minutes and press "Start". When the display shows "Add Food" insert the cooking rack in the bottom position. When the display shows "Turn Food" turn the fillets. When cooking time is complete, remove the tray from the Vortex Oven. Serve hot.

NUTRITION: Calories 206 Carbs 0.2g Fat 8.6g Protein 31.9g

238. BUTTERED SALMON

Basic Recipe
Preparation Time: 5 minutes
Cooking Time: 10 minutes
Serving: 2
INGREDIENTS:
- 2 salmon fillets (6-oz)
- Salt and ground black pepper, as required
- 1 tbsp butter, melted

DIRECTIONS:

Season each salmon fillet with salt and black pepper and then, coat with the butter. Arrange the salmon fillets onto the greased cooking tray. Arrange the drip pan in the bottom of the Cosori Air Fryer Oven cooking chamber. Select "Air Fry" and then adjust the temperature to 360 °F. Set the time for 10 minutes and press "Start". When the display shows "Add Food" insert the cooking tray in the center position. When the display shows "Turn Food" turn the salmon fillets. When cooking time is complete, remove the tray from the Vortex Oven. Serve hot.

NUTRITION: Calories 276 Carbs 0g Fat 16.3g Protein 33.1g

239. BUTTERMILK MARINATED CHICKEN

Basic Recipe
Preparation Time: 10 minutes
Cooking Time: 25 minutes
Serving: 6
INGREDIENTS:
- 3-lb. whole chicken
- 1 tablespoon salt
- 1-pint buttermilk

DIRECTIONS:

Place the whole chicken in a large bowl and Drizzle with salt on top. Pour the buttermilk over it and leave the chicken soaked overnight. Cover the chicken bowl and refrigerate overnight.

Remove the chicken from the marinade and fix it on the rotisserie rod in the Air fryer oven.

Turn the dial to select the "Air Roast" mode.

Hit the Time button and again use the dial to set the cooking time to 25 minutes

Now push the Temp button and rotate the dial to set the temperature at 370 degrees F.

Close its lid and allow the chicken to roast.

Serve warm.

NUTRITION: Calories 284 Fat 7.9 g Carbs 46 g Protein 17.9 g

240. ROASTED TURKEY BREAST

Intermediate Recipe
Preparation Time: 10 minutes
Cooking Time: 50 minutes
Serving: 6
INGREDIENTS:
- 3 lb. boneless turkey breast
- ¼ cup mayonnaise
- 2 teaspoon poultry seasoning
- 1 teaspoon salt
- ½ teaspoon garlic powder
- ¼ teaspoon black pepper

DIRECTIONS:

Whisk all the ingredients, including turkey in a bowl, and coat it well.

Place the boneless turkey breast in the Air fryer basket.

Rotate the dial to select the "Air fry" mode.

Press the Time button and again use the dial to set the cooking time to 50 minutes

Now press the Temp button and rotate the dial to set the temperature at 350 degrees F.

Once preheated, place the air fryer basket in the Ninja oven and Close its lid to bake.

Slice and serve.

NUTRITION: Calories 322 Fat 11.8 Carbs 14.6 g Protein 17.3 g

241. BRINE SOAKED TURKEY

Intermediate Recipe
Preparation Time: 10 minutes
Cooking Time: 45 minutes
Serving: 8
INGREDIENTS:
- 7 lb. bone-in, skin-on turkey breast
- Brine:
- 1/2 cup salt
- 1 lemon
- 1/2 onion
- 3 cloves garlic, smashed
- 5 sprigs fresh thyme
- 3 bay leaves
- Black pepper
- Turkey Breast:
- 4 tablespoon butter, softened
- 1/2 teaspoon black pepper
- 1/2 teaspoon garlic powder
- 1/4 teaspoon dried thyme
- 1/4 teaspoon dried oregano

DIRECTIONS:

Mix the turkey brine ingredients in a pot and soak the turkey in the brine overnight. Next day, remove the soaked turkey from the brine.

Whisk the butter, black pepper, garlic powder, oregano, and thyme. Brush the butter mixture over the turkey then place it in a baking tray.

Press "Power Button" of Air Fry Oven and turn the dial to select the "Air Roast" mode. Press the Time button and again turn the dial to set the cooking time to 45 minutes

Now push the Temp button and rotate the dial to set the temperature at 370 degrees F. Once preheated, place the turkey baking tray in the oven and close its lid.

Slice and serve warm.

NUTRITION: Calories 397 Fat 15.4 g Carbs 58.5 g Protein 7.9 g

242. PARMESAN CHICKEN MEATBALLS

Basic Recipe
Preparation Time: 10 minutes
Cooking Time: 12 minutes
Serving: 4
INGREDIENTS:
- 1-lb. ground chicken
- 1 large egg, beaten
- ½ cup Parmesan cheese, grated
- ½ cup pork rinds, ground
- 1 teaspoon garlic powder

- 1 teaspoon paprika
- 1 teaspoon kosher salt
- ½ teaspoon pepper
- Crust:
- ½ cup pork rinds, ground

DIRECTIONS:

Toss all the meatball ingredients in a bowl and mix well. Make small meatballs out this mixture and roll them in the pork rinds.

Place the coated meatballs in the air fryer basket. Press "Power Button" of Air Fry Oven and turn the dial to select the "Bake" mode.

Press the Time button and again turn the dial to set the cooking time to 12 minutes. Now push the Temp button and rotate the dial to set the temperature at 400 degrees F.

Once preheated, place the air fryer basket inside and close its lid.

Serve warm.

NUTRITION: Calories 529 Fat 17 g Carbs 55 g Protein 41g

243. TURKEY MEATBALLS

Basic Recipe
Preparation Time: 10 minutes
Cooking Time: 20 minutes
Serving: 6
INGREDIENTS:

- 1.5 lb. turkey mince
- 1 red bell pepper, deseeded and chopped
- 1 large egg, beaten
- 4 tablespoons parsley, minced
- 1 tablespoon cilantro, minced
- Salt, to taste
- Black pepper, to taste

DIRECTIONS:

Toss all the meatball ingredients in a bowl and mix well. Make small meatballs out this mixture and place them in the air fryer basket.

Press "Power Button" of Air Fry Oven and turn the dial to select the "Air Fry" mode. Press the Time button and again turn the dial to set the cooking time to 20 minutes

Now push the Temp button and rotate the dial to set the temperature at 375 degrees F.Once preheated, place the air fryer basket inside and close its lid. Serve warm.

NUTRITION: Calories 338 Fat 9.7 g Carbs 32.5 g Protein 10.3 g

244. BREADED COD

Basic Recipe
Preparation Time: 5 minutes
Cooking Time: 10 minutes
Serving: 4
INGREDIENTS:

- 1/3 cup all-purpose flour
- Ground black pepper, as required
- 1 large egg
- 2 tbsp water
- 2/3 cup cornflakes, crushed
- 1 tbsp parmesan cheese, grated
- 1/8 tsp cayenne pepper
- 1 lb. Cod fillets –
- Salt, as required

DIRECTIONS:

In a shallow dish, add the flour and black pepper and mix well. In a second shallow dish, add the egg and water and beat well. In a third shallow dish, add the cornflakes, cheese and cayenne pepper and mix well.

Season the cod fillets with salt evenly. Coat the fillets with flour mixture, then dip into egg mixture and finally coat with the cornflake mixture.

Arrange the cod fillets onto the greased cooking rack. Arrange the drip pan in the bottom of the Cosori Air Fryer Oven cooking chamber. Select "Air Fry" and then adjust the temperature to 400 °F. Set the time for 10

minutes and press "Start".

When the display shows "Add Food" insert the cooking rack in the bottom position. When the display shows "Turn Food" turn the cod fillets. When cooking time is complete, remove the tray from the Vortex Oven. Serve hot.

NUTRITION: Calories 168 Carbs 12.1g Fat 2.7g Protein 23.7g

245. CHICKEN DRUMSTICKS

Basic Recipe
Preparation Time: 10 minutes
Cooking Time: 20 minutes
Serving: 8
INGREDIENTS:

- 8 chicken drumsticks
- 2 tablespoon olive oil
- 1 teaspoon salt
- 1 teaspoon pepper
- 1 teaspoon garlic powder
- 1 teaspoon paprika
- 1/2 teaspoon cumin

DIRECTIONS:

Mix olive oil with salt, black pepper, garlic powder, paprika, and cumin in a bowl.

Rub this mixture liberally over all the drumsticks.

Place these drumsticks in the Air fryer basket.

Turn the dial to select the "Air Fry" mode.

Hit the Time button and again use the dial to set the cooking time to 20 minutes

Now push the Temp button and rotate the dial to set the temperature at 375 degrees F.

Once preheated, place the Air fryer basket inside the oven.

Flip the drumsticks when cooked halfway through.

Resume air frying for another rest of the 10 minutes

Serve warm.

NUTRITION: Calories 212 Fat 11.8 g Carbs 14.6 g Protein 17.3 g

246. SPICY CATFISH

Basic Recipe
Preparation Time: 5 minutes
Cooking Time: 15 minutes
Serving : 4
INGREDIENTS:

- 2 tbsp cornmeal polenta
- 2 tsp cajun seasoning
- ½ tsp paprika
- ½ tsp garlic powder
- Salt, as required
- 2 (6-oz) catfish fillets
- 1 tbsp olive oil

DIRECTIONS:

In a bowl, mix together the cornmeal, Cajun seasoning, paprika, garlic powder, and salt. Add the catfish fillets and coat evenly with the mixture. Now, coat each fillet with oil. Arrange the fish fillets onto a greased cooking rack and spray with cooking spray. Arrange the drip pan in the bottom of the Cosori Air Fryer Oven cooking chamber. Select "Air Fry" and then adjust the temperature to 400 °F. Set the timer for 14 minutes and press "Start". When the display shows "Add Food" insert the cooking rack in the center position. When the display shows "Turn Food" turn the fillets. When cooking time is complete, remove the rack from the Vortex Oven. Serve hot.

NUTRITION: Calories 32 Carbs 6.7g Fat 20.3g Protein 27.3g

247. PRAWNS IN BUTTER SAUCE

Basic Recipe
Preparation Time: 5 minutes

Cooking Time : 6 minutes

Serving: 2

INGREDIENTS:

- ½ lb. Peeled and deveined large prawns
- 1 large garlic clove, minced
- 1 tbsp butter melted
- 1 tsp fresh lemon zest grated

DIRECTIONS:

Add all the ingredients into a bowl and toss to coat well. Set aside at room temperature for about 30 minutes. Arrange the prawn mixture into a baking dish that will fit in the Vortex Air Fryer Oven. Arrange the drip pan in the bottom of the Cosori Air Fryer Oven cooking chamber. Select "Bake" and then adjust the temperature to 450 °F. Set the time for 6 minutes and press "Start".

When the display shows "Add Food" insert the baking dish in the center position. When cooking time is complete, remove the baking dish from the Vortex Oven. When the display shows "Turn Food" do not turn food. When cooking time is complete, remove the baking dish from the Vortex Oven. Serve hot.

NUTRITION: Calories 189 Carbs 2.4g Fat 7.7g Protein 26g

248. TUNA BURGERS

Basic Recipe

Preparation Time: 5 minutes

Cooking Time : 6 minutes

Serving : 4

INGREDIENTS:

- 7 oz canned tuna
- 1 large egg
- ¼ cup breadcrumbs
- 1 tbsp. Mustard
- ¼ tsp garlic powder
- ¼ tsp onion powder
- ¼ tsp cayenne pepper
- Salt and ground black pepper, as required

DIRECTIONS:

Add all the ingredients into a bowl and mix until well combined. Make 4 equal-sized patties from the mixture. Arrange the patties onto a greased cooking rack. Arrange the drip pan in the bottom of the Cosori Air Fryer Oven cooking chamber. Select "Air Fry" and then adjust the temperature to 400 °F. Set the time for 6 minutes and press "Start". When the display shows "Add Food" insert the cooking rack in the center position. When the display shows "Turn Food" turn the burgers. When the cooking time is complete, remove the tray from the Vortex Oven. Serve hot.

NUTRITION: Calories 151 Carbs 6.3g Fat 6.4g Protein 16.4g

249. BBQ CHICKEN RECIPE FROM GREECE

Basic Recipe

Preparation Time: 5 minutes

Cooking Time: 24minutes

Serving: 2

INGREDIENTS:

- 1 (8 ounce) container fat-free plain yogurt
- 2 tablespoons fresh lemon juice
- 2 teaspoons dried oregano
- 1-pound skinless, boneless chicken breast halves - cut into 1-inch pieces
- 1 large red onion, cut into wedges
- 1/2 teaspoon lemon zest
- 1/2 teaspoon salt
- 1 large green bell pepper, cut into 1 1/2-inch pieces
- 1/3 cup crumbled feta cheese with basil and sun-dried tomatoes
- 1/4 teaspoon ground black pepper
- 1/4 teaspoon crushed dried rosemary

DIRECTIONS:

In a shallow dish, mix well rosemary, pepper, salt, oregano, lemon juice, lemon zest, feta cheese, and yogurt. Add chicken and toss well to coat. Marinate in the ref for 3 hours.

Thread bell pepper, onion, and chicken pieces in skewers. Place on skewer rack.

For 12 minutes, cook it on 360oF. Turnover skewers halfway through cooking time. If needed, cook in batches.

Serve and enjoy.

NUTRITION: Calories 242 Carbs 12.3g Protein 31.0g Fat 7.5g

250. VINEGAR HALIBUT

Basic Recipe

Preparation Time: 5 minutes

Cooking Time: 12 minutes

Serving: 2

INGREDIENTS:

- 2 (5-oz) Halibut fillets
- 1 garlic cloves, minced
- 1 tsp fresh rosemary, minced
- 1 tbsp olive oil
- 1 tbsp red wine vinegar
- 1/8 tsp hot sauce

DIRECTIONS:

In a large resealable bag, add all ingredients. Seal the bag and shale well to mix. Refrigerate to marinate for at least 30 minutes Remove the fish fillets from the bag and shake off the excess marinade. Arrange the halibut fillets onto the greased cooking tray.

Arrange the drip pan in the bottom of the Cosori Air Fryer Oven cooking chamber. Select "Bake" and then adjust the temperature to 450 °F. Set the time for 12 minutes and press "Start". When the display shows "Add Food" insert the cooking tray in the center position. When the display shows "Turn Food" turn the halibut fillets. When the cooking time is complete, remove the tray from the Vortex Oven. Serve hot.

NUTRITION: Calories 223 Carbs 1g Fat 10.4g Protein 30g

251. AIR FRIED CHICKEN TENDERLOIN

Basic Recipe

Preparation Time: 5 minutes

Cooking Time: 15 minutes

Serving: 8

INGREDIENTS:

- ½ cup almond flour
- 1 egg, beaten
- 2 tablespoons coconut oil
- 8 chicken tenderloins
- Salt and pepper to taste

DIRECTIONS:

Preheat the air fryer for 5 minutes Season the chicken tenderloin with salt and pepper to taste.

Soak in beaten eggs then dredge in almond flour. Place in the air fryer and brush with coconut oil.

Cook for 15 minutes at 3750F.

Halfway through the cooking time, give the fryer basket a shake to cook evenly.

NUTRITION: Calories 130.3 Carbs 0.7g Protein 8.7 g Fat 10.3 g

252. SIMPLE HADDOCK

Basic Recipe

Preparation Time: 5 minutes

Cooking Time: 10 minutes

Serving: 2

INGREDIENTS:

- 2 (6-oz) haddock fillets
- 1 tbsp olive oil
- Salt and ground black pepper, as required

DIRECTIONS:

Coat the haddock fillets with oil and then, sprinkle with salt and black pepper. Arrange the haddock fillets onto a greased cooking rack and spray with cooking spray. Arrange the drip pan in the bottom of the Cosori Air Fryer Oven cooking chamber. Select "Air Fry" and then adjust the temperature to 355 °F. Set the time for 8 minutes and press "Start". When the display shows "Add Food" insert the cooking rack in the center position. When the display shows "Turn Food" do not turn food. When the cooking time is complete, remove the rack from the Vortex Oven. Serve hot.

NUTRITION: Calories 251 Carbs 0g Fat 8.6g Protein 41.2g

253. ALMOND FLOUR BATTERED CHICKEN CORDON BLEU

Basic Recipe
Preparation Time: 5 minutes
Cooking Time : 30 minutes
Serving: 2
INGREDIENTS:
• ¼ cup almond flour
• 1 slice cheddar cheese
• 1 slice of ham
• 1 small egg, beaten
• 1 teaspoon parsley
• 2 chicken breasts, butterflied
• Salt and pepper to taste

DIRECTIONS:

Season the chicken with parsley, salt and pepper to taste.
Place the cheese and ham in the middle of the chicken and roll. Secure with toothpick.
Soak the rolled-up chicken in egg and dredge in almond flour.
Place in the air fryer.
Cook for 30 minutes at 3500F.
NUTRITION: Calories 1142 Carbs 5.5g Protein 79.4g Fat 89.1g

254. CRISPY HADDOCK

Basic Recipe
Preparation Time: 5 minutes
Cooking Time: 10 minutes
Serving: 3
INGREDIENTS:
• ½ Cup flour
• ½ tsp. Paprika
• 1 egg, beaten
• ¼ cup mayonnaise
• 4 oz salt and vinegar potato chips, crushed finely
• 1 lb haddock fillet cut into 6 pieces

DIRECTION:

In a shallow dish, mix together the flour and paprika. In a second shallow dish, add the egg and mayonnaise and beat well. In a third shallow dish, place the crushed potato chips. Coat the fish pieces with flour mixture, then dip into egg mixture and finally coat with the potato chips. Arrange the fish pieces onto 2 cooking trays. Arrange the drip pan in the bottom of the Cosori Air Fryer Oven cooking chamber. Select "Air Fry" and then adjust the temperature to 370 °F. Set the time for 10 minutes and press "Start". When the display shows "Add Food" insert 1 cooking tray in the top position and another in the bottom position. When the display shows "Turn Food" do not turn the food but switch the position of cooking trays. When cooking time is complete, remove the trays from the Vortex Oven. Serve hot.
NUTRITION: Calories 456 Carbs 40.9g Fat 22.7g Protein 43.5g

255. CRISPY TILAPIA

Basic Recipe
Preparation Time: 5 minutes
Cooking Time: 15 minutes

Serving: 2
INGREDIENTS:
• ¾ cup cornflakes, crushed
• 1 (1-oz.) packet, dry ranch-style dressing mix
• 2½ tbsp vegetable oil
• 2 eggs
• 4 (6-oz) tilapia fillets

DIRECTIONS:

In a shallow bowl, beat the eggs. In another bowl, add the cornflakes, ranch dressing, and oil and mix until a crumbly mixture form. Dip the fish fillets into egg and then, coat with the cornflake mixture.
Arrange the tilapia fillets onto the greased cooking tray. Arrange the drip pan in the bottom of the Cosori Air Fryer Oven cooking chamber. Select "Air Fry" and then adjust the temperature to 355 °F. Set the time for 14 minutes and press "Start".
When the display shows "Add Food" insert the cooking tray in the center position. When the display shows "Turn Food" turn the tilapia fillets. When cooking time is complete, remove the tray from the Vortex Oven. Serve hot.
NUTRITION: Calories 291 Carbs 4.9g Fat 14.6g Protein 34.8g

256. ALMOND FLOUR COCO-MILK BATTERED CHICKEN

Basic Recipe
Preparation Time: 5 minutes
Cooking Time: 30 minutes
Serving: 4
INGREDIENTS:
• ¼ cup coconut milk
• ½ cup almond flour
• 1 ½ tablespoons old bay Cajun seasoning
• 1 egg, beaten
• 4 small chicken thighs
• Salt and pepper to taste

DIRECTIONS:

Preheat the air fryer for 5 minutes
Mix the egg and coconut milk in a bowl.
Soak the chicken thighs in the beaten egg mixture.
In a mixing bowl, combine the almond flour, Cajun seasoning, salt and pepper.
Dredge the chicken thighs in the almond flour mixture.
Place in the air fryer basket.
Cook for 30 minutes at 3500F.
NUTRITION: Calories 590 Carbs 3.2g Protein 32.5 g Fat 38.6g

257. CRISPY PRAWNS

Basic Recipe
Preparation Time: 5 minutes
Cooking Time: 10 minutes
Serving: 4

INGREDIENTS:
• 1 egg
• ½ lb crushed nacho chips
• 12prawns, peeled and deveined

DIRECTIONS:

In a shallow dish, beat the egg. In another shallow dish, place the crushed nacho chips. Coat the prawn into egg and then roll into nacho chips.
Arrange the coated prawns onto 2 cooking trays in a single layer. Arrange the drip pan in the bottom of the Cosori Air Fryer Oven cooking chamber. Select "Air Fry" and then adjust the temperature to 355 °F. Set the time for 8 minutes and press "Start".
When the display shows "Add Food" insert 1 tray in the top position and another in the bottom position. When the display shows "Turn Food" do not turn the food but switch the position of cooking trays. When cooking

time is complete, remove the trays from the Vortex Oven. Serve hot.
NUTRITION: Calories 386 Carbs 36.1g Fat 17g Protein 21g

258. BACON 'N EGG-SUBSTITUTE BAKE

Basic Recipe
Preparation Time: 5 minutes
Cooking Time: 30 minutes
Serving : 4
INGREDIENTS:
• 1 (6 ounce) package Canadian bacon, quartered
• 1/2 cup 2% milk
• 1/4 teaspoon ground mustard
• 1/4 teaspoon salt
• 2 cups shredded Cheddar-Monterey Jack cheese blend
• 3/4 cup and 2 tablespoons egg substitute (such as Egg Beaters® Southwestern Style)
• 4 frozen hash brown patties

DIRECTIONS:
Lightly grease baking pan of air fryer with cooking spray.
Evenly spread hash brown patties on bottom of pan. Top evenly with bacon and then followed by cheese.
In a bowl, whisk well mustard, salt, milk, and egg substitute. Pour over bacon mixture.
Cover air fryer baking pan with foil.
Preheat air fryer to 330oF.
Cook for another 20 minutes, remove foil and continue cooking for another 15 minutes or until eggs are set.
Serve and enjoy.
Nutrition: Calories 459 ,Carbs 21.0g ,Protein 29.4g
Fat 28.5g

259. BAKED RICE, BLACK BEAN AND CHEESE

Intermediate Recipe
Preparation Time: 5 minutes
Cooking Time: 1 hour
Serving: 4
INGREDIENTS:
• 1 cooked skinless boneless chicken breast halves, chopped
• 1 cup shredded Swiss cheese
• 1/2 (15 ounce) can black beans, Dry out
• 1/2 (4 ounce) can diced green chili peppers, Dry out
• 1/2 cup vegetable broth
• 1/2 medium zucchini, thinly sliced
• 1/4 cup sliced mushrooms
• 1/4 teaspoon cumin
• 1-1/2 teaspoons olive oil
• 2 tablespoons and 2 teaspoons diced onion
• 3 tablespoons brown rice
• 3 tablespoons shredded carrots
• Ground cayenne pepper to taste
• Salt to taste

DIRECTIONS:
Lightly grease baking pan of air fryer with cooking spray. Add rice and broth. Cover pan with foil cook for 10 minutes at 390oF. Lower heat to 300oF and fluff rice. Cook for another 10 minutes Let it stand for 10 minutes and transfer to a bowl and set aside.
Add oil to same baking pan. Stir in onion and cook for 5 minutes at 330oF.
Stir in mushrooms, chicken, and zucchini. Mix well and cook for 5 minutes
Stir in cayenne pepper, salt, and cumin. Mix well and cook for another 2 minutes
Stir in ½ of the Swiss cheese, carrots, chilies, beans, and rice. Toss well to mix. Evenly spread in pan. Top with remaining cheese.
Cover pan with foil.
Cook for 15 minutes at 390oF and then remove foil and cook for another

5 to 10 minutes or until tops are lightly browned.
Serve and enjoy.
NUTRITION: Calories 337 Carbs 11.5g Protein 25.3g Fat 21.0g

260. BASIL-GARLIC BREADED CHICKEN BAKE

Intermediate Recipe
Preparation Time: 5 minutes
Cooking Time : 30 minutes
Serving: 2
INGREDIENTS:
• 2 boneless skinless chicken breast halves (4 ounces each)
• 1 tablespoon butter, melted
• 1 large tomato, seeded and chopped
• 2 garlic cloves, minced
• 1 1/2 tablespoons minced fresh basil
• 1/2 tablespoon olive oil
• 1/2 teaspoon salt
• 1/4 cup all-purpose flour
• 1/4 cup egg substitute
• 1/4 cup grated Parmesan cheese
• 1/4 cup dry bread crumbs
• 1/4 teaspoon pepper

DIRECTIONS:
In shallow bowl, whisk well egg substitute and place flour in a separate bowl. Dip chicken in flour, then egg, and then flour. In a small bowl whisk well the butter, bread crumbs and cheese. Sprinkle over chicken.
Lightly grease baking pan of air fryer with cooking spray. Place breaded chicken on bottom of pan. Cover with foil.
For 20 minutes, cook it on 390 F.
Meanwhile, in a bowl whisk well remaining ingredient.
Remove foil from pan and then pour over chicken the remaining Ingredients.
Cook for 8 minutes
Serve and enjoy.
NUTRITION: Calories 311 Carbs 22.0g Protein 31.0g Fat 11.0g

261. CAESAR MARINATED GRILLED CHICKEN

Basic Recipe
Preparation Time: 5 minutes
Cooking Time: 20 minutes
Serving: 3
INGREDIENTS:
• ¼ cup crouton
• 1 teaspoon lemon zest. Form into ovals, skewer and grill.
• 1/2 cup Parmesan
• 1/4 cup breadcrumbs
• 1-pound ground chicken
• 2 tablespoons Caesar dressing and more for drizzling
• 2-4 romaine leaves

DIRECTIONS:
In a shallow dish, mix well chicken, 2 tablespoons Caesar dressing, parmesan, and breadcrumbs. Mix well with hands. Form into 1-inch oval patties.
Thread chicken pieces in skewers. Place on skewer rack in air fryer.
For 12 minutes, cook it on 360oF. Turnover skewers halfway through cooking time. If needed, cook in batches.
Serve and enjoy on a bed of lettuce and sprinkle with croutons and extra dressing.
NUTRITION: Calories 339 Carbs 9.5g Protein 32.6g Fat 18.9g

262. CHEESE STUFFED CHICKEN

Basic Recipe
Preparation Time: 5 minutes
Cooking Time: 25 minutes
Serving : 4

INGREDIENTS:
- 1 tablespoon creole seasoning
- 1 tablespoon olive oil
- 1 teaspoon garlic powder
- 1 teaspoon onion powder
- 4 chicken breasts, butterflied and pounded
- 4 slices Colby cheese
- 4 slices pepper jack cheese

DIRECTIONS:
Preheat the air fryer to 3900F.

Place the grill pan accessory in the air fryer.

Create the dry rub by mixing in a bowl the creole seasoning, garlic powder, and onion powder. Season it with salt and pepper if desired.

Rub the seasoning on to the chicken.

Place the chicken on a working surface and place a slice each of pepper jack and Colby cheese.

Fold the chicken and secure the edges with toothpicks.

Brush chicken with olive oil.

Grill for 30 minutes and make sure to flip the meat every 10 minutes

NUTRITION: Calories 727 Carbs 5.4 g Protein 73.1g Fat 45.9g

263. JUICY CHEESEBURGERS

Basic Recipe
Preparation Time: 5 minutes
Cooking Time: 15 minutes
Servings: 4

INGREDIENTS:
- 1 pound 93% lean ground beef
- 1 teaspoon Worcestershire sauce
- 1 tablespoon burger seasoning
- Salt
- Pepper
- Cooking oil
- 4 slices cheese
- Buns

DIRECTIONS:
In a large bowl, mix the ground beef, Worcestershire, burger seasoning, and salt and pepper to taste until well blended. Spray the air fryer basket with cooking oil. You will need only a quick sprits. The burgers will produce oil as they cook. Shape the mixture into 4 patties. Place the burgers in the air fryer. The burgers should fit without the need to stack, but stacking is okay if necessary.

Pour into the Oven rack/basket. Place the Rack on the middle-shelf of the Air Fryer Oven. Set temperature to 375°F, and set time to 8 minutes Cook for 8 minutes Open the air fryer and flip the burgers. Cook for an additional 3 to 4 minutes Check the inside of the burgers to determine if they have finished cooking. You can stick a knife or fork in the center to examine the color.

Top each burger with a slice of cheese. Cook for an additional minute, or until the cheese has melted

Serve on buns with any additional toppings of your choice.

NUTRITION: Calories 566 Cal Fat 39 g Carbs 0 g Protein 29 g

264. MEAT LOVERS' PIZZA

Intermediate Recipe
Preparation Time: 10 minutes
Cooking Time: 12 minutes
Servings: 2

INGREDIENTS:
- 1 pre-prepared 7-inch pizza pie crust, defrosted if necessary
- 1/3 cup of marinara sauce
- 2 ounces of grilled steak, sliced into bite-sized pieces
- 2 ounces of salami, sliced fine
- 2 ounces of pepperoni, sliced fine
- ¼ cup of American cheese
- ¼ cup of shredded mozzarella cheese

DIRECTIONS:
Preheat the Air Fryer Oven to 350 degrees. Lay the pizza dough flat on a sheet of parchment paper or tin foil, cut large enough to hold the entire pie crust, but small enough that it will leave the edges of the air frying basket uncovered to allow for air circulation. Using a fork, stab the pizza dough several times across the surface – piercing the pie crust will allow air to circulate throughout the crust and ensure even cooking. With a deep soup spoon, ladle the marinara sauce onto the pizza dough, and spread evenly in expanding circles over the surface of the pie-crust. Be sure to leave at least ½ inch of bare dough around the edges, to ensure that extra-crispy crunchy first bite of the crust! Distribute the pieces of steak and the slices of salami and pepperoni evenly over the sauce-covered dough, then sprinkle the cheese in an even layer on top.

Set the air fryer timer to 12 minutes, and place the pizza with foil or paper on the fryer's basket surface. Again, be sure to leave the edges of the basket uncovered to allow for proper air circulation, and don't let your bare fingers touch the hot surface. After 12 minutes, when the Air Fryer Oven shuts off, the cheese should be perfectly melted and lightly crisped, and the pie crust should be golden brown. Using a spatula – or two, if necessary, remove the pizza from the air fryer basket and set on a serving plate. Wait a few minutes until the pie is cool enough to handle, then cut into slices and serve.

NUTRITION: Calories 390 Cal Fat 21 g Carbs 34 g Fiber 3 g

265. COUNTRY FRIED STEAK

Basic Recipe
Preparation Time: 5 minutes
Cooking Time: 12 minutes
Servings: 2

INGREDIENTS:
- 1 tsp. pepper
- 2 C. almond milk
- 2 tbsp. almond flour
- 6 ounces ground sausage meat
- 1 tsp. pepper
- 1 tsp. salt
- 1 tsp. garlic powder
- 1 tsp. onion powder
- 1 C. panko breadcrumbs
- 1 C. almond flour
- 3 beaten eggs
- 6 ounces sirloin steak, pounded till thin

DIRECTIONS:
Season panko breadcrumbs with spices

Dredge steak in flour, then egg, and then seasoned panko mixture.

Place into air fryer basket.

Set temperature to 370°F, and set time to 12 minutes

To make sausage gravy, cook sausage and Dry outof fat, but reserve 2 tablespoons.

Add flour to sausage and mix until incorporated. Gradually mix in milk over medium to high heat till it becomes thick.

Season mixture with pepper and cook 3 minutes longer.

Serve steak topped with gravy and enjoy.

NUTRITION: Calories 395 Cal Fat 11 g Carbs 0 g Protein 39 g

266. AIR FRIED GRILLED STEAK

Basic Recipe
Preparation Time: 5 minutes
Cooking Time: 45 minutes
Servings: 2

INGREDIENTS:
- 2 top sirloin steaks
- 3 tablespoons butter, melted
- 3 tablespoons olive oil
- Salt and pepper to taste

DIRECTIONS:

Preheat the Air Fryer Oven for 5 minutes. Season the sirloin steaks with olive oil, salt and pepper.

Place the beef in the air fryer basket.

Cook for 45 minutes at 350°F.

Once cooked, serve with butter.

NUTRITION: Calories 1536 Fat 123.7 g Carbs 0 g Protein 103.4 g

267. EASY AIR FRIED ROASTED ASPARAGUS

Basic Recipe

Preparation Time: 5 minutes

Cooking Time: 10 minutes

Servings: 4

INGREDIENTS:

- 1 bunch fresh asparagus
- 1 ½ tsp. herbs de provence
- Fresh lemon wedge (optional)
- 1 tablespoon olive oil or cooking spray
- Salt and pepper to taste

DIRECTIONS:

Wash asparagus and trim off hard ends. Drizzle with asparagus with olive oil and add seasonings

Place asparagus in air fryer and cook on 360F for 6 to 10 minutes

Drizzle with squeezed lemon over roasted asparagus.

NUTRITION: Calories 46 Protein 2g Fat 3g Carbs 1g

268. COPYCAT TACO BELL CRUNCH WRAPS

Basic Recipe

Preparation Time: 10 minutes

Cooking Time: 2 minutes

Servings: 6

INGREDIENTS:

- 6 wheat tostadas
- 2 C. sour cream
- 2 C. Mexican blend cheese
- 2 C. shredded lettuce
- 12 ounces low-sodium nacho cheese
- 3 Roma tomatoes
- 6 12-inch wheat tortillas
- 1 1/3 C. water
- 2 packets low-sodium taco seasoning
- 2 pounds of lean ground beef

DIRECTIONS:

Ensure your air fryer is preheated to 400 degrees.

Make beef according to taco seasoning packets.

Place 2/3 C. prepared beef, 4 tbsp. cheese, 1 tostada, 1/3 C. sour cream, 1/3 C. lettuce, 1/6th of tomatoes and 1/3 C. cheese on each tortilla.

Fold up tortillas edges and repeat with remaining ingredients.

Lay the folded sides of tortillas down into the air fryer and spray with olive oil.

Set temperature to 400°F, and set time to 2 minutes Cook 2 minutes till browned.

NUTRITION: Calories 311 Cal Fat 9 g Carbs 0 g Protein 22 g

269. BBQ PINEAPPLE 'N TERIYAKI GLAZED CHICK-EN

Basic Recipe

Preparation Time: 5 minutes

Cooking Time: 20 minutes

Serving: 2

INGREDIENTS:

- ¼ cup pineapple juice
- ¼ teaspoon pepper
- ½ cup brown sugar
- ½ cup soy sauce

- ½ teaspoon salt
- 1 green bell pepper, cut into 1-inch cubes
- 1 red bell pepper, cut into 1-inch cubes
- 1 red onion, cut into 1-inch cubes
- 1 Tablespoon cornstarch
- 1 Tablespoon water
- 1 yellow red bell pepper, cut into 1-inch cubes
- 2 boneless skinless chicken breasts cut into 1-inch cubes
- 2 cups fresh pineapple cut into 1-inch cubes
- 2 garlic cloves, minced
- Green onions, for garnish

DIRECTIONS:

In a saucepan, bring to a boil salt, pepper, garlic, pineapple juice, soy sauce, and brown sugar. In a small bowl whisk well, cornstarch and water. Slowly stir in to mixture in pan while whisking constantly. Simmer until thickened, around 3 minutes. Save ¼ cup of the sauce for basting and set aside.

In shallow dish, mix well chicken and remaining thickened sauce. Toss well to coat. Marinate in the ref for a half hour.

Thread bell pepper, onion, pineapple, and chicken pieces in skewers. Place on skewer rack in air fryer.

For 10 minutes, cook on 360oF. Turnover skewers halfway through cooking time. and baste with sauce. If needed, cook in batches.

Serve and enjoy with a sprinkle of green onions.

NUTRITION: Calories 391 Carbs 58.7g Protein 31.2g Fat 3.4g

270. BEEF & VEGGIE SPRING ROLLS

Basic Recipe

Preparation Time: 5 minutes

Cooking Time: 12 minutes

Servings: 10

INGREDIENTS:

- 2-ounce Asian rice noodles
- 1 tablespoon sesame oil
- 7-ounce ground beef
- 1 small onion, chopped
- 3 garlic cloves, crushed
- 1 cup fresh mixed vegetables
- 1 teaspoon soy sauce
- 1 packet spring roll skins
- 2 tablespoons water
- Olive oil, as required

DIRECTIONS:

Soak the noodles in warm water till soft.

Dry out and cut into small lengths. In a pan heat the oil and add the onion and garlic and sauté for about 4-5 minutes

Add beef and cook for about 4-5 minutes

Add vegetables and cook for about 5-7 minutes or till cooked through.

Stir in soy sauce and remove from the heat.

Immediately, stir in the noodles and keep aside till all the juices have been absorbed.

Preheat the Air Fryer Oven to 350 degrees F.

Place the spring rolls skin onto a smooth surface.

Add a line of the filling diagonally across.

Fold the top point over the filling and then fold in both sides.

On the final point, brush it with water before rolling to seal.

Brush the spring rolls with oil.

Arrange the rolls in batches in the air fryer and Cook for about 8 minutes

Repeat with remaining rolls. Now, place spring rolls onto a baking sheet.

Bake it for about 6 minutes per side.

NUTRITION: Calories 364 Cal Fat 9 g Carbs 39 g Protein 32 g

271. BROCCOLI CREAMY CASSEROLE

Basic Recipe

Preparation Time: 5 minutes

Cooking Time: 30 minutes
Servings: 4
INGREDIENTS:
- 1 cup diced ham
- 1 (14-ounce) bags frozen broccoli
- 4 ounces' cream cheese, softened
- ½ cup plain full-fat greek yogurt
- ¼ cup mayonnaise
- ½ teaspoon garlic salt
- ½ teaspoon onion powder
- ½ teaspoon dried basil
- ½ teaspoon smoked paprika
- ¼ teaspoon rosemary
- ¼ teaspoon thyme
- ½ cup shredded cheese
- ½ cup crushed pork rinds

DIRECTIONS:
Preheat air fryer to 350-degrees F. Spray a 6-inch soufflé dish with non-stick cooking spray; set aside.
Mix the ham, broccoli, cream cheese, yoghurt, mayonnaise, garlic salt, onion powder, basil, smoked paprika, rosemary and thyme in a large bowl.
Pour the batter into a oiled pan and cover the pan with grated cheese and shredded rinds. Bake it for 25 minutes or until the pan is golden and bubbly.
NUTRITION: Calories 273, Fat 17.4g,Carbs 9.7g Protein 17.4g

272. BROCCOLI-RICE 'N CHEESE CASSEROLE
Basic Recipe
Preparation Time: 5 minutes
Cooking Time: 30 minutes
Serving: 4
INGREDIENTS:
- 1 (10 ounce) can chunk chicken, Dry out
- 1 cup uncooked instant rice
- 1 cup water
- 1/2 (10.75 ounce) can condensed cream of chicken soup
- 1/2 (10.75 ounce) can condensed cream of mushroom soup
- 1/2 cup milk
- 1/2 small white onion, chopped
- 1/2-pound processed cheese food
- 2 tablespoons butter
- 8-ounce frozen chopped broccoli

DIRECTIONS:
Lightly grease baking pan of air fryer with cooking spray. Add water and bring to a boil at 390oF. Stir in rice and cook for 3 minutes. Stir in processed cheese, onion, broccoli, milk, butter, chicken soup, mushroom soup, and chicken. Mix well. Cook for 15 minutes at 390oF, fluff mixture and continue cooking for another 10 minutes until tops are browned. Serve and enjoy.
NUTRITION: Calories 752 Carbs 82.7g Protein 36.0g Fat 30.8g

273. SPICY THAI BEEF STIR-FRY
Basic Recipe
Preparation Time: 15 minutes
Cooking Time: 9 minutes
Servings: 4
INGREDIENTS:
- 1-pound sirloin steaks, thinly sliced
- 2 tablespoons lime juice, divided
- ⅓ Cup crunchy peanut butter
- ½ cup beef broth
- 1 tablespoon olive oil
- 1½ cups broccoli florets
- 2 cloves garlic, sliced
- 1 to 2 red chili peppers, sliced

DIRECTIONS:
In a medium bowl, combine the steak with 1 tablespoon of the lime juice. Set aside.
Combine the peanut butter and beef broth in a small bowl and mix well.
Dry out the beef and add the juice from the bowl into the peanut butter mixture.
In a 6-inch metal bowl, combine the olive oil, steak, and broccoli.
Pour into the Oven rack/basket. Place the Rack on the middle-shelf of the Air Fryer Oven. Set temperature to 375°F, and set time to 4 minutes
Cook for 3 to 4 minutes or until the steak is almost cooked and the broccoli is crisp and tender, shaking the basket once during cooking time.
Add the garlic, chili peppers, and the peanut butter mixture and stir.
Cook for 3 to 5 minutes or until the sauce is bubbling and the broccoli is tender.
Serve over hot rice.
NUTRITION: Calories 387 Cal Fat 22 g Carbs 0 g Protein 42 g

274. CHARRED ONIONS AND STEAK CUBE BBQ
Basic Recipe
Preparation Time: 5 minutes
Cooking Time: 40 minutes
Servings: 3
INGREDIENTS:
- 1 cup red onions cut into wedges
- 1 tablespoon dry mustard
- 1 tablespoon olive oil
- 1-pound boneless beef sirloin, cut into cubes
- Salt and pepper to taste

DIRECTIONS:
Preheat the air fryer to 390°F.
Place the grill pan accessory in the air fryer.
Toss all ingredients in a bowl and mix until everything is coated with the seasonings.
Place on the grill pan and cook for 40 minutes
Halfway through the cooking time, give a stir to cook evenly.
NUTRITION: Calories 260 Cal Fat 10.7 g Carbs 0 g Protein 35.5 g

275. BEEF BRISKET RECIPE FROM TEXAS
Basic Recipe
Preparation Time: 15 minutes
Cooking Time: 1 hour and 30 minutes
Servings: 8
INGREDIENTS:
- 1 ½ cup beef stock
- 1 bay leaf
- 1 tablespoon garlic powder
- 1 tablespoon onion powder
- 2 pounds beef brisket, trimmed
- 2 tablespoons chili powder
- 2 teaspoons dry mustard
- 4 tablespoons olive oil
- Salt and pepper to taste

DIRECTIONS:
Preheat the Air Fryer Oven for 5 minutes Place all ingredients in a deep baking dish that will fit in the air fryer.
Bake it for 1 hour and 30 minutes at 400°F.
Stir the beef every after 30 minutes to soak in the sauce.
NUTRITION: Calories 306 Cal Fat 24.1 g Carbs 0 g Protein 18.3 g

276. AIR FRYER ROASTED BROCCOLI
Basic Recipe
Preparation Time: 5 minutes
Cooking Time: 10 minutes
Servings: 4

INGREDIENTS:
- 1 tsp. herbes de provence seasoning (optional)
- 4 cups fresh broccoli
- 1 tablespoon olive oil
- Salt and pepper to taste

DIRECTIONS:

Drizzle with or spray broccoli with olive and sprinkle seasoning throughout

Spray air fryer basket with cooking oil, place broccoli and cook for 5-8 minutes on 360F

Open air fryer and examine broccoli after 5 minutes because different fryer brands cook at different rates.

NUTRITION: Calories 61 Fat 4g Protein 3g Carbs 4g

277. CHEESE AND VEGGIE CUPS

Basic Recipe
Preparation Time: 10 minutes
Cooking Time: 20 minutes
Servings: 4
INGREDIENTS:
- Non-stick cooking spray
- 4 large eggs
- 1 cup diced veggies of choice
- 1 cup shredded cheese
- 4 Tbsp. half and half
- 1 Tbsp. chopped cilantro
- Salt and Pepper

DIRECTIONS:

Grease 4 ramekins

Whisk eggs, vegetables, half the cheese, half and half, cilantro, and salt and pepper together. In a medium bowl and divide between the ramekins

Place ramekins in the air-fryer basket, set temperature to 300 F for 12 minutes

Top the cups with remaining cheese.

Set air-fryer to 400 degrees F, cook 2 minutes until cheese is melted.

NUTRITION: Calories 195kcal Carbs 7g Protein 13g Fat 12g

278. BBQ TURKEY MEATBALLS WITH CRANBERRY SAUCE

Basic Recipe
Preparation Time: 5 minutes
Cooking Time: 20 minutes
Serving: 4
INGREDIENTS:
- 1 ½ tablespoons of water
- 2 teaspoons cider vinegar
- 1 tsp. salt and more to taste
- 1-pound ground turkey
- 1 1/2 tablespoons barbecue sauce
- 1/3 cup cranberry sauce
- 1/4-pound ground bacon

DIRECTIONS:

In a bowl, mix well with hands the turkey, ground bacon and a tsp. of salt. Evenly form into 16 equal sized balls.

In a small saucepan boil cranberry sauce, barbecue sauce, water, cider vinegar, and a dash or two of salt. Mix well and simmer for 3 minutes

Thread meatballs in skewers and baste with cranberry sauce. Place on skewer rack in air fryer.

For 15 minutes, cook it on 360oF. Every after 5 minutes of cooking time, turnover skewers and baste with sauce. If needed, cook in batches.

Serve and enjoy.

NUTRITION: Calories 217 Carbs 11.5g Protein 28.0g Fat 10.9g

279. BEEFY 'N CHEESY SPANISH RICE CASSEROLE

Intermediate Recipe
Preparation Time: 10 minutes

Cooking Time: 50 minutes
Servings: 3
INGREDIENTS:
- 2 tablespoons chopped green bell pepper
- 1 tablespoon chopped fresh cilantro
- 1/2-pound lean ground beef
- 1/2 cup water
- 1/2 teaspoon salt
- 1/2 teaspoon brown sugar
- 1/2 pinch ground black pepper
- 1/3 cup uncooked long grain rice
- 1/4 cup finely chopped onion
- 1/4 cup chili sauce
- 1/4 teaspoon ground cumin
- 1/4 teaspoon Worcestershire sauce
- 1/4 cup shredded Cheddar cheese
- 1/2 (14.5 ounce) can canned tomatoes

DIRECTIONS:

Lightly grease baking pan of air fryer with cooking spray. Add ground beef.

For 10 minutes, cook on 360°F Halfway through cooking time, stir and crumble beef. Discard excess fat,

Stir in pepper, Worcestershire sauce, cumin, brown sugar, salt, chili sauce, rice, water, tomatoes, green bell pepper, and onion. Mix well.

Cover pan with foil and cook for 25 minutes. Stirring occasionally

Give it one last good stir, press down firmly and sprinkle cheese on top. Cook uncovered for 15 minutes at 390°F until tops are lightly browned.

Serve and enjoy with chopped cilantro.

NUTRITION: Calories 346 Cal Fat 19.1 g Carbs 0 g Protein 18.5 g

280. BUTTERED SPINACH-EGG OMELET

Basic Recipe
Preparation Time: 5 minutes
Cooking Time: 10 minutes
Serving: 4
INGREDIENTS:
- ¼ cup coconut milk
- 1 tablespoon melted butter
- 1-pound baby spinach, chopped finely
- 3 tablespoons olive oil
- 4 eggs, beaten
- Salt and pepper to taste

DIRECTIONS:

Preheat the air fryer for 5 minutes. In a mixing bowl, combine the eggs, coconut milk, olive oil, and butter until well-combined.

Add the spinach and season with salt and pepper to taste. Pour all ingredients in a baking dish that will fit in the air fryer. Bake at 3500F for 15 minutes

NUTRITION: Calories 310 Carbs 3.6g Protein 13.6g Fat 26.8g

281. BUFFALO STYLE CHICKEN DIP

Basic Recipe
Preparation Time: 5 minutes
Cooking Time: 10 minutes
Serving: 4
INGREDIENTS:
- 1 (8 ounce) package cream cheese, softened
- 1 tablespoon shredded pepper Jack cheese
- 1/2 pinch cayenne pepper, for garnish
- 1/2 pinch cayenne pepper, or to taste
- 1/4 cup and 2 tablespoons hot pepper sauce (such as Frank's Re-shoot®)
- 1/4 cup blue cheese dressing
- 1/4 cup crumbled blue cheese
- 1/4 cup shredded pepper Jack cheese
- 1/4 teaspoon seafood seasoning (such as Old Bay®)

- 1-1/2 cups diced cooked rotisserie chicken

DIRECTIONS:

Lightly grease baking pan of air fryer with cooking spray. Mix in cayenne pepper, seafood seasoning, crumbled blue cheese, blue cheese dressing, pepper Jack, hot pepper sauce, cream cheese, and chicken.

For 15 minutes, cook it on 390 F.

Let it stand for 5 minutes and garnish with cayenne pepper.

Serve and enjoy.

NUTRITION: Calories 405 Carbs 3.2g Protein 17.1g Fat 35.9g

282. CHIMICHURRI SKIRT STEAK

Basic Recipe

Preparation Time: 10 minutes

Cooking Time: 8 minutes

Servings: 2

INGREDIENTS:

- 2 x 8 oz. skirt steak
- 1 cup finely chopped parsley
- ¼ cup finely chopped mint
- 2 tbsp. fresh oregano (washed & finely chopped)
- 3 finely chopped cloves of garlic
- 1 tsp. red pepper flakes (crushed)
- 1 tbsp. ground cumin
- 1 tsp. cayenne pepper
- 2 tsp. smoked paprika
- 1 tsp. salt
- ¼ tsp. pepper
- ¾ cup oil
- 3 tbsp. red wine vinegar

DIRECTIONS:

Throw all the ingredients in a bowl (besides the steak) and mix well.

Put ¼ cup of the mixture in a plastic baggie with the steak and leave in the fridge overnight (2–24hrs).

Leave the bag out at room temperature for at least 30 min before popping into the air fryer. Preheat for a minute or two to 390° F before cooking until med–rare (8–10 min). Pour into the Oven rack/basket. Place the Rack on the middle-shelf of the Air Fryer Oven. Set temperature to 390°F, and set time to 10 minutes

Put 2 Tbsp. of the chimichurri mix on top of each steak before serving.

NUTRITION: Calories 308.6 Cal Fat 22.6 g Carbs 3 g Protein 23.7 g

283. CHICKEN FRIED RICE

Basic Recipe

Preparation Time: 15 minutes

Cooking Time: 12 minutes

Serving: 4

INGREDIENTS:

- 3 cups Cooked brown rice cold
- 1 cup cooked chicken diced
- 1 cup Cauliflower and carrots
- 6 tablespoons Low sodium soy sauce
- 1 tablespoon Avocado oil
- 1/2 cup Onion diced

DIRECTIONS:

Put the cooked, brown rice in the bowl, add the avocado oil and soy sauce and mix well.

Put the peas & carrots, the diced onion and the diced chicken and mix greatly.

Put the rice mixture into the non-stick pan

Place the pan in the air fryer.

Set the fryer to 360 f with a cooking time of 20 minutes. When the timer is off, remove the pan from the fryer. Serve and enjoy!

NUTRITION: Calories 147 Fat 1.3g Carbs 9.1g Protein 10.1g

284. CREAMY BURGER & POTATO BAKE

Intermediate Recipe

Preparation Time: 5 minutes

Cooking Time: 55 minutes

Servings: 3

INGREDIENTS:

- Salt to taste
- Freshly ground pepper, to taste
- 1/2 (10.75 ounce) can condensed cream of mushroom soup
- 1/2-pound lean ground beef
- 1-1/2 cups peeled and thinly sliced potatoes
- 1/2 cup shredded Cheddar cheese
- 1/4 cup chopped onion
- 1/4 cup and 2 tablespoons milk

DIRECTIONS:

Lightly grease baking pan of air fryer with cooking spray. Add ground beef. For 10 minutes, cook on 360°F

Stir and crumble halfway through cooking time.

Meanwhile, in a bowl, whisk well pepper, salt, milk, onion, and mushroom soup. Mix well.

Dry out fat off ground beef and transfer beef to a plate.

In same air fryer baking pan, layer ½ of potatoes on bottom, then ½ of soup mixture, and then ½ of beef. Repeat process.

Cover pan with foil.

Cook for 30 minutes Remove foil and cook for another 15 minutes or until potatoes are tender.

Serve and enjoy.

NUTRITION: Calories 399 Cal Fat 26.9 g Carbs 0 g Protein 22.1 g

285. AIR FRYER BEEF CASSEROLE

Basic Recipe

Preparation Time: 5 minutes

Cooking Time: 30 minutes

Servings: 4

INGREDIENTS:

- 1 green bell pepper, seeded and chopped
- 1 onion, chopped
- 1-pound ground beef
- 3 cloves of garlic, minced
- 3 tablespoons olive oil
- 6 cups eggs, beaten
- Salt and pepper to taste

DIRECTIONS:

Preheat the Air Fryer Oven for 5 minutes

In a baking dish that will fit in the air fryer, mix the ground beef, onion, garlic, olive oil, and bell pepper. Season it with salt and pepper to taste.

Pour in the beaten eggs and give a good stir.

Place the dish with the beef and egg mixture in the air fryer.

Pour into the Oven rack/basket. Place the Rack on the middle-shelf of the Air Fryer Oven. Set temperature to 325°F, and set time to 30 minutes.

Bake it for 30 minutes

NUTRITION: Calories 1520 Cal Fat 125.11 g Carbs 0 g Protein 87.9 g

286. CHEESEBURGER EGG ROLLS

Basic Recipe

Preparation Time: 10 minutes

Cooking Time: 7 minutes

Servings: 6

INGREDIENTS:

- 6 egg roll wrappers
- 6 chopped dill pickle chips
- 1 tbsp. yellow mustard
- 3 tbsp. cream cheese
- 3 tbsp. shredded cheddar cheese
- ½ C. chopped onion

- ½ C. chopped bell pepper
- ¼ tsp. onion powder
- ¼ tsp. garlic powder
- 8 ounces of raw lean ground beef

DIRECTIONS:

In a skillet, add seasonings, beef, onion, and bell pepper. Stir and crumble beef till fully cooked, and vegetables are soft.

Take skillet off the heat and add cream cheese, mustard, and cheddar cheese, stirring till melted.

Pour beef mixture into a bowl and fold in pickles.

Lay out egg wrappers and place 1/6th of beef mixture into each one.

Moisten egg roll wrapper edges with water. Fold sides to the middle and seal with water.

Repeat with all other egg rolls.

Place rolls into air fryer, one batch at a time.

Pour into the Oven rack/basket. Place the Rack on the middle-shelf of the Air Fryer Oven. Set temperature to 392°F, and set time to 7 minutes

NUTRITION: Calories 153 Cal Fat 4 g Carbs 0 g Protein 12 g

287. CRISPY CHEESY VEGAN QUESARITO

Basic Recipe
Preparation Time: 5 minutes
Cooking Time: 10 minutes
Servings: 4

INGREDIENTS:
- 2 large gluten free tortillas
- 4 tablespoons Vegan Queso (divided)
- 2-3 tablespoons grated cheese
- 3 tablespoons Meaty Crumbles
- 3-4 tablespoons Simple Spanish rice
- 1-2 tablespoons Spicy Almond Sauce
- 1 tablespoon cashew cream or dairy free sour cream
- Added ingredients
- Fresh baby spinach, Fresh bell peppers
- Roasted red peppers

DIRECTIONS:

Lay first tortilla flat on prep surface.

Cut about an inch from around the entire edge of the second tortilla using a knife, making one smaller tortilla and then set aside.

On the first tortilla, spread the vegan queso around the middle of the tortilla, in a circle the size of the smaller tortilla.

Add 3 tablespoons grated cheese to the top of the queso, in an even layer across the small circle (1 tablespoon grated cheese)

Top the queso / cheese circle with the smaller second tortilla, and press down slightly.

Spoon a line of the meaty crumbles onto the middle of the second smaller tortilla, spoon the Spanish rice on top of the meaty crumbles, followed by the tangy cream sauce and cashew cream / sour cream.

Carefully fold and roll burrito tightly. Secure the edge with the reserved 1 tablespoon grated cheese. Place the burrito cheese sealed side down in air fryer basket.

Fry for 6-7 minutes at 370°F, or until lightly golden and crisp.

NUTRITION: Calories 514 Fat 18g Carbs 13g Protein 22g

288. HAM WRAPPED PRAWNS

Basic Recipe
Preparation Time: 15 minutes
Cooking Time: 15 minutes
Servings: 4

INGREDIENTS:
- 2 garlic cloves, minced
- 1 tablespoon paprika
- 8 king prawns, peeled, deveined and chopped
- 4 ham slices, halved
- 2 tablespoons olive oil
- Salt and freshly ground black pepper, to taste

DIRECTIONS:

Preheat the air fryer to 430 degrees F and wrap each prawn with a ham slice.

Arrange in the air fryer basket and cook for about 4 minutes

Dish out and meanwhile place bell pepper in the air fryer basket.

Cook for about 10 minutes and transfer in a bowl.

Cover the bowl with a foil and set aside for 15 minutes

Now, place bell pepper, garlic, paprika and oil in a blender.

Blend till a puree is formed and serve with ham wrapped prawns.

NUTRITION: Calories 553 Fat 33.6g Carbs 2.6g Protein 5g

289. CRISPY INDIAN WRAP

Basic Recipe
Preparation Time: 20 minutes
Cooking Time: 8 minutes
Servings: 4

INGREDIENTS:
- Cilantro Chutney
- 2¾ cups diced potato, cooked until tender
- 2 teaspoons oil (coconut, sunflower, or safflower)
- 3 large garlic cloves, minced or pressed
- 1½ tablespoons fresh lime juice
- 1½ teaspoons cumin powder
- 1 teaspoon onion granules
- 1 teaspoon coriander powder
- ½ teaspoon sea salt
- ½ teaspoon turmeric
- ¼ teaspoon cayenne powder
- 4 large flour tortillas, preferably whole grain or sprouted
- 1 cup cooked garbanzo beans (canned are fine), rinsed and Dry out
- ½ cup finely chopped cabbage
- ¼ cup minced red onion or scallion
- Cooking oil spray (sunflower, safflower, or refined coconut)

DIRECTIONS:

Make the Cilantro Chutney and set aside.

In a large bowl, mash the potatoes well, using a potato masher or large fork. Add the oil, garlic, lime, cumin, onion, coriander, salt, turmeric, and cayenne. Stir very well, until thoroughly combined. Set aside.

Lay the tortillas out flat on the counter. In the middle of each, evenly distribute the potato filling. Add some of the garbanzo beans, cabbage, and red onion to each, on top of the potatoes.

Spray the air fryer basket with oil and set aside. Enclose the Indian wraps by folding the bottom of the tortillas up and over the filling, then folding the sides in—and finally rolling the bottom up to form, essentially, an enclosed burrito.

Place the wraps in the air fryer basket, seam side down. They can touch each other a little bit, but if they're too crowded, you'll need to cook them in batches. Fry for 5 minutes Spray with oil again, flip over, and cook an additional 2 or 3 minutes, until nicely browned and crisp. Serve topped with the Cilantro Chutney.

NUTRITION: Calories 288 Fat 7g Carbs 50g Protein 9g

290. ROASTED AIR FRYER SAVORY CARROTS

Basic Recipe
Preparation Time: 10 minutes
Cooking Time: 20 minutes
Servings: 4

INGREDIENTS:

1 lb. medium sized carrots (washed and peeled)
¼ cup grated parmesan cheese
Fresh chopped parsley (optional)
2 tablespoon olive oil
½ tsp. paprika
½ tsp. garlic powder
Salt and pepper (to taste)

DIRECTIONS:

Place peeled and chopped carrots in a large bowl, add olive oil, and toss in garlic powder and paprika

Put the carrot mix in an air fryer basket and cook on 38 0º F for 10 minutes, shake and cook for another 10 minutes in the same heat.

Once the carrot is done, use parsley and parmesan cheese as topping and add pepper and salt to taste.

NUTRITION: Calories 119 Fat 6g Protein 1g Carbs 17g

291. BANG-BANG CHICKEN

Basic Recipe
Preparation Time: 10 minutes
Cooking Time: 15 minutes
Servings: 4

INGREDIENTS:
- 1 cup Greek Yogurt
- ½ cup Sweet chili sauce
- 2 tablespoons hot sauce
- ⅓ Cup Coconut flour
- 1-pound Chicken breast tenderloins cut into bite-size pieces
- 1 ½ cups Panko bread crumbs
- 2 Green onions, chopped

DIRECTIONS:
Whisk Greek yogurt, sweet chili sauce and hot sauce in a large container. Set the 3/4 cup of the batter aside with a spoon and put the coconut flour in a plastic bag with a large seal.

Add the chicken, close the bag, and mix well to cover. Place the coated chicken pieces with the yoghurt mixture in the large container and stir.

Place the panko breadcrumbs in other big plastic bag with a zipper. Work in batches, place chicken pieces in panko, close and mixed well covered. Preheat an air fryer to 200 ° C. Place as many pieces of chicken as possible in the basket without overfilling them, Cook in an air fryer for at least 10 minutes

Turn around and cook another 5 minutes repetition with the rest of the chicken Transfer the fried chicken to a large container and put the reaming sauce over it.

Sprinkle with spring onions and cover and stir. Serve immediately.

NUTRITION: Calories 303 Fat 15.3g Carbs 10.9g Protein 17.1g

292. AIR FRYER VEGGIE QUESADILLAS

Basic Recipe
Preparation Time: 20 minutes
Cooking Time: 20 minutes
Servings: 4

INGREDIENTS:
- 4 sprouted whole-grain flour tortillas (6-in.)
- 1 cup sliced red bell pepper
- 4 ounces reduced-fat Cheddar cheese, shredded
- 1 cup sliced zucchini
- 1 cup canned black beans, Dry out and rinsed (no salt)
- Cooking spray
- 2 ounces plain 2% reduced-fat Greek yogurt
- 1 teaspoon lime zest
- 1 Tbsp. fresh juice (from 1 lime)
- ¼ tsp. ground cumin
- 2 tablespoons chopped fresh cilantro
- 1/2 cup Dry out refrigerated pico de gallo

DIRECTIONS:
Place tortillas on work surface, sprinkle 2 tablespoons shredded cheese over half of each tortilla and top with cheese on each tortilla with 1/4 cup each red pepper slices, zucchini slices, and black beans. Sprinkle evenly with remaining 1/2 cup cheese.

Fold tortillas over to form half-moon shaped quesadillas, lightly coat with cooking spray, and secure with toothpicks.

Lightly spray air fryer basket with cooking spray. Place 2 quesadillas in the basket, and cook at 400°F for 10 minutes until tortillas are golden brown and slightly crispy, cheese is melted, and vegetables are slightly softened. Turn quesadillas over halfway through cooking.

Repeat with remaining quesadillas. Meanwhile, stir yogurt, lime juice, lime zest and cumin in a small bowl. Cut each quesadilla into wedges and sprinkle with cilantro.

Serve with 1 tablespoon cumin cream and 2 tablespoons pico de gallo each.

NUTRITION: Calories 291 Fat 8g Protein 17g Carbs 36g

293. SWEET AND SPICY AIR FRYER BRUSSELS SPROUTS

Basic Recipe
Preparation Time: 5 minutes
Cooking Time: 20 minutes
Servings: 8

INGREDIENTS:
- 1 Brussels sprout cut into two halves
- 1 ½ tablespoon vegetable oil
- ½ tsp. salt
- 2 tablespoon honey
- 1 tablespoon gochujang

DIRECTIONS:
Mix honey, gochujang, vegetable oil and salt in a bowl and stir properly. Take out 1 tablespoon of the sauce and set it aside then add Brussels sprout to the bowl and stir until the sprout is mixed properly

Place the Brussels sprouts into your Air fryer, set heat at 36 0º F and cook for 15 minutes; shake the basket halfway into cooking time and set the bowl aside when the timer is off.

When the timer goes off, increase the temperature to 39 0º F and cook for another 5 minutes

After 5 minute, put sprouts in a bowl and cover with reserved sauce and stir.

NUTRITION: Calories 128 Fat 4g Carbs 20g Protein 3g

294. AIR FRYER BUFFALO MUSHROOM POPPERS

Basic Recipe
Preparation Time: 30 minutes
Cooking Time: 50 minutes
Servings: 8

INGREDIENTS:
- 1-pound fresh whole button mushrooms
- 1/2 teaspoon kosher salt
- 3 tablespoons 1/3-less-fat cream cheese,
- 1/4 cup all-purpose flour
- Softened 1 jalapeño chili, seeded and minced
- Cooking spray
- 1/4 teaspoon black pepper
- 1 cup panko breadcrumbs
- 2 large eggs, lightly beaten
- 1/4 cup buffalo-style hot sauce
- 2 tablespoons chopped fresh chives
- 1/2 cup low-fat buttermilk
- 1/2 cup plain fat-free yogurt
- 2 ounces blue cheese, crumbled (about 1/2 cup)
- 3 tablespoons apple cider vinegar

DIRECTIONS:
Remove stems from mushroom caps, chop stems and set caps aside. Stir together chopped mushroom stems, cream cheese, jalapeño, salt, and pepper. Stuff about 1 teaspoon of the mixture into each mushroom cap, rounding the filling to form a smooth ball.

Place panko in a bowl, place flour in a second bowl, and eggs in a third Coat mushrooms in flour, dip in egg mixture, and dredge in panko, pressing to adhere. Spray mushrooms well with cooking spray.

Place half of the mushrooms in air fryer basket, and cook for 20 minutes at 350°F. Transfer cooked mushrooms to a large bowl. Drizzle with buffalo sauce over mushrooms; toss to coat then sprinkle with chives.

Stir buttermilk, yogurt, blue cheese, and cider vinegar in a small bowl.
Serve mushroom poppers with blue cheese sauce.
NUTRITION: Calories 133 Fat 4g Protein 7g Carbs 16g

295. RANCH FISH FILLETS
Basic Recipe
Preparation Time: 5 minutes
Cooking Time: 13 minutes
Servings: 4
INGREDIENTS:
- 3/4 cup breadcrumbs or Panko or crushed cornflakes
- 1 packet dry ranch-style dressing mix
- 2 1/2 tablespoons vegetable oil
- 2 eggs beaten
- 4 tilapia salmon or other fish fillets
- Herbs and chilies to garnish

DIRECTIONS:
Preheat the air fryer to 180 degrees F.
Mix ranch dressing with panko in a bowl.
Whisk eggs in a shallow bowl.
Dip each fish fillet in the egg then coat evenly with the panko mixture.
Place the fillets in the air fryer.
Cook for 13 minutes
Serve warm with herbs and chilies.
NUTRITION: Calories 301 Fat 12.2 g Carbs: 15 g Protein 28.8 g

296. CHICKEN, FETA, AND OLIVE CASSEROLE
Basic Recipe
Preparation Time: 5 minutes
Cooking Time: 30 minutes
Servings: 4
INGREDIENTS:
- Chicken Casserole
- 1½ pounds boneless chicken thighs
- Salt and pepper, to taste
- 2 tablespoons butter
- 3 ounces pesto
- 1¼ cups coconut cream
- 3 ounces' green olives
- 5 ounces diced feta cheese
- 1 clove garlic, finely chopped
- For Serving:
- 5 ounces leafy greens
- 4 tablespoons coconut oil
- Salt and pepper, to taste

DIRECTIONS:
Preheat air fryer to 350-degrees F. Spray a 6-inch soufflé dish with non-stick cooking spray; set aside.
Put the butter in a large saucepan. Heat the pan until the butter is melt, then sauté the chicken pieces until golden.
Combine pesto and cream in a container to make the sauce. Put the chicken, olives, feta, and garlic and pesto sauce in a saucepan.
Mix well and Bake it for 30 minutes in air fryer or until the edges are hot and brown
NUTRITION: Calories 643 Fat 56.7g Carbs: 5.7g Protein 28.5g

297. STEAK AND MUSHROOMS
Basic Recipe
Preparation Time: 5 minutes
Cooking Time: 10 minutes
Servings: 4
INGREDIENTS:
- 1-pound Beef sirloin steak, cut into 1-inch cubes
- 8 ounces' Button mushrooms, sliced
- 1/4 cup Worcestershire sauce

- 1 tablespoon Olive oil
- 1 teaspoon Parsley flakes
- 1 teaspoon Paprika
- 1 teaspoon Crushed Chile flakes

DIRECTIONS:
Mix steak, mushrooms, Worcestershire sauce, coconut oil, parsley, paprika and chili flakes in a big bowl.
Cover and freeze for at least 4 hours or overnight. Remove from fridge 30 minutes before cooking.
Preheat the air fryer to 200 ° C. Dry out the marinade of the meat mixture and throw away. Place the steak and mushrooms in the frying basket and cook in the preheated air fryer for 5 minutes
Mix and cook for another 5 minutes Place the steak and mushrooms on a plate and let them rest for 5 minutes
NUTRITION: Calories 269 Fat 10.8g Carbs 5.2g Protein 36.3g

298. PORK LOIN
Basic Recipe
Preparation Time: 5 minutes
Cooking Time: 20 minutes
Servings: 4
INGREDIENTS:
- 1.5 lb. Pork tenderloin,
- Cooking spray
- 2 Small heads roasted garlic
- Salt & pepper

DIRECTIONS:
Pat the Pork loin dry.
Cover all sides lightly with a non-stick coating, salt and pepper on both sides.
Brushing with roasted garlic
Spray the rack and place it to air fryer.
Bake on vortex air fry press, at 350°F at least 10 minutes for each side.
Safely take off from air fryer.
Remove carefully from the air fryer. Coming back to the fryer and Bake it for another 10 minutes
NUTRITION: Calories 220 Fat 10g Carbs 3.9g Protein 27.6g

299. CRISPY PORK CHOPS
Basic Recipe
Preparation Time: 15 minutes
Cooking Time: 10 minutes
Serving: 4
INGREDIENTS:
- 1 1/2 lb. Boneless pork chops
- 1/3 cup Almond Flour
- 1/4 cup Grated Parmesan cheese
- 1 teaspoon Garlic powder
- 1 teaspoon Paprika

DIRECTIONS:
Preheat your air fryer to 350 degrees F.
In the meantime, mix all the ingredients excluding pork chops in a large airtight bag. Place the pork chops in the bag, close them, and shake to cover the pork chops. Discard from the bag and put in one layer in the air fryer.
Cook at least 12 minutes, according to the density of your pork chops.
NUTRITION: Calories 204 Fat 7.4g Carbs 1.9g Protein 31.5g

300. AIR FRYER VEGETABLES
Basic Recipe
Preparation Time: 5 minutes
Cooking Time: 10 minutes
Servings: 4
INGREDIENTS:
- 1/2 lb. broccoli fresh

- 1/2 lb. cauliflower fresh
- 1 tbsp.olive oil
- 1/4 tsp. seasoning
- 1/3 c water

DIRECTIONS:

Mix vegetables, olive oil and seasonings in a medium bowl.
Pour 1/3 c. water in the Air Fryer base to prevent from smoking.
Place vegetables in the air fryer basket.
Cook at 400 degrees for 7-10 minutes
Shake vegetables half way through the 7-10 minutes
NUTRITION: Calories 65kcal Carbs 7g Protein 3g Fat 4g

301. SESAME-CRUSTED COD WITH CAULIFLOWER

Basic Recipe
Preparation Time: 5 minutes
Cooking Time: 20 minutes
Servings: 4

INGREDIENTS:
- 4 (5 ounce) cod fillets
- Salt and ground black pepper to taste
- 3 tablespoons butter, melted
- 2 tablespoons sesame seeds
- Coconut oil
- 1 small head cauliflower
- 3 cloves garlic, thinly sliced
- 1 lemon, cut into wedges

DIRECTIONS:

Gently grease the air fryer basket with coconut oil and preheat to 400 degrees F.
Defrost fish if frozen; dry with kitchen paper, and lightly Season it with salt and pepper.
At the same time mix butter and sesame seeds in a bowl. Keep aside 2 tablespoons of the butter and sesame batter for the fish. Toss cauliflower and garlic with remaining butter batter and put into the air fryer basket.
Cook cauliflower in the preheated air fryer in parts, if required, until just cooked, tossing once, about 10 minutes Remove and keep warm while cooking fish.
Grease fish with 1/2 of the remaining butter batter. Put fillets in air fryer basket. Cook 4 minutes; shift fish. Grease with remaining butter batter. Cook 5 to 6 minutes more or until fish starts to flake when tested with a fork. Serve with cauliflower and lemon wedges.
NUTRITION: Calories 181 Fat 14.7g Carbs 7.2g Protein 7g

302. TUNA STUFFED POTATOES

Basic Recipe
Preparation Time: 15 minutes
Cooking Time: 30 minutes
Servings: 4

INGREDIENTS:
- 1½-pounds tuna, Dry out
- 2 tablespoons plain Greek yogurt
- ½ tablespoon olive oil
- 4 starchy potatoes, soaked for 30 minutes
- 1 tablespoon capers
- 1 teaspoon red chili powder
- 1 scallion, chopped and divided
- Salt and freshly ground black pepper, to taste

DIRECTIONS:

Preheat the air fryer to 355 degrees F.
Place the potatoes in the air fryer basket and cook for about 30 minutes Take out and place on a flat surface.
Meanwhile, add yogurt, tuna, red chili powder, scallion, salt and pepper in a bowl. Mix well.
Cut each potato from top side lengthwise and press the open side of potato halves slightly.
Stuff potato with tuna mixture and sprinkle with capers.

Dish out and serve.
NUTRITION: Calories 1387 Fat 54g Carbs 35.7g Protein 180.7g

303. CAJUN SPICED SALMON

Basic Recipe
Preparation Time: 10 minutes
Cooking Time: 10 minutes
Servings: 8

INGREDIENTS:
- 4 tablespoons Cajun seasoning
- 4 salmon steaks

DIRECTIONS:

Add Cajun seasoning in a bowl and rub salmon evenly with it.
Preheat the air fryer to 385 degrees F.
Arrange air fryer grill pan and place salmon steaks on it.
Cook for about 8 minutes and flip once in the middle way.
Take out and serve hot.
NUTRITION: Calories 118 Fat 5.5g Carbs 0g Protein 17.3g

304. STEAK AND ASPARAGUS BUNDLES

Basic Recipe
Preparation Time: 15 minutes
Cooking Time: 15 minutes
Servings: 4

INGREDIENTS:
- 2 - 2 1/2 pounds Flank steak - cut into 6 pieces
- Kosher salt/black pepper
- 2 cloves Garlic - crushed
- 1-pound Asparagus - trimmed
- 3 Bell peppers - seeded and sliced thinly

1/3 cup Beef broth
2 tablespoons unsalted butter
Olive oil spray

DIRECTIONS:

Season the fillets with salt and pepper and place in a large zippered bag.
Add garlic. Close the bag and massage the fillets so that they are completely covered.
Put in the fridge and marinate at least 1 hour overnight. When you're done, remove the marinade fillets and place them on a chopping board or sheet.
Throw away the marinade. Spread the mass evenly and place the asparagus and peppers in the middle of each steak.
Roll the steak around the vegetables and secure them.
Preheat the fryer. Depending on the size of your air fryer, the packages are stacked in the frying basket.
Spray the vegetables with olive oil. Cook for 5 minutes at 400 degrees.
Remove the meat packaging and let it rest for 5 minutes before serving / cutting. At rest in a small to medium hot pan: balsamic vinegar, broth and butter over medium heat.
Mix and continue cooking until the sauce thicken and halves. Season it with salt and pepper and pour the sauce over the meat packets before serving.
NUTRITION: Calories 220 Fat 10g Carbs 3.8g Protein 27.6g

305. RASPBERRY SMOKED PORK CHOPS

Basic Recipe
Preparation Time: 15 minutes
Cooking Time: 15 minutes
Serving: 4

INGREDIENTS:
- Cooking spray
- 2 Large eggs
- 1/4 cup Coconut milk
- 1 cup Panko bread crumbs
- 1 cup finely chopped walnuts
- 4 Smoked bone-in pork chops (7-1/2 ounces each)

- 1/4 cup Coconut flour
- 2 tablespoons Stevia
- 2 tablespoons Raspberry
- 1 tablespoon Fresh orange juice

DIRECTIONS:

Preheat the fryer to 400 °. Spray some oil in the frying basket.

Mix the eggs and coconut milk in a flat bowl. Mix the panko breadcrumbs with walnuts in another flat bowl and cover the pork chops with the flour. Shake off excess.

Dip into the egg mixture and then into the crumb mixture and tap on it to help it stick. If necessary,

Work in batches and place the chops in a single layer in the basket of the air fryer oven. Spray with oil, cook for 12 to 15 minutes until golden brown, turn after half the cooking time and sprinkle with additional cooking spray.

Remove and keep warm.

Repeat with the remaining chops. In the meantime, put the remaining ingredients in a small saucepan. Bring to a boil. Boil and stir until it gets a little thick, 6-8 minutes. Serve with chops.

NUTRITION: Calories 542 Fat 31.8g Carbs 24.9g Protein 41.3g

306. MUSHROOM, ONION AND FETA FRITTATA

Basic Recipe

Preparation Time: 15 minutes

Cooking Time: 10 minutes

Servings: 4

INGREDIENTS:

- 3 whole eggs
- 2 cup sliced button mushrooms
- ½ red onions
- 1 tbsp. Olive oil
- 3 tbsp crumbled feta
- 1 pinch salt

DIRECTIONS:

Peel and slice half a red onion into ¼ inch thin slices.

Wash button mushrooms; then slice into ¼ inch thin slices.

Place a pan under a medium flame, add olive oil sweat onions and mushrooms and sauté until tender. Take onions and mushrooms off the heat and place on kitchen towel to cool.

Preheat Air fryer to 320°F.

In a mixing bowl crack 3 eggs and whisk thoroughly and vigorously.

Coat the outside and bottom of a 6-ounce ramekin lightly with pan spray. Pour eggs into the ramekin, add ¼ cup onion and mushrooms mixture, and then add cheese.

Place in Air fryer and cook for 10 to 12 minutes

NUTRITION: Calories 90 Fat 4.5g Carbs 8g Protein 13g

307. LEMONY & SPICY COCONUT CRUSTED PRAWNS

Basic Recipe

Preparation Time: 20 minutes

Cooking Time: 7 minutes

Servings: 4

INGREDIENTS:

- ½ cup unsweetened coconut, shredded
- ¼ teaspoon lemon zest
- ¼ teaspoon cayenne pepper
- Vegetable oil, as required
- ¼ teaspoon red pepper flakes, crushed
- ½ cup flour
- ½ cup breadcrumbs
- 1-pound prawns, peeled and de-veined
- 2 egg whites
- Salt and black pepper, to taste

DIRECTIONS:

Take a shallow dish and mix salt, flour and pepper in it.

Crack eggs in another shallow dish. Beat well.

In the third shallow dish, add coconut, breadcrumbs, lime zest, salt and cayenne pepper. Mix well.

Now, preheat the air fryer to 395 degrees F.

Dip shrimp into flour mixture, then in the egg mixture and roll them evenly into the breadcrumb mixture.

Place them in the air fryer basket and Drizzle with vegetable oil over them.

Cook for about 7 minutes and take out.

Serve and enjoy!

NUTRITION: Calories 773 Fat 60.7g Carbs 25.5g Protein 31.5g

308. TANGY SALMON

Basic Recipe

Preparation Time: 10 minutes

Cooking Time: 10 minutes

Servings: 8

INGREDIENTS:

- 4 tablespoons Cajun seasoning
- 8 salmon fillets
- 4 tablespoons fresh lemon juice

DIRECTIONS:

Season salmon fillets with Cajun seasoning and set aside for 15 minutes

Preheat the air fryer to 360 degrees F and arrange grill pan in it.

Place salmon fillets on the grill pan and cook for about 7 minutes

Drizzle with lemon juice and serve.

NUTRITION: Calories 237 Fat 11.1g Carbs 21g Protein 34.7g

309. SEASONED SALMON

Basic Recipe

Preparation Time: 5 minutes

Cooking Time: 10 minutes

Servings: 4

INGREDIENTS:

- 2 wild caught salmon fillets, 1-1/12-inches thick
- 2 teaspoons avocado oil or olive oil
- 2 teaspoons paprika
- Salt and coarse, to taste
- Black pepper, to taste
- Green herbs, to garnish

DIRECTIONS:

Clean the salmon and let it rest for 1 hour at room temperature.

Season the fish with olive oil, salt, pepper, and paprika.

Arrange the fish in the air fryer basket.

Cook for 7 minutes at 390 degrees.

Once done, remove the fish from the fryer.

Garnish with fresh herbs.

Serve warm.

NUTRITION: Calories 249 Fat 11.9 g Carbs 1.8 g Protein 35 g

310. LEMON GARLIC SHRIMP

Basic Recipe

Preparation Time: 5 minutes

Cooking Time: 5 minutes

Servings: 4

INGREDIENTS:

- 1-pound Small shrimp, peeled with tails removed
- 1 tablespoon Olive oil
- 4 Garlic cloves, minced
- 1 Lemon, zested and juiced
- 1 pinch Crushed red pepper flakes (optional)
- 1/4 cup Parsley, chopped
- 1/4 teaspoon Sea salt

DIRECTIONS:

Preheat vortex air fryer to 400 ° F.

In a container, mix the shrimp, olive oil, garlic, salt, lemon zest, and pepper flakes (whether used). Mix to Cover

Put the shrimp in the basket of your air fryer oven. Cook for 6-7 minutes, shake the basket in half or till than the shrimps are done, pour the shrimps into a bowl and mix them with lemon juice and parsley. Season with additional salt.

NUTRITION: Calories 130 Fat 4.6g Carbs 4.7g Protein 20.3g

311. ROASTED HEIRLOOM TOMATO WITH BAKED FETA

Basic Recipe

Preparation Time: 20 minutes

Cooking Time: 14 minutes

Servings: 2

INGREDIENTS:

- 1 ea. Heirloom tomato
- 8 oz. Feta cheese block
- ½ cup red onions (sliced paper thin)
- 1 tbsp. Olive oil
- For Basil Pesto:
- ½ cup parsley (rough chopped)
- ½ cup basil (rough chopped)
- ½ cup parmesan (freshly grated)
- 3 tbsp toasted pine nuts
- 1 ea. Garlic clove
- ½ cup olive oil
- 1 pinch salt

DIRECTIONS:

Preheat the Air fryer to 390°F.

Combine pine nuts, 1 tsp. olive oil, and pinch of salt.

Toss pine nuts into the Air fryer and set timer for 2 minutes Remove and place onto a paper towel and set aside.

Wash and chop one bunch of parsley and one bunch of basil.

Place chopped parsley, basil, fresh grated parmesan, garlic, toasted pine nuts and salt in a small pot over medium-high heat.

Turn on the food processor and Drizzle with in the olive oil.

Remove the pesto and refrigerate.

Slice the tomato into ½ inch thick slices. Slice the feta into ½ inch thick slices. Take a circle cutter and cut the feta the same size as the heirloom tomato.

Stack the feta on top of the tomato, spread 1 tablespoon basil pesto in between.

Slice the red onions paper thin and toss with 1 tablespoon of olive oil and apply to the top of the feta.

Place tomatoes into the Air fryer and cook for 12-14 minutes

Finish with sea salt and basil pesto.

NUTRITION: Calories 322.2 Fat 30.8g Carbs 7.7.G Protein 32g

312. STEVIA –CAJUN CHICKEN THIGHS

Basic Recipe

Preparation Time: 10 minutes

Cooking Time: 25 minutes

Servings: 4

INGREDIENTS:

- 1 ½ pounds skinless, boneless chicken thighs
- ¼ cup coconut flour
- ⅓ cup almond flour
- 2 ½ teaspoons cajun seasoning
- ½ teaspoon garlic powder
- ½ teaspoon stevia powder
- ¼ teaspoon ground paprika
- ⅛ teaspoon cayenne pepper
- ¼ teaspoon salt

DIRECTIONS:

Mix coconut flour, almond flour, Cajun spice, garlic powder, salt, stevia powder, paprika and cayenne pepper in a dish. The thighs distribute the flour mixture. Remove extra flour

Preheat a deep fryer to 175 °C (360 degrees F). Place the chicken legs in the frying basket and let them done within 15 minutes Turn the legs over and done until the chicken legs in the middle are it is no longer pink and the juice comes out clearly for about 10 minutes longer.

A quick reading thermometer in the middle should show at least 74 ° C (165 ° F). Take the chicken legs out of the deep fryer and sprinkle the lemon juice over each leg.

NUTRITION: Calories 121 Fat 9.1g Carbs 3.3g Protein 7.2g

313. LEMON PEPPER SHRIMP

Basic Recipe

Preparation Time: 5 minutes

Cooking Time: 10 minutes

Servings: 4

INGREDIENTS:

- 2 tablespoons Coconut oil
- 2 Lemons, juiced
- 2 teaspoons Black pepper
- 1/2 teaspoon Paprika
- 1/2 teaspoon Minced garlic
- 24 ounces uncooked medium shrimp, peeled and deveined
- 1 Lime, sliced

DIRECTIONS:

Preheat the Vortex air fryer oven to 200 ° C.

Combine coconut oil, lime juice, black pepper, paprika, and garlic mined in a container. Put shrimp and coat till than covered.

Place the shrimp in the Vortex air fryer oven and cook for 7 minutes or till than cooked. Serve with lime slices.

NUTRITION: Calories 234 Fat 9g Carbs 3.8g Protein 37g

314. WARMING WINTER BEEF WITH CELERY

Basic Recipe

Preparation Time: 5 minutes

Cooking Time: 12 minutes

Servings: 4

INGREDIENTS:

- 9 ounces tender beef, chopped
- 1/2 cup leeks, chopped
- 1/2 cup celery stalks, chopped
- 2 cloves garlic, smashed
- 2 tablespoons red cooking wine
- 3/4 cup cream of celery soup
- 2 sprigs rosemary, chopped
- 1/4 teaspoon smoked paprika
- 3/4 teaspoons salt
- 1/4 teaspoon black pepper, or to taste

DIRECTIONS:

Add the beef, leeks, celery, and garlic to the baking dish; cook for about 5 minutes at 390 degrees F.

Once the meat is starting to tender, pour in the wine and soup. Season with rosemary, smoked paprika, salt, and black pepper

Now, cook an additional 7 minutes

NUTRITION: Calories 364 Cal Fat 9 g Carbs 39 g Protein 32 g

315. SESAME SEEDS COATED FISH

Basic Recipe

Preparation Time: 20 minutes

Cooking Time: 20 minutes

Servings: 28

INGREDIENTS:

- ½ cup sesame seeds, toasted
- ½ teaspoon dried rosemary, crushed

- 8 tablespoons olive oil
- 14 frozen fish fillets (white fish of your choice)
- 6 eggs
- ½ cup breadcrumbs
- 8 tablespoons plain flour
- Salt and freshly ground black pepper, to taste

DIRECTIONS:

Take three dishes, place flour in one, crack eggs in the other and mix remaining ingredients except fillets in the third one.

Now, coat fillets in the flour and dip in the beaten eggs.

Then, dredge generously with the sesame seeds mixture.

Meanwhile, preheat the air fryer to 390 degrees F and line the air fryer basket with the foil.

Arrange fillets in the basket and cook for about 14 minutes, flipping once in the middle way.

Take out and serve hot.

NUTRITION: Calories 179 Fat 9.3g Carbs: 15.8g Protein 7.7g

316. MONTREAL FRIED SHRIMP

Basic Recipe
Preparation Time: 5 minutes
Cooking Time: 10 minutes
Servings: 6

INGREDIENTS:

- 1-pound raw shrimp peeled and deveined
- 1 egg white 3 tablespoon
- 1/2 cup all-purpose flour
- 3/4 cup panko breadcrumbs
- 1 teaspoon paprika
- 1 tablespoon McCormick's Grill Mates Montreal Chicken Seasoning or to taste
- Salt and pepper to taste
- Cooking spray

DIRECTIONS:

Preheat the Air Fryer to 400 degrees F.

Toss the shrimp with Montreal seasonings.

Whisk egg whites in a medium sized bowl.

Keep the breadcrumbs and flour in separate bowls.

First dredge each shrimp in the flour, then dip into the egg whites, and then coat with the breadcrumbs.

Place the coated shrimps in the air dryer and spray the cooking oil over them.

Air fry for about 4 minutes then flip the shrimps.

Continue cooking for another 4 minutes

Serve warm.

NUTRITION: Calories 248 Fat 2.4 g Carbs 12.2 g Protein 44.3 g

317. PORK MEATBALLS

Basic Recipe
Preparation Time: 10 minutes
Cooking Time: 20 minutes
Servings: 4

INGREDIENTS:

12 ounces Ground pork
1/2 cup Panko bread crumbs
1 Egg
1 teaspoon Salt
1 teaspoon Dried parsley
1/2 teaspoon Paprika

DIRECTIONS:

Preheat the air fryer oven to 175 ° C. Mix ground pork, panko breadcrumbs, eggs, salt, parsley and paprika in a large bowl and mix well.

Make 12 large meatballs with a scoop of ice cream.

Place the meatballs on a baking sheet, place half of the meatballs in the

basket and cook for 8 minutes

Shake the basket and cook for another 2 minutes Place on a serving plate and let rest for 5 minutes Repeat with the remaining meatballs.

NUTRITION: Calories 64 Fat 1.6g Carbs 3.3g Protein 8.5g

318. ROASTED AIR FRYER SWEET CARROTS

Basic Recipe
Preparation Time: 10 minutes
Cooking Time: 20 minutes
Servings: 4

INGREDIENTS:

- 1 lb. carrots, peeled and chopped into 1-inch pieces
- ¼ tablespoons salt
- 2 tablespoons brown sugar
- 2 tablespoons melted butter

DIRECTIONS:

Place peeled and chopped carrots in a bowl, add melted butter, brown sugar and salt and stir properly until the carrot is properly coated.

Pour coated mixture into an air fryer safe bowl, place it in the air fryer, set heat at 38 0° F and cook for 10 minutes, stir and cook for another 10 minutes

Your sweet carrot is ready to be served.

NUTRITION: Calcium 42mg Vitamin 7mg Fiber 3g Carbs 17g Sodium 275mg

319. CRISPY SALT AND PEPPER TOFU

Basic Recipe
Preparation Time: 5 minutes
Cooking Time: 20 minutes
Servings: 4

INGREDIENTS:

- ¼ cup chickpea flour
- ¼ cup arrowroot (or cornstarch)
- 1 teaspoon sea salt
- 1 teaspoon granulated garlic
- ½ teaspoon freshly grated black pepper
- 1 (15-ounce) package tofu, firm or extra-firm
- Cooking oil spray (sunflower, safflower, or refined coconut)
- Asian Spicy Sweet Sauce, optional

DIRECTIONS:

In a medium bowl, combine the flour, arrowroot, salt, garlic, and pepper. Stir well to combine. Cut the tofu into cubes (no need to press—if it's a bit watery, that's fine!). Place the cubes into the flour mixture. Toss well to coat. Spray the tofu with oil and toss again. (The spray will help the coating better stick to the tofu.)

Spray the air fryer basket with the oil. Place the tofu in a single layer in the air fryer basket (you may have to do this in 2 batches, depending on the size of your appliance) and spray the tops with oil. Fry for 8 minutes Remove the air fryer basket and spray again with oil. Toss gently or turn the pieces over. Spray with oil again and fry for another 7 minutes, or until golden-browned and very crisp. Serve immediately, either plain or with the Asian Spicy Sweet Sauce.

NUTRITION: Calories 148 Fat 5g Carbs 14g Protein 11g

320. NACHO CHIPS CRUSTED PRAWNS

Basic Recipe
Preparation Time: 10 minutes
Cooking Time: 10 minutes
Servings: 8

INGREDIENTS:

- 2 large eggs
- 36 prawns, peeled and deveined
- 1½-pounds Nacho flavored chips, crushed finely

DIRECTIONS:

Add nacho chips in a bowl and crush well.

Add eggs in another bowl and beat well.

Preheat the air fryer to 350 degrees F.

Dip each prawn in the egg mixture and then in the crushed nachos.

Place them in the air fryer and cook for about 8 minutes

Take out and serve hot.

Tip: More crushed nachos will make prawns crispier.

NUTRITION: Calories 1090 Fat 55.2g Carbs 101.9g Protein 49.2g

321. PARSLEY CATFISH

Basic Recipe

Preparation Time: 10 minutes

Cooking Time: 25 minutes

Servings: 4

INGREDIENTS:

- 4 catfish fillets
- 1/4 cup Louisiana Fish fry
- 1 tablespoon olive oil
- 1 tablespoon chopped parsley optional
- 1 lemon, sliced
- Fresh herbs, to garnish

DIRECTIONS:

Preheat air fryer to 400 degrees F.

Rinse the fish fillets and pat them try.

Rub the fillets with the seasoning and coat well.

Spray oil on top of each fillet.

Place the fillets in the air fryer basket.

Cover the lid and cook for 10 minutes

Flip the fillets and cook more for another 10 minutes

Flip the fish and cook for 3 minutes until crispy.

Garnish with parsley, fresh herbs, and lemon.

Serve warm.

NUTRITION: Calories 248 Fat 15.7 g Carbs 0.4 g Protein 24.9 g

322. WONDROUS CREOLE FRIED SHRIMP WITH SRIRACHA SAUCE

Basic Recipe

Preparation Time: 10 minutes

Cooking Time: 10 minutes

Servings: 4

INGREDIENTS:

- 1 pound of peeled and deveined shrimp
- ½ cup of cornmeal
- ½ cup of breadcrumbs
- 1 beaten egg
- 1 tablespoon of hot sauce
- 1 tablespoon of mustard
- 2 tablespoons of creole seasoning
- 1 teaspoon of onion powder
- 1 teaspoon of garlic powder
- 1 teaspoon of black pepper
- 1 teaspoon of salt
- Siracha sauce ingredients
- 1 cup of mayonnaise
- 3 tablespoons of sriracha sauce
- 1 tablespoon of soy sauce
- 1 teaspoon of black pepper

DIRECTIONS:

Turn on your air fryer to 360 degrees Fahrenheit.

Using a bowl, add the eggs, hot sauce, mustard, 1 tablespoon of creole seasoning, onion powder, garlic powder, black pepper, salt, the shrimp and toss until it is properly covered.

Using another bowl, add the breadcrumbs, flour, 1 tablespoon of creole seasoning, and the shrimp and cover it properly.

Grease your air fryer basket with a nonstick cooking spray and add the shrimp.

Cook it for 5 minutes or until it has a golden-brown color, while being careful not to overcook.

Thereafter, carefully remove it from your air fryer and allow it to cool.

Pick a separate bowl, add and mix all the sauce ingredients properly. Serve!

NUTRITION: Calories 200 Fat 12g Protein 15g Carbs 7g

323. BUTTERED SCALLOPS

Basic Recipe

Preparation Time: 10 minutes

Cooking Time: 5 minutes

Servings: 8

INGREDIENTS:

- 4 tablespoons butter, melted
- 3-pounds Sea scallops
- 2 tablespoons fresh thyme, minced
- Salt and freshly ground black pepper, to taste

DIRECTIONS:

Add butter, sea scallops, thyme, salt and pepper in a bowl. Toss to coat well.

Preheat the air fryer to 385 degrees F and grease the air fryer basket.

Place scallops in the basket and cook for 5 minutes

Take out and serve hot.

Tip: Pour melted butter on the scallops to enhance their taste.

NUTRITION: Calories 203 Fat 7.1g Carbs 4.5g Protein 28.7g

324. EASY PEASY PIZZA

Basic Recipe

Preparation Time: 5 minutes

Cooking Time: 10 minutes

Servings: 4

INGREDIENTS:

- Cooking oil spray (coconut, sunflower, or safflower)
- 1 flour tortilla, preferably sprouted or whole grain
- ¼ cup vegan pizza or marinara sauce
- ⅓ Cup grated vegan mozzarella cheese or Cheesy Sauce
- Toppings of your choice

DIRECTIONS:

Spray the air fryer basket with oil. Place the tortilla in the air fryer basket. If the tortilla is a little bigger than the base, no problem! Simply fold the edges up a bit to form a semblance of a "crust."

Pour the sauce in the center, and evenly distribute it around the tortilla "crust" (I like to use the back of a spoon for this purpose).

Sprinkle evenly with vegan cheese, and add your toppings. Bake it for 9 minutes, or until nicely browned. Remove carefully, cut into four pieces, and enjoy.

NUTRITION: Calories 210 Fat 6g Carbs 33g Protein 5g

325. SPICY SHRIMP

Basic Recipe

Preparation Time: 5 minutes

Cooking Time: 5 minutes

Servings: 8

INGREDIENTS:

- 2 teaspoons old bay seasoning
- 1 teaspoon cayenne pepper
- 1 teaspoon smoked paprika
- 4 tablespoons olive oil
- 2-pounds tiger shrimp
- Salt, to taste

DIRECTIONS:

Add all the ingredients in a large bowl. Mix well. Preheat the air fryer to 390 degrees F and grease the air fryer basket.

Place shrimps in the air fryer basket and cook for about 5 minutes. Take out and serve hot.

Tip: Top with chili sauce to enhance its taste.
NUTRITION: Calories 174 Fat 8.3g Carbs 0.3g Protein 23.8g

326. LEMON-GARLIC CHICKEN THIGHS

Basic Recipe
Preparation Time: 10 minutes
Cooking Time: 25 minutes
Servings: 4
INGREDIENTS:
- ¼ cup Lemon juice
- 2 tablespoons Coconut oil
- 1 teaspoon Dijon mustard
- 2 cloves Garlic, minced
- ¼ teaspoon Salt
- ⅛ Teaspoon Ground black pepper
- 4 Skin-on, bone-in chicken thighs
- 4 Lime wedges

DIRECTIONS:
Put lemon juice, coconut oil, Dijon mustard, garlic, salt and pepper in a container and mix well.
Reserve the marinade and put the chicken legs in a large plastic bag with a zipper. Put the marinade over the chicken and close the bag. Make sure all chicken bits are covered. Put in the freeze for at most 120 min.
Preheat an air fryer oven to 175 ° C.
Take the chicken out of the marinade and rub dry with a kitchen towel.
Put the chicken bits in the frying basket and cook as needed.
Roast for 22 to 24 minutes until the chicken in the bone are cooked and the juice is clear.
Press a lime wedge on each slice before serving.
NUTRITION: Calories 222 Fat 16.8g Carbs 1.5g Protein 15.9g

FISH & SEAFOOD RECIPES
327. PARMESAN-CRUSTED HAKE WITH GARLIC SAUCE

Servings: 3
Cooking Time: 10 Minutes
INGREDIENTS:
- Fish:
- 6 tablespoons mayonnaise
- 1 tablespoon fresh lime juice
- 1 teaspoon Dijon mustard
- 1 cup grated Parmesan cheese
- Salt, to taste
- ¼ teaspoon ground black pepper, or more to taste
- 3 hake fillets, patted dry
- Nonstick cooking spray
- Garlic Sauce:
- ¼ cup plain Greek yogurt
- 2 tablespoons olive oil
- 2 cloves garlic, minced
- ½ teaspoon minced tarragon leaves

DIRECTIONS:
Mix the mayo, lime juice, and mustard in a shallow bowl and whisk to combine. In another shallow bowl, stir together the grated Parmesan cheese, salt, and pepper.
Dredge each fillet in the mayo mixture, then roll them in the cheese mixture until they are evenly coated on both sides.
Spray the air fryer basket with nonstick cooking spray. Place the fillets in the pan.
Put the air fryer basket on the baking pan and slide into Rack Position 2, select Air Fry, set temperature to 395ºF (202ºC), and set time to 10 minutes.
Flip the fillets halfway through the cooking time.
Meanwhile, in a small bowl, whisk all the ingredients for the sauce until well incorporated.

When cooking is complete, the fish should flake apart with a fork. Remove the fillets from the oven and serve warm alongside the sauce.

328. GLAZED TUNA AND FRUIT KEBABS

Servings: 4
Cooking Time: 10 Minutes
INGREDIENTS:
- Kebabs:
- 1 pound (454 g) tuna steaks, cut into 1-inch cubes
- ½ cup canned pineapple chunks, drained, juice reserved
- ½ cup large red grapes
- Marinade:
- 1 tablespoon honey
- 1 teaspoon olive oil
- 2 teaspoons grated fresh ginger
- Pinch cayenne pepper
- Special Equipment:
- 4 metal skewers

DIRECTIONS:
Make the kebabs: Thread, alternating tuna cubes, pineapple chunks, and red grapes, onto the metal skewers.
Make the marinade: Whisk together the honey, olive oil, ginger, and cayenne pepper in a small bowl. Brush generously the marinade over the kebabs and allow to sit for 10 minutes.
When ready, transfer the kebabs to the air fryer basket.
Put the air fryer basket on the baking pan and slide into Rack Position 2, select Air Fry, set temperature to 370ºF (188ºC), and set time to 10 minutes.
After 5 minutes, remove from the oven and flip the kebabs and brush with the remaining marinade. Return the pan to the oven and continue cooking for an additional 5 minutes.
When cooking is complete, the kebabs should reach an internal temperature of 145ºF (63ºC) on a meat thermometer. Remove from the oven and discard any remaining marinade. Serve hot.

329. CRISPY CHEESY FISH FINGERS

Servings: 4
Cooking Time: 20 Minutes
INGREDIENTS:
- Large codfish filet, approximately 6-8 ounces, fresh or frozen and thawed, cut into 1 ½-inch strips
- 2 raw eggs
- ½ cup of breadcrumbs (we like Panko, but any brand or home recipe will do)
- 2 tablespoons of shredded or powdered parmesan cheese
- 1 tablespoons of shredded cheddar cheese
- Pinch of salt and pepper

DIRECTIONS:
Preparing the Ingredients. Cover the basket of the Cosori air fryer oven with a lining of tin foil, leaving the edges uncovered to allow air to circulate through the basket.
Preheat the air fryer oven to 350 degrees.
In a large mixing bowl, beat the eggs until fluffy and until the yolks and whites are fully combined.
Dunk all the fish strips in the beaten eggs, fully submerging.
In a separate mixing bowl, combine the bread crumbs with the parmesan, cheddar, and salt and pepper, until evenly mixed.
One by one, coat the egg-covered fish strips in the mixed dry ingredients so that they're fully covered, and place on the foil-lined Oven rack/basket. Place the Rack on the middle-shelf of the Cosori air fryer oven.
Air Frying. Set the air-fryer timer to 20 minutes.
Halfway through the cooking time, shake the handle of the air-fryer so that the breaded fish jostles inside and fry-coverage is even.
After 20 minutes, when the fryer shuts off, the fish strips will be perfectly cooked and their breaded crust golden-brown and delicious! Using tongs, remove from the air fryer oven and set on a serving dish to cool.

330. FLAVORFUL BAKED HALIBUT

Servings: 4
Cooking Time: 12 Minutes
INGREDIENTS:
- 1 lb halibut fillets
- 1/4 tsp garlic powder
- 1/4 tsp paprika
- 1/4 tsp smoked paprika
- 1/4 tsp pepper
- 1/4 cup olive oil
- 1 lemon juice
- 1/2 tsp salt

DIRECTIONS:
FIT THE COSORI OVEN WITH THE RACK IN POSITION
Place fish fillets into the baking dish.
In a small bowl, mix lemon juice, oil, paprika, smoked paprika, garlic powder, and salt.
Brush lemon juice mixture over fish fillets.
Set to bake at 425 F for 17 minutes. After 5 minutes place the baking dish in the preheated oven.
Serve and enjoy.
Nutrition Info: Calories 236 Fat 15.3 g Carbohydrates 0.4 g Sugar 0.1 g Protein 24 g Cholesterol 36 mg

331.   TENDER & JUICY CAJUN COD

Servings: 6
Cooking Time: 15 Minutes

INGREDIENTS:
- 3 cod fillets, cut in half
- 1 tbsp Cajun seasoning
- 1 tbsp garlic, minced
- 1 tbsp olive oil
- 1/4 cup butter, melted
- Pepper
- Salt

DIRECTIONS:
Fit the Cosori oven with the rack in position
Season fish fillets with pepper and salt and place in a 9*13-inch baking dish.
Mix together the remaining ingredients and pour over fish fillets.
Set to bake at 400 F for 20 minutes. After 5 minutes place the baking dish in the preheated oven.
Serve and enjoy.
Nutrition Info: Calories 126 Fat 10.4 g Carbohydrates 0.5 g Sugar 0 g Protein 8.2 g Cholesterol 42 mg

332. EASY SCALLOPS

Servings: 2
Cooking Time: 4 Minutes
INGREDIENTS:
- 12 medium sea scallops, rinsed and patted dry
- 1 teaspoon fine sea salt
- ¾ teaspoon ground black pepper, plus more for garnish
- Fresh thyme leaves, for garnish (optional)
- Avocado oil spray

DIRECTIONS:
Coat the air fryer basket with avocado oil spray.
Place the scallops in a medium bowl and spritz with avocado oil spray. Sprinkle the salt and pepper to season.
Transfer the seasoned scallops to the basket, spacing them apart.
Put the air fryer basket on the baking pan and slide into Rack Position 2, select Air Fry, set temperature to 390°F (199°C), and set time to 4 minutes.
Flip the scallops halfway through the cooking time.
When cooking is complete, the scallops should reach an internal temperature of just 145ºF (63ºC) on a meat thermometer. Sprinkle the pepper and thyme leaves on top for garnish, if desired. Serve immediately.

333. GARLIC-BUTTER CATFISH

Servings: 2
Cooking Time: 20 Minutes

INGREDIENTS:
- 2 catfish fillets
- 2 tsp blackening seasoning
- Juice of 1 lime
- 2 tbsp butter, melted
- 1 garlic clove, mashed
- 2 tbsp cilantro

DIRECTIONS:
In a bowl, blend in garlic, lime juice, cilantro, and butter. Pour half of the mixture over the fillets and sprinkle with blackening seasoning. Place the fillets in the basket and fit in the baking tray; cook for 15 minutes at 360 F on Air Fry function. Serve the fish with remaining sauce.

334. TROPICAL SHRIMP SKEWERS

Servings: 4
Cooking Time: 5 Minutes
INGREDIENTS:
- 1 tbsp. lime juice
- 1 tbsp. honey
- ¼ tsp red pepper flakes
- ¼ tsp pepper
- ¼ tsp ginger
- Nonstick cooking spray
- 1 lb. medium shrimp, peel, devein & leave tails on
- 2 cups peaches, drain & chop
- ½ green bell pepper, chopped fine
- ¼ cup scallions, chopped

DIRECTIONS:
Soak 8 small wooden skewers in water for 15 minutes.
In a small bowl, whisk together lime juice, honey and spices. Transfer 2 tablespoons of the mixture to a medium bowl.
Place the baking pan in position 2 of the oven. Lightly spray fryer basket with cooking spray. Set oven to broil on 400°F for 10 minutes.
Thread 5 shrimp on each skewer and brush both sides with marinade. Place in basket and after 5 minutes, place on the baking pan. Cook 4-5 minutes or until shrimp turn pink.
Add peaches, bell pepper, and scallions to reserved honey mixture, mix well. Divide salsa evenly between serving plates and top with 2 skewers each. Serve immediately.
Nutrition Info: Calories 181, Total Fat 1g, Saturated Fat 0g, Total Carbs 27g, Net Carbs 25g, Protein 16g, Sugar 21g, Fiber 2g, Sodium 650mg, Potassium 288mg, Phosphorus 297mg

335. SPICY ORANGE SHRIMP

Servings: 4
Cooking Time: 12 Minutes
INGREDIENTS:
- ⅓ cup orange juice
- 3 teaspoons minced garlic
- 1 teaspoon Old Bay seasoning
- ¼ to ½ teaspoon cayenne pepper
- 1 pound (454 g) medium shrimp, thawed, deveined, peeled, with tails off, and patted dry
- Cooking spray

DIRECTIONS:

Stir together the orange juice, garlic, Old Bay seasoning, and cayenne pepper in a medium bowl. Add the shrimp to the bowl and toss to coat well.

Cover the bowl with plastic wrap and marinate in the refrigerator for 30 minutes.

Spritz the air fryer basket with cooking spray. Place the shrimp in the pan and spray with cooking spray.

Put the air fryer basket on the baking pan and slide into Rack Position 2, select Air Fry, set temperature to 400ºF (205ºC), and set time to 12 minutes.

Flip the shrimp halfway through the cooking time.

When cooked, the shrimp should be opaque and crisp. Remove from the oven and serve hot.

336. LEMON PEPPER TILAPIA FILLETS

Servings: 4
Cooking Time: 15 Minutes
INGREDIENTS:
- 1 lb tilapia fillets
- 1 tbsp Italian seasoning
- 2 tbsp canola oil
- 2 tbsp lemon pepper
- Salt to taste
- 2-3 butter buds

DIRECTIONS:
Preheat your Cosori oven to 400 F on Bake function. Drizzle tilapia fillets with canola oil. In a bowl, mix salt, lemon pepper, butter buds, and Italian seasoning; spread on the fish. Place the fillet on a baking tray and press Start. Cook for 10 minutes until tender and crispy. Serve warm.

337. TASTY PARMESAN SHRIMP

Servings: 4
Cooking Time: 10 Minutes

INGREDIENTS:
- 1 lb shrimp, peeled and deveined
- 1/4 cup parmesan cheese, grated
- 4 garlic cloves, minced
- 1 tbsp olive oil
- 1/4 tsp oregano
- 1/2 tsp pepper
- 1/2 tsp onion powder
- 1/2 tsp basil

DIRECTIONS:
Fit the Cosori oven with the rack in position 2.
Add all ingredients into the large bowl and toss well.
Add shrimp to the air fryer basket then place an air fryer basket in the baking pan.
Place a baking pan on the oven rack. Set to air fry at 350 F for 10 minutes.
Serve and enjoy.
Nutrition Info: Calories 189 Fat 6.7 g Carbohydrates 3.4 g Sugar 0.1 g Protein 27.9 g Cholesterol 243 mg

338. ROSEMARY GARLIC SHRIMP

Servings: 4
Cooking Time: 10 Minutes
INGREDIENTS:
- 1 lb shrimp, peeled and deveined
- 2 garlic cloves, minced
- 1/2 tbsp fresh rosemary, chopped
- 1 tbsp olive oil
- Pepper
- Salt

DIRECTIONS:

Fit the Cosori oven with the rack in position
Add shrimp and remaining ingredients in a large bowl and toss well.
Pour shrimp mixture into the baking dish.
Set to bake at 400 F for 15 minutes. After 5 minutes place the baking dish in the preheated oven.
Serve and enjoy.
Nutrition Info: Calories 168 Fat 5.5 g Carbohydrates 2.5 g Sugar 0 g Protein 26 g Cholesterol 239 mg

339. SPICY HALIBUT

Servings: 4
Cooking Time: 12 Minutes

INGREDIENTS:
- 1 lb halibut fillets
- 1/2 tsp chili powder
- 1/2 tsp smoked paprika
- 1/4 cup olive oil
- 1/4 tsp garlic powder
- Pepper
- Salt

DIRECTIONS:
Fit the Cosori oven with the rack in position
Place halibut fillets in a baking dish.
In a small bowl, mix oil, garlic powder, paprika, pepper, chili powder, and salt.
Brush fish fillets with oil mixture.
Set to bake at 425 F for 17 minutes. After 5 minutes place the baking dish in the preheated oven.
Serve and enjoy.
Nutrition Info: Calories 236 Fat 15.3 g Carbohydrates 0.5 g Sugar 0.1 g Protein 24 g Cholesterol 36 mg

340. SEAFOOD SPRING ROLLS

Servings: 4
Cooking Time: 20 Minutes
INGREDIENTS:
- 1 tablespoon olive oil
- 2 teaspoons minced garlic
- 1 cup matchstick cut carrots
- 2 cups finely sliced cabbage
- 2 (4-ounce / 113-g) cans tiny shrimp, drained
- 4 teaspoons soy sauce
- Salt and freshly ground black pepper, to taste
- 16 square spring roll wrappers
- Cooking spray

DIRECTIONS:
Spray the air fryer basket with cooking spray. Set aside.
Heat the olive oil in a medium skillet over medium heat until it shimmers.
Add the garlic to the skillet and cook for 30 seconds. Stir in the cabbage and carrots and sauté for about 5 minutes, stirring occasionally, or until the vegetables are lightly tender.
Fold in the shrimp and soy sauce and sprinkle with salt and pepper, then stir to combine. Sauté for another 2 minutes, or until the moisture is evaporated. Remove from the heat and set aside to cool.
Put a spring roll wrapper on a work surface and spoon 1 tablespoon of the shrimp mixture onto the lower end of the wrapper.
Roll the wrapper away from you halfway, and then fold in the right and left sides, like an envelope. Continue to roll to the very end, using a little water to seal the edge. Repeat with the remaining wrappers and filling.
Place the spring rolls in the air fryer basket in a single layer, leaving space between each spring roll. Mist them lightly with cooking spray.
Put the air fryer basket on the baking pan and slide into Rack Position 2, select Air Fry, set temperature to 375ºF (190ºC), and set time to 10 minutes.

Flip the rolls halfway through the cooking time.

When cooking is complete, the spring rolls will be heated through and start to brown. If necessary, continue cooking for 5 minutes more. Remove from the oven and cool for a few minutes before serving.

341. ROASTED HALIBUT STEAKS WITH PARSLEY

Servings: 4
Cooking Time: 10 Minutes
INGREDIENTS:
- 1 pound (454 g) halibut steaks
- ¼ cup vegetable oil
- 2½ tablespoons Worcester sauce
- 2 tablespoons honey
- 2 tablespoons vermouth
- 1 tablespoon freshly squeezed lemon juice
- 1 tablespoon fresh parsley leaves, coarsely chopped
- Salt and pepper, to taste
- 1 teaspoon dried basil

DIRECTIONS:
Put all the ingredients in a large mixing dish and gently stir until the fish is coated evenly. Transfer the fish to the air fryer basket.

Put the air fryer basket on the baking pan and slide into Rack Position 2, select Roast, set temperature to 390ºF (199ºC), and set time to 10 minutes.

Flip the fish halfway through cooking time.

When cooking is complete, the fish should reach an internal temperature of at least 145ºF (63ºC) on a meat thermometer. Remove from the oven and let the fish cool for 5 minutes before serving.

342. GREEK COD WITH ASPARAGUS

Servings: 2
Cooking Time: 20 Minutes
INGREDIENTS:
- 1 lb cod, cut into 4 pieces
- 8 asparagus spears
- 1 leek, sliced
- 1 onion, quartered
- 2 tomatoes, halved
- 1/2 tsp oregano
- 1/2 tsp red chili flakes
- 1/2 cup olives, chopped
- 2 tbsp olive oil
- 1/4 tsp pepper
- 1/4 tsp salt

DIRECTIONS:
Fit the Cosori oven with the rack in position

Arrange fish pieces, olives, asparagus, leek, onion, and tomatoes in a baking dish.

Season with oregano, chili flakes, pepper, and salt and drizzle with olive oil.

Set to bake at 400 F for 25 minutes. After 5 minutes place the baking dish in the preheated oven.

Serve and enjoy.

Nutrition Info: Calories 489 Fat 20.2 g Carbohydrates 22.5 g Sugar 9.1 g Protein 56.6 g Cholesterol 125 mg

343. ROASTED SCALLOPS WITH SNOW PEAS

Servings: 4
Cooking Time: 8 Minutes
INGREDIENTS:
- 1 pound (454 g) sea scallops
- 3 tablespoons hoisin sauce
- ½ cup toasted sesame seeds
- 6 ounces (170 g) snow peas, trimmed

- 3 teaspoons vegetable oil, divided
- 1 teaspoon soy sauce
- 1 teaspoon sesame oil
- 1 cup roasted mushrooms

DIRECTIONS:
Brush the scallops with the hoisin sauce. Put the sesame seeds in a shallow dish. Roll the scallops in the sesame seeds until evenly coated.

Combine the snow peas with 1 teaspoon of vegetable oil, the sesame oil, and soy sauce in a medium bowl and toss to coat.

Grease the baking pan with the remaining 2 teaspoons of vegetable oil. Put the scallops in the middle of the pan and arrange the snow peas around the scallops in a single layer.

Slide the baking pan into Rack Position 2, select Roast, set temperature to 375ºF (190ºC), and set time to 8 minutes.

After 5 minutes, remove the pan and flip the scallops. Fold in the mushrooms and stir well. Return the pan to the oven and continue cooking.

When done, remove from the oven and cool for 5 minutes. Serve warm.

344. FIRED SHRIMP WITH MAYONNAISE SAUCE

Servings: 4
Cooking Time: 7 Minutes
INGREDIENTS:
- Shrimp
- 12 jumbo shrimp
- ½ teaspoon garlic salt
- ¼ teaspoon freshly cracked mixed peppercorns
- Sauce:
- 4 tablespoons mayonnaise
- 1 teaspoon grated lemon rind
- 1 teaspoon Dijon mustard
- 1 teaspoon chipotle powder
- ½ teaspoon cumin powder

DIRECTIONS:
In a medium bowl, season the shrimp with garlic salt and cracked mixed peppercorns.

Place the shrimp in the air fryer basket.

Put the air fryer basket on the baking pan and slide into Rack Position 2, select Air Fry, set temperature to 395ºF (202ºC), and set time to 7 minutes.

After 5 minutes, remove from the oven and flip the shrimp. Return to the oven and continue cooking for 2 minutes more, or until they are pink and no longer opaque.

Meanwhile, stir together all the ingredients for the sauce in a small bowl until well mixed.

When cooking is complete, remove the shrimp from the oven and serve alongside the sauce.

345. BAKED HALIBUT STEAKS WITH PARSLEY

Servings: 4
Cooking Time: 10 Minutes
INGREDIENTS:
- 1 pound (454 g) halibut steaks
- ¼ cup vegetable oil
- 2½ tablespoons Worcester sauce
- 2 tablespoons honey
- 2 tablespoons vermouth
- 1 tablespoon freshly squeezed lemon juice
- 1 tablespoon fresh parsley leaves, coarsely chopped
- Salt and pepper, to taste
- 1 teaspoon dried basil

DIRECTIONS:
Put all the ingredients in a large mixing dish and gently stir until the fish is coated evenly. Transfer the fish to the baking pan.

Slide the baking pan into Rack Position 1, select Convection Bake, set temperature to 375ºF (190ºC), and set time to 10 minutes.

Flip the fish halfway through cooking time.

When cooking is complete, the fish should reach an internal temperature of at least 145ºF (63ºC) on a meat thermometer. Remove from the oven and let the fish cool for 5 minutes before serving.

346. AIR FRYER SALMON
Servings: 2
Cooking Time: 10 Minutes
INGREDIENTS:
- ½ tsp. salt
- ½ tsp. garlic powder
- ½ tsp. smoked paprika
- Salmon

DIRECTIONS:
Preparing the Ingredients. Mix spices and sprinkle onto salmon.
Place seasoned salmon into the Cosori air fryer oven.
Air Frying. Set temperature to 400°F, and set time to 10 minutes.
Nutrition Info: CALORIES: 185; FAT: 11G; PROTEIN:21G; SUGAR:0G

347. SPICY GRILLED HALIBUT
Servings: 4
Cooking Time: 10 Minutes
INGREDIENTS:
- ½ cup fresh lemon juice
- 2 jalapeno peppers, seeded & chopped fine
- 4 6 oz. halibut fillets
- Nonstick cooking spray
- ¼ cup cilantro, chopped

DIRECTIONS:
In a small bowl, combine lemon juice and chilies, mix well.
Place fish in a large Ziploc bag and add marinade. Toss to coat. Refrigerate 30 minutes.
Lightly spray the baking pan with cooking spray. Set oven to broil on 400°F for 15 minutes.
After 5 minutes, lay fish on the pan and place in position 2 of the oven.
Cook 10 minutes, or until fish flakes easily with a fork. Turn fish over and brush with marinade halfway through cooking time.
Sprinkle with cilantro before serving.
Nutrition Info: Calories 328, Total Fat 24g, Saturated Fat 4g, Total Carbs 3g, Net Carbs 3g, Protein 25g, Sugar 1g, Fiber 0g, Sodium 137mg, Potassium 510mg, Phosphorus 284mg

348. BAKED LEMON SWORDFISH
Servings: 2
Cooking Time: 10 Minutes
INGREDIENTS:
- 12 oz swordfish fillets
- 1/8 tsp crushed red pepper
- 1 garlic clove, minced
- 2 tsp fresh parsley, chopped
- 3 tbsp olive oil
- 1/2 tsp lemon zest, grated
- 1/2 tsp ginger, grated

DIRECTIONS:
Fit the Cosori oven with the rack in position
In a small bowl, mix 2 tbsp oil, lemon zest, red pepper, ginger, garlic, and parsley.
Season fish fillets with salt.
Heat remaining oil in a pan over medium-high heat.
Place fish fillets in the pan and cook until browned, about 2-3 minutes.
Transfer fish fillets in a baking dish.
Set to bake at 400 F for 15 minutes. After 5 minutes place the baking dish in the preheated oven.
Pour oil mixture over fish fillets and serve.
Nutrition Info: Calories 449 Fat 29.8 g Carbohydrates 1.1 g Sugar 0.1 g Protein 43.4 g Cholesterol 85 mg

349. PERFECT BAKED COD
Servings: 4
Cooking Time: 15 Minutes
INGREDIENTS:
- 4 cod fillets
- 1 tbsp olive oil
- 1 tsp dried parsley
- 2 tsp paprika
- 3/4 cup parmesan cheese, grated
- 1/4 tsp salt

DIRECTIONS:
Fit the Cosori oven with the rack in position
In a shallow dish, mix parmesan cheese, paprika, parsley, and salt.
Brush fish fillets with oil and coat with parmesan cheese mixture.
Place coated fish fillets into the baking dish.
Set to bake at 400 F for 20 minutes. After 5 minutes place the baking dish in the preheated oven.
Serve and enjoy.
Nutrition Info: Calories 160 Fat 8.1 g Carbohydrates 1.2 g Sugar 0.1 g Protein 21.7 g Cholesterol 56 mg

350. SALMON BEANS & MUSHROOMS
Servings: 6
Cooking Time: 25 Minutes
INGREDIENTS:
- 4 salmon fillets
- 2 tbsp fresh parsley, minced
- 1/4 cup fresh lemon juice
- 1 tsp garlic, minced
- 1 tbsp olive oil
- 1/2 lb mushrooms, sliced
- 1/2 lb green beans, trimmed
- 1/2 cup parmesan cheese, grated
- Pepper
- Salt

DIRECTIONS:
Fit the Cosori oven with the rack in position
Heat oil in a small saucepan over medium-high heat.
Add garlic and sauté for 30 seconds.
Remove from heat and stir in lemon juice, parsley, pepper, and salt.
Arrange fish fillets, mushrooms, and green beans in baking pan and drizzle with oil mixture.
Sprinkle with grated parmesan cheese.
Set to bake at 400 F for 30 minutes. After 5 minutes place the baking pan in the preheated oven.
Serve and enjoy.
Nutrition Info: Calories 225 Fat 11.5 g Carbohydrates 4.7 g Sugar 1.4 g Protein 27.5 g Cholesterol 58 mg

351. EASY SALMON CAKES
Servings: 2
Cooking Time: 15 Minutes + Cooling Time
INGREDIENTS:
- 8 oz salmon, cooked
- 1 ½ oz potatoes, mashed
- A handful of capers
- A handful of parsley, chopped
- Zest of 1 lemon
- 1 ¾ oz plain flour

DIRECTIONS:
Carefully flake the salmon in a bowl. Stir in zest, capers, dill, and mashed potatoes. Shape the mixture into cakes and dust them with flour. Place in the fridge for 60 minutes.
Preheat your Cosori to 350 F on Air Fry function. Remove the cakes from the fridges and arrange them on the greased basket. Fit in the bak-

ing tray and cook for 10 minutes, shaing once halfway through. Serve chilled.

352. FISH SPICY LEMON KEBAB
INGREDIENTS:
- 1 lb. boneless fish roughly chopped
- 3 onions chopped
- 5 green chilies-roughly chopped
- 1 ½ tbsp. ginger paste
- 1 ½ tsp garlic paste
- 1 ½ tsp salt
- 3 tsp lemon juice
- 2 tsp garam masala
- 4 tbsp. chopped coriander
- 3 tbsp. cream
- 2 tbsp. coriander powder
- 4 tbsp. fresh mint chopped
- 3 tbsp. chopped capsicum
- 3 eggs
- 2 ½ tbsp. white sesame seeds

DIRECTIONS:
Take all the ingredients mentioned under the first heading and mix them in a bowl. Grind them thoroughly to make a smooth paste. Take the eggs in a different bowl and beat them. Add a pinch of salt and leave them aside. Take a flat plate and in it mix the sesame seeds and breadcrumbs. Mold the fish mixture into small balls and flatten them into round and flat kebabs. Dip these kebabs in the egg and salt mixture and then in the mixture of breadcrumbs and sesame seeds. Leave these kebabs in the fridge for an hour or so to set.
Pre heat the Cosori oven at 160 degrees Fahrenheit for around 5 minutes. Place the kebabs in the basket and let them cook for another 25 minutes at the same temperature. Turn the kebabs over in between the cooking process to get a uniform cook. Serve the kebabs with mint sauce.

353. SPEEDY FRIED SCALLOPS
Servings: 4
Cooking Time: 5 Minutes
INGREDIENTS:
- 12 fresh scallops
- 3 tbsp flour
- Salt and black pepper to taste
- 1 egg, lightly beaten
- 1 cup breadcrumbs

DIRECTIONS:
Coat the scallops with flour. Dip into the egg, then into the breadcrumbs. Spray with olive oil and arrange them on the basket. Fit in the baking tray and cook for 6 minutes at 360 F on Air Fry function, turning once halfway through cooking. Serve.

354. LOBSTER SPICY LEMON KEBAB
INGREDIENTS:
- 1 lb. lobster (Shelled and cubed)
- 3 onions chopped
- 5 green chilies-roughly chopped
- 1 ½ tbsp. ginger paste
- 1 ½ tsp garlic paste
- 1 ½ tsp salt
- 3 tsp lemon juice
- 2 tsp garam masala
- 4 tbsp. chopped coriander
- 3 tbsp. cream
- 2 tbsp. coriander powder
- 4 tbsp. fresh mint chopped
- 3 tbsp. chopped capsicum

- 3 eggs
- 2 ½ tbsp. white sesame seeds

DIRECTIONS:
Take all the ingredients mentioned under the first heading and mix them in a bowl. Grind them thoroughly to make a smooth paste.
Take the eggs in a different bowl and beat them. Add a pinch of salt and leave them aside.
Take a flat plate and in it mix the sesame seeds and breadcrumbs.
Dip the lobster cubes in the egg and salt mixture and then in the mixture of
breadcrumbs and sesame seeds. Leave these kebabs in the fridge for an hour or so to set.
Pre heat the Cosori oven at 160 degrees Fahrenheit for around 5 minutes. Place the kebabs in the basket and let them cook for another 25 minutes at the same temperature. Turn the kebabs over in between the cooking process to get a uniform cook. Serve the kebabs with mint sauce.

355. PARSLEY CATFISH FILLETS
Servings: 4
Cooking Time: 25 Minutes
INGREDIENTS:
- 4 catfish fillets, rinsed and dried
- ¼ cup seasoned fish fry
- 1 tbsp olive oil
- 1 tbsp fresh parsley, chopped

DIRECTIONS:
Add seasoned fish fry and fillets in a large Ziploc bag; massage well to coat. Place the fillets in the Cosori basket and cook for 14-16 minutes at 360 F on AirFry function. Top with parsley.

356. GRILLED SOY SALMON FILLETS
Servings: 4
Cooking Time: 8 Minutes
INGREDIENTS:
- 4 salmon fillets
- 1/4 teaspoon ground black pepper
- 1/2 teaspoon cayenne pepper
- 1/2 teaspoon salt
- 1 teaspoon onion powder
- 1 tablespoon fresh lemon juice
- 1/2 cup soy sauce
- 1/2 cup water
- 1 tablespoon honey
- 2 tablespoons extra-virgin olive oil

DIRECTIONS:
Preparing the Ingredients. Firstly, pat the salmon fillets dry using kitchen towels. Season the salmon with black pepper, cayenne pepper, salt, and onion powder.
To make the marinade, combine together the lemon juice, soy sauce, water, honey, and olive oil. Marinate the salmon for at least 2 hours in your refrigerator.
Arrange the fish fillets on a grill basket in your Cosori air fryer oven.
Air Frying. Bake at 330 degrees for 8 to 9 minutes, or until salmon fillets are easily flaked with a fork.
Work with batches and serve warm.

357. CHEESE CARP FRIES
INGREDIENTS:
- 1 lb. carp Oregano Fingers
- ingredients for the marinade:
- 1 tbsp. olive oil
- 1 tsp. mixed herbs
- ½ tsp. red chili flakes
- A pinch of salt to taste
- 1 tbsp. lemon juice

- For the garnish:
- 1 cup melted cheddar cheese

DIRECTIONS:

Take all the ingredients mentioned under the heading "For the marinade" and mix them well. Cook the carp Oregano Fingers and soak them in the marinade.

Pre heat the Cosori oven for around 5 minutes at 300 Fahrenheit. Take out the basket of the fryer and place the carp in them. Close the basket. Now keep the fryer at 220 Fahrenheit for 20 or 25 minutes.

In between the process, toss the fries twice or thrice so that they get cooked properly. Towards the end of the cooking process (the last 2 minutes or so), sprinkle the melted cheddar cheese over the fries and serve hot.

358. BASIL TOMATO SALMON

Servings: 2
Cooking Time: 20 Minutes

INGREDIENTS:

- 2 salmon fillets
- 1 tomato, sliced
- 1 tbsp dried basil
- 2 tbsp parmesan cheese, grated
- 1 tbsp olive oil

DIRECTIONS:

Fit the Cosori oven with the rack in position
Place salmon fillets in a baking dish.
Sprinkle basil on top of salmon fillets.
Arrange tomato slices on top of salmon fillets. Drizzle with oil and top with cheese.
Set to bake at 375 F for 25 minutes. After 5 minutes place the baking dish in the preheated oven.
Serve and enjoy.

Nutrition Info: Calories 324 Fat 19.6 g Carbohydrates 1.5 g Sugar 0.8 g Protein 37.1 g Cholesterol 83 mg

359. CARP FLAT CAKES

INGREDIENTS:

- 2 tbsp. garam masala
- 1 lb. fileted carp
- 3 tsp ginger finely chopped
- 1-2 tbsp. fresh coriander leaves
- 2 or 3 green chilies finely chopped
- 1 ½ tbsp. lemon juice
- Salt and pepper to taste

DIRECTIONS:

Mix the ingredients in a clean bowl and add water to it. Make sure that the paste is not too watery but is enough to apply on the sides of the carp filets.

Pre heat the Cosori oven at 160 degrees Fahrenheit for 5 minutes. Place the French Cuisine Galettes in the fry basket and let them cook for another 25 minutes at the same temperature. Keep rolling them over to get a uniform cook. Serve either with mint sauce or ketchup.

360. CRISPY COATED SCALLOPS

Servings: 4
Cooking Time: 10 Minutes

INGREDIENTS:

- Nonstick cooking spray
- 1 lb. sea scallops, patted dry
- 1 teaspoon onion powder
- ½ tsp pepper
- 1 egg
- 1 tbsp. water
- ¼ cup Italian bread crumbs
- Paprika

- 1 tbsp. fresh lemon juice

DIRECTIONS:

Lightly spray fryer basket with cooking spray. Place baking pan in position 2 of the oven.
Sprinkle scallops with onion powder and pepper.
In a shallow dish, whisk together egg and water.
Place bread crumbs in a separate shallow dish.
Dip scallops in egg then bread crumbs coating them lightly. Place in fryer basket and lightly spray with cooking spray. Sprinkle with paprika. Place the basket on the baking pan and set oven to air fryer on 400°F. Bake 10-12 minutes until scallops are firm on the inside and golden brown on the outside. Drizzle with lemon juice and serve.

Nutrition Info: Calories 122, Total Fat 2g, Saturated Fat 1g, Total Carbs 10g, Net Carbs 9g, Protein 16g, Sugar 1g, Fiber 1g, Sodium 563mg, Potassium 282mg, Phosphorus 420mg

361. COCONUT SHRIMP

Servings: 4
Cooking Time: 5 Minutes

INGREDIENTS:

- 1 (8-ounce) can crushed pineapple
- ½ cup sour cream
- ¼ cup pineapple preserves
- 2 egg whites
- ⅔ cup cornstarch
- ⅔ cup sweetened coconut
- 1 cup panko bread crumbs
- 1 pound uncooked large shrimp, thawed if frozen, deveined and shelled
- Olive oil for misting

DIRECTIONS:

Preparing the Ingredients. Drain the crushed pineapple well, reserving the juice. In a small bowl, combine the pineapple, sour cream, and preserves, and mix well. Set aside. In a shallow bowl, beat the egg whites with 2 tablespoons of the reserved pineapple liquid. Place the cornstarch on a plate. Combine the coconut and bread crumbs on another plate. Dip the shrimp into the cornstarch, shake it off, then dip into the egg white mixture and finally into the coconut mixture. Place the shrimp in the air fryer rack/basket and mist with oil.

Air Frying. Air-fry for 5 to 7 minutes or until the shrimp are crisp and golden brown.

Nutrition Info: CALORIES: 524; FAT: 14G; PROTEIN:33G; FIBER:4G

362. OYSTER CLUB SANDWICH

INGREDIENTS:

- 2 slices of white bread
- 1 tbsp. softened butter
- ½ lb. shelled oyster
- 1 small capsicum
- For Barbeque Sauce:
- ¼ tbsp. Worcestershire sauce
- ½ tsp. olive oil
- ½ flake garlic crushed
- ¼ cup chopped onion
- ¼ tsp. mustard powder
- 1 tbsp. tomato ketchup
- ½ tbsp. sugar
- ¼ tbsp. red chili sauce
- ½ cup water.
- A pinch of salt and black pepper to taste

DIRECTIONS:

Take the slices of bread and remove the edges. Now cut the slices horizontally. Cook the ingredients for the sauce and wait till it thickens. Now, add the oyster to the sauce and stir till it obtains the flavors.
Roast the capsicum and peel the skin off. Cut the capsicum into slices. Mix the ingredients together and apply it to the bread slices. Pre-heat

the Cosori oven for 5 minutes at 300 Fahrenheit. Open the basket of the Fryer and place the prepared Classic Sandwiches in it such that no two Classic Sandwiches are touching each other. Now keep the fryer at 250 degrees for around 15 minutes.

Turn the Classic Sandwiches in between the cooking process to cook both slices. Serve the Classic Sandwiches with tomato ketchup or mint sauce.

363. PARMESAN-CRUSTED SALMON PATTIES

Servings: 4
Cooking Time: 13 Minutes
INGREDIENTS:
- 1 pound (454 g) salmon, chopped into ½-inch pieces
- 2 tablespoons coconut flour
- 2 tablespoons grated Parmesan cheese
- 1½ tablespoons milk
- ½ white onion, peeled and finely chopped
- ½ teaspoon butter, at room temperature
- ½ teaspoon chipotle powder
- ½ teaspoon dried parsley flakes
- ⅓ teaspoon ground black pepper
- ⅓ teaspoon smoked cayenne pepper
- 1 teaspoon fine sea salt

DIRECTIONS:
Put all the ingredients for the salmon patties in a bowl and stir to combine well.

Scoop out 2 tablespoons of the salmon mixture and shape into a patty with your palm, about ½ inch thick. Repeat until all the mixture is used. Transfer to the refrigerator for about 2 hours until firm.

When ready, arrange the salmon patties in the baking pan.

Slide the baking pan into Rack Position 1, select Convection Bake, set temperature to 395°F (202°C), and set time to 13 minutes.

Flip the patties halfway through the cooking time.

When cooking is complete, the patties should be golden brown. Remove from the oven and cool for 5 minutes before serving.

364. HONEY GLAZED SALMON

Servings: 4
Cooking Time: 8 Minutes
INGREDIENTS:
- 4 salmon fillets
- 2 tsp soy sauce
- 1 tbsp honey
- Pepper
- Salt

DIRECTIONS:
Fit the Cosori oven with the rack in position 2.

Brush salmon with soy sauce and season with pepper and salt.

Place salmon in the air fryer basket then place an air fryer basket in the baking pan.

Place a baking pan on the oven rack. Set to air fry at 375 F for 8 minutes. Brush salmon with honey and serve.

Nutrition Info: Calories 253 Fat 11 g Carbohydrates 4.6 g Sugar 4.4 g Protein 34.7 g Cholesterol 78 mg

365. LEMON SALMON

Servings: 2
Cooking Time: 20 Minutes
INGREDIENTS:
- 2 salmon fillets
- Salt to taste
- Zest of 1 lemon

DIRECTIONS:
Rub the fillets with salt and lemon zest. Place them in the frying basket and spray with cooking spray. Press Start and cook the salmon in the

preheated Cosori oven for 14 minutes at 360 F on AirFry function. Serve with steamed asparagus and a drizzle of lemon juice.

366. EASY SHRIMP FAJITAS

Servings: 10
Cooking Time: 20 Minutes
INGREDIENTS:
- 1 lb shrimp
- 1 tbsp olive oil
- 2 bell peppers, diced
- 2 tbsp taco seasoning
- 1/2 cup onion, diced

DIRECTIONS:
Fit the Cosori oven with the rack in position 2.

Add shrimp and remaining ingredients into the bowl and toss well.

Add shrimp mixture to the air fryer basket then place an air fryer basket in baking pan.

Place a baking pan on the oven rack. Set to air fry at 390 F for 20 minutes.

Serve and enjoy.

Nutrition Info: Calories 76 Fat 2.2 g Carbohydrates 3 g Sugar 1.4 g Protein 10.6 g Cholesterol 96 mg

367. PANKO-CRUSTED TILAPIA

Servings: 3
Cooking Time: 10 Minutes
INGREDIENTS:
- 2 tsp. Italian seasoning
- 2 tsp. lemon pepper
- 1/3 C. panko breadcrumbs
- 1/3 C. egg whites
- 1/3 C. almond flour
- 3 tilapia fillets
- Olive oil

DIRECTIONS:
Preparing the Ingredients. Place panko, egg whites, and flour into separate bowls. Mix lemon pepper and Italian seasoning in with breadcrumbs.

Pat tilapia fillets dry. Dredge in flour, then egg, then breadcrumb mixture.

Air Frying. Add to the Oven rack/basket and spray lightly with olive oil.

Place the Rack on the middle-shelf of the Cosori air fryer oven.

Cook 10-11 minutes at 400 degrees, making sure to flip halfway through cooking.

Nutrition Info: CALORIES: 256; FAT: 9G; PROTEIN:39G; SUGAR:5G

368. OLD BAY CRAB CAKES

Servings: 4
Cooking Time: 20 Minutes
INGREDIENTS:
- 2 slices dried bread, crusts removed
- Small amount of milk
- 1 tablespoon mayonnaise
- 1 tablespoon Worcestershire sauce
- 1 tablespoon baking powder
- 1 tablespoon parsley flakes
- 1 teaspoon Old Bay® Seasoning
- 1/4 teaspoon salt
- 1 egg
- 1 pound lump crabmeat

DIRECTIONS:
Preparing the Ingredients. Crush your bread over a large bowl until it is broken down into small pieces. Add milk and stir until bread crumbs are moistened. Mix in mayo and Worcestershire sauce. Add remaining ingredients and mix well. Shape into 4 patties.

Air Frying. Cook at 360 degrees for 20 minutes, flip half way through.

Nutrition Info: CALORIES: 165; CARBS:5.8; FAT: 4.5G; PRO-TEIN:24G; FIBER:0G

369. EASY BLACKENED SHRIMP

Servings: 6
Cooking Time: 10 Minutes

INGREDIENTS:
- 1 lb shrimp, deveined
- 1 tbsp olive oil
- 1/4 tsp pepper
- 2 tsp blackened seasoning
- 1/4 tsp salt

DIRECTIONS:
Fit the Cosori oven with the rack in position
Toss shrimp with oil, pepper, blackened seasoning, and salt.
Transfer shrimp into the baking pan.
Set to bake at 400 F for 15 minutes. After 5 minutes place the baking pan in the preheated oven.
Serve and enjoy.
Nutrition Info: Calories 167 Fat 4.3 g Carbohydrates 10.5 g Sugar 0 g Protein 20.6 g Cholesterol 159 mg

370. LOBSTER GRANDMA'S EASY TO COOK WON-TONS

INGREDIENTS:
- 1 ½ cup all-purpose flour
- ½ tsp. salt
- 5 tbsp. water
- For filling:
- 2 cups minced lobster
- 2 tbsp. oil
- 2 tsp. ginger-garlic paste
- 2 tsp. soya sauce
- 2 tsp. vinegar

DIRECTIONS:
Squeeze the dough and cover it with plastic wrap and set aside. Next, cook the ingredients for the filling and try to ensure that the lobster is covered well with the sauce.
Roll the dough and place the filling in the center. Now, wrap the dough to cover the filling and pinch the edges together.
Pre heat the Cosori oven at 200° F for 5 minutes. Place the wontons in the fry basket and close it. Let them cook at the same temperature for another 20 minutes. Recommended sides are chili sauce or ketchup.

371. AIR-FRIED SCALLOPS

Servings: 2
Cooking Time: 12 Minutes

INGREDIENTS:
- ⅓ cup shallots, chopped
- 1½ tablespoons olive oil
- 1½ tablespoons coconut aminos
- 1 tablespoon Mediterranean seasoning mix
- ½ tablespoon balsamic vinegar
- ½ teaspoon ginger, grated
- 1 clove garlic, chopped
- 1 pound (454 g) scallops, cleanedCooking spray
- Belgian endive, for garnish

DIRECTIONS:
Place all the ingredients except the scallops and Belgian endive in a small skillet over medium heat and stir to combine. Let this mixture simmer for about 2 minutes.
Remove the mixture from the skillet to a large bowl and set aside to cool.
Add the scallops, coating them all over, then transfer to the refrigerator to marinate for at least 2 hours.

When ready, place the scallops in the air fryer basket in a single layer and spray with cooking spray.
Put the air fryer basket on the baking pan and slide into Rack Position 2, select Air Fry, set temperature to 345ºF (174ºC), and set time to 10 minutes.
Flip the scallops halfway through the cooking time.
When cooking is complete, the scallops should be tender and opaque. Remove from the oven and serve garnished with the Belgian endive.

372. TILAPIA MEUNIÈRE WITH VEGETABLES

Servings: 4
Cooking Time: 20 Minutes
INGREDIENTS:
- 10 ounces (283 g) Yukon Gold potatoes, sliced ¼-inch thick
- 5 tablespoons unsalted butter, melted, divided
- 1 teaspoon kosher salt, divided
- 4 (8-ounce / 227-g) tilapia fillets
- ½ pound (227 g) green beans, trimmed
- Juice of 1 lemon
- 2 tablespoons chopped fresh parsley, for garnish

DIRECTIONS:
In a large bowl, drizzle the potatoes with 2 tablespoons of melted butter and ¼ teaspoon of kosher salt. Transfer the potatoes to the baking pan.
Slide the baking pan into Rack Position 2, select Roast, set temperature to 375ºF (190ºC), and set time to 20 minutes.
Meanwhile, season both sides of the fillets with ½ teaspoon of kosher salt. Put the green beans in the medium bowl and sprinkle with the remaining ¼ teaspoon of kosher salt and 1 tablespoon of butter, tossing to coat.
After 10 minutes, remove from the oven and push the potatoes to one side. Put the fillets in the middle of the pan and add the green beans on the other side. Drizzle the remaining 2 tablespoons of butter over the fillets. Return the pan to the oven and continue cooking, or until the fish flakes easily with a fork and the green beans are crisp-tender.
When cooked, remove from the oven. Drizzle the lemon juice over the fillets and sprinkle the parsley on top for garnish. Serve hot.

373. ASIAN-INSPIRED SWORDFISH STEAKS

Servings: 4
Cooking Time: 8 Minutes
INGREDIENTS:
- 4 (4-ounce / 113-g) swordfish steaks
- ½ teaspoon toasted sesame oil
- 1 jalapeño pepper, finely minced
- 2 garlic cloves, grated
- 2 tablespoons freshly squeezed lemon juice
- 1 tablespoon grated fresh ginger
- ½ teaspoon Chinese five-spice powder
- ⅛ teaspoon freshly ground black pepper

DIRECTIONS:
On a clean work surface, place the swordfish steaks and brush both sides of the fish with the sesame oil.
Combine the jalapeño, garlic, lemon juice, ginger, five-spice powder, and black pepper in a small bowl and stir to mix well. Rub the mixture all over the fish until completely coated. Allow to sit for 10 minutes.
When ready, arrange the swordfish steaks in the air fryer basket.
Put the air fryer basket on the baking pan and slide into Rack Position 2, select Air Fry, set temperature to 380ºF (193ºC), and set time to 8 minutes.
Flip the steaks halfway through.
When cooking is complete, remove from the oven and cool for 5 minutes before serving.

374. SQUAB OREGANO FINGERS

INGREDIENTS:

- ½ lb. squab Oregano Fingers
- 2 cups of dry breadcrumbs
- 1 cup oil for frying
- 1 ½ tbsp. ginger-garlic paste
- 3 tbsp. lemon juice
- 2 tsp salt
- 1 ½ tsp pepper powder
- 1 tsp red chili flakes or to taste
- 3 eggs
- 5 tbsp. corn flour
- 2 tsp tomato ketchup

DIRECTIONS:

Make the marinade and transfer the Oregano Fingers into the marinade. Leave them on a plate to dry for fifteen minutes. Now cover the Oregano Fingers with the crumbs and set aside to dry for fifteen minutes.

Pre heat the Cosori oven at 160 degrees Fahrenheit for 5 minutes or so. Keep the fish in the fry basket now and close it properly. Let the Oregano Fingers cook at the same temperature for another 25 minutes. In between the cooking process, toss the fish once in a while to avoid burning the food. Serve either with tomato ketchup or chili sauce. Mint sauce also works well with the fish.

375. FLAVORFUL HERB SALMON

Servings: 4
Cooking Time: 15 Minutes
INGREDIENTS:
- 1 lb salmon fillets
- 1/2 tbsp dried rosemary
- 1 tbsp olive oil
- 1/4 tsp dried basil
- 1 tbsp dried chives
- 1/4 tsp dried thyme
- Pepper
- Salt

DIRECTIONS:

Fit the Cosori oven with the rack in position 2.
Place salmon skin side down in air fryer basket then place an air fryer basket in baking pan.
Mix olive oil, thyme, basil, chives, and rosemary in a small bowl.
Brush salmon with oil mixture.
Place a baking pan on the oven rack. Set to air fry at 400 F for 15 minutes.
Serve and enjoy.
Nutrition Info: Calories 182 Fat 10.6 g Carbohydrates 0.4 g Sugar 0 g Protein 22.1 g Cholesterol 50 mg

376. ITALIAN COD

Servings: 4
Cooking Time: 20 Minutes
INGREDIENTS:
- 1 1/2 lbs cod fillet
- 1/4 cup olives, sliced
- 1 lb cherry tomatoes, halved
- 2 garlic cloves, crushed
- 1 small onion, chopped
- 1 tbsp olive oil
- 1/4 cup of water
- 1 tsp Italian seasoning
- Pepper
- Salt

DIRECTIONS:

Fit the Cosori oven with the rack in position
Place fish fillets, olives, tomatoes, garlic, and onion in a baking dish. Drizzle with oil.
Sprinkle with Italian seasoning, pepper, and salt. Pour water into the dish.

Set to bake at 400 F for 25 minutes. After 5 minutes place the baking dish in the preheated oven.
Serve and enjoy.
Nutrition Info: Calories 210 Fat 6.5 g Carbohydrates 7.2 g Sugar 3.8 g Protein 31.7 g Cholesterol 84 mg

377. PRAWN MOMO'S RECIPE

INGREDIENTS:
- 1 ½ cup all-purpose flour
- ½ tsp. salt
- 5 tbsp. water
- For filling:
- 2 cups minced prawn
- 2 tbsp. oil
- 2 tsp. ginger-garlic paste
- 2 tsp. soya sauce
- 2 tsp. vinegar

DIRECTIONS:

Squeeze the dough and cover it with plastic wrap and set aside. Next, cook the ingredients for the filling and try to ensure that the prawn is covered well with the sauce. Roll the dough and cut it into a square.

Place the filling in the center. Now, wrap the dough to cover the filling and pinch the edges together. Pre heat the Cosori oven at 200° F for 5 minutes. Place the wontons in the fry basket and close it. Let them cook at the same temperature for another 20 minutes. Recommended sides are chili sauce or ketchup.

378. AIR FRIED HADDOCK FILETS

Servings: 8
Cooking Time: 20 Minutes
INGREDIENTS:
- Nonstick cooking spray
- 2 egg whites
- ½ tsp dill
- ½ tsp pepper
- 1 cup cornflakes, crushed
- 2 lbs. haddock fillets, cut in 8 pieces

DIRECTIONS:

Place baking pan in position 2 of the oven. Lightly spray fryer basket with cooking spray.
In a shallow bowl, whisk together egg whites, dill, and pepper.
Place crushed cornflakes in a separate shallow dish.
Dip fish in egg mixture, then cornflakes, coating completely. Place in fryer basket.
Place basket on the baking pan and set oven to air fryer on 400°F. Cook 18-20 minutes, turning over halfway through, until fish flakes easily with a fork. Serve.
Nutrition Info: Calories 193, Total Fat 1g, Saturated Fat 0g, Total Carbs 7g, Net Carbs 7g, Protein 39g, Sugar 1g, Fiber 0g, Sodium 568mg, Potassium 692mg, Phosphorus 524mg

379. ORANGE FISH FILLETS

Servings: 2
Cooking Time: 25 Minutes
INGREDIENTS:
- 1 lb salmon fillets
- 1 orange juice
- 1 orange zest, grated
- 2 tbsp honey
- 3 tbsp soy sauce

DIRECTIONS:

Fit the Cosori oven with the rack in position
In a small bowl, whisk together honey, soy sauce, orange juice, and orange zest.

Place salmon fillets in a baking dish and pour honey mixture over salmon fillets.

Set to bake at 425 F for 30 minutes. After 5 minutes place the baking dish in the preheated oven.

Serve and enjoy.

Nutrition Info: Calories 399 Fat 14.1 g Carbohydrates 24.4 g Sugar 21.3 g Protein 45.9 g Cholesterol 100 mg

380. ITALIAN SALMON

Servings: 4
Cooking Time: 20 Minutes
INGREDIENTS:
- 1 3/4 lbs salmon fillet
- 1/4 cup sun-dried tomatoes, drained
- 1 tbsp fresh dill, chopped
- 1/4 cup capers
- 1/4 cup olives, pitted and chopped
- 1/3 cup basil pesto
- 1/3 cup artichoke hearts
- 1 tsp paprika
- 1/4 tsp salt

DIRECTIONS:
Fit the Cosori oven with the rack in position
Arrange salmon fillet in a baking pan and season with paprika and salt. Pour remaining ingredients on top of salmon.
Set to bake at 400 F for 25 minutes. After 5 minutes place the baking pan in the preheated oven.
Serve and enjoy.
Nutrition Info: Calories 286 Fat 13.4 g Carbohydrates 3.6 g Sugar 0.5 g Protein 39.6 g Cholesterol 88 mg

381. DELIGHTFUL CATFISH FILLETS

Servings: 4
Cooking Time: 25 Minutes
INGREDIENTS:
- 4 catfish fillets
- ¼ cup seasoned fish fry
- 1 tbsp olive oil
- 1 tbsp parsley, chopped

DIRECTIONS:
Add seasoned fish fry and catfish fillets in a large Ziploc bag and massage well to coat. Place the fillets in your Cosori Air Fryer basket and fit in the baking tray; cook for 10 minutes at 360 F on Air Fry function. Flip the fish and cook for 2-3 more minutes. Top with parsley and serve.

382. CAJUN AND LEMON PEPPER COD

Servings: 2 Cod Fillets
Cooking Time: 12 Minutes
INGREDIENTS:
- 1 tablespoon Cajun seasoning
- 1 teaspoon salt
- ½ teaspoon lemon pepper
- ½ teaspoon freshly ground black pepper
- 2 (8-ounce / 227-g) cod fillets, cut to fit into the air fryer basket
- Cooking spray
- 2 tablespoons unsalted butter, melted
- 1 lemon, cut into 4 wedges

DIRECTIONS:
Spritz the baking pan with cooking spray.
Thoroughly combine the Cajun seasoning, salt, lemon pepper, and black pepper in a small bowl. Rub this mixture all over the cod fillets until completely coated.
Put the fillets in the prepared pan and brush the melted butter over both sides of each fillet.
Slide the baking pan into Rack Position 1, select Convection Bake, set temperature to 360ºF (182ºC), and set time to 12 minutes.
Flip the fillets halfway through the cooking time.
When cooking is complete, the fish should flake apart with a fork. Remove the fillets from the oven and serve with fresh lemon wedges.

383. SPINACH & TUNA BALLS WITH RICOTTA

Servings: 4
Cooking Time: 20 Minutes
INGREDIENTS:
- 14 oz store-bought crescent dough
- ½ cup spinach, steamed
- 1 cup ricotta cheese, crumbled
- ¼ tsp garlic powder
- 1 tsp fresh oregano, chopped
- ½ cup canned tuna, drained

DIRECTIONS:
Preheat Cosori on AirFry function to 350 F. Roll the dough onto a lightly floured flat surface. Combine the ricotta cheese, spinach, tuna, oregano, salt, and garlic powder together in a bowl.

Cut the dough into 4 equal pieces. Divide the mixture between the dough pieces. Make sure to place the filling in the center. Fold the dough and secure with a fork. Place onto a lined baking dish and press Start. Cook for 12 minutes until lightly browned. Serve.

384. CRISPY CRAB LEGS

Servings: 4
Cooking Time: 15 Minutes
INGREDIENTS:
- 3 pounds crab legs
- ½ cup butter, melted

DIRECTIONS:
Preheat Cosori on Air Fry function to 380 F. Cover the crab legs with salted water and let them stay for a few minutes. Drain, pat them dry, and place the legs in the basket. Fit in the baking tray and brush with some butter; cook for 10 minutes, flipping once. Drizzle with the remaining butter and serve.

385. SPICY BAKED SHRIMP

Servings: 4
Cooking Time: 8 Minutes

INGREDIENTS:
- 2 lbs shrimp, peeled & deveined
- 1/4 tsp cayenne pepper
- 1 tsp garlic powder
- 2 tbsp chili powder
- 2 tbsp olive oil
- 1 tsp kosher salt

DIRECTIONS:
Fit the Cosori oven with the rack in position
Toss shrimp with remaining ingredients.
Transfer shrimp into the baking pan.
Set to bake at 400 F for 13 minutes. After 5 minutes place the baking pan in the preheated oven.
Serve and enjoy.
Nutrition Info: Calories 344 Fat 11.5 g Carbohydrates 6.1 g Sugar 0.5 g Protein 52.3 g Cholesterol 478 mg

386. BAKED BUTTERY SHRIMP

Servings: 4
Cooking Time: 15 Minutes
INGREDIENTS:
- 1 lb shrimp, peel & deveined
- 2 tsp garlic powder

- 2 tsp dry mustard
- 2 tsp cumin
- 2 tsp paprika
- 2 tsp black pepper
- 4 tsp cayenne pepper
- 1/2 cup butter, melted
- 2 tsp onion powder
- 1 tsp dried oregano
- 1 tsp dried thyme
- 3 tsp salt

DIRECTIONS:

Fit the Cosori oven with the rack in position
Add shrimp, butter, and remaining ingredients into the mixing bowl and toss well.
Transfer shrimp mixture into the baking pan.
Set to bake at 400 F for 20 minutes. After 5 minutes place the baking pan in the preheated oven.
Serve and enjoy.
Nutrition Info: Calories 372 Fat 26.2 g Carbohydrates 7.5 g Sugar 1.3 g Protein 27.6 g Cholesterol 300 mg

387. TOMATO GARLIC SHRIMP

Servings: 4
Cooking Time: 25 Minutes
INGREDIENTS:
- 1 lb shrimp, peeled
- 1 tbsp garlic, sliced
- 2 cups cherry tomatoes
- 1 tbsp olive oil
- Pepper
- Salt

DIRECTIONS:

Fit the Cosori oven with the rack in position
Add shrimp, oil, garlic, tomatoes, pepper, and salt into the large bowl and toss well.
Transfer shrimp mixture into the baking dish.
Set to bake at 400 F for 30 minutes. After 5 minutes place the baking dish in the preheated oven.
Serve and enjoy.
Nutrition Info: Calories 184 Fat 5.6 g Carbohydrates 5.9 g Sugar 2.4 g Protein 26.8 gCholesterol 239 mg

388. PAPRIKA SHRIMP

Servings: 4
Cooking Time: 10 Minutes
INGREDIENTS:
- 1 pound (454 g) tiger shrimp
- 2 tablespoons olive oil
- ½ tablespoon old bay seasoning
- ¼ tablespoon smoked paprika
- ¼ teaspoon cayenne pepper
- A pinch of sea salt

DIRECTIONS:

Toss all the ingredients in a large bowl until the shrimp are evenly coated.
Arrange the shrimp in the air fryer basket.
Put the air fryer basket on the baking pan and slide into Rack Position 2, select Air Fry, set temperature to 380°F (193°C), and set time to 10 minutes.
When cooking is complete, the shrimp should be pink and cooked through. Remove from the oven and serve hot.

389. BAKED GARLIC PAPRIKA HALIBUT

Servings: 4
Cooking Time: 12 Minutes

INGREDIENTS:
- 1 lb halibut fillets
- 1/2 tsp smoked paprika
- 1/4 cup olive oil
- 1/4 tsp garlic powder
- Pepper
- Salt

DIRECTIONS:

Fit the Cosori oven with the rack in position
Place fish fillets in a baking dish.
In a small bowl, mix together oil, garlic powder, paprika, pepper, and salt.
Brush fish fillets with oil mixture.
Set to bake at 425 F for 17 minutes. After 5 minutes place the baking dish in the preheated oven.
Serve and enjoy.
Nutrition Info: Calories 235 Fat 15.3 g Carbohydrates 0.3 g Sugar 0.1 g Protein 23.9 g Cholesterol 36 mg

390. LEMON-GARLIC BUTTER LOBSTER

Servings: 2
Cooking Time: 15 Minutes
INGREDIENTS:
- 4 oz lobster tails
- 1 tsp garlic, minced
- 1 tbsp butter
- Salt and black pepper to taste
- ½ tbsp lemon Juice

DIRECTIONS:

Add all the ingredients to a food processor except for lobster and blend well. Wash lobster and halve using a meat knife; clean the skin of the lobster and cover with the marinade.
  Preheat your Cosori to 380 F on Air Fry function. Place the lobster in the cooking basket and fit in the baking tray; cook for 10 minutes. Serve with fresh herbs.

391. SALMON FRITTERS

INGREDIENTS:
- 2 tbsp. garam masala
- 1 lb. fileted Salmon
- 3 tsp ginger finely chopped
- 1-2 tbsp. fresh coriander leaves
- 2 or 3 green chilies finely chopped
- 1 ½ tbsp. lemon juice
- Salt and pepper to taste

DIRECTIONS:

Mix the ingredients in a clean bowl.
Mold this mixture into round and flat French Cuisine Galettes.
Wet the French Cuisine Galettes slightly with water.
Pre heat the Cosori oven at 160 degrees Fahrenheit for 5 minutes. Place the French Cuisine Galettes in the fry basket and let them cook for another 25 minutes at the same temperature. Keep rolling them over to get a uniform cook. Serve either with mint sauce or ketchup.

392. CAJUN SALMON WITH LEMON

Servings: 1
Cooking Time: 10 Minutes
INGREDIENTS:
- 1 salmon fillet
- ¼ tsp brown sugar
- Juice of ½ lemon
- 1 tbsp cajun seasoning
- 2 lemon wedges

- 1 tbsp fresh parsley, chopped

DIRECTIONS:

Preheat Cosori on Bake function to 350 F. Combine sugar and lemon and coat in the salmon. Sprinkle with the Cajun seasoning as well. Place a parchment paper on a baking tray and press Start. Cook for 14-16 minutes. Serve with lemon wedges and chopped parsley.

393. PECAN-CRUSTED CATFISH FILLETS

Servings: 4

Cooking Time: 12 Minutes

INGREDIENTS:

- ½ cup pecan meal
- 1 teaspoon fine sea salt
- ¼ teaspoon ground black pepper
- 4 (4-ounce / 113-g) catfish fillets
- Avocado oil spray
- For Garnish (Optional):
- Fresh oregano
- Pecan halves

DIRECTIONS:

Spray the air fryer basket with avocado oil spray.

Combine the pecan meal, sea salt, and black pepper in a large bowl. Dredge each catfish fillet in the meal mixture, turning until well coated. Spritz the fillets with avocado oil spray, then transfer to the basket.

Put the air fryer basket on the baking pan and slide into Rack Position 2, select Air Fry, set temperature to 375ºF (190ºC), and set time to 12 minutes.

Flip the fillets halfway through the cooking time.

When cooking is complete, the fish should be cooked through and no longer translucent. Remove from the oven and sprinkle the oregano sprigs and pecan halves on top for garnish, if desired. Serve immediately.

394. FISH CLUB CLASSIC SANDWICH

INGREDIENTS:

- 2 slices of white bread
- 1 tbsp. softened butter
- 1 tin tuna
- 1 small capsicum
- For Barbeque Sauce:
- ¼ tbsp. Worcestershire sauce
- ½ tsp. olive oil
- ½ flake garlic crushed
- ¼ cup chopped onion
- ¼ tsp. mustard powder
- ½ tbsp. sugar
- ¼ tbsp. red chili sauce
- 1 tbsp. tomato ketchup
- ½ cup water.
- A pinch of salt and black pepper to taste

DIRECTIONS:

Take the slices of bread and remove the edges. Now cut the slices horizontally. Cook the ingredients for the sauce and wait till it thickens. Now, add the fish to the sauce and stir till it obtains the flavors. Roast the capsicum and peel the skin off. Cut the capsicum into slices.

Mix the ingredients together and apply it to the bread slices. Pre-heat the Cosori oven for 5 minutes at 300 Fahrenheit.

Open the basket of the Fryer and place the prepared Classic Sandwiches in it such that no two Classic Sandwiches are touching each other. Now keep the fryer at 250 degrees for around 15 minutes. Turn the Classic Sandwiches in between the cooking process to cook both slices. Serve the Classic Sandwiches with tomato ketchup or mint sauce.

395. LEMON PEPPER WHITE FISH FILLETS

Servings: 2

Cooking Time: 12 Minutes

INGREDIENTS:

- 12 oz white fish fillets
- 1/2 tsp lemon pepper seasoning
- Pepper
- Salt

DIRECTIONS:

Fit the Cosori oven with the rack in position 2.

Spray fish fillets with cooking spray and season with lemon pepper seasoning, pepper, and salt.

Place fish fillets in the air fryer basket then place an air fryer basket in the baking pan.

Place a baking pan on the oven rack. Set to air fry at 360 F for 12 minutes.

Serve and enjoy.

Nutrition Info: Calories 294 Fat 12.8 g Carbohydrates 0.4 g Sugar 0 g Protein 41.7 g Cholesterol 131 mg

396. BACON-WRAPPED SCALLOPS

Servings: 4

Cooking Time: 10 Minutes

INGREDIENTS:

- 8 slices bacon, cut in half
- 16 sea scallops, patted dry
- Cooking spray
- Salt and freshly ground black pepper, to taste
- 16 toothpicks, soaked in water for at least 30 minutes

DIRECTIONS:

On a clean work surface, wrap half of a slice of bacon around each scallop and secure with a toothpick.

Lay the bacon-wrapped scallops in the air fryer basket in a single layer. Spritz the scallops with cooking spray and sprinkle the salt and pepper to season.

Put the air fryer basket on the baking pan and slide into Rack Position 2, select Air Fry, set temperature to 370ºF (188ºC), and set time to 10 minutes.

Flip the scallops halfway through the cooking time.

When cooking is complete, the bacon should be cooked through and the scallops should be firm. Remove the scallops from the oven to a plate Serve warm.

397. PARMESAN SALMON & ASPARAGUS

Servings: 4

Cooking Time: 20 Minutes

INGREDIENTS:

- 4 salmon fillets
- 1 cup parmesan cheese, shredded
- 1 tbsp garlic, minced
- 3 tbsp olive oil
- 1 lb asparagus, ends trimmed
- 1/4 tsp pepper
- 1/4 tsp salt

DIRECTIONS:

Fit the Cosori oven with the rack in position

Place fish fillets and asparagus in a parchment-lined baking pan.

Brush fish fillets with olive oil. Season with pepper and salt.

Sprinkle with garlic and shredded parmesan cheese on top.

Set to bake at 400 F for 25 minutes. After 5 minutes place the baking pan in the preheated oven.

Serve and enjoy.

Nutrition Info: Calories 424 Fat 26.5 g Carbohydrates 6 g Sugar 2.2 g Protein 44.4 g Cholesterol 95 mg

398. MEDITERRANEAN SOLE

Servings: 6

Cooking Time: 20 Minutes

INGREDIENTS:
- Nonstick cooking spray
- 2 tbsp. olive oil
- 8 scallions, sliced thin
- 2 cloves garlic, diced fine
- 4 tomatoes, chopped
- ½ cup dry white wine
- 2 tbsp. fresh parsley, chopped fine
- 1 tsp oregano
- 1 tsp pepper
- 2 lbs. sole, cut in 6 pieces
- 4 oz. feta cheese, crumbled

DIRECTIONS:

Place the rack in position 1 of the oven. Spray an 8x11-inch baking dish with cooking spray.

Heat the oil in a medium skillet over medium heat. Add scallions and garlic and cook until tender, stirring frequently.

Add the tomatoes, wine, parsley, oregano, and pepper. Stir to mix. Simmer for 5 minutes, or until sauce thickens. Remove from heat.

Pour half the sauce on the bottom of the prepared dish. Lay fish on top then pour remaining sauce over the top. Sprinkle with feta.

Set the oven to bake on 400°F for 25 minutes. After 5 minutes, place the baking dish on the rack and cook 15-18 minutes or until fish flakes easily with a fork. Serve immediately.

Nutrition Info: Calories 220, Total Fat 12g, Saturated Fat 4g, Total Carbs 6g, Net Carbs 4g, Protein 22g, Sugar 4g, Fiber 2g, Sodium 631mg, Potassium 540mg, Phosphorus 478mg

399. MARYLAND CRAB CAKES

Servings: 6

Cooking Time: 10 Minutes

INGREDIENTS:
- Nonstick cooking spray
- 2 eggs
- 1 cup Panko bread crumbs
- 1 stalk celery, chopped
- 3 tbsp. mayonnaise
- 1 tsp Worcestershire sauce
- ¼ cup mozzarella cheese, grated
- 1 tsp Italian seasoning
- 1 tbsp. fresh parsley, chopped
- 1 tsp pepper
- ¾ lb. lump crabmeat, drained

DIRECTIONS:

Place baking pan in position 2 of the oven. Lightly spray the fryer basket with cooking spray.

In a large bowl, combine all ingredients except crab meat, mix well.

Fold in crab carefully so it retains some chunks. Form mixture into 12 patties.

Place patties in a single layer in the fryer basket. Place the basket on the baking pan.

Set oven to air fryer on 350°F for 10 minutes. Cook until golden brown, turning over halfway through cooking time. Serve immediately.

Nutrition Info: Calories 172, Total Fat 8g, Saturated Fat 2g, Total Carbs 14g, Net Carbs 13g, Protein 16g, Sugar 1g, Fiber 1g, Sodium 527mg, Potassium 290mg, Phosphorus 201mg

400. CRUSTY SCALLOPS

Servings: 4

Cooking Time: 20 Minutes

INGREDIENTS:
- 12 fresh scallops
- 3 tbsp flour
- Salt and black pepper to taste
- 1 egg, lightly beaten
- 1 cup breadcrumbs

DIRECTIONS:

Coat the scallops with flour. Dip into the egg, then into the breadcrumbs. Arrange them on the frying basket and spray with cooking spray. Cook for 12 minutes at 360 F on AirFry function.

401. SHRIMP MOMO'S RECIPE

INGREDIENTS:
- 1 ½ cup all-purpose flour
- ½ tsp. salt
- 5 tbsp. water
- For filling:
- 2 cups minced shrimp
- 2 tbsp. oil
- 2 tsp. ginger-garlic paste
- 2 tsp. soya sauce
- 2 tsp. vinegar

DIRECTIONS:

Squeeze the dough and cover it with plastic wrap and set aside. Next, cook the ingredients for the filling and try to ensure that the shrimp is covered well with the sauce. Roll the dough and cut it into a square. Place the filling in the center.

Now, wrap the dough to cover the filling and pinch the edges together. Pre heat the Cosori oven at 200° F for 5 minutes. Place the wontons in the fry basket and close it. Let them cook at the same temperature for another 20 minutes. Recommended sides are chili sauce or ketchup.

402. PAPRIKA BASIL BAKED BASA

Servings: 2

Cooking Time: 30 Minutes

INGREDIENTS:
- 2 basa fish fillets
- 4 lemon slices
- 1/8 tsp lemon juice
- 1/2 tbsp dried basil
- 1/2 tbsp sweet paprika
- 4 tbsp butter, melted
- 1/8 tsp salt

DIRECTIONS:

Fit the Cosori oven with the rack in position

Place fish fillets into the baking dish.

Pour remaining ingredients over fish fillets.

Set to bake at 350 F for 30 minutes. After 5 minutes place the baking dish in the preheated oven.

Serve and enjoy.

Nutrition Info: Calories 433 Fat 35.2 g Carbohydrates 6.5 g Sugar 3.4 g Protein 24.4 g Cholesterol 61 mg

403. GARLICKY COD FILLETS

Servings: 4

Cooking Time: 12 Minutes

INGREDIENTS:
- 1 teaspoon olive oil
- 4 cod fillets
- ¼ teaspoon fine sea salt
- ¼ teaspoon ground black pepper, or more to taste
- 1 teaspoon cayenne pepper
- ½ cup fresh Italian parsley, coarsely chopped
- ½ cup nondairy milk
- 1 Italian pepper, chopped
- 4 garlic cloves, minced
- 1 teaspoon dried basil
- ½ teaspoon dried oregano

DIRECTIONS:

Lightly coat the sides and bottom of the baking pan with the olive oil. Set aside.

In a large bowl, sprinkle the fillets with salt, black pepper, and cayenne pepper.

In a food processor, pulse the remaining ingredients until smoothly puréed.

Add the purée to the bowl of fillets and toss to coat, then transfer to the prepared baking pan.

Slide the baking pan into Rack Position 1, select Convection Bake, set temperature to 380ºF (193ºC), and set time to 12 minutes.

When cooking is complete, the fish should flake when pressed lightly with a fork. Remove from the oven and serve warm.

VEGETABLES RECIPES

404. LEMONY WAX BEANS

Prep time: 5 minutes | Cook time: 12 minutes | Serves 4

- 2 pounds (907 g) wax beans
- 2 tablespoons extra-virgin olive oil
- Salt and freshly ground black pepper, to taste
- Juice of ½ lemon, for serving

Line a baking sheet with aluminum foil.

Toss the wax beans with the olive oil in a large bowl. Lightly season with salt and pepper.

Spread out the wax beans on the sheet pan.

Select Roast, set temperature to 400ºF (205ºC), and set time to 12 minutes. Select Start to begin preheating.

Once preheated, place the baking sheet into the oven.

When done, the beans will be caramelized and tender. Remove from the oven to a plate and serve sprinkled with the lemon juice.

405. LEMONY BRUSSELS SPROUTS AND TOMATOES

Prep time: 15 minutes | Cook time: 20 minutes | Serves 4

- 1 pound (454 g) Brussels sprouts, trimmed and halved
- 1 tablespoon extra-virgin olive oil
- Sea Salt and freshly ground black pepper, to taste
- ½ cup sun-dried tomatoes, chopped
- 2 tablespoons freshly squeezed lemon juice
- 1 teaspoon lemon zest

Line a large baking sheet with aluminum foil.

Toss the Brussels sprouts with the olive oil in a large bowl. Sprinkle with salt and black pepper.

Spread the Brussels sprouts in a single layer on the baking sheet.

Select Roast, set temperature to 400ºF (205ºC), and set time to 20 minutes. Select Start to begin preheating.

Once preheated, place the baking sheet into the oven.

When done, the Brussels sprouts should be caramelized. Remove from the oven to a serving bowl, along with the tomatoes, lemon juice, and lemon zest. Toss to combine. Serve immediately.

406. MAPLE AND PECAN GRANOLA

Prep time: 5 minutes | Cook time: 20 minutes | Serves 4

- 1½ cups rolled oats
- ¼ cup maple syrup
- ¼ cup pecan pieces
- 1 teaspoon vanilla extract
- ½ teaspoon ground cinnamon

Line a baking sheet with parchment paper.

Mix together the oats, maple syrup, pecan pieces, vanilla, and cinnamon in a large bowl and stir until the oats and pecan pieces are completely coated. Spread the mixture evenly on the baking sheet.

Select Bake, set temperature to 300ºF (150ºC), and set time to 20 minutes. Select Start to begin preheating.

Once preheated, place the baking sheet into the oven. Stir once halfway through the cooking time.

When done, remove from the oven and cool for 30 minutes before serving. The granola may still be a bit soft right after removing, but it will gradually firm up as it cools.

407. SWEET AND SPICY BROCCOLI

Prep time: 10 minutes | Cook time: 15 to 20 minutes | Serves 4

- ½ teaspoon olive oil, plus more for greasing
- 1 pound (454 g) fresh broccoli, cut into florets
- ½ tablespoon minced garlic
- Salt, to taste
- Sauce:
- 1½ tablespoons soy sauce
- 2 teaspoons hot sauce or sriracha
- 1½ teaspoons honey
- 1 teaspoon white vinegar
- Freshly ground black pepper, to taste

Grease a perforated pan with olive oil.

Add the broccoli florets, ½ teaspoon of olive oil, and garlic to a large bowl and toss well. Season with salt to taste.

Put the broccoli in the perforated pan in a single layer.

Select Air Fry, set temperature to 400ºF (205ºC), and set time to 15 minutes. Select Start to begin preheating.

Once preheated, place the pan into the oven. Stir the broccoli florets three times during cooking.

Meanwhile, whisk together all the ingredients for the sauce in a small bowl until well incorporated. If the honey doesn't incorporate well, microwave the sauce for 10 to 20 seconds until the honey is melted.

When cooking is complete, the broccoli should be lightly browned and crispy. Continue cooking for 5 minutes, if desired. Remove from the oven to a serving bowl. Pour over the sauce and toss to combine. Add more salt and pepper, if needed. Serve warm.

408. ROASTED VEGETABLES WITH BASIL

Prep time: 15 minutes | Cook time: 20 minutes | Serves 2

- 1 small eggplant, halved and sliced
- 1 yellow bell pepper, cut into thick strips
- 1 red bell pepper, cut into thick strips
- 2 garlic cloves, quartered
- 1 red onion, sliced
- 1 tablespoon extra-virgin olive oil
- Salt and freshly ground black pepper, to taste
- ½ cup chopped fresh basil, for garnish
- Cooking spray

Grease a nonstick baking dish with cooking spray.

Place the eggplant, bell peppers, garlic, and red onion in the greased baking dish. Drizzle with the olive oil and toss to coat well. Spritz any uncoated surfaces with cooking spray.

Select Bake, set temperature to 350ºF (180ºC), and set time to 20 minutes. Select Start to begin preheating.

Once preheated, place the baking dish into the oven. Flip the vegetables halfway through the cooking time.

When done, remove from the oven and sprinkle with salt and pepper. Sprinkle the basil on top for garnish and serve.

409. CINNAMON CELERY ROOTS

Prep time: 10 minutes | Cook time: 20 minutes | Serves 4

- 2 celery roots, peeled and diced
- 1 teaspoon extra-virgin olive oil
- 1 teaspoon butter, melted
- ½ teaspoon ground cinnamon
- Sea salt and freshly ground black pepper, to taste

Line a baking sheet with aluminum foil.

Toss the celery roots with the olive oil in a large bowl until well coated. Transfer them to the prepared baking sheet.

Select Roast, set temperature to 350ºF (180ºC), and set time to 20 minutes. Select Start to begin preheating.

Once preheated, place the baking sheet into the oven.

When done, the celery roots should be very tender. Remove from the oven to a serving bowl. Stir in the butter and cinnamon and mash them with a potato masher until fluffy.

Season with salt and pepper to taste. Serve immediately.

410. CHEESY BROCCOLI TOTS

Prep time: 20 minutes | Cook time: 15 minutes | Serves 4

- 12 ounces (340 g) frozen broccoli, thawed, drained, and patted dry
- 1 large egg, lightly beaten
- ½ cup seasoned whole-wheat bread crumbs
- ¼ cup shredded reduced-fat sharp Cheddar cheese
- ¼ cup grated Parmesan cheese
- 1½ teaspoons minced garlic
- Salt and freshly ground black pepper, to taste
- Cooking spray

Spritz a perforated pan lightly with cooking spray.

Place the remaining ingredients into a food processor and process until the mixture resembles a coarse meal. Transfer the mixture to a bowl.

Using a tablespoon, scoop out the broccoli mixture and form into 24 oval "tater tot" shapes with your hands.

Put the tots in the prepared perforated pan in a single layer, spacing them 1 inch apart. Mist the tots lightly with cooking spray.

Select Air Fry, set temperature to 375ºF (190ºC), and set time to 15 minutes. Select Start to begin preheating.

Once preheated, place the pan into the oven. Flip the tots halfway through the cooking time.

When done, the tots will be lightly browned and crispy. Remove from the oven and serve on a plate.

411. PAPRIKA CAULIFLOWER

Prep time: 10 minutes | Cook time: 20 minutes | Serves 4

- 1 large head cauliflower, broken into small florets
- 2 teaspoons smoked paprika
- 1 teaspoon garlic powder
- Salt and freshly ground black pepper, to taste
- Cooking spray

Spray a perforated pan with cooking spray.

In a medium bowl, toss the cauliflower florets with the smoked paprika and garlic powder until evenly coated. Sprinkle with salt and pepper.

Place the cauliflower florets in the perforated pan and lightly mist with cooking spray.

Select Air Fry, set temperature to 400ºF (205ºC), and set time to 20 minutes. Select Start to begin preheating.

Once preheated, place the pan into the oven. Stir the cauliflower four times during cooking.

Remove the cauliflower from the oven and serve hot.

412. SPICY KUNG PAO TOFU

Prep time: 10 minutes | Cook time: 10 minutes | Serves 4

- ⅓ cup Asian-Style sauce
- 1 teaspoon cornstarch
- ½ teaspoon red pepper flakes, or more to taste
- 1 pound (454 g) firm or extra-firm tofu, cut into 1-inch cubes
- 1 small carrot, peeled and cut into ¼-inch-thick coins
- 1 small green bell pepper, cut into bite-size pieces
- 3 scallions, sliced, whites and green parts separated
- 3 tablespoons roasted unsalted peanuts

In a large bowl, whisk together the sauce, cornstarch, and red pepper flakes. Fold in the tofu, carrot, pepper, and the white parts of the scallions and toss to coat. Spread the mixture evenly on the sheet pan.

Select Roast, set temperature to 375ºF (190ºC), and set time to 10 minutes. Select Start to begin preheating.

Once preheated, place the pan into the oven. Stir the ingredients once halfway through the cooking time.

When done, remove the pan from the oven. Serve sprinkled with the peanuts and scallion greens.

413. ROASTED ASPARAGUS WITH EGGS AND TO-MATOES

Prep time: 10 minutes | Cook time: 12 minutes | Serves 4

- 2 pounds (907 g) asparagus, trimmed
- 3 tablespoons extra-virgin olive oil, divided
- 1 teaspoon kosher salt, divided
- 1 pint cherry tomatoes
- 4 large eggs
- ¼ teaspoon freshly ground black pepper

Put the asparagus on the sheet pan and drizzle with 2 tablespoons of olive oil, tossing to coat. Season with ½ teaspoon of kosher salt.

Select Roast, set temperature to 375ºF (190ºC), and set time to 12 minutes. Select Start to begin preheating.

Once preheated, place the pan into the oven.

Meanwhile, toss the cherry tomatoes with the remaining 1 tablespoon of olive oil in a medium bowl until well coated.

After 6 minutes, remove the pan and toss the asparagus. Evenly spread the asparagus in the middle of the sheet pan. Add the tomatoes around the perimeter of the pan. Return the pan to the oven and continue cooking.

After 2 minutes, remove the pan from the oven.

Carefully crack the eggs, one at a time, over the asparagus, spacing them out. Season with the remaining ½ teaspoon of kosher salt and the pepper. Return the pan to the oven and continue cooking. Cook for an additional 3 to 7 minutes, or until the eggs are cooked to your desired doneness.

When done, divide the asparagus and eggs among four plates. Top each plate evenly with the tomatoes and serve.

414. RATATOUILLE

Prep time: 10 minutes | Cook time: 12 minutes | Serves 6

- 1 medium zucchini, sliced ½-inch thick
- 1 small eggplant, peeled and sliced ½-inch thick
- 2 teaspoons kosher salt, divided
- 4 tablespoons extra-virgin olive oil, divided
- 3 garlic cloves, minced
- 1 small onion, chopped
- 1 small red bell pepper, cut into ½-inch chunks
- 1 small green bell pepper, cut into ½-inch chunks
- ½ teaspoon dried oregano
- ¼ teaspoon freshly ground black pepper
- 1 pint cherry tomatoes

- 2 tablespoons minced fresh basil
- 1 cup panko bread crumbs
- ½ cup grated Parmesan cheese (optional)

Season one side of the zucchini and eggplant slices with ¾ teaspoon of salt. Put the slices, salted side down, on a rack set over a baking sheet. Sprinkle the other sides with ¾ teaspoon of salt. Allow to sit for 10 minutes, or until the slices begin to exude water. When ready, rinse and dry them. Cut the zucchini slices into quarters and the eggplant slices into eighths.

Pour the zucchini and eggplant into a large bowl, along with 2 tablespoons of olive oil, garlic, onion, bell peppers, oregano, and black pepper. Toss to coat well. Arrange the vegetables on the sheet pan.

Select Roast, set temperature to 375ºF (190ºC), and set time to 12 minutes. Select Start to begin preheating.

Once preheated, place the pan into the oven.

Meanwhile, add the tomatoes and basil to the large bowl. Sprinkle with the remaining ½ teaspoon of salt and 1 tablespoon of olive oil. Toss well and set aside.

Stir together the remaining 1 tablespoon of olive oil, panko, and Parmesan cheese (if desired) in a small bowl.

After 6 minutes, remove the pan and add the tomato mixture to the sheet pan and stir to mix well. Scatter the panko mixture on top. Return the pan to the oven and continue cooking for 6 minutes, or until the vegetables are softened and the topping is golden brown.

Cool for 5 minutes before serving.

415. BEAN, SALSA, AND CHEESE TACOS
Prep time: 12 minutes | Cook time: 7 minutes | Serves 4

- 1 (15-ounce / 425-g) can black beans, drained and rinsed
- ½ cup prepared salsa
- 1½ teaspoons chili powder
- 4 ounces (113 g) grated Monterey Jack cheese
- 2 tablespoons minced onion
- 8 (6-inch) flour tortillas
- 2 tablespoons vegetable or extra-virgin olive oil
- Shredded lettuce, for serving

In a medium bowl, add the beans, salsa and chili powder. Coarsely mash them with a potato masher. Fold in the cheese and onion and stir until combined.

Arrange the flour tortillas on a cutting board and spoon 2 to 3 tablespoons of the filling into each tortilla. Fold the tortillas over, pressing lightly to even out the filling. Brush the tacos on one side with half the olive oil and put them, oiled side down, on the sheet pan. Brush the top side with the remaining olive oil.

Select Air Fry, set temperature to 400ºF (205ºC), and set time to 7 minutes. Select Start to begin preheating.

Once preheated, place the pan into the oven. Flip the tacos halfway through the cooking time.

Remove the pan from the oven and allow to cool for 5 minutes. Serve with the shredded lettuce on the side.

416. SPICY THAI-STYLE VEGETABLES
Prep time: 10 minutes | Cook time: 8 minutes | Serves 4

- 1 small head Napa cabbage, shredded, divided
- 1 medium carrot, cut into thin coins
- 8 ounces (227 g) snow peas
- 1 red or green bell pepper, sliced into thin strips
- 1 tablespoon vegetable oil
- 2 tablespoons soy sauce
- 1 tablespoon sesame oil
- 2 tablespoons brown sugar
- 2 tablespoons freshly squeezed lime juice

- 2 teaspoons red or green Thai curry paste
- 1 serrano chile, deseeded and minced
- 1 cup frozen mango slices, thawed
- ½ cup chopped roasted peanuts or cashews

Put half the Napa cabbage in a large bowl, along with the carrot, snow peas, and bell pepper. Drizzle with the vegetable oil and toss to coat. Spread them evenly on the sheet pan.

Select Roast, set temperature to 375ºF (190ºC), and set time to 8 minutes. Select Start to begin preheating.

Once preheated, place the pan into the oven.

Meanwhile, whisk together the soy sauce, sesame oil, brown sugar, lime juice, and curry paste in a small bowl.

When done, the vegetables should be tender and crisp. Remove the pan and put the vegetables back into the bowl. Add the chile, mango slices, and the remaining cabbage. Pour over the dressing and toss to coat. Top with the roasted nuts and serve.

417. BALSAMIC ASPARAGUS
Prep time: 15 minutes | Cook time: 10 minutes | Serves 4

- 4 tablespoons olive oil, plus more for greasing
- 4 tablespoons balsamic vinegar
- 1½ pounds (680 g) asparagus spears, trimmed
- Salt and freshly ground black pepper, to taste

Grease a perforated pan with olive oil.

In a shallow bowl, stir together the 4 tablespoons of olive oil and balsamic vinegar to make a marinade.

Put the asparagus spears in the bowl so they are thoroughly covered by the marinade and allow to marinate for 5 minutes.

Put the asparagus in the greased perforated pan in a single layer and season with salt and pepper.

Select Air Fry, set temperature to 350ºF (180ºC), and set time to 10 minutes. Select Start to begin preheating.

Once preheated, place the pan into the oven. Flip the asparagus halfway through the cooking time.

When done, the asparagus should be tender and lightly browned. Cool for 5 minutes before serving.

418. TORTELLINI WITH VEGGIES AND PARMESAN
Prep time: 10 minutes | Cook time: 16 minutes | Serves 4

- 8 ounces (227 g) sugar snap peas, trimmed
- ½ pound (227 g) asparagus, trimmed and cut into 1-inch pieces
- 2 teaspoons kosher salt or 1 teaspoon fine salt, divided
- 1 tablespoon extra-virgin olive oil
- 1½ cups water
- 1 (20-ounce / 340-g) package frozen cheese tortellini
- 2 garlic cloves, minced
- 1 cup heavy (whipping) cream
- 1 cup cherry tomatoes, halved
- ½ cup grated Parmesan cheese
- ¼ cup chopped fresh parsley or basil

Add the peas and asparagus to a large bowl. Add ½ teaspoon of kosher salt and the olive oil and toss until well coated. Place the veggies in the sheet pan.

Select Bake, set the temperature to 450ºF (235ºC), and set the time for 4 minutes. Select Start to begin preheating.

Once the unit has preheated, place the pan in the oven.

Meanwhile, dissolve 1 teaspoon of kosher salt in the water.

Once cooking is complete, remove the pan from the oven and arrange the tortellini on the pan. Pour the salted water over the tortellini. Transfer the pan back to the oven.

Select Bake, set temperature to 450ºF (235ºC), and set time for 7 minutes. Select Start to begin preheating.

Meantime, stir together the garlic, heavy cream, and remaining ½ teaspoon of kosher salt in a small bowl.

Once cooking is complete, remove the pan from the oven. Blot off any remaining water with a paper towel. Gently stir the ingredients. Drizzle the cream over and top with the tomatoes.

Select Roast, set the temperature to 375ºF (190ºC), and set the time for 5 minutes. Select Start to begin preheating.

Once the unit has preheated, place the pan in the oven.

After 4 minutes, remove the pan from the oven.

Add the Parmesan cheese and stir until the cheese is melted

Serve topped with the parsley.

419. ASIAN-INSPIRED BROCCOLI

Prep time: 5 minutes | Cook time: 10 minutes | Serves 2

- 12 ounces (340 g) broccoli florets
- 2 tablespoons Asian hot chili oil
- 1 teaspoon ground Sichuan peppercorns (or black pepper)
- 2 garlic cloves, finely chopped
- 1 (2-inch) piece fresh ginger, peeled and finely chopped
- Kosher salt and freshly ground black pepper

Toss the broccoli florets with the chili oil, Sichuan peppercorns, garlic, ginger, salt, and pepper in a mixing bowl until thoroughly coated.

Transfer the broccoli florets to a perforated pan.

Select Air Fry, set temperature to 375ºF (190ºC), and set time to 10 minutes. Select Start to begin preheating.

Once preheated, slide the pan into the oven. Stir the broccoli florets halfway through the cooking time.

When cooking is complete, the broccoli florets should be lightly browned and tender. Remove the broccoli from the oven and serve on a plate.

420. SESAME-THYME WHOLE MAITAKE MUSHROOMS

Prep time: 5 minutes | Cook time: 15 minutes | Serves 2

- 1 tablespoon soy sauce
- 2 teaspoons toasted sesame oil
- 3 teaspoons vegetable oil, divided
- 1 garlic clove, minced
- 7 ounces (198 g) maitake (hen of the woods) mushrooms
- ½ teaspoon flaky sea salt
- ½ teaspoon sesame seeds
- ½ teaspoon finely chopped fresh thyme leaves

Whisk together the soy sauce, sesame oil, 1 teaspoon of vegetable oil, and garlic in a small bowl.

Arrange the mushrooms in a perforated pan in a single layer. Drizzle the soy sauce mixture over the mushrooms.

Select Roast, set temperature to 300ºF (150ºC), and set time to 15 minutes. Select Start to begin preheating.

Once preheated, slide the pan into the oven.

After 10 minutes, remove the pan from the oven. Flip the mushrooms and sprinkle the sea salt, sesame seeds, and thyme leaves on top. Drizzle the remaining 2 teaspoons of vegetable oil all over. Return to the oven and continue roasting for an additional 5 minutes.

When cooking is complete, remove the mushrooms from the oven to a plate and serve hot.

421. SWEET-AND-SOUR BRUSSELS SPROUTS

Prep time: 5 minutes | Cook time: 20 minutes | Serves 2

- ¼ cup Thai sweet chili sauce
- 2 tablespoons black vinegar or balsamic vinegar
- ½ teaspoon hot sauce
- 2 small shallots, cut into ¼-inch-thick slices
- 8 ounces (227 g) Brussels sprouts, trimmed (large sprouts halved)
- Kosher salt and freshly ground black pepper, to taste
- 2 teaspoons lightly packed fresh cilantro leaves, for garnish

Place the chili sauce, vinegar, and hot sauce in a large bowl and whisk to combine.

Add the shallots and Brussels sprouts and toss to coat. Sprinkle with the salt and pepper. Transfer the Brussels sprouts and sauce to a baking pan.

Select Roast, set temperature to 390ºF (199ºC), and set time to 20 minutes. Select Start to begin preheating.

Once preheated, place the baking pan in the oven. Stir the Brussels sprouts twice during cooking.

When cooking is complete, the Brussels sprouts should be crisp-tender. Remove from the oven. Sprinkle the cilantro on top for garnish and serve warm.

422. PANKO GREEN BEANS

Prep time: 5 minutes | Cook time: 15 minutes | Serves 4

- ½ cup flour
- 2 eggs
- 1 cup panko bread crumbs
- ½ cup grated Parmesan cheese
- 1 teaspoon cayenne pepper
- Salt and black pepper, to taste
- 1½ pounds (680 g) green beans

In a bowl, place the flour. In a separate bowl, lightly beat the eggs. In a separate shallow bowl, thoroughly combine the bread crumbs, cheese, cayenne pepper, salt, and pepper.

Dip the green beans in the flour, then in the beaten eggs, finally in the bread crumb mixture to coat well. Transfer the green beans to a perforated pan.

Select Air Fry, set temperature to 400ºF (205ºC), and set time to 15 minutes. Select Start to begin preheating.

Once preheated, slide the pan into the oven. Stir the green beans halfway through the cooking time.

When cooking is complete, remove from the oven to a bowl and serve.

423. CHEESY ASPARAGUS AND POTATO PLATTER

Prep time: 5 minutes | Cook time: 26 minutes | Serves 5

- 4 medium potatoes, cut into wedges
- Cooking spray
- 1 bunch asparagus, trimmed
- 2 tablespoons olive oil
- Salt and pepper, to taste
- Cheese Sauce:
- ¼ cup crumbled cottage cheese
- ¼ cup buttermilk
- 1 tablespoon whole-grain mustard
- Salt and black pepper, to taste

Spritz a perforated pan with cooking spray.

Put the potatoes in a perforated pan.

Select Roast of the oven. Set temperature to 400ºF (205ºC) and set time to 20 minutes. Select Start to begin preheating.

Once preheated, slide the pan into the oven. Stir the potatoes halfway through.

When cooking is complete, the potatoes should be golden brown.

Remove the potatoes from the oven to a platter. Cover the potatoes with foil to keep warm. Set aside.

Place the asparagus in a perforated pan and drizzle with the olive oil. Sprinkle with salt and pepper.

Select Roast of the oven. Set temperature to 400ºF (205ºC) and set time to 6 minutes. Stir the asparagus halfway through.

When cooking is complete, the asparagus should be crispy.

Meanwhile, make the cheese sauce by stirring together the cottage cheese, buttermilk, and mustard in a small bowl. Season as needed with salt and pepper.

Transfer the asparagus to the platter of potatoes and drizzle with the cheese sauce. Serve immediately.

424. HERBED BROCCOLI WITH CHEESE
Prep time: 5 minutes | Cook time: 18 minutes | Serves 4

- 1 large-sized head broccoli, stemmed and cut into small florets
- 2½ tablespoons canola oil
- 2 teaspoons dried basil
- 2 teaspoons dried rosemary
- Salt and ground black pepper, to taste
- ⅓ cup grated yellow cheese

Bring a pot of lightly salted water to a boil. Add the broccoli florets to the boiling water and let boil for about 3 minutes.

Drain the broccoli florets well and transfer to a large bowl. Add the canola oil, basil, rosemary, salt, and black pepper to the bowl and toss until the broccoli is fully coated. Place the broccoli in a perforated pan.

Select Air Fry, set temperature to 390°F (199°C), and set time to 15 minutes. Select Start to begin preheating.

Once preheated, slide the pan into the oven. Stir the broccoli halfway through the cooking time.

When cooking is complete, the broccoli should be crisp. Remove the pan from the oven. Serve the broccoli warm with grated cheese sprinkled on top.

425. CHEESY CABBAGE WEDGES
Prep time: 5 minutes | Cook time: 20 minutes | Serves 4

- 4 tablespoons melted butter
- 1 head cabbage, cut into wedges
- 1 cup shredded Parmesan cheese
- Salt and black pepper, to taste
- ½ cup shredded Mozzarella cheese

Brush the melted butter over the cut sides of cabbage wedges and sprinkle both sides with the Parmesan cheese. Season with salt and pepper to taste.

Place the cabbage wedges in a perforated pan.

Select Air Fry, set temperature to 380°F (193°C), and set time to 20 minutes. Select Start to begin preheating.

Once preheated, slide the pan into the oven. Flip the cabbage halfway through the cooking time.

When cooking is complete, the cabbage wedges should be lightly browned. Transfer the cabbage wedges to a plate and serve with the Mozzarella cheese sprinkled on top.

426. CRISPY EGGPLANT SLICES WITH PARSLEY
Prep time: 5 minutes | Cook time: 12 minutes | Serves 4

- 1 cup flour
- 4 eggs
- Salt, to taste
- 2 cups bread crumbs
- 1 teaspoon Italian seasoning
- 2 eggplants, sliced
- 2 garlic cloves, sliced
- 2 tablespoons chopped parsley
- Cooking spray

Spritz a perforated pan with cooking spray. Set aside.

On a plate, place the flour. In a shallow bowl, whisk the eggs with salt. In another shallow bowl, combine the bread crumbs and Italian seasoning. Dredge the eggplant slices, one at a time, in the flour, then in the whisked eggs, finally in the bread crumb mixture to coat well.

Lay the coated eggplant slices in the perforated pan.

Select Air Fry, set temperature to 390°F (199°C), and set time to 12 minutes. Select Start to begin preheating.

Once preheated, slide the pan into the oven. Flip the eggplant slices halfway through the cooking time.

When cooking is complete, the eggplant slices should be golden brown and crispy. Transfer the eggplant slices to a plate and sprinkle the garlic and parsley on top before serving.

427. TERIYAKI CAULIFLOWER
Prep time: 5 minutes | Cook time: 14 minutes | Serves 4

- ½ cup soy sauce
- ⅓ cup water
- 1 tablespoon brown sugar
- 1 teaspoon sesame oil
- 1 teaspoon cornstarch
- 2 cloves garlic, chopped
- ½ teaspoon chili powder
- 1 big cauliflower head, cut into florets

Make the teriyaki sauce: In a small bowl, whisk together the soy sauce, water, brown sugar, sesame oil, cornstarch, garlic, and chili powder until well combined.

Place the cauliflower florets in a large bowl and drizzle the top with the prepared teriyaki sauce and toss to coat well.

Put the cauliflower florets in a perforated pan.

Select Air Fry. Set temperature to 340°F (171°C) and set time to 14 minutes. Select Start to begin preheating.

Once preheated, slide the pan into the oven. Stir the cauliflower halfway through.

When cooking is complete, the cauliflower should be crisp-tender.

Let the cauliflower cool for 5 minutes before serving.

428. ROSEMARY ROASTED SQUASH WITH CHEESE
Prep time: 5 minutes | Cook time: 20 minutes | Serves 2

- 1 pound (454 g) butternut squash, cut into wedges
- 2 tablespoons olive oil
- 1 tablespoon dried rosemary
- Salt, to salt
- 1 cup crumbled goat cheese
- 1 tablespoon maple syrup

Toss the squash wedges with the olive oil, rosemary, and salt in a large bowl until well coated.

Transfer the squash wedges to a perforated pan, spreading them out in as even a layer as possible.

Select Air Fry, set temperature to 350°F (180°C), and set time to 20 minutes. Select Start to begin preheating.

Once preheated, slide the pan into the oven.

After 10 minutes, remove from the oven and flip the squash. Return the pan to the oven and continue cooking for 10 minutes.

When cooking is complete, the squash should be golden brown. Remove the pan from the oven. Sprinkle the goat cheese on top and serve drizzled with the maple syrup.

429. SCALLOPED POTATOES
Prep time: 5 minutes | Cook time: 15 to 20 minutes | Serves 4

- 2 cup sliced frozen potatoes, thawed
- 3 cloves garlic, minced
- Pinch salt

- Freshly ground black pepper, to taste
- ¾ cup heavy cream

Toss the potatoes with the garlic, salt, and black pepper in a baking pan until evenly coated. Pour the heavy cream over the top.

Select Bake, set temperature to 380ºF (193ºC), and set time to 15 minutes. Select Start to begin preheating.

Once preheated, place the baking pan in the oven.

When cooking is complete, the potatoes should be tender and the top golden brown. Check for doneness and bake for another 5 minutes if needed. Remove from the oven and serve hot.

430. HONEY-GLAZED BABY CARROTS
Prep time: 5 minutes | Cook time: 12 minutes | Serves 4

- 1 pound (454 g) baby carrots
- 2 tablespoons olive oil
- 1 tablespoon honey
- 1 teaspoon dried dill
- Salt and black pepper, to taste

Place the carrots in a large bowl. Add the olive oil, honey, dill, salt, and pepper and toss to coat well.

Transfer the carrots to a perforated pan.

Select Roast, set temperature to 350ºF (180ºC), and set time to 12 minutes. Select Start to begin preheating.

Once preheated, slide the pan into the oven. Stir the carrots once during cooking.

When cooking is complete, the carrots should be crisp-tender. Remove from the oven and serve warm.

431. MEDITERRANEAN BAKED EGGS WITH SPINACH
Prep time: 10 minutes | Cook time: 10 minutes | Serves 2

- 2 tablespoons olive oil
- 4 eggs, whisked
- 5 ounces (142 g) fresh spinach, chopped
- 1 medium-sized tomato, chopped
- 1 teaspoon fresh lemon juice
- ½ teaspoon ground black pepper
- ½ teaspoon coarse salt
- ½ cup roughly chopped fresh basil leaves, for garnish

Generously grease a baking pan with olive oil.

Stir together the remaining ingredients except the basil leaves in the greased baking pan until well incorporated.

Select Bake, set temperature to 280ºF (137ºC), and set time to 10 minutes. Select Start to begin preheating.

Once preheated, place the baking pan into the oven.

When cooking is complete, the eggs should be completely set and the vegetables should be tender. Remove from the oven and serve garnished with the fresh basil leaves.

432. VEGETARIAN MEATBALLS
Prep time: 15 minutes | Cook time: 18 minutes | Serves 3

- ½ cup grated carrots
- ½ cup sweet onions
- 2 tablespoons olive oil
- 1 cup rolled oats
- ½ cup roasted cashews
- 2 cups cooked chickpeas
- Juice of 1 lemon
- 2 tablespoons soy sauce
- 1 tablespoon flax meal

- 1 teaspoon garlic powder
- 1 teaspoon cumin
- ½ teaspoon turmeric

Mix the carrots, onions, and olive oil in a baking dish and stir to combine.

Select Roast of the oven. Set temperature to 350ºF (180ºC) and set time to 6 minutes. Select Start to begin preheating.

Once preheated, slide the pan into the oven. Stir the vegetables halfway through.

When cooking is complete, the vegetables should be tender.

Meanwhile, put the oats and cashews in a food processor or blender and pulse until coarsely ground. Transfer the mixture to a large bowl. Add the chickpeas, lemon juice, and soy sauce to the food processor and pulse until smooth. Transfer the chickpea mixture to the bowl of oat and cashew mixture.

Remove the carrots and onions from the oven to the bowl of chickpea mixture. Add the flax meal, garlic powder, cumin, and turmeric and stir to incorporate.

Scoop tablespoon-sized portions of the veggie mixture and roll them into balls with your hands. Transfer the balls to a perforated pan.

Increase the temperature to 370ºF (188ºC) and set time to 12 minutes on Bake. Flip the balls halfway through the cooking time.

When cooking is complete, the balls should be golden brown.

Serve warm.

433. ROASTED VEGETABLES WITH RICE
Prep time: 5 minutes | Cook time: 12 minutes | Serves 4

- 2 teaspoons melted butter
- 1 cup chopped mushrooms
- 1 cup cooked rice
- 1 cup peas
- 1 carrot, chopped
- 1 red onion, chopped
- 1 garlic clove, minced
- Salt and black pepper, to taste
- 2 hard-boiled eggs, grated
- 1 tablespoon soy sauce

Coat a baking dish with melted butter.

Stir together the mushrooms, cooked rice, peas, carrot, onion, garlic, salt, and pepper in a large bowl until well mixed. Pour the mixture into the prepared baking dish.

Select Roast, set temperature to 380ºF (193ºC), and set time to 12 minutes. Select Start to begin preheating.

Once preheated, place the baking dish in the oven.

When cooking is complete, remove from the oven. Divide the mixture among four plates. Serve warm with a sprinkle of grated eggs and a drizzle of soy sauce.

434. ITALIAN BAKED TOFU
Prep time: 5 minutes | Cook time: 10 minutes | Serves 2

- 1 tablespoon soy sauce
- 1 tablespoon water
- ⅓ teaspoon garlic powder
- ⅓ teaspoon onion powder
- ⅓ teaspoon dried oregano
- ⅓ teaspoon dried basil
- Black pepper, to taste
- 6 ounces (170 g) extra firm tofu, pressed and cubed

In a large mixing bowl, whisk together the soy sauce, water, garlic powder, onion powder, oregano, basil, and black pepper. Add the tofu cubes, stirring to coat, and let them marinate for 10 minutes.

Arrange the tofu in a perforated pan.

Select Bake of the oven. Set temperature to 390ºF (199ºC) and set time to 10 minutes. Select Start to begin preheating.

Once preheated, slide the pan into the oven. Flip the tofu halfway through the cooking time.

When cooking is complete, the tofu should be crisp.

Remove from the oven to a plate and serve.

435. TOFU, CARROT AND CAULIFLOWER RICE

Prep time: 10 minutes | Cook time: 22 minutes | Serves 4

- ½ block tofu, crumbled
- 1 cup diced carrot
- ½ cup diced onions
- 2 tablespoons soy sauce
- 1 teaspoon turmeric
- Cauliflower:
- 3 cups cauliflower rice
- ½ cup chopped broccoli
- ½ cup frozen peas
- 2 tablespoons soy sauce
- 1 tablespoon minced ginger
- 2 garlic cloves, minced
- 1 tablespoon rice vinegar
- 1½ teaspoons toasted sesame oil

Mix the tofu, carrot, onions, soy sauce, and turmeric in a baking dish and stir until well incorporated.

Select Roast of the oven. Set temperature to 370ºF (188ºC) and set time to 10 minutes. Select Start to begin preheating.

Once preheated, slide the pan into the oven. Flip the tofu and carrot halfway through the cooking time.

When cooking is complete, the tofu should be crisp.

Meanwhile, in a large bowl, combine all the ingredients for the cauliflower and toss well.

Remove the dish from the oven and add the cauliflower mixture to the tofu and stir to combine.

Return the baking dish to the oven and set time to 12 minutes on Roast.

When cooking is complete, the vegetables should be tender.

Cool for 5 minutes before serving.

436. ROASTED VEGETABLE MÉLANGE WITH HERBS

Prep time: 10 minutes | Cook time: 16 minutes | Serves 4

- 1 (8-ounce / 227-g) package sliced mushrooms
- 1 yellow summer squash, sliced
- 1 red bell pepper, sliced
- 3 cloves garlic, sliced
- 1 tablespoon olive oil
- ½ teaspoon dried basil
- ½ teaspoon dried thyme
- ½ teaspoon dried tarragon

Toss the mushrooms, squash, and bell pepper with the garlic and olive oil in a large bowl until well coated. Mix in the basil, thyme, and tarragon and toss again.

Spread the vegetables evenly in a perforated pan.

Select Roast, set temperature to 350ºF (180ºC), and set time to 16 minutes. Select Start to begin preheating.

Once preheated, slide the pan into the oven.

When cooking is complete, the vegetables should be fork-tender. Remove the pan from the oven. Cool for 5 minutes before serving.

437. SIMPLE RATATOUILLE

Prep time: 15 minutes | Cook time: 16 minutes | Serves 2

- 2 Roma tomatoes, thinly sliced

- 1 zucchini, thinly sliced
- 2 yellow bell peppers, sliced
- 2 garlic cloves, minced
- 2 tablespoons olive oil
- 2 tablespoons herbes de Provence
- 1 tablespoon vinegar
- Salt and black pepper, to taste

Place the tomatoes, zucchini, bell peppers, garlic, olive oil, herbes de Provence, and vinegar in a large bowl and toss until the vegetables are evenly coated. Sprinkle with salt and pepper and toss again. Pour the vegetable mixture into a baking dish.

Select Roast of the oven. Set temperature to 390ºF (199ºC) and set time to 16 minutes. Select Start to begin preheating.

Once preheated, slide the pan into the oven. Stir the vegetables halfway through.

When cooking is complete, the vegetables should be tender.

Let the vegetable mixture stand for 5 minutes in the oven before removing and serving.

438. CARAMELIZED EGGPLANT WITH YOGURT SAUCE

Prep time: 5 minutes | Cook time: 15 minutes | Serves 2

- 1 medium eggplant, quartered and cut crosswise into ½-inch-thick slices
- 2 tablespoons vegetable oil
- Kosher salt and freshly ground black pepper, to taste
- ½ cup plain yogurt (not Greek)
- 2 tablespoons harissa paste
- 1 garlic clove, grated
- 2 teaspoons honey

Toss the eggplant slices with the vegetable oil, salt, and pepper in a large bowl until well coated.

Lay the eggplant slices in a perforated pan.

Select Air Fry, set temperature to 400ºF (205ºC), and set time to 15 minutes. Select Start to begin preheating.

Once preheated, slide the pan into the oven. Stir the slices two to three times during cooking.

Meanwhile, make the yogurt sauce by whisking together the yogurt, harissa paste, and garlic in a small bowl.

When cooking is complete, the eggplant slices should be golden brown. Spread the yogurt sauce on a platter, and pile the eggplant slices over the top. Serve drizzled with the honey.

439. CRISPY FRIED OKRA WITH CHILI

Prep time: 5 minutes | Cook time: 10 minutes | Serves 4

- 3 tablespoons sour cream
- 2 tablespoons flour
- 2 tablespoons semolina
- ½ teaspoon red chili powder
- Salt and black pepper, to taste
- 1 pound (454 g) okra, halved
- Cooking spray

Spray a perforated pan with cooking spray. Set aside.

In a shallow bowl, place the sour cream. In another shallow bowl, thoroughly combine the flour, semolina, red chili powder, salt, and pepper. Dredge the okra in the sour cream, then roll in the flour mixture until evenly coated. Transfer the okra to a perforated pan.

Select Air Fry, set temperature to 400ºF (205ºC), and set time to 10 minutes. Select Start to begin preheating.

Once preheated, slide the pan into the oven. Flip the okra halfway through the cooking time.

When cooking is complete, the okra should be golden brown and crispy. Remove the pan from the oven. Cool for 5 minutes before serving.

440. ROASTED BRUSSELS SPROUTS WITH PARMESAN

Prep time: 10 minutes | Cook time: 20 minutes | Serves 4

- 1 pound (454 g) fresh Brussels sprouts, trimmed
- 1 tablespoon olive oil
- ½ teaspoon salt
- ⅛ teaspoon pepper
- ¼ cup grated Parmesan cheese

In a large bowl, combine the Brussels sprouts with olive oil, salt, and pepper and toss until evenly coated.
Spread the Brussels sprouts evenly in a perforated pan.
Select Air Fry, set temperature to 330ºF (166ºC), and set time to 20 minutes. Select Start to begin preheating.
Once preheated, slide the pan into the oven. Stir the Brussels sprouts twice during cooking.
When cooking is complete, the Brussels sprouts should be golden brown and crisp. Remove the pan from the oven. Sprinkle the grated Parmesan cheese on top and serve warm.

441. CAYENNE TAHINI KALE

Prep time: 5 minutes | Cook time: 15 minutes | Serves 2 to 4

- Dressing:
- ¼ cup tahini
- ¼ cup fresh lemon juice
- 2 tablespoons olive oil
- 1 teaspoon sesame seeds
- ½ teaspoon garlic powder
- ¼ teaspoon cayenne pepper
- Kale:
- 4 cups packed torn kale leaves (stems and ribs removed and leaves torn into palm-size pieces)
- Kosher salt and freshly ground black pepper, to taste

Make the dressing: Whisk together the tahini, lemon juice, olive oil, sesame seeds, garlic powder, and cayenne pepper in a large bowl until well mixed.
Add the kale and massage the dressing thoroughly all over the leaves. Sprinkle the salt and pepper to season.
Place the kale in a perforated pan in a single layer.
Select Air Fry, set temperature to 350ºF (180ºC), and set time to 15 minutes. Select Start to begin preheating.
Once preheated, slide the pan into the oven.
When cooking is complete, the leaves should be slightly wilted and crispy. Remove from the oven and serve on a plate.

442. CHEESE-WALNUT STUFFED MUSHROOMS

Prep time: 5 minutes | Cook time: 10 minutes | Serves 4

- 4 large portobello mushrooms
- 1 tablespoon canola oil
- ½ cup shredded Mozzarella cheese
- ⅓ cup minced walnuts
- 2 tablespoons chopped fresh parsley
- Cooking spray

Spritz a perforated pan with cooking spray.
On a clean work surface, remove the mushroom stems. Scoop out the gills with a spoon and discard. Coat the mushrooms with canola oil. Top each mushroom evenly with the shredded Mozzarella cheese, followed by the minced walnuts.
Arrange the mushrooms in the perforated pan.
Select Roast of the oven. Set temperature to 350ºF (180ºC) and set time

to 10 minutes. Select Start to begin preheating.
Once preheated, slide the pan into the oven.
When cooking is complete, the mushroom should be golden brown.
Transfer the mushrooms to a plate and sprinkle the parsley on top for garnish before serving.

443. EASY CHEESY VEGETABLE QUESADILLA

Prep time: 5 minutes | Cook time: 10 minutes | Serves 1

- 1 teaspoon olive oil
- 2 flour tortillas
- ¼ zucchini, sliced
- ¼ yellow bell pepper, sliced
- ¼ cup shredded gouda cheese
- 1 tablespoon chopped cilantro
- ½ green onion, sliced

Coat a perforated pan with 1 teaspoon of olive oil.
Arrange a flour tortilla in the perforated pan and scatter the top with zucchini, bell pepper, gouda cheese, cilantro, and green onion. Place the other flour tortilla on top.
Select Air Fry, set temperature to 390ºF (199ºC), and set time to 10 minutes. Select Start to begin preheating.
Once preheated, slide the pan into the oven.
When cooking is complete, the tortillas should be lightly browned and the vegetables should be tender. Remove from the oven and cool for 5 minutes before slicing into wedges.

444. CINNAMON-SPICED ACORN SQUASH

Prep time: 5 minutes | Cook time: 15 minutes | Serves 2

- 1 medium acorn squash, halved crosswise and deseeded
- 1 teaspoon coconut oil
- 1 teaspoon light brown sugar
- Few dashes of ground cinnamon
- Few dashes of ground nutmeg

On a clean work surface, rub the cut sides of the acorn squash with coconut oil. Scatter with the brown sugar, cinnamon, and nutmeg.
Put the squash halves in a perforated pan, cut-side up.
Select Air Fry, set temperature to 325ºF (163ºC), and set time to 15 minutes. Select Start to begin preheating.
Once preheated, slide the pan into the oven.
When cooking is complete, the squash halves should be just tender when pierced in the center with a paring knife. Remove the pan from the oven. Rest for 5 to 10 minutes and serve warm.

445. SPICY CABBAGE

Prep time: 5 minutes | Cook time: 7 minutes | Serves 4

- 1 head cabbage, sliced into 1-inch-thick ribbons
- 1 tablespoon olive oil
- 1 teaspoon garlic powder
- 1 teaspoon red pepper flakes
- 1 teaspoon salt
- 1 teaspoon freshly ground black pepper

Toss the cabbage with the olive oil, garlic powder, red pepper flakes, salt, and pepper in a large mixing bowl until well coated.
Transfer the cabbage to a perforated pan.
Select Roast, set temperature to 350ºF (180ºC), and set time to 7 minutes. Select Start to begin preheating.
Once preheated, slide the pan into the oven. Flip the cabbage with tongs halfway through the cooking time.
When cooking is complete, the cabbage should be crisp. Remove from the oven to a plate and serve warm.

446. CREAMY CORN CASSEROLE

Prep time: 5 minutes | Cook time: 15 minutes | Serves 4

- 2 cups frozen yellow corn
- 1 egg, beaten
- 3 tablespoons flour
- ½ cup grated Swiss or Havarti cheese
- ½ cup light cream
- ¼ cup milk
- Pinch salt
- Freshly ground black pepper, to taste
- 2 tablespoons butter, cut into cubes
- Nonstick cooking spray

Spritz a baking pan with nonstick cooking spray.
Stir together the remaining ingredients except the butter in a medium bowl until well incorporated. Transfer the mixture to the prepared baking pan and scatter with the butter cubes.
Select Bake, set temperature to 320°F (160°C), and set time to 15 minutes. Select Start to begin preheating.
Once preheated, place the baking pan in the oven.
When cooking is complete, the top should be golden brown and a toothpick inserted in the center should come out clean. Remove the pan from the oven. Let the casserole cool for 5 minutes before slicing into wedges and serving.

447. BALSAMIC-GLAZED CARROTS

Prep time: 5 minutes | Cook time: 18 minutes | Serves 3

- 3 medium-size carrots, cut into 2-inch × ½-inch sticks
- 1 tablespoon orange juice
- 2 teaspoons balsamic vinegar
- 1 teaspoon maple syrup
- 1 teaspoon avocado oil
- ½ teaspoon dried rosemary
- ¼ teaspoon sea salt
- ¼ teaspoon lemon zest

Put the carrots in a baking pan and sprinkle with the orange juice, balsamic vinegar, maple syrup, avocado oil, rosemary, sea salt, finished by the lemon zest. Toss well.
Select Roast, set temperature to 392°F (200°C), and set time to 18 minutes. Select Start to begin preheating.
Once preheated, place the baking pan in the oven. Stir the carrots several times during the cooking process.
When cooking is complete, the carrots should be nicely glazed and tender. Remove from the oven and serve hot.

448. CHEESY BROCCOLI GRATIN

Prep time: 5 minutes | Cook time: 14 minutes | Serves 2

⅓ cup fat-free milk
1 tablespoon all-purpose or gluten-free flour
½ tablespoon olive oil
½ teaspoon ground sage
¼ teaspoon kosher salt
⅛ teaspoon freshly ground black pepper
2 cups roughly chopped broccoli florets
6 tablespoons shredded Cheddar cheese
2 tablespoons panko bread crumbs
1 tablespoon grated Parmesan cheese
Olive oil spray

Spritz a baking dish with olive oil spray.
Mix the milk, flour, olive oil, sage, salt, and pepper in a medium bowl and whisk to combine. Stir in the broccoli florets, Cheddar cheese, bread crumbs, and Parmesan cheese and toss to coat.
Pour the broccoli mixture into the prepared baking dish.
Select Bake, set temperature to 330°F (166°C), and set time to 14 minutes. Select Start to begin preheating.
Once preheated, place the baking dish in the oven.
When cooking is complete, the top should be golden brown and the broccoli should be tender. Remove from the oven and serve immediately.

449. ROSEMARY ROASTED POTATOES

Prep time: 5 minutes | Cook time: 20 minutes | Serves 4

- 1½ pounds (680 g) small red potatoes, cut into 1-inch cubes
- 2 tablespoons olive oil
- 2 tablespoons minced fresh rosemary
- 1 tablespoon minced garlic
- 1 teaspoon salt, plus additional as needed
- ½ teaspoon freshly ground black pepper, plus additional as needed

Toss the potato cubes with the olive oil, rosemary, garlic, salt, and pepper in a large bowl until thoroughly coated.
Arrange the potato cubes in a perforated pan in a single layer.
Select Roast, set temperature to 400°F (205°C), and set time to 20 minutes. Select Start to begin preheating.
Once preheated, slide the pan into the oven. Stir the potatoes a few times during cooking for even cooking.
When cooking is complete, the potatoes should be tender. Remove from the oven to a plate. Taste and add additional salt and pepper as needed.

450. GARLIC ROASTED ASPARAGUS

Prep time: 5 minutes | Cook time: 10 minutes | Serves 4

- 1 pound (454 g) asparagus, woody ends trimmed
- 2 tablespoons olive oil
- 1 tablespoon balsamic vinegar
- 2 teaspoons minced garlic
- Salt and freshly ground black pepper, to taste

In a large shallow bowl, toss the asparagus with the olive oil, balsamic vinegar, garlic, salt, and pepper until thoroughly coated. Put the asparagus in a perforated pan.
Select Roast, set temperature to 400°F (205°C), and set time to 10 minutes. Select Start to begin preheating.
Once preheated, slide the pan into the oven. Flip the asparagus with tongs halfway through the cooking time.
When cooking is complete, the asparagus should be crispy. Remove the pan from the oven and serve warm.

451. BUTTERNUT SQUASH CROQUETTES

Prep time: 5 minutes | Cook time: 17 minutes | Serves 4

- ⅓ butternut squash, peeled and grated
- ⅓ cup all-purpose flour
- 2 eggs, whisked
- 4 cloves garlic, minced
- 1½ tablespoons olive oil
- 1 teaspoon fine sea salt
- ⅓ teaspoon freshly ground black pepper, or more to taste
- ⅓ teaspoon dried sage
- A pinch of ground allspice

Line a perforated pan with parchment paper. Set aside.
In a mixing bowl, stir together all the ingredients until well combined.
Make the squash croquettes: Use a small cookie scoop to drop table-

spoonfuls of the squash mixture onto a lightly floured surface and shape into balls with your hands. Transfer them to the perforated pan.

Select Air Fry, set temperature to 345ºF (174ºC), and set time to 17 minutes. Select Start to begin preheating.

Once preheated, slide the pan into the oven.

When cooking is complete, the squash croquettes should be golden brown. Remove from the oven to a plate and serve warm.

452. SIMPLE ZUCCHINI CRISPS
Prep time: 5 minutes | Cook time: 14 minutes | Serves 4

- 2 zucchini, sliced into ¼- to ½-inch-thick rounds (about 2 cups)
- ¼ teaspoon garlic granules
- ⅛ teaspoon sea salt
- Freshly ground black pepper, to taste (optional)
- Cooking spray

Spritz a perforated pan with cooking spray.

Put the zucchini rounds in the perforated pan, spreading them out as much as possible. Top with a sprinkle of garlic granules, sea salt, and black pepper (if desired). Spritz the zucchini rounds with cooking spray.

Select Roast, set temperature to 392ºF (200ºC), and set time to 14 minutes. Select Start to begin preheating.

Once preheated, slide the pan into the oven. Flip the zucchini rounds halfway through.

When cooking is complete, the zucchini rounds should be crisp-tender. Remove from the oven. Let them rest for 5 minutes and serve.

453. CHILI C ORN ON THE COB
Prep time: 10 minutes | Cook time: 15 minutes | Serves 4

- 2 tablespoon olive oil, divided
- 2 tablespoons grated Parmesan cheese
- 1 teaspoon garlic powder
- 1 teaspoon chili powder
- 1 teaspoon ground cumin
- 1 teaspoon paprika
- 1 teaspoon salt
- ¼ teaspoon cayenne pepper (optional)
- 4 ears fresh corn, shucked

Grease a perforated pan with 1 tablespoon of olive oil. Set aside.

Combine the Parmesan cheese, garlic powder, chili powder, cumin, paprika, salt, and cayenne pepper (if desired) in a small bowl and stir to mix well.

Lightly coat the ears of corn with the remaining 1 tablespoon of olive oil. Rub the cheese mixture all over the ears of corn until completely coated.

Arrange the ears of corn in the greased perforated pan in a single layer.

Select Air Fry, set temperature to 400ºF (205ºC), and set time to 15 minutes. Select Start to begin preheating.

Once preheated, slide the pan into the oven. Flip the ears of corn halfway through the cooking time.

When cooking is complete, they should be lightly browned. Remove from the oven and let them cool for 5 minutes before serving.

454. SWEET BRUSSELS SPROUTS
Prep time: 10 minutes | Cook time: 11 minutes | Serves 4

- 2½ cups trimmed Brussels sprouts
- Sauce:
- 1½ teaspoons mellow white miso
- 1½ tablespoons maple syrup
- 1 teaspoon toasted sesame oil
- 1 teaspoons tamari or shoyu
- 1 teaspoon grated fresh ginger
- 2 large garlic cloves, finely minced
- ¼ to ½ teaspoon red chili flakes
- Cooking spray

Spritz a perforated pan with cooking spray.

Arrange the Brussels sprouts in the perforated pan and spray them with cooking spray.

Select Air Fry, set temperature to 392ºF (200ºC), and set time to 11 minutes. Select Start to begin preheating.

Once preheated, slide the pan into the oven.

After 6 minutes, remove the pan from the oven. Flip the Brussels sprouts and spritz with cooking spray again. Return to the oven and continue cooking for 5 minutes more.

Meanwhile, make the sauce: Stir together the miso and maple syrup in a medium bowl. Add the sesame oil, tamari, ginger, garlic, and red chili flakes and whisk to combine.

When cooking is complete, the Brussels sprouts should be crisp-tender. Transfer the Brussels sprouts to the bowl of sauce, tossing to coat well. If you prefer a saltier taste, you can add additional ½ teaspoon tamari to the sauce. Serve immediately.

455. CREAM CHEESE STUFFED BELL PEPPERS
Prep time: 5 minutes | Cook time: 15 minutes | Serves 2

- 2 bell peppers, tops and seeds removed
- Salt and pepper, to taste
- ⅔ cup cream cheese
- 2 tablespoons mayonnaise
- 1 tablespoon chopped fresh celery stalks
- Cooking spray

Spritz a perforated pan with cooking spray.

Place the peppers in a perforated pan.

Select Roast of the oven. Set temperature to 400ºF (205ºC) and set time to 10 minutes. Select Start to begin preheating.

Once preheated, slide the pan into the oven. Flip the peppers halfway through.

When cooking is complete, the peppers should be crisp-tender.

Remove from the oven to a plate and season with salt and pepper.

Mix the cream cheese, mayo, and celery in a small bowl and stir to incorporate. Evenly stuff the roasted peppers with the cream cheese mixture with a spoon. Serve immediately.

456. STUFFED SQUASH WITH TOMATOES AND PO-BLANO
Prep time: 5 minutes | Cook time: 30 minutes | Serves 4

- 1 pound (454 g) butternut squash, ends trimmed
- 2 teaspoons olive oil, divided
- 6 grape tomatoes, halved
- 1 poblano pepper, cut into strips
- Salt and black pepper, to taste
- ¼ cup grated Mozzarella cheese

Using a large knife, cut the squash in half lengthwise on a flat work surface. This recipe just needs half of the squash. Scoop out the flesh to make room for the stuffing. Coat the squash half with 1 teaspoon of olive oil.

Put the squash half in a perforated pan.

Select Bake of the oven. Set temperature to 350ºF (180ºC) and set time to 15 minutes. Select Start to begin preheating.

Once preheated, slide the pan into the oven. Flip the squash halfway through.

When cooking is complete, the squash should be tender.

Meanwhile, thoroughly combine the tomatoes, poblano pepper, remaining 1 teaspoon of olive oil, salt, and pepper in a bowl.

Remove the pan from the oven and spoon the tomato mixture into the squash. Return to the oven.

Select Roast of the oven. Set time to 15 minutes.

After 12 minutes, remove the pan from the oven. Scatter the Mozzarella cheese on top. Return the pan to the oven and continue cooking.

When cooking is complete, the tomatoes should be soft and the cheese should be melted.

Cool for 5 minutes before serving.

457. VEGETABLE AND CHEESE STUFFED TOMATOES

Prep time: 10 minutes | Cook time: 18 minutes | Serves 4

- 4 medium beefsteak tomatoes, rinsed
- ½ cup grated carrot
- 1 medium onion, chopped
- 1 garlic clove, minced
- 2 teaspoons olive oil
- 2 cups fresh baby spinach
- ¼ cup crumbled low-sodium feta cheese
- ½ teaspoon dried basil

On your cutting board, cut a thin slice off the top of each tomato. Scoop out a ¼- to ½-inch-thick tomato pulp and place the tomatoes upside down on paper towels to drain. Set aside.

Stir together the carrot, onion, garlic, and olive oil in a baking pan.

Select Bake of the oven. Set temperature to 350ºF (180ºC) and set time to 5 minutes. Select Start to begin preheating.

Once preheated, slide the pan into the oven. Stir the vegetables halfway through.

When cooking is complete, the carrot should be crisp-tender.

Remove the pan from the oven and stir in the spinach, feta cheese, and basil.

Spoon ¼ of the vegetable mixture into each tomato and transfer the stuffed tomatoes to the oven. Set time to 13 minutes.

When cooking is complete, the filling should be hot and the tomatoes should be lightly caramelized.

Let the tomatoes cool for 5 minutes and serve.

458. ROASTED BELL PEPPERS WITH GARLIC

Prep time: 10 minutes | Cook time: 22 minutes | Serves 4

- 1 green bell pepper, sliced into 1-inch strips
- 1 red bell pepper, sliced into 1-inch strips
- 1 orange bell pepper, sliced into 1-inch strips
- 1 yellow bell pepper, sliced into 1-inch strips
- 2 tablespoons olive oil, divided
- ½ teaspoon dried marjoram
- Pinch salt
- Freshly ground black pepper, to taste
- 1 head garlic

Toss the bell peppers with 1 tablespoon of olive oil in a large bowl until well coated. Season with the marjoram, salt, and pepper. Toss again and set aside.

Cut off the top of a head of garlic. Place the garlic cloves on a large square of aluminum foil. Drizzle the top with the remaining 1 tablespoon of olive oil and wrap the garlic cloves in foil.

Transfer the garlic to a perforated pan.

Select Roast of the oven. Set temperature to 330ºF (166ºC) and set time to 15 minutes. Select Start to begin preheating.

Once preheated, slide the pan into the oven.

After 15 minutes, remove the perforated pan from the oven and add the bell peppers. Return to the oven and set time to 7 minutes.

When cooking is complete or until the garlic is soft and the bell peppers are tender.

TRANSFER THE COOKED BELL PEPPERS TO A PLATE. REMOVE THE GARLIC AND UNWRAP THE FOIL. LET THE GARLIC REST FOR A FEW MINUTES. ONCE COOLED, SQUEEZE THE ROASTED GARLIC CLOVES OUT OF THEIR SKINS AND ADD THEM TO THE PLATE OF BELL PEPPERS. STIR WELL AND SERVE IMMEDIATELY.

459. SPICY BROCCOLI WITH HOT SAUCE

Prep time: 5 minutes | Cook time: 14 minutes | Serves 6

- Broccoli:
- 1 medium-sized head broccoli, cut into florets
- 1½ tablespoons olive oil
- 1 teaspoon shallot powder
- 1 teaspoon porcini powder
- ½ teaspoon freshly grated lemon zest
- ½ teaspoon hot paprika
- ½ teaspoon granulated garlic
- ⅓ teaspoon fine sea salt
- ⅓ teaspoon celery seeds
- Hot Sauce:
- ½ cup tomato sauce
- 1 tablespoon balsamic vinegar
- ½ teaspoon ground allspice

In a mixing bowl, combine all the ingredients for the broccoli and toss to coat. Transfer the broccoli to a perforated pan.

Select Air Fry, set temperature to 360ºF (182ºC), and set time to 14 minutes. Select Start to begin preheating.

Once preheated, slide the pan into the oven.

Meanwhile, make the hot sauce by whisking together the tomato sauce, balsamic vinegar, and allspice in a small bowl.

When cooking is complete, remove the broccoli from the oven and serve with the hot sauce.

460. BLISTERED SHISHITO PEPPERS WITH LIME JUICE

Prep time: 5 minutes | Cook time: 9 minutes | Serves 3

- ½ pound (227 g) shishito peppers, rinsed
- Cooking spray
- Sauce:
- 1 tablespoon tamari or shoyu
- 2 teaspoons fresh lime juice
- 2 large garlic cloves, minced

Spritz a perforated pan with cooking spray.

Place the shishito peppers in the perforated pan and spritz them with cooking spray.

Select Roast, set temperature to 392ºF (200ºC), and set time to 9 minutes. Select Start to begin preheating.

Once preheated, slide the pan into the oven.

Meanwhile, whisk together all the ingredients for the sauce in a large bowl. Set aside.

After 3 minutes, remove the pan from the oven. Flip the peppers and spritz them with cooking spray. Return to the oven and continue cooking.

After another 3 minutes, remove the pan from the oven. Flip the peppers and spray with cooking spray. Return to the oven and continue roasting for 3 minutes more, or until the peppers are blistered and nicely browned.

When cooking is complete, remove the peppers from the oven to the bowl of sauce. Toss to coat well and serve immediately.

461. CRISPY ZUCCHINI STICKS

Prep time: 5 minutes | Cook time: 14 minutes | Serves 4

- 2 small zucchini, cut into 2-inch × ½-inch sticks
- 3 tablespoons chickpea flour
- 2 teaspoons arrowroot (or cornstarch)
- ½ teaspoon garlic granules
- ¼ teaspoon sea salt
- ⅛ teaspoon freshly ground black pepper
- 1 tablespoon water
- Cooking spray

Combine the zucchini sticks with the chickpea flour, arrowroot, garlic granules, salt, and pepper in a medium bowl and toss to coat. Add the water and stir to mix well.
Spritz a perforated pan with cooking spray and spread out the zucchini sticks in the pan. Mist the zucchini sticks with cooking spray.
Select Air Fry, set temperature to 392ºF (200ºC), and set time to 14 minutes. Select Start to begin preheating.
Once preheated, slide the pan into the oven. Stir the sticks halfway through the cooking time.
When cooking is complete, the zucchini sticks should be crispy and nicely browned. Remove from the oven and serve warm.

462. CRISPY TOFU STICKS
Prep time: 5 minutes | Cook time: 14 minutes | Serves 4

- 2 tablespoons olive oil, divided
- ½ cup flour
- ½ cup crushed cornflakes
- Salt and black pepper, to taste
- 14 ounces (397 g) firm tofu, cut into ½-inch-thick strips

Grease a perforated pan with 1 tablespoon of olive oil.
Combine the flour, cornflakes, salt, and pepper on a plate.
Dredge the tofu strips in the flour mixture until they are completely coated. Transfer the tofu strips to the greased perforated pan.
Drizzle the remaining 1 tablespoon of olive oil over the top of tofu strips.
Select Air Fry, set temperature to 360ºF (182ºC), and set time to 14 minutes. Select Start to begin preheating.
Once preheated, slide the pan into the oven. Flip the tofu strips halfway through the cooking time.
When cooking is complete, the tofu strips should be crispy. Remove from the oven and serve warm.

463. BAKED TURNIP AND ZUCCHINI
Prep time: 5 minutes | Cook time: 18 minutes | Serves 4

- 3 turnips, sliced
- 1 large zucchini, sliced
- 1 large red onion, cut into rings
- 2 cloves garlic, crushed
- 1 tablespoon olive oil
- Salt and black pepper, to taste

Put the turnips, zucchini, red onion, and garlic in a baking pan. Drizzle the olive oil over the top and sprinkle with the salt and pepper.
Select Bake, set temperature to 330ºF (166ºC), and set time to 18 minutes. Select Start to begin preheating.
Once preheated, slide the pan into the oven.
When cooking is complete, the vegetables should be tender. Remove from the oven and serve on a plate.

464. CASHEW CAULIFLOWER WITH YOGURT SAUCE
Prep time: 5 minutes | Cook time: 12 minutes | Serves 2

- 4 cups cauliflower florets (about half a large head)
- 1 tablespoon olive oil
- 1 teaspoon curry powder
- Salt, to taste
- ½ cup toasted, chopped cashews, for garnish
- Yogurt Sauce:
- ¼ cup plain yogurt
- 2 tablespoons sour cream
- 1 teaspoon honey
- 1 teaspoon lemon juice
- Pinch cayenne pepper
- Salt, to taste
- 1 tablespoon chopped fresh cilantro, plus leaves for garnish

In a large mixing bowl, toss the cauliflower florets with the olive oil, curry powder, and salt.
Place the cauliflower florets in a perforated pan.
Select Air Fry. Set temperature to 400ºF (205ºC) and set time to 12 minutes. Select Start to begin preheating.
Once preheated, slide the pan into the oven. Stir the cauliflower florets twice during cooking.
When cooking is complete, the cauliflower should be golden brown. Meanwhile, mix all the ingredients for the yogurt sauce in a small bowl and whisk to combine.
Remove the cauliflower from the oven and drizzle with the yogurt sauce. Scatter the toasted cashews and cilantro on top and serve immediately.

465. GARLIC STUFFED MUSHROOMS
Prep time: 5 minutes | Cook time: 12 minutes | Serves 2

- 18 medium-sized white mushrooms
- 1 small onion, peeled and chopped
- 4 garlic cloves, peeled and minced
- 2 tablespoons olive oil
- 2 teaspoons cumin powder
- A pinch ground allspice
- Fine sea salt and freshly ground black pepper, to taste

On a clean work surface, remove the mushroom stems. Using a spoon, scoop out the mushroom gills and discard.
Thoroughly combine the onion, garlic, olive oil, cumin powder, allspice, salt, and pepper in a mixing bowl. Stuff the mushrooms evenly with the mixture.
Place the stuffed mushrooms in a perforated pan.
Select Roast of the oven. Set temperature to 345ºF (174ºC) and set time to 12 minutes. Select Start to begin preheating.
Once preheated, slide the pan into the oven.
When cooking is complete, the mushroom should be browned.
Cool for 5 minutes before serving.

466. STUFFED PORTOBELLOS WITH PEPPERS AND C HEESE
Prep time: 15 minutes | Cook time: 15 minutes | Serves 4

- 4 tablespoons sherry vinegar or white wine vinegar
- 6 garlic cloves, minced, divided
- 1 tablespoon fresh thyme leaves
- 1 teaspoon Dijon mustard
- 1 teaspoon kosher salt, divided
- ¼ cup plus 3¼ teaspoons extra-virgin olive oil, divided
- 8 portobello mushroom caps, each about 3 inches across, patted dry
- 1 small red or yellow bell pepper, thinly sliced
- 1 small green bell pepper, thinly sliced
- 1 small onion, thinly sliced
- ¼ teaspoon red pepper flakes
- Freshly ground black pepper, to taste

- 4 ounces (113 g) shredded Fontina cheese

Stir together the vinegar, 4 minced garlic cloves, thyme, mustard, and ½ teaspoon of kosher salt in a small bowl. Slowly pour in ¼ cup of olive oil, whisking constantly, or until an emulsion is formed. Reserve 2 tablespoons of the marinade and set aside.

Put the mushrooms in a resealable plastic bag and pour in the marinade. Seal and shake the bag, coating the mushrooms in the marinade. Transfer the mushrooms to the sheet pan, gill-side down.

Put the remaining 2 minced garlic cloves, bell peppers, onion, red pepper flakes, remaining ½ teaspoon of salt, and black pepper in a medium bowl. Drizzle with the remaining 3¼ teaspoons of olive oil and toss well. Transfer the bell pepper mixture to the sheet pan.

Select Roast, set temperature to 375ºF (190ºC), and set time to 12 minutes. Select Start to begin preheating.

Once preheated, place the pan into the oven.

After 7 minutes, remove the pan and stir the peppers and flip the mushrooms. Return the pan to the oven and continue cooking for 5 minutes.

Remove the pan from the oven and place the pepper mixture onto a cutting board and coarsely chop.

Brush both sides of the mushrooms with the reserved 2 tablespoons marinade. Stuff the caps evenly with the pepper mixture. Scatter the cheese on top.

Select Broil, set temperature to High, and set time to 3 minutes. Select Start to begin preheating.

Once preheated, slide the pan into the oven.

When done, the mushrooms should be tender and the cheese should be melted.

Serve warm.

467. STUFFED P ORTOBELLO MUSHROOMS WITH VEGETABLES

Prep time: 5 minutes | Cook time: 8 minutes | Serves 4

- 4 portobello mushrooms, stem removed
- 1 tablespoon olive oil
- 1 tomato, diced
- ½ green bell pepper, diced
- ½ small red onion, diced
- ½ teaspoon garlic powder
- Salt and black pepper, to taste
- ½ cup grated Mozzarella cheese

Using a spoon to scoop out the gills of the mushrooms and discard them. Brush the mushrooms with the olive oil.

In a mixing bowl, stir together the remaining ingredients except the Mozzarella cheese. Using a spoon to stuff each mushroom with the filling and scatter the Mozzarella cheese on top.

Arrange the mushrooms in a perforated pan.

Select Roast of the oven. Set temperature to 330ºF (166ºC) and set time to 8 minutes. Select Start to begin preheating.

Once preheated, slide the pan into the oven.

When cooking is complete, the cheese should be melted.

Serve warm.

468. STUFFED PEPPERS WITH BEANS AND RICE

Prep time: 10 minutes | Cook time: 18 minutes | Serves 4

- 4 medium red, green, or yellow bell peppers, halved and deseeded
- 4 tablespoons extra-virgin olive oil, divided
- ½ teaspoon kosher salt, divided
- 1 (15-ounce / 425-g) can chickpeas
- 1½ cups cooked white rice
- ½ cup diced roasted red peppers
- ¼ cup chopped parsley
- ½ small onion, finely chopped

- 3 garlic cloves, minced
- ½ teaspoon cumin
- ¼ teaspoon freshly ground black pepper
- ¾ cup panko bread crumbs

Brush the peppers inside and out with 1 tablespoon of olive oil. Season the insides with ¼ teaspoon of kosher salt. Arrange the peppers on the sheet pan, cut side up.

Place the chickpeas with their liquid into a large bowl. Lightly mash the beans with a potato masher. Sprinkle with the remaining ¼ teaspoon of kosher salt and 1 tablespoon of olive oil. Add the rice, red peppers, parsley, onion, garlic, cumin, and black pepper to the bowl and stir to incorporate.

Divide the mixture among the bell pepper halves.

Stir together the remaining 2 tablespoons of olive oil and panko in a small bowl. Top the pepper halves with the panko mixture.

Select Roast, set temperature to 375ºF (190ºC), and set time to 18 minutes. Select Start to begin preheating.

Once preheated, place the pan into the oven.

When done, the peppers should be slightly wrinkled , and the panko should be golden brown.

Remove from the oven and serve on a plate.

469. AIR FRIED WINTER VEGETABLE S

Prep time: 5 minutes | Cook time: 16 minutes | Serves 2

- 1 parsnip, sliced
- 1 cup sliced butternut squash
- 1 small red onion, cut into wedges
- ½ chopped celery stalk
- 1 tablespoon chopped fresh thyme
- 2 teaspoons olive oil
- Salt and black pepper, to taste

Toss all the ingredients in a large bowl until the vegetables are well coated.

Transfer the vegetables to a perforated pan.

Select Air Fry, set temperature to 380ºF (193ºC), and set time to 16 minutes. Select Start to begin preheating.

Once preheated, slide the pan into the oven. Stir the vegetables halfway through the cooking time.

When cooking is complete, the vegetables should be golden brown and tender. Remove from the oven and serve warm.

470. CRISPY VEG GIES WITH HALLOUMI

Prep time: 5 minutes | Cook time: 14 minutes | Serves 2

- 2 zucchinis, cut into even chunks
- 1 large eggplant, peeled, cut into chunks
- 1 large carrot, cut into chunks
- 6 ounces (170 g) halloumi cheese, cubed
- 2 teaspoons olive oil
- Salt and black pepper, to taste
- 1 teaspoon dried mixed herbs

Combine the zucchinis, eggplant, carrot, cheese, olive oil, salt, and pepper in a large bowl and toss to coat well.

Spread the mixture evenly in a perforated pan.

Select Air Fry, set temperature to 340ºF (171ºC), and set time to 14 minutes. Select Start to begin preheating.

Once preheated, slide the pan into the oven. Stir the mixture once during cooking.

When cooking is complete, they should be crispy and golden. Remove from the oven and serve topped with mixed herbs.

471. CRUSTED BRUSSELS SPROUTS WITH SAGE

Prep time: 5 minutes | Cook time: 15 minutes | Serves 4

- 1 pound (454 g) Brussels sprouts, halved
- 1 cup bread crumbs
- 2 tablespoons grated Grana Padano cheese
- 1 tablespoon paprika
- 2 tablespoons canola oil
- 1 tablespoon chopped sage

Line a perforated pan with parchment paper. Set aside.

In a small bowl, thoroughly mix the bread crumbs, cheese, and paprika.

In a large bowl, place the Brussels sprouts and drizzle the canola oil over the top. Sprinkle with the bread crumb mixture and toss to coat.

Transfer the Brussels sprouts to the prepared perforated pan.

Select Roast, set temperature to 400°F (205°C), and set time to 15 minutes. Select Start to begin preheating.

Once preheated, slide the pan into the oven. Stir the Brussels a few times during cooking.

When cooking is complete, the Brussels sprouts should be lightly browned and crisp. Transfer the Brussels sprouts to a plate and sprinkle the sage on top before serving.

472. BUTTERED BROCCOLI WITH PARMESAN
Prep time: 5 minutes | Cook time: 4 minutes | Serves 4

- 1 pound (454 g) broccoli florets
- 1 medium shallot, minced
- 2 tablespoons olive oil
- 2 tablespoons unsalted butter, melted
- 2 teaspoons minced garlic
- ¼ cup grated Parmesan cheese

Combine the broccoli florets with the shallot, olive oil, butter, garlic, and Parmesan cheese in a medium bowl and toss until the broccoli florets are thoroughly coated.

Place the broccoli florets in a perforated pan in a single layer.

Select Roast, set temperature to 360°F (182°C), and set time to 4 minutes. Select Start to begin preheating.

Once preheated, slide the pan into the oven.

When cooking is complete, the broccoli florets should be crisp-tender. Remove from the oven and serve warm.

473. GARLICKY SESAME CARROTS
Prep time: 5 minutes | Cook time: 16 minutes | Serves 4 to 6

- 1 pound (454 g) baby carrots
- 1 tablespoon sesame oil
- ½ teaspoon dried dill
- Pinch salt
- Freshly ground black pepper, to taste
- 6 cloves garlic, peeled
- 3 tablespoons sesame seeds

In a medium bowl, drizzle the baby carrots with the sesame oil. Sprinkle with the dill, salt, and pepper and toss to coat well.

Place the baby carrots in a perforated pan.

Select Roast, set temperature to 380°F (193°C), and set time to 16 minutes. Select Start to begin preheating.

Once preheated, slide the pan into the oven.

After 8 minutes, remove the pan from the oven and stir in the garlic. Return the pan to the oven and continue roasting for 8 minutes more.

When cooking is complete, the carrots should be lightly browned. Remove the pan from the oven and serve sprinkled with the sesame seeds.

474. FRIED ROOT VEGETABLE MEDLEY WITH THYME

Prep time: 10 minutes | Cook time: 22 minutes | Serves 4

- 2 carrots, sliced
- 2 potatoes, cut into chunks
- 1 rutabaga, cut into chunks
- 1 turnip, cut into chunks
- 1 beet, cut into chunks
- 8 shallots, halved
- 2 tablespoons olive oil
- Salt and black pepper, to taste
- 2 tablespoons tomato pesto
- 2 tablespoons water
- 2 tablespoons chopped fresh thyme

Toss the carrots, potatoes, rutabaga, turnip, beet, shallots, olive oil, salt, and pepper in a large mixing bowl until the root vegetables are evenly coated.

Place the root vegetables in a perforated pan.

Select Air Fry. Set temperature to 400°F (205°C) and set time to 22 minutes. Select Start to begin preheating.

Once preheated, slide the pan into the oven. Stir the vegetables twice during cooking.

When cooking is complete, the vegetables should be tender.

Meanwhile, in a small bowl, whisk together the tomato pesto and water until smooth.

When ready, remove the root vegetables from the oven to a platter. Drizzle with the tomato pesto mixture and sprinkle with the thyme. Serve immediately.

475. HEARTY ROASTED VEGGIE SALAD
Prep time: 5 minutes | Cook time: 20 minutes | Serves 2

- 1 potato, chopped
- 1 carrot, sliced diagonally
- 1 cup cherry tomatoes
- ½ small beetroot, sliced
- ¼ onion, sliced
- ½ teaspoon turmeric
- ½ teaspoon cumin
- ¼ teaspoon sea salt
- 2 tablespoons olive oil, divided
- A handful of arugula
- A handful of baby spinach
- Juice of 1 lemon
- 3 tablespoons canned chickpeas, for serving
- Parmesan shavings, for serving

Combine the potato, carrot, cherry tomatoes, beetroot, onion, turmeric, cumin, salt, and 1 tablespoon of olive oil in a large bowl and toss until well coated.

Arrange the veggies in a perforated pan.

Select Roast of the oven. Set temperature to 370°F (188°C) and set time to 20 minutes. Select Start to begin preheating.

Once preheated, slide the pan into the oven. Stir the vegetables halfway through.

When cooking is complete, the potatoes should be golden brown.

Let the veggies cool for 5 to 10 minutes in the oven.

Put the arugula, baby spinach, lemon juice, and remaining 1 tablespoon of olive oil in a salad bowl and stir to combine. Mix in the roasted veggies and toss well.

Scatter the chickpeas and Parmesan shavings on top and serve immediately.

476. CHEESY RICE AND OLIVES STUFFED PEPPERS
Prep time: 5 minutes | Cook time: 16 to 17 minutes | Serves 4

- 4 red bell peppers, tops sliced off
- 2 cups cooked rice
- 1 cup crumbled feta cheese
- 1 onion, chopped
- ¼ cup sliced kalamata olives
- ¾ cup tomato sauce
- 1 tablespoon Greek seasoning
- Salt and black pepper, to taste
- 2 tablespoons chopped fresh dill, for serving

Microwave the red bell peppers for 1 to 2 minutes until tender.
When ready, transfer the red bell peppers to a plate to cool.
Mix the cooked rice, feta cheese, onion, kalamata olives, tomato sauce, Greek seasoning, salt, and pepper in a medium bowl and stir until well combined.
Divide the rice mixture among the red bell peppers and transfer to a greased baking dish.
Select Bake of the oven. Set temperature to 360ºF (182ºC) and set time to 15 minutes. Select Start to begin preheating.
Once preheated, slide the pan into the oven.
When cooking is complete, the rice should be heated through and the vegetables should be soft.
Remove from the oven and serve with the dill sprinkled on top.

VEGETABLE SIDES

477. BAKED POTATOES WITH YOGURT AND CHIVES
Prep time: 5 minutes | Cook time: 35 minutes | Serves 4

- 4 (7-ounce / 198-g) russet potatoes, rinsed
- Olive oil spray
- ½ teaspoon kosher salt, divided
- ½ cup 2% plain Greek yogurt
- ¼ cup minced fresh chives
- Freshly ground black pepper, to taste

Pat the potatoes dry and pierce them all over with a fork. Spritz the potatoes with olive oil spray. Sprinkle with ¼ teaspoon of the salt.
Transfer the potatoes to a perforated pan.
Select Bake, set temperature to 400ºF (205ºC), and set time to 35 minutes. Select Start to begin preheating.
Once preheated, slide the pan into the oven.
When cooking is complete, the potatoes should be fork-tender. Remove from the oven and split open the potatoes. Top with the yogurt, chives, the remaining ¼ teaspoon of salt, and finish with the black pepper. Serve immediately.

478. PARMESAN ASPARAGUS FRIES
Prep time: 15 minutes | Cook time: 6 minutes | Serves 4 ·

- 2 egg whites
- ¼ cup water
- ¼ cup plus 2 tablespoons grated Parmesan cheese, divided
- ¾ cup panko bread crumbs
- ¼ teaspoon salt
- 12 ounces (340 g) fresh asparagus spears , woody ends trimmed
- Cooking spray

In a shallow dish , whisk together the egg whites and water until slightly foamy. In a separate shallow dish, thoroughly combine ¼ cup of Parmesan cheese, bread crumbs, and salt.
Dip the asparagus in the egg white, then roll in the cheese mixture to coat well.
Place the asparagus in a perforated pan in a single layer, leaving space between each spear. Spritz the asparagus with cooking spray.

Select Air Fry, set temperature to 390ºF (199ºC), and set time to 6 minutes. Select Start to begin preheating.
Once preheated, slide the pan into the oven.
When cooking is complete, the asparagus should be golden brown and crisp. Remove the pan from the oven. Sprinkle with the remaining 2 tablespoons of cheese and serve hot.

479. PARMESAN ZUCCHINI CHIPS
Prep time: 5 minutes | Cook time: 14 minutes | Serves 4

- 2 egg whites
- Salt and black pepper, to taste
- ½ cup seasoned bread crumbs
- 2 tablespoons grated Parmesan cheese
- ¼ teaspoon garlic powder
- 2 medium zucchini, sliced
- Cooking spray

Spritz a perforated pan with cooking spray.
In a bowl, beat the egg whites with salt and pepper. In a separate bowl, thoroughly combine the bread crumbs, Parmesan cheese, and garlic powder.
Dredge the zucchini slices in the egg white, then coat in the bread crumb mixture.
Arrange the zucchini slices in the perforated pan.
Select Air Fry of the oven. Set temperature to 400ºF (205ºC) and set time to 14 minutes. Select Start to begin preheating.
Once preheated, slide the pan into the oven. Flip the zucchini halfway through.
When cooking is complete, the zucchini should be tender.
Remove from the oven to a plate and serve.

480. ROSEMARY BEETS WITH BALSAMIC GLAZE
Prep time: 5 minutes | Cook time: 10 minutes | Serves 2

- Beet:
- 2 beets, cubed
- 2 tablespoons olive oil
- 2 springs rosemary, chopped
- Salt and black pepper, to taste
- Balsamic Glaze:
- ⅓ cup balsamic vinegar
- 1 tablespoon honey

Combine the beets, olive oil, rosemary, salt, and pepper in a mixing bowl and toss until the beets are completely coated.
Place the beets in a perforated pan.
Select Air Fry of the oven. Set temperature to 400ºF (205ºC) and set time to 10 minutes. Select Start to begin preheating.
Once preheated, slide the pan into the oven. Stir the vegetables halfway through.
When cooking is complete, the beets should be crisp and browned at the edges.
Meanwhile, make the balsamic glaze: Place the balsamic vinegar and honey in a small saucepan and bring to a boil over medium heat. When the sauce boils, reduce the heat to medium-low heat and simmer until the liquid is reduced by half.
When ready, remove the beets from the oven to a platter. Pour the balsamic glaze over the top and serve immediately.

481. CHARRED GREEN BEANS WITH SESAME SEEDS
Prep time: 5 minutes | Cook time: 8 minutes | Serves 4

- 1 tablespoon reduced-sodium soy sauce or tamari
- ½ tablespoon Sriracha sauce

- 4 teaspoons toasted sesame oil, divided
- 12 ounces (340 g) trimmed green beans
- ½ tablespoon toasted sesame seeds

Whisk together the soy sauce, Sriracha sauce, and 1 teaspoon of sesame oil in a small bowl until smooth. Set aside.

Toss the green beans with the remaining sesame oil in a large bowl until evenly coated.

Place the green beans in a perforated pan in a single layer.

Select Air Fry, set temperature to 375ºF (190ºC), and set time to 8 minutes. Select Start to begin preheating.

Once preheated, slide the pan into the oven. Stir the green beans halfway through the cooking time.

When cooking is complete, the green beans should be lightly charred and tender. Remove from the oven to a platter. Pour the prepared sauce over the top of green beans and toss well. Serve sprinkled with the toasted sesame seeds.

482. TAMARIND SWEET POTATOES
Prep time: 5 minutes | Cook time: 22 minutes | Serves 4

- 5 garnet sweet potatoes, peeled and diced
- 1½ tablespoons fresh lime juice
- 1 tablespoon butter, melted
- 2 teaspoons tamarind paste
- 1½ teaspoon ground allspice
- ⅓ teaspoon white pepper
- ½ teaspoon turmeric powder
- A few drops liquid stevia

In a large mixing bowl, combine all the ingredients and toss until the sweet potatoes are evenly coated. Place the sweet potatoes in a perforated pan.

Select Air Fry, set temperature to 400ºF (205ºC), and set time to 22 minutes. Select Start to begin preheating.

Once preheated, slide the pan into the oven. Stir the potatoes twice during cooking.

When cooking is complete, the potatoes should be crispy on the outside and soft on the inside. Let the potatoes cool for 5 minutes before serving.

483. HONEY-GLAZED ROASTED VEGGIES
Prep time: 15 minutes | Cook time: 20 minutes | Makes 3 cups

Glaze:
- 2 tablespoons raw honey
- 2 teaspoons minced garlic
- ¼ teaspoon dried marjoram
- ¼ teaspoon dried basil
- ¼ teaspoon dried oregano
- ⅛ teaspoon dried sage
- ⅛ teaspoon dried rosemary
- ⅛ teaspoon dried thyme
- ½ teaspoon salt
- ¼ teaspoon ground black pepper

Veggies:
- 3 to 4 medium red potatoes, cut into 1- to 2-inch pieces
- 1 small zucchini, cut into 1- to 2-inch pieces
- 1 small carrot, sliced into ¼-inch rounds
- 1 (10.5-ounce / 298-g) package cherry tomatoes, halved
- 1 cup sliced mushrooms
- 3 tablespoons olive oil

Combine the honey, garlic, marjoram, basil, oregano, sage, rosemary, thyme, salt, and pepper in a small bowl and stir to mix well. Set aside.

Place the red potatoes, zucchini, carrot, cherry tomatoes, and mushroom in a large bowl. Drizzle with the olive oil and toss to coat.

Pour the veggies into a perforated pan.

Select Roast of the oven. Set temperature to 380ºF (193ºC) and set time to 15 minutes. Select Start to begin preheating.

Once preheated, slide the pan into the oven. Stir the veggies halfway through.

When cooking is complete, the vegetables should be tender.

When ready, transfer the roasted veggies to the large bowl. Pour the honey mixture over the veggies, tossing to coat.

Spread out the veggies in a baking pan and place in the oven.

Increase the temperature to 390ºF (199ºC) and set time to 5 minutes on Roast.

When cooking is complete, the veggies should be tender and glazed. Serve warm.

MEATLESS RECIPES

484. MUSHROOM CLUB SANDWICH
INGREDIENTS:
- ¼ tbsp. Worcestershire sauce
- ½ tsp. olive oil
- ½ flake garlic crushed
- ¼ cup chopped onion
- ¼ tbsp. red chili sauce
- ½ cup water
- 2 slices of white bread
- 1 tbsp. softened butter
- 1 cup minced mushroom
- 1 small capsicum

DIRECTIONS:
Take the slices of bread and remove the edges. Now cut the slices horizontally.

Cook the ingredients for the sauce and wait till it thickens. Now, add the mushroom to the sauce and stir till it obtains the flavors. Roast the capsicum and peel the skin off. Cut the capsicum into slices. Apply the sauce on the slices.

Pre-heat the Cosori oven for 5 minutes at 300 Fahrenheit. Open the basket of the Fryer and place the prepared Classic Sandwiches in it such that no two Classic Sandwiches are touching each other. Now keep the fryer at 250 degrees for around 15 minutes. Turn the Classic Sandwiches in between the cooking process to cook both slices. Serve the Classic Sandwiches with tomato ketchup or mint sauce.

485. PANKO GREEN BEANS
Servings: 4
Cooking Time: 15 Minutes
INGREDIENTS:
- ½ cup flour
- 2 eggs
- 1 cup panko bread crumbs
- ½ cup grated Parmesan cheese
- 1 teaspoon cayenne pepper
- Salt and black pepper, to taste
- 1½ pounds (680 g) green beans

DIRECTIONS:
In a bowl, place the flour. In a separate bowl, lightly beat the eggs. In a separate shallow bowl, thoroughly combine the bread crumbs, cheese, cayenne pepper, salt, and pepper.

Dip the green beans in the flour, then in the beaten eggs, finally in the bread crumb mixture to coat well. Transfer the green beans to the air fryer basket.

Put the air fryer basket on the baking pan and slide into Rack Position 2, select Air Fry, set temperature to 400ºF (205ºC), and set time to 15 minutes.

Stir the green beans halfway through the cooking time.

When cooking is complete, remove from the oven to a bowl and serve.

486. ROASTED VEGETABLES SALAD

Servings: 5
Cooking Time: 85 Minutes
INGREDIENTS:
- 3 eggplants
- 1 tbsp of olive oil
- 3 medium zucchini
- 1 tbsp of olive oil
- 4 large tomatoes, cut them in eighths
- 4 cups of one shaped pasta
- 2 peppers of any color
- 1 cup of sliced tomatoes cut into small cubes
- 2 teaspoon of salt substitute
- 8 tbsp of grated parmesan cheese
- ½ cup of Italian dressing
- Leaves of fresh basil

DIRECTIONS:
Preparing the Ingredients. Wash your eggplant and slice it off then discard the green end. Make sure not to peel.
Slice your eggplant into1/2 inch of thick rounds. 1/2 inch)
Pour 1tbsp of olive oil on the eggplant round.
Air Frying. Put the eggplants in the basket of the Cosori air fryer oven and then toss it in the air fryer oven. Cook the eggplants for 40 minutes. Set the heat to 360 ° F
Meanwhile, wash your zucchini and slice it then discard the green end. But do not peel it.
Slice the Zucchini into thick rounds of ½ inch each. Toss your ingredients
Add 1 tbsp of olive oil.
Air Frying. Cook the zucchini for 25 minutes on a heat of 360° F and when the time is off set it aside.
Wash and cut the tomatoes.
Air Frying. Arrange your tomatoes in the basket of the Cosori air fryer oven. Set the timer to 30 minutes. Set the heat to 350° F
When the time is off, cook your pasta according to the pasta guiding directions, empty it into a colander. Run the cold water on it and wash it and drain the pasta and put it aside.
Meanwhile, wash and chop your peppers and place it in a bow
Wash and thinly slice your cherry tomatoes and add it to the bowl. Add your roasted veggies.
Add the pasta, a pinch of salt, the topping dressing, add the basil and the parm and toss everything together. (It is better to mix with your hands).
Set the ingredients together in the refrigerator, and let it chill
Serve your salad and enjoy it!

487. VEGGIE & GARLIC BAKE

Servings: 4
Cooking Time: 20 Minutes
INGREDIENTS:
- 1 lb turnips, sliced
- 1 large red onion, cut into rings
- 1 large zucchini, sliced
- Salt and black pepper to taste
- 2 cloves garlic, crushed
- 1 bay leaf, cut in 6 pieces
- 1 tbsp olive oil

DIRECTIONS:
Place turnips, onion, and zucchini in a bowl. Toss with olive oil and season with salt and pepper. Preheat Cosori on AirFry function to 330 F. Place the veggies into a baking pan.
Slip the bay leaves in the different parts of the slices and tuck the garlic cloves in between the slices. Press Start and cook for 15 minutes. Serve warm with as a side to a meat dish or salad.

488. VEGAN MEATLOAF

Servings: 8
Cooking Time: 65 Minutes
INGREDIENTS:
- Nonstick cooking spray
- 3 1/3 cups chickpeas, cooked
- 1 onion, chopped fine
- 2 stalks celery, chopped
- 2 carrots, chopped fine
- 2 cloves garlic diced fine
- 2 cups panko bread crumbs
- ½ cup almond milk, unsweetened
- 3 tbsp. vegan Worcestershire sauce
- 3 tbsp. soy sauce, divided
- 2 tbsp. olive oil
- 2 tbsp. flax seeds, ground
- ¼ cup + 2 tbsp. tomato paste
- 1 tsp liquid smoke
- ¼ tsp pepper
- 2 tbsp. maple syrup
- 2 tbsp. apple cider vinegar
- 1 tsp paprika

DIRECTIONS:
Place rack in position Lightly spray a 9-inch loaf pan with cooking spray. Place chickpeas, onion, celery, carrots, cloves, bread crumbs, milk, Worcestershire, 2 tablespoons soy sauce, oil, flax seeds, 2 tablespoons tomato paste, liquid smoke, and pepper in a food processor, you may need to do this in batches. Pulse until ingredients are combined but don't over blend. Transfer each batch to a large bowl, then mix together.
Set oven to bake on 375°F for 35 minutes.
Press mixture into the prepared pan. After the oven has preheated 5 minutes, add loaf pan to the oven and bake 30 minutes.
In a small bowl, whisk together remaining tomato paste and soy sauce, along with the syrup, vinegar, and paprika until smooth.
When the timer goes off, remove the loaf from the oven. Spoon glaze over top and bake another 20-25 minutes. Let cool 10 minutes before slicing and serving.
Nutrition Info: Calories 623, Total Fat 11g, Saturated Fat 2g, Total Carbs 83g, Net Carbs 70g, Protein 23g, Sugar 18g, Fiber 13g, Sodium 501mg, Potassium 969mg, Phosphorus 317mg

489. CAULIFLOWER BITES

Servings: 4
Cooking Time: 18 Minutes
INGREDIENTS:
- 1 Head Cauliflower, cut into small florets
- Tsps Garlic Powder
- Pinch of Salt and Pepper
- 1 Tbsp Butter, melted
- 1/2 Cup Chili Sauce
- Olive Oil

DIRECTIONS:
Preparing the Ingredients. Place cauliflower into a bowl and pour oil over florets to lightly cover.
Season florets with salt, pepper, and the garlic powder and toss well.
Air Frying. Place florets into the Cosori air fryer oven at 350 degrees for 14 minutes.
Remove cauliflower from the Air fryer oven.
Combine the melted butter with the chili sauce
Pour over the florets so that they are well coated.
Return to the Cosori air fryer oven and cook for additional 3 to 4 minutes
Serve as a side or with ranch or cheese dip as a snack.

490. ROASTED BELL PEPPERS WITH GARLIC

Servings: 4
Cooking Time: 22 Minutes

INGREDIENTS:

- 1 green bell pepper, sliced into 1-inch strips
- 1 red bell pepper, sliced into 1-inch strips
- 1 orange bell pepper, sliced into 1-inch strips
- 1 yellow bell pepper, sliced into 1-inch strips
- 2 tablespoons olive oil, divided
- ½ teaspoon dried marjoram
- Pinch salt
- Freshly ground black pepper, to taste
- 1 head garlic

DIRECTIONS:

Toss the bell peppers with 1 tablespoon of olive oil in a large bowl until well coated. Season with the marjoram, salt, and pepper. Toss again and set aside.

Cut off the top of a head of garlic. Place the garlic cloves on a large square of aluminum foil. Drizzle the top with the remaining 1 tablespoon of olive oil and wrap the garlic cloves in foil.

Transfer the garlic to the air fryer basket.

Put the air fryer basket on the baking pan and slide into Rack Position 2, select Roast, set temperature to 330ºF (166ºC) and set time to 15 minutes.

After 15 minutes, remove from the oven and add the bell peppers. Return to the oven and set time to 7 minutes.

When cooking is complete or until the garlic is soft and the bell peppers are tender.

Transfer the cooked bell peppers to a plate. Remove the garlic and unwrap the foil. Let the garlic rest for a few minutes. Once cooled, squeeze the roasted garlic cloves out of their skins and add them to the plate of bell peppers. Stir well and serve immediately.

491. VEGAN BEETROOT CHIPS

Servings: 2
Cooking Time: 9 Minutes

INGREDIENTS:

- 4 cups golden beetroot slices
- 2 tbsp olive oil
- 1 tbsp yeast flakes
- 1 tsp vegan seasoning
- Salt to taste

DIRECTIONS:

In a bowl, add the oil, beetroot slices, vegan seasoning, and yeast and mix well. Dump the coated chips in the basket. Set the heat to 370 F and press Start. Cook on AirFry function for14-16 minutes, shaking once halfway through. Serve.

492. CHEESY CABBAGE WEDGES

Servings: 4
Cooking Time: 25 Minutes

INGREDIENTS:

- ½ head cabbage, cut into wedges
- 2 cups Parmesan cheese, chopped
- 4 tbsp melted butter
- Salt and black pepper to taste
- ½ cup blue cheese sauce

DIRECTIONS:

Brush the cabbage wedges with butter and coat with mozzarella cheese. Place the coated wedges in the greased basket and fit in the baking tray; cook for 20 minutes at 380 F on Air Fry setting. Serve with blue cheese sauce.

493. OKRA FLAT CAKES

INGREDIENTS:

- 2 or 3 green chilies finely chopped
- 1 ½ tbsp. lemon juice

- Salt and pepper to taste
- 2 tbsp. garam masala
- 2 cups sliced okra
- 3 tsp. ginger finely chopped
- 1-2 tbsp. fresh coriander leaves

DIRECTIONS:

Mix the ingredients in a clean bowl and add water to it. Make sure that the

paste is not too watery but is enough to apply on the okra.

Pre heat the Cosori oven at 160 degrees Fahrenheit for 5 minutes. Place the French Cuisine Galettes in the fry basket and let them cook for another 25 minutes at the same temperature. Keep rolling them over to get a uniform cook. Serve either with mint sauce or ketchup.

494. CAYENNE TAHINI KALE

Servings: 2 To 4
Cooking Time: 15 Minutes

INGREDIENTS:

Dressing:

- ¼ cup tahini
- ¼ cup fresh lemon juice
- 2 tablespoons olive oil
- 1 teaspoon sesame seeds
- ½ teaspoon garlic powder
- ¼ teaspoon cayenne pepper

Kale:

- 4 cups packed torn kale leaves (stems and ribs removed and leaves torn into palm-size pieces)
- Kosher salt and freshly ground black pepper, to taste

DIRECTIONS:

Make the dressing: Whisk together the tahini, lemon juice, olive oil, sesame seeds, garlic powder, and cayenne pepper in a large bowl until well mixed.

Add the kale and massage the dressing thoroughly all over the leaves. Sprinkle the salt and pepper to season.

Place the kale in the air fryer basket in a single layer.

Put the air fryer basket on the baking pan and slide into Rack Position 2, select Air Fry, set temperature to 350ºF (180ºC), and set time to 15 minutes.

When cooking is complete, the leaves should be slightly wilted and crispy. Remove from the oven and serve on a plate.

495. BLACK GRAM FRENCH CUISINE GALETTE

INGREDIENTS:

- 2 or 3 green chilies finely chopped
- 1 ½ tbsp. lemon juice
- Salt and pepper to taste
- 2 cup black gram
- 2 medium potatoes boiled and mashed
- 1 ½ cup coarsely crushed peanuts
- 3 tsp. ginger finely chopped
- 1-2 tbsp. fresh coriander leaves

DIRECTIONS:

Mix the ingredients in a clean bowl.

Mold this mixture into round and flat French Cuisine Galettes.

Wet the French Cuisine Galettes slightly with water.

Pre heat the Cosori oven at 160 degrees Fahrenheit for 5 minutes. Place the French Cuisine Galettes in the fry basket and let them cook for another 25 minutes at the same temperature. Keep rolling them over to get a uniform cook. Serve either with mint sauce or ketchup.

496. CAYENNE SPICY GREEN BEANS

Servings: 4
Cooking Time: 20 Minutes
INGREDIENTS:

- 1 cup panko breadcrumbs
- 2 whole eggs, beaten
- ½ cup Parmesan cheese, grated
- ½ cup flour
- 1 tsp cayenne pepper
- 1 ½ pounds green beans
- Salt to taste

DIRECTIONS:

In a bowl, mix panko breadcrumbs, Parmesan cheese, cayenne pepper, salt, and pepper. Roll the green beans in flour and dip in eggs. Dredge beans in the parmesan-panko mix. Place the prepared beans in the greased cooking basket and fit in the baking tray; cook for 15 minutes on Air Fry function at 350 F, shaking once. Serve and enjoy!

497. GHERKINS FLAT CAKES
INGREDIENTS:
- 2 or 3 green chilies finely chopped
- 1 ½ tbsp. lemon juice
- Salt and pepper to taste
- 2 tbsp. garam masala
- 2 cups sliced gherkins
- 3 tsp. ginger finely chopped
- 1-2 tbsp. fresh coriander leaves

DIRECTIONS:

Mix the ingredients in a clean bowl and add water to it. Make sure that the paste is not too watery but is enough to apply on the gherkin.
Pre heat the Cosori oven at 160 degrees Fahrenheit for 5 minutes. Place the French Cuisine Galettes in the fry basket and let them cook for another 25 minutes at the same temperature. Keep rolling them over to get a uniform cook. Serve either with mint sauce or ketchup.

498. CABBAGE FLAT CAKES
INGREDIENTS:
- 2 or 3 green chilies finely chopped
- 1 ½ tbsp. lemon juice
- Salt and pepper to taste
- 2 tbsp. garam masala
- 2 cups halved cabbage leaves
- 3 tsp. ginger finely chopped
- 1-2 tbsp. fresh coriander leaves

DIRECTIONS:

Mix the ingredients in a clean bowl and add water to it. Make sure that the paste is not too watery but is enough to apply on the cabbage.
Pre heat the Cosori oven at 160 degrees Fahrenheit for 5 minutes. Place the French Cuisine Galettes in the fry basket and let them cook for another 25 minutes at the same temperature. Keep rolling them over to get a uniform cook. Serve either with mint sauce or ketchup.

499. ASIAN-INSPIRED BROCCOLI
Servings: 2
Cooking Time: 10 Minutes
INGREDIENTS:
- 12 ounces (340 g) broccoli florets
- 2 tablespoons Asian hot chili oil
- 1 teaspoon ground Sichuan peppercorns (or black pepper)
- 2 garlic cloves, finely chopped
- 1 (2-inch) piece fresh ginger, peeled and finely chopped
- Kosher salt and freshly ground black pepper

DIRECTIONS:

Toss the broccoli florets with the chili oil, Sichuan peppercorns, garlic, ginger, salt, and pepper in a mixing bowl until thoroughly coated.
Transfer the broccoli florets to the air fryer basket.
Put the air fryer basket on the baking pan and slide into Rack Position 2, select Air Fry, set temperature to 375ºF (190ºC), and set time to 10 minutes.
Stir the broccoli florets halfway through the cooking time.
When cooking is complete, the broccoli florets should be lightly browned and tender. Remove the broccoli from the oven and serve on a plate.

500. MINT FRENCH CUISINE GALETTE
INGREDIENTS:
- 1-2 tbsp. fresh coriander leaves
- 2 or 3 green chilies finely chopped
- 1 ½ tbsp. lemon juice
- Salt and pepper to taste
- 2 cups mint leaves (Sliced fine)
- 2 medium potatoes boiled and mashed
- 1 ½ cup coarsely crushed peanuts
- 3 tsp. ginger finely chopped

DIRECTIONS:

Mix the sliced mint leaves with the rest of the ingredients in a clean bowl.
Mold this mixture into round and flat French Cuisine Galettes.
Wet the French Cuisine Galettes slightly with water. Coat each French Cuisine Galette with the crushed peanuts.
Pre heat the Cosori oven at 160 degrees Fahrenheit for 5 minutes. Place the French Cuisine Galettes in the fry basket and let them cook for another 25 minutes at the same temperature. Keep rolling them over to get a uniform cook. Serve either with mint sauce or ketchup.

501. STUFFED PORTOBELLO MUSHROOMS WITH VEGETABLES
Servings: 4
Cooking Time: 8 Minutes

INGREDIENTS:
- 4 portobello mushrooms, stem removed
- 1 tablespoon olive oil
- 1 tomato, diced
- ½ green bell pepper, diced
- ½ small red onion, diced
- ½ teaspoon garlic powder
- Salt and black pepper, to taste
- ½ cup grated Mozzarella cheese

DIRECTIONS:

Using a spoon to scoop out the gills of the mushrooms and discard them. Brush the mushrooms with the olive oil.
In a mixing bowl, stir together the remaining ingredients except the Mozzarella cheese. Using a spoon to stuff each mushroom with the filling and scatter the Mozzarella cheese on top.
Arrange the mushrooms in the air fryer basket.
Put the air fryer basket on the baking pan and slide into Rack Position 2, select Roast, set temperature to 330ºF (166ºC) and set time to 8 minutes.
When cooking is complete, the cheese should be melted.
Serve warm.

502. COTTAGE CHEESE GNOCCHI'S
INGREDIENTS:
- 2 tsp. ginger-garlic paste
- 2 tsp. soya sauce
- 2 tsp. vinegar
- 1 ½ cup all-purpose flour
- ½ tsp. salt
- 5 tbsp. water
- 2 cups grated cottage cheese
- 2 tbsp. oil

DIRECTIONS:

Squeeze the dough and cover it with plastic wrap and set aside. Next, cook the ingredients for the filling and try to ensure that the cottage cheese is covered well with the sauce.

Roll the dough and place the filling in the center. Now, wrap the dough to cover the filling and pinch the edges together.

Pre heat the Cosori oven at 200° F for 5 minutes. Place the gnocchi's in the fry basket and close it. Let them cook at the same temperature for another 20 minutes. Recommended sides are chili sauce or ketchup.

503. COTTAGE CHEESE FRENCH CUISINE GALETTE
INGREDIENTS:
- 1-2 tbsp. fresh coriander leaves
- 2 or 3 green chilies finely chopped
- 1 ½ tbsp. lemon juice
- Salt and pepper to taste
- 2 tbsp. garam masala
- 2 cups grated cottage cheese
- 1 ½ cup coarsely crushed peanuts
- 3 tsp. ginger finely chopped

DIRECTIONS:
Mix the ingredients in a clean bowl.
Mold this mixture into round and flat French Cuisine Galettes.
Wet the French Cuisine Galettes slightly with water. Coat each French Cuisine Galette with the crushed peanuts.
Pre heat the Cosori oven at 160 degrees Fahrenheit for 5 minutes. Place the French Cuisine Galettes in the fry basket and let them cook for another 25 minutes at the same temperature. Keep rolling them over to get a uniform cook. Serve either with mint sauce or ketchup.

504. RADISH FLAT CAKES
INGREDIENTS:
- 1-2 tbsp. fresh coriander leaves
- 2 or 3 green chilies finely chopped
- 1 ½ tbsp. lemon juice
- Salt and pepper to taste
- 2 tbsp. garam masala
- 2 cups sliced radish
- 3 tsp. ginger finely chopped

DIRECTIONS:
Mix the ingredients in a clean bowl and add water to it. Make sure that the paste is not too watery but is enough to apply on the radish.
Pre heat the Cosori oven at 160 degrees Fahrenheit for 5 minutes. Place the French Cuisine Galettes in the fry basket and let them cook for another 25 minutes at the same temperature. Keep rolling them over to get a uniform cook. Serve either with mint sauce or ketchup.

505. STUFFED MUSHROOMS
Servings: 12
Cooking Time: 8 Minutes
INGREDIENTS:
- 2 Rashers Bacon, Diced
- ½ Onion, Diced
- ½ Bell Pepper, Diced
- 1 Small Carrot, Diced
- 24 Medium Size Mushrooms (Separate the caps & stalks)
- 1 cup Shredded Cheddar Plus Extra for the Top
- ½ cup Sour Cream

DIRECTIONS:
Preparing the Ingredients. Chop the mushrooms stalks finely and fry them up with the bacon, onion, pepper and carrot at 350 ° for 8 minutes. When the veggies are fairly tender, stir in the sour cream & the cheese. Keep on the heat until the cheese has melted and everything is mixed nicely.
Now grab the mushroom caps and heap a plop of filling on each one.

Place in the fryer basket and top with a little extra cheese.

506. CHEESY FRITTATA WITH VEGETABLES
Servings: 2
Cooking Time: 25 Minutes
INGREDIENTS:
- 1 cup baby spinach
- ⅓ cup sliced mushrooms
- 1 zucchini, sliced with a 1-inch thickness
- 1 small red onion, sliced
- ¼ cup chopped chives
- ¼ lb asparagus, trimmed and sliced thinly
- 2 tsp olive oil
- 4 eggs, cracked into a bowl
- ⅓ cup milk
- Salt and black pepper to taste
- ⅓ cup grated Cheddar cheese
- ⅓ cup crumbled Feta cheese

DIRECTIONS:
Preheat Cosori on Bake function to 320 F. Line a baking dish with parchment paper. Mix the beaten eggs with milk, salt, and pepper.
Heat olive oil in a skillet over medium heat add stir-fry asparagus, zucchini, onion, mushrooms, and baby spinach for 5 minutes. Pour the veggies into the baking dish and top with the egg mixture. Sprinkle with feta and cheddar cheeses. Cook for 15 minutes. Garnish with chives.

507. CHEESE-WALNUT STUFFED MUSHROOMS
Servings: 4
Cooking Time: 10 Minutes
INGREDIENTS:
- 4 large portobello mushrooms
- 1 tablespoon canola oil
- ½ cup shredded Mozzarella cheese
- ⅓ cup minced walnuts
- 2 tablespoons chopped fresh parsley
- Cooking spray

DIRECTIONS:
Spritz the air fryer basket with cooking spray.
On a clean work surface, remove the mushroom stems. Scoop out the gills with a spoon and discard. Coat the mushrooms with canola oil. Top each mushroom evenly with the shredded Mozzarella cheese, followed by the minced walnuts.
Arrange the mushrooms in the basket.
Put the air fryer basket on the baking pan and slide into Rack Position 2, select Roast, set temperature to 350°F (180°C) and set time to 10 minutes.
When cooking is complete, the mushroom should be golden brown.
Transfer the mushrooms to a plate and sprinkle the parsley on top for garnish before serving.

508. COTTAGE CHEESE FINGERS
INGREDIENTS:
- 2 tsp. salt
- 1 tsp. pepper powder
- 1 tsp. red chili powder
- 6 tbsp. corn flour
- 4 eggs
- 2 cups cottage cheese Oregano Fingers
- 2 cup dry breadcrumbs
- 2 tsp. oregano
- 1 ½ tbsp. ginger-garlic paste
- 4 tbsp. lemon juice

DIRECTIONS:
Mix all the ingredients for the marinade and put the chicken Oregano Fingers inside and let it rest overnight.

Mix the breadcrumbs, oregano and red chili flakes well and place the marinated Oregano Fingers on this mixture. Cover it with plastic wrap and leave it till right before you serve to cook.

Pre heat the Cosori oven at 160 degrees Fahrenheit for 5 minutes. Place the Oregano Fingers in the fry basket and close it. Let them cook at the same temperature for another 15 minutes or so. Toss the Oregano Fingers well so that they are cooked uniformly.

509. LEMONY BRUSSELS SPROUTS AND TOMATOES

Servings: 4
Cooking Time: 20 Minutes
INGREDIENTS:
- 1 pound (454 g) Brussels sprouts, trimmed and halved
- 1 tablespoon extra-virgin olive oil
- Sea Salt and freshly ground black pepper, to taste
- ½ cup sun-dried tomatoes, chopped
- 2 tablespoons freshly squeezed lemon juice
- 1 teaspoon lemon zest

DIRECTIONS:
Line the air fryer basket with aluminum foil.
Toss the Brussels sprouts with the olive oil in a large bowl. Sprinkle with salt and black pepper.
Spread the Brussels sprouts in a single layer in the basket.
Put the air fryer basket on the baking pan and slide into Rack Position 2, select Roast, set temperature to 400ºF (205ºC), and set time to 20 minutes.
When done, the Brussels sprouts should be caramelized. Remove from the oven to a serving bowl, along with the tomatoes, lemon juice, and lemon zest. Toss to combine. Serve immediately.

510. CILANTRO ROASTED CARROTS WITH CUMIN SEEDS

Servings: 4
Cooking Time: 15 Minutes
INGREDIENTS:
- 1 lb carrots, julienned
- 1 tbsp olive oil
- 1 tsp cumin seeds
- 2 tbsp fresh cilantro, chopped

DIRECTIONS:
Preheat Cosori on AirFry function to 350 F. In a bowl, mix oil, carrots, and cumin seeds. Gently stir to coat the carrots well. Place the carrots in a baking tray and press Star. Cook for 10 minutes. Scatter fresh coriander over the carrots and serve.

511. COTTAGE CHEESE SPICY LEMON KEBAB

INGREDIENTS:
- 3 tsp. lemon juice
- 2 tbsp. coriander powder
- 3 tbsp. chopped capsicum
- 2 tbsp. peanut flour
- 2 cups cubed cottage cheese
- 3 onions chopped
- 5 green chilies-roughly chopped
- 1 ½ tbsp. ginger paste
- 1 ½ tsp. garlic paste
- 1 ½ tsp. salt
- 3 eggs

DIRECTIONS:
Coat the cottage cheese cubes with the corn flour and mix the other ingredients in a bowl. Make the mixture into a smooth paste and coat the cheese cubes with the mixture. Beat the eggs in a bowl and add a little salt to them.
Dip the cubes in the egg mixture and coat them with sesame seeds and

leave them in the refrigerator for an hour.
Pre heat the Cosori oven at 290 Fahrenheit for around 5 minutes. Place the kebabs in the basket and let them cook for another 25 minutes at the same temperature. Turn the kebabs over in between the cooking process to get a uniform cook. Serve the kebabs with mint sauce.

512. AIR FRIED WINTER VEGETABLES

Servings: 2
Cooking Time: 16 Minutes
INGREDIENTS:
- 1 parsnip, sliced
- 1 cup sliced butternut squash
- 1 small red onion, cut into wedges
- ½ chopped celery stalk
- 1 tablespoon chopped fresh thyme
- 2 teaspoons olive oil
- Salt and black pepper, to taste

DIRECTIONS:
Toss all the ingredients in a large bowl until the vegetables are well coated.
Transfer the vegetables to the air fryer basket.
Put the air fryer basket on the baking pan and slide into Rack Position 2, select Air Fry, set temperature to 380ºF (193ºC), and set time to 16 minutes.
Stir the vegetables halfway through the cooking time.
When cooking is complete, the vegetables should be golden brown and tender. Remove from the oven and serve warm.

513. SPINACH ENCHILADAS WITH MOZZARELLA

Servings: 4
Cooking Time: 20 Minutes
INGREDIENTS:
- 8 corn tortillas, warm
- 2 cups mozzarella cheese, shredded
- 1 cup ricotta cheese, crumbled
- 1 package frozen spinach
- 1 garlic clove, minced
- ½ cup sliced onions
- ½ cup sour cream
- 1 tbsp butter
- 1 can enchilada sauce

DIRECTIONS:
In a saucepan, heat oil and sauté garlic and onion for 3 minutes. Stir in the spinach and cook for 5 more minutes. Remove and stir in the ricotta cheese, sour cream and some mozzarella.
Spoon ¼ cup of spinach mixture in the middle of a tortilla. Roll up and place seam side down in the basket. Repeat the process with the remaining tortillas.
Pour the enchilada sauce all over and sprinkle with the remaining mozzarella. Cook for 15 minutes at 380 F on AirFry function.

514. WHITE LENTIL FRENCH CUISINE GALETTE

INGREDIENTS:
- 1 ½ tbsp. lemon juice
- Salt and pepper to taste
- 2 cup white lentil soaked
- 3 tsp. ginger finely chopped
- 1-2 tbsp. fresh coriander leaves
- 2 or 3 green chilies finely chopped

DIRECTIONS:
Wash the soaked lentils and mix it with the rest of the ingredients in a clean bowl.
Mold this mixture into round and flat French Cuisine Galettes.

Wet the French Cuisine Galettes slightly with water.

Pre heat the Cosori oven at 160 degrees Fahrenheit for 5 minutes. Place the French Cuisine Galettes in the fry basket and let them cook for another 25 minutes at the same temperature. Keep rolling them over to get a uniform cook. Serve either with mint sauce or ketchup.

515. TORTELLINI WITH VEGGIES AND PARMESAN

Servings: 4
Cooking Time: 16 Minutes
INGREDIENTS:
- 8 ounces (227 g) sugar snap peas, trimmed
- ½ pound (227 g) asparagus, trimmed and cut into 1-inch pieces
- 2 teaspoons kosher salt or 1 teaspoon fine salt, divided
- 1 tablespoon extra-virgin olive oil
- 1½ cups water
- 1 (20-ounce / 340-g) package frozen cheese tortellini
- 2 garlic cloves, minced
- 1 cup heavy (whipping) cream
- 1 cup cherry tomatoes, halved
- ½ cup grated Parmesan cheese
- ¼ cup chopped fresh parsley or basil
- Add the peas and asparagus to a large bowl. Add ½ teaspoon of kosher salt and the olive oil and toss until well coated. Place the veggies in the baking pan.

DIRECTIONS:
Slide the baking pan into Rack Position 1, select Convection Bake, set the temperature to 450°F (235°C), and set the time for 4 minutes.
Meanwhile, dissolve 1 teaspoon of kosher salt in the water.
Once cooking is complete, remove the pan from the oven and place the tortellini in the pan. Pour the salted water over the tortellini. Put the pan back to the oven.
Slide the baking pan into Rack Position 1, select Convection Bake, set temperature to 450°F (235°C), and set time for 7 minutes.
Meantime, stir together the garlic, heavy cream, and remaining ½ teaspoon of kosher salt in a small bowl.
Once cooking is complete, remove the pan from the oven. Blot off any remaining water with a paper towel. Gently stir the ingredients. Drizzle the cream over and top with the tomatoes.
Slide the baking pan into Rack Position 2, select Roast, set the temperature to 375°F (190°C), and set the time for 5 minutes.
After 4 minutes, remove from the oven.
Add the Parmesan cheese and stir until the cheese is melted
Serve topped with the parsley.

516. VEGETABLE SPICY LEMON KEBAB

INGREDIENTS:
- 1 ½ tsp. salt
- 3 tsp. lemon juice
- 2 tsp. garam masala
- 4 tbsp. chopped coriander
- 3 tbsp. cream
- 3 tbsp. chopped capsicum
- 2 cups mixed vegetables
- 3 onions chopped
- 5 green chilies-roughly chopped
- 1 ½ tbsp. ginger paste
- 1 ½ tsp. garlic paste
- 3 eggs
- 2 ½ tbsp. white sesame seeds

DIRECTIONS:
Grind the ingredients except for the egg and form a smooth paste. Coat the vegetables in the paste. Now, beat the eggs and add a little salt to it. Dip the coated vegetables in the egg mixture and then transfer to the sesame seeds and coat the vegetables well. Place the vegetables on a stick. Pre heat the Cosori oven at 160 degrees Fahrenheit for around 5 minutes. Place the sticks in the basket and let them cook for another 25 minutes at the same temperature. Turn the sticks over in between the cooking process to get a uniform cook.

517. WINTER VEGETARIAN FRITTATA

Servings: 4
Cooking Time: 30 Minutes
INGREDIENTS:
- 1 leek, peeled and thinly sliced into rings
- 2 cloves garlic, finely minced
- 3 medium-sized carrots, finely chopped
- 2 tablespoons olive oil
- 6 large-sized eggs
- Sea salt and ground black pepper, to taste
- 1/2 teaspoon dried marjoram, finely minced
- 1/2 cup yellow cheese of choice

DIRECTIONS:
Preparing the Ingredients. Sauté the leek, garlic, and carrot in hot olive oil until they are tender and fragrant; reserve.
In the meantime, preheat your Cosori air fryer oven to 330 degrees F.
In a bowl, whisk the eggs along with the salt, ground black pepper, and marjoram.
Then, grease the inside of your baking dish with a nonstick cooking spray. Pour the whisked eggs into the baking dish. Stir in the sautéed carrot mixture. Top with the cheese shreds.
Air Frying. Place the baking dish in the Cosori air fryer oven cooking basket. Cook about 30 minutes and serve warm

518. CHILI COTTAGE CHEESE

INGREDIENTS:
- 2 tbsp. olive oil
- 1 capsicum. Cut into thin and long pieces (lengthwise).
- 2 small onions. Cut them into halves.
- 1 ½ tsp. ginger garlic paste.
- ½ tbsp. red chili sauce.
- 2 tbsp. tomato ketchup.
- 1 ½ tbsp. sweet chili sauce.
- 2 tsp. vinegar.
- 2 tsp. soya sauce.
- A few drops of edible red food coloring.
- 1-2 tbsp. honey.
- 2 cups cubed cottage cheese
- 2 ½ tsp. ginger-garlic paste
- 1 tsp. red chili sauce
- ¼ tsp. salt
- ¼ tsp. red chili powder/black pepper
- A few drops of edible orange food coloring
- ¼ tsp. Ajinomoto.
- A pinch of black pepper powder.
- 1-2 tsp. red chili flakes.
- For the garnish, use the greens of spring onions and sesame seeds.

DIRECTIONS:
Create the mix for the cottage cheese cubes and coat the chicken well with it.
Pre heat the Cosori oven at 250 Fahrenheit for 5 minutes or so. Open the basket of the Fryer. Place the Oregano Fingers inside the basket. Now let the fryer stay at 290 Fahrenheit for another 20 minutes. Keep tossing the Oregano Fingers periodically through the cook to get a uniform cook.
Add the ingredients to the sauce and cook it with the vegetables till it thickens. Add the Oregano Fingers to the sauce and cook till the flavors have blended.

519. MUSHROOM MARINADE CUTLET

INGREDIENTS:
- 2 cup fresh green coriander
- ½ cup mint leaves

- 4 tsp. fennel
- 2 tbsp. ginger-garlic paste
- 1 small onion
- 6-7 flakes garlic (optional)
- Salt to taste
- 2 cups sliced mushrooms
- 1 big capsicum (Cut this capsicum into big cubes)
- 1 onion (Cut it into quarters. Now separate the layers carefully.)
- 5 tbsp. gram flour
- A pinch of salt to taste
- 3 tbsp. lemon juice

DIRECTIONS: **TAKE A CLEAN AND DRY CONTAINER. PUT INTO IT THE CORIANDER, MINT, FENNEL, AND GINGER, ONION/GARLIC, SALT AND LEMON JUICE. MIX THEM.**
Pour the mixture into a grinder and blend until you get a thick paste. Slit the mushroom almost till the end and leave them aside. Now stuff all the pieces with the paste and set aside. Take the sauce and add to it the gram flour and some salt. Mix them together properly. Rub this mixture all over the stuffed mushroom.

Now, to the leftover sauce, add the capsicum and onions. Apply the sauce generously on each of the pieces of capsicum and onion. Now take satay sticks and arrange the cottage cheese pieces and vegetables on separate sticks.

Pre heat the Cosori oven at 290 Fahrenheit for around 5 minutes. Open the basket. Arrange the satay sticks properly. Close the basket. Keep the sticks with the mushroom at 180 degrees for around half an hour while the sticks with the vegetables are to be kept at the same temperature for only 7 minutes. Turn the sticks in between so that one side does not get burnt and also to provide a uniform cook.

520. ASIAN TOFU "MEATBALLS"
Servings: 4
Cooking Time: 10 Minutes
INGREDIENTS:
- 3 dried shitake mushrooms
- Nonstick cooking spray
- 14 oz. firm tofu, drained & pressed
- ¼ cup carrots, cooked
- ¼ cup bamboo shoots, sliced thin
- ½ cup Panko bread crumbs
- 2 tbsp. corn starch
- 3 ½ tablespoon soy sauce, divided
- 1 tsp garlic powder
- ¼ tsp salt
- 1/8 tsp pepper
- 1 tbsp. olive oil
- 2 tbsp. garlic, diced fine
- 2 tbsp. ketchup
- 2 tsp sugar

DIRECTIONS:
Place the shitake mushrooms in a bowl and add just enough water to cover. Let soak 20 minutes until soft. Drain well and chop.
Place the baking pan in position Lightly spray the fryer basket with cooking spray.
Place mushrooms, tofu, carrots, bamboo shoots, bread crumbs, corn starch, 1 ½ tablespoons soy sauce, and seasonings in a food processor. Pulse until thoroughly combined. Form mixture into 1-inch balls.
Place balls in fryer basket, these may need to be cooked in batches, and place in oven. Set to air fry on 380°F for 10 minutes. Turn the balls around halfway through cooking time.
Heat oil in a saucepan over medium heat. Add garlic and cook 1 minute. Stir in remaining soy sauce, ketchup, and sugar. Bring to a simmer and cook until sauce thickens, 3-5 minutes.
When the meatballs are done, add them to sauce and stir to coat. Serve immediately.
Nutrition Info: Calories 305, Total Fat 13g, Saturated Fat 2g, Total Carbs 28g, Net Carbs 24g, Protein 20g, Sugar 5g, Fiber 4g, Sodium 789mg, Potassium 470mg, Phosphorus 260mg

521. MAPLE AND PECAN GRANOLA
Servings: 4
Cooking Time: 20 Minutes
INGREDIENTS:
- 1½ cups rolled oats
- ¼ cup maple syrup
- ¼ cup pecan pieces
- 1 teaspoon vanilla extract
- ½ teaspoon ground cinnamon

DIRECTIONS:
Line a baking sheet with parchment paper.
Mix together the oats, maple syrup, pecan pieces, vanilla, and cinnamon in a large bowl and stir until the oats and pecan pieces are completely coated. Spread the mixture evenly in the baking pan.
Slide the baking pan into Rack Position 1, select Convection Bake, set temperature to 300ºF (150ºC), and set time to 20 minutes.
Stir once halfway through the cooking time.
When done, remove from the oven and cool for 30 minutes before serving. The granola may still be a bit soft right after removing, but it will gradually firm up as it cools.

522. VEGETABLE AU GRATIN
Servings: 3
Cooking Time: 30 Minutes
INGREDIENTS:
- 1 cup cubed eggplant
- ¼ cup chopped red pepper
- ¼ cup chopped green pepper
- ¼ cup chopped onion
- ⅓ cup chopped tomatoes
- 1 clove garlic, minced
- 1 tbsp sliced pimiento-stuffed olives
- 1 tsp capers
- ¼ tsp dried basil
- ¼ tsp dried marjoram
- Salt and black pepper to taste
- ¼ cup grated mozzarella cheese
- 1 tbsp breadcrumbs

DIRECTIONS:
In a bowl, add eggplant, peppers, onion, tomatoes, olives, garlic, basil, marjoram, capers, salt, and black pepper. Lightly grease a baking tray with cooking spray. Add in the vegetable mixture and spread it evenly. Sprinkle mozzarella cheese on top and cover with breadcrumbs. Cook in your Cosori for 20 minutes on Bake function at 360 F. Serve.

523. COTTAGE CHEESE AND MUSHROOM MEXICAN BURRITOS
INGREDIENTS:
- ½ cup mushrooms thinly sliced
- 1 cup cottage cheese cut in too long and slightly thick
- Oregano
- Fingers
- A pinch of salt to taste
- ½ tsp. red chili flakes
- 1 tsp. freshly ground peppercorns
- ½ cup pickled jalapenos
- 1-2 lettuce leaves shredded.
- ½ cup red kidney beans (soaked overnight)
- ½ small onion chopped
- 1 tbsp. olive oil
- 2 tbsp. tomato puree

- ¼ tsp. red chili powder
- 1 tsp. of salt to taste
- 4-5 flour tortillas
- 1 or 2 spring onions chopped finely. Also cut the greens.
- Take one tomato. Remove the seeds and chop it into small pieces.
- 1 green chili chopped.
- 1 cup of cheddar cheese grated.
- 1 cup boiled rice (not necessary).
- A few flour tortillas to put the filing in.

DIRECTIONS:

Cook the beans along with the onion and garlic and mash them finely.

Now, make the sauce you will need for the burrito. Ensure that you create a slightly thick sauce.

For the filling, you will need to cook the ingredients well in a pan and ensure that the vegetables have browned on the outside.

To make the salad, toss the ingredients together. Place the tortilla and add a layer of sauce, followed by the beans and the filling at the center. Before you roll it, you will need to place the salad on top of the filling.

Pre-heat the Cosori oven for around 5 minutes at 200 Fahrenheit. Open the fry basket and keep the burritos inside. Close the basket properly. Let the Air

Fryer remain at 200 Fahrenheit for another 15 minutes or so. Halfway through, remove the basket and turn all the burritos over in order to get a uniform cook.

524. MUSHROOM POPS

INGREDIENTS:
- 1 tsp. dry basil
- 1 tsp. lemon juice
- 1 tsp. red chili flakes
- 1 cup whole mushrooms
- 1 ½ tsp. garlic paste
- Salt and pepper to taste
- 1 tsp. dry oregano

DIRECTIONS:

Add the ingredients into a separate bowl and mix them well to get a consistent mixture.

Dip the mushrooms in the above mixture and leave them aside for some time.

Pre heat the Cosori oven at 180° C for around 5 minutes. Place the coated cottage cheese pieces in the fry basket and close it properly. Let them cook at the same temperature for 20 more minutes. Keep turning them over in the basket so that they are cooked properly. Serve with tomato ketchup.

525. TASTY POLENTA CRISPS

Servings: 4
Cooking Time: 25 Minutes + Chilling Time
INGREDIENTS:
- 2 cups milk
- 1 cup instant polenta
- Salt and black pepper to taste
- fresh thyme, chopped

DIRECTIONS:

Fill a saucepan with milk and 2 cups of water and place over low heat. Bring to a simmer. Keep whisking as you pour in the polenta. Continue to whisk until polenta thickens and bubbles; season to taste. Add polenta to a lined with parchment paper baking tray and spread out.

Refrigerate for 45 minutes. Slice, set polenta into batons, and spray with olive oil. Arrange polenta chips into the basket and fit in the baking tray; cook for 16 minutes at 380 F on Air Fry function, turning once halfway through. Make sure the fries are golden and crispy. Serve.

526. COTTAGE CHEESE BEST HOMEMADE CRO-QUETTE

INGREDIENTS:
- 1 big capsicum (Cut this capsicum into big cubes)
- 1 onion (Cut it into quarters. Now separate the layers carefully.)
- 5 tbsp. gram flour
- A pinch of salt to taste
- 2 cup fresh green coriander
- ½ cup mint leaves
- 4 tsp. fennel
- 1 small onion
- 2 tbsp. ginger-garlic paste
- 6-7 garlic flakes (optional)
- 3 tbsp. lemon juice
- 2 cups cottage cheese cut into slightly thick and long pieces (similar to
- French fries)
- Salt

DIRECTIONS:

Take a clean and dry container. Put into it the coriander, mint, fennel, and ginger, onion/garlic, salt and lemon juice. Mix them.

Pour the mixture into a grinder and blend until you get a thick paste. Now move on to the cottage cheese pieces.

Slit these pieces almost till the end and leave them aside. Now stuff all the pieces with the paste that was obtained from the previous step. Now leave the stuffed cottage cheese aside. Take the sauce and add to it the gram flour and some salt.

Mix them together properly. Rub this mixture all over the stuffed cottage cheese pieces. Now leave the cottage cheese aside. Now, to the leftover sauce, add the capsicum and onions. Apply the sauce generously on each of the pieces of capsicum and onion.

Now take satay sticks and arrange the cottage cheese pieces and vegetables on separate sticks. Pre heat the Cosori oven at 290 Fahrenheit for around 5 minutes. Open the basket. Arrange the satay sticks properly. Close the basket.

Keep the sticks with the cottage cheese at 180 degrees for around half an hour while the sticks with the vegetables are to be kept at the same temperature for only 7 minutes. Turn the sticks in between so that one side does not get burnt and also to provide a uniform cook.

527. TRADITIONAL JACKET POTATOES

Servings: 4
Cooking Time: 30 Minutes
INGREDIENTS:
- 4 potatoes, well washed
- 2 garlic cloves, minced
- Salt and black pepper to taste
- 1 tsp rosemary
- 1 tsp butter

DIRECTIONS:

Preheat your Cosori Oven to 360 F on Air Fry function. Prick the potatoes with a fork. Place them into your Air fryer basket and fit in the baking tray; cook for 25 minutes. Cut the potatoes in half and top with butter and rosemary; season with salt and pepper. Serve immediately.

528. CAULIFLOWER SPICY LEMON KEBAB

INGREDIENTS:
- 3 tsp. lemon juice
- 2 tsp. garam masala
- 3 eggs
- 2 ½ tbsp. white sesame seeds
- 2 cups cauliflower florets
- 3 onions chopped
- 5 green chilies-roughly chopped
- 1 ½ tbsp. ginger paste
- 1 ½ tsp. garlic paste
- 1 ½ tsp. salt

DIRECTIONS:

Grind the ingredients except for the egg and form a smooth paste. Coat the florets in the paste. Now, beat the eggs and add a little salt to it.

Dip the coated florets in the egg mixture and then transfer to the sesame seeds and coat the florets well. Place the vegetables on a stick.

Pre heat the Cosori oven at 160 degrees Fahrenheit for around 5 minutes. Place the sticks in the basket and let them cook for another 25 minutes at the same temperature. Turn the sticks over in between the cooking process to get a uniform cook.

529. FETA & SCALLION TRIANGLES

Servings: 4
Cooking Time: 20 Minutes
INGREDIENTS:
- 4 oz feta cheese, crumbled
- 2 sheets filo pastry
- 1 egg yolk, beaten
- 2 tbsp fresh parsley, finely chopped
- 1 scallion, finely chopped
- 2 tbsp olive oil
- Salt and black pepper to taste

DIRECTIONS:
In a bowl, mix the yolk with the cheese, parsley, and scallion. Season with salt and black pepper. Cut each filo sheet in 3 strips. Put a teaspoon of the feta mixture on the bottom. Roll the strip in a spinning spiral way until the filling of the inside mixture is completely wrapped in a triangle. Preheat Cosori on Bake function to 360 F. Brush the surface of filo with olive oil. Place up to 5 triangles in the oven and press Start. Cook for 5 minutes. Lower the temperature to 330 F, cook for 3 more minutes or until golden brown.

530. VEGGIE MIX FRIED CHIPS

Servings: 4
Cooking Time: 45 Minutes
INGREDIENTS:
- 1 large eggplant, cut into strips
- 5 potatoes, peeled and cut into strips
- 3 zucchinis, cut into strips
- ½ cup cornstarch
- ½ cup olive oil
- Salt to taste

DIRECTIONS:
Preheat Cosori on AirFry function to 390 F. In a bowl, stir cornstarch, ½ cup of water, salt, pepper, olive oil, eggplants, zucchini, and potatoes. Place the veggie mixture in the basket and press Start. Cook for 12 minutes. Serve warm.

531. ROASTED VEGETABLES WITH RICE

Servings: 4
Cooking Time: 12 Minutes
INGREDIENTS:
- 2 teaspoons melted butter
- 1 cup chopped mushrooms
- 1 cup cooked rice
- 1 cup peas
- 1 carrot, chopped
- 1 red onion, chopped
- 1 garlic clove, minced
- Salt and black pepper, to taste
- 2 hard-boiled eggs, grated
- 1 tablespoon soy sauce

DIRECTIONS:
Coat the baking pan with melted butter.
Stir together the mushrooms, cooked rice, peas, carrot, onion, garlic, salt, and pepper in a large bowl until well mixed. Pour the mixture into the prepared baking pan.

Slide the baking pan into Rack Position 2, select Roast, set temperature to 380°F (193°C), and set time to 12 minutes.

When cooking is complete, remove from the oven. Divide the mixture among four plates. Serve warm with a sprinkle of grated eggs and a drizzle of soy sauce.

532. ASPARAGUS FRENCH CUISINE GALETTE

INGREDIENTS:
- 1 ½ tbsp. lemon juice
- Salt and pepper to taste
- 2 cups minced asparagus
- 3 tsp. ginger finely chopped
- 1-2 tbsp. fresh coriander leaves
- 2 or 3 green chilies finely chopped

DIRECTIONS:
Mix the ingredients in a clean bowl.
Mold this mixture into round and flat French Cuisine Galettes.
Wet the French Cuisine Galettes slightly with water.
Pre heat the Cosori oven at 160 degrees Fahrenheit for 5 minutes. Place the French Cuisine Galettes in the fry basket and let them cook for another 25 minutes at the same temperature. Keep rolling them over to get a uniform cook. Serve either with mint sauce or ketchup.

533. RATATOUILLE

Servings: 6
Cooking Time: 12 Minutes
INGREDIENTS:
- 1 medium zucchini, sliced ½-inch thick
- 1 small eggplant, peeled and sliced ½-inch thick
- 2 teaspoons kosher salt, divided
- 4 tablespoons extra-virgin olive oil, divided
- 3 garlic cloves, minced
- 1 small onion, chopped
- 1 small red bell pepper, cut into ½-inch chunks
- 1 small green bell pepper, cut into ½-inch chunks
- ½ teaspoon dried oregano
- ¼ teaspoon freshly ground black pepper
- 1 pint cherry tomatoes
- 2 tablespoons minced fresh basil
- 1 cup panko bread crumbs
- ½ cup grated Parmesan cheese (optional)

DIRECTIONS:
Season one side of the zucchini and eggplant slices with ¾ teaspoon of salt. Put the slices, salted side down, on a rack set over a baking sheet. Sprinkle the other sides with ¾ teaspoon of salt. Allow to sit for 10 minutes, or until the slices begin to exude water. When ready, rinse and dry them. Cut the zucchini slices into quarters and the eggplant slices into eighths.

Pour the zucchini and eggplant into a large bowl, along with 2 tablespoons of olive oil, garlic, onion, bell peppers, oregano, and black pepper. Toss to coat well. Arrange the vegetables in the air fryer basket.

Put the air fryer basket on the baking pan and slide into Rack Position 2, select Roast, set temperature to 375°F (190°C), and set time to 12 minutes.

Meanwhile, add the tomatoes and basil to the large bowl. Sprinkle with the remaining ½ teaspoon of salt and 1 tablespoon of olive oil. Toss well and set aside.

Stir together the remaining 1 tablespoon of olive oil, panko, and Parmesan cheese (if desired) in a small bowl.

After 6 minutes, remove from the oven and add the tomato mixture and stir to mix well. Scatter the panko mixture on top. Return to the oven and continue cooking for 6 minutes, or until the vegetables are softened and the topping is golden brown.

Cool for 5 minutes before serving.

534. BUTTER BURGERS

Servings: 4
Cooking Time: 30 Minutes
INGREDIENTS:
- Nonstick cooking spray
- ½ cup black beans, rinsed & drained
- 12 oz. mushrooms, sliced
- 1 ½ cup brown rice, cooked
- ½ cup oats
- 1 tsp salt
- ½ tsp pepper
- 1 tsp garlic powder
- 1 tsp onion powder
- ¼ tsp red pepper flakes
- ¼ cup Vegan butter
- 2 cups onions, sliced

DIRECTIONS:
Place baking pan in position 2 in the oven. Lightly spray fryer basket with cooking spray.
Pat the beans with paper towel to get them as dry as possible.
Heat a medium skillet over med-high heat. Add mushrooms and cook, stirring frequently, until almost no moisture remains.
Add mushrooms, beans, rice, oats, and seasonings to a food processor. Pulse to chop and combine ingredients. Do not over blend. Let mixture rest 20 minutes.
Melt butter in a large skillet over medium heat. Add onions and cook until browned and tender.
Form mushroom mixture into 4 patties and place in the fryer basket.
Place in oven and set to air fry on 350°F for 10 minutes. Cook burgers 8-10 minutes, until nicely browned, turning over halfway through cooking time.
Serve on toasted buns topped with cooked onions.
Nutrition Info: Calories 351, Total Fat 15g, Saturated Fat 8g, Total Carbs 44g, Net Carbs 37g, Protein 10g, Sugar 4g, Fiber 7g, Sodium 704mg, Potassium 604mg, Phosphorus 286mg

535. POTATO FRIED BAKED PASTRY
INGREDIENTS:
- 1 tsp. powdered ginger
- 1 or 2 green chilies that are finely chopped or mashed
- ½ tsp. cumin
- 1 tsp. coarsely crushed coriander
- 1 dry red chili broken into pieces
- A small amount of salt (to taste)
- 2 tbsp. unsalted butter
- 1 ½ cup all-purpose flour
- A pinch of salt to taste
- Add as much water as required to make the dough stiff and firm
- 2-3 big potatoes boiled and mashed
- ¼ cup boiled peas
- ½ tsp. dried mango powder
- ½ tsp. red chili power.
- 1-2 tbsp. coriander.

DIRECTIONS:
Mix the dough for the outer covering and make it stiff and smooth. Leave it to rest in a container while making the filling. Cook the ingredients in a pan and stir them well to make a thick paste. Roll the paste out.
Roll the dough into balls and flatten them. Cut them in halves and add the filling. Use water to help you fold the edges to create the shape of a cone.
Pre-heat the Cosori oven for around 5 to 6 minutes at 300 Fahrenheit.
Place all the samosas in the fry basket and close the basket properly. Keep the Cosori oven at 200 degrees for another 20 to 25 minutes. Around the halfway point, open the basket and turn the samosas over for uniform cooking. After this, fry at 250 degrees for around 10 minutes in order to give them the desired golden-brown color. Serve hot. Recommended sides are tamarind or mint sauce.

53b. CASHEW CAULIFLOWER WITH YOGURT SAUCE
Servings: 2
Cooking Time: 12 Minutes
INGREDIENTS:
- 4 cups cauliflower florets (about half a large head)
- 1 tablespoon olive oil
- 1 teaspoon curry powder
- Salt, to taste
- ½ cup toasted, chopped cashews, for garnish
- Yogurt Sauce:
- ¼ cup plain yogurt
- 2 tablespoons sour cream
- 1 teaspoon honey
- 1 teaspoon lemon juice
- Pinch cayenne pepper
- Salt, to taste
- 1 tablespoon chopped fresh cilantro, plus leaves for garnish

DIRECTIONS:
In a large mixing bowl, toss the cauliflower florets with the olive oil, curry powder, and salt.
Place the cauliflower florets in the air fryer basket.
Put the air fryer basket on the baking pan and slide into Rack Position 2, select Air Fry, set temperature to 400ºF (205ºC) and set time to 12 minutes.
Stir the cauliflower florets twice during cooking.
When cooking is complete, the cauliflower should be golden brown.
Meanwhile, mix all the ingredients for the yogurt sauce in a small bowl and whisk to combine.
Remove the cauliflower from the oven and drizzle with the yogurt sauce.
Scatter the toasted cashews and cilantro on top and serve immediately.

537. CRISPY EGGPLANT SLICES WITH PARSLEY
Servings: 4
Cooking Time: 12 Minutes
INGREDIENTS:
- 1 cup flour
- 4 eggs
- Salt, to taste
- 2 cups bread crumbs
- 1 teaspoon Italian seasoning
- 2 eggplants, sliced
- 2 garlic cloves, sliced
- 2 tablespoons chopped parsley
- Cooking spray

DIRECTIONS:
Spritz the air fryer basket with cooking spray. Set aside.
On a plate, place the flour. In a shallow bowl, whisk the eggs with salt. In another shallow bowl, combine the bread crumbs and Italian seasoning.
Dredge the eggplant slices, one at a time, in the flour, then in the whisked eggs, finally in the bread crumb mixture to coat well.
Lay the coated eggplant slices in the basket.
Put the air fryer basket on the baking pan and slide into Rack Position 2, select Air Fry, set temperature to 390ºF (199ºC), and set time to 12 minutes.
Flip the eggplant slices halfway through the cooking time.
When cooking is complete, the eggplant slices should be
golden brown and crispy. Transfer the eggplant slices to a plate and sprinkle the garlic and parsley on top before serving.

538. BROCCOLI MARINADE CUTLET
INGREDIENTS:
- 1 ½ tsp. salt
- 3 tsp. lemon juice
- 2 tsp. garam masala

- 3 eggs
- 2 ½ tbsp. white sesame seeds
- 2 cups broccoli florets
- 3 onions chopped
- 5 green chilies-roughly chopped
- 1 ½ tbsp. ginger paste
- 1 ½ tsp. garlic paste

DIRECTIONS:

Grind the ingredients except for the egg and form a smooth paste. Coat the florets in the paste. Now, beat the eggs and add a little salt to it.

Dip the coated florets in the egg mixture and then transfer to the sesame seeds and coat the florets well. Place the vegetables on a stick.

Pre heat the Cosori oven at 160 degrees Fahrenheit for around 5 minutes. Place the sticks in the basket and let them cook for another 25 minutes at the same temperature. Turn the sticks over in between the cooking process to get a uniform cook.

539. CAULIFLOWER RICE WITH TOFU & PEAS

Servings: 4
Cooking Time: 30 Minutes
INGREDIENTS:
- Tofu:
- ½ block tofu, crumbled
- ½ cup diced onion
- 2 tbsp soy sauce
- 1 tsp turmeric
- 1 cup diced carrot
- Cauliflower:
- 3 cups cauliflower rice
- 2 tbsp soy sauce
- ½ cup chopped broccoli
- 2 garlic cloves, minced
- 1 ½ tsp toasted sesame oil
- 1 tbsp minced ginger
- ½ cup frozen peas
- 1 tbsp rice vinegar

DIRECTIONS:

Preheat Cosori on Air Fry function to 370 F. Combine all the tofu ingredients in a greased baking dish. Cook for 10 minutes.

Meanwhile, place all cauliflower ingredients in a large bowl and mix to combine. Stir the cauliflower mixture in the tofu baking dish and return to the oven; cook for 12 minutes. Serve.

540. ROSEMARY ROASTED SQUASH WITH CHEESE

Servings: 2
Cooking Time: 20 Minutes
INGREDIENTS:
- 1 pound (454 g) butternut squash, cut into wedges
- 2 tablespoons olive oil
- 1 tablespoon dried rosemary
- Salt, to salt
- 1 cup crumbled goat cheese
- 1 tablespoon maple syrup

DIRECTIONS:

Toss the squash wedges with the olive oil, rosemary, and salt in a large bowl until well coated.

Transfer the squash wedges to the air fryer basket, spreading them out in as even a layer as possible.

Put the air fryer basket on the baking pan and slide into Rack Position 2, select Air Fry, set temperature to 350ºF (180ºC), and set time to 20 minutes.

After 10 minutes, remove from the oven and flip the squash. Return the pan to the oven and continue cooking for 10 minutes.

When cooking is complete, the squash should be golden brown. Remove from the oven. Sprinkle the goat cheese on top and serve drizzled with the maple syrup.

541. CHINESE SPRING ROLLS

Servings: 4
Cooking Time: 15 Minutes
INGREDIENTS:
- ½ head cabbage, grated
- 2 carrots, grated
- 1 tsp fresh ginger, minced
- 1 garlic clove, minced
- 1 tsp sesame oil
- 1 tsp soy sauce
- 1 tsp sesame seeds
- ½ tsp salt
- 1 tsp olive oil
- 1 package spring roll wrappers

DIRECTIONS:

Combine all ingredients in a bowl. Divide the mixture between the roll sheets and roll them up; arrange on a baking tray. Press Start and cook in the Cosori for 5 minutes on Bake function at 370 F.

542. SPEEDY VEGETABLE PIZZA

Servings: 1
Cooking Time: 15 Minutes
INGREDIENTS:
- 1 ½ tbsp tomato paste
- ¼ cup grated cheddar cheese
- ¼ cup grated mozzarella cheese
- 1 tbsp cooked sweet corn
- 4 zucchini slices
- 4 eggplant slices
- 4 red onion rings
- ½ green bell pepper, chopped
- 3 cherry tomatoes, quartered
- 1 pizza crust
- ¼ tsp basil
- ¼ tsp oregano

DIRECTIONS:

Preheat Cosori on Bake function to 350 F. Spread the tomato paste on the pizza crust. Top with zucchini and eggplant slices first, then green peppers, and onion rings. Cover with cherry tomatoes and scatter the corn. Sprinkle with oregano and basil and sprinkle with cheddar and mozzarella cheeses. Cook for 10-12 minutes until golden brown on top. Serve.

543. MOZZARELLA EGGPLANT PATTIES

Servings: 1
Cooking Time: 10 Minutes
INGREDIENTS:
- 1 hamburger bun
- 1 eggplant, sliced
- 1 mozzarella slice, chopped
- 1 red onion cut into 3 rings
- 1 lettuce leaf
- ½ tbsp tomato sauce
- 1 pickle, sliced

DIRECTIONS:

Preheat Cosori on Bake function to 330 F. Place the eggplant slices in a greased baking tray and cook for 6 minutes. Take out the tray and top the eggplant with mozzarella cheese and cook for 30 more seconds. Spread tomato sauce on one half of the bun. Place the lettuce leaf on top of the sauce. Place the cheesy eggplant on top of the lettuce. Top with onion rings and pickles and then with the other bun half to serve.

544. COCONUT VEGAN FRIES

Servings: 2
Cooking Time: 20 Minutes
INGREDIENTS:

- 2 potatoes, spiralized
- 1 tbsp tomato ketchup
- 2 tbsp olive oil
- Salt and black pepper to taste
- 2 tbsp coconut oil

DIRECTIONS:

In a bowl, mix olive oil, coconut oil, salt, and pepper. Add in the potatoes and toss to coat. Place them in the basket and fit in the baking tray; cook for 15 minutes on Air Fry function at 360 F. Serve with ketchup and enjoy!

545. TOMATO & FETA BITES WITH PINE NUTS

Servings: 2
Cooking Time: 25 Minutes
INGREDIENTS:
- 1 heirloom tomato, sliced
- 1 (4- oz) block Feta cheese, sliced
- 1 small red onion, thinly sliced
- 1 clove garlic
- 2 tsp + ¼ cup olive oil
- 1 ½ tbsp toasted pine nuts
- ¼ cup fresh parsley, chopped
- ¼ cup grated Parmesan cheese
- ¼ cup chopped basil

DIRECTIONS:

Add basil, pine nuts, garlic, and salt to a food processor. Process while slowly adding ¼ cup of olive oil. Once finished, pour basil pesto into a bowl and refrigerate for 30 minutes.
Preheat Cosori oven on AirFry function to 390 F. Spread some pesto on each slice of tomato.
Top with feta cheese and onion and drizzle with the remaining olive oil. Place in the frying basket and press Start. Cook for 12 minutes. Top with the remaining pesto and serve.

546. SIMPLE RATATOUILLE

Servings: 2
Cooking Time: 16 Minutes
INGREDIENTS:
- 2 Roma tomatoes, thinly sliced
- 1 zucchini, thinly sliced
- 2 yellow bell peppers, sliced
- 2 garlic cloves, minced
- 2 tablespoons olive oil
- 2 tablespoons herbes de Provence
- 1 tablespoon vinegar
- Salt and black pepper, to taste

DIRECTIONS:

Place the tomatoes, zucchini, bell peppers, garlic, olive oil, herbes de Provence, and vinegar in a large bowl and toss until the vegetables are evenly coated. Sprinkle with salt and pepper and toss again. Pour the vegetable mixture into the baking pan.
Slide the baking pan into Rack Position 2, select Roast, set temperature to 390ºF (199ºC) and set time to 16 minutes.
Stir the vegetables halfway through.
When cooking is complete, the vegetables should be tender.
Let the vegetable mixture stand for 5 minutes in the oven before removing and serving.

547. CHEESE FRENCH FRIES

INGREDIENTS:
- 2 medium sized potatoes peeled and cut into thick pieces lengthwise
- 1 tsp. mixed herbs
- ½ tsp. red chili flakes
- A pinch of salt to taste
- 1 tbsp. lemon juice

- 1 cup melted cheddar cheese (You could put this into a piping bag and
- 1 tbsp. olive oil
- create a pattern of it on the fries.)

DIRECTIONS:

Take all the ingredients mentioned under the heading "For the marinade" and mix them well. Now pour into a container 3 cups of water.
Add a pinch of salt into this water. Bring it to the boil. Now blanch the pieces of potato for around 5 minutes. Drain the water using a sieve. Dry the potato pieces on a towel and then place them on another dry towel. Coat these potato Oregano Fingers with the marinade made in the previous step. Pre heat the Cosori oven for around 5 minutes at 300 Fahrenheit. Take out the basket of the fryer and place the potato Oregano Fingers in them.
Close the basket. Now keep the fryer at 220 Fahrenheit for 20 or 25 minutes. In between the process, toss the fries twice or thrice so that they get cooked properly. Towards the end of the cooking process (the last 2 minutes or so), sprinkle the cut coriander leaves on the fries. Add the melted cheddar cheese over the fries and serve hot.

548. MEDITERRANEAN BAKED EGGS WITH SPINACH

Servings: 2
Cooking Time: 10 Minutes
INGREDIENTS:
- 2 tablespoons olive oil
- 4 eggs, whisked
- 5 ounces (142 g) fresh spinach, chopped
- 1 medium-sized tomato, chopped
- 1 teaspoon fresh lemon juice
- ½ teaspoon ground black pepper
- ½ teaspoon coarse salt
- ½ cup roughly chopped fresh basil leaves, for garnish

DIRECTIONS:

Generously grease the baking pan with olive oil.
Stir together the remaining ingredients except the basil leaves in the greased baking pan until well incorporated.
Slide the baking pan into Rack Position 1, select Convection Bake, set temperature to 280ºF (137ºC), and set time to 10 minutes.
When cooking is complete, the eggs should be completely set and the vegetables should be tender. Remove from the oven and serve garnished with the fresh basil leaves.

549. CHICKPEA FRITTERS

Servings: 4
Cooking Time: 10 Minutes
INGREDIENTS:
- Nonstick cooking spray
- 1 cup chickpeas, cooked
- 1 onion, chopped
- ¼ tsp salt
- ¼ tsp pepper
- ¼ tsp turmeric
- ¼ tsp coriander

DIRECTIONS:

Place the baking pan in position 2. Lightly spray the fryer basket with cooking spray.
Add the onion to a food processor and pulse until finely diced.
Add remaining ingredients and pulse until combined but not pureed.
Form the mixture into 8 patties and place them in the fryer basket, these may need to be cooked in two batches.
Place the basket in the oven and set to air fry on 350°F for 10 minutes. Cook fritters until golden brown and crispy, turning over halfway through cooking time. Serve with your favorite dipping sauce.
Nutrition Info: Calories 101, Total Fat 1g, Saturated Fat 0g, Total Carbs

14g, Net Carbs 10g, Protein 4g, Sugar 3g, Fiber 4g, Sodium 149mg, Potassium 159mg, Phosphorus 77mg

550. SPICY THAI-STYLE VEGETABLES

Servings: 4
Cooking Time: 8 Minutes
INGREDIENTS:

- 1 small head Napa cabbage, shredded, divided
- 1 medium carrot, cut into thin coins
- 8 ounces (227 g) snow peas
- 1 red or green bell pepper, sliced into thin strips
- 1 tablespoon vegetable oil
- 2 tablespoons soy sauce
- 1 tablespoon sesame oil
- 2 tablespoons brown sugar
- 2 tablespoons freshly squeezed lime juice
- 2 teaspoons red or green Thai curry paste
- 1 serrano chile, deseeded and minced
- 1 cup frozen mango slices, thawed
- ½ cup chopped roasted peanuts or cashews

DIRECTIONS:

Put half the Napa cabbage in a large bowl, along with the carrot, snow peas, and bell pepper. Drizzle with the vegetable oil and toss to coat. Spread them evenly in the air fryer basket.

Put the air fryer basket on the baking pan and slide into Rack Position 2, select Roast, set temperature to 375ºF (190ºC), and set time to 8 minutes. Meanwhile, whisk together the soy sauce, sesame oil, brown sugar, lime juice, and curry paste in a small bowl.

When done, the vegetables should be tender and crisp. Remove from the oven and put the vegetables back into the bowl. Add the chile, mango slices, and the remaining cabbage. Pour over the dressing and toss to coat. Top with the roasted nuts and serve.

551. BROCCOLI MOMO'S RECIPE

INGREDIENTS:

- 2 tbsp. oil
- 2 tsp. ginger-garlic paste
- 2 tsp. soya sauce
- 2 tsp. vinegar
- 1 ½ cup all-purpose flour
- ½ tsp. salt
- 5 tbsp. water
- 2 cups grated broccoli

DIRECTIONS:

Squeeze the dough and cover it with plastic wrap and set aside. Next, cook the ingredients for the filling and try to ensure that the broccoli is covered well with the sauce.

Roll the dough and cut it into a square. Place the filling in the center. Now, wrap the dough to cover the filling and pinch the edges together. Pre heat the Cosori oven at 200° F for 5 minutes. Place the gnocchi's in the fry basket and close it. Let them cook at the same temperature for another 20 minutes. Recommended sides are chili sauce or ketchup.

552. GARLIC STUFFED MUSHROOMS

Servings: 2
Cooking Time: 12 Minutes
INGREDIENTS:

- 18 medium-sized white mushrooms
- 1 small onion, peeled and chopped
- 4 garlic cloves, peeled and minced
- 2 tablespoons olive oil
- 2 teaspoons cumin powder
- A pinch ground allspice
- Fine sea salt and freshly ground black pepper, to taste

DIRECTIONS:

On a clean work surface, remove the mushroom stems. Using a spoon, scoop out the mushroom gills and discard.

Thoroughly combine the onion, garlic, olive oil, cumin powder, allspice, salt, and pepper in a mixing bowl. Stuff the mushrooms evenly with the mixture.

Place the stuffed mushrooms in the air fryer basket.

Put the air fryer basket on the baking pan and slide into Rack Position 2, select Roast, set temperature to 345ºF (174ºC) and set time to 12 minutes.

When cooking is complete, the mushroom should be browned.

Cool for 5 minutes before serving.

553. HOMEMADE BLOOMING ONIONS

Servings: 4
Cooking Time: 40 Minutes
INGREDIENTS:

- 4 onions
- 3 tbsp butter, melted
- 1 tbsp olive oil

DIRECTIONS:

Peel the onions and slice off the root bottom so it can sit well. Cut slices into the onion to make it look like a blooming flower, make sure not to go all the way through; four cuts will do.

Preheat Cosori on AirFry function to 350 F. Drizzle the onions with olive oil and butter and press Start. Cook for about 30 minutes. Serve with garlic mayo dip.

554. VEGETABLE SKEWER

INGREDIENTS:

- 3 tbsp. cream
- 3 eggs
- 2 cups mixed vegetables
- 3 onions chopped
- 5 green chilies
- 1 ½ tbsp. ginger paste
- 1 ½ tsp. garlic paste
- 1 ½ tsp. salt
- 2 ½ tbsp. white sesame seeds

DIRECTIONS:

Grind the ingredients except for the egg and form a smooth paste. Coat the vegetables in the paste. Now, beat the eggs and add a little salt to it. Dip the coated vegetables in the egg mixture and then transfer to the sesame seeds and coat the vegetables well. Place the vegetables on a stick. Pre heat the Cosori oven at 160 degrees Fahrenheit for around 5 minutes. Place the sticks in the basket and let them cook for another 25 minutes at the same temperature. Turn the sticks over in between the cooking process to get a uniform cook.

555. VEG MOMO'S RECIPE

INGREDIENTS:

- 2 tsp. ginger-garlic paste
- 2 tsp. soya sauce
- 2 tsp. vinegar
- 1 ½ cup all-purpose flour
- ½ tsp. salt or to taste
- 5 tbsp. water
- 2 cup carrots grated
- 2 cup cabbage grated
- 2 tbsp. oil

DIRECTIONS:

Squeeze the dough and cover it with plastic wrap and set aside. Next, cook the ingredients for the filling and try to ensure that the vegetables are covered well with the sauce.

Roll the dough and cut it into a square. Place the filling in the center.

Now, wrap the dough to cover the filling and pinch the edges together. Pre heat the Cosori oven at 200° F for 5 minutes. Place the gnocchi's in the fry basket and close it. Let them cook at the same temperature for another 20 minutes. Recommended sides are chili sauce or ketchup.

556. POTATO WEDGES

INGREDIENTS:

- 1 tsp. mixed herbs
- ½ tsp. red chili flakes
- A pinch of salt to taste
- 1 tbsp. lemon juice
- 2 medium sized potatoes (Cut into wedges)
- ingredients for the marinade:
- 1 tbsp. olive oil

DIRECTIONS:

Boil the potatoes and blanch them. Mix the ingredients for the marinade and add the potato Oregano Fingers to it making sure that they are coated well.

Pre heat the Cosori oven for around 5 minutes at 300 Fahrenheit. Take out the basket of the fryer and place the potato Oregano Fingers in them. Close the basket.

Now keep the fryer at 200 Fahrenheit for 20 or 25 minutes. In between the process, toss the fries twice or thrice so that they get cooked properly.

557. GREEN CHILI FLAT CAKES

INGREDIENTS:

- 2 or 3 green chilies finely chopped
- 1 ½ tbsp. lemon juice
- Salt and pepper to taste
- 2 tbsp. garam masala
- 10–12 green chilies
- 3 tsp. ginger finely chopped
- 1-2 tbsp. fresh coriander leaves

DIRECTIONS:

Mix the ingredients in a clean bowl and add water to it. Make sure that the paste is not too watery but is enough to apply to the green chilies. Pre heat the Cosori oven at 160 degrees Fahrenheit for 5 minutes. Place the French Cuisine Galettes in the fry basket and let them cook for another 25 minutes at the same temperature. Keep rolling them over to get a uniform cook. Serve either with mint sauce or ketchup.

558. TOFU & PEA CAULI RICE

Servings: 4
Cooking Time: 30 Minutes
INGREDIENTS:

- Tofu:
- ½ block tofu
- ½ cup onions, chopped
- 2 tbsp soy sauce
- 1 tsp turmeric
- 1 cup carrots, chopped
- Cauliflower:
- 3 cups cauliflower rice
- 2 tbsp soy sauce
- ½ cup broccoli, chopped
- 2 garlic cloves, minced
- 1 ½ tsp toasted sesame oil
- 1 tbsp fresh ginger, minced
- ½ cup frozen peas
- 1 tbsp rice vinegar

DIRECTIONS:

Preheat Cosori on AirFry function to 370 F. Crumble the tofu and combine it with all tofu ingredients. Place in a baking dish and cook for 10 minutes.

Meanwhile, place all cauliflower ingredients in a large bowl; mix to combine. Add the cauliflower mixture to the tofu and stir to combine. Press Start and cook for 12 minutes. Serve.

559. MACARONI FRIED BAKED PASTRY

INGREDIENTS:

- 2 carrot sliced
- 2 cabbage sliced
- 2 tbsp. soya sauce
- 2 tsp. vinegar
- Some salt and pepper to taste
- 2 tbsp. olive oil
- ½ tsp. axiomata
- 1 cup all-purpose flour
- 2 tbsp. unsalted butter
- A pinch of salt to taste
- Take the amount of water sufficient enough to make a stiff dough
- 3 cups boiled macaroni
- 2 onion sliced
- 2 capsicum sliced
- 2 tbsp. ginger finely chopped
- 2 tbsp. garlic finely chopped
- 2 tbsp. green chilies finely chopped
- 2 tbsp. ginger-garlic paste

DIRECTIONS:

Mix the dough for the outer covering and make it stiff and smooth. Leave it to rest in a container while making the filling. Cook the ingredients in a pan and stir them well to make a thick paste. Roll the paste out.
Roll the dough into balls and flatten them. Cut them in halves and add the filling. Use water to help you fold the edges to create the shape of a cone. Pre-heat the Cosori oven for around 5 to 6 minutes at 300 Fahrenheit. Place all the samosas in the fry basket and close the basket properly. Keep the Cosori oven at 200 degrees for another 20 to 25 minutes. Around the halfway point, open the basket and turn the samosas over for uniform cooking. After this, fry at 250 degrees for around 10 minutes in order to give them the desired golden-brown color. Serve hot. Recommended sides are tamarind or mint sauce.

560. BAKED CHICKPEA STARS

INGREDIENTS:

- 4 tbsp. roasted sesame seeds
- 2 small onion finely chopped
- ½ tsp. coriander powder
- ½ tsp. cumin powder
- Use olive oil for greasing purposes
- 1 cup white chick peas soaked overnight
- 1 tsp. ginger-garlic paste
- 4 tbsp. chopped coriander leaves
- 2 green chilies finely chopped
- 4 tbsp. thick curd
- Pinches of salt and pepper to taste
- 1 tsp. dry mint

DIRECTIONS:

Since the chickpeas have been soaked you will first have to drain them. Add a pinch of salt and pour water until the chickpeas are submerged. Put this container in a pressure cooker and let the chickpeas cook for around 25 minutes until they turn soft. Remove the cooker from the flame. Now mash the chickpeas.

Take another container. Into it add the ginger garlic paste, onions, coriander leaves, coriander powder, cumin powder, green chili, salt and pepper, and 1 tbsp. Use your hands to mix these ingredients Pour this mixture into the container with the mashed chickpeas and mix. Spread this mixture over a flat surface to about a half-inch thickness.

Cut star shapes out of this layer. Make a mixture of curd and mint leaves and spread this over the surface of the star shaped cutlets. Coat all the sides with sesame seeds. Pre heat the Cosori oven at 200-degree Fahrenheit for 5 minutes. Open the basket of the Fryer and put the stars inside. Close the basket properly. Continue to cook the stars for around half an hour. Periodically turn over the stars in the basket in order to prevent overcooking one side. Serve either with mint sauce or tomato ketchup.

MEAT RECIPES

561. CHICKEN BURGER PATTIES

Servings: 4
Cooking Time: 25 Minutes

INGREDIENTS:
- 1 lb ground chicken
- 1 egg, lightly beaten
- 1 cup cheddar cheese, shredded
- 1 cup carrot, grated
- 1 cup cauliflower, grated
- 1/8 tsp red pepper flakes
- 2 garlic cloves, minced
- 1/2 cup onion, minced
- 3/4 cup breadcrumbs
- Pepper
- Salt

DIRECTIONS:
Fit the Cosori oven with the rack in position
Add all ingredients into the bowl and mix until well combined.
Make small patties and place them in a parchment-lined baking pan.
Set to bake at 400 F for 30 minutes. After 5 minutes place the baking pan in the preheated oven.
Serve and enjoy.
Nutrition Info: Calories 451 Fat 20 g Carbohydrates 20.9 g Sugar 4.1 g Protein 44.9 g Cholesterol 172 mg

562. PAPRIKA PORK TENDERLOIN

Servings: 6
Cooking Time: 30 Minutes
INGREDIENTS:
- 2 lbs pork tenderloin
- For rub:
- 1 tbsp smoked paprika
- 1/2 tsp chili powder
- 1 tbsp garlic powder
- 1 tbsp onion powder
- 1/2 tsp salt

DIRECTIONS:
Fit the Cosori oven with the rack in position
In a small bowl, mix all rub ingredients.
Coat pork tenderloin with the rub and place in baking pan.
Set to bake at 425 F for 35 minutes. After 5 minutes place the baking pan in the preheated oven.
Slice and serve.
Nutrition Info: Calories 229 Fat 5.5 g Carbohydrates 2.7 g Sugar 0.9 g Protein 40.1 g Cholesterol 110 mg

563. DRUMSTICKS WITH BARBECUE-HONEY SAUCE

Servings: 5
Cooking Time: 18 Minutes
INGREDIENTS:
- 1 tablespoon olive oil
- 10 chicken drumsticks
- Chicken seasoning or rub, to taste
- Salt and ground black pepper, to taste
- 1 cup barbecue sauce
- ¼ cup honey

DIRECTIONS:
Grease the basket with olive oil.
Rub the chicken drumsticks with chicken seasoning or rub, salt and ground black pepper on a clean work surface.
Arrange the chicken drumsticks in the basket.
Put the air fryer basket on the baking pan and slide into Rack Position 2, select Air Fry, set temperature to 390ºF (199ºC) and set time to 18 minutes.
Flip the drumsticks halfway through.
When cooking is complete, the drumsticks should be lightly browned.
Meanwhile, combine the barbecue sauce and honey in a small bowl. Stir to mix well.
Remove the drumsticks from the oven and baste with the sauce mixture to serve.

564. CRISPY CRUSTED CHICKEN

Servings: 4
Cooking Time: 30 Minutes
INGREDIENTS:
- 4 chicken breasts, skinless and boneless
- 2 tbsp butter, melted
- 3 cups corn flakes, crushed
- 1 tsp poultry seasoning
- 1 tsp water
- 1 egg, lightly beaten
- Pepper
- Salt

DIRECTIONS:
Fit the Cosori oven with the rack in position
Season chicken with poultry seasoning, pepper, and salt.
In a shallow dish, whisk together egg and water.
In a separate shallow dish, mix crushed cornflakes and melted butter.
Dip chicken into the egg mixture then coats with crushed cornflakes.
Place the coated chicken into the parchment-lined baking pan.
Set to bake at 400 F for 35 minutes. After 5 minutes place the baking pan in the preheated oven.
Serve and enjoy.
Nutrition Info: Calories 421 Fat 17.7 g Carbohydrates 18.6 g Sugar 1.5 g Protein 45.1 g Cholesterol 186 mg

565. HAM & CHEESE STUFFED CHICKEN BREASTS

Servings: 4
Cooking Time: 40 Minutes
INGREDIENTS:
- 4 skinless and boneless chicken breasts
- 4 slices ham
- 4 slices Swiss cheese
- 3 tbsp all-purpose flour
- 4 tbsp butter
- 1 tbsp paprika
- 1 tbsp chicken bouillon granules
- ½ cup dry white wine
- 1 cup heavy whipping cream

DIRECTIONS:
Preheat Cosori on Air Fry function to 380 F. Pound the chicken breasts and top with a slice of ham and Swiss cheese. Fold the edges of the chicken over the filling and secure the borders with toothpicks. In a medium bowl, combine the paprika and flour and coat in the chicken rolls. Fry the chicken in your Cosori for 20 minutes, turning once.
In a large skillet over low heat, melt the butter and add the heavy cream, bouillon granules, and wine; bring to a boil. Add in the chicken and let simmer for around 5-10 minutes. Serve.

566. BAKED SWEET & TANGY PORK CHOPS

Servings: 2

Cooking Time: 35 Minutes

INGREDIENTS:

- 2 pork chops
- 2 tbsp brown sugar
- 2 tbsp ketchup
- 2 onion sliced
- Pepper
- Salt

DIRECTIONS:

Fit the Cosori oven with the rack in position

Season pork chops with pepper and salt.

Place pork chops in a baking dish.

Mix ketchup and brown sugar and pour over pork chops.

Top with onion slices.

Set to bake at 375 F for 40 minutes. After 5 minutes place the baking dish in the preheated oven.

Serve and enjoy.

Nutrition Info: Calories 308 Fat 19.9 g Carbohydrates 13.5 g Sugar 12.5 g Protein 18.4 g Cholesterol 69 mg

567. CHICKEN SKEWERS WITH CORN SALAD

Servings: 4

Cooking Time: 10 Minutes

INGREDIENTS:

- 1 pound (454 g) boneless, skinless chicken breast, cut into
- 1½-inch chunks
- 1 green bell pepper, deseeded and cut into 1-inch pieces
- 1 red bell pepper, deseeded and cut into 1-inch pieces
- 1 large onion, cut into large chunks
- 2 tablespoons fajita seasoning
- 3 tablespoons vegetable oil, divided
- 2 teaspoons kosher salt, divided
- 2 cups corn, drained
- ¼ teaspoon granulated garlic
- 1 teaspoon freshly squeezed lime juice
- 1 tablespoon mayonnaise
- 3 tablespoons grated Parmesan cheese
- Special Equipment:
- 12 wooden skewers, soaked in water for at least 30 minutes

DIRECTIONS:

Place the chicken, bell peppers, and onion in a large bowl. Add the fajita seasoning, 2 tablespoons of vegetable oil, and 1½ teaspoons of kosher salt. Toss to coat evenly.

Alternate the chicken and vegetables on the skewers, making about 12 skewers.

Place the corn in a medium bowl and add the remaining vegetable oil. Add the remaining kosher salt and the garlic, and toss to coat. Place the corn in an even layer in the baking pan and place the skewers on top.

Slide the baking pan into Rack Position 2, select Roast, set temperature to 375°F (190°C), and set time to 10 minutes.

After about 5 minutes, remove from the oven and turn the skewers. Return to the oven and continue cooking.

When cooking is complete, remove from the oven. Place the skewers on a platter. Put the corn back to the bowl and combine with the lime juice, mayonnaise, and Parmesan cheese. Stir to mix well. Serve the skewers with the corn.

568. LAMB SPICY LEMON KEBAB

INGREDIENTS:

- 3 tsp lemon juice
- 2 tsp garam masala
- 4 tbsp. chopped coriander
- 3 tbsp. cream
- 1 lb. of lamb
- 3 onions chopped
- 5 green chilies-roughly chopped
- 1 ½ tbsp. ginger paste

- 1 ½ tsp garlic paste
- 1 ½ tsp salt
- 4 tbsp. fresh mint chopped
- 3 tbsp. chopped capsicum
- 3 eggs
- 2 ½ tbsp. white sesame seeds

DIRECTIONS:

Cut the lamb into medium sized chunks. Marinate these chunks overnight in any marinade of your choice. You can use any of the marinades mentioned in this book. Take all the ingredients mentioned under the first heading and mix them in a bowl. Grind them thoroughly to make a smooth paste.

Take the eggs in a different bowl and beat them. Add a pinch of salt and leave them aside. Take a flat plate and in it mix the sesame seeds and breadcrumbs. Mold the lamb mixture into small balls and flatten them into round and flat kebabs.

Dip these kebabs in the egg and salt mixture and then in the mixture of breadcrumbs and sesame seeds. Leave these kebabs in the fridge for an hour or so to set. Pre heat the Cosori oven at 160 degrees Fahrenheit for around 5 minutes. Place the kebabs in the basket and let them cook for another 25 minutes at the same temperature. Turn the kebabs over in between the cooking process to get a uniform cook. Serve the kebabs with mint sauce.

569. BACON-WRAPPED CHICKEN BREASTS ROLLS

Servings: 4

Cooking Time: 15 Minutes

INGREDIENTS:

- ¼ cup chopped fresh chives
- 2 tablespoons lemon juice
- 1 teaspoon dried sage
- 1 teaspoon fresh rosemary leaves
- ½ cup fresh parsley leaves
- 4 cloves garlic, peeled
- 1 teaspoon ground fennel
- 3 teaspoons sea salt
- ½ teaspoon red pepper flakes
- 4 (4-ounce / 113-g) boneless, skinless chicken breasts, pounded to ¼ inch thick
- 8 slices bacon
- Sprigs of fresh rosemary, for garnish
- Cooking spray

DIRECTIONS:

Spritz the air fryer basket with cooking spray.

Put the chives, lemon juice, sage, rosemary, parsley, garlic, fennel, salt, and red pepper flakes in a food processor, then pulse to purée until smooth.

Unfold the chicken breasts on a clean work surface, then brush the top side of the chicken breasts with the sauce.

Roll the chicken breasts up from the shorter side, then wrap each chicken rolls with 2 bacon slices to cover. Secure with toothpicks.

Arrange the rolls in the basket.

Put the air fryer basket on the baking pan and slide into Rack Position 2, select Air Fry, set temperature to 340°F (171°C) and set time to 10 minutes.

Flip the rolls halfway through.

After 10 minutes, increase temperature to 390°F (199°C) and set time to 5 minutes.

When cooking is complete, the bacon should be browned and crispy.

Transfer the rolls to a large plate. Discard the toothpicks and spread with rosemary sprigs before serving.

570. BEEF CHIMICHANGAS

Servings: 4

Cooking Time: 10 Minutes

INGREDIENTS:

- 1 lb. ground beef
- 1 tbsp. taco seasoning
- 1/3 cup salsa
- 4 flour tortillas
- 16 oz. refried beans
- 1 cup Mexican cheese blend, grated
- 1 cup lettuce, shredded
- 1 tbsp. olive oil

DIRECTIONS:

Heat a medium skillet over medium heat. Add beef and taco seasoning and cook, breaking up with spatula, until meat is no longer pink. Stir in salsa and remove from heat.

Place tortillas, one at a time, on work surface and spread with 1/3 cup beans, leaving a 1-inch border.

Top with beef mixture, cheese and lettuce. Fold one edge of the tortilla to the middle, then the opposite edge so they overlap slightly. Fold other two ends towards middle until you have a rectangular pocket.

Place the baking pan in position 2 of the oven. Lightly brush Chimichangas with oil and place in fryer basket. Place on baking pan.

Set oven to air fry on 400°F for 10 minutes. Cook until Chimichangas are golden brown and crispy. Serve immediately with your favorite toppings.

Nutrition Info: Calories 638, Total Fat 22g, Saturated Fat 9g, Total Carbs 58g, Net Carbs 42g, Protein 52g, Sugar 3g, Fiber 12g, Sodium 928mg, Potassium 1045mg, Phosphorus 650mg

571. HERB TURKEY TENDERLOIN

Servings: 4

Cooking Time: 40 Minutes

INGREDIENTS:

- 24 oz turkey tenderloin
- 1 tbsp dried rosemary
- 1 tbsp dried sage
- Pepper
- Salt

DIRECTIONS:

Fit the Cosori oven with the rack in position

Rub turkey tenderloin with rosemary, sage, pepper, and salt.

Place turkey tenderloin into the baking pan.

Set to bake at 350 F for 45 minutes. After 5 minutes place the baking pan in the preheated oven.

Slice and serve.

Nutrition Info: Calories 185 Fat 2.4 g Carbohydrates 0.9 g Sugar 0 g Protein 42.3 g Cholesterol 68 mg

572. CHILI LIME WHOLE CHICKEN

Servings: 4

Cooking Time: 50 Minutes + Marinating Time

INGREDIENTS:

- 1 (2 ½ lb) whole chicken
- Salt and black pepper to taste
- 1 tsp chili powder
- 1 tsp garlic powder
- 1 tsp oregano
- 1 tsp cilantro powder
- 1 tsp cumin powder
- 4 tbsp olive oil
- 1 tsp paprika
- 1 lime, juiced

DIRECTIONS:

In a bowl, mix oregano, garlic powder, chili powder, cilantro, paprika, cumin, pepper, salt, and olive oil. Mix well to create a rub for the chicken and rub onto it. Refrigerate for 20 minutes.

Preheat Cosori on AirFry function to 350 F. Place the chicken in the basket. Cook for 30-35 minutes. Let it rest for 10 minutes. Drizzle lime

juice over and serve carved with green salad.

573. BEER CORNED BEEF WITH CARROTS

Servings: 4

Cooking Time: 35 Minutes

INGREDIENTS:

- 1 tbsp beef spice
- 1 white onion, chopped
- 2 carrots, chopped
- 12 oz bottle beer
- 1 ½ cups chicken broth
- 4 pounds corned beef

DIRECTIONS:

Cover beef with beer and let sit in the fridge for 30 minutes. Transfer to a pot over medium heat and add in chicken broth, carrots, and onion. Bring to a boil and simmer for 10 minutes. Drain boiled meat and veggies and place them in a baking dish. Sprinkle with beef spice. Select Bake function, adjust the temperature to 400 F, and press Start. Cook for 30 minutes.

574. CHEESY CHICKEN ESCALLOPS

Servings: 4

Cooking Time: 10 Minutes

INGREDIENTS:

- 4 skinless chicken breasts
- 2 ½ oz panko breadcrumbs
- 1 ounce Parmesan cheese, grated
- 6 sage leaves, chopped
- 1 ¼ ounces flour
- 2 beaten eggs

DIRECTIONS:

Place the chicken breasts between a cling film, beat well using a rolling pin until a ½ inch thickness is achieved.

In a bowl, add Parmesan cheese, sage, and breadcrumbs. Dredge the chicken into the seasoned flour and then into the eggs. Finally, coat in the breadcrumbs.

Spray the chicken breasts with cooking spray and cook in your Cosori oven for 14-16 minutes at 350 F on Air Fry function.

575. JUICY & TENDER CHICKEN BREAST

Servings: 4

Cooking Time: 20 Minutes

INGREDIENTS:

- 4 chicken breasts, skinless & boneless
- 1/4 tsp pepper
- 1/4 tsp onion powder
- 1/4 tsp garlic powder
- 1 tsp paprika
- 1 tsp Italian seasoning
- 1 tbsp brown sugar
- 3 tbsp butter, melted
- 1 tsp salt

DIRECTIONS:

Fit the Cosori oven with the rack in position

In a small bowl, mix paprika, brown sugar, Italian seasoning, garlic powder, onion powder, pepper, and salt.

Brush chicken with melted butter and rub with spice mixture.

Place chicken into the baking dish.

Set to bake at 425 F for 25 minutes. After 5 minutes place the baking dish in the preheated oven.

Serve and enjoy.

Nutrition Info: Calories 369 Fat 19.9 g Carbohydrates 3 g Sugar 2.4 g Protein 42.5 g Cholesterol 154 mg

576. AIR FRIED BEEF AND MUSHROOM STROGANOFF

Prep time: 15 minutes | Cook time: 14 minutes | Serves 4

- 1 pound (454 g) beef steak, thinly sliced
- 8 ounces (227 g) mushrooms, sliced
- 1 whole onion, chopped
- 2 cups beef broth
- 1 cup sour cream
- 4 tablespoons butter, melted
- 2 cups cooked egg noodles

Combine the mushrooms, onion, beef broth, sour cream and butter in a bowl until well blended. Add the beef steak to another bowl.
Spread the mushroom mixture over the steak and let marinate for 10 minutes.
Pour the marinated steak in a baking pan.
Select Bake of the oven. Set temperature to 400°F (205°C) and set time to 14 minutes. Press Start to begin preheating.
Once preheated, place the pan into the oven. Flip the steak halfway through the cooking time.
When cooking is complete, the steak should be browned and the vegetables should be tender.
Serve hot with the cooked egg noodles.

577. CAJUN BURGER PATTIES

Servings: 2
Cooking Time: 10 Minutes
INGREDIENTS:
- 1 egg, lightly beaten
- 1/2 lb ground pork
- 1/2 cup breadcrumbs
- 1 tbsp Cajun seasoning
- Pepper
- Salt

DIRECTIONS:
Fit the Cosori oven with the rack in position 2.
Line the air fryer basket with parchment paper.
Add all ingredients into the large bowl and mix until well combined.
Make two equal shapes of patties from meat mixture and place in the air fryer basket then place an air fryer basket in the baking pan.
Place a baking pan on the oven rack. Set to air fry at 360 F for 10 minutes.
Serve and enjoy.
Nutrition Info: Calories 300 Fat 7.6 g Carbohydrates 19.6 g Sugar 1.8 g Protein 36.1 g Cholesterol 165 mg

578. AIR FRYER TURKEY BREAST

Servings: 6
Cooking Time: 60 Minutes
INGREDIENTS:
- Pepper and salt
- 1 oven-ready turkey breast
- Turkey seasonings of choice

DIRECTIONS:
Preparing the Ingredients. Preheat the Cosori air fryer oven to 350 degrees.
Season turkey with pepper, salt, and other desired seasonings.
Place turkey in the Oven rack/basket. Place the Rack on the middle-shelf of the Cosori air fryer oven.
Air Frying. Set temperature to 350°F, and set time to 60 minutes. Cook 60 minutes. The meat should be at 165 degrees when done.
Allow to rest 10-15 minutes before slicing. Enjoy!
Nutrition Info: CALORIES: 212; FAT: 12G; PROTEIN:24G; SUGAR:0G

579. FRIED CHICKEN TENDERLOINS

Servings: 4
Cooking Time: 15 Minutes
INGREDIENTS:
- 8 chicken tenderloins
- 2 tbsp butter, softened
- 2 oz breadcrumbs
- 1 large egg, whisked

DIRECTIONS:
Preheat Cosori on Air Fry function to 380 F. Combine butter and breadcrumbs in a bowl. Keep mixing and stirring until the mixture gets crumbly. Dip the chicken in the egg, then in the crumb mix. Place in the greased basket and fit in the baking tray; cook for 10 minutes, flipping once until crispy. Set on Broil function for crispier taste. Serve.

580. MEATBALLS

Servings: 6
Cooking Time: 20 Minutes
INGREDIENTS:
- 2 lbs ground beef
- 1 egg, lightly beaten
- 1 tsp cinnamon
- 2 tsp cumin
- 2 tsp coriander
- 1 tsp garlic, minced
- 1 tbsp fresh basil, chopped
- 1/4 cup fresh parsley, minced
- 1 tsp smoked paprika
- 1 tsp oregano
- 1 onion, grated
- 1/4 tsp pepper
- 1/2 tsp salt

DIRECTIONS:
Fit the Cosori oven with the rack in position
Add all ingredients into the large mixing bowl and mix until well combined.
Make small balls from the meat mixture and place it into the parchment-lined baking pan.
Set to bake at 400 F for 25 minutes. After 5 minutes place the baking pan in the preheated oven.
Serve and enjoy.
Nutrition Info: Calories 306 Fat 10.4 g Carbohydrates 3.1 g Sugar 0.9 g Protein 47.3 g Cholesterol 162 mg

581. MINTY CHICKEN-FRIED PORK CHOPS

Servings: 6
Cooking Time: 30 Minutes
INGREDIENTS:
- 4 medium-sized pork chops, approximately 3.5 ounces each
- 1 cup of breadcrumbs (Panko brand works well)
- 2 medium-sized eggs
- Pinch of salt and pepper
- ½ tablespoon of mint, either dried and ground; or fresh, rinsed and finely chopped

DIRECTIONS:
Preparing the Ingredients. Cover the basket of the Cosori air fryer oven with a lining of tin foil, leaving the edges uncovered to allow air to circulate through the basket. Preheat the Cosori air fryer oven to 350 degrees.
In a mixing bowl, beat the eggs until fluffy and until the yolks and whites are fully combined, and set aside.
In a separate mixing bowl, combine the breadcrumbs, mint, salt, and pepper, and set aside. One by one, dip each raw pork chop into the bowl with dry ingredients, coating all sides; then submerge into the bowl with wet ingredients, then dip again into the dry ingredients. This double coating will ensure an extra crisp air-fry. Lay the coated pork chops on the

foil covering the Oven rack/basket, in a single flat layer. Place the Rack on the middle-shelf of the Cosori air fryer oven.

Air Frying. Set the Cosori air fryer oven timer for 15 minutes. After 15 minutes, the Cosori air fryer oven will turn off, and the pork should be mid-way cooked and the breaded coating starting to brown. Using tongs, turn each piece of steak over to ensure a full all-over fry. Reset the air fryer oven to 320 degrees for 15 minutes.

After 15 minutes, when the air fryer shuts off, remove the fried pork chops using tongs and set on a serving plate. Eat as soon as cool enough to handle – and enjoy!

582. CHICKEN MEXICAN BURRITOS

INGREDIENTS:
- ½ lb. chicken (You will need to cut the chicken into small pieces)
- 2 carrots (Cut in to long thin slices)
- 1-2 lettuce leaves shredded.
- 1 or 2 spring onions chopped finely. Also cut the greens.
- Take one tomato. Remove the seeds and chop it into small
- pieces.
- 1 green chili chopped.
- 1 tbsp. Olive oil
- 1 medium onion finely sliced
- 3 flakes garlic crushed
- 1 tsp. white wine
- A pinch of salt to taste
- ½ tsp. red chili flakes
- 1 cup of cheddar cheese grated.
- 1 cup boiled rice (not necessary).
- A few flour tortillas to put the filing in.
- ½ small onion chopped
- 1 tbsp. olive oil
- 2 tbsp. tomato puree
- ¼ tsp. red chili powder
- 1 tsp. of salt to taste
- 4-5 flour tortillas

DIRECTIONS:
Cook the chicken, onions and garlic in two cups of water. You will need to cook till the chicken pieces have turned very soft. Now, mash the beans very fine.

In a pan, add oil and a few more onions to the pan and cook till the onions have turned translucent. Add the tomato puree and the cooked chicken and stir. Add the chili powder and salt to the pan and continue to cook till you get a thick paste. Set it aside.

For the filling, you will need to sauté the onions and garlic in oil. Add the French beans and the chopped carrots. You will need to stir-fry for a few minutes and add the remaining ingredients for the filling. Cook for another ten minutes and take the pan off the flame.

Mix it well and add the jalapenos. To make the salad, toss the ingredients together. Place a tortilla and add a layer of the French beans to it.

Cover the edges using the chicken paste. Put the filling in the center of the tortilla along with the salad and some boiled rice. Roll up the tortilla using the chicken sauce to help you hold it together. Pre-heat the Cosori oven for around 5 minutes at 200 Fahrenheit. Open the fry basket and keep the burritos inside. Close the basket properly.

Let the Cosori oven remain at 200 Fahrenheit for another 15 minutes or so. Halfway through, remove the basket and turn all the burritos over in order to get a uniform cook. You can either serve the burritos as they are or you can cut them into pieces so that they are easier to eat. Recommended sides are salsa or some salad.

583. TERIYAKI PORK RIBS WITH TOMATO SAUCE

Servings: 3
Cooking Time: 20 Minutes + Marinating Time
INGREDIENTS:
- 1 pound pork ribs
- Salt and black pepper to taste

- 1 tbsp sugar
- 1 tsp ginger juice
- 1 tsp five-spice powder
- 1 tbsp teriyaki sauce
- 1 tbsp soy sauce
- 1 garlic clove, minced
- 2 tbsp honey
- 1 tbsp tomato sauce
- 1 tbsp olive oil

DIRECTIONS:
In a bowl, mix pepper, sugar, five-spice powder, salt, ginger juice, and teriyaki sauce. Add pork ribs to the marinade and let sit for 2 hours.

Add ribs to the greased basket and fit in the baking tray; cook for 8 minutes on Air Fry function at 350 F. In a separate bowl, mix soy sauce, garlic, honey, 1 tbsp of water, and tomato sauce.

In a pan over medium heat, heat olive oil and fry garlic for 30 seconds. Add fried pork ribs and pour in the sauce. Stir-fry for a few minutes and serve.

584. EASY BBQ CHICKEN DRUMSTICKS

Servings: 4
Cooking Time: 25 Minutes
INGREDIENTS:
- 4 chicken drumsticks
- 1/4 tsp paprika
- 1/2 tsp garlic powder
- 2 tbsp olive oil
- 1/2 cup BBQ sauce
- 1/2 tsp onion powder
- Pepper
- Salt

DIRECTIONS:
Fit the Cosori oven with the rack in position 2.

In a mixing bowl, add chicken drumsticks, onion powder, garlic powder, olive oil, paprika, pepper, and salt and toss well.

Add chicken drumsticks to the air fryer basket then place an air fryer basket in baking pan.

Place a baking pan on the oven rack. Set to air fry at 400 F for 20 minutes.

Brush chicken drumsticks with BBQ sauce and air fry for 5 minutes. Serve and enjoy.

Nutrition Info: Calories 187 Fat 9.7 g Carbohydrates 11.9 g Sugar 8.4 g Protein 12.8 g Cholesterol 40 mg

585. QUAIL CHILI

INGREDIENTS:
- 1 lb. quail (Cut into cubes)
- 2 ½ tsp. ginger-garlic paste
- 1 tsp. red chili sauce
- 2 tbsp. tomato ketchup
- 2 tsp. soya sauce
- 1-2 tbsp. honey
- ¼ tsp. Ajinomoto
- ¼ tsp. salt
- ¼ tsp. red chili powder/black pepper
- A few drops of edible orange food coloring
- 2 tbsp. olive oil
- 1 ½ tsp. ginger garlic paste
- ½ tbsp. red chili sauce
- 1-2 tsp. red chili flakes

DIRECTIONS:
Mix all the ingredients for the marinade and put the quail cubes inside and let it rest overnight.

Mix the breadcrumbs, oregano and red chili flakes well and place the marinated Oregano Fingers on this mixture. Cover it with plastic wrap and leave it till right before you serve to cook.

Pre heat the Cosori oven at 160 degrees Fahrenheit for 5 minutes. Place the Oregano Fingers in the fry basket and close it. Let them cook at the same temperature for another 15 minutes or so. Toss the Oregano Fingers well so that they are cooked uniformly.

586. LAMB KOFTA
Prep time: 25 minutes | Cook time: 10 minutes | Serves 4

- 1 pound (454 g) ground lamb
- 1 tablespoon ras el hanout (North African spice)
- ½ teaspoon ground coriander
- 1 teaspoon onion powder
- 1 teaspoon garlic powder
- 1 teaspoon cumin
- 2 tablespoons mint, chopped
- Salt and ground black pepper, to taste

Special Equipment:
4 bamboo skewers
Combine the ground lamb, ras el hanout, coriander, onion powder, garlic powder, cumin, mint, salt, and ground black pepper in a large bowl. Stir to mix well.
Transfer the mixture into sausage molds and sit the bamboo skewers in the mixture. Refrigerate for 15 minutes.
Spritz a perforated pan with cooking spray. Place the lamb skewers in the pan and spritz with cooking spray.
Select Air Fry of the oven. Set temperature to 380°F (193°C) and set time to 10 minutes. Press Start to begin preheating.
Once preheated, place the pan into the oven. Flip the lamb skewers halfway through.
When cooking is complete, the lamb should be well browned.
Serve immediately.

587. LEMON MUSTARD CHICKEN
Servings: 4
Cooking Time: 20 Minutes
INGREDIENTS:
- 1 lbs chicken tenders
- 1 garlic clove, minced
- 1/2 oz fresh lemon juice
- 1/2 tsp pepper
- 2 tbsp fresh tarragon, chopped
- 1/2 cup whole grain mustard
- 1/2 tsp paprika
- 1/4 tsp kosher salt

DIRECTIONS:
Fit the Cosori oven with the rack in position
Add all ingredients except chicken to the large bowl and mix well.
Add chicken to the bowl and stir until well coated.
Place chicken in a baking dish.
Set to bake at 425 F for 25 minutes. After 5 minutes place the baking dish in the preheated oven.
Serve and enjoy.
Nutrition Info: Calories 242 Fat 9.5 g Carbohydrates 3.1 g Sugar 0.1 g Protein 33.2 g Cholesterol 101 mg

588. TURKEY BURGER CUTLETS
INGREDIENTS:
- ½ lb. minced turkey
- ½ cup breadcrumbs
- A pinch of salt to taste
- ¼ tsp. ginger finely chopped
- 1 green chili finely chopped
- 1 tsp. lemon juice
- 1 tbsp. fresh coriander leaves. Chop them finely
- ¼ tsp. red chili powder
- ½ cup of boiled peas
- ¼ tsp. cumin powder
- ¼ tsp. dried mango powder

DIRECTIONS:
Take a container and into it pour all the masalas, onions, green chilies, peas, coriander leaves, lemon juice, ginger and 1-2 tbsp. breadcrumbs. Add the minced turkey as well. Mix all the ingredients well. Mold the mixture into round Cutlets. Press them gently. Now roll them out carefully. Pre heat the Cosori oven at 250 Fahrenheit for 5 minutes.
Open the basket of the Fryer and arrange the Cutlets in the basket. Close it carefully.
Keep the fryer at 150 degrees for around 10 or 12 minutes. In between the cooking process, turn the Cutlets over to get a uniform cook. Serve hot with mint sauce.

589. BACON WITH ROSEMARY POTATOES
Servings: 4
Cooking Time: 40 Minutes
INGREDIENTS:
- 2 lb potatoes, halved
- 2 garlic cloves, minced
- 4 bacon slices, chopped
- 1 tbsp fresh rosemary, chopped
- 2 tbsp olive oil

DIRECTIONS:
In a mixing bowl, mix garlic, bacon, olive oil, and rosemary; toss in potatoes. Place the mixture in a baking dish Roast in the preheated Cosori for 25-30 minutes at 400 F on AirFry function.

590. BEEF AND TOMATO SAUCE MEATLOAF
Prep time: 15 minutes | Cook time: 25 minutes | Serves 4

- 1½ pounds (680 g) ground beef
- 1 cup tomato sauce
- ½ cup breadcrumbs
- 2 egg whites
- ½ cup grated Parmesan cheese
- 1 diced onion
- 2 tablespoons chopped parsley
- 2 tablespoons minced ginger
- 2 garlic cloves, minced
- ½ teaspoon dried basil
- 1 teaspoon cayenne pepper
- Salt and ground black pepper, to taste
- Cooking spray

Spritz a meatloaf pan with cooking spray.
Combine all the ingredients in a large bowl. Stir to mix well.
Pour the meat mixture in the prepared meatloaf pan and press with a spatula to make it firm.
Select Bake of the oven. Set temperature to 360°F (182°C) and set time to 25 minutes. Press Start to begin preheating.
Once preheated, place the pan into the oven.
When cooking is complete, the beef should be well browned.
Serve immediately.

591. BO LUC LAC
Prep time: 50 minutes | Cook time: 4 minutes | Serves 4

For the Meat:
- 2 teaspoons soy sauce
- 4 garlic cloves, minced
- 1 teaspoon kosher salt
- 2 teaspoons sugar
- ¼ teaspoon ground black pepper
- 1 teaspoon toasted sesame oil
- 1½ pounds (680 g) top sirloin steak, cut into 1-inch cubes
- Cooking spray

For the Salad:
- 1 head Bibb lettuce, leaves separated and torn into large pieces
- ¼ cup fresh mint leaves
- ½ cup halved grape tomatoes
- ½ red onion, halved and thinly sliced
- 2 tablespoons apple cider vinegar
- 1 garlic clove, minced
- 2 teaspoons sugar
- ¼ teaspoon kosher salt
- ¼ teaspoon ground black pepper
- 2 tablespoons vegetable oil
- For Serving:
- Lime wedges, for garnish
- Coarse salt and freshly cracked black pepper, to taste

Combine the ingredients for the meat, except for the steak, in a large bowl. Stir to mix well.

Dunk the steak cubes in the bowl and press to coat. Wrap the bowl in plastic and marinate under room temperature for at least 30 minutes.

Spritz a perforated pan with cooking spray.

Discard the marinade and transfer the steak cubes in the prepared perforated pan.

Select Air Fry of the oven. Set temperature to 450ºF (235ºC) and set time to 4 minutes. Press Start to begin preheating.

Once preheated, place the pan into the oven. Flip the steak cubes halfway through.

When cooking is complete, the steak cubes should be lightly browned but still have a little pink.

Meanwhile, combine the ingredients for the salad in a separate large bowl. Toss to mix well.

Pour the salad in a large serving bowl and top with the steak cubes. Squeeze the lime wedges over and sprinkle with salt and black pepper before serving.

592. CARAWAY CRUSTED BEEF STEAKS

Prep time: 5 minutes | Cook time: 10 minutes | Serves 4

- 4 beef steaks
- 2 teaspoons caraway seeds
- 2 teaspoons garlic powder
- Sea salt and cayenne pepper, to taste
- 1 tablespoon melted butter
- ⅓ cup almond flour
- 2 eggs, beaten

Add the beef steaks to a large bowl and toss with the caraway seeds, garlic powder, salt and pepper until well coated.

Stir together the melted butter and almond flour in a bowl. Whisk the eggs in a different bowl.

Dredge the seasoned steaks in the eggs, then dip in the almond and butter mixture.

Arrange the coated steaks in the perforated pan.

Select Air Fry of the oven. Set temperature to 355ºF (179ºC) and set time to 10 minutes. Press Start to begin preheating.

Once preheated, place the pan into the oven. Flip the steaks once halfway through to ensure even cooking.

When cooking is complete, the internal temperature of the beef steaks should reach at least 145ºF (63ºC) on a meat thermometer.

Transfer the steaks to plates. Let cool for 5 minutes and serve hot.

593. CARNE ASADA

Prep time: 5 minutes | Cook time: 15 minutes | Serves 4

- 3 chipotle peppers in adobo, chopped
- ⅓ cup chopped fresh oregano
- ⅓ cup chopped fresh parsley
- 4 cloves garlic, minced
- Juice of 2 limes
- 1 teaspoon ground cumin seeds
- ⅓ cup olive oil
- 1 to 1½ pounds (454 g to 680 g) flank steak
- Salt, to taste

Combine the chipotle, oregano, parsley, garlic, lime juice, cumin, and olive oil in a large bowl. Stir to mix well.

Dunk the flank steak in the mixture and press to coat well. Wrap the bowl in plastic and marinate under room temperature for at least 30 minutes.

Discard the marinade and place the steak in the perforated pan. Sprinkle with salt.

Select Air Fry of the oven. Set temperature to 390ºF (199ºC) and set time to 15 minutes. Press Start to begin preheating.

Once preheated, place the pan into the oven. Flip the steak halfway through the cooking time.

When cooking is complete, the steak should be medium-rare or reach your desired doneness.

Remove the steak from the oven and slice to serve.

594. ITALIAN STEAK AND SPINACH ROLLS

Prep time: 50 minutes | Cook time: 9 minutes | Serves 4

- 2 teaspoons dried Italian seasoning
- 2 cloves garlic, minced
- 1 tablespoon vegetable oil
- 1 teaspoon kosher salt
- 1 teaspoon ground black pepper
- 1 pound (454 g) flank steak, ¼ to ½ inch thick
- 1 (10-ounce / 284-g) package frozen spinach, thawed and squeezed dry
- ½ cup diced jarred roasted red pepper
- 1 cup shredded Mozzarella cheese
- Cooking spray

Combine the Italian seasoning, garlic, vegetable oil, salt, and ground black pepper in a large bowl. Stir to mix well.

Dunk the steak in the seasoning mixture and toss to coat well. Wrap the bowl in plastic and marinate under room temperature for at least 30 minutes.

Spritz a perforated pan with cooking spray.

Remove the marinated steak from the bowl and unfold on a clean work surface, then spread the top of the steak with a layer of spinach, a layer of red pepper and a layer of cheese. Leave a ¼-inch edge uncovered.

Roll the steak up to wrap the filling, then secure with 3 toothpicks. Cut the roll in half and transfer the rolls in the prepared perforated pan, seam side down.

Select Air Fry of the oven. Set temperature to 400ºF (205ºC) and set time to 9 minutes. Press Start to begin preheating.

Once preheated, place the pan into the oven. Flip the rolls halfway through the cooking.

When cooking is complete, the steak should be lightly browned and the internal temperature reaches at least 145ºF (63ºC).

Remove the rolls from the oven and slice to serve.

595. LUSH SALISBURY STEAK WITH MUSHROOM GRAVY

Prep time: 20 minutes | Cook time: 33 minutes | Serves 2

- For the Mushroom Gravy:
- ¾ cup sliced button mushrooms
- ¼ cup thinly sliced onions
- ¼ cup unsalted butter, melted
- ½ teaspoon fine sea salt
- ¼ cup beef broth
- For the Steaks:

- ½ pound (227 g) ground beef (85% lean)
- 1 tablespoon dry mustard
- 2 tablespoons tomato paste
- ¼ teaspoon garlic powder
- ½ teaspoon onion powder
- ½ teaspoon fine sea salt
- ¼ teaspoon ground black pepper
- Chopped fresh thyme leaves, for garnish

Toss the mushrooms and onions with butter in a baking pan to coat well, then sprinkle with salt.

Select Bake of the oven. Set temperature to 390ºF (199ºC) and set time to 8 minutes. Press Start to begin preheating.

Once preheated, place the pan into the oven. Stir the mixture halfway through the cooking.

When cooking is complete, the mushrooms should be tender.

Pour the broth in the baking pan and set time to 10 more minutes to make the gravy.

Meanwhile, combine all the ingredients for the steaks, except for the thyme leaves, in a large bowl. Stir to mix well. Shape the mixture into two oval steaks.

Arrange the steaks over the gravy and set time to 15 minutes. When cooking is complete, the patties should be browned. Flip the steaks halfway through.

Transfer the steaks onto a plate and pour the gravy over. Sprinkle with fresh thyme and serve immediately.

596. MEAT AND RICE STUFFED BELL PEPPERS
Prep time: 20 minutes | Cook time: 18 minutes | Serves 4

- ¾ pound (340 g) lean ground beef
- 4 ounces (113 g) lean ground pork
- ¼ cup onion, minced
- 1 (15-ounce / 425-g) can crushed tomatoes
- 1 teaspoon Worcestershire sauce
- 1 teaspoon barbecue seasoning
- 1 teaspoon honey
- ½ teaspoon dried basil
- ½ cup cooked brown rice
- ½ teaspoon garlic powder
- ½ teaspoon oregano
- ½ teaspoon salt
- 2 small bell peppers, cut in half, stems removed, deseeded
- Cooking spray

Spritz a baking pan with cooking spray.

Arrange the beef, pork, and onion in the baking pan.

Select Bake of the oven. Set temperature to 360ºF (182ºC) and set time to 8 minutes. Press Start to begin preheating.

Once preheated, place the pan into the oven. Break the ground meat into chunks halfway through the cooking.

When cooking is complete, the ground meat should be lightly browned.

Meanwhile, combine the tomatoes, Worcestershire sauce, barbecue seasoning, honey, and basil in a saucepan. Stir to mix well.

Transfer the cooked meat mixture to a large bowl and add the cooked rice, garlic powder, oregano, salt, and ¼ cup of the tomato mixture. Stir to mix well.

Stuff the pepper halves with the mixture, then arrange the pepper halves in the perforated pan.

Select Air Fry of the oven. Set time to 10 minutes. Place the pan into the oven.

When cooking is complete, the peppers should be lightly charred.

Serve the stuffed peppers with the remaining tomato sauce on top.

597. MUSHROOM IN BACON-WRAPPED FILETS MIGNONS

Prep time: 10 minutes | Cook time: 13 minutes | Serves 8

- 1 ounce (28 g) dried porcini mushrooms
- ½ teaspoon granulated white sugar
- ½ teaspoon salt
- ½ teaspoon ground white pepper
- 8 (4-ounce / 113-g) filets mignons or beef tenderloin steaks
- 8 thin-cut bacon strips

Put the mushrooms, sugar, salt, and white pepper in a spice grinder and grind to combine.

On a clean work surface, rub the filets mignons with the mushroom mixture, then wrap each filet with a bacon strip. Secure with toothpicks if necessary.

Arrange the bacon-wrapped filets mignons in the perforated pan, seam side down.

Select Air Fry of the oven. Set temperature to 400ºF (205ºC) and set time to 13 minutes. Press Start to begin preheating.

Once preheated, place the pan into the oven. Flip the filets halfway through.

When cooking is complete, the filets should be medium rare.

Serve immediately.

598. AIR FRIED BEEF SATAY WITH PEANUT DIPPING SAUCE
Prep time: 30 minutes | Cook time: 5 minutes | Serves 4

- 8 ounces (227 g) London broil, sliced into 8 strips
- 2 teaspoons curry powder
- ½ teaspoon kosher salt
- Cooking spray
- Peanut Dipping sauce:
- 2 tablespoons creamy peanut butter
- 1 tablespoon reduced-sodium soy sauce
- 2 teaspoons rice vinegar
- 1 teaspoon honey
- 1 teaspoon grated ginger

Special Equipment:
4 bamboo skewers, cut into halves and soaked in water for 20 minutes to keep them from burning while cooking

Spritz a perforated pan with cooking spray.

In a bowl, place the London broil strips and sprinkle with the curry powder and kosher salt to season. Thread the strips onto the soaked skewers. Arrange the skewers in the prepared perforated pan and spritz with cooking spray.

Select Air Fry of the oven. Set temperature to 360ºF (182ºC) and set time to 5 minutes. Press Start to begin preheating.

Once preheated, place the pan into the oven. Flip the beef halfway through the cooking time.

When cooking is complete, the beef should be well browned.

In the meantime, stir together the peanut butter, soy sauce, rice vinegar, honey, and ginger in a bowl to make the dipping sauce.

Transfer the beef to the serving dishes and let rest for 5 minutes. Serve with the peanut dipping sauce on the side.

599. AIR FRIED LONDON BROIL
Prep time: 8 hours 5 minutes | Cook time: 25 minutes | Serves 6

- 2 tablespoons Worcestershire sauce
- 2 tablespoons minced onion
- ¼ cup honey
- ⅔ cup ketchup
- 2 tablespoons apple cider vinegar
- ½ teaspoon paprika

- ¼ cup olive oil
- 1 teaspoon salt
- 1 teaspoon freshly ground black pepper
- 2 pounds (907 g) London broil, top round (about 1-inch thick)

Combine all the ingredients, except for the London broil, in a large bowl. Stir to mix well.

Pierce the meat with a fork generously on both sides, then dunk the meat in the mixture and press to coat well.

Wrap the bowl in plastic and refrigerate to marinate for at least 8 hours. Discard the marinade and transfer the London broil to the perforated pan.

Select Air Fry of the oven. Set temperature to 400°F (205°C) and set time to 25 minutes. Press Start to begin preheating.

Once preheated, place the pan into the oven. Flip the meat halfway through the cooking time.

When cooking is complete, the meat should be well browned.

Transfer the cooked London broil on a plate and allow to cool for 5 minutes before slicing to serve.

600. NEW YORK STRIP WITH HONEY-MUSTARD BUTTER

Prep time: 5 minutes | Cook time: 14 minutes | Serves 4

- 2 pounds (907 g) New York Strip
- 1 teaspoon cayenne pepper
- 1 tablespoon honey
- 1 tablespoon Dijon mustard
- ½ stick butter, softened
- Sea salt and freshly ground black pepper, to taste
- Cooking spray

Spritz a perforated pan with cooking spray.

Sprinkle the New York Strip with cayenne pepper, salt, and black pepper on a clean work surface.

Arrange the New York Strip in the prepared pan and spritz with cooking spray.

Select Air Fry of the oven. Set temperature to 400°F (205°C) and set time to 14 minutes. Press Start to begin preheating.

Once preheated, place the pan into the oven. Flip the New York Strip halfway through.

When cooking is complete, the strips should be browned.

Meanwhile, combine the honey, mustard, and butter in a small bowl. Stir to mix well.

Transfer the air fried New York Strip onto a plate and baste with the honey-mustard butter before serving.

601. BEEF MEATBALLS WITH ZESTY MARINARA SAUCE

Prep time: 5 minutes | Cook time: 8 minutes | Serves 4

- 1 pound (454 g) lean ground sirloin beef
- 2 tablespoons seasoned breadcrumbs
- ¼ teaspoon kosher salt
- 1 large egg, beaten
- 1 cup marinara sauce, for serving
- Cooking spray

Spritz a perforated pan with cooking spray.

Mix all the ingredients, except for the marinara sauce, into a bowl until well blended. Shape the mixture into sixteen meatballs.

Arrange the meatballs in the prepared perforated pan and mist with cooking spray.

Select Air Fry of the oven. Set temperature to 360°F (182°C) and set time to 8 minutes. Press Start to begin preheating.

Once preheated, place the pan into the oven. Flip the meatballs halfway through.

When cooking is complete, the meatballs should be well browned.

Divide the meatballs among four plates and serve warm with the marinara sauce.

602. PANKO CRUSTED CALF'S LIVER STRIPS

Prep time: 15 minutes | Cook time: 5 minutes | Serves 4

- 1 pound (454 g) sliced calf's liver, cut into ½-inch wide strips
- 2 eggs
- 2 tablespoons milk
- ½ cup whole wheat flour
- 2 cups panko breadcrumbs
- Salt and ground black pepper, to taste
- Cooking spray

Spritz a perforated pan with cooking spray.

Rub the calf's liver strips with salt and ground black pepper on a clean work surface.

Whisk the eggs with milk in a large bowl. Pour the flour in a shallow dish. Pour the panko on a separate shallow dish.

Dunk the liver strips in the flour, then in the egg mixture. Shake the excess off and roll the strips over the panko to coat well.

Arrange the liver strips in the preheated pan and spritz with cooking spray.

Select Air Fry of the oven. Set temperature to 390°F (199°C) and set time to 5 minutes. Press Start to begin preheating.

Once preheated, place the pan into the oven. Flip the strips halfway through.

When cooking is complete, the strips should be browned.

Serve immediately.

603. REUBEN BEEF ROLLS WITH THOUSAND IS-LAND SAUCE

Prep time: 15 minutes | Cook time: 10 minutes | Makes 10 rolls

- ½ pound (227 g) cooked corned beef, chopped
- ½ cup drained and chopped sauerkraut
- 1 (8-ounce / 227-g) package cream cheese, softened
- ½ cup shredded Swiss cheese
- 20 slices prosciutto
- Cooking spray
- Thousand Island Sauce:
- ¼ cup chopped dill pickles
- ¼ cup tomato sauce
- ¾ cup mayonnaise
- Fresh thyme leaves, for garnish
- 2 tablespoons sugar
- ⅛ teaspoon fine sea salt
- Ground black pepper, to taste

Spritz a perforated pan with cooking spray.

Combine the beef, sauerkraut, cream cheese, and Swiss cheese in a large bowl. Stir to mix well.

Unroll a slice of prosciutto on a clean work surface, then top with another slice of prosciutto crosswise. Scoop up 4 tablespoons of the beef mixture in the center.

Fold the top slice sides over the filling as the ends of the roll, then roll up the long sides of the bottom prosciutto and make it into a roll shape. Overlap the sides by about 1 inch. Repeat with remaining filling and prosciutto.

Arrange the rolls in the prepared pan, seam side down, and spritz with cooking spray.

Select Air Fry of the oven. Set temperature to 400°F (205°C) and set time to 10 minutes. Press Start to begin preheating.

Once preheated, place the pan into the oven. Flip the rolls halfway through.

When cooking is complete, the rolls should be golden and crispy.
Meanwhile, combine the ingredients for the sauce in a small bowl. Stir to mix well.
Serve the rolls with the dipping sauce.

604. CINNAMON-BEEF KOFTA

Prep time: 10 minutes | Cook time: 13 minutes | Makes 12 koftas

- 1½ pounds (680 g) lean ground beef
- 1 teaspoon onion powder
- ¾ teaspoon ground cinnamon
- ¾ teaspoon ground dried turmeric
- 1 teaspoon ground cumin
- ¾ teaspoon salt
- ¼ teaspoon cayenne
- 12 (3½- to 4-inch-long) cinnamon sticks
- Cooking spray

Spritz a perforated pan with cooking spray.
Combine all the ingredients, except for the cinnamon sticks, in a large bowl. Toss to mix well.
Divide and shape the mixture into 12 balls, then wrap each ball around each cinnamon stick and leave a quarter of the length uncovered.
Arrange the beef-cinnamon sticks in the prepared pan and spritz with cooking spray.
Select Air Fry of the oven. Set temperature to 375ºF (190ºC) and set time to 13 minutes. Press Start to begin preheating.
Once preheated, place the pan into the oven. Flip the sticks halfway through the cooking.
When cooking is complete, the beef should be browned.
Serve immediately.

605. SALSA BEEF MEATBALLS

Prep time: 10 minutes | Cook time: 10 minutes | Serves 4

- 1 pound (454 g) ground beef (85% lean)
- ½ cup salsa
- ¼ cup diced green or red bell peppers
- 1 large egg, beaten
- ¼ cup chopped onions
- ½ teaspoon chili powder
- 1 clove garlic, minced
- ½ teaspoon ground cumin
- 1 teaspoon fine sea salt
- Lime wedges, for serving
- Cooking spray

Spritz a perforated pan with cooking spray.
Combine all the ingredients in a large bowl. Stir to mix well.
Divide and shape the mixture into 1-inch balls. Arrange the balls in the pan and spritz with cooking spray.
Select Air Fry of the oven. Set temperature to 350ºF (180ºC) and set time to 10 minutes. Press Start to begin preheating.
Once preheated, place the pan into the oven. Flip the balls with tongs halfway through.
When cooking is complete, the balls should be well browned.
Transfer the balls on a plate and squeeze the lime wedges over before serving.

606. SIMPLE GROUND BEEF WITH ZUCCHINI

Prep time: 5 minutes | Cook time: 12 minutes | Serves 4

- 1½ pounds (680 g) ground beef
- 1 pound (454 g) chopped zucchini
- 2 tablespoons extra-virgin olive oil
- 1 teaspoon dried oregano
- 1 teaspoon dried basil

- 1 teaspoon dried rosemary
- 2 tablespoons fresh chives, chopped

In a large bowl, combine all the ingredients, except for the chives, until well blended.
Place the beef and zucchini mixture in the baking pan.
Select Bake of the oven. Set temperature to 400ºF (205ºC) and set time to 12 minutes. Press Start to begin preheating.
Once preheated, place the pan into the oven.
When cooking is complete, the beef should be browned and the zucchini should be tender.
Divide the beef and zucchini mixture among four serving dishes. Top with fresh chives and serve hot.

607. SPICE-COATED STEAKS WITH CUCUMBER AND SNAP PEA SALAD

Prep time: 15 minutes | Cook time: 15 minutes | Serves 4

- 1 (1½-pound / 680-g) boneless top sirloin steak, trimmed and halved crosswise
- 1½ teaspoons chili powder
- 1½ teaspoons ground cumin
- ¾ teaspoon ground coriander
- ⅛ teaspoon cayenne pepper
- ⅛ teaspoon ground cinnamon
- 1¼ teaspoons plus ⅛ teaspoon salt, divided
- ½ teaspoon plus ⅛ teaspoon ground black pepper, divided
- 1 teaspoon plus 1½ tablespoons extra-virgin olive oil, divided
- 3 tablespoons mayonnaise
- 1½ tablespoons white wine vinegar
- 1 tablespoon minced fresh dill
- 1 small garlic clove, minced
- 8 ounces (227 g) sugar snap peas, strings removed and cut in half on bias
- ½ English cucumber, halved lengthwise and sliced thin
- 2 radishes, trimmed, halved and sliced thin
- 2 cups baby arugula

In a bowl, mix chili powder, cumin, coriander, cayenne pepper, cinnamon, 1¼ teaspoons salt and ½ teaspoon pepper until well combined.
Add the steaks to another bowl and pat dry with paper towels. Brush with 1 teaspoon oil and transfer to the bowl of spice mixture. Roll over to coat thoroughly.
Arrange the coated steaks in the perforated pan, spaced evenly apart.
Select Air Fry of the oven. Set temperature to 400ºF (205ºC) and set time to 15 minutes. Press Start to begin preheating.
Once preheated, place the pan into the oven. Flip the steak halfway through to ensure even cooking.
When cooking is complete, an instant-read thermometer inserted in the thickest part of the meat should register at least 145ºF (63ºC).
Transfer the steaks to a clean work surface and wrap with aluminum foil. Let stand while preparing salad.
Make the salad: In a large bowl, stir together 1½ tablespoons olive oil, mayonnaise, vinegar, dill, garlic, ⅛ teaspoon salt, and ⅛ teaspoon pepper. Add snap peas, cucumber, radishes and arugula. Toss to blend well.
Slice the steaks and serve with the salad.

608. SUMPTUOUS BEEF AND PORK SAUSAGE MEATLOAF

Prep time: 10 minutes | Cook time: 25 minutes | Serves 4

- ¾ pound (340 g) ground chuck
- 4 ounces (113 g) ground pork sausage
- 2 eggs, beaten
- 1 cup Parmesan cheese, grated
- 1 cup chopped shallot

- 3 tablespoons plain milk
- 1 tablespoon oyster sauce
- 1 tablespoon fresh parsley
- 1 teaspoon garlic paste
- 1 teaspoon chopped porcini mushrooms
- ½ teaspoon cumin powder
- Seasoned salt and crushed red pepper flakes, to taste

In a large bowl, combine all the ingredients until well blended.

Place the meat mixture in the baking pan. Use a spatula to press the mixture to fill the pan.

Select Bake of the oven. Set temperature to 360ºF (182ºC) and set time to 25 minutes. Press Start to begin preheating.

Once preheated, place the pan into the oven.

When cooking is complete, the meatloaf should be well browned.

Let the meatloaf rest for 5 minutes. Transfer to a serving dish and slice. Serve warm.

609. EASY LAMB CHOPS WITH ASPARAGUS

Prep time: 10 minutes | Cook time: 15 minutes | Serves 4

- 4 asparagus spears, trimmed
- 2 tablespoons olive oil, divided
- 1 pound (454 g) lamb chops
- 1 garlic clove, minced
- 2 teaspoons chopped fresh thyme, for serving
- Salt and ground black pepper, to taste

Spritz a perforated pan with cooking spray.

On a large plate, brush the asparagus with 1 tablespoon olive oil, then sprinkle with salt. Set aside.

On a separate plate, brush the lamb chops with remaining olive oil and sprinkle with salt and ground black pepper.

Arrange the lamb chops in the pan.

Select Air Fry of the oven. Set temperature to 400ºF (205ºC) and set time to 15 minutes. Press Start to begin preheating.

Once preheated, place the pan into the oven. Flip the lamb chops and add the asparagus and garlic halfway through.

When cooking is complete, the lamb should be well browned and the asparagus should be tender.

Serve them on a plate with thyme on top.

610. GOLDEN LAMB CHOPS

Prep time: 5 minutes | Cook time: 25 minutes | Serves 4

- 1 cup all-purpose flour
- 2 teaspoons dried sage leaves
- 2 teaspoons garlic powder
- 1 tablespoon mild paprika
- 1 tablespoon salt
- 4 (6-ounce / 170-g) bone-in lamb shoulder chops, fat trimmed
- Cooking spray

Spritz a perforated pan with cooking spray.

Combine the flour, sage leaves, garlic powder, paprika, and salt in a large bowl. Stir to mix well. Dunk in the lamb chops and toss to coat well.

Arrange the lamb chops in the pan and spritz with cooking spray.

Select Air Fry of the oven. Set temperature to 375ºF (190ºC) and set time to 25 minutes. Press Start to begin preheating.

Once preheated, place the pan into the oven. Flip the chops halfway through.

When cooking is complete, the chops should be golden brown and reaches your desired doneness.

Serve immediately.

611. TUSCAN AIR FRIED VEAL LOIN

Prep time: 1 hour 10 minutes | Cook time: 12 minutes | Makes 3 veal

chops

- 1½ teaspoons crushed fennel seeds
- 1 tablespoon minced fresh rosemary leaves
- 1 tablespoon minced garlic
- 1½ teaspoons lemon zest
- 1½ teaspoons salt
- ½ teaspoon red pepper flakes
- 2 tablespoons olive oil
- 3 (10-ounce / 284-g) bone-in veal loin, about ½ inch thick

Combine all the ingredients, except for the veal loin, in a large bowl. Stir to mix well.

Dunk the loin in the mixture and press to submerge. Wrap the bowl in plastic and refrigerate for at least an hour to marinate.

Arrange the veal loin in the perforated pan.

Select Air Fry of the oven. Set temperature to 400ºF (205ºC) and set time to 12 minutes. Press Start to begin preheating.

Once preheated, place the pan into the oven. Flip the veal halfway through.

When cooking is complete, the internal temperature of the veal should reach at least 145ºF (63ºC) for medium rare.

Serve immediately.

612. AIR FRIED CRISPY VENISON

Prep time: 10 minutes | Cook time: 10 minutes | Serves 4

- 2 eggs
- ¼ cup milk
- 1 cup whole wheat flour
- ½ teaspoon salt
- ¼ teaspoon ground black pepper
- 1 pound (454 g) venison backstrap, sliced
- Cooking spray

Spritz a perforated pan with cooking spray.

Whisk the eggs with milk in a large bowl. Combine the flour with salt and ground black pepper in a shallow dish.

Dredge the venison in the flour first, then into the egg mixture. Shake the excess off and roll the venison back over the flour to coat well.

Arrange the venison in the pan and spritz with cooking spray.

Select Air Fry of the oven. Set temperature to 360ºF (182ºC) and set time to 10 minutes. Press Start to begin preheating.

Once preheated, place the pan into the oven. Flip the venison halfway through.

When cooking is complete, the internal temperature of the venison should reach at least 145 ºF (63 ºC) for medium rare.

Serve immediately.

613. LAHMACUN (TURKISH PIZZA)

Prep time: 20 minutes | Cook time: 10 minutes | Serves 4

- 4 (6-inch) flour tortillas

For the Meat Topping:
- 4 ounces (113 g) ground lamb or 85% lean ground beef
- ¼ cup finely chopped green bell pepper
- ¼ cup chopped fresh parsley
- 1 small plum tomato, deseeded and chopped
- 2 tablespoons chopped yellow onion
- 1 garlic clove, minced
- 2 teaspoons tomato paste
- ¼ teaspoon sweet paprika
- ¼ teaspoon ground cumin
- ⅛ to ¼ teaspoon red pepper flakes
- ⅛ teaspoon ground allspice
- ⅛ teaspoon kosher salt
- ⅛ teaspoon black pepper

For Serving:

- ¼ cup chopped fresh mint
- 1 teaspoon extra-virgin olive oil
- 1 lemon, cut into wedges

Combine all the ingredients for the meat topping in a medium bowl until well mixed.

Lay the tortillas on a clean work surface. Spoon the meat mixture on the tortillas and spread all over.

Place the tortillas in the perforated pan.

Select Air Fry of the oven. Set temperature to 400°F (205°C) and set time to 10 minutes. Press Start to begin preheating.

Once preheated, place the pan into the oven.

When cooking is complete, the edge of the tortilla should be golden and the meat should be lightly browned.

Transfer them to a serving dish. Top with chopped fresh mint and drizzle with olive oil. Squeeze the lemon wedges on top and serve.

614. LAMB LOIN CHOPS WITH HORSERADISH CREAM SAUCE
Prep time: 10 minutes | Cook time: 13 minutes | Serves 4

For the Lamb:
- 4 lamb loin chops
- 2 tablespoons vegetable oil
- 1 clove garlic, minced
- ½ teaspoon kosher salt
- ½ teaspoon black pepper

For the Horseradish Cream Sauce:
- 1 to 1½ tablespoons prepared horseradish
- 1 tablespoon Dijon mustard
- ½ cup mayonnaise
- 2 teaspoons sugar
- Cooking spray

Spritz a perforated pan with cooking spray.

Place the lamb chops on a plate. Rub with the oil and sprinkle with the garlic, salt and black pepper. Let sit to marinate for 30 minutes at room temperature.

Make the horseradish cream sauce: Mix the horseradish, mustard, mayonnaise, and sugar in a bowl until well combined. Set half of the sauce aside until ready to serve.

Arrange the marinated chops in the perforated pan.

Select Air Fry of the oven. Set temperature to 325°F (163°C) and set time to 10 minutes. Press Start to begin preheating.

Once preheated, place the pan into the oven. Flip the lamb chops halfway through.

When cooking is complete, the lamb should be lightly browned.

Transfer the chops from the oven to the bowl of the horseradish sauce. Roll to coat well.

Put the coated chops back in the perforated pan in the oven. Set the temperature to 400°F (205°C) and the time to 3 minutes.

When cooking is complete, the internal temperature should reach 145°F (63°C) on a meat thermometer (for medium-rare). Flip the lamb halfway through.

Serve hot with the horseradish cream sauce.

615. LAMB RACK WITH PISTACHIO
Prep time: 10 minutes | Cook time: 20 minutes | Serves 2

- ½ cup finely chopped pistachios
- 1 teaspoon chopped fresh rosemary
- 3 tablespoons panko breadcrumbs
- 2 teaspoons chopped fresh oregano

- 1 tablespoon olive oil
- Salt and freshly ground black pepper, to taste
- 1 lamb rack, bones fat trimmed and frenched
- 1 tablespoon Dijon mustard

Put the pistachios, rosemary, breadcrumbs, oregano, olive oil, salt, and black pepper in a food processor. Pulse to combine until smooth.

Rub the lamb rack with salt and black pepper on a clean work surface, then place it in the perforated pan.

Select Air Fry of the oven. Set temperature to 380°F (193°C) and set time to 12 minutes. Press Start to begin preheating.

Once preheated, place the pan into the oven. Flip the lamb halfway through.

When cooking is complete, the lamb should be lightly browned.

Transfer the lamb on a plate and brush with Dijon mustard on the fat side, then sprinkle with the pistachios mixture over the lamb rack to coat well.

Put the lamb rack back to the oven and air fry for 8 more minutes or until the internal temperature of the rack reaches at least 145°F (63°C).

Remove the lamb rack from the oven with tongs and allow to cool for 5 minutes before slicing to serve.

616. ROASTED LAMB CHOPS WITH POTATOES
Prep time: 10 minutes | Cook time: 20 minutes | Serves 4

- 8 (½-inch thick) lamb loin chops (about 2 pounds / 907 g)
- 2 teaspoons kosher salt or 1 teaspoon fine salt, divided
- ¾ cup plain whole milk yogurt
- 2 garlic cloves, minced or smashed
- 1 tablespoon freshly grated ginger (1- or 2-inch piece) or 1 teaspoon ground ginger
- 1 teaspoon curry powder
- 1 teaspoon smoked paprika
- ½ teaspoon cayenne pepper
- 12 ounces (340 g) small red potatoes, quartered
- Cooking spray

Sprinkle the lamb chops on both sides with 1 teaspoon of kosher salt and set aside.

Meanwhile, make the marinade by stirring together the yogurt, garlic, ginger, curry powder, paprika, cayenne pepper, and remaining 1 teaspoon of kosher salt in a large bowl.

Transfer 2 tablespoons of the marinade to a resealable plastic bag, leaving those 2 tablespoons in the bowl. Place the lamb chops in the bag. Squeeze out as much air as possible and squish the bag around so that the chops are well coated with the marinade. Set aside.

Add the potatoes to the bowl and toss until well coated. Spritz the sheet pan with cooking spray. Arrange the potatoes in the pan.

Select Roast, set temperature to 375°F (190°C), and set time to 10 minutes. Select Start to begin preheating.

Once the unit has preheated, place the pan in the oven.

Once cooking is complete, remove the pan from the oven.

Remove the chops from the marinade, draining off all but a thin coat. Return them to the baking pan.

Select Broil, set the temperature to High, and set the time for 10 minutes. Select Start to begin preheating.

Once the unit has preheated, place the pan in the oven. After 5 minutes, remove the pan from the oven and turn over the chops and potatoes. Slide the pan into the oven and continue cooking until the lamb read 145°F (63°C) on a meat thermometer. If you want it more well done, continue cooking for another few
minutes.

Remove the pan from the oven and serve.

617. AIR FRIED GOLDEN WASABI SPAM
Prep time: 5 minutes | Cook time: 12 minutes | Serves 3

- ⅔ cup all-purpose flour
- 2 large eggs
- 1½ tablespoons wasabi paste
- 2 cups panko breadcrumbs
- 6 ½-inch-thick spam slices
- Cooking spray

Spritz a perforated pan with cooking spray.

Pour the flour in a shallow plate. Whisk the eggs with wasabi in a large bowl. Pour the panko in a separate shallow plate.

Dredge the spam slices in the flour first, then dunk in the egg mixture, and then roll the spam over the panko to coat well. Shake the excess off.

Arrange the spam slices in the pan and spritz with cooking spray.

Select Air Fry of the oven. Set temperature to 400°F (205°C) and set time to 12 minutes. Press Start to begin preheating.

Once preheated, place the pan into the oven. Flip the spam slices halfway through.

When cooking is complete, the spam slices should be golden and crispy. Serve immediately.

618. APPLE-GLAZED PORK

Prep time: 15 minutes | Cook time: 19 minutes | Serves 4

- 1 sliced apple
- 1 small onion, sliced
- 2 tablespoons apple cider vinegar, divided
- ½ teaspoon thyme
- ½ teaspoon rosemary
- ¼ teaspoon brown sugar
- 3 tablespoons olive oil, divided
- ¼ teaspoon smoked paprika
- 4 pork chops
- Salt and ground black pepper, to taste

Combine the apple slices, onion, 1 tablespoon of vinegar, thyme, rosemary, brown sugar, and 2 tablespoons of olive oil in a baking pan. Stir to mix well.

Select Bake of the oven. Set temperature to 350°F (180°C) and set time to 4 minutes. Press Start to begin preheating.

Once preheated, place the pan into the oven. Stir the mixture halfway through.

Meanwhile, combine the remaining vinegar and olive oil, and paprika in a large bowl. Sprinkle with salt and ground black pepper. Stir to mix well. Dredge the pork in the mixture and toss to coat well.

Place the pork in the perforated pan.

When cooking is complete, remove the baking pan from the oven and place in the perforated pan.

Select Air Fry of the oven and set time to 10 minutes. Flip the pork chops halfway through.

When cooking is complete, the pork should be lightly browned.

Remove the pork from the oven and baste with baked apple mixture on both sides. Put the pork back to the oven and air fry for an additional 5 minutes. Flip halfway through.

Serve immediately.

619. ASPARAGUS AND PROSCIUTTO TART

Prep time: 10 minutes | Cook time: 25 minutes | Serves 4

- All-purpose flour, for dusting
- 1 sheet (½ package) frozen puff pastry, thawed
- ½ cup grated Parmesan cheese
- 1 pound (454 g) (or more) asparagus, trimmed
- 8 ounces (227 g) thinly sliced prosciutto, sliced into ribbons about ½-inch wide
- 2 teaspoons aged balsamic vinegar

On a lightly floured cutting board, unwrap and unfold the puff pastry and roll it lightly with a rolling pin so as to press the folds together. Place it on the sheet pan.

Roll about ½ inch of the pastry edges up to form a ridge around the perimeter. Crimp the corners together to create a solid rim around the pastry. Using a fork, pierce the bottom of the pastry all over. Scatter the cheese over the bottom of the pastry.

Arrange the asparagus spears on top of the cheese in a single layer with 4 or 5 spears pointing one way, the next few pointing the opposite direction. You may need to trim them so they fit within the border of the pastry shell. Lay the prosciutto on top more or less evenly.

Select Bake, set temperature to 375°F (190°C), and set time to 25 minutes. Select Start to begin preheating.

Once the unit has preheated, place the pan in the oven.

After about 15 minutes, check the tart, rotating the pan if the crust is not browning evenly and continue cooking until the pastry is golden brown and the edges of the prosciutto pieces are browned.

Remove the pan from the oven. Allow to cool for 5 minutes before slicing.

Drizzle with the balsamic vinegar just before serving.

620. THAI CURRY BEEF MEATBALLS

Prep time: 5 minutes | Cook time: 15 minutes | Serves 4

- 1 pound (454 g) ground beef
- 1 tablespoon sesame oil
- 2 teaspoons chopped lemongrass
- 1 teaspoon red Thai curry paste
- 1 teaspoon Thai seasoning blend
- Juice and zest of ½ lime
- Cooking spray

Spritz a perforated pan with cooking spray.

In a medium bowl, combine all the ingredients until well blended.

Shape the meat mixture into 24 meatballs and arrange them in the pan.

Select Air Fry of the oven. Set temperature to 380°F (193°C) and set time to 15 minutes. Press Start to begin preheating.

Once preheated, place the pan into the oven. Flip the meatballs halfway through.

When cooking is complete, the meatballs should be browned.

Transfer the meatballs to plates. Let cool for 5 minutes before serving.

621. BACON-WRAPPED SAUSAGE WITH TOMATO RELISH

Prep time: 1 hour 15 minutes | Cook time: 32 minutes | Serves 4

- 8 pork sausages
- 8 bacon strips
- Relish:
- 8 large tomatoes, chopped
- 1 small onion, peeled
- 1 clove garlic, peeled
- 1 tablespoon white wine vinegar
- 3 tablespoons chopped parsley
- 1 teaspoon smoked paprika
- 2 tablespoons sugar
- Salt and ground black pepper, to taste

Purée the tomatoes, onion, and garlic in a food processor until well mixed and smooth.

Pour the purée in a saucepan and drizzle with white wine vinegar. Sprinkle with salt and ground black pepper. Simmer over medium heat for 10 minutes.

Add the parsley, paprika, and sugar to the saucepan and cook for 10 more minutes or until it has a thick consistency. Keep stirring during the cooking. Refrigerate for an hour to chill.

Wrap the sausage with bacon strips and secure with toothpicks, then place them in the perforated pan.

Select Air Fry of the oven. Set temperature to 350°F (180°C) and set time to 12 minutes. Press Start to begin preheating.

Once preheated, place the pan into the oven. Flip the bacon-wrapped sausage halfway through.

When cooking is complete, the bacon should be crispy and browned.

Transfer the bacon-wrapped sausage on a plate and baste with the relish or just serve with the relish alongside.

622. STUFFED BEEF TENDERLOIN WITH FETA CHEESE

Prep time: 10 minutes | Cook time: 10 minutes | Serves 4

- 1½ pounds (680 g) beef tenderloin, pounded to ¼ inch thick
- 3 teaspoons sea salt
- 1 teaspoon ground black pepper
- 2 ounces (57 g) creamy goat cheese
- ½ cup crumbled feta cheese
- ¼ cup finely chopped onions
- 2 cloves garlic, minced
- Cooking spray

Spritz a perforated pan with cooking spray.

Unfold the beef tenderloin on a clean work surface. Rub the salt and pepper all over the beef tenderloin to season.

Make the filling for the stuffed beef tenderloins: Combine the goat cheese, feta, onions, and garlic in a medium bowl. Stir until well blended. Spoon the mixture in the center of the tenderloin. Roll the tenderloin up tightly like rolling a burrito and use some kitchen twine to tie the tenderloin.

Arrange the tenderloin in the perforated pan.

Select Air Fry of the oven. Set temperature to 400°F (205°C) and set time to 10 minutes. Press Start to begin preheating.

Once preheated, place the pan into the oven. Flip the tenderloin halfway through.

When cooking is complete, the instant-read thermometer inserted in the center of the tenderloin should register 135°F (57°C) for medium-rare. Transfer to a platter and serve immediately.

623. TERIYAKI RUMP STEAK WITH BROCCOLI AND CAPSICUM

Prep time: 5 minutes | Cook time: 13 minutes | Serves 4

- ½ pound (227 g) rump steak
- ⅓ cup teriyaki marinade
- 1½ teaspoons sesame oil
- ½ head broccoli, cut into florets
- 2 red capsicums, sliced
- Fine sea salt and ground black pepper, to taste
- Cooking spray

Toss the rump steak in a large bowl with teriyaki marinade. Wrap the bowl in plastic and refrigerate to marinate for at least an hour.

Spritz a perforated pan with cooking spray.

Discard the marinade and transfer the steak in the pan. Spritz with cooking spray.

Select Air Fry of the oven. Set temperature to 400°F (205°C) and set time to 13 minutes. Press Start to begin preheating.

Once preheated, place the pan into the oven. Flip the steak halfway through.

When cooking is complete, the steak should be well browned.

Meanwhile, heat the sesame oil in a nonstick skillet over medium heat. Add the broccoli and capsicum. Sprinkle with salt and ground black pepper. Sauté for 5 minutes or until the broccoli is tender.

Transfer the air fried rump steak on a plate and top with the sautéed broccoli and capsicum. Serve hot.

624. CHAR SIU

Prep time: 8 hours 10 minutes | Cook time: 15 minutes | Serves 4

- ¼ cup honey
- 1 teaspoon Chinese five-spice powder
- 1 tablespoon Shaoxing wine (rice cooking wine)
- 1 tablespoon hoisin sauce
- 2 teaspoons minced garlic
- 2 teaspoons minced fresh ginger
- 2 tablespoons soy sauce
- 1 tablespoon sugar
- 1 pound (454 g) fatty pork shoulder, cut into long, 1-inch-thick pieces
- Cooking spray

Combine all the ingredients, except for the pork should, in a microwave-safe bowl. Stir to mix well. Microwave until the honey has dissolved. Stir periodically.

Pierce the pork pieces generously with a fork, then put the pork in a large bowl. Pour in half of the honey mixture. Set the remaining sauce aside until ready to serve.

Press the pork pieces into the mixture to coat and wrap the bowl in plastic and refrigerate to marinate for at least 8 hours.

Spritz a perforated pan with cooking spray.

Discard the marinade and transfer the pork pieces in the perforated pan.

Select Air Fry of the oven. Set temperature to 400°F (205°C) and set time to 15 minutes. Press Start to begin preheating.

Once preheated, place the pan into the oven. Flip the pork halfway through.

When cooking is complete, the pork should be well browned.

Meanwhile, microwave the remaining marinade on high for a minute or until it has a thick consistency. Stir periodically.

Remove the pork from the oven and allow to cool for 10 minutes before serving with the thickened marinade.

625. CITRUS CARNITAS

Prep time: 1 hour 10 minutes | Cook time: 25 minutes | Serves 6

- 2½ pounds (1.1 kg) boneless country-style pork ribs, cut into 2-inch pieces
- 3 tablespoons olive brine
- 1 tablespoon minced fresh oregano leaves
- ⅓ cup orange juice
- 1 teaspoon ground cumin
- 1 tablespoon minced garlic
- 1 teaspoon salt
- 1 teaspoon ground black pepper
- Cooking spray

Combine all the ingredients in a large bowl. Toss to coat the pork ribs well. Wrap the bowl in plastic and refrigerate for at least an hour to marinate.

Spritz a perforated pan with cooking spray.

Arrange the marinated pork ribs in the pan and spritz with cooking spray.

Select Air Fry of the oven. Set temperature to 400°F (205°C) and set time to 25 minutes. Press Start to begin preheating.

Once preheated, place the pan into the oven. Flip the ribs halfway through.

When cooking is complete, the ribs should be well browned.

Serve immediately.

626. CLASSIC WALLISER SCHNITZEL

Prep time: 5 minutes | Cook time: 14 minutes | Serves 2

- ½ cup pork rinds
- ½ tablespoon fresh parsley

- ½ teaspoon fennel seed
- ½ teaspoon mustard
- ⅓ tablespoon cider vinegar
- 1 teaspoon garlic salt
- ⅓ teaspoon ground black pepper
- 2 eggs
- 2 pork schnitzel, halved
- Cooking spray

Spritz a perforated pan with cooking spray.
Put the pork rinds, parsley, fennel seeds, and mustard in a food processor. Pour in the vinegar and sprinkle with salt and ground black pepper. Pulse until well combined and smooth.
Pour the pork rind mixture in a large bowl. Whisk the eggs in a separate bowl.
Dunk the pork schnitzel in the whisked eggs, then dunk in the pork rind mixture to coat well. Shake the excess off.
Arrange the schnitzel in the pan and spritz with cooking spray.
Select Air Fry of the oven. Set temperature to 350ºF (180ºC) and set time to 14 minutes. Press Start to begin preheating.
Once preheated, place the pan into the oven.
After 7 minutes, remove the pan from the oven. Flip the schnitzel. Return the pan to the oven and continue cooking.
When cooking is complete, the schnitzel should be golden and crispy. Serve immediately.

627. CRISPY PORK TENDERLOIN
Prep time: 5 minutes | Cook time: 10 minutes | Serves 6

- 2 large egg whites
- 1½ tablespoons Dijon mustard
- 2 cups crushed pretzel crumbs
- 1½ pounds (680 g) pork tenderloin, cut into ¼-pound (113-g) sections
- Cooking spray

Spritz a perforated pan with cooking spray.
Whisk the egg whites with Dijon mustard in a bowl until bubbly. Pour the pretzel crumbs in a separate bowl.
Dredge the pork tenderloin in the egg white mixture and press to coat. Shake the excess off and roll the tenderloin over the pretzel crumbs.
Arrange the well-coated pork tenderloin in the pan and spritz with cooking spray.
Select Air Fry of the oven. Set temperature to 350ºF (180ºC) and set time to 10 minutes. Press Start to begin preheating.
Once preheated, place the pan into the oven.
After 5 minutes, remove the pan from the oven. Flip the pork. Return the pan to the oven and continue cooking.
When cooking is complete, the pork should be golden brown and crispy. Serve immediately.

628. HOMEMADE TERIYAKI PORK RIBS
Prep time: 5 minutes | Cook time: 30 minutes | Serves 4

- ¼ cup soy sauce
- ¼ cup honey
- 1 teaspoon garlic powder
- 1 teaspoon ground dried ginger
- 4 (8-ounce / 227-g) boneless country-style pork ribs
- Cooking spray

Spritz a perforated pan with cooking spray.
Make the teriyaki sauce: combine the soy sauce, honey, garlic powder, and ginger in a bowl. Stir to mix well.
Brush the ribs with half of the teriyaki sauce, then arrange the ribs in the pan. Spritz with cooking spray.
Select Air Fry of the oven. Set temperature to 350ºF (180ºC) and set time

to 30 minutes. Press Start to begin preheating.
Once preheated, place the pan into the oven.
After 15 minutes, remove the pan from the oven. Flip the ribs and brush with remaining teriyaki sauce. Return the pan to the oven and continue cooking.
When cooking is complete, the internal temperature of the ribs should reach at least 145ºF (63ºC).
Serve immediately.

629. KIELBASA SAUSAGE WITH PINEAPPLE AND BELL PEPPERS
Prep time: 15 minutes | Cook time: 10 minutes | Serves 2 to 4

- ¾ pound (340 g) kielbasa sausage, cut into ½-inch slices
- 1 (8-ounce / 227-g) can pineapple chunks in juice, drained
- 1 cup bell pepper chunks
- 1 tablespoon barbecue seasoning
- 1 tablespoon soy sauce
- Cooking spray

Spritz a perforated pan with cooking spray.
Combine all the ingredients in a large bowl. Toss to mix well.
Pour the sausage mixture in the perforated pan.
Select Air Fry of the oven. Set temperature to 390ºF (199ºC) and set time to 10 minutes. Press Start to begin preheating.
Once preheated, place the pan into the oven.
After 5 minutes, remove the pan from the oven. Stir the sausage mixture. Return the pan to the oven and continue cooking.
When cooking is complete, the sausage should be lightly browned and the bell pepper and pineapple should be soft.
Serve immediately.

630. LEMONY PORK LOIN CHOP SCHNITZEL
Prep time: 15 minutes | Cook time: 15 minutes | Serves 4

- 4 thin boneless pork loin chops
- 2 tablespoons lemon juice
- ½ cup flour
- ¼ teaspoon marjoram
- 1 teaspoon salt
- 1 cup panko breadcrumbs
- 2 eggs
- Lemon wedges, for serving
- Cooking spray

On a clean work surface, drizzle the pork chops with lemon juice on both sides.
Combine the flour with marjoram and salt on a shallow plate. Pour the breadcrumbs on a separate shallow dish. Beat the eggs in a large bowl.
Dredge the pork chops in the flour, then dunk in the beaten eggs to coat well. Shake the excess off and roll over the breadcrumbs. Arrange the pork chops in the perforated pan and spritz with cooking spray.
Select Air Fry of the oven. Set temperature to 400ºF (205ºC) and set time to 15 minutes. Press Start to begin preheating.
Once preheated, place the pan into the oven.
After 7 minutes, remove the pan from the oven. Flip the pork. Return the pan to the oven and continue cooking.
When cooking is complete, the pork should be crispy and golden.
Squeeze the lemon wedges over the fried chops and serve immediately.

631. MACADAMIA NUTS CRUSTED PORK RACK
Prep time: 5 minutes | Cook time: 35 minutes | Serves 2

- 1 clove garlic, minced
- 2 tablespoons olive oil
- 1 pound (454 g) rack of pork

- 1 cup chopped macadamia nuts
- 1 tablespoon breadcrumbs
- 1 tablespoon rosemary, chopped
- 1 egg
- Salt and ground black pepper, to taste

Combine the garlic and olive oil in a small bowl. Stir to mix well.

On a clean work surface, rub the pork rack with the garlic oil and sprinkle with salt and black pepper on both sides.

Combine the macadamia nuts, breadcrumbs, and rosemary in a shallow dish. Whisk the egg in a large bowl.

Dredge the pork in the egg, then roll the pork over the macadamia nut mixture to coat well. Shake the excess off.

Arrange the pork in the perforated pan.

Select Air Fry of the oven. Set temperature to 350°F (180°C) and set time to 30 minutes. Press Start to begin preheating.

Once preheated, place the pan into the oven.

After 30 minutes, remove the pan from the oven. Flip the pork rack. Return the pan to the oven and increase temperature to 390°F (199°C) and set time to 5 minutes. Keep cooking.

When cooking is complete, the pork should be browned.

Serve immediately.

632. PORK, BELL PEPPER, AND PINEAPPLE SKEWERS

Prep time: 10 minutes | Cook time: 12 minutes | Serves 4

- ¼ teaspoon kosher salt or ⅛ teaspoon fine salt
- 1 medium pork tenderloin (about 1 pound / 454 g), cut into 1½-inch chunks
- 1 green bell pepper, seeded and cut into 1-inch pieces
- 1 red bell pepper, seeded and cut into 1-inch pieces
- 2 cups fresh pineapple chunks
- ¾ cup Teriyaki Sauce or store-bought variety, divided

Special Equipment:
12 (9- to 12-inch) wooden skewers, soaked in water for about 30 minutes

Sprinkle the pork cubes with the salt.

Thread the pork, bell peppers, and pineapple onto a skewer. Repeat until all skewers are complete. Brush the skewers generously with about half of the Teriyaki Sauce. Place them on the sheet pan.

Select Roast, set temperature to 375°F (190°C), and set time to 10 minutes. Select Start to begin preheating.

Once the unit has preheated, place the pan in the oven.

After about 5 minutes, remove the pan from the oven. Turn over the skewers and brush with the remaining half of Teriyaki Sauce. Transfer the pan back to the oven and continue cooking until the vegetables are tender and browned in places and the pork is browned and cooked through.

Remove the pan from the oven and serve.

633. PORK AND TRICOLOR VEGETABLES KEBABS

Prep time: 1 hour 20 minutes | Cook time: 8 minutes | Serves 4

For the Pork:
- 1 pound (454 g) pork steak, cut in cubes
- 1 tablespoon white wine vinegar
- 3 tablespoons steak sauce
- ¼ cup soy sauce
- 1 teaspoon powdered chili
- 1 teaspoon red chili flakes
- 2 teaspoons smoked paprika
- 1 teaspoon garlic salt

For the Vegetable:
- 1 green squash, deseeded and cut in cubes
- 1 yellow squash, deseeded and cut in cubes

- 1 red pepper, cut in cubes
- 1 green pepper, cut in cubes
- Salt and ground black pepper, to taste
- Cooking spray

Special Equipment:
4 bamboo skewers, soaked in water for at least 30 minutes

Combine the ingredients for the pork in a large bowl. Press the pork to dunk in the marinade. Wrap the bowl in plastic and refrigerate for at least an hour.

Spritz a perforated pan with cooking spray.

Remove the pork from the marinade and run the skewers through the pork and vegetables alternatively. Sprinkle with salt and pepper to taste.

Arrange the skewers in the pan and spritz with cooking spray.

Select Air Fry of the oven. Set temperature to 380°F (193°C) and set time to 8 minutes. Press Start to begin preheating.

Once preheated, place the pan into the oven.

After 4 minutes, remove the pan from the oven. Flip the skewers. Return the pan to the oven and continue cooking.

When cooking is complete, the pork should be browned and the vegetables should be lightly charred and tender.

Serve immediately.

634. BACON-WRAPPED HOT DOGS WITH MAYO-KETCHUP SAUCE

Prep time: 5 minutes | Cook time: 10 minutes | Serves 5

- 10 thin slices of bacon
- 5 pork hot dogs, halved
- 1 teaspoon cayenne pepper
- Sauce:
- ¼ cup mayonnaise
- 4 tablespoons low-carb ketchup
- 1 teaspoon rice vinegar
- 1 teaspoon chili powder

Arrange the slices of bacon on a clean work surface. One by one, place the halved hot dog on one end of each slice, season with cayenne pepper and wrap the hot dog with the bacon slices and secure with toothpicks as needed.

Place wrapped hot dogs in the perforated pan.

Select Air Fry of the oven. Set temperature to 390°F (199°C) and set time to 10 minutes. Press Start to begin preheating.

Once preheated, place the pan into the oven. Flip the bacon-wrapped hot dogs halfway through.

When cooking is complete, the bacon should be crispy and browned.

Make the sauce: Stir all the ingredients for the sauce in a small bowl. Wrap the bowl in plastic and set in the refrigerator until ready to serve.

Transfer the hot dogs to a platter and serve hot with the sauce.

635. HAWAIIAN CHICKEN BITES

Prep time: 1 hour 15 minutes | Cook time: 15 minutes | Serves 4
- ½ cup pineapple juice
- 2 tablespoons apple cider vinegar
- ½ tablespoon minced ginger
- ½ cup ketchup
- 2 garlic cloves, minced
- ½ cup brown sugar
- 2 tablespoons sherry
- ½ cup soy sauce
- 4 chicken breasts, cubed
- Cooking spray

Combine the pineapple juice, cider vinegar, ginger, ketchup, garlic, and sugar in a saucepan. Stir to mix well. Heat over low heat for 5 minutes or until thickened. Fold in the sherry and soy sauce.

Dunk the chicken cubes in the mixture. Press to submerge. Wrap the bowl in plastic and refrigerate to marinate for at least an hour.
Spritz a perforated pan with cooking spray.
Remove the chicken cubes from the marinade. Shake the excess off and put in the perforated pan. Spritz with cooking spray.
Select Air Fry of the oven. Set temperature to 360ºF (182ºC) and set time to 15 minutes. Press Start to begin preheating.
Once preheated, place the pan into the oven. Flip the chicken cubes at least three times during the air frying.
When cooking is complete, the chicken cubes should be glazed and well browned.
Serve immediately.

636. HONEY GLAZED CHICKEN BREASTS

Prep time: 5 minutes | Cook time: 10 minutes | Serves 4

- 4 (4-ounce / 113-g) boneless, skinless chicken breasts
- Chicken seasoning or rub, to taste
- Salt and ground black pepper, to taste
- ¼ cup honey
- 2 tablespoons soy sauce
- 2 teaspoons grated fresh ginger
- 2 garlic cloves, minced
- Cooking spray

Spritz a perforated pan with cooking spray.
Rub the chicken breasts with chicken seasoning, salt, and black pepper on a clean work surface.
Arrange the chicken breasts in the perforated pan and spritz with cooking spray.
Select Air Fry of the oven. Set temperature to 400ºF (205ºC) and set time to 10 minutes. Press Start to begin preheating.
Once preheated, place the pan into the oven. Flip the chicken breasts halfway through.
When cooking is complete, the internal temperature of the thickest part of the chicken should reach at least 165ºF (74ºC).
Meanwhile, combine the honey, soy sauce, ginger, and garlic in a saucepan and heat over medium-high heat for 3 minutes or until thickened. Stir constantly.
Remove the chicken from the oven and serve with the honey glaze.

637. ITALIAN CHICKEN BREASTS WITH TOMATOES

Prep time: 10 minutes | Cook time: 35 minutes | Serves 8

- 3 pounds (1.4 kg) chicken breasts, bone-in
- 1 teaspoon minced fresh basil
- 1 teaspoon minced fresh rosemary
- 2 tablespoons minced fresh parsley
- 1 teaspoon cayenne pepper
- ½ teaspoon salt
- ½ teaspoon freshly ground black pepper
- 4 medium Roma tomatoes, halved
- Cooking spray

Spritz a perforated pan with cooking spray.
Combine all the ingredients, except for the chicken breasts and tomatoes, in a large bowl. Stir to mix well.
Dunk the chicken breasts in the mixture and press to coat well.
Transfer the chicken breasts in the perforated pan.
Select Air Fry of the oven. Set temperature to 370ºF (188ºC) and set time to 20 minutes. Press Start to begin preheating.
Once preheated, place the pan into the oven. Flip the breasts halfway through the cooking time.
When cooking is complete, the internal temperature of the thickest part of the breasts should reach at least 165 ºF (74 ºC).
Remove the cooked chicken breasts from the oven and adjust the temperature to 350ºF (180ºC).
Place the tomatoes in the perforated pan and spritz with cooking spray. Sprinkle with a touch of salt.
Set time to 10 minutes. Stir the tomatoes halfway through the cooking time.
When cooking is complete, the tomatoes should be tender.
Serve the tomatoes with chicken breasts on a large serving plate.

638. CHICKEN SCHNITZEL

Prep time: 15 minutes | Cook time: 5 minutes | Serves 4

- ½ cup all-purpose flour
- 1 teaspoon marjoram
- ½ teaspoon thyme
- 1 teaspoon dried parsley flakes
- ½ teaspoon salt
- 1 egg
- 1 teaspoon lemon juice
- 1 teaspoon water
- 1 cup breadcrumbs
- 4 chicken tenders, pounded thin, cut in half lengthwise
- Cooking spray

Spritz a perforated pan with cooking spray.
Combine the flour, marjoram, thyme, parsley, and salt in a shallow dish. Stir to mix well.
Whisk the egg with lemon juice and water in a large bowl. Pour the breadcrumbs in a separate shallow dish.
Roll the chicken halves in the flour mixture first, then in the egg mixture, and then roll over the breadcrumbs to coat well. Shake the excess off.
Arrange the chicken halves in the perforated pan and spritz with cooking spray on both sides.
Select Air Fry of the oven. Set temperature to 390ºF (199ºC) and set time to 5 minutes. Press Start to begin preheating.
Once preheated, place the pan into the oven. Flip the halves halfway through.
When cooking is complete, the chicken halves should be golden brown and crispy.
Serve immediately.

639. PORK BUTT WITH GARLICKY CORIAN-DER-PARSLEY SAUCE

Prep time: 1 hour 15 minutes | Cook time: 30 minutes | Serves 4

- 1 teaspoon golden flaxseeds meal
- 1 egg white, well whisked
- 1 tablespoon soy sauce
- 1 teaspoon lemon juice, preferably freshly squeezed
- 1 tablespoon olive oil
- 1 pound (454 g) pork butt, cut into pieces 2-inches long
- Salt and ground black pepper, to taste
- Garlicky Coriander-Parsley Sauce:
- 3 garlic cloves, minced
- ⅓ cup fresh coriander leaves
- ⅓ cup fresh parsley leaves
- 1 teaspoon lemon juice
- ½ tablespoon salt
- ⅓ cup extra-virgin olive oil

Combine the flaxseeds meal, egg white, soy sauce, lemon juice, salt, black pepper, and olive oil in a large bowl. Dunk the pork strips in and press to submerge.
Wrap the bowl in plastic and refrigerate to marinate for at least an hour.
Arrange the marinated pork strips in the perforated pan.
Select Air Fry of the oven. Set temperature to 380ºF (193ºC) and set time to 30 minutes. Press Start to begin preheating.

Once preheated, place the pan into the oven.

After 15 minutes, remove the pan from the oven. Flip the pork. Return the pan to the oven and continue cooking.

When cooking is complete, the pork should be well browned.

Meanwhile, combine the ingredients for the sauce in a small bowl. Stir to mix well. Arrange the bowl in the refrigerator to chill until ready to serve.

Serve the air fried pork strips with the chilled sauce.

640. PORK SAUSAGE WITH CAULIFLOWER MASH

Prep time: 5 minutes | Cook time: 27 minutes | Serves 6

- 1 pound (454 g) cauliflower, chopped
- 6 pork sausages, chopped
- ½ onion, sliced
- 3 eggs, beaten
- ⅓ cup Colby cheese
- 1 teaspoon cumin powder
- ½ teaspoon tarragon
- ½ teaspoon sea salt
- ½ teaspoon ground black pepper
- Cooking spray

Spritz the baking pan with cooking spray.

In a saucepan over medium heat, boil the cauliflower until tender. Place the boiled cauliflower in a food processor and pulse until puréed. Transfer to a large bowl and combine with remaining ingredients until well blended.

Pour the cauliflower and sausage mixture into the pan.

Select Bake of the oven. Set temperature to 365ºF (185ºC) and set time to 27 minutes. Press Start to begin preheating.

Once preheated, place the pan into the oven.

When cooking is complete, the sausage should be lightly browned.

Divide the mixture among six serving dishes and serve warm.

641. PORK SCHNITZELS WITH SOUR CREAM AND DILL SAUCE

Prep time: 5 minutes | Cook time: 4 minutes | Serves 4 to 6

- ½ cup flour
- 1½ teaspoons salt
- Freshly ground black pepper, to taste
- 2 eggs
- ½ cup milk
- 1½ cups toasted breadcrumbs
- 1 teaspoon paprika
- 6 boneless, center cut pork chops (about 1½ pounds / 680 g), fat trimmed, pound to ½-inch thick
- 2 tablespoons olive oil
- 3 tablespoons melted butter
- Lemon wedges, for serving
- Sour Cream and Dill Sauce:
- 1 cup chicken stock
- 1½ tablespoons cornstarch
- ⅓ cup sour cream
- 1½ tablespoons chopped fresh dill
- Salt and ground black pepper, to taste

Combine the flour with salt and black pepper in a large bowl. Stir to mix well. Whisk the egg with milk in a second bowl. Stir the breadcrumbs and paprika in a third bowl.

Dredge the pork chops in the flour bowl, then in the egg milk, and then into the breadcrumbs bowl. Press to coat well. Shake the excess off.

Arrange the pork chop in the perforated pan, then brush with olive oil and butter on all sides.

Select Air Fry of the oven. Set temperature to 400ºF (205ºC) and set time

to 4 minutes. Press Start to begin preheating.

Once preheated, place the pan into the oven.

After 2 minutes, remove the pan from the oven. Flip the pork. Return the pan to the oven and continue cooking.

When cooking is complete, the pork chop should be golden brown and crispy.

Meanwhile, combine the chicken stock and cornstarch in a small saucepan and bring to a boil over medium-high heat. Simmer for 2 more minutes.

Turn off the heat, then mix in the sour cream, fresh dill, salt, and black pepper.

Remove the schnitzels from the oven to a plate and baste with sour cream and dill sauce. Squeeze the lemon wedges over and slice to serve.

642. SIMPLE PORK MEATBALLS WITH RED CHILI

Prep time: 5 minutes | Cook time: 15 minutes | Serves 4

- 1 pound (454 g) ground pork
- 2 cloves garlic, finely minced
- 1 cup scallions, finely chopped
- 1½ tablespoons Worcestershire sauce
- ½ teaspoon freshly grated ginger root
- 1 teaspoon turmeric powder
- 1 tablespoon oyster sauce
- 1 small sliced red chili, for garnish
- Cooking spray

Spritz a perforated pan with cooking spray.

Combine all the ingredients, except for the red chili in a large bowl. Toss to mix well.

Shape the mixture into equally sized balls, then arrange them in the perforated pan and spritz with cooking spray.

Select Air Fry of the oven. Set temperature to 350ºF (180ºC) and set time to 15 minutes. Press Start to begin preheating.

Once preheated, place the pan into the oven.

After 7 minutes, remove the pan from the oven. Flip the balls. Return the pan to the oven and continue cooking.

When cooking is complete, the balls should be lightly browned.

Serve the pork meatballs with red chili on top.

643. SMOKY PAPRIKA PORK AND VEGETABLE KABOBS

Prep time: 25 minutes | Cook time: 15 minutes | Serves 4

- 1 pound (454 g) pork tenderloin, cubed
- 1 teaspoon smoked paprika
- Salt and ground black pepper, to taste
- 1 green bell pepper, cut into chunks
- 1 zucchini, cut into chunks
- 1 red onion, sliced
- 1 tablespoon oregano
- Cooking spray

Special Equipment:

Small bamboo skewers, soaked in water for 20 minutes to keep them from burning while cooking

Spritz a perforated pan with cooking spray.

Add the pork to a bowl and season with the smoked paprika, salt and black pepper. Thread the seasoned pork cubes and vegetables alternately onto the soaked skewers. Arrange the skewers in the pan.

Select Air Fry of the oven. Set temperature to 350ºF (180ºC) and set time to 15 minutes. Press Start to begin preheating.

Once preheated, place the pan into the oven.

After 7 minutes, remove the pan from the oven. Flip the pork skewers. Return the pan to the oven and continue cooking.

When cooking is complete, the pork should be browned and vegetables are tender.

Transfer the skewers to the serving dishes and sprinkle with oregano. Serve hot.

644. SPICY PORK CHOPS WITH CARROTS AND MUSHROOMS

Prep time: 10 minutes | Cook time: 15 minutes | Serves 4

- 2 carrots, cut into sticks
- 1 cup mushrooms, sliced
- 2 garlic cloves, minced
- 2 tablespoons olive oil
- 1 pound (454 g) boneless pork chops
- 1 teaspoon dried oregano
- 1 teaspoon dried thyme
- 1 teaspoon cayenne pepper
- Salt and ground black pepper, to taste
- Cooking spray

In a mixing bowl, toss together the carrots, mushrooms, garlic, olive oil and salt until well combined.

Add the pork chops to a different bowl and season with oregano, thyme, cayenne pepper, salt and black pepper.

Lower the vegetable mixture in the greased perforated pan. Place the seasoned pork chops on top.

Select Air Fry of the oven. Set temperature to 360ºF (182ºC) and set time to 15 minutes. Press Start to begin preheating.

Once preheated, place the pan into the oven.

After 7 minutes, remove the pan from the oven. Flip the pork and stir the vegetables. Return the pan to the oven and continue cooking.

When cooking is complete, the pork chops should be browned and the vegetables should be tender.

Transfer the pork chops to the serving dishes and let cool for 5 minutes. Serve warm with vegetable on the side.

645. PORK LEG ROAST WITH CANDY ONIONS

Prep time: 10 minutes | Cook time: 52 minutes | Serves 4

- 2 teaspoons sesame oil
- 1 teaspoon dried sage, crushed
- 1 teaspoon cayenne pepper
- 1 rosemary sprig, chopped
- 1 thyme sprig, chopped
- Sea salt and ground black pepper, to taste
- 2 pounds (907 g) pork leg roast, scored
- ½ pound (227 g) candy onions, sliced
- 4 cloves garlic, finely chopped
- 2 chili peppers, minced

In a mixing bowl, combine the sesame oil, sage, cayenne pepper, rosemary, thyme, salt and black pepper until well mixed. In another bowl, place the pork leg and brush with the seasoning mixture.

Place the seasoned pork leg in a baking pan. Select Air Fry of the oven. Set temperature to 400ºF (205ºC) and set time to 40 minutes. Press Start to begin preheating.

Once preheated, place the pan into the oven.

After 20 minutes, remove the pan from the oven. Flip the pork leg. Return the pan to the oven and continue cooking.

After another 20 minutes, add the candy onions, garlic, and chili peppers to the pan and air fry for another 12 minutes.

When cooking is complete, the pork leg should be browned.

Transfer the pork leg to a plate. Let cool for 5 minutes and slice. Spread the juices left in the pan over the pork and serve warm with the candy onions.

646. TONKATSU

Prep time: 5 minutes | Cook time: 10 minutes | Serves 4

- ⅔ cup all-purpose flour
- 2 large egg whites
- 1 cup panko breadcrumbs
- 4 (4-ounce / 113-g) center-cut boneless pork loin chops (about ½ inch thick)
- Cooking spray

Pour the flour in a bowl. Whisk the egg whites in a separate bowl. Spread the breadcrumbs on a large plate.

Dredge the pork loin chops in the flour first, press to coat well, then shake the excess off and dunk the chops in the eggs whites, and then roll the chops over the breadcrumbs. Shake the excess off.

Arrange the pork chops in the perforated pan and spritz with cooking spray.

Select Air Fry of the oven. Set temperature to 375ºF (190ºC) and set time to 10 minutes. Press Start to begin preheating.

Once preheated, place the pan into the oven.

After 5 minutes, remove the pan from the oven. Flip the pork chops. Return the pan to the oven and continue cooking.

When cooking is complete, the pork chops should be crunchy and lightly browned.

Serve immediately.

647. APPLE AND PORK BAKE

Prep time: 10 minutes | Cook time: 45 minutes | Serves 4

- 2 apples, peeled, cored, and sliced
- 1 teaspoon ground cinnamon, divided
- 4 boneless pork chops (½-inch thick)
- Salt and freshly ground black pepper, to taste
- 3 tablespoons brown sugar
- ¾ cup water
- 1 tablespoon olive oil

Layer apples in bottom of a baking pan. Sprinkle with ½ teaspoon of cinnamon.

Trim fat from pork chops. Lay on top of the apple slices. Sprinkle with salt and pepper.

In a small bowl, combine the brown sugar, water, and remaining cinnamon. Pour the mixture over the chops. Drizzle chops with 1 tablespoon of olive oil.

Select Bake of the oven. Set temperature to 375ºF (190ºC) and set time to 45 minutes. Press Start to begin preheating.

Once preheated, place the pan into the oven.

When cooking is complete, an instant-read thermometer inserted in the pork should register 165 ºF (74 ºC).

Allow to rest for 3 minutes before serving.

648. BEEF AND SPINACH MEATLOAVES

Prep time: 15 minutes | Cook time: 45 minutes | Serves 2

- 1 large egg, beaten
- 1 cup frozen spinach
- ⅓ cup almond meal
- ¼ cup chopped onion
- ¼ cup plain Greek milk
- ¼ teaspoon salt
- ¼ teaspoon dried sage
- 2 teaspoons olive oil, divided
- Freshly ground black pepper, to taste
- ½ pound (227 g) extra-lean ground beef
- ¼ cup tomato paste
- 1 tablespoon granulated stevia
- ¼ teaspoon Worcestershire sauce
- Cooking spray

Coat a shallow baking pan with cooking spray.

In a large bowl, combine the beaten egg, spinach, almond meal, onion, milk, salt, sage, 1 teaspoon of olive oil, and pepper.

Crumble the beef over the spinach mixture. Mix well to combine. Divide the meat mixture in half. Shape each half into a loaf. Place the loaves in the prepared pan.

In a small bowl, whisk together the tomato paste, stevia, Worcestershire sauce, and remaining 1 teaspoon of olive oil. Spoon half of the sauce over each meatloaf.

Select Bake of the oven. Set the temperature to 350°F (180°C) and set the time to 40 minutes. Press Start to begin preheating.

Once preheated, place the pan into the oven.

When cooking is complete, an instant-read thermometer inserted in the center of the meatloaves should read at least 165 °F (74 °C).

Serve immediately.

649. CALF'S LIVER GOLDEN STRIPS

Prep time: 15 minutes | Cook time: 4 to 5 minutes | Serves 4

- 1 pound (454 g) sliced calf's liver, cut into about ½-inch-wide strips
- Salt and ground black pepper, to taste
- 2 eggs
- 2 tablespoons milk
- ½ cup whole wheat flour
- 1½ cups panko bread crumbs
- ½ cup plain bread crumbs
- ½ teaspoon salt
- ¼ teaspoon ground black pepper
- Cooking spray

Sprinkle the liver strips with salt and pepper.

Beat together the egg and milk in a bowl. Place wheat flour in a shallow dish. In a second shallow dish, mix panko, plain bread crumbs, ½ teaspoon salt, and ¼ teaspoon pepper.

Dip liver strips in flour, egg wash, and then bread crumbs, pressing in coating slightly to make crumbs stick.

Spritz a perforated pan with cooking spray. Place strips in a single layer in the perforated pan.

Select Air Fry of the oven. Set the temperature to 400°F (205°C) and set the time to 4 minutes. Press Start to begin preheating.

Once preheated, place the pan into the oven.

After 2 minutes, remove the pan from the oven. Flip the strips with tongs. Return the pan to the oven and continue cooking.

When cooking is complete, the liver strips should be crispy and golden. Serve immediately.

650. CHUCK AND SAUSAGE SUBS

Prep time: 15 minutes | Cook time: 24 minutes | Serves 4

- 1 large egg
- ¼ cup whole milk
- 24 saltines, crushed but not pulverized
- 1 pound (454 g) ground chuck
- 1 pound (454 g) Italian sausage, casings removed
- 4 tablespoons grated Parmesan cheese, divided
- 1 teaspoon kosher salt
- 4 sub rolls, split
- 1 cup Marinara sauce
- ¾ cup shredded Mozzarella cheese

In a large bowl, whisk the egg into the milk, then stir in the crackers. Let sit for 5 minutes to hydrate.

With your hands, break the ground chuck and sausage into the milk mixture, alternating beef and sausage. When you've added half of the meat, sprinkle 2 tablespoons of the grated Parmesan and the salt over

it, then continue breaking up the meat until it's all in the bowl. Gently mix everything together. Try not to overwork the meat, but get it all combined.

Form the mixture into balls about the size of a golf ball. You should get about 24 meatballs. Flatten the balls slightly to prevent them from rolling, then place them on a baking pan, about 2 inches apart.

Select Roast, set temperature to 400°F (205°C), and set time to 20 minutes. Press Start to begin preheating.

Once preheated, place the pan into the oven.

After 10 minutes, remove the pan from the oven and turn over the meatballs. Return the pan to the oven and continue cooking.

When cooking is complete, remove the pan from the oven. Place the meatballs on a rack. Wipe off the baking pan.

Open the rolls, cut-side up, on the baking pan. Place 3 to 4 meatballs on the base of each roll, and top each sandwich with ¼ cup of marinara sauce. Divide the Mozzarella among the top halves of the buns and sprinkle the remaining Parmesan cheese over the Mozzarella.

Select Broil, set temperature to High, and set time to 4 minutes. Press Start to begin preheating.

Once preheated, place the pan into the oven. Check the sandwiches after 2 minutes; the Mozzarella cheese should be melted and bubbling slightly. When cooking is complete, remove the pan from the oven. Close the sandwiches and serve.

651. DIJON PORK TENDERLOIN

Prep time: 15 minutes | Cook time: 15 minutes | Serves 4

- 3 tablespoons Dijon mustard
- 3 tablespoons honey
- 1 teaspoon dried rosemary
- 1 tablespoon olive oil
- 1 pound (454 g) pork tenderloin, rinsed and drained
- Salt and freshly ground black pepper, to taste

In a small bowl, combine the Dijon mustard, honey, and rosemary. Stir to combine.

Rub the pork tenderloin with salt and pepper on all sides on a clean work surface.

Heat the olive oil in an oven-safe skillet over high heat. Sear the pork loin on all sides in the skillet for 6 minutes or until golden brown. Flip the pork halfway through.

Remove from the heat and spread honey-mustard mixture evenly to coat the pork loin.

Select Bake of the oven, set temperature to 425°F (220°C) and set time to 15 minutes. Press Start to begin preheating.

Once preheated, place the pan into the oven.

When cooking is complete, an instant-read thermometer inserted in the pork should register at least 145 °F (63 °C).

Remove from the oven and allow to rest for 3 minutes. Slice the pork into ½-inch slices and serve.

652. EASY PORK CHOP ROAST

Prep time: 5 minutes | Cook time: 20 minutes | Serves 2

- 2 (10-ounce / 284-g) bone-in, center cut pork chops, 1-inch thick
- 2 teaspoons Worcestershire sauce
- Salt and ground black pepper, to taste
- Cooking spray

Rub the Worcestershire sauce on both sides of pork chops.

Season with salt and pepper to taste.

Spritz a perforated pan with cooking spray and place the chops in the perforated pan side by side.

Select Roast of the oven. Set the temperature to 350°F (180°C) and set the time to 20 minutes. Press Start to begin preheating.

Once preheated, place the pan into the oven.

After 10 minutes, remove the pan from the oven. Flip the pork chops with tongs. Return the pan to the oven and continue cooking.

When cooking is complete, the pork should be well browned on both sides.

Let rest for 5 minutes before serving.

653. GOLD CUTLETS WITH ALOHA SALSA

Prep time: 20 minutes | Cook time: 7 minutes | Serves 4

- 2 eggs
- 2 tablespoons milk
- ¼ cup all-purpose flour
- ¼ cup panko bread crumbs
- 4 teaspoons sesame seeds
- 1 pound (454 g) boneless, thin pork cutlets (½-inch thick)
- ¼ cup cornstarch
- Salt and ground lemon pepper, to taste
- Cooking spray
- Aloha Salsa:
- 1 cup fresh pineapple, chopped in small pieces
- ¼ cup red bell pepper, chopped
- ½ teaspoon ground cinnamon
- 1 teaspoon soy sauce
- ¼ cup red onion, finely chopped
- ⅛ teaspoon crushed red pepper
- ⅛ teaspoon ground black pepper

In a medium bowl, stir together all ingredients for salsa. Cover and refrigerate while cooking the pork.

Beat together eggs and milk in a large bowl. In another bowl, mix the flour, panko, and sesame seeds. Pour the cornstarch in a shallow dish.

Sprinkle pork cutlets with lemon pepper and salt. Dip pork cutlets in cornstarch, egg mixture, and then panko coating. Spritz both sides with cooking spray.

Select Air Fry of the oven. Set the temperature to 400ºF (205ºC) and set the time to 7 minutes. Press Start to begin preheating.

Once preheated, place the pan into the oven.

After 3 minutes, remove the pan from the oven. Flip the cutlets with tongs. Return the pan to the oven and continue cooking.

When cooking is complete, the pork should be crispy and golden brown on both sides.

Serve the fried cutlets with the Aloha salsa on the side.

654. HEARTY MUSHROOM AND SAUSAGE CALZONES

Prep time: 10 minutes | Cook time: 24 minutes | Serves 4

- 2 links Italian sausages (about ½ pound / 227 g)
- 1 pound (454 g) pizza dough, thawed
- 3 tablespoons olive oil, divided
- ¼ cup Marinara sauce
- ½ cup roasted mushrooms
- 1 cup shredded Mozzarella cheese

Place the sausages in a baking pan.

Select Roast, set temperature to 375ºF (190ºC), and set time to 12 minutes. Press Start to begin preheating.

Once preheated, place the pan into the oven.

After 6 minutes, remove the pan from the oven and turn over the sausages. Return the pan to the oven and continue cooking.

While the sausages cook, divide the pizza dough into 4 equal pieces. One at a time, place a piece of dough onto a square of parchment paper 9 inches in diameter. Brush the dough on both sides with ¾ teaspoon of olive oil, then top the dough with another piece of parchment. Press the dough into a 7-inch circle. Remove the top piece of parchment and set aside. Repeat with the remaining pieces of dough.

When cooking is complete, remove the pan from the oven. Place the sausages on a cutting board. Let them cool for several minutes, then slice into ¼-inch rounds and cut each round into 4 pieces.

One at a time, spread a tablespoon of marinara sauce over half of a dough circle, leaving a ½-inch border at the edges. Cover with a quarter of the sausage pieces and add a quarter of the mushrooms. Sprinkle with ¼ cup of cheese. Pull the other side of the dough over the filling and pinch the edges together to seal. Transfer from the parchment to the baking pan. Repeat with the other rounds of dough, sauce, sausage, mushrooms, and cheese.

Brush the tops of the calzones with 1 tablespoon of olive oil.

Select Roast, set temperature to 450ºF (235ºC), and set time to 12 minutes. Press Start to begin preheating.

Once preheated, place the pan into the oven.

After 6 minutes, remove the pan from the oven. The calzones should be golden brown. Turn over the calzones and brush the tops with the remaining olive oil. Return the pan to the oven and continue cooking.

When cooking is complete, the crust should be a deep golden brown on both sides. Remove the pan from the oven. The center should be molten; let cool for several minutes before serving.

655. ITALIAN SAUSAGES AND RED GRAPES

Prep time: 10 minutes | Cook time: 20 minutes | Serves 6

- 2 pounds (905 g) seedless red grapes
- 3 shallots, sliced
- 2 teaspoons fresh thyme
- 2 tablespoons olive oil
- ½ teaspoon kosher salt
- Freshly ground black pepper, to taste
- 6 links (about 1½ pounds / 680 g) hot Italian sausage
- 3 tablespoons balsamic vinegar

Place the grapes in a large bowl. Add the shallots, thyme, olive oil, salt, and pepper. Gently toss. Place the grapes in a baking pan. Arrange the sausage links evenly in the pan.

Select Roast, set temperature to 375ºF (190ºC), and set time to 20 minutes. Press Start to begin preheating.

Once preheated, place the pan into the oven.

After 10 minutes, remove the pan. Turn over the sausages and sprinkle the vinegar over the sausages and grapes. Gently toss the grapes and move them to one side of the pan. Return the pan to the oven and continue cooking.

When cooking is complete, the grapes should be very soft and the sausages browned. Serve immediately.

656. RAVIOLI WITH BEEF-MARINARA SAUCE

Prep time: 10 minutes | Cook time: 10 minutes | Serves 4

- 1 (20-ounce / 567-g) package frozen cheese ravioli
- 1 teaspoon kosher salt
- 1¼ cups water
- 6 ounces (170 g) cooked ground beef
- 2½ cups Marinara sauce
- ¼ cup grated Parmesan cheese, for garnish

Place the ravioli in an even layer on a baking pan. Stir the salt into the water until dissolved and pour it over the ravioli.

Select Bake, set temperature to 450ºF (235ºC), and set time to 10 minutes. Press Start to begin preheating.

Once preheated, place the pan into the oven.

While the ravioli is cooking, mix the ground beef into the marinara sauce in a medium bowl.

After 6 minutes, remove the pan from the oven. Blot off any remaining water, or drain the ravioli and return them to the pan. Pour the meat sauce over the ravioli. Return the pan to the oven and continue cooking.

When cooking is complete, remove the pan from the oven. The ravioli should be tender and sauce heated through. Gently stir the ingredients. Serve the ravioli with the Parmesan cheese, if desired.

657. PORK WITH BUTTERNUT SQUASH AND APPLES

Prep time: 15 minutes | Cook time: 13 minutes | Serves 4

- 4 boneless pork loin chops, ¾- to 1-inch thick
- 1 teaspoon kosher salt, divided
- 2 tablespoons Dijon mustard
- 2 tablespoons brown sugar
- 1 pound (454 g) butternut squash, cut into 1-inch cubes
- 1 large apple, peeled and cut into 12 to 16 wedges
- 1 medium onion, thinly sliced
- ½ teaspoon dried thyme
- ¼ teaspoon freshly ground black pepper
- 1 tablespoon unsalted butter, melted
- ½ cup chicken stock

Sprinkle the pork chops on both sides with ½ teaspoon of kosher salt. In a small bowl, whisk together the mustard and brown sugar. Baste about half of the mixture on one side of the pork chops. Place the chops, basted-side up, on a baking pan.
Place the squash in a large bowl. Add the apple, onion, thyme, remaining kosher salt, pepper, and butter and toss to coat. Arrange the squash-fruit mixture around the chops on the pan. Pour the chicken stock over the mixture, avoiding the chops.
Select Roast, set temperature to 350°F (180°C), and set time to 13 minutes. Press Start to begin preheating.
Once preheated, place the pan into the oven.
After about 7 minutes, remove the pan from the oven. Gently toss the squash mixture and turn over the chops. Baste the chops with the remaining mustard mixture. Return the pan to the oven and continue cooking.
When cooking is complete, the pork chops should register at least 145°F (63°C) in the center on a meat thermometer, and the squash and apples should be tender. If necessary, continue cooking for up to 3 minutes more.
Remove the pan from the oven. Spoon the squash and apples onto four plates, and place a pork chop on top. Serve immediately.

658. PORK FRIED RICE WITH SCRAMBLED EGG

Prep time: 10 minutes | Cook time: 12 minutes | Serves 4

- 3 scallions, diced (about ½ cup)
- ½ red bell pepper, diced (about ½ cup)
- 2 teaspoons sesame oil
- ½ pound (227 g) pork tenderloin, diced
- ½ cup frozen peas, thawed
- ½ cup roasted mushrooms
- ½ cup soy sauce
- 2 cups cooked rice
- 1 egg, beaten

Place the scallions and red pepper on a baking pan. Drizzle with the sesame oil and toss the vegetables to coat them in the oil.
Select Roast, set temperature to 375°F (190°C), and set time to 12 minutes. Press Start to begin preheating.
Once preheated, place the pan into the oven.
While the vegetables are cooking, place the pork in a large bowl. Add the peas, mushrooms, soy sauce, and rice and toss to coat the ingredients with the sauce.
After about 4 minutes, remove the pan from the oven. Place the pork mixture on the pan and stir the scallions and peppers into the pork and rice. Return the pan to the oven and continue cooking.
After another 6 minutes, remove the pan from the oven. Move the rice

mixture to the sides to create an empty circle in the middle of the pan. Pour the egg in the circle. Return the pan to the oven and continue cooking.
When cooking is complete, remove the pan from the oven and stir the egg to scramble it. Stir the egg into the fried rice mixture. Serve immediately.

659. SIRLOIN STEAK AND PEPPER FAJITAS

Prep time: 10 minutes | Cook time: 15 minutes | Serves 4

- 8 (6-inch) flour tortillas
- 1 pound (454 g) top sirloin steak, sliced ¼-inch thick
- 1 red bell pepper, deseeded and sliced ½-inch thick
- 1 green bell pepper, deseeded and sliced ½-inch thick
- 1 jalapeño, deseeded and sliced thin
- 1 medium onion, sliced ½-inch thick
- 2 tablespoons vegetable oil
- 2 tablespoons Mexican seasoning
- 1 teaspoon kosher salt
- 2 tablespoons salsa
- 1 small avocado, sliced

Line a baking pan with aluminum foil. Place the tortillas on the foil in two stacks and wrap in the foil.
Select Roast, set temperature to 325°F (163°C), and set time to 6 minutes. Press Start to begin preheating.
Once preheated, place the pan into the oven. After 3 minutes, remove the pan from the oven and flip the packet of tortillas over. Return the pan to the oven and continue cooking.
While the tortillas warm, place the steak, bell peppers, jalapeño, and onion in a large bowl and drizzle the oil over. Sprinkle with the Mexican seasoning and salt, and toss to coat.
When cooking is complete, remove the pan from the oven and place the packet of tortillas on top of the oven to keep warm. Place the beef and peppers mixture on the baking pan, spreading out into a single layer as much as possible.
Select Roast, set temperature to 375°F (190°C), and set time to 9 minutes. Press Start to begin preheating.
Once preheated, place the pan into the oven.
After about 5 minutes, remove the pan from the oven and stir the ingredients. Return the pan to the oven and continue cooking.
When cooking is complete, the vegetables will be soft and browned in places, and the beef will be browned on the outside and barely pink inside. Remove the pan from the oven. Unwrap the tortillas and spoon the fajita mixture into the tortillas. Serve with salsa and avocado slices.

660. SPICY PORK LETTUCE WRAPS

Prep time: 10 minutes | Cook time: 12 minutes | Serves 4

- 1 (1-pound / 454-g) medium pork tenderloin, silver skin and external fat trimmed
- ⅔ cup soy sauce, divided
- 1 teaspoon cornstarch
- 1 medium jalapeño, deseeded and minced
- 1 can diced water chestnuts
- ½ large red bell pepper, deseeded and chopped
- 2 scallions, chopped, white and green parts separated
- 1 head butter lettuce
- ½ cup roasted, chopped almonds
- ¼ cup coarsely chopped cilantro

Cut the tenderloin into ¼-inch slices and place them on a baking pan. Baste with about 3 tablespoons of soy sauce. Stir the cornstarch into the remaining sauce and set aside.
Select Roast, set temperature to 375°F (190°C), and set time to 12 minutes. Press Start to begin preheating.

Once preheated, place the pan into the oven.

After 5 minutes, remove the pan from the oven. Place the pork slices on a cutting board. Place the jalapeño, water chestnuts, red pepper, and the white parts of the scallions on the baking pan and pour the remaining sauce over. Stir to coat the vegetables with the sauce. Return the pan to the oven and continue cooking.

While the vegetables cook, chop the pork into small pieces. Separate the lettuce leaves, discarding any tough outer leaves and setting aside the small inner leaves for another use. You'll want 12 to 18 leaves, depending on size and your appetites.

After 5 minutes, remove the pan from the oven. Add the pork to the vegetables, stirring to combine. Return the pan to the oven and continue cooking for the remaining 2 minutes until the pork is warmed back up and the sauce has reduced slightly.

When cooking is complete, remove the pan from the oven. Place the pork and vegetables in a medium serving bowl and stir in half the green parts of the scallions. To serve, spoon some pork and vegetables into each of the lettuce leaves. Top with the remaining scallion greens and garnish with the nuts and cilantro.

661. SRIRACHA BEEF AND BROCCOLI

Prep time: 10 minutes | Cook time: 15 minutes | Serves 4

- 12 ounces (340 g) broccoli, cut into florets (about 4 cups)
- 1 pound (454 g) flat iron steak, cut into thin strips
- ½ teaspoon kosher salt
- ¾ cup soy sauce
- 1 teaspoon Sriracha sauce
- 3 tablespoons freshly squeezed orange juice
- 1 teaspoon cornstarch
- 1 medium onion, thinly sliced

Line a baking pan with aluminum foil. Place the broccoli on top and sprinkle with 3 tablespoons of water. Seal the broccoli in the foil in a single layer.

Select Roast, set temperature to 375ºF (190ºC), and set time to 6 minutes. Press Start to begin preheating.

Once preheated, place the pan into the oven.

While the broccoli steams, sprinkle the steak with the salt. In a small bowl, whisk together the soy sauce, Sriracha, orange juice, and cornstarch. Place the onion and beef in a large bowl.

When cooking is complete, remove the pan from the oven. Open the packet of broccoli and use tongs to transfer the broccoli to the bowl with the beef and onion, discarding the foil and remaining water. Pour the sauce over the beef and vegetables and toss to coat. Place the mixture in the baking pan.

Select Roast, set temperature to 375ºF (190ºC), and set time to 9 minutes. Press Start to begin preheating.

Once preheated, place the pan into the oven.

After about 4 minutes, remove the pan from the oven and gently toss the ingredients. Return the pan to oven and continue cooking.

When cooking is complete, the sauce should be thickened, the vegetables tender, and the beef barely pink in the center. Serve warm.

662. WORCESTERSHIRE RIBEYE STEAKS

Prep time: 35 minutes | Cook time: 10 to 12 minutes | Serves 2 to 4

- 2 (8-ounce / 227-g) boneless ribeye steaks
- 4 teaspoons Worcestershire sauce
- ½ teaspoon garlic powder
- Salt and ground black pepper, to taste
- 4 teaspoons olive oil

Brush the steaks with Worcestershire sauce on both sides. Sprinkle with garlic powder and coarsely ground black pepper. Drizzle the steaks with olive oil. Allow steaks to marinate for 30 minutes.

Transfer the steaks in the perforated pan.

Select Roast of the oven. Set the temperature to 400ºF (205ºC) and set time to 4 minutes. Press Start to begin preheating.

Once preheated, place the pan into the oven.

After 2 minutes, remove the pan from the oven. Flip the steaks. Return the pan to the oven and continue cooking.

When cooking is complete, the steaks should be well browned.

Remove the steaks from the perforated pan and let sit for 5 minutes. Salt and serve.

POULTRY RECIPES

663. AIR FRIED CHICKEN POTATOES WITH SUN-DRIED TOMATO

Prep time: 15 minutes | Cook time: 25 minutes | Serves 2

- 2 teaspoons minced fresh oregano, divided
- 2 teaspoons minced fresh thyme, divided
- 2 teaspoons extra-virgin olive oil, plus extra as needed
- 1 pound (454 g) fingerling potatoes, unpeeled
- 2 (12-ounce / 340-g) bone-in split chicken breasts, trimmed
- 1 garlic clove, minced
- ¼ cup oil-packed sun-dried tomatoes, patted dry and chopped
- 1½ tablespoons red wine vinegar
- 1 tablespoon capers, rinsed and minced
- 1 small shallot, minced
- Salt and ground black pepper, to taste

Combine 1 teaspoon of oregano, 1 teaspoon of thyme, ¼ teaspoon of salt, ¼ teaspoon of ground black pepper, 1 teaspoons of olive oil in a large bowl. Add the potatoes and toss to coat well.

Combine the chicken with remaining thyme, oregano, and olive oil. Sprinkle with garlic, salt, and pepper. Toss to coat well.

Place the potatoes in the perforated pan, then arrange the chicken on top of the potatoes.

Select Air Fry of the oven. Set temperature to 350ºF (180ºC) and set time to 25 minutes. Press Start to begin preheating.

Once preheated, place the pan into the oven. Flip the chicken and potatoes halfway through.

When cooking is complete, the internal temperature of the chicken should reach at least 165 °F (74 °C) and the potatoes should be wilted.

Meanwhile, combine the sun-dried tomatoes, vinegar, capers, and shallot in a separate large bowl. Sprinkle with salt and ground black pepper. Toss to mix well.

Remove the chicken and potatoes from the oven and allow to cool for 10 minutes. Serve with the sun-dried tomato mix.

664. AIR FRIED CHICKEN WINGS WITH BUFFALO SAUCE

Prep time: 10 minutes | Cook time: 20 minutes | Serves 6

- 16 chicken drumettes (party wings)
- Chicken seasoning or rub, to taste
- 1 teaspoon garlic powder
- Ground black pepper, to taste
- ¼ cup buffalo wings sauce
- Cooking spray

Spritz a perforated pan with cooking spray.

Rub the chicken wings with chicken seasoning, garlic powder, and ground black pepper on a clean work surface.

Arrange the chicken wings in the perforated pan. Spritz with cooking spray.

Select Air Fry of the oven. Set temperature to 400ºF (205ºC) and set time to 10 minutes. Press Start to begin preheating.

Once preheated, place the pan into the oven. Flip the chicken wings halfway through.

When cooking is complete, the chicken wings should be lightly browned. Transfer the chicken wings in a large bowl, then pour in the buffalo wings sauce and toss to coat well.

Put the wings back to the oven and set time to 7 minutes. Flip the wings halfway through.

When cooking is complete, the wings should be heated through. Serve immediately.

665. APRICOT-GLAZED CHICKEN DRUMSTICKS

Prep time: 15 minutes | Cook time: 30 minutes | Makes 6 drumsticks

For the Glaze:
- ½ cup apricot preserves
- ½ teaspoon tamari
- ¼ teaspoon chili powder
- 2 teaspoons Dijon mustard

For the Chicken:
- 6 chicken drumsticks
- ½ teaspoon seasoning salt
- 1 teaspoon salt
- ½ teaspoon ground black pepper
- Cooking spray

Make the glaze:
Combine the ingredients for the glaze in a saucepan, then heat over low heat for 10 minutes or until thickened.
Turn off the heat and sit until ready to use.

Make the Chicken:
Spritz a perforated pan with cooking spray.
Combine the seasoning salt, salt, and pepper in a small bowl. Stir to mix well.
Place the chicken drumsticks in the perforated pan. Spritz with cooking spray and sprinkle with the salt mixture on both sides.
Select Air Fry of the oven. Set temperature to 370°F (188°C) and set time to 20 minutes. Press Start to begin preheating.
Once preheated, place the pan into the oven. Flip the chicken halfway through.
When cooking is complete, the chicken should be well browned.
Baste the chicken with the glaze and air fry for 2 more minutes or until the chicken tenderloin is glossy.
Serve immediately.

666. BELL PEPPER STUFFED CHICKEN ROLL-UPS

Prep time: 10 minutes | Cook time: 12 minutes | Serves 4

- 2 (4-ounce / 113-g) boneless, skinless chicken breasts, slice in half horizontally
- 1 tablespoon olive oil
- Juice of ½ lime
- 2 tablespoons taco seasoning
- ½ green bell pepper, cut into strips
- ½ red bell pepper, cut into strips
- ¼ onion, sliced

Unfold the chicken breast slices on a clean work surface. Rub with olive oil, then drizzle with lime juice and sprinkle with taco seasoning.
Top the chicken slices with equal amount of bell peppers and onion. Roll them up and secure with toothpicks.
Arrange the chicken roll-ups in the perforated pan.
Select Air Fry of the oven. Set temperature to 400°F (205°C) and set time to 12 minutes. Press Start to begin preheating.

Once preheated, place the pan into the oven. Flip the chicken roll-ups halfway through.

When cooking is complete, the internal temperature of the chicken should reach at least 165°F (74°C).

Remove the chicken from the oven. Discard the toothpicks and serve immediately.

667. BACON-WRAPPED AND CHEESE-STUFFED CHICKEN

Prep time: 10 minutes | Cook time: 20 minutes | Serves 4

- 4 (5-ounce / 142-g) boneless, skinless chicken breasts, pounded to ¼ inch thick
- 1 cup cream cheese
- 2 tablespoons chopped fresh chives
- 8 slices thin-cut bacon
- Sprig of fresh cilantro, for garnish
- Cooking spray

Spritz a perforated pan with cooking spray.
On a clean work surface, slice the chicken horizontally to make a 1-inch incision on top of each chicken breast with a knife, then cut into the chicken to make a pocket. Leave a ½-inch border along the sides and bottom.
Combine the cream cheese and chives in a bowl. Stir to mix well, then gently pour the mixture into the chicken pockets.
Wrap each stuffed chicken breast with 2 bacon slices, then secure the ends with toothpicks.
Arrange them in the perforated pan.
Select Air Fry of the oven. Set temperature to 400°F (205°C) and set time to 20 minutes. Press Start to begin preheating.
Once preheated, place the pan into the oven. Flip the bacon-wrapped chicken halfway through the cooking time.
When cooking is complete, the bacon should be browned and crispy.
Transfer them on a large plate and serve with cilantro on top.

668. BACON-WRAPPED CHICKEN BREASTS ROLLS

Prep time: 10 minutes | Cook time: 15 minutes | Serves 4

- ¼ cup chopped fresh chives
- 2 tablespoons lemon juice
- 1 teaspoon dried sage
- 1 teaspoon fresh rosemary leaves
- ½ cup fresh parsley leaves
- 4 cloves garlic, peeled
- 1 teaspoon ground fennel
- 3 teaspoons sea salt
- ½ teaspoon red pepper flakes
- 4 (4-ounce / 113-g) boneless, skinless chicken breasts, pounded to ¼ inch thick
- 8 slices bacon
- Sprigs of fresh rosemary, for garnish
- Cooking spray

Spritz a perforated pan with cooking spray.
Put the chives, lemon juice, sage, rosemary, parsley, garlic, fennel, salt, and red pepper flakes in a food processor, then pulse to purée until smooth.
Unfold the chicken breasts on a clean work surface, then brush the top side of the chicken breasts with the sauce.
Roll the chicken breasts up from the shorter side, then wrap each chicken rolls with 2 bacon slices to cover. Secure with toothpicks.
Arrange the rolls in the perforated pan.
Select Air Fry of the oven. Set temperature to 340°F (171°C) and set time to 10 minutes. Press Start to begin preheating.
Once preheated, place the pan into the oven. Flip the rolls halfway

through.

After 10 minutes, increase temperature to 390°F (199°C) and set time to 5 minutes.

When cooking is complete, the bacon should be browned and crispy.

Transfer the rolls to a large plate. Discard the toothpicks and spread with rosemary sprigs before serving.

669. BARBECUE CHICKEN AND COLESLAW TOSTADAS

Prep time: 15 minutes | Cook time: 10 minutes | Makes 4 tostadas

Coleslaw:
- ¼ cup sour cream
- ¼ small green cabbage, finely chopped
- ½ tablespoon white vinegar
- ½ teaspoon garlic powder
- ½ teaspoon salt
- ¼ teaspoon ground black pepper

Tostadas:
- 2 cups pulled rotisserie chicken
- ½ cup barbecue sauce
- 4 corn tortillas
- ½ cup shredded Mozzarella cheese
- Cooking spray

Make the Coleslaw:

Combine the ingredients for the coleslaw in a large bowl. Toss to mix well.

Refrigerate until ready to serve.

Make the Tostadas:

Spritz a perforated pan with cooking spray.

Toss the chicken with barbecue sauce in a separate large bowl to combine well. Set aside.

Place one tortilla in the perforated pan and spritz with cooking spray.

Select Air Fry of the oven. Set temperature to 370°F (188°C) and set time to 10 minutes. Press Start to begin preheating.

Once preheated, place the pan into the oven. Flip the tortilla and spread the barbecue chicken and cheese over halfway through.

When cooking is complete, the tortilla should be browned and the cheese should be melted.

Serve the tostadas with coleslaw on top.

670. BRUSCHETTA CHICKEN

Prep time: 10 minutes | Cook time: 10 minutes | Serves 4

- Bruschetta Stuffing:
- 1 tomato, diced
- 3 tablespoons balsamic vinegar
- 1 teaspoon Italian seasoning
- 2 tablespoons chopped fresh basil
- 3 garlic cloves, minced
- 2 tablespoons extra-virgin olive oil
- Chicken:
- 4 (4-ounce / 113-g) boneless, skinless chicken breasts, cut 4 slits each
- 1 teaspoon Italian seasoning
- Chicken seasoning or rub, to taste
- Cooking spray

Spritz a perforated pan with cooking spray.

Combine the ingredients for the bruschetta stuffing in a bowl. Stir to mix well. Set aside.

Rub the chicken breasts with Italian seasoning and chicken seasoning on a clean work surface.

Arrange the chicken breasts, slits side up, in the perforated pan and spritz

with cooking spray.

Select Air Fry of the oven. Set temperature to 370°F (188°C) and set time to 10 minutes. Press Start to begin preheating.

Once preheated, place the pan into the oven. Flip the breast and fill the slits with the bruschetta stuffing halfway through.

When cooking is complete, the chicken should be well browned.

Serve immediately.

671. CHEESE-ENCRUSTED CHICKEN TENDERLOINS WITH PEANUTS

Prep time: 10 minutes | Cook time: 12 minutes | Serves 4

- ½ cup grated Parmesan cheese
- ½ teaspoon garlic powder
- 1 teaspoon red pepper flakes
- Sea salt and ground black pepper, to taste
- 2 tablespoons peanut oil
- 1½ pounds (680 g) chicken tenderloins
- 2 tablespoons peanuts, roasted and roughly chopped
- Cooking spray

Spritz a perforated pan with cooking spray.

Combine the Parmesan cheese, garlic powder, red pepper flakes, salt, black pepper, and peanut oil in a large bow. Stir to mix well.

Dip the chicken tenderloins in the cheese mixture, then press to coat well. Shake the excess off.

Transfer the chicken tenderloins in the perforated pan.

Select Air Fry of the oven. Set temperature to 360°F (182°C) and set time to 12 minutes. Press Start to begin preheating.

Once preheated, place the pan into the oven. Flip the tenderloin halfway through.

When cooking is complete, the tenderloin should be well browned.

Transfer the chicken tenderloins on a large plate and top with roasted peanuts before serving.

672. LECHON KAWALI

Prep time: 10 minutes | Cook time: 30 minutes | Serves 4

- 1 pound (454 g) pork belly, cut into three thick chunks
- 6 garlic cloves
- 2 bay leaves
- 2 tablespoons soy sauce
- 1 teaspoon kosher salt
- 1 teaspoon ground black pepper
- 3 cups water
- Cooking spray

Put all the ingredients in a pressure cooker, then put the lid on and cook on high for 15 minutes.

Natural release the pressure and release any remaining pressure, transfer the tender pork belly on a clean work surface. Allow to cool under room temperature until you can handle.

Generously spritz a perforated pan with cooking spray.

Cut each chunk into two slices, then put the pork slices in the pan.

Select Air Fry of the oven. Set temperature to 400°F (205°C) and set time to 15 minutes. Press Start to begin preheating.

Once preheated, place the pan into the oven.

After 7 minutes, remove the pan from the oven. Flip the pork. Return the pan to the oven and continue cooking.

When cooking is complete, the pork fat should be crispy.

Serve immediately.

673. CHEESY PEPPERONI AND CHICKEN PIZZA

Prep time: 15 minutes | Cook time: 15 minutes | Serves 6
- 2 cups cooked chicken, cubed
- 1 cup pizza sauce
- 20 slices pepperoni

- ¼ cup grated Parmesan cheese
- 1 cup shredded Mozzarella cheese
- Cooking spray

Spritz a baking pan with cooking spray.

Arrange the chicken cubes in the prepared baking pan, then top the cubes with pizza sauce and pepperoni. Stir to coat the cubes and pepperoni with sauce. Scatter the cheeses on top.

Select Air Fry of the oven. Set temperature to 375ºF (190ºC) and set time to 15 minutes. Press Start to begin preheating.

Once preheated, place the pan into the oven.

When cooking is complete, the pizza should be frothy and the cheeses should be melted.

Serve immediately.

674. CHICKEN AND HAM MEATBALLS WITH DIJON SAUCE

Prep time: 10 minutes | Cook time: 15 minutes | Serves 4

Meatballs:
- ½ pound (227 g) ham, diced
- ½ pound (227 g) ground chicken
- ½ cup grated Swiss cheese
- 1 large egg, beaten
- 3 cloves garlic, minced
- ¼ cup chopped onions
- 1½ teaspoons sea salt
- 1 teaspoon ground black pepper
- Cooking spray

Dijon Sauce:
- 3 tablespoons Dijon mustard
- 2 tablespoons lemon juice
- ¼ cup chicken broth, warmed
- ¾ teaspoon sea salt
- ¼ teaspoon ground black pepper
- Chopped fresh thyme leaves, for garnish

Spritz a perforated pan with cooking spray.

Combine the ingredients for the meatballs in a large bowl. Stir to mix well, then shape the mixture in twelve 1½-inch meatballs.

Arrange the meatballs in the perforated pan.

Select Air Fry of the oven. Set temperature to 390ºF (199ºC) and set time to 15 minutes. Press Start to begin preheating.

Once preheated, place the pan into the oven. Flip the balls halfway through.

When cooking is complete, the balls should be lightly browned.

Meanwhile, combine the ingredients, except for the thyme leaves, for the sauce in a small bowl. Stir to mix well.

Transfer the cooked meatballs on a large plate, then baste the sauce over. Garnish with thyme leaves and serve.

675. CHICKEN ROCHAMBEAU WITH MUSHROOM SAUCE

Prep time: 25 minutes | Cook time: 30 minutes | Serves 4

- 1 tablespoon melted butter
- ¼ cup all-purpose flour
- 4 chicken tenders, cut in half crosswise
- 4 slices ham, ¼-inch thick, large enough to cover an English muffin
- 2 English muffins, split in halves
- Salt and ground black pepper, to taste
- Cooking spray
- Mushroom Sauce:
- 2 tablespoons butter
- ½ cup chopped mushrooms
- ½ cup chopped green onions
- 2 tablespoons flour

- 1 cup chicken broth
- 1½ teaspoons Worcestershire sauce
- ¼ teaspoon garlic powder

Put the butter in a baking pan. Combine the flour, salt, and ground black pepper in a shallow dish. Roll the chicken tenders over to coat well.

Arrange the chicken in the baking pan and flip to coat with the melted butter.

Select Broil of the oven. Set temperature to 390ºF (199ºC) and set time to 10 minutes. Press Start to begin preheating.

Once preheated, place the pan into the oven. Flip the tenders halfway through.

When cooking is complete, the juices of chicken tenders should run clear. Meanwhile, make the mushroom sauce: melt 2 tablespoons of butter in a saucepan over medium-high heat.

Add the mushrooms and onions to the saucepan and sauté for 3 minutes or until the onions are translucent.

Gently mix in the flour, broth, Worcestershire sauce, and garlic powder until smooth.

Reduce the heat to low and simmer for 5 minutes or until it has a thick consistency. Set the sauce aside until ready to serve.

When broiling is complete, remove the baking pan from the oven and set the ham slices into the perforated pan.

Select Air Fry of the oven. Set time to 5 minutes. Press Start. Flip the ham slices halfway through.

When cooking is complete, the ham slices should be heated through.

Remove the ham slices from the oven and set in the English muffin halves and warm for 1 minute.

Arrange each ham slice on top of each muffin half, then place each chicken tender over the ham slice.

Transfer to the oven and set time to 2 minutes on Air Fry.

Serve with the sauce on top.

676. CHICKEN THIGHS IN WAFFLES

Prep time: 1 hour 20 minutes | Cook time: 20 minutes | Serves 4

For the chicken:
- 4 chicken thighs, skin on
- 1 cup low-fat buttermilk
- ½ cup all-purpose flour
- ½ teaspoon garlic powder
- ½ teaspoon mustard powder
- 1 teaspoon kosher salt
- ½ teaspoon freshly ground black pepper
- ¼ cup honey, for serving
- Cooking spray

For the waffles:
- ½ cup all-purpose flour
- ½ cup whole wheat pastry flour
- 1 large egg, beaten
- 1 cup low-fat buttermilk
- 1 teaspoon baking powder
- 2 tablespoons canola oil
- ½ teaspoon kosher salt
- 1 tablespoon granulated sugar

Combine the chicken thighs with buttermilk in a large bowl. Wrap the bowl in plastic and refrigerate to marinate for at least an hour.

Spritz a perforated pan with cooking spray.

Combine the flour, mustard powder, garlic powder, salt, and black pepper in a shallow dish. Stir to mix well.

Remove the thighs from the buttermilk and pat dry with paper towels. Sit the bowl of buttermilk aside.

Dip the thighs in the flour mixture first, then into the buttermilk, and then into the flour mixture. Shake the excess off.

Arrange the thighs in the perforated pan and spritz with cooking spray.

Select Air Fry of the oven. Set temperature to 360°F (182°C) and set time to 20 minutes. Press Start to begin preheating.

Once preheated, place the pan into the oven. Flip the thighs halfway through.

When cooking is complete, an instant-read thermometer inserted in the thickest part of the chicken thighs should register at least 165 °F (74 °C). Meanwhile, make the waffles: combine the ingredients for the waffles in a large bowl. Stir to mix well, then arrange the mixture in a waffle iron and cook until a golden and fragrant waffle forms.

Remove the waffles from the waffle iron and slice into 4 pieces. Remove the chicken thighs from the oven and allow to cool for 5 minutes.

Arrange each chicken thigh on each waffle piece and drizzle with 1 tablespoon of honey. Serve warm.

677. CRISPY CHICKEN SKIN

Prep time: 5 minutes | Cook time: 6 minutes | Serves 4
- 1 pound (454 g) chicken skin, cut into slices
- 1 teaspoon melted butter
- ½ teaspoon crushed chili flakes
- 1 teaspoon dried dill
- Salt and ground black pepper, to taste

Combine all the ingredients in a large bowl. Toss to coat the chicken skin well.

Transfer the skin in the perforated pan.

Select Air Fry of the oven. Set temperature to 360°F (182°C) and set time to 6 minutes. Press Start to begin preheating.

Once preheated, place the pan into the oven. Stir the skin halfway through.

When cooking is complete, the skin should be crispy. Serve immediately.

678. SAUSAGE RATATOUILLE

Prep time: 10 minutes | Cook time: 25 minutes | Serves 4

- 4 pork sausages
- Ratatouille:
- 2 zucchinis, sliced
- 1 eggplant, sliced
- 15 ounces (425 g) tomatoes, sliced
- 1 red bell pepper, sliced
- 1 medium red onion, sliced
- 1 cup canned butter beans, drained
- 1 tablespoon balsamic vinegar
- 2 garlic cloves, minced
- 1 red chili, chopped
- 2 tablespoons fresh thyme, chopped
- 2 tablespoons olive oil

Place the sausages in the perforated pan.

Select Air Fry of the oven. Set temperature to 390°F (199°C) and set time to 10 minutes. Press Start to begin preheating.

Once preheated, place the pan into the oven.

After 7 minutes, remove the pan from the oven. Flip the sausages. Return the pan to the oven and continue cooking.

When cooking is complete, the sausages should be lightly browned.

Meanwhile, make the ratatouille: arrange the vegetable slices on the prepared baking pan alternatively, then add the remaining ingredients on top.

Transfer the air fried sausage to a plate, then arrange the baking pan in the oven.

Select Bake. Set time to 15 minutes and bake until the vegetables are tender. Give the vegetables a stir halfway through the baking.

Serve the ratatouille with the sausage on top.

679. KOREAN FLAVOR GLAZED CHICKEN WINGS

Prep time: 10 minutes | Cook time: 25 minutes | Serves 4

Wings:
- 2 pounds (907 g) chicken wings
- 1 teaspoon salt
- 1 teaspoon ground black pepper

Sauce:
- 2 tablespoons gochujang
- 1 tablespoon mayonnaise
- 1 tablespoon minced ginger
- 1 tablespoon minced garlic
- 1 teaspoon agave nectar
- 2 packets Splenda
- 1 tablespoon sesame oil

For Garnish:
- 2 teaspoons sesame seeds
- ¼ cup chopped green onions

Line a baking pan with aluminum foil, then arrange the rack on the pan. On a clean work surface, rub the chicken wings with salt and ground black pepper, then arrange the seasoned wings on the rack.

Select Air Fry of the oven. Set temperature to 400°F (205°C) and set time to 20 minutes. Press Start to begin preheating.

Once preheated, place the pan into the oven. Flip the wings halfway through.

When cooking is complete, the wings should be well browned.

Meanwhile, combine the ingredients for the sauce in a small bowl. Stir to mix well. Reserve half of the sauce in a separate bowl until ready to serve.

Remove the air fried chicken wings from the oven and toss with remaining half of the sauce to coat well.

Place the wings back to the oven. Select Air Fry. Set time to 5 minutes.

When cooking is complete, the internal temperature of the wings should reach at least 165°F (74°C).

Remove the wings from the oven and place on a large plate. Sprinkle with sesame seeds and green onions. Serve with reserved sauce.

680. LETTUCE CHICKEN TACOS WITH PEANUT SAUCE

Prep time: 10 minutes | Cook time: 6 minutes | Serves 4

- 1 pound (454 g) ground chicken
- 2 cloves garlic, minced
- ¼ cup diced onions
- ¼ teaspoon sea salt
- Cooking spray
- Peanut Sauce:
- ¼ cup creamy peanut butter, at room temperature
- 2 tablespoons tamari
- 1½ teaspoons hot sauce
- 2 tablespoons lime juice
- 2 tablespoons grated fresh ginger
- 2 tablespoons chicken broth
- 2 teaspoons sugar

For Serving:
- 2 small heads butter lettuce, leaves separated
- Lime slices (optional)

Spritz a baking pan with cooking spray.

Combine the ground chicken, garlic, and onions in the baking pan, then sprinkle with salt. Use a fork to break the ground chicken and combine them well.

Select Bake of the oven. Set temperature to 350°F (180°C) and set time to 5 minutes. Press Start to begin preheating.

Once preheated, place the pan into the oven. Stir them halfway through the cooking time.

When cooking is complete, the chicken should be lightly browned.

Meanwhile, combine the ingredients for the sauce in a small bowl. Stir to mix well.

Pour the sauce in the pan of chicken, then bake for 1 more minute or until heated through.

Unfold the lettuce leaves on a large serving plate, then divide the chicken mixture on the lettuce leaves. Drizzle with lime juice and serve immediately.

681. LIME CHICKEN WITH CILANTRO

Prep time: 35 minutes | Cook time: 10 minutes | Serves 4

- 4 (4-ounce / 113-g) boneless, skinless chicken breasts
- ½ cup chopped fresh cilantro
- Juice of 1 lime
- Chicken seasoning or rub, to taste
- Salt and ground black pepper, to taste
- Cooking spray

Put the chicken breasts in the large bowl, then add the cilantro, lime juice, chicken seasoning, salt, and black pepper. Toss to coat well.

Wrap the bowl in plastic and refrigerate to marinate for at least 30 minutes.

Spritz a perforated pan with cooking spray.

Remove the marinated chicken breasts from the bowl and place in the perforated pan. Spritz with cooking spray.

Select Air Fry of the oven. Set temperature to 400ºF (205ºC) and set time to 10 minutes. Press Start to begin preheating.

Once preheated, place the pan into the oven. Flip the breasts halfway through.

When cooking is complete, the internal temperature of the chicken should reach at least 165 ºF (74 ºC).

Serve immediately.

682. NICE GOULASH

Prep time: 5 minutes | Cook time: 17 minutes | Serves 2

- 2 red bell peppers, chopped
- 1 pound (454 g) ground chicken
- 2 medium tomatoes, diced
- ½ cup chicken broth
- Salt and ground black pepper, to taste
- Cooking spray

Spritz a baking pan with cooking spray.

Set the bell pepper in the baking pan.

Select Broil of the oven. Set temperature to 365ºF (185ºC) and set time to 5 minutes. Press Start to begin preheating.

Once preheated, place the pan into the oven. Stir the bell pepper halfway through.

When broiling is complete, the bell pepper should be tender.

Add the ground chicken and diced tomatoes in the baking pan and stir to mix well.

Set the time of oven to 12 minutes. Press Start. Stir the mixture and mix in the chicken broth, salt and ground black pepper halfway through.

When cooking is complete, the chicken should be well browned.

Serve immediately.

683. EASY CHICKEN FINGERS

Prep time: 20 minutes | Cook time: 10 minutes | Makes 12 chicken fingers

- ½ cup all-purpose flour
- 2 cups panko breadcrumbs

- 2 tablespoons canola oil
- 1 large egg
- 3 boneless and skinless chicken breasts, each cut into 4 strips
- Kosher salt and freshly ground black pepper, to taste
- Cooking spray

Spritz a perforated pan with cooking spray.

Pour the flour in a large bowl. Combine the panko and canola oil on a shallow dish. Whisk the egg in a separate bowl.

Rub the chicken strips with salt and ground black pepper on a clean work surface, then dip the chicken in the bowl of flour. Shake the excess off and dunk the chicken strips in the bowl of whisked egg, then roll the strips over the panko to coat well.

Arrange the strips in the perforated pan.

Select Air Fry of the oven. Set temperature to 360ºF (182ºC) and set time to 10 minutes. Press Start to begin preheating.

Once preheated, place the pan into the oven. Flip the strips halfway through.

When cooking is complete, the strips should be crunchy and lightly browned.

Serve immediately.

684. CHICKEN WITH ASPARAGUS, BEAN S, AND ARUGULA

Prep time: 20 minutes | Cook time: 25 minutes | Serves 2

- 1 cup canned cannellini beans, rinsed
- 1½ tablespoons red wine vinegar
- 1 garlic clove, minced
- 2 tablespoons extra-virgin olive oil, divided
- Salt and ground black pepper, to taste
- ½ red onion, sliced thinly
- 8 ounces (227 g) asparagus, trimmed and cut into 1-inch lengths
- 2 (8-ounce / 227-g) boneless, skinless chicken breasts, trimmed
- ¼ teaspoon paprika
- ½ teaspoon ground coriander
- 2 ounces (57 g) baby arugula, rinsed and drained

Warm the beans in microwave for 1 minutes and combine with red wine vinegar, garlic, 1 tablespoon of olive oil, ¼ teaspoon of salt, and ¼ teaspoon of ground black pepper in a bowl. Stir to mix well.

Combine the onion with ⅛ teaspoon of salt, ⅛ teaspoon of ground black pepper, and 2 teaspoons of olive oil in a separate bowl. Toss to coat well. Place the onion in a perforated pan.

Select Air Fry of the oven. Set temperature to 400ºF (205ºC) and set time to 2 minutes. Press Start to begin preheating.

Once preheated, place the pan into the oven.

After 2 minutes, add the asparagus and set time to 8 minutes. Stir the vegetable halfway through.

When cooking is complete, the asparagus should be tender.

Transfer the onion and asparagus to the bowl with beans.

Set aside.

Toss the chicken breasts with remaining ingredients, except for the baby arugula, in a large bowl.

Put the chicken breasts in the perforated pan.

Select Air Fry of the oven. Set time to 14 minutes. Place the pan into the oven. Flip the breasts halfway through.

When cooking is complete, the internal temperature of the chicken reaches at least 165 ºF (74 ºC).

Remove the chicken from the oven and serve on an aluminum foil with asparagus, beans, onion, and arugula. Sprinkle with salt and ground black pepper. Toss to serve.

685. DRUMSTICKS WITH BARBECUE-HONEY SAUCE

Prep time: 5 minutes | Cook time: 18 minutes | Serves 5

- 1 tablespoon olive oil
- 10 chicken drumsticks
- Chicken seasoning or rub, to taste
- Salt and ground black pepper, to taste
- 1 cup barbecue sauce
- ¼ cup honey

Grease the perforated pan with olive oil.

Rub the chicken drumsticks with chicken seasoning or rub, salt and ground black pepper on a clean work surface.

Arrange the chicken drumsticks in the perforated pan.

Select Air Fry of the oven. Set temperature to 390ºF (199ºC) and set time to 18 minutes. Press Start to begin preheating.

Once preheated, place the pan into the oven. Flip the drumsticks halfway through.

When cooking is complete, the drumsticks should be lightly browned.

Meanwhile, combine the barbecue sauce and honey in a small bowl. Stir to mix well.

Remove the drumsticks from the oven and baste with the sauce mixture to serve.

686. MUTTON FRENCH CUISINE GALETTE

INGREDIENTS:
- 2 tbsp. garam masala
- 1 lb. minced mutton
- 3 tsp ginger finely chopped
- 1-2 tbsp. fresh coriander leaves
- 2 or 3 green chilies finely chopped
- 1 ½ tbsp. lemon juice
- Salt and pepper to taste

DIRECTIONS:

Mix the ingredients in a clean bowl. Mold this mixture into round and flat French Cuisine Galettes. Wet the French Cuisine Galettes slightly with water.

Pre heat the Cosori oven at 160 degrees Fahrenheit for 5 minutes. Place the French Cuisine Galettes in the fry basket and let them cook for another 25 minutes at the same temperature. Keep rolling them over to get a uniform cook. Serve either with mint sauce or ketchup.

687. GOLD LIVERS

Prep time: 10 minutes | Cook time: 10 minutes | Serves 4

- 2 eggs
- 2 tablespoons water
- ¾ cup flour
- 2 cups panko breadcrumbs
- 1 teaspoon salt
- ½ teaspoon ground black pepper
- 20 ounces (567 g) chicken livers
- Cooking spray

Spritz a perforated pan with cooking spray.

Whisk the eggs with water in a large bowl. Pour the flour in a separate bowl. Pour the panko on a shallow dish and sprinkle with salt and pepper. Dredge the chicken livers in the flour. Shake the excess off, then dunk the livers in the whisked eggs, and then roll the livers over the panko to coat well.

Arrange the livers in the perforated pan and spritz with cooking spray.

Select Air Fry of the oven. Set temperature to 390ºF (199ºC) and set time to 10 minutes. Press Start to begin preheating.

Once preheated, place the pan into the oven. Flip the livers halfway through.

When cooking is complete, the livers should be golden and crispy.
Serve immediately.

688. SIMPLE WHOLE CHICKEN BAKE

Prep time: 10 minutes | Cook time: 1 hour | Serves 2 to 4

- ½ cup melted butter
- 3 tablespoons garlic, minced
- Salt, to taste
- 1 teaspoon ground black pepper
- 1 (1-pound / 454-g) whole chicken

Combine the butter with garlic, salt, and ground black pepper in a small bowl.

Brush the butter mixture over the whole chicken, then place the chicken in a perforated pan, skin side down.

Select Bake of the oven. Set temperature to 350ºF (180ºC) and set time to 60 minutes. Press Start to begin preheating.

Once preheated, place the pan into the oven. Flip the chicken halfway through.

When cooking is complete, an instant-read thermometer inserted in the thickest part of the chicken should register at least 165 ºF (74 ºC).

Remove the chicken from the oven and allow to cool for 15 minutes before serving.

689. SPICY CHICKEN SKEWERS WITH SATAY SAUCE

Prep time: 5 minutes | Cook time: 10 minutes | Serves 4

- 4 (6-ounce / 170-g) boneless, skinless chicken breasts, sliced into strips
- 1 teaspoon sea salt
- 1 teaspoon paprika
- Cooking spray
- Satay Sauce:
- ¼ cup creamy almond butter
- ½ teaspoon hot sauce
- 1½ tablespoons coconut vinegar
- 2 tablespoons chicken broth
- 1 teaspoon peeled and minced fresh ginger
- 1 clove garlic, minced
- 1 teaspoon sugar
For Serving:
- ¼ cup chopped cilantro leaves
- Red pepper flakes, to taste
- Thinly sliced red, orange, or / and yellow bell peppers
Special Equipment:
16 wooden or bamboo skewers, soaked in water for 15 minutes

Spritz a perforated pan with cooking spray.

Run the bamboo skewers through the chicken strips, then arrange the chicken skewers in the perforated pan and sprinkle with salt and paprika.

Select Air Fry of the oven. Set temperature to 400ºF (205ºC) and set time to 10 minutes. Press Start to begin preheating.

Once preheated, place the pan into the oven. Flip the chicken skewers halfway during the cooking.

When cooking is complete, the chicken should be lightly browned.

Meanwhile, combine the ingredients for the sauce in a small bowl. Stir to mix well.

Transfer the cooked chicken skewers on a large plate, then top with cilantro, sliced bell peppers, red pepper flakes. Serve with the sauce or just baste the sauce over before serving.

690. SPICY TANDOORI CHICKEN DRUMSTICKS

Prep time: 70 minutes | Cook time: 14 minutes | Serves 4

- 8 (4- to 5-ounce / 113- to 142-g) skinless bone-in chicken drumsticks
- ½ cup plain full-fat or low-fat yogurt

- ¼ cup buttermilk
- 2 teaspoons minced garlic
- 2 teaspoons minced fresh ginger
- 2 teaspoons ground cinnamon
- 2 teaspoons ground coriander
- 2 teaspoons mild paprika
- 1 teaspoon salt
- 1 teaspoon Tabasco hot red pepper sauce

In a large bowl, stir together all the ingredients except for chicken drumsticks until well combined. Add the chicken drumsticks to the bowl and toss until well coated. Cover in plastic and set in the refrigerator to marinate for 1 hour, tossing once.

Arrange the marinated drumsticks in a perforated pan, leaving enough space between them.

Select Air Fry of the oven. Set temperature to 375ºF (190ºC) and set time to 14 minutes. Press Start to begin preheating.

Once preheated, place the pan into the oven. Flip the drumsticks once halfway through to ensure even cooking.

When cooking is complete, the internal temperature of the chicken drumsticks should reach 160ºF (71ºC) on a meat thermometer.

Transfer the drumsticks to plates. Rest for 5 minutes before serving.

691. GOLDEN CHICKEN CUTLETS
Prep time: 15 minutes | Cook time: 15 minutes | Serves 4

- 2 tablespoons panko breadcrumbs
- ¼ cup grated Parmesan cheese
- ⅛ tablespoon paprika
- ½ tablespoon garlic powder
- 2 large eggs
- 4 chicken cutlets
- 1 tablespoon parsley
- Salt and ground black pepper, to taste
- Cooking spray

Spritz a perforated pan with cooking spray.

Combine the breadcrumbs, Parmesan, paprika, garlic powder, salt, and ground black pepper in a large bowl. Stir to mix well. Beat the eggs in a separate bowl.

Dredge the chicken cutlets in the beaten eggs, then roll over the breadcrumbs mixture to coat well. Shake the excess off.

Transfer the chicken cutlets in the perforated pan and spritz with cooking spray.

Select Air Fry of the oven. Set temperature to 400ºF (205ºC) and set time to 15 minutes. Press Start to begin preheating.

Once preheated, place the pan into the oven. Flip the cutlets halfway through.

When cooking is complete, the cutlets should be crispy and golden brown.

Serve with parsley on top.

692. SPANISH CHICKEN AND PEPPER BAGUETTE
Prep time: 10 minutes | Cook time: 20 minutes | Serves 2

- 1¼ pounds (567 g) assorted small chicken parts, breasts cut into halves
- ¼ teaspoon salt
- ¼ teaspoon ground black pepper
- 2 teaspoons olive oil
- ½ pound (227 g) mini sweet peppers
- ¼ cup light mayonnaise
- ¼ teaspoon smoked paprika
- ½ clove garlic, crushed
- Baguette, for serving
- Cooking spray

Spritz a perforated pan with cooking spray.

Toss the chicken with salt, ground black pepper, and olive oil in a large bowl.

Arrange the sweet peppers and chicken in the perforated pan.

Select Air Fry of the oven. Set temperature to 375ºF (190ºC) and set time to 20 minutes. Press Start to begin preheating.

Once preheated, place the pan into the oven. Flip the chicken and transfer the peppers on a plate halfway through.

When cooking is complete, the chicken should be well browned.

Meanwhile, combine the mayo, paprika, and garlic in a small bowl. Stir to mix well.

Assemble the baguette with chicken and sweet pepper, then spread with mayo mixture and serve.

693. SWEET-AND-SOUR CHICKEN NUGGETS
Prep time: 15 minutes | Cook time: 15 minutes | Serves 4

- 1 cup cornstarch
- Chicken seasoning or rub, to taste
- Salt and ground black pepper, to taste
- 2 eggs
- 2 (4-ounce/ 113-g) boneless, skinless chicken breasts, cut into 1-inch pieces
- 1½ cups sweet-and-sour sauce
- Cooking spray

Spritz a perforated pan with cooking spray.

Combine the cornstarch, chicken seasoning, salt, and pepper in a large bowl. Stir to mix well. Whisk the eggs in a separate bowl.

Dredge the chicken pieces in the bowl of cornstarch mixture first, then in the bowl of whisked eggs, and then in the cornstarch mixture again.

Arrange the well-coated chicken pieces in the perforated pan. Spritz with cooking spray.

Select Air Fry of the oven. Set temperature to 360ºF (182ºC) and set time to 15 minutes. Press Start to begin preheating.

Once preheated, place the pan into the oven. Flip the chicken halfway through.

When cooking is complete, the chicken should be golden brown and crispy.

Transfer the chicken pieces on a large serving plate, then baste with sweet-and-sour sauce before serving.

694. EASY CAJUN CHICKEN DRUMSTICKS
Prep time: 5 minutes | Cook time: 18 minutes | Serves 5
- 1 tablespoon olive oil
- 10 chicken drumsticks
- 1½ tablespoons Cajun seasoning
- Salt and ground black pepper, to taste

Grease the perforated pan with olive oil.

On a clean work surface, rub the chicken drumsticks with Cajun seasoning, salt, and ground black pepper.

Arrange the seasoned chicken drumsticks in the perforated pan.

Select Air Fry of the oven. Set temperature to 390ºF (199ºC) and set time to 18 minutes. Press Start to begin preheating.

Once preheated, place the pan into the oven. Flip the drumsticks halfway through.

When cooking is complete, the drumsticks should be lightly browned.

Remove the chicken drumsticks from the oven. Serve immediately.

695. TERIYAKI CHICKEN THIGHS WITH LEMONY SNOW PEAS

Prep time: 30 minutes | Cook time: 34 minutes | Serves 4

- ¼ cup chicken broth
- ½ teaspoon grated fresh ginger
- ⅛ teaspoon red pepper flakes
- 1½ tablespoons soy sauce
- 4 (5-ounce / 142-g) bone-in chicken thighs, trimmed
- 1 tablespoon mirin
- ½ teaspoon cornstarch
- 1 tablespoon sugar
- 6 ounces (170 g) snow peas, strings removed
- ⅛ teaspoon lemon zest
- 1 garlic clove, minced
- ¼ teaspoon salt
- Ground black pepper, to taste
- ½ teaspoon lemon juice

Combine the broth, ginger, pepper flakes, and soy sauce in a large bowl. Stir to mix well.

Pierce 10 to 15 holes into the chicken skin. Put the chicken in the broth mixture and toss to coat well. Let sit for 10 minutes to marinate.

Transfer the marinated chicken on a plate and pat dry with paper towels. Scoop 2 tablespoons of marinade in a microwave-safe bowl and combine with mirin, cornstarch and sugar. Stir to mix well. Microwave for 1 minute or until frothy and has a thick consistency. Set aside.

Arrange the chicken in a perforated pan, skin side up.

Select Air Fry of the oven. Set temperature to 400°F (205°C) and set time to 25 minutes. Press Start to begin preheating.

Once preheated, place the pan into the oven. Flip the chicken halfway through.

When cooking is complete, brush the chicken skin with marinade mixture. Air fry the chicken for 5 more minutes or until glazed.

Remove the chicken from the oven. Allow the chicken to cool for 10 minutes.

Meanwhile, combine the snow peas, lemon zest, garlic, salt, and ground black pepper in a small bowl. Toss to coat well.

Transfer the snow peas in the perforated pan.

Select Air Fry of the oven. Set temperature to 400°F (205°C) and set time to 3 minutes.

When cooking is complete, the peas should be soft.

Remove the peas from the oven and toss with lemon juice.

Serve the chicken with lemony snow peas.

696. YAKITORI

Prep time: 10 minutes | Cook time: 15 minutes | Serves 4

- ½ cup mirin
- ¼ cup dry white wine
- ½ cup soy sauce
- 1 tablespoon light brown sugar
- 1½ pounds (680 g) boneless, skinless chicken thighs, cut into 1½-inch pieces, fat trimmed
- 4 medium scallions, trimmed, cut into 1½-inch pieces
- Cooking spray

Special Equipment:

4 (4-inch) bamboo skewers, soaked in water for at least 30 minutes

Combine the mirin, dry white wine, soy sauce, and brown sugar in a saucepan. Bring to a boil over medium heat. Keep stirring.

Boil for another 2 minutes or until it has a thick consistency. Turn off the heat.

Spritz a perforated pan with cooking spray.

Run the bamboo skewers through the chicken pieces and scallions alternatively.

Arrange the skewers in the perforated pan, then brush with mirin mixture on both sides. Spritz with cooking spray.

Select Air Fry of the oven. Set temperature to 400°F (205°C) and set time

to 10 minutes. Press Start to begin preheating.

Once preheated, place the pan into the oven. Flip the skewers halfway through.

When cooking is complete, the chicken and scallions should be glossy. Serve immediately.

697. CHINA SPICY TURKEY THIGHS

Prep time: 10 minutes | Cook time: 25 minutes | Serves 6

- 2 pounds (907 g) turkey thighs
- 1 teaspoon Chinese five-spice powder
- ¼ teaspoon Sichuan pepper
- 1 teaspoon pink Himalayan salt
- 1 tablespoon Chinese rice vinegar
- 1 tablespoon mustard
- 1 tablespoon chili sauce
- 2 tablespoons soy sauce
- Cooking spray

Spritz a perforated pan with cooking spray.

Rub the turkey thighs with five-spice powder, Sichuan pepper, and salt on a clean work surface.

Put the turkey thighs in the perforated pan and spritz with cooking spray.

Select Air Fry of the oven. Set temperature to 360°F (182°C) and set time to 22 minutes. Press Start to begin preheating.

Once preheated, place the pan into the oven. Flip the thighs at least three times during the cooking.

When cooking is complete, the thighs should be well browned.

Meanwhile, heat the remaining ingredients in a saucepan over medium-high heat. Cook for 3 minutes or until the sauce is thickened and reduces to two thirds.

Transfer the thighs onto a plate and baste with sauce before serving.

698. HERBED TURKEY BREAST WITH SIMPLE DIJON SAUCE

Prep time: 5 minutes | Cook time: 30 minutes | Serves 4

- 1 teaspoon chopped fresh sage
- 1 teaspoon chopped fresh tarragon
- 1 teaspoon chopped fresh thyme leaves
- 1 teaspoon chopped fresh rosemary leaves
- 1½ teaspoons sea salt
- 1 teaspoon ground black pepper
- 1 (2-pound / 907-g) turkey breast
- 3 tablespoons Dijon mustard
- 3 tablespoons butter, melted
- Cooking spray

Spritz a perforated pan with cooking spray.

Combine the herbs, salt, and black pepper in a small bowl. Stir to mix well. Set aside.

Combine the Dijon mustard and butter in a separate bowl. Stir to mix well.

Rub the turkey with the herb mixture on a clean work surface, then brush the turkey with Dijon mixture.

Arrange the turkey in the perforated pan.

Select Air Fry of the oven. Set temperature to 390°F (199°C) and set time to 30 minutes. Press Start to begin preheating.

Once preheated, place the pan into the oven. Flip the turkey breast halfway through.

When cooking is complete, an instant-read thermometer inserted in the thickest part of the turkey breast should reach at least 165 °F (74 °C).

Transfer the cooked turkey breast on a large plate and slice to serve.

699. LETTUCE-WRAPPED TURKEY AND MUSH-

ROOM MEATBALLS

Prep time: 10 minutes | Cook time: 15 minutes | Serves 6

Sauce:
- 2 tablespoons tamari
- 2 tablespoons tomato sauce
- 1 tablespoon lime juice
- ¼ teaspoon peeled and grated fresh ginger
- 1 clove garlic, smashed to a paste
- ½ cup chicken broth
- ⅓ cup sugar
- 2 tablespoons toasted sesame oil
- Cooking spray

Meatballs:
- 2 pounds (907 g) ground turkey
- ¾ cup finely chopped button mushrooms
- 2 large eggs, beaten
- 1½ teaspoons tamari
- ¼ cup finely chopped green onions, plus more for garnish
- 2 teaspoons peeled and grated fresh ginger
- 1 clove garlic, smashed
- 2 teaspoons toasted sesame oil
- 2 tablespoons sugar

For Serving:
- Lettuce leaves, for serving
- Sliced red chiles, for garnish (optional)
- Toasted sesame seeds, for garnish (optional)

Spritz a perforated pan with cooking spray.

Combine the ingredients for the sauce in a small bowl. Stir to mix well. Set aside.

Combine the ingredients for the meatballs in a large bowl. Stir to mix well, then shape the mixture in twelve 1½-inch meatballs.

Arrange the meatballs in the perforated pan, then baste with the sauce.

Select Air Fry of the oven. Set temperature to 350ºF (180ºC) and set time to 15 minutes. Press Start to begin preheating.

Once preheated, place the pan into the oven. Flip the balls halfway through.

When cooking is complete, the meatballs should be golden brown.

Unfold the lettuce leaves on a large serving plate, then transfer the cooked meatballs on the leaves. Spread the red chiles and sesame seeds over the balls, then serve.

700.ROSEMARY TURKEY BREAST

Prep time: 2 hours 20 minutes | Cook time: 30 minutes | Serves 6

- ½ teaspoon dried rosemary
- 2 minced garlic cloves
- 2 teaspoons salt
- 1 teaspoon ground black pepper
- ¼ cup olive oil
- 2½ pounds (1.1 kg) turkey breast
- ¼ cup pure maple syrup
- 1 tablespoon stone-ground brown mustard
- 1 tablespoon melted vegan butter

Combine the rosemary, garlic, salt, ground black pepper, and olive oil in a large bowl. Stir to mix well.

Dunk the turkey breast in the mixture and wrap the bowl in plastic. Refrigerate for 2 hours to marinate.

Remove the bowl from the refrigerator and let sit for half an hour before cooking.

Spritz a perforated pan with cooking spray.

Remove the turkey from the marinade and place in the perforated pan.

Select Air Fry of the oven. Set temperature to 400ºF (205ºC) and set time

to 20 minutes. Press Start to begin preheating.

Once preheated, place the pan into the oven. Flip the breast halfway through.

When cooking is complete, the breast should be well browned.

Meanwhile, combine the remaining ingredients in a small bowl. Stir to mix well.

Pour half of the butter mixture over the turkey breast in the oven and air fry for 10 more minutes. Flip the breast and pour the remaining half of butter mixture over halfway through.

Transfer the turkey on a plate and slice to serve.

701. SWEET MARINADED PORK CHOPS

Servings: 3
Cooking Time: 15 Minutes
INGREDIENTS:
- 3 pork chops, ½-inch thick
- Salt and black pepper to taste to season
- 1 tbsp maple syrup
- 1 ½ tbsp minced garlic
- 3 tbsp mustard

DIRECTIONS:

In a bowl, add maple syrup, garlic, mustard, salt, and pepper; mix well. Add in the pork and toss to coat. Slide-out the basket and place the chops inside. Fit in the baking tray and cook in your Cosori at 350 F for 6 minutes on Air Fry function.

Flip the chops with a spatula and cook further for 6 minutes. Once ready, remove them to a platter and serve with steamed asparagus.

702. STRAWBERRY-GLAZED TURKEY

Prep time: 15 minutes | Cook time: 37 minutes | Serves 2

- 2 pounds (907 g) turkey breast
- 1 tablespoon olive oil
- Salt and ground black pepper, to taste
- 1 cup fresh strawberries

Rub the turkey bread with olive oil on a clean work surface, then sprinkle with salt and ground black pepper.

Transfer the turkey in a perforated pan and spritz with cooking spray.

Select Air Fry of the oven. Set temperature to 375ºF (190ºC) and set time to 30 minutes. Press Start to begin preheating.

Once preheated, place the pan into the oven. Flip the turkey breast halfway through.

Meanwhile, put the strawberries in a food processor and pulse until smooth.

When cooking is complete, spread the puréed strawberries over the turkey and fry for 7 more minutes.

Serve immediately.

703. TURKEY AND CAULIFLOWER MEATLOAF

Prep time: 15 minutes | Cook time: 50 minutes | Serves 6

- 2 pounds (907 g) lean ground turkey
- 1⅓ cups riced cauliflower
- 2 large eggs, lightly beaten
- ¼ cup almond flour
- ⅔ cup chopped yellow or white onion
- 1 teaspoon ground dried turmeric
- 1 teaspoon ground cumin
- 1 teaspoon ground coriander
- 1 tablespoon minced garlic
- 1 teaspoon salt
- 1 teaspoon ground black pepper
- Cooking spray

Spritz a loaf pan with cooking spray.

Combine all the ingredients in a large bowl. Stir to mix well. Pour half of the mixture in the prepared loaf pan and press with a spatula to coat the bottom evenly. Spritz the mixture with cooking spray.

Select Bake of the oven. Set temperature to 350ºF (180ºC) and set time to 25 minutes. Press Start to begin preheating.

Once preheated, place the pan into the oven.

When cooking is complete, the meat should be well browned and the internal temperature should reach at least 165 ºF (74 ºC).

Remove the loaf pan from the oven and serve immediately.

704. DEEP FRIED DUCK LEG QUARTERS

Prep time: 5 minutes | Cook time: 45 minutes | Serves 4

- 4 (½-pound / 227-g) skin-on duck leg quarters
- 2 medium garlic cloves, minced
- ½ teaspoon salt
- ½ teaspoon ground black pepper

Spritz a perforated pan with cooking spray.

On a clean work surface, rub the duck leg quarters with garlic, salt, and black pepper.

Arrange the leg quarters in the perforated pan and spritz with cooking spray.

Select Air Fry of the oven. Set temperature to 300ºF (150ºC) and set time to 30 minutes. Press Start to begin preheating.

Once preheated, place the pan into the oven.

After 30 minutes, remove the pan from the oven. Flip the leg quarters. Increase temperature to 375ºF (190ºC) and set time to 15 minutes. Return the pan to the oven and continue cooking.

When cooking is complete, the leg quarters should be well browned and crispy.

Remove the duck leg quarters from the oven and allow to cool for 10 minutes before serving.

705. DUCK BREASTS WITH MARMALADE BALSAMIC GLAZE

Prep time: 5 minutes | Cook time: 13 minutes | Serves 4

- 4 (6-ounce / 170-g) skin-on duck breasts
- 1 teaspoon salt
- ¼ cup orange marmalade
- 1 tablespoon white balsamic vinegar
- ¾ teaspoon ground black pepper

Cut 10 slits into the skin of the duck breasts, then sprinkle with salt on both sides.

Place the breasts in a perforated pan, skin side up.

Select Air Fry of the oven. Set temperature to 400ºF (205ºC) and set time to 10 minutes. Press Start to begin preheating.

Once preheated, place the pan into the oven.

Meanwhile, combine the remaining ingredients in a small bowl. Stir to mix well.

When cooking is complete, brush the duck skin with the marmalade mixture. Flip the breast and air fry for 3 more minutes or until the skin is crispy and the breast is well browned.

Serve immediately.

706. GLAZED DUCK WITH CHERRY SAUCE

Prep time: 20 minutes | Cook time: 32 minutes | Serves 12

- 1 whole duck (about 5 pounds / 2.3 kg in total), split in half, back and rib bones removed, fat trimmed
- 1 teaspoon olive oil
- Salt and freshly ground black pepper, to taste
- Cherry Sauce:
- 1 tablespoon butter

- 1 shallot, minced
- ½ cup sherry
- 1 cup chicken stock
- 1 teaspoon white wine vinegar
- ¾ cup cherry preserves
- 1 teaspoon fresh thyme leaves
- Salt and freshly ground black pepper, to taste

On a clean work surface, rub the duck with olive oil, then sprinkle with salt and ground black pepper to season.

Place the duck in a perforated pan, breast side up.

Select Air Fry of the oven. Set temperature to 400ºF (205ºC) and set time to 25 minutes. Press Start to begin preheating.

Once preheated, place the pan into the oven. Flip the ducks halfway through the cooking time.

Meanwhile, make the cherry sauce: Heat the butter in a skillet over medium-high heat or until melted.

Add the shallot and sauté for 5 minutes or until lightly browned.

Add the sherry and simmer for 6 minutes or until it reduces in half.

Add the chicken stick, white wine vinegar, and cherry preserves. Stir to combine well. Simmer for 6 more minutes or until thickened.

Fold in the thyme leaves and sprinkle with salt and ground black pepper. Stir to mix well.

When the cooking of the duck is complete, glaze the duck with a quarter of the cherry sauce, then air fry for another 4 minutes.

Flip the duck and glaze with another quarter of the cherry sauce. Air fry for an additional 3 minutes.

Transfer the duck on a large plate and serve with remaining cherry sauce.

707. ROASTED PEPPER CHICKEN THIGHS

Servings: 4

Cooking Time: 55 Minutes

INGREDIENTS:

- 8 chicken thighs
- 1 1/2 lbs potatoes, cut into small chunks
- 6 garlic cloves, crushed
- 1/4 cup capers, drained
- 10 oz jar roasted red peppers, drained and sliced
- 2 cups grape tomatoes
- 4 tbsp olive oil
- 1 tsp dried oregano
- Pepper
- Salt

DIRECTIONS:

Fit the Cosori oven with the rack in position

Season chicken with pepper and salt.

Heat 2 tablespoons of olive oil in a pan over medium heat.

Add chicken to the pan and sear until brown from all the sides.

Transfer chicken in baking pan.

Add tomato, potatoes, capers, oregano, garlic, and red peppers around the chicken. Drizzle with remaining olive oil.

Set to bake at 400 F for 60 minutes. After 5 minutes place the baking pan in the preheated oven.

Serve and enjoy.

Nutrition Info: Calories 542 Fat 21.9 g Carbohydrates 45.1 g Sugar 4.4 g Protein 35.6 g Cholesterol 89 mg

708. THAI GAME HENS WITH CUCUMBER AND CHILE SALAD

Prep time: 25 minutes | Cook time: 25 minutes | Serves 6

- 2 (1¼-pound / 567-g) Cornish game hens, giblets discarded
- 1 tablespoon fish sauce
- 6 tablespoons chopped fresh cilantro
- 2 teaspoons lime zest

- 1 teaspoon ground coriander
- 2 garlic cloves, minced
- 2 tablespoons packed light brown sugar
- 2 teaspoons vegetable oil
- Salt and ground black pepper, to taste
- 1 English cucumber, halved lengthwise and sliced thin
- 1 Thai chile, stemmed, deseeded, and minced
- 2 tablespoons chopped dry-roasted peanuts
- 1 small shallot, sliced thinly
- 1 tablespoon lime juice
- Lime wedges, for serving
- Cooking spray

Arrange a game hen on a clean work surface, remove the backbone with kitchen shears, then pound the hen breast to flat. Cut the breast in half. Repeat with the remaining game hen.

Loose the breast and thigh skin with your fingers, then pat the game hens dry and pierce about 10 holes into the fat deposits of the hens. Tuck the wings under the hens.

Combine 2 teaspoons of fish sauce, ¼ cup of cilantro, lime zest, coriander, garlic, 4 teaspoons of sugar, 1 teaspoon of vegetable oil, ½ teaspoon of salt, and ⅛ teaspoon of ground black pepper in a small bowl. Stir to mix well.

Rub the fish sauce mixture under the breast and thigh skin of the game hens, then let sit for 10 minutes to marinate.

Spritz a perforated pan with cooking spray.

Arrange the marinated game hens in the preheated perforated pan, skin side down.

Select Air Fry of the oven. Set temperature to 400ºF (205ºC) and set time to 25 minutes. Press Start to begin preheating.

Once preheated, place the pan into the oven. Flip the game hens halfway through the cooking time.

When cooking is complete, the hen skin should be golden brown and the internal temperature of the hens should read at least 165 ºF (74 ºC). Meanwhile, combine all the remaining ingredients, except for the lime wedges, in a large bowl and sprinkle with salt and black pepper. Toss to mix well.

Transfer the fried hens on a large plate, then sit the salad aside and squeeze the lime wedges over before serving.

709. BACON-WRAPPED TURKEY WITH CARROTS
Prep time: 10 minutes | Cook time: 25 minutes | Serves 4

- 2 (12-ounce / 340-g) turkey tenderloins
- 1 teaspoon kosher salt, divided
- 6 slices bacon
- 3 tablespoons balsamic vinegar
- 2 tablespoons honey
- 1 tablespoon Dijon mustard
- ½ teaspoon dried thyme
- 6 large carrots, peeled and cut into ¼-inch rounds
- 1 tablespoon olive oil

Sprinkle the turkey with ¾ teaspoon of the salt. Wrap each tenderloin with 3 strips of bacon, securing the bacon with toothpicks. Place the turkey in a baking pan.

In a small bowl, mix the balsamic vinegar, honey, mustard, and thyme. Place the carrots in a medium bowl and drizzle with the oil. Add 1 tablespoon of the balsamic mixture and ¼ teaspoon of kosher salt and toss to coat. Place these on the pan around the turkey tenderloins. Baste the tenderloins with about one-half of the remaining balsamic mixture.

Select Roast, set temperature to 375ºF (190ºC), and set time to 25 minutes. Press Start to begin preheating.

Once preheated, place the pan into the oven.

After 13 minutes, remove the pan from the oven. Gently stir the carrots. Flip the tenderloins and baste with the remaining balsamic mixture. Return the pan to the oven and continue cooking.

When cooking is complete, the carrots should tender and the center of the tenderloins should register 165 ºF (74 ºC) on a meat thermometer. Remove the pan from the oven. Slice the turkey and serve with the carrots.

710. BALSAMIC CHICKEN BREAST ROAST
Prep time: 35 minutes | Cook time: 40 minutes | Serves 2

- ¼ cup balsamic vinegar
- 2 teaspoons dried oregano
- 2 garlic cloves, minced
- 1 tablespoon olive oil
- ⅛ teaspoon salt
- ½ teaspoon freshly ground black pepper
- 2 (4-ounce / 113-g) boneless, skinless, chicken-breast halves
- Cooking spray

In a small bowl, add the vinegar, oregano, garlic, olive oil, salt, and pepper. Mix to combine.

Put the chicken in a resealable plastic bag. Pour the vinegar mixture in the bag with the chicken, seal the bag, and shake to coat the chicken. Refrigerate for 30 minutes to marinate.

Spritz a baking pan with cooking spray. Put the chicken in the prepared baking pan and pour the marinade over the chicken.

Select Bake. Set temperature to 400ºF (205ºC) and set time to 40 minutes. Press Start to begin preheating.

Once preheated, place the pan into the oven.

After 20 minutes, remove the pan from the oven. Flip the chicken. Return the pan to the oven and continue cooking.

When cooking is complete, the internal temperature of the chicken should registers at least 165ºF (74ºC).

Let sit for 5 minutes, then serve.

711. BRAISED CHICKEN WITH HOT PEPPERS
Prep time: 10 minutes | Cook time: 27 minutes | Serves 4

- 4 bone-in, skin-on chicken thighs (about 1½ pounds / 680 g)
- 1½ teaspoon kosher salt, divided
- 1 link sweet Italian sausage (about 4 ounces / 113 g), whole
- 8 ounces (227 g) miniature bell peppers, halved and deseeded
- 1 small onion, thinly sliced
- 2 garlic cloves, minced
- 1 tablespoon olive oil
- 4 hot pickled cherry peppers, deseeded and quartered, along with 2 tablespoons pickling liquid from the jar
- ¼ cup chicken stock
- Cooking spray

Salt the chicken thighs on both sides with 1 teaspoon of kosher salt. Spritz a baking pan with cooking spray and place the thighs skin-side down on the pan. Add the sausage.

Select Roast, set temperature to 375ºF (190ºC), and set time to 27 minutes. Press Start to begin preheating.

Once preheated, place the pan into the oven.

While the chicken and sausage cook, place the bell peppers, onion, and garlic in a large bowl. Sprinkle with the remaining kosher salt and add the olive oil. Toss to coat.

After 10 minutes, remove the pan from the oven and flip the chicken thighs and sausage. Add the pepper mixture to the pan. Return the pan to the oven and continue cooking.

After another 10 minutes, remove the pan from the oven and add the pickled peppers, pickling liquid, and stock. Stir the pickled peppers into the peppers and onion. Return the pan to the oven and continue cooking.

When cooking is complete, the peppers and onion should be soft and the chicken should read 165ºF (74ºC) on a meat thermometer. Remove the pan from the oven. Slice the sausage into thin pieces and stir it into the pepper mixture. Spoon the peppers over four plates. Top with a chicken thigh.

712. CHEESY MARINARA CHICKEN BREASTS

Prep time: 30 minutes | Cook time: 1 hour | Serves 2

- 1 large egg
- ¼ cup almond meal
- 2 (6-ounce / 170-g) boneless, skinless chicken breast halves
- 1 (8-ounce / 227-g) jar marinara sauce, divided
- 4 tablespoons shredded Mozzarella cheese, divided
- 4 tablespoons grated Parmesan cheese, divided
- 4 tablespoons chopped fresh basil, divided
- Salt and freshly ground black pepper, to taste
- Cooking spray

Spritz a perforated pan with cooking spray.

In a shallow bowl, beat the egg.

In a separate shallow bowl, place the almond meal.

Dip 1 chicken breast half into the egg, then into the almond meal to coat. Place the coated chicken in the perforated pan. Repeat with the remaining 1 chicken breast half.

Select Bake. Set temperature to 350ºF (180ºC) and set time to 40 minutes. Press Start to begin preheating.

Once preheated, place the perforated pan in the oven.

After 20 minutes, remove the pan from the oven and flip the chicken. Return the pan to oven and continue cooking.

When cooking is complete, the chicken should no longer pink and the juices run clear.

In a baking pan, pour half of marinara sauce.

Place the cooked chicken in the sauce. Cover with the remaining marinara.

Sprinkle 2 tablespoons of Mozzarella cheese and 2 tablespoons of soy Parmesan cheese on each chicken breast. Top each with 2 tablespoons of basil.

Place the baking pan back in the oven and set the baking time to 20 minutes. Flip the chicken halfway through the cooking time.

When cooking is complete, an instant-read thermometer inserted into the center of the chicken should read at least 165ºF (74ºC).

Remove the pan from oven and divide between 2 plates. Season with salt and pepper and serve.

713. CHEESY TURKEY BURGERS

Prep time: 10 minutes | Cook time: 25 minutes | Serves 4

- 2 medium yellow onions
- 1 tablespoon olive oil
- 1½ teaspoons kosher salt, divided
- 1¼ pound (567 g) ground turkey
- ⅓ cup mayonnaise
- 1 tablespoon Dijon mustard
- 2 teaspoons Worcestershire sauce
- 4 slices sharp Cheddar cheese (about 4 ounces / 113 g in total)
- 4 hamburger buns, sliced

Trim the onions and cut them in half through the root. Cut one of the halves in half. Grate one quarter. Place the grated onion in a large bowl. Thinly slice the remaining onions and place in a medium bowl with the oil and ½ teaspoon of kosher salt. Toss to coat. Place the onions in a single layer on a baking pan.

Select Roast, set temperature to 350ºF (180ºC), and set time to 10 minutes. Press Start to begin preheating.

Once preheated, place the pan into the oven.

While the onions are cooking, add the turkey to the grated onion. Add the remaining kosher salt, mayonnaise, mustard, and Worcestershire sauce. Mix just until combined, being careful not to overwork the turkey. Divide the mixture into 4 patties, each about ¾-inch thick.

When cooking is complete, remove the pan from the oven. Move the

onions to one side of the pan and place the burgers on the pan. Poke your finger into the center of each burger to make a deep indentation.

Select Broil, set temperature to High, and set time to 12 minutes. Press Start to begin preheating.

Once preheated, place the pan into the oven. After 6 minutes, remove the pan. Turn the burgers and stir the onions. Return the pan to the oven and continue cooking. After about 4 minutes, remove the pan and place the cheese slices on the burgers. Return the pan to the oven and continue cooking for about 1 minute, or until the cheese is melted and the center of the burgers has reached at least 165 ºF (74 ºC) on a meat thermometer. When cooking is complete, remove the pan from the oven. Loosely cover the burgers with foil.

Lay out the buns, cut-side up, on the oven rack. Select Broil; set temperature to High, and set time to 3 minutes. Select Start to begin. Check the buns after 2 minutes; they should be lightly browned.

Remove the buns from the oven. Assemble the burgers and serve.

714. CHICKEN AND SWEET POTATO CURRY

Prep time: 10 minutes | Cook time: 20 minutes | Serves 4

- 1 pound (454 g) boneless, skinless chicken thighs
- 1 teaspoon kosher salt, divided
- ¼ cup unsalted butter, melted
- 1 tablespoon curry powder
- 2 medium sweet potatoes, peeled and cut in 1-inch cubes
- 12 ounces (340 g) Brussels sprouts, halved

Sprinkle the chicken thighs with ½ teaspoon of kosher salt. Place them in the single layer on a baking pan.

In a small bowl, stir together the butter and curry powder.

Place the sweet potatoes and Brussels sprouts in a large bowl. Drizzle half the curry butter over the vegetables and add the remaining kosher salt. Toss to coat. Transfer the vegetables to the baking pan and place in a single layer around the chicken. Brush half of the remaining curry butter over the chicken.

Select Roast, set temperature to 400ºF (205ºC), and set time to 20 minutes. Press Start to begin preheating.

Once preheated, place the pan into the oven.

After 10 minutes, remove the pan from the oven and turn over the chicken thighs. Baste them with the remaining curry butter. Return the pan to the oven and continue cooking.

Cooking is complete when the sweet potatoes are tender and the chicken is cooked through and reads 165ºF (74ºC) on a meat thermometer.

715. CHICKEN CIABATTA SANDWICHES

Prep time: 12 minutes | Cook time: 13 minutes | Serves 4

- 2 (8-ounce / 227-g) boneless, skinless chicken breasts
- 1 teaspoon kosher salt, divided
- 1 cup all-purpose flour
- 1 teaspoon Italian seasoning
- 2 large eggs
- 2 tablespoons plain yogurt
- 2 cups panko bread crumbs
- 1⅓ cups grated Parmesan cheese, divided
- 2 tablespoons olive oil
- 4 ciabatta rolls, split in half
- ½ cup marinara sauce
- ½ cup shredded Mozzarella cheese

Lay the chicken breasts on a cutting board and cut each one in half parallel to the board so you have 4 fairly even, flat fillets. Place a piece of plastic wrap over the chicken pieces and use a rolling pin to gently pound them to an even thickness, about ½-inch thick. Season the chicken on both sides with ½ teaspoon of kosher salt.

Place the flour on a plate and add the remaining kosher salt and the Italian seasoning. Mix with a fork to distribute evenly. In a wide bowl, whisk together the eggs with the yogurt. In a small bowl combine the panko, 1 cup of Parmesan cheese, and olive oil. Place this in a shallow bowl.

Lightly dredge both sides of the chicken pieces in the seasoned flour, and then dip them in the egg wash to coat completely, letting the excess drip off. Finally, dredge the chicken in the bread crumbs. Carefully place the breaded chicken pieces in the perforated pan.

Select Air Fry, set temperature to 375°F (190°C), and set time to 10 minutes. Press Start to begin preheating.

Once preheated, place the perforated pan into the oven.

After 5 minutes, remove the perforated pan from the oven. Carefully turn the chicken over. Return the perforated pan to the oven and continue cooking. When cooking is complete, remove the perforated pan from the oven.

Unfold the rolls on the perforated pan and spread each half with 1 tablespoon of marinara sauce. Place a chicken breast piece on the bottoms of the buns and sprinkle the remaining Parmesan cheese over the chicken pieces. Divide the Mozzarella among the top halves of the buns.

Select Broil, set temperature to High, and set time to 3 minutes. Press Start to begin preheating.

Once preheated, place the perforated pan into the oven. Check the sandwiches halfway through. When cooking is complete, the Mozzarella cheese should be melted and bubbly.

Remove the perforated pan from the oven. Close the sandwiches and serve.

716. CHICKEN SHAWARMA

Prep time: 10 minutes | Cook time: 18 minutes | Serves 4

1½ pounds (680 g) boneless, skinless chicken thighs
1¼ teaspoon kosher salt, divided
2 tablespoons plus 1 teaspoon olive oil, divided
⅔ cup plus 2 tablespoons plain Greek yogurt, divided
2 tablespoons freshly squeezed lemon juice (about 1 medium lemon)
4 garlic cloves, minced, divided
1 tablespoon Shawarma Seasoning
4 pita breads, cut in half
2 cups cherry tomatoes
½ small cucumber, peeled, deseeded, and chopped
1 tablespoon chopped fresh parsley

Sprinkle the chicken thighs on both sides with 1 teaspoon of kosher salt. Place in a resealable plastic bag and set aside while you make the marinade.

In a small bowl, mix 2 tablespoons of olive oil, 2 tablespoons of yogurt, the lemon juice, 3 garlic cloves, and Shawarma Seasoning until thoroughly combined. Pour the marinade over the chicken. Seal the bag, squeezing out as much air as possible. And massage the chicken to coat it with the sauce. Set aside.

Wrap 2 pita breads each in two pieces of aluminum foil and place on a baking pan.

Select Bake, set temperature to 300°F (150°C), and set time to 6 minutes. Press Start to begin preheating.

Once the oven has preheated, place the pan into the oven. After 3 minutes, remove the pan from the oven and turn over the foil packets. Return the pan to the oven and continue cooking. When cooking is complete, remove the pan from the oven and place the foil-wrapped pitas on the top of the oven to keep warm.

Remove the chicken from the marinade, letting the excess drip off into the bag. Place them on the baking pan. Arrange the tomatoes around the sides of the chicken. Discard the marinade.

Select Broil, set temperature to High, and set time to 12 minutes. Press Start to begin preheating.

Once preheated, place the pan into the oven.

After 6 minutes, remove the pan from the oven and turn over the chicken. Return the pan to the oven and continue cooking.

Wrap the cucumber in a paper towel to remove as much moisture as possible. Place them in a small bowl. Add the remaining yogurt, kosher salt, olive oil, garlic clove, and parsley. Whisk until combined.

When cooking is complete, the chicken should be browned, crisp along

its edges, and sizzling. Remove the pan from the oven and place the chicken on a cutting board. Cut each thigh into several pieces. Unwrap the pitas. Spread a tablespoon of sauce into a pita half. Add some chicken and add 2 roasted tomatoes. Serve.

717. CHICKEN SKEWERS WITH CORN SALAD

Prep time: 17 minutes | Cook time: 10 minutes | Serves 4

- 1 pound (454 g) boneless, skinless chicken breast, cut into 1½-inch chunks
- 1 green bell pepper, deseeded and cut into 1-inch pieces
- 1 red bell pepper, deseeded and cut into 1-inch pieces
- 1 large onion, cut into large chunks
- 2 tablespoons fajita seasoning
- 3 tablespoons vegetable oil, divided
- 2 teaspoons kosher salt, divided
- 2 cups corn, drained
- ¼ teaspoon granulated garlic
- 1 teaspoon freshly squeezed lime juice
- 1 tablespoon mayonnaise
- 3 tablespoons grated Parmesan cheese

Special Equipment:
12 wooden skewers, soaked in water for at least 30 minutes

Place the chicken, bell peppers, and onion in a large bowl. Add the fajita seasoning, 2 tablespoons of vegetable oil, and 1½ teaspoons of kosher salt. Toss to coat evenly.

Alternate the chicken and vegetables on the skewers, making about 12 skewers.

Place the corn in a medium bowl and add the remaining vegetable oil. Add the remaining kosher salt and the garlic, and toss to coat. Place the corn in an even layer on a baking pan and place the skewers on top.

Select Roast, set temperature to 375°F (190°C), and set time to 10 minutes. Press Start to begin preheating.

Once preheated, place the pan into the oven.

After about 5 minutes, remove the pan from the oven and turn the skewers. Return the pan to the oven and continue cooking.

When cooking is complete, remove the pan from the oven. Place the skewers on a platter. Put the corn back to the bowl and combine with the lime juice, mayonnaise, and Parmesan cheese. Stir to mix well. Serve the skewers with the corn.

718. CHICKEN THIGHS WITH RADISH SLAW

Prep time: 10 minutes | Cook time: 27 minutes | Serves 4

- 4 bone-in, skin-on chicken thighs
- 1½ teaspoon kosher salt, divided
- 1 tablespoon smoked paprika
- ½ teaspoon granulated garlic
- ½ teaspoon dried oregano
- ¼ teaspoon freshly ground black pepper
- 3 cups shredded cabbage
- ½ small red onion, thinly sliced
- 4 large radishes, julienned
- 3 tablespoons red wine vinegar
- 2 tablespoons olive oil
- Cooking spray

Salt the chicken thighs on both sides with 1 teaspoon of kosher salt. In a small bowl, combine the paprika, garlic, oregano, and black pepper. Sprinkle half this mixture over the skin sides of the thighs. Spritz a baking pan with cooking spray and place the thighs skin-side down on the pan. Sprinkle the remaining spice mixture over the other sides of the chicken pieces.

Select Roast, set temperature to 375°F (190°C), and set time to 27 minutes. Press Start to begin preheating.

Once preheated, place the pan into the oven.

After 10 minutes, remove the pan from the oven and turn over the chicken thighs. Return the pan to the oven and continue cooking.

While the chicken cooks, place the cabbage, onion, and radishes in a large bowl. Sprinkle with the remaining kosher salt, vinegar, and olive oil. Toss to coat.

After another 9 to 10 minutes, remove the pan from the oven and place the chicken thighs on a cutting board. Place the cabbage mixture in the pan and toss with the chicken fat and spices.

Spread the cabbage in an even layer on the pan and place the chicken on it, skin-side up. Return the pan to the oven and continue cooking. Roast for another 7 to 8 minutes.

When cooking is complete, the cabbage is just becoming tender. Remove the pan from the oven. Taste and adjust the seasoning if necessary. Serve.

719. CHICKEN WITH POTATOES AND CORN

Prep time: 10 minutes | Cook time: 25 minutes | Serves 4

- 4 bone-in, skin-on chicken thighs
- 2 teaspoons kosher salt, divided
- 1 cup Bisquick baking mix
- ½ cup butter, melted, divided
- 1 pound (454 g) small red potatoes, quartered
- 3 ears corn, shucked and cut into rounds 1- to 1½-inches thick
- ⅓ cup heavy whipping cream
- ½ teaspoon freshly ground black pepper

Sprinkle the chicken on all sides with 1 teaspoon of kosher salt. Place the baking mix in a shallow dish. Brush the thighs on all sides with ¼ cup of butter, then dredge them in the baking mix, coating them all on sides. Place the chicken in the center of a baking pan.

Place the potatoes in a large bowl with 2 tablespoons of butter and toss to coat. Place them on one side of the chicken on the pan.

Place the corn in a medium bowl and drizzle with the remaining butter. Sprinkle with ¼ teaspoon of kosher salt and toss to coat. Place on the pan on the other side of the chicken.

Select Roast, set temperature to 375ºF (190ºC), and set time to 25 minutes. Press Start to begin preheating.

Once preheated, place the pan into the oven.

After 20 minutes, remove the pan from the oven and transfer the potatoes back to the bowl. Return the pan to oven and continue cooking.

As the chicken continues cooking, add the cream, black pepper, and remaining kosher salt to the potatoes. Lightly mash the potatoes with a potato masher.

When cooking is complete, the corn should be tender and the chicken cooked through, reading 165ºF (74ºC) on a meat thermometer. Remove the pan from the oven and serve the chicken with the smashed potatoes and corn on the side.

720. CREOLE HENS

Prep time: 10 minutes | Cook time: 40 minutes | Serves 4

- ½ tablespoon Creole seasoning
- ½ tablespoon garlic powder
- ½ tablespoon onion powder
- ½ tablespoon freshly ground black pepper
- ½ tablespoon paprika
- 2 tablespoons olive oil
- 2 Cornish hens
- Cooking spray

Spritz a perforated pan with cooking spray.

In a small bowl, mix the Creole seasoning, garlic powder, onion powder, pepper, and paprika.

Pat the Cornish hens dry and brush each hen all over with the olive oil. Rub each hen with the seasoning mixture. Place the Cornish hens in the perforated pan.

Select Air Fry of the oven. Set the temperature to 375ºF (190ºC) and set the time to 30 minutes. Press Start to begin preheating.

Once preheated, place the pan in the oven.

After 15 minutes, remove the pan from the oven. Flip the hens over and baste it with any drippings collected in the bottom drawer of the oven. Return the pan to the oven and continue cooking.

When cooking is complete, a thermometer inserted into the thickest part of the hens should reach at least 165ºF (74ºC).

Let the hens rest for 10 minutes before carving.

721. GNOCCHI WITH CHICKEN AND SPINACH

Prep time: 10 minutes | Cook time: 13 minutes | Serves 4

- 1 (1-pound / 454-g) package shelf-stable gnocchi
- 1¼ cups chicken stock
- ½ teaspoon kosher salt
- 1 pound (454 g) chicken breast, cut into 1-inch chunks
- 1 cup heavy whipping cream
- 2 tablespoons sun-dried tomato purée
- 1 garlic clove, minced
- 1 cup frozen spinach, thawed and drained
- 1 cup grated Parmesan cheese

Place the gnocchi in an even layer on a baking pan. Pour the chicken stock over the gnocchi.

Select Bake, set temperature to 450ºF (235ºC), and set time to 7 minutes. Press Start to begin preheating.

Once preheated, place the pan into the oven.

While the gnocchi are cooking, sprinkle the salt over the chicken pieces. In a small bowl, mix the cream, tomato purée, and garlic.

When cooking is complete, blot off any remaining stock, or drain the gnocchi and return it to the pan. Top the gnocchi with the spinach and chicken. Pour the cream mixture over the ingredients in the pan.

Select Roast, set temperature to 400ºF (205ºC), and set time to 6 minutes. Press Start to begin preheating.

Once preheated, place the pan into the oven.

After 4 minutes, remove the pan from the oven and gently stir the ingredients. Return the pan to the oven and continue cooking.

When cooking is complete, the gnocchi should be tender and the chicken should be cooked through. Remove the pan from the oven. Stir in the Parmesan cheese until it's melted and serve.

722. GOLDEN CHICKEN FRIES

Prep time: 20 minutes | Cook time: 6 minutes | Serves 4 to 6

- 1 pound (454 g) chicken tenders, cut into about ½-inch-wide strips
- Salt, to taste
- ¼ cup all-purpose flour
- 2 eggs
- ¾ cup panko bread crumbs
- ¾ cup crushed organic nacho cheese tortilla chips
- Cooking spray
- Seasonings:
- ½ teaspoon garlic powder
- 1 tablespoon chili powder
- ½ teaspoon onion powder
- 1 teaspoon ground cumin

Stir together all seasonings in a small bowl and set aside.

Sprinkle the chicken with salt. Place strips in a large bowl and sprinkle with 1 tablespoon of the seasoning mix. Stir well to distribute seasonings.

Add flour to chicken and stir well to coat all sides.

Beat eggs in a separate bowl.

In a shallow dish, combine the panko, crushed chips, and the remaining 2 teaspoons of seasoning mix.

Dip chicken strips in eggs, then roll in crumbs. Mist with oil or cooking spray. Arrange the chicken strips in a single layer in the perforated pan.

Select Air Fry of the oven. Set the temperature to 400°F (205°C) and set the time to 6 minutes. Press Start to begin preheating.

Once preheated, place the pan in the oven.

After 4 minutes, remove the pan from the oven. Flip the strips with tongs. Return the pan to the oven and continue cooking.

When cooking is complete, the chicken should be crispy and its juices should be run clear.

Allow to cool under room temperature before serving.

723. PEACH AND CHERRY CHICKEN

Prep time: 8 minutes | Cook time: 15 minutes | Serves 4

- ⅓ cup peach preserves
- 1 teaspoon ground rosemary
- ½ teaspoon black pepper
- ½ teaspoon salt
- ½ teaspoon marjoram
- 1 teaspoon light olive oil
- 1 pound (454 g) boneless chicken breasts, cut in 1½-inch chunks
- 1 (10-ounce / 284-g) package frozen dark cherries, thawed and drained
- Cooking spray

In a medium bowl, mix peach preserves, rosemary, pepper, salt, marjoram, and olive oil.

Stir in chicken chunks and toss to coat well with the preserve mixture.

Spritz a perforated pan with cooking spray and lay chicken chunks in the perforated pan.

Select Bake of the oven. Set the temperature to 400°F (205°C) and set the time to 15 minutes. Press Start to begin preheating.

Once preheated, place the pan in the oven.

After 7 minutes, remove the pan from the oven. Flip the chicken chunks. Return the pan to the oven and continue cooking.

When cooking is complete, the chicken should no longer pink and the juices should run clear.

Scatter the cherries over and cook for an additional minute to heat cherries.

Serve immediately.

724. PINEAPPLE CHICKEN

Prep time: 10 minutes | Cook time: 10 minutes | Serves 6

- 1½ pounds (680 g) boneless, skinless chicken breasts, cut into 1-inch chunks
- ¾ cup soy sauce
- 2 tablespoons ketchup
- 2 tablespoons brown sugar
- 2 tablespoons rice vinegar
- 1 red bell pepper, cut into 1-inch chunks
- 1 green bell pepper, cut into 1-inch chunks
- 6 scallions, cut into 1-inch pieces
- 1 cup (¾-inch chunks) fresh pineapple, rinsed and drained
- Cooking spray

Place the chicken in a large bowl. Add the soy sauce, ketchup, brown sugar, vinegar, red and green peppers, and scallions. Toss to coat.

Spritz a baking pan with cooking spray and place the chicken and vegetables on the pan.

Select Roast, set temperature to 375°F (190°C), and set time to 10 minutes. Press Start to begin preheating.

Once preheated, place the pan into the oven.

After 6 minutes, remove the pan from the oven. Add the pineapple chunks to the pan and stir. Return the pan to the oven and continue cooking.

When cooking is complete, remove the pan from the oven. Serve with steamed rice, if desired.

725. RITZY CHICKEN ROAST

Prep time: 15 minutes | Cook time: 1 hour | Serves 6

- 1 teaspoon Italian seasoning
- ½ teaspoon garlic powder
- ½ teaspoon paprika
- 1 teaspoon salt
- ½ teaspoon freshly ground black pepper
- ½ teaspoon onion powder
- 2 tablespoons olive oil
- 1 (3-pound / 1.4-kg) whole chicken, giblets removed, pat dry
- Cooking spray

Spritz a perforated pan with cooking spray.

In a small bowl, mix the Italian seasoning, garlic powder, paprika, salt, pepper, and onion powder.

Brush the chicken with the olive oil and rub it with the seasoning mixture.

Tie the chicken legs with butcher's twine. Place the chicken in the perforated pan, breast side down.

Select Air Fry of the oven. Set the temperature to 350°F (180°C) and set the time to an hour. Press Start to begin preheating.

Once preheated, place the pan in the oven.

After 30 minutes, remove the pan from the oven. Flip the chicken over and baste it with any drippings collected in the bottom drawer of the oven. Return the pan to the oven and continue cooking.

When cooking is complete, a thermometer inserted into the thickest part of the thigh should reach at least 165°F (74°C).

Let the chicken rest for 10 minutes before carving and serving.

726. SIMPLE HERBED HENS

Prep time: 2 hours 15 minutes | Cook time: 30 minutes | Serves 8

- 4 (1¼-pound / 567-g) Cornish hens, giblets removed, split lengthwise
- 2 cups white wine, divided
- 2 garlic cloves, minced
- 1 small onion, minced
- ½ teaspoon celery seeds
- ½ teaspoon poultry seasoning
- ½ teaspoon paprika
- ½ teaspoon dried oregano
- ¼ teaspoon freshly ground black pepper

Place the hens, cavity side up, on a rack in a baking pan. Pour 1½ cups of the wine over the hens; set aside.

In a shallow bowl, combine the garlic, onion, celery seeds, poultry seasoning, paprika, oregano, and pepper. Sprinkle half of the combined seasonings over the cavity of each split half. Cover and refrigerate. Allow the hens to marinate for 2 hours.

Transfer the hens in the perforated pan. Select Bake, set temperature to 350°F (180°C) and set time to 90 minutes. Press Start to begin preheating.

Once preheated, place the pan into the oven.

Remove the pan from the oven halfway through the baking, turn breast side up, and remove the skin. Pour the remaining ½ cup of wine over the top, and sprinkle with the remaining seasonings.

When cooking is complete, the inner temperature of the hens should be at least 165 °F (74 °C). Transfer the hens to a serving platter and serve hot.

727. SUPER LEMON CHICKEN

Prep time: 5 minutes | Cook time: 35 minutes | Serves 6

- 3 (8-ounce / 227-g) boneless, skinless chicken breasts, halved,

rinsed
- 1 cup dried bread crumbs
- ¼ cup olive oil
- ¼ cup chicken broth
- Zest of 1 lemon
- 3 medium garlic cloves, minced
- ½ cup fresh lemon juice
- ½ cup water
- ¼ cup minced fresh oregano
- 1 medium lemon, cut into wedges
- ¼ cup minced fresh parsley, divided
- Cooking spray

Pour the bread crumbs in a shadow dish, then roll the chicken breasts in the bread crumbs to coat.

Spritz a skillet with cooking spray, and brown the coated chicken breasts over medium heat about 3 minutes on each side. Transfer the browned chicken to a baking pan.

In a small bowl, combine the remaining ingredients, except the lemon and parsley. Pour the sauce over the chicken.

Select Bake of the oven. Set the temperature to 325ºF (163ºC) and set the time to 30 minutes. Press Start to begin preheating.

Once preheated, place the pan in the oven.

After 15 minutes, remove the pan from the oven. Flip the breasts. Return the pan to the oven and continue cooking.

When cooking is complete, the chicken should no longer pink.

Transfer to a serving platter, and spoon the sauce over the chicken. Garnish with the lemon and parsley.

728. THAI DRUMSTICKS WITH GREEN BEANS

Prep time: 5 minutes | Cook time: 25 minutes | Serves 4

- 8 skin-on chicken drumsticks
- 1 teaspoon kosher salt, divided
- 1 pound (454 g) green beans, trimmed
- 2 garlic cloves, minced
- 2 tablespoons vegetable oil
- ⅓ cup Thai sweet chili sauce

Salt the drumsticks on all sides with ½ teaspoon of kosher salt. Let sit for a few minutes, then blot dry with a paper towel. Place on a baking pan.

Select Roast, set temperature to 375ºF (190ºC), and set time to 25 minutes. Press Start to begin preheating.

Once preheated, place the pan into the oven.

While the chicken cooks, place the green beans in a large bowl. Add the remaining kosher salt, the garlic, and oil. Toss to coat.

After 15 minutes, remove the pan from the oven. Brush the drumsticks with the sweet chili sauce. Place the green beans in the pan. Return the pan to the oven and continue cooking.

When cooking is complete, the green beans should be sizzling and browned in spots and the chicken cooked through, reading 165ºF (74ºC) on a meat thermometer. Serve the chicken with the green beans on the side.

729. TURKEY AND BEAN STUFFED PEPPERS

Prep time: 20 minutes | Cook time: 15 minutes | Serves 4

- ½ pound (227 g) lean ground turkey
- 4 medium bell peppers
- 1 (15-ounce / 425-g) can black beans, drained and rinsed
- 1 cup shredded Cheddar cheese
- 1 cup cooked long-grain brown rice
- 1 cup mild salsa
- 1¼ teaspoons chili powder
- 1 teaspoon salt
- ½ teaspoon ground cumin

- ½ teaspoon freshly ground black pepper
- Chopped fresh cilantro, for garnish
- Cooking spray

In a large skillet over medium-high heat, cook the turkey, breaking it up with a spoon, until browned, about 5 minutes. Drain off any excess fat. Cut about ½ inch off the tops of the peppers and then cut in half lengthwise. Remove and discard the seeds and set the peppers aside.

In a large bowl, combine the browned turkey, black beans, Cheddar cheese, rice, salsa, chili powder, salt, cumin, and black pepper. Spoon the mixture into the bell peppers.

Lightly spray the perforated pan with cooking spray. Arrange the bell peppers in the pan.

Select Air Fry of the oven. Set the temperature to 350ºF (180ºC) and set the time to 15 minutes. Press Start to begin preheating.

Once preheated, place the pan in the oven.

When cooking is complete, the stuffed peppers should be lightly charred and wilted.

Allow to cool for a few minutes and garnish with cilantro before serving.

730. TURKEY AND CARROT MEATLOAVES

Prep time: 6 minutes | Cook time: 24 minutes | Serves 4

- ¼ cup grated carrot
- 2 garlic cloves, minced
- 2 tablespoons ground almonds
- ⅓ cup minced onion
- 2 teaspoons olive oil
- 1 teaspoon dried marjoram
- 1 egg white
- ¾ pound (340 g) ground turkey breast

In a medium bowl, stir together the carrot, garlic, almonds, onion, olive oil, marjoram, and egg white.

Add the ground turkey. Mix until combined.

Double 16 foil muffin cup liners to make 8 cups. Divide the turkey mixture evenly among the liners.

Select Bake. Set temperature to 400ºF (205ºC) and set time to 24 minutes. Press Start to begin preheating.

Once preheated, place the muffin cups on the perforated pan in the oven. When cooking is complete, the meatloaves should reach an internal temperature of 165ºF (74ºC) on a meat thermometer.

Serve immediately.

731. SAGE SAUSAGE BALLS

Servings: 4

Cooking Time: 20 Minutes

INGREDIENTS:
- 6 oz pork sausages, sliced
- Salt and black pepper to taste
- 1 cup onions, chopped
- 3 tbsp breadcrumbs
- ½ tsp garlic puree
- 1 tsp sage

DIRECTIONS:

In a bowl, mix onions, sausages, sage, garlic puree, salt, and pepper. Form balls out of the mixture and roll in breadcrumbs. Add the balls to the cooking basket and fit in the baking tray; cook for 15 minutes on Air Fry function at 340 F, shaking once. Serve and enjoy!

732. POMEGRANATE CHICKEN WITH COUSCOUS SALAD

Prep time: 25 minutes | Cook time: 20 minutes | Serves 4
- 3 tablespoons plus 2 teaspoons pomegranate molasses
- ½ teaspoon ground cinnamon

- 1 teaspoon minced fresh thyme
- Salt and ground black pepper, to taste
- 2 (12-ounce / 340-g) bone-in split chicken breasts, trimmed
- ¼ cup chicken broth
- ¼ cup water
- ½ cup couscous
- 1 tablespoon minced fresh parsley
- 2 ounces (57 g) cherry tomatoes, quartered
- 1 scallion, white part minced, green part sliced thin on bias
- 1 tablespoon extra-virgin olive oil
- 1 ounce (28 g) feta cheese, crumbled
- Cooking spray

Spritz a perforated pan with cooking spray.
Combine 3 tablespoons of pomegranate molasses, cinnamon, thyme, and ⅛ teaspoon of salt in a small bowl. Stir to mix well. Set aside.
Place the chicken breasts in the perforated pan, skin side down, and spritz with cooking spray. Sprinkle with salt and ground black pepper.
Select Air Fry of the oven. Set temperature to 350ºF (180ºC) and set time to 20 minutes. Press Start to begin preheating.
Once preheated, place the pan into the oven. Flip the chicken and brush with pomegranate molasses mixture halfway through.
Meanwhile, pour the broth and water in a pot and bring to a boil over medium-high heat. Add the couscous and sprinkle with salt. Cover and simmer for 7 minutes or until the liquid is almost absorbed.
Combine the remaining ingredients, except for the cheese, with cooked couscous in a large bowl. Toss to mix well. Scatter with the feta cheese.
When cooking is complete, remove the chicken from the oven and allow to cool for 10 minutes. Serve with vegetable and couscous salad.

733. SIMPLE AIR FRIED CHICKEN WINGS
Prep time: 10 minutes | Cook time: 15 minutes | Serves 4

- 1 tablespoon olive oil
- 8 whole chicken wings
- Chicken seasoning or rub, to taste
- 1 teaspoon garlic powder
- Freshly ground black pepper, to taste

Grease the perforated pan with olive oil.
On a clean work surface, rub the chicken wings with chicken seasoning and rub, garlic powder, and ground black pepper.
Arrange the well-coated chicken wings in the perforated pan.
Select Air Fry of the oven. Set temperature to 400ºF (205ºC) and set time to 15 minutes. Press Start to begin preheating.
Once preheated, place the pan into the oven. Flip the chicken wings halfway through.
When cooking is complete, the internal temperature of the chicken wings should reach at least 165ºF (74ºC).
Remove the chicken wings from the oven. Serve immediately.

734. SIMPLE CHICKEN NUGGETS
Prep time: 10 minutes | Cook time: 8 minutes | Serves 4

- 1 pound (454 g) boneless, skinless chicken breasts, cut into 1-inch pieces
- 2 tablespoons panko breadcrumbs
- 6 tablespoons breadcrumbs
- Chicken seasoning or rub, to taste
- Salt and ground black pepper, to taste
- 2 eggs
- Cooking spray

Spritz a perforated pan with cooking spray.
Combine the breadcrumbs, chicken seasoning, salt, and black pepper in a large bowl. Stir to mix well. Whisk the eggs in a separate bowl.

Dunk the chicken pieces in the egg mixture, then in the breadcrumb mixture. Shake the excess off.
Arrange the well-coated chicken pieces in the perforated pan. Spritz with cooking spray.
Select Air Fry of the oven. Set temperature to 400ºF (205ºC) and set time to 8 minutes. Press Start to begin preheating.
Once preheated, place the pan into the oven. Flip the chicken halfway through.
When cooking is complete, the chicken should be crispy and golden brown.
Serve immediately.

735. TEX-MEX TURKEY BURGERS
Servings: 4
Cooking Time: 15 Minutes
INGREDIENTS:
- ⅓ cup finely crushed corn tortilla chips
- 1 egg, beaten
- ¼ cup salsa
- ⅓ cup shredded pepper Jack cheese
- Pinch salt
- Freshly ground black pepper
- 1 pound ground turkey
- 1 tablespoon olive oil
- 1 teaspoon paprika

DIRECTIONS:

PREPARING THE INGREDIENTS. IN A MEDIUM BOWL, COMBINE THE TORTILLA CHIPS, EGG, SALSA, CHEESE, SALT, AND PEPPER, AND MIX WELL.
Add the turkey and mix gently but thoroughly with clean hands.
Form the meat mixture into patties about ½ inch thick. Make an indentation in the center of each patty with your thumb, so the burgers don't puff up while cooking.
Brush the patties on both sides with the olive oil and sprinkle with paprika.
Air Frying. Put in the Oven rack/basket. Place the Rack on the middle-shelf of the Cosori air fryer oven. Grill for 14 to 16 minutes or until the meat registers at least 165°F.
Nutrition Info: CALORIES: 354; FAT: 21G; PROTEIN:36G; FIBER:2G

736. BEEF FRIED BAKED PASTRY
INGREDIENTS:
- 2 tbsp. unsalted butter
- 1 ½ cup all-purpose flour
- ½ tsp cumin
- 1 tsp coarsely crushed whole coriander
- 1 dry red chili broken into pieces
- A pinch of salt to taste
- Add as much water as required to make the dough stiff and firm
- 2 cups minced beef
- ¼ cup boiled peas
- 1 or 2 green chilies that are finely chopped or mashed
- A small amount of salt
- 1 tsp. coriander seeds

DIRECTIONS:
You will first need to make the outer covering. In a large bowl, add the flour, butter and enough water to knead it into dough that is stiff. Transfer this to a container and leave it to rest for five minutes.
Place a pan on medium flame and add the oil. Roast the mustard seeds and once roasted, add the coriander seeds and the chopped dry red chilies. Add all the dry ingredients for the filling and mix the ingredients well. Add a little water and continue to stir the ingredients. Make small balls out of the dough and roll them out. Cut the rolled-out dough into halves and apply a little water on the edges to help you fold the halves into a cone. Add the filling to the cone and close up the samosa. Pre-heat

the Cosori oven for around 5 to 6 minutes at 300 Fahrenheit. Place all the samosas in the fry basket and close the basket properly.

Keep the Cosori oven at 200 degrees for another 20 to 25 minutes. Around the halfway point, open the basket and turn the samosas over for uniform cooking. After this, fry at 250 degrees for around 10 minutes in order to give them the desired golden-brown color. Serve hot. Recommended sides are tamarind or mint sauce.

737. CHICKEN WITH VEGETABLES

Servings: 4
Cooking Time: 35 Minutes
INGREDIENTS:
*   1 lb chicken breasts, skinless, boneless and cut into pieces
*   3 cups potatoes cut into pieces
*   4 cups Brussels sprouts, trimmed and quartered
*   1 lemon juice
*   1/3 cup vinaigrette dressing
*   1 onion, diced
*   1/4 cup olives, quartered
*   1 tsp oregano
*   1 1/2 tsp Dijon mustard
*   1/4 tsp pepper
*   1/4 tsp salt

DIRECTIONS:
Fit the Cosori oven with the rack in position
Place chicken in the center of the baking pan.
Place potatoes, sprouts, and onions around the chicken.
In a small bowl, mix vinaigrette, oregano, mustard, lemon juice, and salt and pour over chicken and vegetables.
Sprinkle olives and season with pepper.
Set to bake at 400 F for 40 minutes. After 5 minutes place the baking pan in the preheated oven.
Serve and enjoy.
Nutrition Info: Calories 397 Fat 13 g Carbohydrates 31.4 g Sugar 6.7 g Protein 38.3 g Cholesterol 101 mg

738. STRAWBERRY-GLAZED TURKEY

Servings: 2
Cooking Time: 37 Minutes
INGREDIENTS:
*   2 pounds (907 g) turkey breast
*   1 tablespoon olive oil
*   Salt and ground black pepper, to taste
*   1 cup fresh strawberries

DIRECTIONS:
Rub the turkey bread with olive oil on a clean work surface, then sprinkle with salt and ground black pepper.
Transfer the turkey in the air fryer basket and spritz with cooking spray.
Put the air fryer basket on the baking pan and slide into Rack Position 2, select Air Fry, set temperature to 375ºF (190ºC) and set time to 30 minutes.
Flip the turkey breast halfway through.
Meanwhile, put the strawberries in a food processor and pulse until smooth.
When cooking is complete, spread the puréed strawberries over the turkey and fry for 7 more minutes.
Serve immediately.

739. ROSEMARY TURKEY SCOTCH EGGS

Prep time: 15 minutes | Cook time: 12 minutes | Serves 4

*   1 egg
*   1 cup panko breadcrumbs
*   ½ teaspoon rosemary
*   1 pound (454 g) ground turkey

*   4 hard-boiled eggs, peeled
*   Salt and ground black pepper, to taste
*   Cooking spray

Spritz a perforated pan with cooking spray.
Whisk the egg with salt in a bowl. Combine the breadcrumbs with rosemary in a shallow dish.
Stir the ground turkey with salt and ground black pepper in a separate large bowl, then divide the ground turkey into four portions.
Wrap each hard-boiled egg with a portion of ground turkey. Dredge in the whisked egg, then roll over the breadcrumb mixture.
Place the wrapped eggs in the perforated pan and spritz with cooking spray.
Select Air Fry of the oven. Set temperature to 400ºF (205ºC) and set time to 12 minutes. Press Start to begin preheating.
Once preheated, place the pan into the oven. Flip the eggs halfway through.
When cooking is complete, the scotch eggs should be golden brown and crunchy.
Serve immediately.

740. MUSTARD CHICKEN TENDERS

Servings: 4
Cooking Time: 20 Minutes
INGREDIENTS:
*   ½ C. coconut flour
*   1 tbsp. spicy brown mustard
*   2 beaten eggs
*   1 pound of chicken tenders

DIRECTIONS:
Preparing the Ingredients. Season tenders with pepper and salt.
Place a thin layer of mustard onto tenders and then dredge in flour and dip in egg.
Air Frying. Add to the Cosori air fryer oven, set temperature to 390ºF, and set time to 20 minutes.
Nutrition Info: CALORIES: 403; FAT: 20G; PROTEIN:22G; SUGAR:4G

741. CHICKEN THIGHS WITH RADISH SLAW

Servings: 4
Cooking Time: 27 Minutes
INGREDIENTS:
*   4 bone-in, skin-on chicken thighs
*   1½ teaspoon kosher salt, divided
*   1 tablespoon smoked paprika
*   ½ teaspoon granulated garlic
*   ½ teaspoon dried oregano
*   ¼ teaspoon freshly ground black pepper
*   3 cups shredded cabbage
*   ½ small red onion, thinly sliced
*   4 large radishes, julienned
*   3 tablespoons red wine vinegar
*   2 tablespoons olive oil
*   Cooking spray

DIRECTIONS:
Salt the chicken thighs on both sides with 1 teaspoon of kosher salt. In a small bowl, combine the paprika, garlic, oregano, and black pepper. Sprinkle half this mixture over the skin sides of the thighs. Spritz the baking pan with cooking spray and place the thighs skin-side down in the pan. Sprinkle the remaining spice mixture over the other sides of the chicken pieces.
Slide the baking pan into Rack Position 2, select Roast, set temperature to 375ºF (190ºC), and set time to 27 minutes.
   After 10 minutes, remove from the oven and turn over the chicken thighs. Return to the oven and continue cooking.

While the chicken cooks, place the cabbage, onion, and radishes in a large bowl. Sprinkle with the remaining kosher salt, vinegar, and olive oil. Toss to coat.

After another 9 to 10 minutes, remove from the oven and place the chicken thighs on a cutting board. Place the cabbage mixture in the pan and toss with the chicken fat and spices.

Spread the cabbage in an even layer on the pan and place the chicken on it, skin-side up. Return the pan to the oven and continue cooking. Roast for another 7 to 8 minutes.

When cooking is complete, the cabbage is just becoming tender. Remove from the oven. Taste and adjust the seasoning if necessary. Serve.

742. SEAFOOD GRANDMA'S EASY TO COOK WON-TONS
INGREDIENTS:
- 1 ½ cup all-purpose flour
- ½ tsp. salt
- 5 tbsp. water
- For filling:
- 2 cups minced seafood (prawns, shrimp, oysters, scallops)
- 2 tbsp. oil
- 2 tsp. ginger-garlic paste
- 2 tsp. soya sauce
- 2 tsp. vinegar

DIRECTIONS:
Squeeze the dough and cover it with plastic wrap and set aside. Next, cook the ingredients for the filling and try to ensure that the seafood is covered well with the sauce. Roll the dough and place the filling in the center. Now, wrap the dough to cover the filling and pinch the edges together. Pre heat the Cosori oven at 200° F for 5 minutes.

Place the wontons in the fry basket and close it. Let them cook at the same temperature for another 20 minutes. Recommended sides are chili sauce or ketchup.

743. BAKED PORK RIBS
Servings: 8
Cooking Time: 30 Minutes
INGREDIENTS:
- 2 lbs pork ribs, boneless
- 1 tbsp onion powder
- 1 1/2 tbsp garlic powder
- Pepper
- Salt

DIRECTIONS:
Fit the Cosori oven with the rack in position
Place pork ribs in baking pan and season with onion powder, garlic powder, pepper, and salt.
Set to bake at 350 F for 35 minutes. After 5 minutes place the baking pan in the preheated oven.
Serve and enjoy.
Nutrition Info: Calories 318 Fat 20.1 g Carbohydrates 1.9 g Sugar 0.7 g Protein 30.4 g Cholesterol 117 mg

744. PROVENÇAL CHICKEN WITH PEPPERS
Servings: 2
Cooking Time: 20 Minutes
INGREDIENTS:
- 2 chicken tenders
- Salt and black pepper to taste
- ½ tsp herbs de Provence
- 1 tbsp butter, softened
- 2 mini red peppers, sliced

- 1 onion, sliced
DIRECTIONS:
Preheat Cosori on AirFry function to 390 F. Lay a foil on a flat surface. Place the chicken, red peppers, and onion on the foil, sprinkle with herbs de Provence and brush with butter. Season with salt and black pepper. Wrap the foil around the breasts.
Place the wrapped chicken in the basket and press Start; cook for 12 minutes. Remove and carefully unwrap. Serve with the sauce extract and veggies.

745. LAMB CHEESE HOMEMADE FRIED STICKS
INGREDIENTS:
- 2 cups lamb (Cut the lamb into long strips)
- 1 cup cheddar cheese
- 1 big lemon-juiced
- 4 or 5 tbsp. corn flour
- 1 cup of water
- 1 tbsp. ginger-garlic paste
- For seasoning, use salt and red chili powder in small amounts
- ½ tsp. carom
- One or two poppadums'

DIRECTIONS:
Make a mixture of lemon juice, red chili powder, salt, ginger garlic paste and carom to use as a marinade. Let the lamb pieces marinate in the mixture for some time and then roll them in dry corn flour. Leave them aside for around 20 minutes. Take the poppadum into a pan and roast them. Once they are cooked, crush them into very small pieces.

Now take another container and pour around 100 ml of water into it. Dissolve 2 tbsp. of corn flour in this water. Dip the cottage cheese pieces in this solution of corn flour and roll them on to the pieces of crushed poppadum so that the poppadum sticks to the lamb. Pre heat the Cosori oven for 10 minutes at 300 Fahrenheit.

Then open the basket of the fryer and place the lamb pieces inside it. Close the basket properly. Let the fryer stay at 250 degrees for another 20 minutes. Halfway through, open the basket and toss the lamb around a bit to allow for uniform cooking. Once they are done, you can serve it either with ketchup or mint sauce. Another recommended side is mint sauce.

746. RITZY CHICKEN ROAST
Servings: 6
Cooking Time: 1 Hour
INGREDIENTS:
- 1 teaspoon Italian seasoning
- ½ teaspoon garlic powder
- ½ teaspoon paprika
- 1 teaspoon salt
- ½ teaspoon freshly ground black pepper
- ½ teaspoon onion powder
- 2 tablespoons olive oil
- 1 (3-pound / 1.4-kg) whole chicken, giblets removed, pat dry
- Cooking spray

DIRECTIONS:
Spritz the air fryer basket with cooking spray.
In a small bowl, mix the Italian seasoning, garlic powder, paprika, salt, pepper, and onion powder.
Brush the chicken with the olive oil and rub it with the seasoning mixture.
Tie the chicken legs with butcher's twine. Place the chicken in the basket, breast side down.
Put the air fryer basket on the baking pan and slide into Rack Position 2, select Air Fry, set the temperature to 350ºF (180ºC) and set the time to an hour.
After 30 minutes, remove from the oven. Flip the chicken over and baste it with any drippings collected in the bottom drawer of the oven. Return to the oven and continue cooking.

When cooking is complete, a thermometer inserted into the thickest part of the thigh should reach at least 165ºF (74ºC).

Let the chicken rest for 10 minutes before carving and serving.

747. LAMB BARBECUE CLUB SANDWICH
INGREDIENTS:
- 2 slices of white bread
- 1 tbsp. softened butter
- ½ lb. cut lamb (Get the meat cut into cubes)
- ¼ cup chopped onion
- ½ tbsp. sugar
- 1 small capsicum
- For Barbeque Sauce:
- ¼ tbsp. Worcestershire sauce
- ½ tsp. olive oil
- ½ flake garlic crushed
- ¼ tbsp. red chili sauce

DIRECTIONS:
Take the slices of bread and remove the edges. Now cut the slices horizontally. Cook the ingredients for the sauce and wait till it thickens. Now, add the lamb to the sauce and stir till it obtains the flavors. Roast the capsicum and peel the skin off. Cut the capsicum into slices. Mix the ingredients together and apply it to the bread slices.

Pre-heat the Cosori oven for 5 minutes at 300 Fahrenheit. Open the basket of the Fryer and place the prepared Classic Sandwiches in it such that no two Classic Sandwiches are touching each other. Now keep the fryer at 250 degrees for around 15 minutes. Turn the Classic Sandwiches in between the cooking process to cook both slices. Serve the Classic Sandwiches with tomato ketchup or mint sauce.

748. SPANISH CHICKEN AND PEPPER BAGUETTE
Servings: 2
Cooking Time: 20 Minutes
INGREDIENTS:
- 1¼ pounds (567 g) assorted small chicken parts, breasts cut into halves
- ¼ teaspoon salt
- ¼ teaspoon ground black pepper
- 2 teaspoons olive oil
- ½ pound (227 g) mini sweet peppers
- ¼ cup light mayonnaise
- ¼ teaspoon smoked paprika
- ½ clove garlic, crushed
- Baguette, for serving
- Cooking spray

DIRECTIONS:
SPRITZ THE AIR FRYER BASKET WITH COOKING SPRAY.
Toss the chicken with salt, ground black pepper, and olive oil in a large bowl.
Arrange the sweet peppers and chicken in the basket.
Put the air fryer basket on the baking pan and slide into Rack Position 2, select Air Fry, set temperature to 375ºF (190ºC) and set time to 20 minutes.
Flip the chicken and transfer the peppers on a plate halfway through.
When cooking is complete, the chicken should be well browned.
Meanwhile, combine the mayo, paprika, and garlic in a small bowl. Stir to mix well.
Assemble the baguette with chicken and sweet pepper, then spread with mayo mixture and serve.

749. GARLIC BUTTER WINGS
Servings: 4
Cooking Time: 25 Minutes
INGREDIENTS:
- 1 lb chicken wings

- 1 tsp garlic powder
- 1/4 tsp pepper
- 1/2 tsp Italian seasoning
- 1/2 tsp salt
- For sauce:
- 1 tbsp butter, melted
- 1/8 tsp garlic powder

DIRECTIONS:
Fit the Cosori oven with the rack in position 2.
In a large bowl, toss chicken wings with Italian seasoning, garlic powder, pepper, and salt.
Arrange chicken wings in the air fryer basket then place an air fryer basket in the baking pan.
Place a baking pan on the oven rack. Set to air fry at 390 F for 25 minutes.
In a bowl, mix melted butter and garlic powder.
Add chicken wings and toss until well coated.
Serve and enjoy.
Nutrition Info: Calories 246 Fat 11.5 g Carbohydrates 0.7 g Sugar 0.2 g Protein 33 g Cholesterol 109 mg

750. LAMB KOFTA
Servings: 4
Cooking Time: 10 Minutes
INGREDIENTS:
- 1 pound (454 g) ground lamb
- 1 tablespoon ras el hanout (North African spice)
- ½ teaspoon ground coriander
- 1 teaspoon onion powder
- 1 teaspoon garlic powder
- 1 teaspoon cumin
- 2 tablespoons mint, chopped
- Salt and ground black pepper, to taste
- Special Equipment:
- 4 bamboo skewers

DIRECTIONS:
Combine the ground lamb, ras el hanout, coriander, onion powder, garlic powder, cumin, mint, salt, and ground black pepper in a large bowl. Stir to mix well.
Transfer the mixture into sausage molds and sit the bamboo skewers in the mixture. Refrigerate for 15 minutes.
Spritz the air fryer basket with cooking spray. Place the lamb skewers in the pan and spritz with cooking spray.
Put the air fryer basket on the baking pan and slide into Rack Position 2, select Air Fry, set temperature to 380ºF (193ºC) and set time to 10 minutes.
Flip the lamb skewers halfway through.
When cooking is complete, the lamb should be well browned.
Serve immediately.

751. SRIRACHA CHICKEN WINGS
Servings: 4
Cooking Time: 30 Minutes
INGREDIENTS:
- 1 lb chicken wings
- 2 tbsp sriracha sauce
- 1/4 cup honey
- 1 tbsp butter
- 1 1/2 tbsp soy sauce
- Pepper
- Salt

DIRECTIONS:
Fit the Cosori oven with the rack in position 2.
Season chicken wings with pepper and salt.
Add chicken wings to the air fryer basket then place an air fryer basket in the baking pan.

Place a baking pan on the oven rack. Set to air fry at 360 F for 30 minutes.

Meanwhile, add butter, soy sauce, sriracha sauce, and honey in a saucepan and cook for 3 minutes.

Add chicken wings into the bowl.

Pour sauce over chicken wings and toss until well coated.

Serve and enjoy.

Nutrition Info: Calories 359 Fat 16.3 g Carbohydrates 18.4 g Sugar 18 g Protein 33.3 g Cholesterol 114 mg

752. BARBECUE FLAVORED PORK RIBS

Servings: 6

Cooking Time: 15 Minutes

INGREDIENTS:

- ¼ cup honey, divided
- ¾ cup BBQ sauce
- 2 tablespoons tomato ketchup
- 1 tablespoon Worcestershire sauce
- 1 tablespoon soy sauce
- ½ teaspoon garlic powder
- Freshly ground white pepper, to taste
- 1¾ pound pork ribs

DIRECTIONS:

Preparing the Ingredients. In a large bowl, mix together 3 tablespoons of honey and remaining ingredients except pork ribs.

Refrigerate to marinate for about 20 minutes.

Preheat the Cosori air fryer oven to 355 degrees F.

Place the ribs in an Air fryer rack/basket.

Air Frying. Cook for about 13 minutes.

Remove the ribs from the Cosori air fryer oven and coat with remaining honey.

Serve hot.

753. LECHON KAWALI

Servings: 4

Cooking Time: 30 Minutes

INGREDIENTS:

- 1 pound (454 g) pork belly, cut into three thick chunks
- 6 garlic cloves
- 2 bay leaves
- 2 tablespoons soy sauce
- 1 teaspoon kosher salt
- 1 teaspoon ground black pepper
- 3 cups water
- Cooking spray

DIRECTIONS:

Put all the ingredients in a pressure cooker, then put the lid on and cook on high for 15 minutes.

Natural release the pressure and release any remaining pressure, transfer the tender pork belly on a clean work surface. Allow to cool under room temperature until you can handle.

Generously Spritz the air fryer basket with cooking spray.

Cut each chunk into two slices, then put the pork slices in the pan.

Put the air fryer basket on the baking pan and slide into Rack Position 2, select Air Fry, set temperature to 400°F (205°C) and set time to 15 minutes.

After 7 minutes, remove from the oven. Flip the pork. Return to the oven and continue cooking.

When cooking is complete, the pork fat should be crispy.

Serve immediately.

754. CHICKEN PASTA BROCCOLI CASSEROLE

Servings: 8

Cooking Time: 35 Minutes

INGREDIENTS:

- 2 lbs chicken breasts, cut into large chunks
- 16 oz pasta, cooked and drained
- 12 oz frozen broccoli, thawed
- 1/2 cup cheddar cheese, shredded
- 1 can cream of chicken condensed soup
- 1 tbsp olive oil
- Pepper
- Salt

DIRECTIONS:

Fit the Cosori oven with the rack in position

Heat oil in a pan over medium heat.

Season chicken with pepper and salt and place into the pan. Cook chicken until lightly browned, about 3-4 minutes on each side.

Remove pan from heat and set aside.

Add chicken and remaining ingredients into the mixing bowl and mix well.

Pour chicken mixture into the 9*13-inch greased casserole dish.

Set to bake at 400 F for 40 minutes. After 5 minutes place the casserole dish in the preheated oven.

Serve and enjoy.

Nutrition Info: Calories 446 Fat 14.2 g Carbohydrates 35.2 g Sugar 0.9 g Protein 42.4 g Cholesterol 151 mg

755. PERFECT CHICKEN PARMESAN

Servings: 2

Cooking Time: 25 Minutes

INGREDIENTS:

- 2 large white meat chicken breasts, approximately 5-6 ounces
- 1 cup of breadcrumbs (Panko brand works well)
- 2 medium-sized eggs
- Pinch of salt and pepper
- 1 tablespoon of dried oregano
- 1 cup of marinara sauce (store-bought or homemade will
- do equally well)
- 2 slices of provolone cheese
- 1 tablespoon of parmesan cheese

DIRECTIONS:

Preparing the Ingredients. Cover the basket of the Cosori air fryer oven with a lining of tin foil, leaving the edges uncovered to allow air to circulate through the basket.

Preheat the air fryer oven to 350 degrees.

In a mixing bowl, beat the eggs until fluffy and until the yolks and whites are fully combined, and set aside.

In a separate mixing bowl, combine the breadcrumbs, oregano, salt and pepper, and set aside.

One by one, dip the raw chicken breasts into the bowl with dry ingredients, coating both sides; then submerge into the bowl with wet ingredients, then dip again into the dry ingredients. This double coating will ensure an extra crisp-and-delicious air-fry!

Lay the coated chicken breasts on the foil covering the Oven rack/basket, in a single flat layer. Place the Rack on the middle-shelf of the Cosori air fryer oven.

Air Frying. Set the Cosori air fryer oven timer for 10 minutes.

After 10 minutes, the air fryer will turn off and the chicken should be mid-way cooked and the breaded coating starting to brown.

Using tongs, turn each piece of chicken over to ensure a full all-over fry. Reset the air fryer oven to 320 degrees for another 10 minutes.

While the chicken is cooking, pour half the marinara sauce into a 7-inch heat-safe pan.

After 15 minutes, when the air fryer shuts off, remove the fried chicken breasts using tongs and set in the marinara-covered pan. Drizzle the rest of the marinara sauce over the fried chicken, then place the slices of provolone cheese atop both of them and sprinkle the parmesan cheese over the entire pan.

Reset the air fryer oven to 350 degrees for 5 minutes.

After 5 minutes, when the air fryer shuts off, remove the dish from the air fryer using tongs or oven mitts. The chicken will be perfectly crisped and the cheese melted and lightly toasted. Serve while hot!

756. CRISPY CAJUN CHICKEN BREAST

Servings: 2
Cooking Time: 25 Minutes
INGREDIENTS:
- 2 chicken breasts
- 3/4 cup breadcrumbs
- 1 tsp garlic powder
- 1 tsp paprika
- 1 tsp Cajun seasoning
- 2 tbsp mayonnaise
- 1/2 tsp pepper
- 1/2 tsp salt

DIRECTIONS:
Fit the Cosori oven with the rack in position
In a shallow dish, mix breadcrumbs, Cajun seasoning, paprika, garlic powder, pepper, and salt.
Brush chicken with mayonnaise and coat with breadcrumbs.
Place coated chicken breasts into the baking pan.
Set to bake at 425 F for 30 minutes. After 5 minutes place the baking pan in the preheated oven.
Serve and enjoy.
Nutrition Info: Calories 504 Fat 18.1 g Carbohydrates 34.6 g Sugar 3.9 g Protein 48.3 g Cholesterol 134 mg

757. DIJON GARLIC PORK TENDERLOIN

Servings: 6
Cooking Time: 10 Minutes
INGREDIENTS:
- 1 C. breadcrumbs
- Pinch of cayenne pepper
- 3 crushed garlic cloves
- 2 tbsp. ground ginger
- 2 tbsp. Dijon mustard
- 2 tbsp. raw honey
- 4 tbsp. water
- 2 tsp. salt
- 1 pound pork tenderloin, sliced into 1-inch rounds

DIRECTIONS:
Preparing the Ingredients. With pepper and salt, season all sides of tenderloin.
Combine cayenne pepper, garlic, ginger, mustard, honey, and water until smooth.
Dip pork rounds into the honey mixture and then into breadcrumbs, ensuring they all get coated well.
Place coated pork rounds into your Cosori air fryer oven.
Air Frying. Set temperature to 400°F, and set time to 10 minutes. Cook 10 minutes at 400 degrees. Flip and then cook an additional 5 minutes until golden in color.
Nutrition Info: CALORIES: 423; FAT: 18G; PROTEIN:31G; SUGAR:3G

758. DELICIOUS COCONUT CHICKEN CASSEROLE

Servings: 4
Cooking Time: 20 Minutes
INGREDIENTS:
- 2 large eggs, beaten
- 2 tbsp garlic powder
- Salt and black pepper to taste
- ¾ cup breadcrumbs
- ¾ cup shredded coconut
- 1 pound chicken tenders

DIRECTIONS:

Preheat your Cosori on Air Fry function to 400 F. Spray a baking sheet with cooking spray. In a deep dish, whisk garlic powder, eggs, pepper, and salt. In another bowl, mix the breadcrumbs and coconut. Dip your chicken tenders in egg mixture, then in the coconut mix; shake off any excess. Place the prepared chicken tenders in the greased basket and fit in the baking tray; cook for 12-14 minutes until golden brown. Serve.

759. VORTEX MEATBALLS

Servings: 4
Cooking Time: 25 Minutes
INGREDIENTS:
- 1 lb ground beef
- 1 tsp fresh rosemary, chopped
- 1 tbsp garlic, chopped
- 1/2 tsp pepper
- 1 tsp garlic powder
- 1 tsp onion powder
- 1/4 cup breadcrumbs
- 2 eggs
- 1 lb ground pork
- 1/2 tsp pepper
- 1 tsp sea salt

DIRECTIONS:
Fit the Cosori oven with the rack in position
Add all ingredients into the mixing bowl and mix until well combined. Make small balls from the meat mixture and place it into the parchment-lined baking pan.
Set to bake at 400 F for 30 minutes. After 5 minutes place the baking pan in the preheated oven.
Serve and enjoy.
Nutrition Info: Calories 441 Fat 13.7 g Carbohydrates 7.2 g Sugar 1 g Protein 68.1 g Cholesterol 266 mg

760. SHRIMP PASTE CHICKEN

Servings: 2
Cooking Time: 30 Minutes
INGREDIENTS:
- 6 chicken wings
- ½ tbsp sugar
- 2 tbsp cornflour
- 1 tbsp white wine
- 1 tbsp shrimp paste
- 1 tbsp grated ginger
- ½ tbsp olive oil

DIRECTIONS:
In a bowl, mix shrimp paste, olive oil, ginger, white wine, and sugar. Cover the chicken wings with the prepared marinade and roll in the flour. Place the chicken in the greased baking dish and cook in your Cosori for 20 minutes at 350 F on Air Fry function. Serve.

761. SIMPLE BURGER PATTIES

Servings: 4
Cooking Time: 8 Minutes
INGREDIENTS:
- 1 lb ground beef
- 1/2 tsp garlic powder
- 1/4 tsp onion powder
- 1 tbsp soy sauce
- Pepper
- Salt

DIRECTIONS:
Fit the Cosori oven with the rack in position 2.
Line the air fryer basket with parchment paper.
Add all ingredients into the mixing bowl and mix until well combined.
Make four equal shape patties from the meat mixture and place in the air

fryer basket then place an air fryer basket in the baking pan.

Place a baking pan on the oven rack. Set to air fry at 375 F for 8 minutes. Serve and enjoy.

Nutrition Info: Calories 215 Fat 7.1 g Carbohydrates 0.7 g Sugar 0.2 g Protein 34.7 g Cholesterol 101 mg

762. SPINACH TURKEY MEATBALLS

Servings: 6
Cooking Time: 20 Minutes
INGREDIENTS:

- 2 lbs ground turkey
- 1/2 cup breadcrumbs
- 1 egg, lightly beaten
- 1/4 cup fresh parsley, chopped
- 1 cup spinach, chopped
- 1 tbsp fresh mint, chopped
- 1/4 tsp cumin
- 1/2 tsp oregano
- 4 oz feta cheese
- 1/2 tsp pepper
- 1/2 tsp onion powder
- Salt

DIRECTIONS:

Fit the Cosori oven with the rack in position

Add all ingredients into the large bowl and mix until well combined.

Make small balls from the meat mixture and place it into the parchment-lined baking pan.

Set to bake at 375 F for 25 minutes. After 5 minutes place the baking pan in the preheated oven.

Serve and enjoy.

Nutrition Info: Calories 395 Fat 21.9 g Carbohydrates 8.1 g Sugar 1.5 g Protein 46.5 g Cholesterol 198 mg

763. HERBY STUFFED TURKEY BREAST

Servings: 4
Cooking Time: 35 Minutes

INGREDIENTS:

- 1 pound turkey breast
- 1 ham slice
- 1 slice cheddar cheese
- 2 oz breadcrumbs
- 1 tbsp cream cheese
- ½ tsp garlic powder
- 1 tbsp fresh thyme, chopped
- 1 tbsp fresh tarragon, chopped
- 1 egg, beaten
- Salt and black pepper to taste

DIRECTIONS:

Preheat Cosori on Air Fry function to 350 F. Cut the turkey in the middle; that way so you can add ingredients in the center. Season with salt, pepper, thyme, and tarragon. Combine cream cheese and garlic powder in a bowl.

Spread the mixture on the inside of the breast. Place half cheddar slice and half ham slice in the center of each breast. Dip in the egg first, then sprinkle with breadcrumbs. Cook on the baking tray for 30 minutes, flipping once.

764. STICKY CHINESE-STYLE CHICKEN

Servings: 3
Cooking Time: 25 Minutes
INGREDIENTS:

- 1 lb chicken wingettes
- 1 tbsp cilantro leaves, chopped
- Salt and black pepper, to taste

- 1 tbsp roasted peanuts, chopped
- ½ tbsp apple cider vinegar
- 1 garlic clove, minced
- ½ tbsp chili sauce
- 1 ginger, minced
- 1 ½ tbsp soy sauce
- 2 ½ tbsp honey

DIRECTIONS:

In a bowl, mix ginger, garlic, chili sauce, honey, soy sauce, cilantro, salt, pepper, and vinegar. Add in the chicken toss to coat. Place the prepared chicken onto the greased basket and fit in the baking tray; cook for 20 minutes at 360 F on Air Fry function. Serve sprinkled with peanuts.

765. VEAL PATTI WITH BOILED PEAS

INGREDIENTS:

- ½ lb. minced veal
- ½ cup breadcrumbs
- A pinch of salt to taste
- ½ cup of boiled peas
- ¼ tsp. ginger finely chopped
- 1 green chili finely chopped
- 1 tsp. lemon juice
- 1 tbsp. fresh coriander leaves. Chop them finely
- ¼ tsp. red chili powder
- ¼ tsp. cumin powder
- ¼ tsp. dried mango powder

DIRECTIONS:

Take a container and into it pour all the masalas, onions, green chilies, peas, coriander leaves, lemon juice, and ginger and 1-2 tbsp. breadcrumbs. Add the minced veal as well. Mix all the ingredients well. Mold the mixture into round patties. Press them gently. Now roll them out carefully.

Pre heat the Cosori oven at 250 Fahrenheit for 5 minutes. Open the basket of the Fryer and arrange the patties in the basket. Close it carefully. Keep the fryer at 150 degrees for around 10 or 12 minutes. In between the cooking process, turn the patties over to get a uniform cook. Serve hot with mint sauce.

766. CRUNCHY PARMESAN PORK CHOPS

Servings: 4
Cooking Time: 10 Minutes
INGREDIENTS:

- 4 pork chops, boneless
- 2 tbsp olive oil
- 1/4 tsp pepper
- 1/2 tsp garlic powder
- 1 tsp dried parsley
- 1/4 tsp smoked paprika
- 2 tbsp breadcrumbs
- 1/4 cup parmesan cheese, grated

DIRECTIONS:

Fit the Cosori oven with the rack in position

In a shallow dish, mix breadcrumbs, paprika, parmesan cheese, garlic powder, parsley, and pepper.

Brush pork chops with oil and coat with breadcrumb mixture.

Place coated pork chops into the baking pan.

Set to bake at 450 F for 15 minutes. After 5 minutes place the baking pan in the preheated oven.

Serve and enjoy.

Nutrition Info: Calories 350 Fat 28.3 g Carbohydrates 3.1 g Sugar 0.3 g Protein 20.4 g Cholesterol 73 mg

767. PORK FRIED RICE WITH SCRAMBLED EGG

Servings: 4
Cooking Time: 12 Minutes

INGREDIENTS:

- 3 scallions, diced (about ½ cup)
- ½ red bell pepper, diced (about ½ cup)
- 2 teaspoons sesame oil
- ½ pound (227 g) pork tenderloin, diced
- ½ cup frozen peas, thawed
- ½ cup roasted mushrooms
- ½ cup soy sauce
- 2 cups cooked rice
- 1 egg, beaten

DIRECTIONS:

Place the scallions and red pepper in the baking pan. Drizzle with the sesame oil and toss the vegetables to coat them in the oil.

Slide the baking pan into Rack Position 2, select Roast, set temperature to 375ºF (190ºC), and set time to 12 minutes.

While the vegetables are cooking, place the pork in a large bowl. Add the peas, mushrooms, soy sauce, and rice and toss to coat the ingredients with the sauce.

After about 4 minutes, remove from the oven. Place the pork mixture on the pan and stir the scallions and peppers into the pork and rice. Return the pan to the oven and continue cooking.

After another 6 minutes, remove from the oven. Move the rice mixture to the sides to create an empty circle in the middle of the pan. Pour the egg in the circle. Return the pan to the oven and continue cooking.

When cooking is complete, remove from the oven and stir the egg to scramble it. Stir the egg into the fried rice mixture. Serve immediately.

768. CORN FLOUR LAMB FRIES WITH RED CHILI

INGREDIENTS:

- 2 tsp. salt
- 1 tsp. pepper powder
- 1 lb. boneless lamb cut into Oregano Fingers
- 2 cup dry breadcrumbs
- 2 tsp. oregano
- 2 tsp. red chili flakes
- 1 ½ tbsp. ginger-garlic paste
- 4 tbsp. lemon juice
- 1 tsp. red chili powder
- 6 tbsp. corn flour
- 4 eggs

DIRECTIONS:

Mix all the ingredients for the marinade and put the lamb Oregano Fingers inside and let it rest overnight.

Mix the breadcrumbs, oregano and red chili flakes well and place the marinated Oregano Fingers on this mixture. Cover it with plastic wrap and leave it till right before you serve to cook.

Pre heat the Cosori oven at 160 degrees Fahrenheit for 5 minutes. Place the Oregano Fingers in the fry basket and close it. Let them cook at the same temperature for another 15 minutes or so. Toss the Oregano Fingers well so that they are cooked uniformly.

769. CARNE ASADA

Servings: 4
Cooking Time: 15 Minutes
INGREDIENTS:

- 3 chipotle peppers in adobo, chopped
- ⅓ cup chopped fresh oregano
- ⅓ cup chopped fresh parsley
- 4 cloves garlic, minced
- Juice of 2 limes
- 1 teaspoon ground cumin seeds
- ⅓ cup olive oil
- 1 to 1½ pounds (454 g to 680 g) flank steak
- Salt, to taste

DIRECTIONS:

Combine the chipotle, oregano, parsley, garlic, lime juice, cumin, and olive oil in a large bowl. Stir to mix well.

Dunk the flank steak in the mixture and press to coat well. Wrap the bowl in plastic and marinate under room temperature for at least 30 minutes.

Discard the marinade and place the steak in the basket. Sprinkle with salt.

Put the air fryer basket on the baking pan and slide into Rack Position 2, select Air Fry, set temperature to 390ºF (199ºC) and set time to 15 minutes.

Flip the steak halfway through the cooking time.

When cooking is complete, the steak should be medium-rare or reach your desired doneness.

Remove the steak from the oven and slice to serve.

770. FESTIVE STUFFED PORK CHOPS

Servings: 4
Cooking Time: 40 Minutes
INGREDIENTS:

- 4 pork chops
- Salt and black pepper to taste
- 4 cups stuffing mix
- 2 tbsp olive oil
- 4 garlic cloves, minced
- 2 tbsp fresh sage leaves, chopped

DIRECTIONS:

Cut a hole in pork chops and fill chops with stuffing mix. In a bowl, mix sage, garlic, oil, salt, and pepper. Rub the chops with the marinade and let sit for 10 minutes.

Preheat Cosori on Bake function to 380 F. Put the chops in a baking tray and place in the oven. Press Start and cook for 25 minutes. Serve and enjoy!

771. TAMARIND PORK CHOPS WITH GREEN BEANS

Servings: 4
Cooking Time: 30 Minutes + Marinating Time
INGREDIENTS:

- 2 tbsp tamarind paste
- ½ lb green beans, trimmed
- 1 tbsp garlic, minced
- ½ cup green mole sauce
- 3 tbsp corn syrup
- 1 tbsp olive oil
- 2 tbsp molasses
- 4 tbsp southwest seasoning
- 2 tbsp ketchup
- 4 pork chops

DIRECTIONS:

In a bowl, mix all the ingredients, except for potatoes, pork chops, and mole sauce. Add in 2 tbsp of water. Let the pork chops marinate in the mixture for 30 minutes.

Place pork chops in the basket and fit in the baking tray; cook for 25 minutes on Air Fry function at 350 F. Blanch the green beans in salted water in a pot over medium heat for 2-3 minutes until tender. Drain and season with salt and pepper. Serve the pork with green beans and mole sauce.

772. GREEK CHICKEN PAILLARD

Servings: 8
Cooking Time: 25 Minutes
INGREDIENTS:

- 4 chicken breasts, skinless and boneless
- 1/2 cup olives, diced
- 1 small onion, sliced
- 1 fennel bulb, sliced
- 28 oz can tomatoes, diced

- 1/4 cup fresh basil, chopped
- 1/4 cup fresh parsley, chopped
- 1/4 cup pine nuts
- 2 tbsp olive oil
- Pepper
- Salt

DIRECTIONS:

Fit the Cosori oven with the rack in position

Season chicken with pepper and salt and place in baking dish. Drizzle with oil.

In a bowl, mix together olives, tomatoes, pine nuts, onion, fennel, pepper, and salt.

Pour olive mixture over chicken.

Set to bake at 450 F for 30 minutes. After 5 minutes place the baking dish in the preheated oven.

Garnish with basil and parsley and serve.

Nutrition Info: Calories 242 Fat 12.8 g Carbohydrates 9.3 g Sugar 3.9 g Protein 23.2 g Cholesterol 65 mg

773. PORK NECK WITH SALAD

Servings: 2

Cooking Time: 12 Minutes

INGREDIENTS:

For Pork:
- 1 tablespoon soy sauce
- 1 tablespoon fish sauce
- ½ tablespoon oyster sauce
- ½ pound pork neck

For Salad:
- 1 ripe tomato, sliced tickly
- 8-10 Thai shallots, sliced
- 1 scallion, chopped
- 1 bunch fresh basil leaves
- 1 bunch fresh cilantro leaves

For Dressing:
- 3 tablespoons fish sauce
- 2 tablespoons olive oil
- 1 teaspoon apple cider vinegar
- 1 tablespoon palm sugar
- 2 bird eye chili
- 1 tablespoon garlic, minced

DIRECTIONS:

Preparing the Ingredients. For pork in a bowl, mix together all ingredients except pork.

Add pork neck and coat with marinade evenly. Refrigerate for about 2-3 hours.

Preheat the Cosori air fryer oven to 340 degrees F.

Air Frying. Place the pork neck onto a grill pan. Cook for about 12 minutes.

Meanwhile, in a large salad bowl, mix together all salad ingredients.

In a bowl, add all dressing ingredients and beat till well combined.

Remove pork neck from Air fryer oven and cut into desired slices.

Place pork slices over salad.

774. TURKEY AND CAULIFLOWER MEATLOAF

Servings: 6

Cooking Time: 50 Minutes

INGREDIENTS:
- 2 pounds (907 g) lean ground turkey
- 1⅓ cups riced cauliflower
- 2 large eggs, lightly beaten
- ¼ cup almond flour
- ⅔ cup chopped yellow or white onion
- 1 teaspoon ground dried turmeric
- 1 teaspoon ground cumin
- 1 teaspoon ground coriander

- 1 tablespoon minced garlic
- 1 teaspoon salt
- 1 teaspoon ground black pepper
- Cooking spray

DIRECTIONS:

Spritz the baking pan with cooking spray.

Combine all the ingredients in a large bowl. Stir to mix well. Pour half of the mixture in the prepared pan and press with a spatula to coat the bottom evenly. Spritz the mixture with cooking spray.

Slide the baking pan into Rack Position 1, select Convection Bake, set temperature to 350ºF (180ºC) and set time to 25 minutes.

When cooking is complete, the meat should be well browned and the internal temperature should reach at least 165ºF (74ºC).

Remove the pan from the oven and serve immediately.

775. AIR FRYER JUICY PORK CHOPS

Servings: 2

Cooking Time: 12 Minutes

INGREDIENTS:
- 2 pork chops
- 2 tbsp brown sugar
- 1 tbsp olive oil
- 1/4 tsp garlic powder
- 1/2 tsp onion powder
- 1 tsp ground mustard
- 1 tbsp paprika
- Pepper
- Salt

DIRECTIONS:

Fit the Cosori oven with the rack in position 2.

Add all dry ingredients into the small bowl and mix well.

Brush pork chops with oil and rub with spice mixture.

Place pork chops in the air fryer basket then place an air fryer basket in the baking pan.

Place a baking pan on the oven rack. Set to air fry at 400 F for 12 minutes.

Serve and enjoy.

Nutrition Info: Calories 371 Fat 27.8 g Carbohydrates 12.1 g Sugar 9.5 g Protein 19 g Cholesterol 69 mg

776. CREOLE HENS

Servings: 4

Cooking Time: 40 Minutes

INGREDIENTS:
- ½ tablespoon Creole seasoning
- ½ tablespoon garlic powder
- ½ tablespoon onion powder
- ½ tablespoon freshly ground black pepper
- ½ tablespoon paprika
- 2 tablespoons olive oil
- 2 Cornish hens
- Cooking spray

DIRECTIONS:

Spritz the air fryer basket with cooking spray.

In a small bowl, mix the Creole seasoning, garlic powder, onion powder, pepper, and paprika.

Pat the Cornish hens dry and brush each hen all over with the olive oil.

Rub each hen with the seasoning mixture. Place the Cornish hens in the basket.

Put the air fryer basket on the baking pan and slide into Rack Position 2, select Air Fry, set the temperature to 375ºF (190ºC) and set the time to 30 minutes.

After 15 minutes, remove from the oven. Flip the hens over and baste it with any drippings collected in the bottom drawer of the oven. Return to the oven and continue cooking.

When cooking is complete, a thermometer inserted into the thickest part of the hens should reach at least 165ºF (74ºC).

Let the hens rest for 10 minutes before carving.

777. SPICY CHICKEN SKEWERS WITH SATAY SAUCE

Servings: 4

Cooking Time: 10 Minutes

INGREDIENTS:

- 4 (6-ounce / 170-g) boneless, skinless chicken breasts, sliced into strips
- 1 teaspoon sea salt
- 1 teaspoon paprika
- Cooking spray
- Satay Sauce:
- ¼ cup creamy almond butter
- ½ teaspoon hot sauce
- 1½ tablespoons coconut vinegar
- 2 tablespoons chicken broth
- 1 teaspoon peeled and minced fresh ginger
- 1 clove garlic, minced
- 1 teaspoon sugar
- For Serving:
- ¼ cup chopped cilantro leaves
- Red pepper flakes, to taste
- Thinly sliced red, orange, or / and yellow bell peppers
- Special Equipment:
- 16 wooden or bamboo skewers, soaked in water for 15 minutes

DIRECTIONS:

Spritz the air fryer basket with cooking spray.

Run the bamboo skewers through the chicken strips, then arrange the chicken skewers in the basket and sprinkle with salt and paprika.

Put the air fryer basket on the baking pan and slide into Rack Position 2, select Air Fry, set temperature to 400ºF (205ºC) and set time to 10 minutes.

Flip the chicken skewers halfway during the cooking.

When cooking is complete, the chicken should be lightly browned.

Meanwhile, combine the ingredients for the sauce in a small bowl. Stir to mix well.

Transfer the cooked chicken skewers on a large plate, then top with cilantro, sliced bell peppers, red pepper flakes. Serve with the sauce or just baste the sauce over before serving.

778. STEAK SEARED IN BROWNED BUTTER

INGREDIENTS:

- 2 (1-lb) steaks, 1 inch thick
- 1 Tbsp extra-virgin olive oil
- 3 Tbsp unsalted butter, divided
- 1 lb. Yukon gold potatoes, sliced about ½-inch thick
- 2 fresh rosemary sprigs
- Salt and freshly ground black pepper, to taste
- ½ cup beef broth

DIRECTIONS:

Let the steaks rest at room temperature for 30 minutes.

In Cosori oven over medium-high heat, heat the oil and 1 Tbsp of butter. Add the potatoes and rosemary and cook for 5 minutes, until fork tender. Season with salt and pepper. Remove from the pot and set aside.

Season the steak with salt and pepper. Add the steak to Cosori oven over high heat and cook for 5 minutes on each side for medium-rare, or longer if desired. Remove the steaks and let them rest on a cutting board.

Melt the remaining 2 Tbsp of butter over medium heat, stirring often. Add the broth when the butter starts to brown. Keep stirring and scraping up the browned bits using a wooden spoon.

Add the potatoes to the pan and heat through, about 5 minutes. Cut the steaks in half, spoon the potatoes and browned butter over each steak, and serve.

779. ROSEMARY TURKEY SCOTCH EGGS

Servings: 4

Cooking Time: 12 Minutes

INGREDIENTS:

- 1 egg
- 1 cup panko bread crumbs
- ½ teaspoon rosemary
- 1 pound (454 g) ground turkey
- 4 hard-boiled eggs, peeled
- Salt and ground black pepper, to taste
- Cooking spray

DIRECTIONS:

Spritz the air fryer basket with cooking spray.

Whisk the egg with salt in a bowl. Combine the bread crumbs with rosemary in a shallow dish.

Stir the ground turkey with salt and ground black pepper in a separate large bowl, then divide the ground turkey into four portions.

Wrap each hard-boiled egg with a portion of ground turkey. Dredge in the whisked egg, then roll over the breadcrumb mixture.

Place the wrapped eggs in the basket and spritz with cooking spray.

Put the air fryer basket on the baking pan and slide into Rack Position 2, select Air Fry, set temperature to 400ºF (205ºC) and set time to 12 minutes.

Flip the eggs halfway through.

When cooking is complete, the scotch eggs should be golden brown and crunchy.

Serve immediately.

780. SWEET HONEY THIGHS

Servings: 4

Cooking Time: 30 Minutes

INGREDIENTS:

- 4 thighs, skin-on
- 3 tbsp honey
- 2 tbsp Dijon mustard
- ½ tbsp garlic powder
- Salt and black pepper to taste

DIRECTIONS:

In a bowl, mix honey, mustard, garlic, salt, and pepper. Coat the thighs in the mixture and arrange them on the basket. Cook for 16-20 minutes at 400 F on AirFry function. Serve warm.

781. EASY PORK BITES

Servings: 4

Cooking Time: 15 Minutes

INGREDIENTS:

- 1 lb pork belly, cut into 3/4-inch cubes
- 1/2 tsp onion powder
- 1/2 tsp garlic powder
- 1 tsp soy sauce
- Pepper
- Salt

DIRECTIONS:

Fit the Cosori oven with the rack in position 2.

In a mixing bowl, toss pork cubes with onion powder, garlic powder, soy sauce, pepper, and salt.

Place pork cubes in the air fryer basket then place an air fryer basket in the baking pan.

Place a baking pan on the oven rack. Set to air fry at 400 F for 15 minutes.

Serve and enjoy.

Nutrition Info: Calories 526 Fat 30.5 g Carbohydrates 0.6 g Sugar 0.2 g Protein 52.5 g Cholesterol 131 mg

QUICK & EASY RECIPES FOR EVERYDAY

782. SIMPLE CHEESY SHRIMPS

Prep time: 10 minutes | Cook time: 8 minutes | Serves 4 to 6

- ⅔ cup grated Parmesan cheese
- 4 minced garlic cloves
- 1 teaspoon onion powder
- ½ teaspoon oregano
- 1 teaspoon basil
- 1 teaspoon ground black pepper
- 2 tablespoons olive oil
- 2 pounds (907 g) cooked large shrimps, peeled and deveined
- Lemon wedges, for topping
- Cooking spray

Spritz a perforated pan with cooking spray.

Combine all the ingredients, except for the shrimps, in a large bowl. Stir to mix well.

Dunk the shrimps in the mixture and toss to coat well. Shake the excess off. Arrange the shrimps in the perforated pan.

Select Air Fry. Set temperature to 350ºF (180ºC) and set time to 8 minutes. Select Start to begin preheating.

Once the oven has preheated, slide the pan into the oven. Flip the shrimps halfway through the cooking time.

When cooking is complete, the shrimps should be opaque. Remove the pan from the oven.

Transfer the cooked shrimps on a large plate and squeeze the lemon wedges over before serving.

783. SPANAKOPITA

Prep time: 10 minutes | Cook time: 8 minutes | Serves 6

- ½ (10-ounce / 284-g) package frozen spinach, thawed and squeezed dry
- 1 egg, lightly beaten
- ¼ cup pine nuts, toasted
- ¼ cup grated Parmesan cheese
- ¾ cup crumbled feta cheese
- ⅛ teaspoon ground nutmeg
- ½ teaspoon salt
- Freshly ground black pepper, to taste
- 6 sheets phyllo dough
- ½ cup butter, melted

Combine all the ingredients, except for the phyllo dough and butter, in a large bowl. Whisk to combine well. Set aside.

Place a sheet of phyllo dough on a clean work surface. Brush with butter then top with another layer sheet of phyllo. Brush with butter, then cut the layered sheets into six 3-inch-wide strips.

Top each strip with 1 tablespoon of the spinach mixture, then fold the bottom left corner over the mixture towards the right strip edge to make a triangle. Keep folding triangles until each strip is folded over.

Brush the triangles with butter and repeat with remaining strips and phyllo dough.

Place the triangles in the baking pan.

Select Air Fry. Set temperature to 350ºF (180ºC) and set time to 8 minutes. Select Start to begin preheating.

Once the oven has preheated, place the pan into the oven. Flip the triangles halfway through the cooking time.

When cooking is complete, the triangles should be golden brown. Remove the pan from the oven.

Serve immediately.

784. SPICY AIR FRIED OLD BAY SHRIMP

Prep time: 10 minutes | Cook time: 10 minutes | Makes 2 cups

- ½ teaspoon Old Bay Seasoning

- 1 teaspoon ground cayenne pepper
- ½ teaspoon paprika
- 1 tablespoon olive oil
- ⅛ teaspoon salt
- ½ pound (227 g) shrimps, peeled and deveined
- Juice of half a lemon

Combine the Old Bay Seasoning, cayenne pepper, paprika, olive oil, and salt in a large bowl, then add the shrimps and toss to coat well.

Put the shrimps in a perforated pan.

Select Air Fry. Set temperature to 390ºF (199ºC) and set time to 10 minutes. Select Start to begin preheating.

Once preheated, slide the pan into the oven. Flip the shrimps halfway through the cooking time.

When cooking is complete, the shrimps should be opaque. Remove the pan from the oven.

Serve the shrimps with lemon juice on top.

785. TRADITIONAL LATKES

Prep time: 15 minutes | Cook time: 10 minutes | Makes 4 latkes

- 1 egg
- 2 tablespoons all-purpose flour
- 2 medium potatoes, peeled and shredded, rinsed and drained
- ¼ teaspoon granulated garlic
- ½ teaspoon salt
- Cooking spray

Spritz a perforated pan with cooking spray.

Whisk together the egg, flour, potatoes, garlic, and salt in a large bowl. Stir to mix well.

Divide the mixture into four parts, then flatten them into four circles. Arrange the circles onto the perforated pan and spritz with cooking spray.

Select Air Fry. Set temperature to 380ºF (193ºC) and set time to 10 minutes. Select Start to begin preheating.

Once the oven has preheated, slide the pan into the oven. Flip the latkes halfway through.

When cooked, the latkes will be golden brown and crispy. Remove the pan from the oven.

Serve immediately.

786. GARLICKY SPIRALIZED ZUCCHINI AND SQUASH

Prep time: 10 minutes | Cook time: 10 minutes | Serves 4

- 2 large zucchini, peeled and spiralized
- 2 large yellow summer squash, peeled and spiralized
- 1 tablespoon olive oil, divided
- ½ teaspoon kosher salt
- 1 garlic clove, whole
- 2 tablespoons fresh basil, chopped
- Cooking spray

Spritz a perforated pan with cooking spray.

Combine the zucchini and summer squash with 1 teaspoon of the olive oil and salt in a large bowl. Toss to coat well.

Transfer the zucchini and summer squash to the perforated pan and add the garlic.

Select Air Fry. Set temperature to 360ºF (182ºC) and set time to 10 minutes. Select Start to begin preheating.

Once preheated, place the pan into the oven. Stir the zucchini and summer squash halfway through the cooking time.

When cooked, the zucchini and summer squash will be tender and fragrant. Transfer the cooked zucchini and summer squash onto a plate and set aside.

Remove the garlic from the oven and allow to cool for 5 minutes. Mince the garlic and combine with remaining olive oil in a small bowl. Stir to mix well.

Drizzle the spiralized zucchini and summer squash with garlic oil and sprinkle with basil. Toss to serve.

787. AIR FRIED CRISPY BRUSSELS SPROUTS

Prep time: 5 minutes | Cook time: 20 minutes | Serves 4

- ¼ teaspoon salt
- ⅛ teaspoon ground black pepper
- 1 tablespoon extra-virgin olive oil
- 1 pound (454 g) Brussels sprouts, trimmed and halved
- Lemon wedges, for garnish

Combine the salt, black pepper, and olive oil in a large bowl. Stir to mix well.

Add the Brussels sprouts to the bowl of mixture and toss to coat well.

Arrange the Brussels sprouts in a perforated pan.

Select Air Fry. Set temperature to 350°F (180°C) and set time to 20 minutes. Select Start to begin preheating.

Once preheated, place the pan into the oven. Stir the Brussels sprouts two times during cooking.

When cooked, the Brussels sprouts will be lightly browned and wilted. Remove the pan from the oven.

Transfer the cooked Brussels sprouts to a large plate and squeeze the lemon wedges on top to serve.

788. LEMONY AND GARLICKY ASPARAGUS

Prep time: 5 minutes | Cook time: 10 minutes | Makes 10 spears

- 10 spears asparagus (about ½ pound / 227 g in total), snap the ends off
- 1 tablespoon lemon juice
- 2 teaspoons minced garlic
- ½ teaspoon salt
- ¼ teaspoon ground black pepper
- Cooking spray

Line a perforated pan with parchment paper.

Put the asparagus spears in a large bowl. Drizzle with lemon juice and sprinkle with minced garlic, salt, and ground black pepper. Toss to coat well.

Transfer the asparagus to the perforated pan and spritz with cooking spray.

Select Air Fry. Set temperature to 400°F (205°C) and set time to 10 minutes. Select Start to begin preheating.

Once the oven has preheated, slide the pan into the oven. Flip the asparagus halfway through cooking.

When cooked, the asparagus should be wilted and soft. Remove the pan from the oven.

Serve immediately.

789. BAKED CHERRY TOMATOES WITH BASIL

Prep time: 5 minutes | Cook time: 5 minutes | Serves 2

- 2 cups cherry tomatoes
- 1 clove garlic, thinly sliced
- 1 teaspoon olive oil
- ⅛ teaspoon kosher salt
- 1 tablespoon freshly chopped basil, for topping
- Cooking spray

Spritz a baking pan with cooking spray and set aside.

In a large bowl, toss together the cherry tomatoes, sliced garlic, olive oil, and kosher salt. Spread the mixture in an even layer in the prepared pan.

Select Bake. Set temperature to 360°F (182°C) and set time to 5 minutes.

Select Start to begin preheating.

Once the oven has preheated, slide the pan into the oven.

When cooking is complete, the tomatoes should be the soft and wilted.

Transfer to a bowl and rest for 5 minutes. Top with the chopped basil and serve warm.

790. FAST CINNAMON TOAST

Prep time: 5 minutes | Cook time: 5 minutes | Serves 6

- 1½ teaspoons cinnamon
- 1½ teaspoons vanilla extract
- ½ cup sugar
- 2 teaspoons ground black pepper
- 2 tablespoons melted coconut oil
- 12 slices whole wheat bread

Combine all the ingredients, except for the bread, in a large bowl. Stir to mix well.

Dunk the bread in the bowl of mixture gently to coat and infuse well. Shake the excess off. Arrange the bread slices in a perforated pan.

Select Air Fry. Set temperature to 400°F (205°C) and set time to 5 minutes. Select Start to begin preheating.

Once the oven has preheated, place the pan into the oven. Flip the bread halfway through.

When cooking is complete, the bread should be golden brown.

Remove the bread slices from the oven and slice to serve.

791. BUTTERNUT SQUASH WITH HAZELNUTS

Prep time: 10 minutes | Cook time: 23 minutes | Makes 3 cups

- 2 tablespoons whole hazelnuts
- 3 cups butternut squash, peeled, deseeded and cubed
- ¼ teaspoon kosher salt
- ¼ teaspoon freshly ground black pepper
- 2 teaspoons olive oil
- Cooking spray

Spritz a perforated pan with cooking spray. Spread the hazelnuts in the pan.

Select Air Fry. Set temperature to 300°F (150°C) and set time to 3 minutes. Select Start to begin preheating.

Once preheated, slide the pan into the oven.

When done, the hazelnuts should be soft. Remove from the oven. Chopped the hazelnuts roughly and transfer to a small bowl. Set aside.

Put the butternut squash in a large bowl, then sprinkle with salt and pepper and drizzle with olive oil. Toss to coat well. Transfer the squash to the lightly greased perforated pan.

Select Air Fry. Set temperature to 360°F (182°C) and set time to 20 minutes.

Place the pan into the oven. Flip the squash halfway through the cooking time.

When cooking is complete, the squash will be soft. Transfer the squash to a plate and sprinkle with the chopped hazelnuts before serving.

792. LEMONY SHISHITO PEPPERS

Prep time: 5 minutes | Cook time: 5 minutes | Serves 4

- ½ pound (227 g) shishito peppers (about 24)
- 1 tablespoon olive oil
- Coarse sea salt, to taste
- Lemon wedges, for serving
- Cooking spray

Spritz a perforated pan with cooking spray.

Toss the peppers with olive oil in a large bowl to coat well.

Arrange the peppers in the perforated pan.

Select Air Fry. Set temperature to 400°F (205°C) and set time to 5 minutes. Select Start to begin preheating.

Once preheated, place the pan into the oven. Flip the peppers and sprinkle the peppers with salt halfway through the cooking time.

When cooked, the peppers should be blistered and lightly charred. Transfer the peppers onto a plate and squeeze the lemon wedges on top before serving.

793. KALE CHIPS WITH SOY SAUCE

Prep time: 5 minutes | Cook time: 5 minutes | Serves 2

- 4 medium kale leaves, about 1 ounce (28 g) each, stems removed, tear the leaves in thirds
- 2 teaspoons soy sauce
- 2 teaspoons olive oil

Toss the kale leaves with soy sauce and olive oil in a large bowl to coat well. Place the leaves in the baking pan.

Select Air Fry. Set temperature to 400°F (205°C) and set time to 5 minutes. Select Start to begin preheating.

Once the oven has preheated, slide the pan into the oven. Flip the leaves with tongs gently halfway through.

When cooked, the kale leaves should be crispy. Remove the pan from the oven.

Serve immediately.

794. POTATO CHIPS WITH LEMONY CREAM DIP

Prep time: 20 minutes | Cook time: 15 minutes | Serves 2 to 4

- 2 large russet potatoes, sliced into ⅛-inch slices, rinsed
- Sea salt and freshly ground black pepper, to taste
- Cooking spray
- Lemony Cream Dip:
- ½ cup sour cream
- ¼ teaspoon lemon juice
- 2 scallions, white part only, minced
- 1 tablespoon olive oil
- ¼ teaspoon salt
- Freshly ground black pepper, to taste

Soak the potato slices in water for 10 minutes, then pat dry with paper towels.

Transfer the potato slices in a perforated pan. Spritz the slices with cooking spray.

Select Air Fry. Set temperature to 300°F (150°C) and set time to 15 minutes. Select Start to begin preheating.

Once the oven has preheated, place the pan into the oven. Stir the potato slices three times during cooking. Sprinkle with salt and ground black pepper in the last minute.

Meanwhile, combine the ingredients for the dip in a small bowl. Stir to mix well.

When cooking is complete, the potato slices will be crispy and golden brown. Remove the pan from the oven.

Serve the potato chips immediately with the dip.

795. SIMPLE AIR FRIED EDAMAME

Prep time: 5 minutes | Cook time: 7 minutes | Serves 6

- 1½ pounds (680 g) unshelled edamame
- 2 tablespoons olive oil
- 1 teaspoon sea salt

Place the edamame in a large bowl, then drizzle with olive oil. Toss to coat well. Transfer the edamame to a perforated pan.

Select Air Fry. Set temperature to 400°F (205°C) and set time to 7 minutes. Select Start to begin preheating.

Once preheated, place the pan into the oven. Stir the edamame at least three times during cooking.

When done, the edamame will be tender and warmed through.

Transfer the cooked edamame onto a plate and sprinkle with salt. Toss to combine well and set aside for 3 minutes to infuse before serving.

796. SOUTHWEST CORN AND BELL PEPPER ROAST

Prep time: 10 minutes | Cook time: 10 minutes | Serves 4

- Corn:
- 1½ cups thawed frozen corn kernels
- 1 cup mixed diced bell peppers
- 1 jalapeño, diced
- 1 cup diced yellow onion
- ½ teaspoon ancho chile powder
- 1 tablespoon fresh lemon juice
- 1 teaspoon ground cumin
- ½ teaspoon kosher salt
- Cooking spray
- For Serving:
- ¼ cup feta cheese
- ¼ cup chopped fresh cilantro
- 1 tablespoon fresh lemon juice

Spritz a perforated pan with cooking spray.

Combine the ingredients for the corn in a large bowl. Stir to mix well. Pour the mixture into the perforated pan.

Select Air Fry. Set temperature to 375°F (190°C) and set time to 10 minutes. Select Start to begin preheating.

Once the oven has preheated, slide the pan into the oven. Stir the mixture halfway through the cooking time.

When done, the corn and bell peppers should be soft.

Transfer them onto a large plate, then spread with feta cheese and cilantro. Drizzle with lemon juice and serve.

797. GOLDEN SALMON AND CARROT CROQUETTES

Prep time: 15 minutes | Cook time: 10 minutes | Serves 6

- 2 egg whites
- 1 cup almond flour
- 1 cup panko bread crumbs
- 1 pound (454 g) chopped salmon fillet
- ⅔ cup grated carrots
- 2 tablespoons minced garlic cloves
- ½ cup chopped onion
- 2 tablespoons chopped chives
- Cooking spray

Spritz a perforated pan with cooking spray.

Whisk the egg whites in a bowl. Put the flour in a second bowl. Pour the bread crumbs in a third bowl. Set aside.

Combine the salmon, carrots, garlic, onion, and chives in a large bowl. Stir to mix well.

Form the mixture into balls with your hands. Dredge the balls into the flour, then egg, and then bread crumbs to coat well.

Arrange the salmon balls on the perforated pan and spritz with cooking spray.

Select Air Fry. Set temperature to 350°F (180°C) and set time to 10 minutes. Select Start to begin preheating.

Once preheated, slide the pan into the oven. Flip the salmon balls halfway through cooking.

When cooking is complete, the salmon balls will be crispy and browned. Remove the pan from the oven.

Serve immediately.

798. SWEET AIR FRIED PECANS

Prep time: 5 minutes | Cook time: 10 minutes | Makes 4 cups

- 2 egg whites
- 1 tablespoon cumin
- 2 teaspoons smoked paprika
- ½ cup brown sugar
- 2 teaspoons kosher salt
- 1 pound (454 g) pecan halves
- Cooking spray

Spritz a perforated pan with cooking spray.
Combine the egg whites, cumin, paprika, sugar, and salt in a large bowl. Stir to mix well. Add the pecans to the bowl and toss to coat well.
Transfer the pecans to the perforated pan.
Select Air Fry. Set temperature to 300°F (150°C) and set time to 10 minutes. Select Start to begin preheating.
Once the oven has preheated, place the pan into the oven. Stir the pecans at least two times during the cooking.
When cooking is complete, the pecans should be lightly caramelized. Remove the pan from the oven.
Serve immediately.

799. CRISPY ZUCCHINI STICKS

Prep time: 5 minutes | Cook time: 10 minutes | Serves 4
- 1 medium zucchini, cut into 48 sticks
- ¼ cup seasoned bread crumbs
- 1 tablespoon melted buttery spread
- Cooking spray

Spritz a perforated pan with cooking spray and set aside.
In 2 different shallow bowls, add the seasoned bread crumbs and the buttery spread.
One by one, dredge the zucchini sticks into the buttery spread, then roll in the bread crumbs to coat evenly. Arrange the crusted sticks in the perforated pan.
Select Air Fry. Set temperature to 360°F (182°C) and set time to 10 minutes. Select Start to begin preheating.
When preheated, slide the pan into the oven. Stir the sticks halfway through the cooking time.
When done, the sticks should be golden brown and crispy. Transfer the fries to a plate. Rest for 5 minutes and serve warm.

800. CITRUS AVOCADO WEDGE FRIES

Prep time: 10 minutes | Cook time: 8 minutes | Makes 12 fries

- 1 cup all-purpose flour
- 3 tablespoons lime juice
- ¾ cup orange juice
- 1¼ cups plain dried bread crumbs
- 1 cup yellow cornmeal
- 1½ tablespoons chile powder
- 2 large Hass avocados, peeled, pitted, and cut into wedges
- Coarse sea salt, to taste
- Cooking spray

Spritz a perforated pan with cooking spray.
Pour the flour in a bowl. Mix the lime juice with orange juice in a second bowl. Combine the bread crumbs, cornmeal, and chile powder in a third bowl.
Dip the avocado wedges in the bowl of flour to coat well, then dredge the wedges into the bowl of juice mixture, and then dunk the wedges in the bread crumbs mixture. Shake the excess off.
Arrange the coated avocado wedges in a single layer in the perforated pan. Spritz with cooking spray.
Select Air Fry. Set temperature to 400°F (205°C) and set time to 8 minutes. Select Start to begin preheating.

Once preheated, slide the pan into the oven. Stir the avocado wedges and sprinkle with salt halfway through the cooking time.
When cooking is complete, the avocado wedges should be tender and crispy.
Serve immediately.

801. AIR FRIED BACON PINWHEELS

Prep time: 5 minutes | Cook time: 10 minutes | Makes 8 pinwheels

- 1 sheet puff pastry
- 2 tablespoons maple syrup
- ¼ cup brown sugar
- 8 slices bacon
- Ground black pepper, to taste
- Cooking spray

Spritz a perforated pan with cooking spray.
Roll the puff pastry into a 10-inch square with a rolling pin on a clean work surface, then cut the pastry into 8 strips.
Brush the strips with maple syrup and sprinkle with sugar, leaving a 1-inch far end uncovered.
Arrange each slice of bacon on each strip, leaving a ⅛-inch length of bacon hang over the end close to you. Sprinkle with black pepper.
From the end close to you, roll the strips into pinwheels, then dab the uncovered end with water and seal the rolls.
Arrange the pinwheels in the perforated pan and spritz with cooking spray.
Select Air Fry. Set temperature to 360°F (182°C) and set time to 10 minutes. Select Start to begin preheating.
Once preheated, slide the pan into the oven. Flip the pinwheels halfway through.
When cooking is complete, the pinwheels should be golden brown. Remove the pan from the oven.
Serve immediately.

802. CRUNCHY AND BEERY ONION RINGS

Prep time: 10 minutes | Cook time: 16 minutes | Serves 2 to 4

- ⅔ cup all-purpose flour
- 1 teaspoon paprika
- ½ teaspoon baking soda
- 1 teaspoon salt
- ½ teaspoon freshly ground black pepper
- 1 egg, beaten
- ¾ cup beer
- 1½ cups bread crumbs
- 1 tablespoons olive oil
- 1 large Vidalia onion, peeled and sliced into ½-inch rings
- Cooking spray

Spritz a perforated pan with cooking spray.
Combine the flour, paprika, baking soda, salt, and ground black pepper in a bowl. Stir to mix well.
Combine the egg and beer in a separate bowl. Stir to mix well.
Make a well in the center of the flour mixture, then pour the egg mixture in the well. Stir to mix everything well.
Pour the bread crumbs and olive oil in a shallow plate. Stir to mix well.
Dredge the onion rings gently into the flour and egg mixture, then shake the excess off and put into the plate of bread crumbs. Flip to coat the both sides well. Arrange the onion rings in the perforated pan.
Select Air Fry. Set temperature to 360°F (182°C) and set time to 16 minutes. Select Start to begin preheating.
Once preheated, slide the pan into the oven. Flip the rings and put the bottom rings to the top halfway through.
When cooked, the rings will be golden brown and crunchy. Remove the

pan from the oven.
Serve immediately.

803. CORN ON THE COB WITH MAYONNAISE
Prep time: 10 minutes | Cook time: 10 minutes | Serves 4

- 2 tablespoons mayonnaise
- 2 teaspoons minced garlic
- ½ teaspoon sea salt
- 1 cup panko bread crumbs
- 4 (4-inch length) ears corn on the cob, husk and silk removed
- Cooking spray

Spritz a perforated pan with cooking spray.
Combine the mayonnaise, garlic, and salt in a bowl. Stir to mix well.
Pour the panko on a plate.
Brush the corn on the cob with mayonnaise mixture, then roll the cob in the bread crumbs and press to coat well.
Transfer the corn on the cob in the perforated pan and spritz with cooking spray.
Select Air Fry. Set temperature to 400°F (205°C) and set time to 10 minutes. Select Start to begin preheating.
Once the oven has preheated, place the pan into the oven. Flip the corn on the cob at least three times during the cooking.
When cooked, the corn kernels on the cob should be almost browned. Remove the pan from the oven.
Serve immediately.

804. BUTTERY KNOTS WITH PARSLEY
Prep time: 5 minutes | Cook time: 5 minutes | Makes 8 knots

- 1 teaspoon dried parsley
- ¼ cup melted butter
- 2 teaspoons garlic powder
- 1 (11-ounce / 312-g) tube refrigerated French bread dough, cut into 8 slices

Combine the parsley, butter, and garlic powder in a bowl. Stir to mix well.
Place the French bread dough slices on a clean work surface, then roll each slice into a 6-inch long rope. Tie the ropes into knots and arrange them on a plate.
Transfer the knots into a baking pan. Brush the knots with butter mixture.
Select Air Fry. Set temperature to 350°F (180°C) and set time to 5 minutes. Select Start to begin preheating.
Once the oven has preheated, slide the pan into the oven. Flip the knots halfway through the cooking time.
When done, the knots should be golden brown. Remove the pan from the oven.
Serve immediately.

805. CLASSIC WORCESTERSHIRE POUTINE
Prep time: 15 minutes | Cook time: 33 minutes | Serves 2

- 2 russet potatoes, scrubbed and cut into ½-inch sticks
- 2 teaspoons vegetable oil
- 2 tablespoons butter
- ¼ onion, minced
- ¼ teaspoon dried thyme
- 1 clove garlic, smashed
- 3 tablespoons all-purpose flour
- 1 teaspoon tomato paste
- 1½ cups beef stock
- 2 teaspoons Worcestershire sauce
- Salt and freshly ground black pepper, to taste
- ⅔ cup chopped string cheese

Bring a pot of water to a boil, then put in the potato sticks and blanch for 4 minutes.
Drain the potato sticks and rinse under running cold water, then pat dry with paper towels.
Transfer the sticks in a large bowl and drizzle with vegetable oil. Toss to coat well. Place the potato sticks in a perforated pan.
Select Air Fry. Set temperature to 400°F (205°C) and set time to 25 minutes. Select Start to begin preheating.
Once preheated, place the pan into the oven. Stir the potato sticks at least three times during cooking.
Meanwhile, make the gravy: Heat the butter in a saucepan over medium heat until melted.
Add the onion, thyme, and garlic and sauté for 5 minutes or until the onion is translucent.
Add the flour and sauté for an additional 2 minutes. Pour in the tomato paste and beef stock and cook for 1 more minute or until lightly thickened.
Drizzle the gravy with Worcestershire sauce and sprinkle with salt and ground black pepper. Reduce the heat to low to keep the gravy warm until ready to serve.
  When done, the sticks should be golden brown. Remove the pan from the oven. Transfer the fried potato sticks onto a plate, then sprinkle with salt and ground black pepper. Scatter with string cheese and pour the gravy over. Serve warm.

806. SWEET CINNAMON CHICKPEAS
Prep time: 10 minutes | Cook time: 10 minutes | Serves 2

- 1 tablespoon cinnamon
- 1 tablespoon sugar
- 1 cup chickpeas, soaked in water overnight, rinsed and drained

Combine the cinnamon and sugar in a bowl. Stir to mix well.
Add the chickpeas to the bowl, then toss to coat well.
Pour the chickpeas in a perforated pan.
Select Air Fry. Set temperature to 390°F (199°C) and set time to 10 minutes. Select Start to begin preheating.
Once the oven has preheated, slide the pan into the oven. Stir the chickpeas three times during cooking.
When cooked, the chickpeas should be golden brown and crispy. Remove the pan from the oven.
Serve immediately.

807. CRUNCHY GREEN TOMATOES SLICES
Prep time: 10 minutes | Cook time: 8 minutes | Makes 12 slices

- ½ cup all-purpose flour
- 1 egg
- ½ cup buttermilk
- 1 cup cornmeal
- 1 cup panko
- 2 green tomatoes, cut into ¼-inch-thick slices, patted dry
- ½ teaspoon salt
- ½ teaspoon ground black pepper
- Cooking spray

Spritz a baking sheet with cooking spray.
Pour the flour in a bowl. Whisk the egg and buttermilk in a second bowl. Combine the cornmeal and panko in a third bowl.
Dredge the tomato slices in the bowl of flour first, then into the egg mixture, and then dunk the slices into the cornmeal mixture. Shake the excess off.
Transfer the well-coated tomato slices in the baking sheet and sprinkle with salt and ground black pepper. Spritz the tomato slices with cooking spray.

Select Air Fry. Set temperature to 400ºF (205ºC) and set time to 8 minutes. Select Start to begin preheating.

Once preheated, slide the baking sheet into the oven. Flip the slices halfway through the cooking time.

When cooking is complete, the tomato slices should be crispy and lightly browned. Remove the baking sheet from the oven.

Serve immediately.

808. CRISPY CHEESE WAFER

Prep time: 5 minutes | Cook time: 5 minutes | Serves 2

- 1 cup shredded aged Manchego cheese
- 1 teaspoon all-purpose flour
- ½ teaspoon cumin seeds
- ¼ teaspoon cracked black pepper

Line a perforated pan with parchment paper.

Combine the cheese and flour in a bowl. Stir to mix well. Spread the mixture in the pan into a 4-inch round.

Combine the cumin and black pepper in a small bowl. Stir to mix well. Sprinkle the cumin mixture over the cheese round.

Select Air Fry. Set temperature to 375ºF (190ºC) and set time to 5 minutes. Select Start to begin preheating.

Once preheated, place the pan into the oven.

When cooked, the cheese will be lightly browned and frothy.

Use tongs to transfer the cheese wafer onto a plate and slice to serve.

809. SALTY TORTILLA CHIPS

Prep time: 5 minutes | Cook time: 10 minutes | Serves 4

- 4 six-inch corn tortillas, cut in half and slice into thirds
- 1 tablespoon canola oil
- ¼ teaspoon kosher salt
- Cooking spray

Spritz a perforated pan with cooking spray.

On a clean work surface, brush the tortilla chips with canola oil, then transfer the chips to the perforated pan.

Select Air Fry. Set temperature to 360ºF (182ºC) and set time to 10 minutes. Select Start to begin preheating.

Once preheated, slide the pan into the oven. Flip the chips and sprinkle with salt halfway through the cooking time.

When cooked, the chips will be crunchy and lightly browned. Transfer the chips to a plate lined with paper towels. Serve immediately.

810. SIMPLE AIR FRIED OKRA CHIPS

Prep time: 5 minutes | Cook time: 16 minutes | Serves 6

- 2 pounds (907 g) fresh okra pods, cut into 1-inch pieces
- 2 tablespoons canola oil
- 1 teaspoon coarse sea salt

Stir the oil and salt in a bowl to mix well. Add the okra and toss to coat well. Place the okra in a perforated pan.

Select Air Fry. Set temperature to 400ºF (205ºC) and set time to 16 minutes. Select Start to begin preheating.

Once the oven has preheated, slide the pan into the oven. Flip the okra at least three times during cooking.

When cooked, the okra should be lightly browned. Remove the pan from the oven.

Serve immediately.

811. SIMPLE BAKED GREEN BEANS

Prep time: 5 minutes | Cook time: 10 minutes | Makes 2 cups

- ½ teaspoon lemon pepper
- 2 teaspoons granulated garlic

- ½ teaspoon salt
- 1 tablespoon olive oil
- 2 cups fresh green beans, trimmed and snapped in half

Combine the lemon pepper, garlic, salt, and olive oil in a bowl. Stir to mix well.

Add the green beans to the bowl of mixture and toss to coat well.

Arrange the green beans in a perforated pan.

Select Bake. Set temperature to 370ºF (188ºC) and set time to 10 minutes. Select Start to begin preheating.

Once preheated, slide the pan into the oven. Stir the green beans halfway through the cooking time.

When cooking is complete, the green beans will be tender and crispy. Remove the pan from the oven.

Serve immediately.

812. BARTLETT PEARS WITH LEMONY RICOTTA

Prep time: 10 minutes | Cook time: 8 minutes | Serves 4

- 2 large Bartlett pears, peeled, cut in half, cored
- 3 tablespoons melted butter
- ½ teaspoon ground ginger
- ¼ teaspoon ground cardamom
- 3 tablespoons brown sugar
- ½ cup whole-milk ricotta cheese
- 1 teaspoon pure lemon extract
- 1 teaspoon pure almond extract
- 1 tablespoon honey, plus additional for drizzling

Toss the pears with butter, ginger, cardamom, and sugar in a large bowl. Toss to coat well. Arrange the pears in a baking pan, cut side down.

Select Air Fry. Set temperature to 375ºF (190ºC) and set time to 8 minutes. Select Start to begin preheating.

Once preheated, place the pan into the oven.

After 5 minutes, remove the pan and flip the pears. Return the pan to the oven and continue cooking.

When cooking is complete, the pears should be soft and browned. Remove the pan from the oven.

In the meantime, combine the remaining ingredients in a separate bowl. Whip for 1 minute with a hand mixer until the mixture is puffed.

Divide the mixture into four bowls, then put the pears over the mixture and drizzle with more honey to serve.

813. APPLE FRITTERS WITH SUGARY GLAZE

Prep time: 10 minutes | Cook time: 8 minutes | Makes 15 fritters

- Apple Fritters:
- 2 firm apples, peeled, cored, and diced
- ½ teaspoon cinnamon
- Juice of 1 lemon
- 1 cup all-purpose flour
- 1½ teaspoons baking powder
- ½ teaspoon kosher salt
- 2 eggs
- ¼ cup milk
- 2 tablespoons unsalted butter, melted
- 2 tablespoons granulated sugar
- Cooking spray
- Glaze:
- ½ teaspoon vanilla extract
- 1¼ cups powdered sugar, sifted
- ¼ cup water

Line a perforated pan with parchment paper.

Combine the apples with cinnamon and lemon juice in a small bowl. Toss to coat well.

Combine the flour, baking powder, and salt in a large bowl. Stir to mix well.

Whisk the egg, milk, butter, and sugar in a medium bowl. Stir to mix well.

Make a well in the center of the flour mixture, then pour the egg mixture into the well and stir to mix well. Mix in the apple until a dough forms.

Use an ice cream scoop to scoop 15 balls from the dough onto the pan. Spritz with cooking spray.

Select Air Fry. Set temperature to 360°F (182°C) and set time to 8 minutes. Select Start to begin preheating.

Once the oven has preheated, place the pan into the oven. Flip the apple fritters halfway through the cooking time.

Meanwhile, combine the ingredients for the glaze in a separate small bowl. Stir to mix well.

When cooking is complete, the apple fritters will be golden brown. Serve the fritters with the glaze on top or use the glaze for dipping.

814. HOT WINGS
Prep time: 5 minutes | Cook time: 15 minutes | Makes 16 wings

- 16 chicken wings
- 3 tablespoons hot sauce
- Cooking spray

Spritz a perforated pan with cooking spray.

Arrange the chicken wings in the perforated pan.

Select Air Fry. Set temperature to 360°F (182°C) and set time to 15 minutes. Select Start to begin preheating.

Once preheated, place the pan into the oven. Flip the wings at lease three times during cooking.

When cooking is complete, the chicken wings will be well browned. Remove the pan from the oven.

Transfer the air fried wings to a plate and serve with hot sauce.

815. PARSNIP FRIES WITH GARLIC-YOGURT DIP
Prep time: 10 minutes | Cook time: 10 minutes | Serves 4

- 3 medium parsnips, peeled, cut into sticks
- ¼ teaspoon kosher salt
- 1 teaspoon olive oil
- 1 garlic clove, unpeeled
- Cooking spray
Dip:
- ¼ cup plain Greek yogurt
- ⅛ teaspoon garlic powder
- 1 tablespoon sour cream
- ¼ teaspoon kosher salt
- Freshly ground black pepper, to taste

Spritz a perforated pan with cooking spray.

Put the parsnip sticks in a large bowl, then sprinkle with salt and drizzle with olive oil.

Transfer the parsnip into the perforated pan and add the garlic.

Select Air Fry. Set temperature to 360°F (182°C) and set time to 10 minutes. Select Start to begin preheating.

Once preheated, place the pan into the oven. Stir the parsnip halfway through the cooking time.

Meanwhile, peel the garlic and crush it. Combine the crushed garlic with the ingredients for the dip. Stir to mix well.

When cooked, the parsnip sticks should be crisp. Remove the parsnip fries from the oven and serve with the dipping sauce.

816. ROASTED CARROT CHIPS
Prep time: 5 minutes | Cook time: 15 minutes | Makes 3 cups

- 3 large carrots, peeled and sliced into long and thick chips diagonally

- 1 tablespoon granulated garlic
- 1 teaspoon salt
- ¼ teaspoon ground black pepper
- 1 tablespoon olive oil
- 1 tablespoon finely chopped fresh parsley

Toss the carrots with garlic, salt, ground black pepper, and olive oil in a large bowl to coat well. Place the carrots in a perforated pan.

Select Roast. Set temperature to 360°F (182°C) and set time to 15 minutes. Select Start to begin preheating.

Once the oven has preheated, slide the pan into the oven. Stir the carrots halfway through the cooking time.

When cooking is complete, the carrot chips should be soft. Remove the pan from the oven.

Serve the carrot chips with parsley on top.

817. PARMESAN CAULIFLOWER FRITTERS
Prep time: 5 minutes | Cook time: 8 minutes | Serves 6

- 2 cups cooked cauliflower
- 1 cup panko bread crumbs
- 1 large egg, beaten
- ½ cup grated Parmesan cheese
- 1 tablespoon chopped fresh chives
- Cooking spray

Spritz a perforated pan with cooking spray.

Put the cauliflower, panko bread crumbs, egg, Parmesan, and chives in a food processor, then pulse to lightly mash and combine the mixture until chunky and thick.

Shape the mixture into 6 flat patties, then arrange them in the perforated pan and spritz with cooking spray.

Select Air Fry. Set temperature to 390°F (199°C) and set time to 8 minutes. Select Start to begin preheating.

Once preheated, place the pan into the oven. Flip the patties halfway through the cooking time.

When done, the patties should be crispy and golden brown. Remove the pan from the oven.

Serve immediately.

818. CHEDDAR JALAPEÑO CORNBREAD
Prep time: 10 minutes | Cook time: 20 minutes | Serves 8

- ⅔ cup cornmeal
- ⅓ cup all-purpose flour
- ¾ teaspoon baking powder
- 2 tablespoons buttery spread, melted
- ½ teaspoon kosher salt
- 1 tablespoon granulated sugar
- ¾ cup whole milk
- 1 large egg, beaten
- 1 jalapeño pepper, thinly sliced
- ⅓ cup shredded sharp Cheddar cheese
- Cooking spray

Spritz a baking pan with cooking spray.

Combine all the ingredients in a large bowl. Stir to mix well. Pour the mixture in the baking pan.

Select Bake. Set temperature to 300°F (150°C) and set time to 20 minutes. Select Start to begin preheating.

Once preheated, slide the pan into the oven.

When the cooking is complete, a toothpick inserted in the center of the bread should come out clean.

Remove the baking pan from the oven and allow the bread to cool for 5 minutes before slicing to serve.

819. TRADITIONAL FRENCH FRIES

Prep time: 5 minutes | Cook time: 25 minutes | Serves 2

- 2 russet potatoes, peeled and cut into ½-inch sticks
- 2 teaspoons olive oil
- Salt, to taste
- ¼ cup ketchup, for serving

Bring a pot of salted water to a boil. Put the potato sticks into the pot and blanch for 4 minutes.

Rinse the potatoes under running cold water and pat dry with paper towels.

Put the potato sticks in a large bowl and drizzle with olive oil. Toss to coat well.

Transfer the potato sticks to a perforated pan.

Select Air Fry. Set temperature to 400°F (205°C) and set time to 25 minutes. Select Start to begin preheating.

Once the oven has preheated, slide the pan into the oven. Stir the potato sticks and sprinkle with salt halfway through.

When cooked, the potato sticks will be crispy and golden brown. Remove the French fries from the oven and serve with ketchup.

820. SOUTH CAROLINA SHRIMP AND CORN BAKE

Prep time: 10 minutes | Cook time: 18 minutes | Serves 2

- 1 ear corn, husk and silk removed, cut into 2-inch rounds
- 8 ounces (227 g) red potatoes, unpeeled, cut into 1-inch pieces
- 2 teaspoons Old Bay Seasoning, divided
- 2 teaspoons vegetable oil, divided
- ¼ teaspoon ground black pepper
- 8 ounces (227 g) large shrimps (about 12 shrimps), deveined
- 6 ounces (170 g) andouille or chorizo sausage, cut into 1-inch pieces
- 2 garlic cloves, minced
- 1 tablespoon chopped fresh parsley

Put the corn rounds and potatoes in a large bowl. Sprinkle with 1 teaspoon of Old Bay seasoning and drizzle with vegetable oil. Toss to coat well.

Transfer the corn rounds and potatoes onto a baking pan.

Select Bake. Set temperature to 400°F (205°C) and set time to 18 minutes. Select Start to begin preheating.

Once preheated, place the pan into the oven.

After 6 minutes, remove the pan from the oven. Stir the corn rounds and potatoes. Return the pan to the oven and continue cooking.

Meanwhile, cut slits into the shrimps but be careful not to cut them through. Combine the shrimps, sausage, remaining Old Bay seasoning, and remaining vegetable oil in the large bowl. Toss to coat well.

After 6 minutes, remove the pan from the oven. Add the shrimps and sausage to the pan. Return the pan back to the oven and continue cooking for 6 minutes. Stir the shrimp mixture halfway through the cooking time.

When done, the shrimps should be opaque. Remove the pan from the oven.

Transfer the dish to a plate and spread with parsley before serving.

821. SWEET AND SOUR PEANUTS

Prep time: 5 minutes | Cook time: 5 minutes | Serves 9

- 3 cups shelled raw peanuts
- 1 tablespoon hot red pepper sauce
- 3 tablespoons granulated white sugar

Put the peanuts in a large bowl, then drizzle with hot red pepper sauce and sprinkle with sugar. Toss to coat well.

Pour the peanuts in a perforated pan.

Select Air Fry. Set temperature to 400°F (205°C) and set time to 5 minutes. Select Start to begin preheating.

Once preheated, slide the pan into the oven. Stir the peanuts halfway through the cooking time.

When cooking is complete, the peanuts will be crispy and browned. Remove the pan from the oven.

Serve immediately.

SNACK & DESSERT RECIPES

822. BUTTERED DINNER ROLLS

Servings: 12
Cooking Time: 30 Minutes
INGREDIENTS:
- 1 cup milk
- 3 cups plain flour
- 7½ tablespoons unsalted butter
- 1 tablespoon coconut oil
- 1 tablespoon olive oil
- 1 teaspoon yeast
- Salt and black pepper, to taste

DIRECTIONS:
Preheat the Air fryer to 360 degree F and grease an Air fryer basket.

Put olive oil, milk and coconut oil in a pan and cook for about 3 minutes. Remove from the heat and mix well.

Mix together plain flour, yeast, butter, salt and black pepper in a large bowl.

Knead well for about 5 minutes until a dough is formed.

Cover the dough with a damp cloth and keep aside for about 5 minutes in a warm place.

Knead the dough for about 5 minutes again with your hands.

Cover the dough with a damp cloth and keep aside for about 30 minutes in a warm place.

Divide the dough into 12 equal pieces and roll each into a ball.

Arrange 6 balls into the Air fryer basket in a single layer and cook for about 15 minutes.

Repeat with the remaining balls and serve warm.

Nutrition Info: Calories: 208, Fat: 10.3g, Carbohydrates: 25g, Sugar: 1g, Protein: 4.1g, Sodium: 73mg

823. SHRIMP AND ARTICHOKE PUFFS

INGREDIENTS:
- 1 (10-ounce) package frozen artichoke hearts, thawed
- 1 (3-ounce) package cream cheese, softened
- 1 cup shredded Coda cheese
- ½ cup mayonnaise
- 1 tablespoon lemon juice
- 1 teaspoon dried basil leaves
- 6 slices whole wheat bread
- 2 shallots, chopped
- 1 tablespoon olive oil
- ½ pound cooked shrimp

DIRECTIONS:
Preheat oven to 300°F. Using a 2-inch cookie cutter, cut rounds from bread slices. Place rounds on a baking sheet and bake at 300°F for 7 to 9 minutes, or until crisp, turning once. Remove from oven and cool on wire racks.

In a heavy skillet, cook shallots in olive oil over medium heat until tender. Remove from heat. Chop shrimp and add to skillet along with thawed, drained, and chopped artichoke hearts. Add both cheeses, mayonnaise, lemon juice, and basil; stir well to blend.

Spoon 1 tablespoon shrimp mixture onto each bread round, covering the top and mounding the filling. Flash freeze on baking sheets. When frozen solid, pack in rigid containers, with waxed paper between layers. Label puffs and freeze.

To reheat: Place frozen puffs on a baking sheet and bake at 400°F for 10 to 12 minutes or until topping is hot and bubbling.

824. HOMEMADE DOUGHNUTS

Servings: 4
Cooking Time: 25 Minutes
INGREDIENTS:
- 8 oz self-rising flour
- 1 tsp baking powder
- ½ cup milk
- 2 ½ tbsp butter
- 1 egg
- 2 oz brown sugar

DIRECTIONS:

Preheat Cosori on Bake function to 350 F. Beat the butter with the sugar until smooth. Whisk in the egg and milk. In a bowl, combine flour with baking powder. Fold in the butter mixture.

Form donut shapes and cut off the center with cookie cutters. Arrange on a lined baking sheet and cook in for 15 minutes. Serve with whipped cream or icing.

825. EGGLESS BROWNIES

Servings: 8
Cooking Time: 40 Minutes
INGREDIENTS:
- 1/4 cup walnuts, chopped
- 1/3 cup cocoa powder
- 2 tsp baking powder
- 1 cup of sugar
- 1 cup all-purpose flour
- 1/2 cup chocolate chips
- 2 tsp vanilla
- 1 tbsp milk
- 3/4 cup yogurt
- 1/2 cup butter, melted
- 1/4 tsp salt

DIRECTIONS:

Fit the Cosori oven with the rack in position
In a large mixing bowl, sift flour, cocoa powder, baking powder, and salt. Mix well and set aside.
In another bowl, add butter, vanilla, milk, and yogurt and whisk until well combined.
Add flour mixture into the butter mixture and mix until just combined.
Fold in walnuts and chocolate chips.
Pour batter into the prepared baking dish.
Set to bake at 350 F for 45 minutes. After 5 minutes place the baking dish in the preheated oven.
Slice and serve.
Nutrition Info: Calories 363 Fat 18 g Carbohydrates 48 g Sugar 32.4 g Protein 5.5 g Cholesterol 34 mg

826. APRICOT CRUMBLE WITH BLACKBERRIES

Servings: 4
Cooking Time: 30 Minutes
INGREDIENTS:
- 2 ½ cups fresh apricots, de-stoned and cubed
- 1 cup fresh blackberries
- ½ cup sugar
- 2 tbsp lemon Juice
- 1 cup flour
- 5 tbsp butter

DIRECTIONS:

Preheat Cosori on Bake function to 360 F. Add the apricot cubes to a bowl and mix with lemon juice, 2 tbsp sugar, and blackberries. Scoop the mixture into a greased dish and spread it evenly.

In another bowl, mix flour and remaining sugar. Add 1 tbsp of cold water and butter and keep mixing until you have a crumbly mixture. Pour over the fruit mixture and cook for 20 minutes.

827. SWEET CREAM CHEESE WONTONS

Servings: 16
Cooking Time: 5 Minutes
INGREDIENTS:
- 1 egg mixed with a bit of water
- Wonton wrappers
- ½ C. powdered erythritol
- 8 ounces softened cream cheese
- Olive oil

DIRECTIONS:

Preparing the Ingredients. Mix sweetener and cream cheese together.
Lay out 4 wontons at a time and cover with a dish towel to prevent drying out.
Place ½ of a teaspoon of cream cheese mixture into each wrapper.
Dip finger into egg/water mixture and fold diagonally to form a triangle. Seal edges well.
Repeat with remaining ingredients.
Air Frying. Place filled wontons into the Cosori air fryer oven and cook 5 minutes at 400 degrees, shaking halfway through cooking.
Nutrition Info: CALORIES: 303; FAT:3G; PROTEIN:0.5G; SUGAR:4G

828. COOKIE CUSTARDS

INGREDIENTS:
- 2 tbsp. margarine
- A pinch of baking soda and baking powder
- 1 cup all-purpose flour
- ½ cup icing sugar
- ½ cup custard powder

DIRECTIONS:

Cream the margarine and sugar together. Add the remaining ingredients and fold them together.
Prepare a baking tray by greasing it with butter. Make balls out of the dough, coat them with flour and place them in the tray.
Preheat the fryer to 300 Fahrenheit for five minutes. You will need to place the baking tray in the basket and cover it. Cook till you find that the balls have turned golden brown. Remove the tray and leave it to cool outside for half an hour. Store in an airtight container.

829. ITALIAN PORK SKEWERS

INGREDIENTS:
- ¼ cup finely minced onion
- 1 teaspoon dried Italian seasoning
- ½ teaspoon salt
- teaspoon pepper
- 2 pounds pork tenderloin
- ¼ cup balsamic vinegar
- ¼ cup olive oil

DIRECTIONS:

Trim excess fat from tenderloin. Cut pork, on a slant, into ¼-inch-thick slices, each about 4 inches long. In large bowl, combine remaining ingredients and mix well with wire whisk. Add tenderloin slices and mix gently to coat. Cover and refrigerate for 2 to 3 hours. Meanwhile, soak 8-inch wooden skewers in cold water.

Remove pork from marinade and thread onto soaked skewers. Flash freeze on baking sheet in single layer. When frozen solid, pack skewers in rigid containers, with layers separated by waxed paper. Label skewers and freeze.

To thaw and reheat: Thaw overnight in refrigerator. Cook skewers 4 to 6 inches from medium coals on grill, or broil 4 to 6 inches from heat source, for about 4 to 6 minutes or until cooked (160ºF on an instant-read thermometer), turning once.

830. MARGHERITA PIZZA

Servings: 4

Cooking Time: 18 Minutes

INGREDIENTS:
- 1 whole-wheat pizza crust
- 1/2 cup mozzarella cheese, grated
- 1/2 cup can tomatoes
- 2 tbsp olive oil
- 3 Roma tomatoes, sliced
- 10 basil leaves

DIRECTIONS:

Fit the Cosori oven with the rack in position

Roll out whole wheat pizza crust using a rolling pin. Make sure the crust is ½-inch thick.

Sprinkle olive oil on top of pizza crust.

Spread can tomatoes over pizza crust.

Arrange sliced tomatoes and basil on pizza crust. Sprinkle grated cheese on top.

Place pizza on top of the oven rack and set to bake at 425 F for 23 minutes.

Slice and serve.

Nutrition Info: Calories 126 Fat 7.9 g Carbohydrates 11.3 g Sugar 4.2 g Protein 3.6 g Cholesterol 2 mg

831. APPLE WEDGES WITH APRICOTS

Servings: 4

Cooking Time: 15 To 18 Minutes

INGREDIENTS:
- 4 large apples, peeled and sliced into 8 wedges
- 2 tablespoons olive oil
- ½ cup dried apricots, chopped
- 1 to 2 tablespoons sugar
- ½ teaspoon ground cinnamon

DIRECTIONS:

Toss the apple wedges with the olive oil in a mixing bowl until well coated.

Place the apple wedges in the air fryer basket.

Put the air fryer basket on the baking pan and slide into Rack Position 2, select Air Fry, set temperature to 350°F (180°C), and set time to 15 minutes.

After about 12 minutes, remove from the oven. Sprinkle with the dried apricots and air fry for another 3 minutes.

Meanwhile, thoroughly combine the sugar and cinnamon in a small bowl.

Remove the apple wedges from the oven to a plate. Serve sprinkled with the sugar mixture.

832. OATMEAL CAKE

Servings: 8

Cooking Time: 40 Minutes

INGREDIENTS:
- 2 eggs, beaten
- 1 tbsp cocoa powder
- 1/2 tsp salt
- 1 tsp baking soda
- 1/2 cup butter, softened
- 1 cup granulated sugar
- 1 cup brown sugar
- 1 3/4 cups flour
- 1 cup quick oats
- 3/4 cup mix nuts, chopped
- 2 cups chocolate chips
- 1 3/4 cup boiling water

DIRECTIONS:

Fit the Cosori oven with the rack in position

Combine together boiling water and oats in a large bowl.

Add butter and sugar stir until butter melted.

Add flour, baking soda, salt, cocoa powder, 1 cup chocolate chips, half chopped nuts, and egg. Mix until combine.

Pour batter into the greased cake pan and sprinkle remaining nuts and chocolate chips over the top of cake batter.

Set to bake at 350 F for 45 minutes. After 5 minutes place the baking dish in the preheated oven.

Slice and serve.

Nutrition Info: Calories 699 Fat 30.6 g Carbohydrates 97.9 g Sugar 4.1 g Protein 64.8 g Cholesterol 81 mg

833. GARLIC CHEESE DIP

Servings: 10

Cooking Time: 15 Minutes

INGREDIENTS:
- 1 lb. mozzarella; shredded
- 6 garlic cloves; minced
- 3 tbsp. olive oil
- 1 tbsp. thyme; chopped.
- 1 tsp. rosemary; chopped.
- A pinch of salt and black pepper

DIRECTIONS:

In a pan that fits your air fryer, mix all the ingredients, whisk really well, introduce in the air fryer and cook at 370°F for 10 minutes.

Divide into bowls and serve right away.

Nutrition Info: Calories: 184; Fat: 11g; Fiber: 3g; Carbs: 5g; Protein: 7g

834. LEMON-RASPBERRY MUFFINS

Servings: 6

Cooking Time: 15 Minutes

INGREDIENTS:
- 2 cups almond flour
- ¾ cup Swerve
- 1¼ teaspoons baking powder
- ⅓ teaspoon ground allspice
- ⅓ teaspoon ground anise star
- ½ teaspoon grated lemon zest
- ¼ teaspoon salt
- 2 eggs
- 1 cup sour cream
- ½ cup coconut oil
- ½ cup raspberries

DIRECTIONS:

Line a muffin pan with 6 paper liners.

In a mixing bowl, mix the almond flour, Swerve, baking powder, allspice, anise, lemon zest, and salt.

In another mixing bowl, beat the eggs, sour cream, and coconut oil until well mixed. Add the egg mixture to the flour mixture and stir to combine. Mix in the raspberries.

Scrape the batter into the prepared muffin cups, filling each about three-quarters full.

Put the muffin pan into Rack Position 1, select Convection Bake, set temperature to 345°F (174°C), and set time to 15 minutes.

When cooking is complete, the tops should be golden and a toothpick inserted in the middle should come out clean.

Allow the muffins to cool for 10 minutes in the muffin pan before removing and serving.

835. ALMOND PECAN COOKIES

Servings: 16

Cooking Time: 20 Minutes

INGREDIENTS:
- 1/2 cup butter
- 1 tsp vanilla

- 2 tsp gelatin
- 2/3 cup Swerve
- 1 cup pecans
- 1/3 cup coconut flour
- 1 cup almond flour

DIRECTIONS:

Fit the Cosori oven with the rack in position

Add butter, vanilla, gelatin, swerve, coconut flour, and almond flour into the food processor and process until crumbs form.

Add pecans and process until chopped.

Make cookies from prepared mixture and place onto a parchment-lined baking pan.

Set to bake at 350 F for 25 minutes. After 5 minutes place the baking pan in the preheated oven.

Serve and enjoy.

Nutrition Info: Calories 101 Fat 10.2 g Carbohydrates 1.4 g Sugar 0.3 g Protein 1.8 g Cholesterol 15 mg

836. RADISH CHIPS

Servings: 6
Cooking Time: 18 Minutes
INGREDIENTS:
- Garlic powder
- Avocado oil
- Radish slices, 1 lb.
- Pepper
- Onion powder
- Salt

DIRECTIONS:

Toss the washed radish slices with oil, salt, pepper, onion powder, and garlic powder.

Spread these slices in the air fryer basket and return the basket to the fryer.

Air fry them for 5 minutes at 370 degrees F then toss them well.

Air fry the slices again for 5 more minutes.

Adjust seasoning with more spices and cooking oil.

Air fry these slices again for 5 minutes then toss them.

Cook for another 3 minutes and serve.

Nutrition Info: Calories: 72 Fat: 6.6 g Carbs: 3.6 g Protein: 0.8 g

837. EASY SWEET POTATO FRIES

Servings: 2
Cooking Time: 16 Minutes
INGREDIENTS:
- 2 sweet potatoes, peeled and cut into fries shape
- 1 tbsp olive oil
- Salt

DIRECTIONS:

Fit the Cosori oven with the rack in position 2.

Toss sweet potato fries with oil and salt and place in the air fryer basket then place the air fryer basket in the baking pan.

Place a baking pan on the oven rack. Set to air fry at 375 F for 16 minutes.

Serve and enjoy.

Nutrition Info: Calories 178 Fat 7.2 Carbohydrates 27.9 g Sugar 0.5 g Protein 1.5 g Cholesterol 0 mg

838. TURKEY BACON-WRAPPED DATES

Servings: 16 Appetizers
Cooking Time: 6 Minutes
INGREDIENTS:
- 16 whole dates, pitted
- 16 whole almonds
- 6 to 8 strips turkey bacon, cut in half
- Special Equipment:

- 16 toothpicks, soaked in water for at least 30 minutes

DIRECTIONS:

On a flat work surface, stuff each pitted date with a whole almond.

Wrap half slice of bacon around each date and secure it with a toothpick. Place the bacon-wrapped dates in the air fryer basket.

Put the air fryer basket on the baking pan and slide into Rack Position 2, select Air Fry, set temperature to 390ºF (199ºC), and set time to 6 minutes.

When cooking is complete, transfer the dates to a paper towel-lined plate to drain. Serve hot.

839. AIR FRIED CHICKEN TENDERS

Servings: 4
Cooking Time: 10 Minutes
INGREDIENTS:
- 12 oz chicken breasts, cut into tenders
- 1 egg white
- 1/8 cup flour
- ½ cup panko bread crumbs
- Salt and black pepper, to taste

DIRECTIONS:

PREHEAT THE AIR FRYER TO 350 DEGREE F AND GREASE AN AIR FRYER BASKET.

Season the chicken tenders with salt and black pepper.

Coat the chicken tenders with flour, then dip in egg whites and then dredge in the panko bread crumbs.

Arrange in the Air fryer basket and cook for about 10 minutes.

Dish out in a platter and serve warm.

Nutrition Info: Calories: 220, Fat: 17.1g, Carbohydrates: 6g, Sugar: 3.5g, Protein: 12.8g, Sodium: 332mg

840. CINNAMON CHEESECAKE BARS

Servings: 12
Cooking Time: 30 Minutes
INGREDIENTS:
- Nonstick cooking spray
- 16 oz. cream cheese, soft
- 1 tsp vanilla
- 1 ¼ cups sugar, divided
- 2 tubes refrigerated crescent rolls
- 1 tsp cinnamon
- ¼ cup butter

DIRECTIONS:

Place the rack in position Spray the bottom of an 8x11-inch pan with cooking spray.

In a medium bowl, beat cream cheese, vanilla, and ¾ cup sugar until smooth.

Roll out one can of crescent rolls on the bottom of prepared pan, sealing the perforations and pressing partway up the sides.

Spread cream cheese mixture evenly over crescents.

Roll out second can of crescents over the top of cheese mixture, sealing the perforations.

In a small bowl, stir together cinnamon and remaining sugar. Melt the butter.

Set oven to bake on 375°F for 35 minutes.

Sprinkle the cinnamon sugar over the top of the crescents and drizzle with melted butter.

After the oven has preheated for 5 minutes, place the pan in the oven and bake 30 minutes until the top is golden brown.

Cool completely. Cover and refrigerate at least 2 hours before slicing and serving.

Nutrition Info: Calories 332, Total Fat 18g, Saturated Fat 10g, Total Carbs 35g, Net Carbs 35g, Protein 5g, Sugar 23g, Fiber 0g, Sodium 278mg, Potassium 87mg, Phosphorus 70mg

841. BROWNIES

INGREDIENTS:
- ½ cup condensed milk
- 1 tbsp. unsalted butter
- 2 tbsp. water
- ½ cup chopped nuts
- 3 tbsp. melted dark chocolate
- 1 cup all-purpose flour

DIRECTIONS:

Add the ingredients together and whisk till you get a smooth mixture. Prepare a tin by greasing it with butter. Transfer the mixture into the tin. Preheat the fryer to 300 Fahrenheit for five minutes. You will need to place the tin in the basket and cover it. Check whether the brownies have been cooked using a knife or a toothpick and remove the tray. When the brownies have cooled, cut them and serve with a dollop of ice cream.

842. VANILLA PEANUT BUTTER CAKE

Servings: 8
Cooking Time: 30 Minutes
INGREDIENTS:
- 1 1/2 cups all-purpose flour
- 1/3 cup vegetable oil
- 1 tsp baking soda
- 1/2 cup peanut butter powder
- 1 tsp vanilla
- 1 tbsp apple cider vinegar
- 1 cup of water
- 1 cup of sugar
- 1/2 tsp salt

DIRECTIONS:

Fit the Cosori oven with the rack in position

In a large mixing bowl, mix together flour, baking soda, peanut butter powder, sugar, and salt.

In a small bowl, whisk together oil, vanilla, vinegar, and water.

Pour oil mixture into the flour mixture and stir until well combined.

Pour batter into the greased cake pan.

Set to bake at 350 F for 35 minutes. After 5 minutes place the cake pan in the preheated oven.

Slice and serve.

Nutrition Info: Calories 264 Fat 1.8 g Carbohydrates 43.2 g Sugar 25.3 g Protein 2.6 g Cholesterol 0 mg

843. KETO MIXED BERRY CRUMBLE POTS

Servings: 6
Cooking Time: 15 Minutes
INGREDIENTS:
- 2 ounces unsweetened mixed berries
- 1/2 cup granulated swerve
- 2 tablespoons golden flaxseed meal
- 1/4 teaspoon ground star anise
- 1/2 teaspoon ground cinnamon
- 1 teaspoon xanthan gum
- 2/3 cup almond flour
- 1 cup powdered swerve
- 1/2 teaspoon baking powder
- 1/3 cup unsweetened coconut, finely shredded
- 1/2 stick butter, cut into small pieces

DIRECTIONS:

Toss the mixed berries with the granulated swerve, golden flaxseed meal, star anise, cinnamon, and xanthan gum. Divide between six custard cups coated with cooking spray.

In a mixing dish, thoroughly combine the remaining ingredients. Sprinkle over the berry mixture.

Bake in the preheated Air Fryer at 330 degrees F for 35 minutes. Work in batches if needed.

Nutrition Info: 155 Calories; 13g Fat; 1g Carbs; 1g Protein; 8g Sugars; 6g Fiber

844. CHEESY BEEF DIP

Servings: 12
Cooking Time: 25 Minutes
INGREDIENTS:
- 1 lb corned beef, diced
- ¾ cup mayonnaise
- 14 oz can sauerkraut, drained
- 8 oz Swiss cheese, shredded
- Pepper
- Salt

DIRECTIONS:

Fit the Cosori oven with the rack in position

Add all ingredients into the bowl and mix well and pour into the greased baking dish.

Set to bake at 400 F for 30 minutes. After 5 minutes place the baking dish in the preheated oven.

Serve and enjoy.

Nutrition Info: Calories 283 Fat 25 g Carbohydrates 3 g Sugar 1 g Protein 12 g Cholesterol 62 mg

845. COFFEE CHOCOLATE CAKE

Servings: 8
Cooking Time: 30 Minutes
INGREDIENTS:
- Dry Ingredients:
- 1½ cups almond flour
- ½ cup coconut meal
- ⅔ cup Swerve
- 1 teaspoon baking powder
- ¼ teaspoon salt
- Wet Ingredients:
- 1 egg
- 1 stick butter, melted
- ½ cup hot strongly brewed coffee
- Topping:
- ½ cup confectioner's Swerve
- ¼ cup coconut flour
- 3 tablespoons coconut oil
- 1 teaspoon ground cinnamon
- ½ teaspoon ground cardamom

DIRECTIONS:

In a medium bowl, combine the almond flour, coconut meal, Swerve, baking powder, and salt.

In a large bowl, whisk the egg, melted butter, and coffee until smooth.

Add the dry mixture to the wet and stir until well incorporated. Transfer the batter to a greased baking pan.

Stir together all the ingredients for the topping in a small bowl. Spread the topping over the batter and smooth the top with a spatula.

Slide the baking pan into Rack Position 1, select Convection Bake, set temperature to 330ºF (166ºC), and set time to 30 minutes.

When cooking is complete, the cake should spring back when gently pressed with your fingers.

Rest for 10 minutes before serving.

846. CARAMELIZED PEACHES

Servings: 4
Cooking Time: 10 To 13 Minutes
INGREDIENTS:
- 2 tablespoons sugar
- ¼ teaspoon ground cinnamon
- 4 peaches, cut into wedges
- Cooking spray

DIRECTIONS:

Toss the peaches with the sugar and cinnamon in a medium bowl until evenly coated.

Lightly spray the air fryer basket with cooking spray. Place the peaches in the basket in a single layer. Lightly mist the peaches with cooking spray.

Put the air fryer basket on the baking pan and slide into Rack Position 2, select Air Fry, set temperature to 350ºF (180ºC), and set time to 10 minutes.

After 5 minutes, remove from the oven and flip the peaches. Return to the oven and continue cooking for 5 minutes.

When cooking is complete, the peaches should be caramelized. If necessary, continue cooking for 3 minutes. Remove from the oven. Let the peaches cool for 5 minutes and serve warm.

847. NUTTY PARMESAN HOMEMADE FRIED STICKS
INGREDIENTS:
- ½ cup grated Parmesan cheese
- Teas
- 1 package frozen puff pastry sheets, thawed
- ½ cup ground almonds

DIRECTIONS:

Preheat oven to 375ºF. In a small bowl, combine almonds, cheese, and pepper; blend well. Sprinkle half of this mixture over work surface and cover with one sheet puff pastry. Using a rolling pin, gently press pastry into cheese mixture. Turn pastry over and press cheese mixture into other side of pastry. Repeat with other half of cheese mixture and second sheet of puff pastry.

Using pastry cutter or sharp knife, cut pastry into ½-inch strips. Place on parchment paper- or foil-lined baking sheets, twisting each strip several times. Bake at 375ºF for 10 to 15 minutes or until browned and crisp, being careful not to burn sticks. Remove from baking sheet and cool completely on wire racks. Pack carefully into rigid containers, separating layers with waxed paper. Label containers and freeze.

To thaw and reheat: Thaw sticks at room temperature and serve, or carefully place frozen sticks on baking sheet and bake at 350ºF for 4 to 5 minutes or until hotpot cayenne pepper

848. MINI PANCAKES
INGREDIENTS:
- 2 tsp. dried parsley
- Salt and Pepper to taste
- 3 tbsp. Butter
- 1 ½ cups almond flour
- 3 eggs
- 2 tsp. dried basil

DIRECTIONS:

Preheat the air fryer to 250 Fahrenheit.

In a small bowl, mix the ingredients together. Ensure that the mixture is smooth and well balanced.

Take a pancake mold and grease it with butter. Add the batter to the mold and place it in the air fryer basket. Cook till both the sides of the pancake have browned on both sides and serve with maple syrup.

849. EASY BACON BITES
Servings: 4
Cooking Time: 10 Minutes
INGREDIENTS:
- 4 bacon strips, cut into small pieces
- 1/4 cup hot sauce
- 1/2 cup pork rinds, crushed
-

DIRECTIONS:

Fit the Cosori oven with the rack in position 2.
Add bacon pieces in a bowl.

Add hot sauce and toss well.

Add crushed pork rinds and toss until bacon pieces are well coated.

Transfer bacon pieces in the air fryer basket then place an air fryer basket in the baking pan.

Place a baking pan on the oven rack. Set to air fry at 350 F for 10 minutes.

Serve and enjoy.

Nutrition Info: Calories 123 Fat 10.4 g Carbohydrates 0.3 g Sugar 0.2 g Protein 6.5 g Cholesterol 5 mg

850. ALMOND BUTTER COOKIES
Servings: 12
Cooking Time: 12 Minutes

INGREDIENTS:
- 1 teaspoon vanilla extract
- 1 cup almond butter, soft
- 1 egg
- 2 tablespoons erythritol

DIRECTIONS:

In a bowl, mix all the ingredients and whisk really well.

Spread this on a cookie sheet that fits the air fryer lined with parchment paper, introduce in the fryer and cook at 350 degrees F and bake for 12 minutes.

Cool down and serve.

Nutrition Info: calories 130, fat 12, fiber 1, carbs 3, protein 5

CPSIA information can be obtained
at www.ICGtesting.com
Printed in the USA
BVHW061219190521
607713BV00012B/1091

9 781802 571240